standard catalog of ®
FIREBIRD
1967-2002

John Gunnell

Published by

700 East State Street • Iola, WI 54990-0001
715/445-2214 • FAX: 715/445-4087   www.krause.com

Please call or write for our free catalog of publications. Our toll-free
number to place an order or obtain a free catalog is (800) 258-0929.

Library of Congress Catalog Number: 2002105082
ISBN: 0-87349-494-6

Thanks

No project of this scope would be possible without the help and support of Firebird
enthusiasts to check facts and proofread priliminary manuscripts. Those involved in
this project included Dave Doern of Chicago, Illinois; Jerry Heasley of Pampa, Texas;
Jim Mattison of Pontiac Historic Services, Sterling Heights, Michigan; Rocky Rotella
of LaVista, Nebraska; John Sawruk of White Lake, Michigan; Eric Vicker of Bethel
Park, Maryland, and John and Matthew Witzke of Council Bluffs, Iowa.

Foreword

The concept behind Krause Publications' *Standard Catalogs of American Cars* is to compile massive amounts of information about motor vehicles and present it in a standard format that the hobbyist, collector or professional dealer can use to answer some commonly asked questions.

Those questions include: What year, make and model is my vehicle? What did it sell for when it was new? How rare is it? What is special about it? In our general automotive catalogs, some answers are provided by photos and others are provided by the fact-filled text. In one-marque catalogs such as *The Standard Catalog of Firebird 1967-2002,* additional information such as identification number charts and interesting facts about Pontiac history are included throughout the book.

Chester L. Krause of Krause Publications is responsible for the basic concept of creating the *Standard Catalog of American Cars* series. Automotive historian David V. Brownell undertook preliminary work on the concept while editing *Old Cars Weekly* in the 1970s. John A. Gunnell edited the first of the *Standard Catalogs of American Cars.*

No claims are made that these catalogs are infallible. They are not repair manuals or "bibles" for motor vehicle enthusiasts. They are meant as a contribution to the pursuit of greater knowledge about many wonderful vehicles. They are much larger in size, broader in scope and more deluxe in format than most other collector guides, buyer's guides or price guides.

The long-range goal of Krause Publications is to make all of our *Standard Catalogs of American Cars* as nearly perfect as possible. At the same time, we expect they will always raise new questions and bring forth new facts that were not previously unearthed. We maintain an ongoing file of new research, corrections and additional photos that are used, regularly, to refine and expand standard catalogs.

This first edition of *The Standard Catalog of Firebird 1967-2002* was compiled by the experienced editorial team at Krause Publication's books department. In this edition we have put particular emphasis on refining the Firebird vehicle identification number (VIN) information, better organizing the Firebird engine options and reducing the number of codes and abbreviations used so that the overall book is more "reader friendly."

Should you have knowledge you wish to see in future editions of this book, please don't hesitate to contact the editors at *The Standard Catalog of Firebird 1967-2002,* editorial department, 700 East State Street, Iola, WI 54990.

The 1994 Pontiac Trans Am

Contents

EDITOR'S NOTE: VIN Numbers data from General Motors Corp. Vehicle Registration Data Cards and some country of origin data and restraint system data may not apply specifically to Firebirds.

Introduction

Some of my greatest experiences with GM design staff were at Pontiac. Twenty years of my career were devoted to coaching and guiding a very gifted and talented team to many successes.

Returning from Australia in late 1969 after an assignment with GM Holden's, I was given the task of running the advanced Chevrolet II studio (which is another story). However, at the end of my tour at Holden's, I developed a great desire for a Jerry Titus Racing Pontiac Trans Am. White, blue stripes, big wheels and tires, low to the ground and best of all, a large motor — how could it get any better? Of course, I wanted one like the Titus car for my street machine. Finally, after much investigating and thought and disappointment, I scrapped the idea as being very impractical.

In late '71 I got my dream-come-true assignment: to head the Pontiac II design studio. Now, with a great team, we could bring some of that passion to market.

One of my many exciting concepts that we worked on was the graphics of the Trans Am. We converted a Formula into a Trans Am by hanging on fender flairs, keeping the shaker hood and rear spoiler and, of course, painting it bright red. We worked with our graphics department to develop a large graphic of our bird emblem. Remember, the 1970 Trans Am had a bird decal at the beginning of the hood stripe on the Endura front bumper. The new bird was to be sculptured around the shaker hood, which was fitting with the power of the bird and machine.

In the studio we thought it was a knockout. Some thought I would get fired or in trouble, but in my head I knew it was right for the times.

Then came the task of selling the idea to Pontiac and design staff management, vice president William Mitchell, and executive in charge Chuck Jordan. After a review with our management, we got the thumbs-up approval. The Pontiac review was tough, with some liking and some thinking it was a bad joke. You can't please them all.

One evening in spring I took this wild-looking bird beast out on Woodward Avenue in Detroit to test the reaction. First, the old Totem Pole Restaurant, up Woodward Avenue, through several gas stations and drive-ins. You don't have to be a brain surgeon to guess the reaction and results. Guys and girls were in their hot cars, giving thumbs-up and shouting questions about where they could get theirs.

The great reaction to our bird was sort of like hands-on marketing. We reviewed it with Jordan and Mitchell and director Hank Hager. The vote was unanimous to take the concept forward. Pontiac was less receptive at this point, although very interested. It was like "we did a nice job, got everyone excited, but so what?"

It was decided that we would have a show with all the top brass at Pontiac, especially the movers and shakers — general manager James McDonald, chief engineer Steve Malone, the list went on. The team picked red, white and blue for American racing colors to display our new bird graphics. 3-M, under the leadership of ex-Marine Jack Smith, helped us develop our concepts.

The show day came and we were pumped with excitement — three beautiful machines in all their glory. Two important players didn't like the bird decal because they thought it was not a true racing graphic, but in the end general manager James McDonald saved the day. The design got his vote and he said we "had something good and Pontiac ought to give it a chance. Instead of standard equipment, let's offer it as an option and let our customers decide if it's what they want."

Our team was a little disappointed that the Trans Am would be just an option package, but at least we knew we had a chance. When the bird went into production and the sales went wild for the large bird graphics, you would have thought we had invented ice cream. 3-M could not make the decal fast enough. The theme was a bull's eye for our customers and the company.

At one point a used car dealer named Joe Sonk from Warren, Michigan, said "Do not bring a Trans Am in for sale without the bird. Go get a bird for your hood, bring it back, now you have a real Trans Am."

I'd like to make one clarification about the history of the large bird decal. It was very clear that our studio developed the large hood bird and all its colors without any prior knowledge of other attempts. When someone says that our team "resurrected" this idea, my answer is that success has many fathers and failures have none.

And then there were the wheels.

Car enthusiasts love wheels, and two that stand out

in my mind were the cast-aluminum snowflake and the turbo torque designs.

The snowflake wheel was created by designer Jim Shook. We took a lot of weight out of the design by opening up ports and extending the snowflake design out to the rim. When the moment of truth came and we had to show the design, we decided to place the wheel on the desktop in the office. The desktop was bright red, and we placed a spotlight directly above the wheel to light it up.

Then the fun part started. Jim Shook could make terrific car sounds with his mouth. After a great review about the new Firebird design with the design big guys, I mentioned to our vice president, William Mitchell, that I had something special to show him. I opened the door of my office, Jim made some racecar sounds, and the spotlight was turned on. Mitchell stopped in his tracks, his eyes lit up with excitement, and he moved in for a closer look. "Beautiful!" he exclaimed. "It looks like a diamond cutter made this wheel. Let's make a set for our updated Banshee show car."

Pontiac was so impressed that design staff paid to tool up a limited number of these wheels that it put together a plan for a production version for our 1977 Firebirds.

My favorite wheel, though, was the turbo torque because I hold the patent for it. More than that, I liked that wheel because it was an entirely new concept for a cast-aluminum wheel. It was asymmetrical rather than symmetrical.

The first sketch for the turbo torque was turned over to my assistant chief engineer, Richard Shell, and he quickly adjusted it and added the right touches to allow for a production proposal. He was great at that kind of thing. Chuck Hagar liked what he saw and decided we could go forward.

Home runs in design are few and far between. That day we hit one out of the park.

The tough part was convincing Pontiac brass that the wheel was appropriate. Steve Malone, the chief engineer, sent his special projects engineer, Lefty West, down to design staff to convince me that road wheels must be symmetrical, like gears. After an hour of excellent design and engineering debate, Lefty realized we could retain the asymmetrical design. The wheel design was approved at the next Pontiac management meeting and the rest is history.

When it comes to new ideas, not only do you have to possess the passion and ability for design, you must have the commitment and conviction to sell its virtue to make things happen.

With our great teams we produced some of the greatest designs in GM history. My congratulations to all my past Pontiac teams.

— John Schinella,
former director of Pontiac brand character

1979 Trans Am

A.C. Bogarty photo

This gold coupe was one of more than 64,000 1967 Firebirds equipped with a V-8.

1967

The Firebird Arrives

Ford rocked the automotive world with its mid-1964 introduction of the Mustang and took the industry by surprise. General Motors wasn't able to field a true competitor until three years later, when it introduced the Firebird on Feb. 23. It was Pontiac's version of Chevy's new Camaro dressed up with a Poncho-style split grille, different engines and transmissions and a few suspension tweaks.

Pontiac offered the sporty "shorty" in five flavors – base, Sprint, 326, 326 H.O. and 400 — created by tacking regular production options onto the same basic car. The options created distinctive packages that were merchandised as separate models. Bucket seats were standard in all Firebirds. Design characteristics of the '67s included vent windows and three vertical air slots on the rear fenders.

Sprints featured a 215-hp overhead cam six with a four-barrel carburetor. A floor-mounted three-speed manual gearbox and heavy-duty suspension were standard. A Firebird Sprint convertible cost $3,019 and a coupe was $2,782.

Firebird 326s featured a 250-hp version of the 326-cid Tempest V-8 with two-barrel carburetion. The convertible cost $2,998 and the coupe was $2,761. Firebird 326-H.O.s used a 285-hp version of the same V-8 with a 10.5:1 compression ratio and four-barrel carburetor. A column-shift three-speed manual transmission, dual exhausts, H.O. stripes, a heavy-duty battery and wide-oval tires were standard. The H.O.

A.C. Bogarty photo

The base 400 engine produced 325 hp.

convertible cost $3,062 and the coupe cost $2,825.

The performance version of the 1967 Firebird was the 400. It featured a 325-hp version of the 400-cid GTO V-8. Standard equipment included a dual-scoop hood, chrome engine parts, three-speed heavy-duty floor shift and sport-type suspension. Prices were about $100 higher than a comparable 326 H.O. Options included Ram-Air induction, which gave 325 hp and cost over $600.

BASE FIREBIRD - (OHC-6) SERIES 223

Standard equipment included bucket seats, vinyl upholstery, nylon-blend carpets, woodgrain dash trim and E70-14 wide oval tires. The base engine was a regular-fuel OHC six with a monojet carburetor. Two body styles were offered and came with any of the Tempest or GTO power trains. However, the two body styles were marketed in five "models" created by adding regular production options (UPCs) in specific combinations. The models were the base Firebird, Firebird Sprint, Firebird 326, Firebird 326 H.O. and the Firebird 400.

COLORS

C=Cameo Ivory, D=Montreaux Blue, E=Fathom Blue, F=Tyrol Blue, G=Signet Gold, H=Linden Green, K=Gulf Turquoise, L=Mariner Turquoise, M=Plum Mist, N=Burgundy, P=Silverglaze, R=Regimental Red, S=Champagne and T=Montego Cream.

I.D. NUMBERS

VIN stamped on a plate attached to the left front door pillar. First symbol indicates GM division: 2=Pontiac. The second and third symbols indicate series: 23=Firebird. The fourth and fifth symbols indicate the body style: 37=two-door sport coupe (hardtop), 67=two-door convertible. The sixth symbol indicates model year: 7=1967. The seventh symbol indicates the assembly plant: U=Lordstown, Ohio. The last six symbols are the sequential production number starting with 600001 for six-cylinder Firebirds and 100001 for V-8 Firebirds at each assembly plant. Body/style number plate under hood tells manufacturer, build date, Fisher style number, assembly plant, trim code, paint code, accessory codes. The build date takes the form 01A where the two digits indicate month (01=January) and the letter indicates week of the month (A=first week). The style number takes the form 67-22367 where the prefix 67=1967, the first symbol 2=Pontiac, the second and third symbols 23=Firebird series and the fourth and fifth symbols indicate body style (37=Sport Coupe and 67=convertible). The assembly plant code LOR=Lordstown, Ohio (where all Firebirds were made). The Fisher body plate also carries trim and paint codes. VIN appears on front of engine at right-hand cylinder bank along with an alpha-numerical engine production code. Firebird engine production codes included: [230-cid, 155-hp OHC six] ZF-ZG. [230-cid, 165-hp OHC six] ZK-ZS-ZN-ZM. [230-cid, 215-hp OHC six] ZD-ZE-ZR-ZL. [326-cid, 250-hp V-8] WC-WH-XI-YJ. [326-cid, 285-hp V-8] WK-WO-XO-YM. [400-cid, 325-hp V-8] WI-WQ-WU-WZ-XN-YT. [400-cid, 335-hp V-8] WE-WD-XH.

Model Number	Body/Style Number	Body Type & Seating	Factory Price	Shipping Weight	Production Total
223	37	2d sport coupe-5P	$2,666	2,955 lbs.	Note 1
223	67	2d convertible-5P	$2,903	3,247 lbs.	Note 1

Note 1: Production by body style (all models) included 67,032 sport coupes and 15,528 convertibles.

Note 2: Production records were also recorded by the number of sixes and V-8s built with standard or deluxe appointments as listed in the table below:

	Synchromesh	Automatic	Total
Standard OHC six Firebirds	5,258	5,597	10,855
Standard V-8 Firebirds	8,224	15,301	23,525
Deluxe OHC six Firebirds	2,963	3,846	6,809
Deluxe V-8 Firebirds	11,526	29,845	41,371
Totals	27,971	54,589	82,560

Pontiac built more than 82,000 beautiful new Firebirds in 1967.

John DeLorean was a driving influence behind the Firebird.

FIREBIRD SPRINT - (OHC-6) SERIES 223

Sprint models featured a 215-hp OHC six with a four-barrel carburetor. A floor-mounted three-speed manual gearbox and heavy-duty suspension were standard. The Sprint version of the OHC six also featured a racier cam and a tuned exhaust manifold. Body still moldings with "3.8-Litre Overhead Cam" emblems were seen. Body side racing stripes were a popular and heavily-promoted Sprint option.

Model Number	Body/Style Number	Body Type & Seating	Factory Price	Shipping Weight	Production Total
223	37	2d sport coupe-5P	$2,782	3,260 lbs.	Note 3
223	67	2d convertible-5P	$3,019	3,571 lbs.	Note 3

Note 3: See notes 1 and 2.

FIREBIRD 326 - (V-8) - SERIES 223

Firebird 326s featured a 250-hp version of the base Tempest V-8 with two-barrel carburetion. A three-speed transmission with column-mounted shifter was standard equipment. The 326 V-8 also used lettering on the rear edge of the hood bulge for model identification. In this case the model call-outs read "326." E70-14 tires were standard.

Model Number	Body/Style Number	Body Type & Seating	Factory Price	Shipping Weight	Production Total
223	37	2d sport coupe-5P	$2,761	3,323 lbs.	Note 4
223	67	2d convertible-5P	$2,998	3,615 lbs.	Note 4

Note 4: See notes 1 and 2.

FIREBIRD 326 H.O. - (V-8) SERIES 223

Firebird 326 H.O. models featured a 285-hp version of the base Tempest V-8 with 10.5:1 compression and four-barrel carburetion. A three-speed manual transmission with column shift, a dual exhaust system, H.O. side stripes, a heavy-duty battery and F70 x 14 wide oval tires were standard. The Firebird 326 H.O. convertible was priced $3,062 and the Firebird 326 H.O. coupe was priced $2,825.

Model Number	Body/Style Number	Body Type & Seating	Factory Price	Shipping Weight	Production Total
223	37	2d sport coupe-5P	$2,825	3,323 lbs.	Note 5
223	67	2d convertible-5P	$3,062	3,615 lbs.	Note 5

Note 5: See notes 1 and 2.

FIREBIRD 400 - (V-8) - SERIES 223

Firebird 400s used a 325-hp version of the GTO V-8 with four-barrel carburetion. Standard equipment included a dual scoop hood, chrome engine parts, a three-speed heavy-duty floor shifter and a sport-type suspension. The letters "400" appeared on the right-hand side of the deck lid. Options included a Ram Air induction setup that gave 325 hp at a higher rpm peak and cost over $600 extra.

Model Number	Body/Style Number	Body Type & Seating	Factory Price	Shipping Weight	Production Total
223	37	2d sport coupe-5P	$2,777	3,549 lbs.	Note 6
223	67	2d convertible-5P	$3,177	3,855 lbs.	Note 6

Note 6: See notes 1 and 2.

ENGINES

OHC inline six-cylinder: Overhead valves. Overhead camshaft. Cast-iron block. Displacement: 230 cid. Bore & stroke: 3.85 x 3.25 in. Compression ratio: 7.6:1. Brake horsepower: 155 Hydraulic valve lifters. Carburetor: Rochester one-barrel. Engine codes: ZF with three-speed manual transmission; ZG with automatic transmission.

OHC inline six-cylinder: Overhead valves. Overhead camshaft. Cast-iron block. Displacement: 230 cid. Bore & stroke: 3.85 x 3.25 in. Compression ratio: 9.0:1. Brake horsepower: 165 at 4700 rpm. Torque: 216 ft. lbs. at 2600 rpm. Hydraulic valve lifters. Carburetor: Rochester model 7027167 one-barrel. Engine codes: ZK-ZS with three-speed manual transmission; ZM-ZN with automatic transmission.

Tempest OHC Sprint inline six-cylinder [UPC W53]: Overhead valves. Overhead camshaft. Cast-iron block. Displacement: 230 cid. Bore & stroke: 3.85 x 3.25 in. Compression ratio: 10.5:1. Brake horsepower: 215 at 5200 rpm. Torque: 240 ft. lbs. at 3800 rpm. Hydraulic valve lifters. Carburetor: Rochester four-barrel. Engine codes: ZD-ZR with three-speed manual transmission; ZE-ZL with automatic transmission.

326 V-8 [UPC L30]: Overhead valves. Cast-iron block. Displacement: 326 cid. Bore & stroke: 3.718 x 3.75 in. Compression ratio: 9.2:1. Brake horsepower: 250 at 4600 rpm. Torque: 333 ft.-lbs. at 3800 rpm. Hydraulic valve lifters. Carburetion: Rochester model 7025071 two-barrel. Engine codes: WC-WH with manual transmission; XI-YJ with automatic transmission.

326 V-8. H.O. [UPC L76]: Overhead valves. Cast-iron block. Displacement: 326 cid. Bore & stroke: 3.718 x 3.75 in. Compression ratio: 10.5:1. Brake horsepower: 285 at 5000 rpm. Torque: 359 ft. lbs. at 3200 rpm. Hydraulic valve lifters. Carburetion: Four-barrel. Engine codes: WK-WO with manual transmission; XO-YM with automatic transmission.

400 V-8 [UPC W66]: Overhead valves. Cast-iron block. Displacement: 400 cid. Bore & stroke: 4.125 x 3.75 in. Compression ratio: 10.75:1. Brake horsepower: 325 at 4800 rpm. Torque: 410 ft. lbs. at 3400 rpm. Five main bearings. Hydraulic valve lifters. Carburetor: Four-barrel. Engine codes: WI-WQ-WU-WZ with manual transmission; XN-YT with automatic transmission.

Ram Air V-8 [UPC L67]: Overhead valves. Cast-iron block. Displacement: 400 cid. Bore & stroke: 4.125 x 3.75 in. Compression ratio: 10.75:1. Brake horsepower: 335 at 5200 rpm. Torque: 410 ft. lbs. at 3600 rpm. Five main bearings. Hydraulic valve lifters. Carburetor: Rochester model 7027071 four-barrel.

CHASSIS

Wheelbase: 108.1 in. Overall length: 188.8 in. Front tread: 59 in. Rear tread: 60 in. Standard tires: E70 x 14.

TECHNICAL

Body and frame: Integral body and frame with separate bolted-on sub-frame for engine and front suspension. Front suspension: Independent with upper and lower control arms, coil springs, tubular shocks and stabilizer bar. Rear suspension: Hotchkiss solid axle with single-leaf rear springs and tubular shocks. Firebirds with V-8s had traction bars and anti-windup feature (one traction bar with automatic transmission and two traction bars with manual transmission). Steering: Optional power assist coaxial re-circulating ball bearing. Turning diameter: 38.4 ft. curb to curb. Turns lock to lock: 3.0. Fuel tank: 18.5 gal.

OPTIONS

382 door edge guards (price unavailable). 631 front floor mats (price unavailable). 632 rear floor mats (price unavailable). 502 power brakes with pedal trim ($41.60). 501 17.5:1 ratio power steering ($94.79). 551 power windows ($100.05). 401 luggage lamp (price unavailable). 402 ignition switch lamp (price unavailable). 421 underhood lamp (price unavailable). 582 custom air conditioning ($355.98). 374 rear window defogger/blower ($21.06). 531 all Soft-Ray glass ($30.54). 532 Soft-Ray windshield ($21.06). 441 cruise control with automatic transmission only ($52.66). 442 Safeguard speedometer (price unavailable). 654 carpet-back rear fold-down seat ($36.86). 544 power convertible top ($52.66). 474 electric clock ($15.80). 394 remote-control outside rearview mirror (price unavailable). 391 visor vanity mirror (price unavailable). 572 bench or bucket seat headrest ($52.66) 342 push-button radio with manual antenna ($61.09). Manual rear antenna instead of regular front antenna ($9.48). 344 push-button AM/FM

Pontiac sold 15,528 new Firebird convertibles in 1967.

The '67s came with seven engine choices.

radio with manual antenna ($133.76). 351 rear radio speaker ($15.80). 354 Delco stereo tape player ($128.49). Stereo multiplex adaptor (UPC unknown, price unavailable). 462 deluxe steering wheel (price unavailable). 471 custom sports steering wheel (price unavailable). 504 tilt steering wheel, not available with standard steering, three-speed column shift or Turbo-Hydra-Matic transmission without console (price unavailable). 731 Saf-T-Track differential (price unavailable). 491 rally stripes (price unavailable). 444 rally stripes ($31.60). 704 hood-mounted tachometer ($63.19). 524 custom shift knob (price unavailable). 472 console with bucket seats and floor shift ($47.39). 481 dual exhausts, standard with 400-cid V-8 ($30.23). 481 tailpipe extensions (price unavailable). 621 Ride & Handling package, standard with 326 H.O. and Firebird 400 ($9.32). 431 front and rear custom seat belts (price unavailable). 434 front seat shoulder belts (price unavailable). 521 front disc brakes, 502 recommended ($63.19). Hood retainer pins (UPC unknown, price unavailable). 494 dual horns, standard with custom trim (price unavailable). 738 rear axle options (no cost). OBC-SVT vinyl roof for sport coupe ($84.26). OBC custom trim option ($108.48). OBC Strato-Bench front seat ($31.60). 684 heavy-duty fan, base Sprint ($8.43). 514 heavy-duty thermo fan for 326 H.O. ($15.80). 674 heavy-duty

alternatror, standard with air conditioning ($15.80). 681 heavy-duty radiator, standard with air conditioning ($14.74). 361 heavy-duty dual-stage air cleaner ($9.43). 678 heavy-duty battery, included with 674 ($3.48). 453 Rally II wheels, available with 521 (with custom trim $55.81; with standard trim $72.67). 454 Rally I wheels, available with 521 (with custom trim $40.02; with standard trim $56.87). 461 deluxe wheel discs (price unavailable). 458 custom wheel discs (price unavailable). 452 wire wheel discs ($69.51). Two-tone paint in standard colors ($31.07). Two-tone paint in custom colors ($114.27). 185R-14 radial whitewall tires, on 400 ($10.53); on other models ($42.13). E70-14 red line or white sidewall tires, on 400 (no cost); on other models ($31.60).

Historical footnotes

Racecar builder and driver John Fitch marketed a performance-oriented "Fitchbird" package. In magazine road tests, the stock 1967 Firebird Sprint hardtop with 215 hp did 0 to 60 mph in 10 seconds and the quarter mile in 17.5 seconds. With the 325-hp Firebird 400 option, the times went down to 6.4 and 14.3 seconds. A second test driver clocked the Firebird 400 hardtop with the 325-hp motor at 14.7 seconds and 98 mph in the quarter mile.

A 1967 convertible 400 with automatic transmission and manual top.

Thomas Glatch Productions photo

The 1967 Sprint interior was all vinyl
with a standard manual 3-speed
on-the-floor transmission.

Thomas Glatch photo

The stylish Sprint featured a 215-hp,
overhead cam, four-barrel, 230-cid
engine.

Thomas Glatch Productions photo

The body stripes were a popular option on the 1967 Sprint.

Jim Thomson photo

The Firebird 400 convertible was a head turner in 1968.

Subtle Variations

The Firebird arrived so late in 1967, Pontiac had no time to make big changes for 1968. Or maybe they didn't want to. The vent windows went the way of the do-do bird and were replaced by one-piece side glass. Suspension upgrades included bias-mounted rear shocks and multi-leaf rear springs. Pontiac built 90,152 coupes (base price $2,781) and 16,960 ragtops (base price $2,996).

The $116 Sprint option included a three-speed manual gearbox with floor shift, an overhead-cam six, Sprint emblems, body sill moldings and four F70 x 14 tires. The 250-cid engine had a single four-barrel carburetor and 215 hp.

The appeal of the new $106 Firebird 350 option was a 265-hp V-8. The 350 H.O. option included three-speed manual transmission with column shift, dual exhausts, H.O. side stripes, a heavy-duty battery and four F70 x 14 tires.

The Firebird 400 option ($351-$435) added chrome engine parts, a sports suspension, dual exhausts, 400 emblems and a dual-scoop hood. Its 400-cid four-barrel V-8 produced 330 hp. The Ram Air 400 was about the same, except for its de-clutching fan and *functional* hood scoops. The Ram Air V-8 produced 335 hp and did 0 to 60 in 7.6 seconds. A quarter mile took 15.4 seconds.

Jim Thomson photo

The twin hood scoops identified the 400 engine. Most of the styling was unchanged from 1967.

COLORS

C=Cameo Ivory, D=Alpine Blue, E=Aegean Blue, F=Nordic Blue, G=April Gold, K=Meridian Turquoise, L=Aleutian Blue, N=Flambeau Burgundy, P=Springmist Green, Q=Verdoro Green, R=Solar Red, T=Primavera Beige, V=Nightshade Green, Y=Mayfair Maize.

I.D. NUMBERS

VIN stamped on a plate attached to the top of the dashboard. First symbol indicates GM division: 2=Pontiac. The second and third symbols indicate series: 23=Firebird. The fourth and fifth symbols indicate the body style: 37=two-door sport coupe (hardtop), 67=two-door convertible. The sixth symbol indicates model year: 8=1968. The seventh symbol indicates the assembly plant: U=Lordstown, Ohio; L=Van Nuys, California. The last six symbols are the sequential production number starting with 600001 for six-cylinder Firebirds and 100001 for V-8 Firebirds at each assembly plant. Body/style number plate under hood tells manufacturer, build date, Fisher style number, assembly plant, trim code, paint code and accessory codes. The build date takes the form 01A where the two digits indicate month (01=January) and the letter indicates week of the month (A=first week). The style number takes the form 68-22367 where the prefix 68=1968, the first symbol 2=Pontiac, the second and third symbols 23=Firebird series and the fourth and fifth symbols indicate body style (37=sport coupe and 67=convertible). The assembly plant code LOR=Lordstown, Ohio, or LOS=Van Nuys, California. The body number is the same as the sequential production number in the VIN. The Fisher body plate also carries trim and paint codes. VIN appears on front of engine at right-hand cylinder bank along with an alpha-numerical engine production code. Firebird engine production codes included: [250-cid, 175-hp OHC six] ZK-ZN. [250-cid, 215-hp OHC six] ZD-ZE. [350-cid, 265-hp V-8] WC-YJ. [350-cid, 320-hp V-8] YM-WK. [400-cid, 330-hp V-8] YT. [400-cid, 335-hp] WZ-WQ-YW. [Ram Air I 400-cid, 335-hp] WI-XN. [Ram Air II 400-cid, 345-hp] WU/XT.

FIREBIRD - (OHC-6) - SERIES 223

Base Firebird equipment included the standard GM safety features, front bucket seats, vinyl upholstery, a simulated burl woodgrain dashboard, an outside rearview mirror, side marker lights, E70 x 14 black sidewall wide-oval tires with a Space Saver spare and a larger-displacement 250-cid, 175-hp OHC six-cylinder engine. Styling was nearly identical to the 1967 1/2 Firebird except that the 1967 model's vent windows were replaced with one-piece side door glass. Technical changes included bias-mounted rear shock absorbers and multi-leaf rear springs.

Model Number	Body/Style Number	Body Type & Seating	Factory Price	Shipping Weight	Production Total
223	37	2d sport coupe-5P	$2,781	3,061 lbs.	Note 1
223	67	2d convertible-5P	$2,996	3,346 lbs.	Note 1

Note 1: Production by body style (all models) included 90,152 sport coupes and 16,960 convertibles.
Note 2: Production records were also recorded by the number of sixes and V-8s built with standard or deluxe appointments as listed in the next table.

FIREBIRD PRODUCTION NOTES

Model No.	Engine/Trim	Synchromesh	Automatic	Total
Model 223	Standard OHC six	7,528	8,441	15,969
Model 223	Standard V-8	16,632	39,250	55,882
Model 223	Deluxe OHC six	1,216	1,309	2,525
Model 223	Deluxe V-8	7,534	25,202	32,736
Totals		32,910	74,202	107,112

FIREBIRD SPRINT - (OHC-6) - SERIES 223

Sprint models featured a 215-hp OHC six with a four-barrel carburetor. A floor-mounted three-speed manual gearbox and heavy-duty suspension were standard. The Sprint version of the OHC six also featured a racier cam. Body still moldings with "3.8 Litre Overhead Cam" emblems were seen. Body side racing stripes were a popular and heavily-promoted Sprint option.

Model Number	Body/Style Number	Body Type & Seating	Factory Price	Shipping Weight	Production Total
223	37	2d sport coupe-5P	$2,897	3,010 lbs.	Note 3
223	67	2d convertible-5P	$3,112	3,302 lbs.	Note 3

Note 3: See notes 1 and 2.

FIREBIRD 350 - (V-8) - SERIES 223

The new Firebird 350 model featured a three-speed manual transmission with column shift and F70 x 14 tires. The 350-cid V-8 had a 3.88 x 3.75 bore and stroke, a 9.2:1 compression ratio, a Rochester two-barrel carburetor and 265 hp at 4600 rpm. Although the Pontiac V-8 heads had the same compression ratio, they had been redesigned with deeper, smoother combustion chambers and larger, more upright valves to promote a controlled combustion environment. They were part of Pontiac's emissions program, as was a new, thermostatically controlled carburetor pre-heating system.

Model Number	Body/Style Number	Body Type & Seating	Factory Price	Shipping Weight	Production Total
223	37	2d sport coupe-5P	$2,887	3,061 lbs.	Note 4

The base Firebird and Sprint came with an overhead cam straight six.

The 400 H.O. convertible was the top of the line for 1968 Firebirds.

223	67	2d convertible-5P	$3,102	3,346 lbs.	Note 4

Note 4: See notes 1 and 2 above.

FIREBIRD 350 H.O. - (V-8) SERIES 223

Standard equipment on the hot-performing H.O. version of the Firebird 350 included a three-speed manual transmission with column shift, a dual exhaust system, H.O. side stripes, a heavy-duty battery and four F70 x 14 tires. The engine was a 350-cid V-8 with 10.5:1 compression, a Rochester four-barrel carburetor and 320 hp at 5100 rpm. The price of the 350 H.O. was $181 over base model cost.

Model Number	Body/Style Number	Body Type & Seating	Factory Price	Shipping Weight	Production Total
223	22337	2d sport coupe-5P	$2,962	3,061 lbs.	Note 5
223	22367	2d convertible-5P	$3,177	3,346 lbs.	Note 5

Note 5: See notes 1 and 2.

FIREBIRD 400 - (V-8) - SERIES 223

The Firebird 400's standard equipment included a three-speed manual transmission with floor-mounted gear shifter, a chrome air cleaner, chrome rocker arm covers, a chrome oil cap, sports type springs and shock absorbers, a heavy-duty battery, dual exhausts, a hood emblem and dual scoop hood, F70 x 14 red line or white sidewall tires and a Power Flex variable pitch cooling fan.

Model Number	Body/Style Number	Body Type & Seating	Factory Price	Shipping Weight	Production Total
223	37	2d sport coupe-5P	$3,216	3,076 lbs.	Note 6

223	67	2d convertible-5P	$3,431	3,361 lbs.	Note 6

Note 6: See notes 1 and 2.
Note 7: Prices were $84 lower for cars with optional four-speed manual or Turbo-Hydra-Matic transmission.

FIREBIRD RAM AIR 400 - (V-8) SERIES 223

The Ram Air 400 model had the same inclusions as the Firebird 400, except for the addition of a de-clutching cooling fan and twin functional hood scoops. The engine was a 400-cid V-8 with 10.75:1 compression ratio, a Rochester four-barrel carburetor and 335 hp at 5000 rpm. It had a special high-lift camshaft, forged aluminum pistons, an Armasteel crankshaft, new push rods and guides, tulip-head valves and dual high-rate valve springs.

Model Number	Body/Style Number	Body Type & Seating	Factory Price	Shipping Weight	Production Total
223	37	2d sport coupe-5P	$3,412	3,061 lbs.	90,152
223	67	2d convertible-5P	$3,627	3,346 lbs.	16,960

Note 8: See notes 1 and 2.

ENGINES

Inline six-cylinder: Overhead valves. Cast-iron block. Displacement: 250 cu. in. Bore & stroke: 3.875 x 3.531 in. Compression ratio: 9.0:1. Brake horsepower: 175 at 4800 rpm. Torque: 240 ft. lbs. at 3800 rpm. Hydraulic valve lifters. Carburetor: Rochester model 7028065 one-barrel. Engine code: ZN with automatic transmission; ZK with manual transmission.

Inline six-cylinder [UPC L53]: Overhead valves.

Cast-iron block. Displacement: 250 cu. in. Bore & stroke: 3.875 x 3.531 in. Compression ratio: 10.5:1. Brake horsepower: 215 at 4800 rpm. Torque: 255 ft. lbs. at 3800 rpm. Hydraulic valve lifters. Carburetor: Rochester. Engine code: ZE with automatic transmission; ZD with manual transmission.

350 V-8 [UPC L30]: Overhead valves. Cast-iron block. Displacement: 350 cu. in. Bore & stroke: 3.875 x 3.75 in. Compression ratio: 9.2:1. Brake horsepower: 265 at 4600 rpm. Torque: 355 ft. lbs. at 2800 rpm. Hydraulic valve lifters. Carburetor: Rochester model 7028071 two-barrel. Engine code: YJ with automatic transmission; WC with manual transmission.

350 H.O. V-8 [UPC L76]: Overhead valves. Cast-iron block. Displacement: 350 cid. Bore & stroke: 3.875 x 3.75 in. Compression ratio: 10.5:1. Brake horsepower: 320 at 5100 rpm. Torque: 380 ft. lbs. at 3200 rpm. Hydraulic valve lifters. Carburetor: Rochester. Engine code: YM with automatic transmission; WK with manual transmission.

400 V-8 [UPC W66]: Overhead valves. Cast-iron block. Displacement: 400 cid. Bore & stroke: 4.125 x 3.75 in. Compression ratio: 10.75:1. Brake horsepower: 330 at 4800 rpm. Torque: 430 ft. lbs. at 3300 rpm. Five main bearings. Hydraulic valve lifters. Carburetor: Rochester four-barrel. Engine code: YW-YN with automatic transmission; WZ with manual transmission.

400 H.O. V-8 [UPC L74]: Overhead valves. Cast iron block. Displacement: 400 cid. Bore & stroke: 4.125 x 3.75 in. Compression ratio: 10.75:1. Brake horsepower: 335 at 5300 rpm. Torque: 430 ft. lbs. at 3400 rpm. Five main bearings. Hydraulic valve lifters. Carburetor: Rochester four-barrel. Engine code: YW with automatic transmission; WQ with manual transmission.

V-8 Ram Air I [UPC L67]: Overhead valves. Cast-iron block. Displacement: 400 cid. Bore & stroke: 4.125 x 3.75 in. Compression ratio: 10.75:1. Brake horsepower: 335 at 5000 rpm. Torque: 430 ft.-lbs. at 3600 rpm. Five main bearings. Hydraulic valve lifters. Carburetor: Rochester four-barrel. Engine code: XN with automatic transmission; WI with manual transmission.

V-8 Ram Air I [UPC L67]: Overhead valves. Cast-iron block. Displacement: 400 cid. Bore & stroke: 4.125 x 3.75 in. Compression ratio: 10.75:1. Brake horsepower: 340 at 5300 rpm. Torque: 430 ft. lbs. at 3600 rpm. Five main bearings. Hydraulic valve lifters. Carburetor: Rochester four-barrel. Engine code: XT with automatic transmission; WU with manual transmission.

CHASSIS

Wheelbase: 108.1 in. Overall length: 188.8 in. Front tread: 60 in. Rear tread: 60 in.

TECHNICAL

Body and frame: Integral body and frame with separate bolted-on sub frame for engine and front suspension. Front suspension: Independent with upper and lower control arms, coil springs, tubular shocks and stabilizer bar. Rear suspension: Hotchkiss solid axle with traction bars, anti-windup feature, single-leaf rear springs and tubular shocks. Steering: Optional power assist coaxial re-circulating ball bearing. Turning diameter: 38.4 ft. curb to curb. Turns lock to lock: 3.0. Fuel tank: 18.5 gal.

OPTIONS

591 speedometer gear adapter ($11.59). 731 heavy-duty air cleaner ($9.48). 582 custom air conditioner ($360.20). 701 heavy-duty battery, standard with four-barrel carburetor; OHC six without 582 ($15.80). 474 electric clock, not available with 394 ($15.80). 514 heavy-duty clutch and seven-blade fan, with V-8; without 582 ($15.80). 472 console, not available with contour bench seat ($50.55). 441

A Firebird coupe with the 350 V-8 came with a base price of $2,887 when it was new.

A.C. Bogarty photo

Dee Sherrow photo

This sharp 1968 Sprint convertible features a wood steering wheel, power top, dual exhaust, four-barrel OHC six and Rallye II wheels.

cruise control, not available with manual transmission ($52.66). 492 remote-control deck lid ($13.69). 404 rear window defogger, except convertible ($21.06). 361 Safe-T-Track differential ($42.13). 361 heavy-duty Safe-T-Track differential, with H, K, P, S axles ($63.19). 521 front disc brakes ($63.19). 342 four-barrel OHC Sprint six, without 582 ($116.6). 343 two-barrel 350-cid V-8 ($105.60). 344 four-barrel 350 H.O. V-8 ($180.58). 345 four-barrel 400-cid V-8 with 351, 354, 358 ($273.83); without 351, 354, 358 ($358.09). 347 four-barrel 400-cid Ram Air V-8, with 351, 354, 358; not available with 582 ($616.12). 348 four-barrel 400 H.O. V-8 with 351, 354, 358 ($350.72). 481 dual exhausts with 343 ($30.54). 482 exhaust extensions with 341, 342, 343 ($10.53); with 481, 344, 345, 347, 348 ($21.06). 444 auxiliary gauge cluster ($31.60). 531 all tinted glass ($30.54). 532 tinted windshield ($21.06). 412 door edge guards ($6.24). 571 contoured head restraints ($52.66). 414 dual horns ($4.21). 524 custom gearshift knob for cars with manual transmission and floor shifter ($4.21). 671 under-hood lamp ($3.16). 672 ignition switch lamp ($2.11). 652 luggage lamp ($3.16). 631 front floor mats ($6.85). 632 rear floor mats ($8.43). 732 trunk mat ($8.43). 422 right- and left-hand visor vanity mirrors ($4.21). 421 right-hand visor vanity mirror, except with 422 ($2.11). 424 left-hand remote-controlled outside rearview mirror ($9.48). SPS special solid paint, except code A black ($83.20). STT special two-tone paint, coupe ($114.80). RTT two-tone paint, standard color on coupe ($31.60). SPR special paint code, code A black only ($10.53). 502 power brakes ($42.13). 561 full-width four-way power bench seat ($69.51). 501 power steering ($94.79). 564 left-hand four-way power bucket seat ($69.51). 544 power convertible top ($52.66). 551 power windows ($100.05). 381 manually operated rear antenna ($9.48). 394 stereo tape player, not available with 391 or 392 ($133.76). 382 push-button radio with antenna ($61.09). 384 push-button AM/FM radio and manual antenna ($133.76). 391 rear seat speaker ($15.80). 494 rally side stripes, not available with 344 ($14.74). 431 front and rear seat custom seat belts ($9.48). 432 rear shoulder belts with 431 or 754 ($26.33). 754 front seat shoulder belts, with 431 ($26.33); without 431 ($23.17). 568 contour bench seat ($31.60). 604 rear folding seat ($42.13). 634 adjustable front and rear shock absorbers ($52.66).

442 Safeguard speedometer ($10.53). 621 Ride & Handling package without 345 ($9.48). Ride & Handling package with 345 ($4.21). 471 custom sport steering wheel, with 554 ($30.54); without 554 ($45.29). 462 deluxe steering wheel ($14.74). 504 tilt wheel, not available with three-speed column shift or Hydra-Matic without console; power steering required ($42.13). 434 hood-mounted tachometer ($63.19). 402 spare tire cover ($5.27). SVT Cordova vinyl top on coupe ($84.26). 351 Turbo-Hydra-Matic with 345, 347, 348 ($236.97). 352 automatic with 341, 342, 343, 344 ($194.84). 354 four-speed manual transmission with floor shift, without 37S axle ($184.31). 355 heavy-duty three-speed with floor shift with 343, 344 ($84.26); with 345, 348 (no cost). 356 heavy-duty three-speed with floor shift, use with 472, include with 342 ($42.13). 358 close-ratio four-speed manual transmission with floor shift, mandatory with 37S axle ($184.31). 534 custom pedal trim, not available with 554 ($5.27). 458 custom wheel discs, with 554 ($20.01); without 554 ($73.72). 453 Rally II rims with 554 ($63.19); without 554 ($84.26). 321 front foam cushion ($86.37). 554 custom trim option, includes dual horns, deluxe wheel discs, deluxe steering wheel, custom trim pedal plates, front and rear wheel opening moldings, roof rail moldings, windshield pillar garnish moldings and custom seat, door and quarter panel trim ($114.88). 332 lamp group ($5.25). 331 mirror group, except convertible ($13.22). 322 rear window defogger-protection group ($55.25). THC E70-14 red stripe tires with 341 engine ($31.60). THD E70-14 white stripe tires with 341 engine ($31.60). THE E70-14 black sidewall tires with 341 (no charge). TKM 195R-14 white sidewall rayon radial tires, not available with 461; with 341 engine ($56.87); with 342, 343, 344 engine ($42.13); with 345, 347, 348 engines ($10.53). TMC F70-14 redline nylon tires, with 341 engine ($46.34); with 342, 343, 344 engine ($31.60); with 345, 347, 348 engines (no cost). TME F70-14 black sidewall nylon tires, with 341 engine ($14.74); with 342, 343, 344 engine (no cost).

HISTORICAL FOOTNOTES

Production started Aug. 21, 1967. The model introductions were Sept. 21, 1967. Model year output was 107,112 Firebirds. Model year sales stood at 96,510 Firebirds. Calendar year sales hit 91,813 Firebirds

This car was a pilot version of the soon-to-be-released 1969 Trans Am.

Midyear Motivation

Flatter wheel openings, front fender wind splits, new rooflines and a creased lower beltline characterized 1969 Firebirds. The gas filler moved behind the rear license plate and a rectangular Pontiac-style split bumper grille was used. Square body-colored Endura bezels held the headlamps. Headlines were made when the Trans Am arrived March 8, 1969, at the Chicago Auto Show. It was the slinkiest Firebird model-option up to this point.

Standard equipment for Firebirds included vinyl bucket seats, grained dashboards, carpeting, outside mirrors and side marker lamps. The hardtop listed for $2,831 and the ragtop for $3,045. Model options included Sprint ($121 extra), 350 ($111 extra), 350 H.O. ($186 extra), 400 ($275-$358 extra), 400 H.O. ($351-$435 extra) and Ram Air 400 ($832 extra), plus the Trans Am.

The features of each model were similar to 1968. The Trans Am included a heavy-duty three-speed manual gear box with floor shifter, 3.55:1 axle, glass-belted tires, heavy-duty shocks and springs, 1-inch stabilizer bar, power front disc brakes, variable-ratio power steering, engine-air extractors, a rear-deck air foil, a black-textured grille, full-length body stripes, white-and-blue finish, a leather-covered steering wheel and special identification decals. The new Trans Am hardtop had a base price of $3,556 and a production run of just 689 units. The convertible cost some $150 additional and only eight were built.

The Trans Am grew out of the Sports Car Club of America's Trans-American sedan racing series. Pontiac paid the SCCA a $5 royalty per car to use the name. The T/A was originally planned with a special super-high-performance 303-cid small-block V-8 that would have made it race eligible. About 25 cars were fitted with the short-stroke 303-cid tunnel-port V-8s, but these were used exclusively for SCCA Trans-Am racing. Production models could have either a 335-hp 400 H.O. (a.k.a. Ram Air III) V-8 or an optional 345-hp Ram Air IV engine. Quarter-miles times for Trans Ams were in the 14- to 14.5-second bracket.

I.D. NUMBERS

The VIN is on the left top of the instrument panel, visible through windshield. The first symbol indicates the GM division: 2=Pontiac. The second and third symbols indicate series: 23=Firebird. The fourth and fifth symbols indicate body style: 37=two-door sport coupe (hardtop), 67=two-door convertible. The sixth symbol indicates model year: 9=1969. The seventh symbol tells assembly plant: U=Lordstown, Ohio; L=Van Nuys, California; N=Norwood, Ohio. The last six symbols are the sequential production number starting with 600001 for six-cylinder Firebirds and 100001 for V-8 Firebirds at each assembly plant. Body/style number plate under hood tells the manufacturer, the Fisher style number, the assembly plant, the trim code, the paint code and build date. The style number takes the form 69-22337 where the prefix 69=1969, the first symbol 2=Pontiac, the second and third symbols 23=Firebird series and the fourth and fifth symbols indicate body style (37=sport coupe and 67=convertible). The assembly plant codes are: LOR=Lordstown, Ohio; LOS=Los Angeles (Van Nuys), California; NOR=Norwood, Ohio. The VIN appears on front of engine at right-hand cylinder bank along with an alpha-numerical engine production code. Engine production codes included: [250-cid, 175-hp OHC six] ZC-ZF-ZK-ZN. [250-cid, 215-hp OHC six] ZL-ZE. [250-cid, 230-hp OHC six] ZH-ZD. [350-cid, 265-hp

V-8] WM-XB-XL-YE-WC-YJ. [350-cid, 325-hp V-8]
WN-XC-XD-XG-WK. [400-cid, 330-hp V-8]. WZ-YT.
[400-cid, 335-hp] WQ. [400-cid, 345-hp] WH-XN.

COLORS

40=Mayfair Maize, 50=Cameo Ivory, 51=Liberty
Blue, 52=Matador Red, 53=Warwick Blue, 55=Crystal
Turquoise, 57=Midnight Green, 59=Limelight Green,
61=Expresso Brown, 63=Champagne, 65=Antique
Gold, 67=Burgundy, 69=Palladium Silver, 72=Carousel Red, 73=Verdoro Green, 76=Goldenrod Yellow
and 87=Windward Blue.

BASE FIREBIRD - (OHC-6) SERIES 223

Standard equipment for base Firebirds included
vinyl bucket seats, a camera case grained dashboard,
carpeting, outside mirrors, a heater and defroster,
side marker lamps, small hubcaps, a 250-cid OHC six-cylinder engine, a three-speed manual transmission
with column-mounted gearshift, E70 x 14 tires and a
Space Saver spare tire. An optional Custom Trim
package added breathable knit-style vinyl upholstery,
bright roof rail interior moldings, woodgrain dashboard trim, a molded trunk mat, integral front armrests, padded door panels, a passenger assist grip and
assorted interior and exterior trim items.

Model Number	Body/Style Number	Body Type & Seating	Factory Price	Shipping Weight	Production Total
223	37	2d sport coupe-5P	$2,830	3,080 lbs.	75,362
223	67	2d convertible-5P	$3,044	3,330 lbs.	11,649

Note 1: The production totals shown are for all Firebird sport coupes and convertibles including Trans Am. There are no breakouts by option package except for Trans Am.

FIREBIRD SPRINT - (OHC-6) SERIES 223

The Sprint Six package was an extra-cost option
UPC 342. It included the UPC W53 Sprint version of
the 250-cid OHC six-cylinder engine (with a higher
compression ratio, larger valves, a hotter cam grind
and a four-barrel carburetor), a low-restriction
exhaust system, a three-speed manual transmission
with floor-mounted shifter, red Sprint badges on the
rocker panel moldings and a heavy-duty suspension..

Model Number	Body/Style Number	Body Type & Seating	Factory Price	Shipping Weight	Production Total
223	37	2d sport coupe-5P	$2,951	3,080 lbs.	Note 2
223	67	2d convertible-5P	$3,165	3,330 lbs.	Note 2

Note 2: See note 1.

FIREBIRD 350 - (V-8) - SERIES 223

The Firebird 350 option (UPC L30) included a
three-speed manual transmission with column shift
and F70 x 14 tires. The engine was a 350-cid V-8 with
a 9.2:1 compression ratio, a Rochester two-barrel carburetor and 265 hp at 4600 rpm.

Model Number	Body/Style Number	Body Type & Seating	Factory Price	Shipping Weight	Production Total
223	37	2d sport coupe-5P	$2,941	—	Note 3
223	67	2d convertible-5P	$3,155	—	Note 3

Note 3: See note 1.
Note 4: The Firebird 350 package retailed for $110.88, but a contemporary *Motor Trend* road test showed a vehicle price of $2,814.

FIREBIRD 350 H.O. - (V-8) SERIES 223

This option package (UPC 344; engine code L-76)
included a three-speed manual transmission with column shift, a dual exhaust system and a heavy-duty
battery. Side stripes were no longer available for cars

Firebird coupes could still be had for less than $3,000 in 1969.

This Firebird 400 convertible included a special hood with twin air scoops, which were functional on the 400 H.O. model.

with the H.O. option. The engine was a 350-cid V-8 with a 10.5:1 compression ratio, a Rochester four-barrel carburetor and 325 hp at 5100 rpm.

Model Number	Body/Style Number	Body Type & Seating	Factory Price	Shipping Weight	Production Total
223	37	2d sport coupe-5P	$3,137	—	Note 5
223	67	2d convertible-5P	$3,230	—	Note 5

Note 5: See note 1.

FIREBIRD 400 - (V-8) - SERIES 223

This option package (UPC 345; engine code WS6) included chrome engine parts, a dual exhaust system, a heavy-duty battery, a three-speed manual transmission with floor shifter, F70 x 14 red stripe or white sidewall tires and a variable pitch cooling fan. The engine was a 400-cid V-8 with a 10.75:1 compression ratio, a Rochester four-barrel carburetor and 330 hp at 4800 rpm. A special hood is used on the Firebird 400 and incorporates non-functional air scoops. Also, a Ride & Handling package was required. Price: $275-$358 over base model cost depending on transmission.

Model Number	BodyStyle Number	Body Type & Seating	Factory Price	Shipping Weight	Production Total
223	37	2d sport coupe-5P	$3,262	—	Note 6
223	67	2d convertible-5P	$3,460	—	Note 6

Note 6: See note 1.
Note 7: Package price varied according to body style and transmission. Prices shown based on coupe and convertible without Turbo-Hydra-Matic.

FIREBIRD RAM AIR 400 - (V-8) SERIES 223

This option (UPC 348; engine code L-74) included the same features as the Firebird 400, except for addition of de-clutching cooling fan and twin functional hood scoops with operating mechanism. The package price was $558.20.

Model Number	Body/Style Number	Body Type & Seating	Factory Price	Shipping Weight	Production Total
223	37	2d sport coupe-5P	$3,388	—	Note 8
223	67	2d convertible-5P	$3,602	—	Note 8

Note 8: See note 1.

FIREBIRD RAM AIR IV - (V-8) SERIES 223

This option (UPC 347; engine code L-67) includes the same features as the Ram Air 400, plus special hood scoop emblems. The engine is a 400-cid V-8 with a special camshaft and valve train, a 10.75:1 compression ratio, a Rochester four-barrel carburetor and 345 hp at 5400 rpm. Price: $832 over base model cost. Specific transmissions were required. A 3.90:1 ratio rear axle was standard and a 4.33:1 ratio rear axle was optional.

Model Number	Body/Style Number	Body Type & Seating	Factory Price	Shipping Weight	Production Total
223	37	2d sport coupe-5P	$3,662	—	Note 9
223	67	2d convertible-5P	$3,876	—	Note 9

Note 9: See note 1.

TRANS AM - (V-8) - SERIES 223

The option (sales code 322; UPC WS4; engine code L74) included a heavy-duty three-speed manual gearbox with a floor-mounted gearshift, a 3.55:1 rear axle, fiberglass-belted tires, heavy-duty shock absorbers, heavy-duty springs, a one-inch stabilizer bar, power front disc brakes, variable ratio power steering, engine air exhaust louvers on sides of fender, a rear deck lid air foil, a black textured grille, full-length body stripes, white and blue finish, a leather covered steering wheel and special identification decals. The engine was the UPC L74 400 H.O. V-8 with 335 hp. Certain features listed as "standard equipment" in the first printing of sales literature were not used on production Trans Ams. They included a driver-controlled hood scoop, a chrome air cleaner cover and a leather-grained sport steering wheel. According to Firebird expert Eric J. Vicker, Jr., the price listed on the Pontiac build sheet for a standard Trans Am was $1,025 over base model cost. Apparently, the retail price of the Trans Am over the Firebird 400 was $1,163.74. That included $508.70 for the Ram Air V-8, $232.76 for mandatory options including power front disc brakes, variable-ratio power steering and a 3.55:1 ratio rear axle and $421.28 for the other Trans Am goodies. Adding the Ram Air IV V-8 required the expenditure of an additional $558.20.

Model Number	Body/Style Number	Body Type & Seating	Factory Price	Shipping Weight	Production Total
223	37	2d Sport Coupe-5P	$3,556	—	689
223	67	2d Convertible-5P	$3,770	—	8

Note 10: Trans Am production breakout shown here is also included in figures above explained by Note 1.

The 400 H.O. was definitely geared to the fast-paced crowd.

ENGINES

Inline six-cylinder:. Overhead camshaft. Cast-iron block. Displacement: 250 cid. Bore & stroke: 3.875 x 3.531 in. Compression ratio: 9.0:1. Brake horsepower: 175 at 4800 rpm. Torque: 240 ft. lbs. at 2600 rpm. Hydraulic valve lifters. Carburetor: Rochester model 7028065 one-barrel.

Inline Sprint six-cylinder [UPC W53]: Overhead camshaft. Cast-iron block. Displacement: 250 cid. Bore & stroke: 3.875 x 3.531 in. Compression ratio: 10.5:1. Brake horsepower: 215 at 5200 rpm. Torque: 255 ft. lbs. at 3800 rpm. Hydraulic valve lifters. Carburetor: Rochester four-barrel.

303 V-8 Competition only [UPC L32]: Overhead camshaft. Cast-iron block. Displacement: 303 cid. Bore & stroke: 4.12 x 2.83 in. Compression ratio: 12.8:1. Brake horsepower: 475 at 8000 rpm. Solid valve lifters. Carburetor: Rochester four-barrel.

350 V-8 [UPC L30]: Overhead valves. Cast-iron block. Displacement: 350 cid. Bore & stroke: 3.875 x 3.75 in. Compression ratio: 9.2:1. Brake horsepower: 265 at 4600 rpm. Torque: 355 ft. lbs. at 2800 rpm. Hydraulic valve lifters. Carburetor: Rochester two-barrel.

350 H.O. V-8 [UPC L76]: Overhead valves. Cast-iron block. Displacement: 350 cid. Bore & stroke: 3.875 x 3.75 in. Compression ratio: 10.5:1. Brake horsepower: 325 at 5100 rpm. Torque: 380 ft. lbs. at

3200 rpm. Hydraulic valve lifters. Carburetor: Rochester four-barrel.

400 V-8 [UPC W66]: Overhead valves. Cast-iron block. Displacement: 400 cid. Bore & stroke: 4.125 x 3.75 in. Compression ratio: 10.75:1. Brake horsepower: 330 at 4800 rpm. Torque: 430 ft. lbs. at 3300 rpm. Five main bearings. Hydraulic valve lifters. Carburetor: Rochester four-barrel.

400 H.O. V-8 [UPC L74]: Overhead valves. Cast-iron block. Displacement: 400 cid. Bore & stroke: 4.125 x 3.75 in. Compression ratio: 10.75:1. Brake horsepower: 335 at 5000 rpm. Torque: 430 ft. lbs. at 3400 rpm. Five main bearings. Hydraulic valve lifters. Carburetor: Rochester four-barrel.

400 Ram Air IV V-8 [UPC L67]: Overhead valves. Cast-iron block. Displacement: 400 cid. Bore & stroke: 4.125 x 3.75 in. Compression ratio: 10.75:1. Brake horsepower: 345 at 5400 rpm. Torque: 430 ft. lbs. at 3700 rpm. Five main bearings. Hydraulic valve lifters. Carburetor: Rochester four-barrel.

CHASSIS

Wheelbase: 108.1 in. Overall length: 191.1 in. Overall width: 73.9 in. Overall height: 49.6 in. Front tread: 60 in. Rear tread: 60 in.

TECHNICAL

All except Trans Am: Body and frame: Integral body and frame with separate bolted-on sub-frame for engine and front suspension. Front suspension: Independent with upper and lower control arms, coil springs, tubular shocks and stabilizer bar. Rear suspension: Hotchkiss solid axle with traction bars, anti-windup feature, single-leaf rear springs and tubular shocks. Steering: Optional power assist coaxial re-circulating ball bearing. Turning diameter: 38.4 ft. curb to curb. Turns lock to lock: 3.0. Fuel tank: 18.5 gal.

Trans Am: Body and frame: Integral body and frame with separate bolted-on sub-frame for engine and front suspension. Front suspension: Independent with upper and lower control arms, heavy-duty coil springs, heavy-duty tubular shocks and one-inch-diameter stabilizer bar. Rear suspension: Hotchkiss solid axle with traction bars, anti-windup feature, heavy-duty rear springs and heavy-duty tubular shocks. Steering: Saginaw variable-ratio steering with power assist. Ratios: 16.1 to 12.4:1. Turning diameter: 38.5 ft. curb-to-curb. Fuel tank: 18.5 gal.

OPTIONS

582/C60 custom air conditioning, not available with Sprint or Ram Air ($375.99). 731/K45 heavy-duty dual-stage air cleaner ($9.48). 682/K82 heavy-duty 55-amp alternator with 341 or 342 ($15.80). 688/K82 heavy-duty 55-amp alternator, V-8 only, not available with 582 (with 343 or 344 price is $26.33; with 345, 347 or 348 price is $15.80). 672/UA1 heavy-duty battery standard with 344, 345, 347, 348 and 582; ($4.21 with others). 474/U35 electric clock, included with 484 and not available with 444 ($15.80). 472/D55 console with bucket seats ($53.71). SVT/G08 Cordova top on coupe ($89.52). 441/K30 cruise control for cars with automatic trans-

The 1969 Trans Am was a bold new 'Bird.

mission and V-8 ($57.93). 492/A90 remote-control deck lid release ($14.74). 404/C50 rear window defogger, not available with convertible ($22.12). 481/N10 dual exhausts, available with 343 ($30.54). 691/KB2 heavy-duty Power Flex fan, for all without 582 ($10.53); for V-8 with 582 (no cost). 534/M09 gear knob for floor-shifted manual transmission ($5.27). 532/A02 tinted windshield ($22.12). 531/A01 all-tinted glass ($32.65). 412/B93 door edge guards ($6.24). 414/U05 dual horns ($4.21). 694/V64 Instant-Aire pump, not available with 347 or 611 ($15.80). 652/U25 luggage lamp ($3.16). 671/U26 underhood lamp ($4.21). 631/B32 front floor mats ($6.85). 632/B33 rear floor mats ($6.32). 424/D33 right-hand visor vanity mirror ($2.11). 422/DH5 left-hand visor vanity mirror ($2.11). SPO special solid colors, for coupe without vinyl top ($115.85); for convertible or for coupe with vinyl top ($100.05). RTT standard two-tone color, except convertible ($31.60). SPR special color codes F, T, W ($12.64). 514/JL1 custom pedal trim plates ($5.27). 501/N41 variable-ratio power steering ($105.32). 564/A46 left-hand power bucket seat ($73.72). 544/C06 power convertible top ($52.66). 551/A31 power windows ($105.32). 502/J50 power brakes, not available with 345, 347 or 348 ($42.13). 511/JL2 power front disc brakes ($64.25). 588/C57 Power-Flow ventilation, not available teamed with 582 ($42.13). 701/V01 heavy-duty radiator, not available with 582 ($14.74). 382/U63 AM radio with manual antenna ($61.09). 384/U69 AM/FM radio with manual antenna ($133.76). 388/U58 AM/FM stereo radio with manual antenna ($239.08). 484/W63 rally gauge cluster with clock, without 442 or 444 ($47.39). 444/U30 rally gauge cluster and tachometer, without 442, 474 or 484 ($84.26). 621/Y96 Ride & Handling springs and shocks, (with 345, 347 and 348 price was $4.21; with 341, 342, 343 and 344 price was $9.48). 604/A67 rear folding seat ($42.13). 431/WS1 custom front seat belts, includes shoulder straps, in coupe ($12.64); in convertible ($36.86). 432/WS2 custom front seat belts, includes front and rear shoulder straps, in coupe ($38.97); in convertible ($63.19). 438/AS1 front shoulder straps, convertible only ($10.53). 708/N65 Space Saver spare tire, without

454 ($15.80); with 454 (no cost). 402/P17 spare tire cover, not available with 708 ($5.27). 504/N33 tilt steering, not available with manual steering or column-shifted manual transmission ($45.29). 391/U80 rear speaker, not available in 388 or 394 ($15.80), 442/U15 Safeguard speedometer, not available with 484 or 444 ($11.59). 461/N30 deluxe steering wheel ($15.80). 462/N34 custom sports steering wheel, with 342 ($34.76); without 342 ($50.55). 394/U57 stereo tape player, not available with 391 ($133.76). 471/UB5 hood-mounted tachometer ($63.19). 554/W54 Custom trim option, for coupe with knit-vinyl bench seat ($110.99). 554/W54 Custom trim option, for coupe with bucket seats ($780.99). 554/W54 Custom trim option, for coupe with leather bucket seats ($199.05). 452/P02 Custom wheel covers ($20.01 with 324; $41.07 without 324). 451/P01 Deluxe wheel covers ($21.06). 453/N95 wire wheel covers ($52.66 with 324; $73.72 without 324). 454/N98 Rally II wheels ($63.19 with 324; $84.26 without 324). 321/Y88 Basic group ($113.75). 324/Y86 Décor group ($62.14). 331/WS6 power-assist group with 341 or 342 ($364.93); with 343 ($375.49); with 344, 345, 347 or 348 ($396.61). 332/WS5 turnpike cruise group, with Turbo-Hydra-Matic, V-8 and 505 ($176.94). 334/W58 Rally group all 345, 347, 348 with 324 ($149.55). 334/W58 Rally group all 345, 347, 348 without 324 ($186.41). 334/W58 Rally group all 341, 342, 343, 344 with 324 ($154.82). 334/W58 Rally group all 341, 342, 343, 344 without 324 ($191.68). 342/W53 Sprint Sport option, without 582 ($129.54). 343/L30 Firebird 350 Sport option ($110.59). 344/W66 Firebird 400 Sport option, for coupe with 351, 354 or 358 ($347.56). 344/W66 Firebird 400 Sport option, for convertible with 351, 354 or 358 ($331.76). 344/W66 Firebird 400 Sport option, for coupe without 351, 354 or 358 ($431.81). 344/W66 Firebird 400 Sport option, for convertible without 351, 354 or 358 ($416.01). 322/WS4 Trans Am option, with 354 only ($724.60). 341/STD OHC six-cylinder engine with one-barrel carburetor (no cost). 348/L74 400-cid V-8 engine with Ram Air induction and four-barrel carburetor, with 345 ($358). 348/L74 400-cid V-8 engine with Ram Air IV

induction and four-barrel carburetor, with 345 ($558.20). 361/G80 Safe-T-Track rear axle, regular ($42.13). 361/G80 Safe-T-Track rear axle, heavy-duty ($63.19). 364/G95-G97 economy axle ($2.11). 368/G90-G92 performance axle ($2.11). 362/G94-G83 special order axle ($2.11). 359/M38 Turbo-Hydra-Matic transmission, with 341 or 342 ($195.36); with 343 ($205.92). 351/M40 heavy-duty Turbo-Hydra-Matic transmission with 344, 345, 347 or 348 ($227.04). 352/M31 two-speed automatic transmission, with 341 ($163.68); with 343 ($174.24). 353/standard. Three-speed manual transmission with column shift, with 341, 343 or 344 (no cost). 354/M20 four-speed manual transmission with floor shift, with all except 347, V-8; with 3.90 axle ($195.36). 355/M13 heavy-duty three-speed manual transmission with floor shift, with 343 or 344 ($84.26). 356/M12 three-speed manual transmission with floor shift, with 341 ($42.13); with 342 (no cost). 358/M21 close-ratio four-speed manual transmission with floor shift, with 390 ($195.36). HR/PL3 E78-14 white sidewall tires, with 341 ($26.33 extra). GF/PX5 F78-14 black sidewall tires ($14.74 extra). GR/PX6 F78-14 white sidewall tires ($28.44 extra). MT/PY5 F70-14 red sidewall tires ($74.78 extra). MT/PY4 F70-14 white sidewall tires ($74.78 extra).

GROUP OPTIONS

BASIC GROUP: [Sales code 321; UPC Y88] included a push-button radio, foam front seat cushion and rear foam seat cushion. Dealer cost $87.83. Retail price: $113.75.

CUSTOM TRIM: [Sales code 554; UPC W54] For Firebirds with bucket seats, included woodgrain instrument panel inserts, an instrument panel passenger assist grip, bright roof rail moldings, bright interior side moldings, Custom knit vinyl upholstery, Custom door and quarter panel trim and a molded trunk mat. Dealer cost: $62.49. Retail price: $78.99.

LEATHER CUSTOM TRIM: [Sales code 554; UPC W54] For Firebirds with bucket seats, included woodgrain instrument panel inserts, an instrument panel passenger assist grip, bright roof rail moldings, bright interior side moldings, custom knit vinyl upholstery, custom door and quarter panel trim, a molded trunk mat, gold leather and expanded Morrokide seat surfaces. Dealer cost: $157.47. Retail price: $199.05.

DÉCOR GROUP: [Sales code 324; UPC Y86] Included deluxe wheel covers, a deluxe steering wheel, a brake pedal trim package, décor moldings and dual horns. Dealer cost: $98.32 in coupe; $97.48 in convertible. Retail price: $124.28 in coupe; $123.32 in convertible.

POWER ASSIST GROUP: [Sales code 331; UPC WS6] Included Turbo-Hydra-Matic transmission, variable-ratio power steering and front power disc brakes. Retail price: $365-$397, included in Trans Am model option.

RALLY GROUP: [Sales code 334; UPC WS8] Included custom sport steering wheel, Rally II wheel rims, Rally gauge cluster and clock and Ride & Handling package. Dealer cost $118.31 or $147.47 when teamed with Décor group option. Retail price $149.55 or $186.41 when teamed with Décor group option. Standard in Trans Am.

TURNPIKE CRUISE GROUP: [Sales code 332; UPC W55] Included cruise control, tilt steering wheel, power-operated bench seat or left-hand bucket seat. Dealer cost $139.98. Retail price: $176.94.

HISTORICAL FOOTNOTES

Calendar-year sales of Firebirds came to 55,402 cars for a 0.65 percent market share. The high-performance Trans Am was introduced March 8, 1969. Because of slow sales and late introductions of next-year models, 1969 Firebirds left in stock were carried over and sold through the following fall. A total of 87,709 Firebirds and Trans Ams were built during the 1969 model year. Of these: 20,840 Firebirds and Trans Ams had synchromesh transmission and 66,868 had automatic transmission. 114 Trans Ams had the L-74 Ram Air III V-8 and Turbo-Hydra-Matic. 520 Trans Ams had the L-74 Ram Air V-8 and synchromesh. Eight Trans Am convertibles were made. All Trans Am convertibles had the L74 V-8; four had manual transmission. Nine Trans Am coupes had the L67 Ram Air IV engine and Turbo-Hydra-Matic transmission. Forty-six Trans Am coupes had the L67 Ram Air IV engine and manual transmission.

Full-length body stripes made the new 1969 Trans Ams easy to spot.

The menacing T/A hood hid either a 335-hp H.O. V-8 or 345-HP Ram Air V-8.

The Trans Ams had plenty of power with either the Ram Air IV or Ram Air 400 engines.

They Called It The "Beginning of Tomorrow"

The 1970 Firebirds arrived late, but were worth the wait. Car magazines raved about the Maserati-inspired Endura nose with twin recessed grilles. Standard equipment on base Firebirds included a 250-cid, 155-hp six, glass-belted tires, front bucket seats, vinyl upholstery, a woodgrained dash, carpeting, an outside mirror, manual front disc brakes, wide wheel rims and door pockets. There was only a hardtop model with a $2,875 base price and 18,874 were built.

Styling changes for the 1970 Firebird began at the front, where there was a new Endura rubber front end with dual recessed grilles and single headlights. Split side marker lamps, enlarged wheel openings, flush door handles and smooth, clean, curvy body panels brought Pontiac's sports-compact car up to date. Firebird lettering and engine badges were behind the front wheel cutouts.

A new Firebird model had chrome "Esprit" signatures on its roof pillars, knit-vinyl upholstery, a deluxe steering wheel, dual sport mirrors, concealed wipers and antenna, trunk floor mats, wheel trim rings, decor moldings and a 350-cid two-barrel V-8. Esprits sold for $3,241 and 18,961 were built.

The performance-oriented Firebird 400 became the Formula 400. It included fat stabilizer bars, high-rate springs, wind-up rear axle controls, bias-belted tires, extra-wide wheel rims, manual front disc brakes and rear drums, carpet, vinyl interiors, front and rear bucket type seats, dual outside sport mirrors, concealed wipers and antennas and a deluxe steering wheel. Power came from a 400-cid four-barrel V-8 with 10.25:1 compression and 265 hp and a three-

speed Hurst floor shift. The Formula 400 had extra-long twin hood scoops and model nameplates. It sold for $3,370 and just 7,708 were built.

The second Trans Am was all new, but basically similar in features to the 1969 1/2 version. Front air dams, front and rear spoilers, a shaker hood, side air extractors, a rear-end spoiler and aerodynamic outside mirrors gave it an exotic sports car look. It included front and rear stabilizers, heavy-duty shock absorbers and springs, engine-turned dash inserts, a rally gauge cluster, concealed wipers, bucket seats, carpets, vinyl upholstery, power brakes and steering and 11-inch wide, 15-inch diameter Rally rims with wide F60-15 white-letter tires. Trans Ams had white or blue finish with contrasting racing stripes. They were base priced at $4,305 and had a production run of 3,196 units.

The standard V-8 in the new Trans Am was a 400-cid 335-hp Ram Air HO (Ram Air III) V-8. An improved Ram Air IV with 370 hp was available for $390. A wide-ratio four-speed manual gearbox with Hurst floor shift was standard. The Ram Air III T/A did 0 to 60 mph in 6.0 seconds and the quarter mile in 14.6. *Hot Rod* magazine road tested a white 1970 Trans Am with the 400-cid Ram Air IV V-8, a four-speed manual transmission and 3.73:1 gears and recorded a 13.90-second quarter mile at 102 mph.

I.D. NUMBERS

The VIN is on the left top of the instrument panel, visible through windshield. The first symbol indicates the GM division: 2=Pontiac. The second and third symbols indicate series: 23=Base Firebird; 24=Firebird Esprit; 26=Formula Firebird; 28=Trans Am. The fourth and fifth symbols indicate body style: 87=two-door sport coupe (hardtop). The sixth symbol indicates model year: 0=1970. The seventh symbol tells assembly plant: L=Van Nuys, California; N=Norwood,

Ohio. The last six symbols are the sequential production number starting with 600001 for six-cylinder Firebirds and 100001 for V-8 Firebirds at each assembly plant. Body/style number plate under hood tells the manufacturer, the Fisher style number, the assembly plant, the trim code, the paint code and build date. The style number takes the form 70-22387 where the prefix 70=1970, the first symbol 2=Pontiac, the second and third symbols indicate 23=Firebird series and the fourth and fifth symbols indicate body style (87=sport coupe). The assembly plant codes are: LOS=Los Angeles (Van Nuys), California, NOR=Norwood, Ohio. Engine production codes included: [250-cid, 155-hp six] ZB-ZG. [350-cid, 255-hp V-8] WU-YU. [400-cid, 265-hp V-8] XX. [400-cid, 330-hp] WT-YS. [400-cid, 335-hp] WS-YZ. [400-cid, 345-hp V-8] WW (manual)-XP (automatic).

COLORS

10=Polar White, 14=Palladium Silver, 25=Bermuda Blue, 26=Lucerne Blue, 28=Atoll Blue, 43=Keylime Green, 45=Palisade Green, 47=Verdoro Green, 51=Goldenrod Yellow, 53=Coronado Gold, 58=Granada Gold, 63=Palomino Copper, 65=Carousel Red, 67=Castillian Bronze and 75=Cardinal Red.

BASE FIREBIRD - (SIX/V-8) SERIES 223

Styling changes included Endura rubber front ends with dual recessed grilles, single headlights, split side marker lamps, enlarged wheel openings, flush door handles and smooth, clean, curvy body panels. Firebird lettering and engine badges appeared behind front wheel cutouts. The only body type offered was a sleek-looking sports coupe. Standard equipment on base Firebirds included a 250-cid 155-hp six, an Endura front bumper, E78-14 black sidewall fiberglass tires, front bucket seats, rear bucket type seats, a front stabilizer bar, side marker lights, all-vinyl upholstery, a woodgrained dashboard, carpeting, an outside rearview mirror, manual front disc/rear drum brakes, six-inch wheel rims and door storage pockets. A 350-cid 255-hp V-8 was optional.

Model Number	Body/Style Number	Body Type & Seating	Factory Price	Shipping Weight	Production Total
223	87	2d sport coupe-4P	$2,875	3,140 lbs.	18,874

Note 1: 2,899 base Firebirds had manual transmission and 15,975 had automatic transmission.

Note 2: 3,134 base Firebirds were built with six-cylinder engines.

FIREBIRD ESPRIT - (V-8) SERIES 224

The Esprit was outwardly identified by model script on the rear roof pillar, bright roof rail and wheel opening moldings, V-8 displacement badges under front fender Firebird lettering and bird emblems above the grille. Standard equipment included all found on base models, plus custom interior option with knit vinyl upholstery, a vinyl-covered deluxe steering wheel, dual body-color outside sport mirrors, concealed windshield wipers, a concealed radio antenna, trunk floor mats, wheel trim rings, custom trim, decor moldings, higher rate springs and a 350-cid two-barrel V-8 with 8.8:1 compression and 255-hp at 4600 rpm. A three-speed manual gearbox with floor-mounted shift lever was regular equipment.

Model Number	Body/Style Number	Body Type & Seating	Factory Price	Shipping Weight	Production Total
224	87	2d sport coupe-4P	$3,241	3,435 lbs.	18,961

Note 3: 2,104 Firebird Esprits had manual transmission and 16,857 had automatic transmission.

FIREBIRD FORMULA 400 - (V-8) SERIES 226

Standard equipment on the Formula 400 included all GM safety features, fiberglass twin hood scoop,

As in 1969, Trans Ams were available only in blue with white stripes, or white with blue stripes for 1970, and again had plenty of exterior goodies to set them apart.

1 1/8- front and 5/8-in. rear stabilizer bars, F70 x 14 bias-belted black sidewall tires, 7-inch wheel rims, manual front disc/rear drum brakes, carpets, an all-vinyl interior, front bucket seats, rear bucket type seats, dual outside sport mirrors, concealed windshield wipers, a concealed radio antenna and a deluxe steering wheel. The Formula had the same springs as the base Firebird with heavy-duty "Firm Control" shocks. The Trans Am suspension was optional. Power came from a 400-cid four-barrel V-8 with 10.25:1 compression and 330 hp at 4800 rpm. The base engine was linked to a three-speed Hurst floor shift. External distinctions included extra-long twin hood scoops and Formula 400 nameplates. The 335-hp L74 Ram Air III V-8 was optional. No Formulas were equipped with the Ram Air IV V-8.

Model Number	Body/Style Number	Body Type & Seating	Factory Price	Shipping Weight	Production Total
226	87	2d sport coupe-4P	$3,370	3,470 lbs.	7,708

Note 4: 2,777 Firebird Formula 400s had manual transmission and 4,931 had automatic transmission.

TRANS AM - (V-8) - SERIES 228

The Trans Am had all GM safety features, plus front air dams, front and rear spoilers, a shaker hood, side air extractors, a rear deck lid spoiler, aerodynamically styled outside mirrors with left-hand remote contro, a 1 1/4-in. front stabilizer bar, a 7/8-in. rear stabilizer bar, heavy-duty Firm Control shock absorbers, heavy-duty springs, an engine-turned instrument panel insert, a Rally gauge cluster, concealed windshield wipers, bucket seats, carpets, all-vinyl upholstery, power brakes, power steering, 15 x 7-in. Rally wheel rims and F60-15 white letter tires. The standard V-8 in the Trans Am was a 335-hp Ram Air 400 engine. The factory called this the Ram Air H.O., but it is best known as the Ram Air III V-8. It had a 10.5:1 compression ratio and developed peak power at 5000 rpm. The base transmission was a wide-ratio four-speed manual gearbox with Hurst floor shift. The Trans Am came only with white or blue finish with contrasting racing stripes.

Model Number	Body/Style Number	Body Type & Seating	Factory Price	Shipping Weight	Production Total
228	87	2d sport coupe-5P	$4,305	3,550 lbs.	3,196

Note 5: 1,828 Trans Ams had manual transmission and 1,368 had automatic transmission.
Note 6: 3,108 Trans Ams were L74s (1,769 with manual transmission and 1,339 with automatic transmission).
Note 7: 88 Trans Ams were LS1s (59 with manual transmission and 29 with automatic transmission).

ENGINES

Inline six-cylinder [UPC L22]: Overhead valves. Cast-iron block. Displacement: 250 cid. Bore & stroke: 3.875 x 3.531 in. Compression ratio: 8.5:1. Brake horsepower: 155 at 4200 rpm. Torque: 235 ft. lbs. at 1600 rpm. Hydraulic valve lifters. Carburetor: One-barrel. Engine code: ZB with manual transmission; ZG with automatic transmission.

350 V-8 [UPC L30]: Overhead valves. Cast-iron block. Displacement: 350 cid. Bore & stroke: 3.875 x 3.75 in. Compression ratio: 8.8:1. Brake horsepower: 255 at 4600 rpm. Torque: 355 ft. lbs. at 2800 rpm. Hydraulic valve lifters. Carburetor: Two-barrel. Engine code: WU with manual transmission; YU with automatic transmission.

The Firebird series was redesigned in 1970, which included a new grille and headlight setup.

400 V-8 [UPC L65]: Overhead valves. Cast-iron block. Displacement: 400 cid. Bore & stroke: 4.125 x 3.75 in. Compression ratio: 8.8:1. Brake horsepower: 265 at 4600 rpm. Torque: 397 ft. lbs. at 2400 rpm. Five main bearings. Hydraulic valve lifters. Carburetor: Two-barrel. Engine code: XX with automatic transmission only.

400 V-8 [UPC L78]: Overhead valves. Cast-iron block. Displacement: 400 cid. Bore & stroke: 4.125 x 3.75 in. Compression ratio: 10.25:1. Brake horsepower: 330 at 4800 rpm. Torque: 430 ft. lbs. at 3000 rpm. Five main bearings. Hydraulic valve lifters. Carburetor: Four-barrel. Engine code: WT with manual transmission; YS with automatic transmission.

Ram Air III V-8 [UPC L74]: Also called H.O. V-8 Overhead valves. Cast-iron block. Displacement: 400 cid. Bore & stroke: 4.125 x 3.75 in. Compression ratio: 10.75:1. Brake horsepower: 335 at 5000 rpm. Torque: 430 ft. lbs. at 3400 rpm. Five main bearings. Hydraulic valve lifters. Carburetor: Rochester four-barrel. Engine code: WS with manual transmission; YZ with automatic transmission.

Ram Air IV V-8 [UPC LS1]: Overhead valves. Cast-iron block. Displacement: 400 cid. Bore & stroke: 4.125 x 3.75 in. Compression ratio: 10.75:1. Brake horsepower: 345 at 5400 rpm. Torque: 430 ft. lbs. at 3700 rpm. Five main bearings. Hydraulic valve lifters. Carburetor: Rochester four-barrel. Engine code: WW with manual transmission; XP with automatic transmission. (Note: All Trans Ams with the LS1 V-8 had a 3.73:1 ratio rear axle regardless of transmission attachments).

CHASSIS

Base six: Wheelbase: 108.0 in. Overall Length: 191.6 in. Overall width: 73.4 in. Overall height: 50.4 in. Front tread: 61.3 in. Rear tread: 60 in.

Base V-8, Esprit, Formula: Wheelbase: 108.0 in. Overall Length: 191.6 in. Overall width: 73.4 in. Overall height: 50.4 in. Front tread: 61.6 in. Rear tread: 60.3 in.

Trans Am: Wheelbase: 108.0 in. Overall Length: 191.6 in. Overall width: 73.4 in. Overall height: 50.4 in. Front tread: 61.7 in. Rear tread: 60.4 in.

TECHNICAL

Base/Esprit: Body and frame: Integral body and frame with separate bolted-on sub-frame for engine and front suspension. Front suspension: Independent with upper and lower control arms, coil springs, tubular shocks and .938-in. diameter stabilizer bar. Rear suspension: Hotchkiss solid axle, multi-leaf rear springs and tubular shocks. Steering: Optional power assist co-axial re-circulating ball bearing.

Formula: Body and frame: Integral body and frame with separate ladder-type front frame section. Front suspension: Independent with upper and lower control arms, heavy-duty coil springs, heavy-duty Firm Control tubular shocks and 1.125-in. diameter stabilizer bar. Rear suspension: Hotchkiss solid axle, multi-leaf rear springs, .620-in. stabilizer bar and heavy-duty Firm Control tubular shocks. Steering: Optional power assist co-axial re-circulating ball bearing. Fuel tank: 18.5 gal.

Trans Am: Body and frame: Integral body and frame with separate ladder-type front frame section. Front suspension: Independent with upper and lower control arms, heavy-duty coil springs, heavy-duty tubular shocks and 1.250-in. diameter stabilizer bar. Rear suspension: Hotchkiss solid axle, multi-leaf rear springs, 7/8-in. stabilizer bar and tubular shocks. Steering: Saginaw variable-ratio steering with power assist. Ratios: 13:1 to 15:1 variable-ratio. Turning diameter: 36.5 ft. curb-to-curb. Fuel tank: 18.5 gal.

OPTIONS

591 speedometer gear adapter ($11.59). 731 heavy-duty air cleaner, except Trans Am and not available with 348 ($9.48). 582 custom air conditioner; not available with six-cylinder engine ($375.99). 368 performance axle ($10.53). 692 heavy-duty battery ($4.21). 451 custom seat belts, front and rear and front shoulder type ($12.64). 452 custom seat/shoulder belts front and rear ($38.97). 492 electric clock, except Trans Am and not available with 652 ($15.80). 488 Rally gauge cluster with clock, except Trans Am and not available with 341, 484 or 652 ($47.39). 484 Rally gauge cluster with clock, standard Trans Am and not available with 341, 484 or 652 ($94.79). 494 front console, not available in six-cylinder with three-speed manual transmission ($58.98). 402 spare tire cover ($5.27). 481 cruise control ($57.93). 541 rear window defogger ($26.33). 534 electric rear window defogger, with V-8 only ($52.66). 361 Safe-T-Track rear axle, standard with Trans Am, requires specific axle ($42.13). 343 350-cid two-barrel V-8, standard with Esprit, not available with 351 or 358 ($110.59). 400-cid Ram Air V-8, in Esprit with code 350 ($52.66); standard with Trans Am and not available with 352, 359, 754 ($168.51). 711 evaporative emissions control, required in California ($36.86). 531 Soft-Ray tinted glass, all windows ($32.65). 532 Soft-Ray tinted glass, windshield only ($26.33). 684 door edge guards ($6.32). 674 dual horns in base Firebird, standard in others ($4.21). 661 convenience lamps

The "chicken" logo was right up front in 1970.

($11.59). 521 front floor mats, pair ($6.85). 522 rear floor mats, pair ($6.32). 524 fitted trunk floor mats, standard in Esprit and included with 731 ($8.43). 434 dual body-colored sport-type outside rearview mirrors on base Firebird ($26.33). 441 left-hand visor vanity mirror ($2.11). 431 décor moldings on 22387 and 22687, standard other models except not available on Trans Am ($47.49). 741 roof drip moldings, standard on 22487 ($31.60). 754 mountain performance axles, for 22387 and 22487 without 582 ($16.85); for 22487 with 343 or 352 and 22387 and 22487 with 582 ($2.11). 502 Wonder Touch power brakes, standard in 22887 ($42.13). 554 remote-control deck lid release ($14.74). 552 power door locks and seatback locks, not available with 734 ($68.46). 734 power door locks only ($45.29). 501 variable-ratio power steering, standard with 22887 ($105.32). 551 power side windows, all with 494 ($105.32). 401 AM push-button radio ($61.09). 402 AM/FM push-button radio ($133.76). 404 AM/FM stereo radio ($239.08). 412 stereo tape player, requires a radio and not available with 411 ($133.76). 411 rear speaker; not included in 404 and 412 ($15.80). SVT Cordova vinyl top for 22387 and 22687 without 431 ($89.52); for 22387 and 22687 with 431 and 22487 ($73.72). 461 deluxe steering wheel for 22387 ($15.80). 464 Formula steering wheel, in 22487 and 22687 with 501 only ($42.13); in 22387 with 501 only ($57.93); in 22887 (no cost). 504 tilt steering wheel, requires 501 and not available with column-mounted gearshift ($45.19). 351 Turbo-Hydra-Matic transmission, in 22487 and 22687; not available with 341 or 343 ($227.04). 352 two-speed automatic transmission with six-cylinder ($163.68); with 350-cid two-barrel V-8 ($174.24). 354 four-speed manual transmission with floor shift, requires V-8 and not available with 754 ($195.36). 355 heavy-duty three-speed manual transmission with floor shift, without 341, standard in 22687 ($84.26). Close-ratio four-speed manual transmission with floor shift, in Formula with 37R axle, requires 361 ($195.36). 359 Turbo-Hydra-Matic in 22387 and 22487 with 343 engine ($205.92); in 22387 with 341 six-cylinder engine ($195.36). 473 wire wheel discs on 22487 ($52.66); in 22387 and 22687 ($73.72). 474 Rally II wheel rims, on 22487 ($63.19); on 22387 and 22687 includes 471 ($84.26). 471 wheel trim rings, on 22387 and 22687 without 454 ($21.06). 432 recessed windshield wipers on 22387 and 22687 ($18.96). 321 basic group, on all except 22887, includes AM radio, electric clock, visor-vanity mirror, outside rearview mirror, remote-control mirror, remote deck lid release on 2887 and heavy-duty air cleaner ($103.22). 731 Custom trim

Vinyl was still the material of choice for Firebird interiors for 1970.

group, includes instrument panel assist strap, bright roof rail side interior moldings, custom front seat, door and quarter panel interior trim and molded trunk floor mat ($77.94). 331 Power assist group, includes Turbo-Hydra-Matic transmission, power steering and power brakes, in 22387 with 341 six-cylinder engine ($342.81); in 22387 and 22487 with 343 350-cid two-barrel V-8 ($353.37); in 22487 with 400-cid V-8 and 22687 ($374.49). 652 warning lamp group, includes warning lamps for low fuel, low washer fluid, seat belts and headlights, all except 22387 and not with 484 or 488 ($36.86). TGR F78-14 white sidewall tires on 22387 and 22487, not available with 484 or 488 ($36.86 extra). THR E78-14 white sidewall tires, on 22387 and 22487 with 341, 343 or 346 ($43.18 extra). TMF F70-14 black sidewall tires, on 22387 and 22487 with 341, 343 or 346 ($35.81 extra). TML F70-14 raised white letter tires, on 22387 and 22487 with 341, 343 or 346 ($64.25 extra); on 22687 ($28.44 extra). TNL F60-15 raised white letter tires, on 22687 includes 15-in. Rally II wheels ($146.39 extra). 704 Space Saver spare tire, except 22887, standard with 474 or TNL ($15.80).

HISTORICAL FOOTNOTES

Pontiacs were introduced Sept. 18, 1969, and the all-new second-generation Firebird bowed Feb. 26, 1970. Calendar-year output was 422,212 Pontiacs, giving the company sixth place in the sales rankings. James McDonald became the new general manager of Pontiac Motor Division, replacing John Z. DeLorean, who moved to Chevrolet.

The 1971 455 H.O. Trans Am was the most muscular Pontiac around.

Minor Changes

There was no need to change the beautiful Firebird for 1971, and Pontiac hardly did. A careful look would reveal new high-back seats and new wheel covers (except on Trans Ams). Simulated louvers appeared behind the front wheel cutouts.

Base Firebird prices started at $3,047 and 23,022 were built. Some 20,185 buyers paid $400 more to get an Esprit coupe. Formula prices started in the Esprit bracket, but only 7,802 examples of this model were made.

Standard equipment on Trans Ams was about the same as 1970. The exotic sports car version of the Firebird got the new high-back seats, revised grille trim, new optional honeycomb wheels and a rarely ordered rear console. A chrome engine dress-up kit was no longer standard. A new LS5 455 HO engine with four-barrel carburetion and 8.4:1 compression producing 335 hp was standard with a heavy-duty three-speed manual gearbox and floor shifter. The Trans Am price tag started at $4,594 and only 2,116 T/As were built.

I.D. NUMBERS

The VIN was stamped on a plate on top of dashboard at the left-hand side and was viewable through the windshield. The first symbol indicates the GM division: 2=Pontiac. The second and third symbols indicate the series: 23=Firebird, 24=Esprit, 26=Formula 400, 28=Trans Am. The fourth and fifth symbols indicate the body style: 87=two-door sport coupe. The sixth symbol indicates model year: 1=1971. The seventh symbol indicates assembly plant: L=Van Nuys, California, N=Norwood, Ohio. The last six symbols are the sequential production number starting with 600001 for six-cylinder Firebirds and 100001 for V-8 Firebirds at each assembly plant. Body/style number plate under hood tells the manufacturer, the Fisher style number, the assembly plant, the trim code, the paint code and build date. The style number takes the form 71-22487 where the prefix 71=1971, the first symbol 2=Pontiac, the second and third symbols indicate 24=Firebird Esprit series and the fourth and fifth symbols indicate body style (87=sport coupe). The assembly plant codes are: LOS=Los Angeles (Van Nuys), California, NOR=Norwood, Ohio. Engine production codes included: [250-cid, 145-hp six] CAA-CAB-. [350-cid, 255-hp V-8] WR-WU-XR-YU. [400-cid, 265-hp V-8] XX. [400-cid, 300-hp] WX-WS-WT-YS. [400-cid, 325-hp] YC. [455-cid, 335-hp V-8] WC-WL-YE.

COLORS

11=Cameo White, 13=Nordic Silver, 24=Adriatic Blue, 26=Lucerne Blue, 42=Limekist Green, 43=Tropical Lime, 49=Laurentian Green, 53=Quezal Gold, 59=Aztek Gold, 61=Sandalwood, 62=Canyon Copper, 67=Castillian Bronze, 75=Cardinal Red and 78=Rosewood.

BASE FIREBIRD - (SIX/V-8) SERIES 223

Standard equipment on the basic Firebird included vinyl bucket seats, a woodgrain instrument panel insert, a deluxe steering wheel, an Endura front bumper, bright grille moldings, standard hubcaps, narrow rocker panel moldings, front disc/rear drum brakes and E78-14 tires. An inline 250-cid 145-hp overhead-valve six-cylinder Chevrolet-built engine and three-speed manual transmission were standard.

Model Number	Body/Style Number	Body Type & Seating	Factory Price	Shipping Weight	Production Total
223	87	2d sport coupe-4P	$3,047	3,164 lbs.	23,022

Note 1: 2,778 base Firebirds had manual transmission and 20,244 had automatic transmission.
Note 2: 2,975 base Firebirds were built with six-cylinder power plants.

FIREBIRD ESPRIT - (V-8) SERIES 224

Esprits included custom trim features with knit vinyl upholstery, a custom cushion steering wheel, a trunk mat, bright roof drip moldings, wheel opening moldings, concealed windshield wipers, twin body-colored outside rearview mirrors, wheel trim rings and dual horns as standard extras. Power was supplied by the two-barrel 350-cid V-8 with 8.0:1 compression and 250 hp at 4400 rpm. A floor-mounted three-speed manual transmission was the standard gearbox.

Model Number	Body/Style Number	Body Type & Seating	Factory Price	Shipping Weight	Production Total
224	87	2d sport coupe-4P	$3,416	3,423 lbs.	20,185

Note 3: 947 Firebird Esprits had manual transmission and 19,238 had automatic transmission.

FIREBIRD FORMULA - (V-8) SERIES 226

Standard equipment on Formula Firebirds included all-vinyl bucket seats, a custom cushion steering wheel, a flame chestnut woodgrain appearance instrument panel insert, right and left body-colored outside rearview mirrors, (left-hand remote-controlled), an Endura rubber front bumper, a fiberglass hood with simulated twin air scoops, a black-textured grille insert, bright grille moldings, dual horns, front disc/rear drum brakes, a handling package, dual exhausts with chrome extensions and a heavy-duty three-speed manual transmission. Also featured were standard hubcaps, F70-14 black sidewall tires and Formula 350 or 400 or 455 identification. Engine choices were the two-barrel 350-cid V-8, the four-barrel 400-cid V-8, the four-barrel 455-cid V-8 and the 455 H.O. V-8.

Model Number	Body/Style Number	Body Type & Seating	Factory Price	Shipping Weight	Production Total
FIREBIRD FORMULA 350 - SERIES 226 - (V-8)					
226	87	2d sport coupe-4P	$3,440	3,473 lbs.	Note 4
FIREBIRD FORMULA 400 - SERIES 226 - (V-8)					
226	87	2d sport coupe-4P	$3,540	3,473 lbs.	Note 4
FIREBIRD FORMULA 455 - SERIES 226 - (V-8)					
226	87	2d sport coupe-4P	$3,625	3,473 lbs.	Note 4

Note 4: Production of all Formula Firebirds combined was 7,802.
Note 5: 1,860 Formula Firebirds had manual transmission and 5,942 had automatic transmission.

TRANS AM - (V-8) - SERIES 228

Standard equipment on Trans Ams included all-vinyl bucket seats, a Rally gauge cluster (with a clock and a tachometer), an Endura front bumper, a Formula steering wheel, twin body-color outside rearview mirrors (left-hand mirror remote controlled), special honeycomb wheels, functional front fender air extractors, a rear deck lid spoiler, a black textured grille insert, bright grille moldings, front and rear wheel opening air spoilers, concealed windshield wipers, Trans Am identification markings, a performance dual exhaust system with tailpipe extensions, a special air cleaner with rear-facing cold air intake on hood controlled by throttle, a power-flex cooling fan, power steering, a Saf-T-Track differential, a handling package, dual horns, power front disc/rear drum brakes and F60-15 white lettered tires. The UPC LS5 455 H.O. engine with four-barrel carburetion, 8.4:1 compression and 335 hp at 4800 rpm was standard in all Trans Ams, as was a four-speed manual gearbox with floor shifter. As in the past, the Trans Am was offered only in a limited number of exterior finish colors. Cars done in "Cameo White" had blue stripes on a black base. Also available was "Lucerne Blue" body finish with white stripes on a black base. One minor change was the absence of a chrome engine dress-up kit on the standard equipment list.

Model Number	Body/Style Number	Body Type & Seating	Factory Price	Shipping Weight	Production Total
228	87	2d sport coupe-4P	$4,464	3,578 lbs.	2,116

Note 6: 885 Trans Ams had manual transmission and 1,231 had automatic transmission.

ENGINES

Inline six-cylinder [UPC L22]: Overhead valves. Cast-iron block. Displacement: 250 cid. Bore & stroke: 3.875 x 3.531 in. Compression ratio: 8.5:1. Brake horsepower: 155 at 4200 rpm. Torque: 235 ft.-lbs. at 1600 rpm. Hydraulic valve lifters. Carburetor: One-barrel. Engine code: CAA or CAB.

350 V-8 [UPC L30]: Overhead valves. Cast-iron block. Displacement: 350 cid. Bore & stroke: 3.875 x 3.75 in. Compression ratio: 8.2:1. Brake horsepower: 255 at 4600 rpm. Torque: 355 ft. lbs. at 2800 rpm. Hydraulic valve lifters. Carburetor: Two-barrel. Engine code: WR, WU, XR and YU.

400 V-8 [UPC L65]: V-8. Overhead valves. Cast-iron block. Displacement: 400 cid. Bore & stroke: 4.125 x 3.75 in. Compression ratio: 8.2:1. Brake horsepower: 265 at 4400 rpm. Torque: 400 ft. lbs. at

Trans Ams went largely unchanged in the looks department for 1971.

2400 rpm. Five main bearings. Hydraulic valve lifters. Carburetor: Four-barrel. Engine code: XX with automatic transmission only.

400 V-8 [UPC L78]: Overhead valves. Cast-iron block. Displacement: 400 cid. Bore & stroke: 4.125 x 3.75 in. Compression ratio: 8.2:1. Brake horsepower: 300 at 4800 rpm. Torque: 400 ft. lbs. at 3600 rpm. Five main bearings. Hydraulic valve lifters. Carburetor: Four-barrel. Engine code: WK, WT and YS.

455 V-8 [UPC L75]: Overhead valves. Cast-iron block. Displacement: 455 cid. Bore & stroke: 4.15 x 4.21 in. Compression ratio: 8.2:1. Brake horsepower: 325 at 4400 rpm. Torque: 455 ft. lbs. at 3200 rpm. Five main bearings. Hydraulic valve lifters. Carburetor: Four-barrel. Engine code: YC.

455 H.O. V-8 [UPC LS5]: Overhead valves. Cast-iron block. Displacement: 455 cid. Bore & stroke: 4.15 x 4.21 in. Compression ratio: 8.4:1. Brake horsepower: 335 at 4800 rpm. Torque: 480 ft. lbs. at 3600 rpm. Five main bearings. Hydraulic valve lifters. Carburetor: Rochester four-barrel. Engine code: WC, WL and YE.

CHASSIS

Base V-8, Esprit, Formula: Wheelbase: 108.0 in. Overall Length: 191.6 in. Overall width: 73.4 in. Overall height: 50.4 in. Front tread: 61.3 in. with 6-inch rims; 61.6 in. with 7-inch rims. Rear tread: 60 in. with 6-inch rims; 60.3 in. with 7-inch rims.

Trans Am: Wheelbase: 108.0 in. Overall Length: 191.6 in. Overall width: 73.4 in. Overall height: 50.4 in. Front tread: 61.7 in. Rear tread: 60.4 in.

TECHNICAL

Base/Esprit: Body and frame: Integral body and frame with separate bolted-on sub-frame for engine and front suspension. Front suspension: Independent with upper and lower control arms, coil springs, tubular shocks and .938-in. diameter stabilizer bar. Rear suspension: Hotchkiss solid axle, multi-leaf rear springs and tubular shocks. Steering: Optional power assist coaxial re-circulating ball bearing.

Formula 350: Body and frame: Integral body and frame with separate ladder-type front frame section. Front suspension: Independent with upper and lower control arms, heavy-duty coil springs, heavy-duty tubular shocks and .938-in. diameter stabilizer bar. Rear suspension: Hotchkiss solid axle, multi-leaf rear springs, .620-in. stabilizer bar and tubular shocks. Steering: Optional power assist coaxial re-circulating ball bearing.

Formula 400/455/455 H.O.: Body and frame: Integral body and frame with separate ladder-type front frame section. Front suspension: Independent with upper and lower control arms, heavy-duty coil springs, heavy-duty tubular shocks and 1.125-in. diameter stabilizer bar. Rear suspension: Hotchkiss solid axle, multi-leaf rear springs, .620-in. stabilizer bar and tubular shocks. Steering: Optional power assist coaxial re-circulating ball bearing.

Trans Am: Body and frame: Integral body and frame with separate ladder-type front frame section. Front suspension: Independent with upper and lower control arms, heavy-duty coil springs, heavy-duty tubular shocks and 1.250-in. diameter stabilizer bar. Rear suspension: Hotchkiss solid axle, multi-leaf rear springs, .875-in. stabilizer bar and tubular shocks. Steering: Saginaw variable-ratio steering with power assist.

OPTIONS

321/Y88 basic group includes AM radio with windshield antenna, Turbo-Hydra-Matic transmission, standard size white sidewall tires, custom wheel trim rings and power steering, standard on Trans Am; on 2387 six ($448.17); on 2387 V-8 ($458.73); on 2487 V-8 ($432.40); on 2687 with 350-cid V-8 ($471.36); on 2687 with optional V-8s ($492.48). 321/Y88 basic group includes AM/FM radio with windshield antenna, Turbo-Hydra-Matic transmission, standard size white sidewall tires, custom wheel trim rings and power steering, on Trans Am only ($66.35). 331/Y96 Handling package, on Formula, includes honeycomb wheels, F60-15 white letter tires, heavy-duty front and rear stabilizer bars and heavy-duty front and rear springs. ($205.37). 34D(x)/L30 350-cid two-barrel V-8, base Firebird ($121.12). 34G/L65 400-cid two-barrel V-8 in Esprit ($52.66). 34L/L78 400-cid four-barrel V-8 in Formula ($100.05). 34P/L75 455-cid four-barrel V-8 in Formula ($157.98). 34U/LS5 455-cid H.O. four-barrel V-8 in Formula ($236.97). 35K/M38 three-speed Turbo-Hydra-Matic transmission with six-cylinder engine ($175.26). 35L/M40 three-speed Turbo-Hydra-Matic transmission with V-8 engines ($201.48). 35J/M53 two-speed automatic transmission with six-cylinder ($148.92); with 350-cid two-barrel V-8 ($190). 35A standard three-speed manual transmission with column shift, six-cylinder only (no cost). 35B/M12 three-speed manual transmission with floor shift, six-cylinder or 350-cid two-barrel V-8 only ($10.53). 35C/M13 heavy-duty three-speed manual transmission with floor shift, not available with six-cylinder or 400-cid two-barrel V-8 ($84.26). 35E/M20 four-speed manual transmission with floor shift, requires V-8 and not available with six-cylinder or Trans Am ($205.97). 35G/M22 close-ratio four-speed manual transmission with floor shift, not available with six-cylinder or 350-cid two-barrel V-8; standard in Trans Am ($237.65). 361/G80 Safe-T-Track rear axle, standard with Trans Am ($46.34). 368/G90-2 performance axle ($10.53). 401/U63 AM push-button radio with windshield antenna ($66.35). 403/U69 AM/FM radio and windshield antenna ($139.02). 405/U58 AM/FM stereo radio and windshield antenna, not available with rear seat speaker ($238.08). 411/U80 rear speaker, not available with U58, U55 or U57 ($18.96). 412/U57 stereo eight-track tape player, requires a radio and not available with 411 or 414 ($133.76). 414/U55 cassette tape player, not available with U80 or U57 ($133.76). 421/A90 remote deck lid release ($14.74). 422/K45 dual-stage air cleaner, not available on Trans Am ($9.48). 424/D58 rear console ($26.33). 431/D55 front console, with floor shift only ($58.98). 434/D35 dual body-colored sport-type outside rearview mirrors, left-hand remote-controlled, on base Firebird ($26.33). 441/D34 right-hand visor van-

Lucerne Blue was one of 14 Firebird colors in '71.

ity mirror ($3.16). 451/AK1 custom seat belts ($15.80). 461/N30 custom cushion steering wheel, for Formula; standard in Esprit, not available on Trans Am ($15.80). 464/NK3 Formula steering wheel, in 22487 and 22687 with 501 only ($42.13); in 22387 with 501 only ($57.93); in 22887 (no cost). 471/P06 wheel trim rings, standard on Esprit ($26.33). 472/P02 custom wheel covers for base Firebird and Formula ($31.60); for Esprit ($5.27) (Note: Wire wheel covers were no longer available as a factory-installed option, but were available as a dealer-installed accessory). 474/N98 Rally II wheels on Firebird and Formula ($89.52); on Esprit ($63.19); on Trans Am (no cost). NL/PM7 Rally II wheel and F60-15 white letter tires on Formula, standard on Trans Am ($162.19). 478/P05 honeycomb wheels, on Firebird and Formula ($126.38); on Esprit ($100.05); on Trans Am ($36.86). NL/PM7 Honeycomb wheels and F60-15 white letter tires on Formula, standard on Trans Am ($199.05). 481/B80 roof drip moldings, standard on Esprit, included with vinyl tops ($15.80). 484/B85 belt reveal moldings, standard in Esprit ($21.06). 491/B96 front and rear wheel opening moldings, standard on Esprit, not available on Trans Am ($21.06). 492/B93 door edge guards ($6.32). 494/B84 vinyl body side moldings, black, not available with Trans Am ($31.60). 501/N41 variable-ratio power steering, standard in Trans Am ($115.85). 502 Wonder Touch power brakes, standard in Trans Am ($7.39). 504 tilt steering wheel, not available with manual steering or column-mounted gearshift ($45.29). 521/B32 front floor mats, pair ($7.37). 522/B33 rear floor mats, pair ($6.32). 524 fitted trunk floor mats, standard in Esprit ($8.43). 531/A01 Soft-Ray tinted glass, all windows ($37.92). 532/A02 Soft-Ray tinted glass, windshield only ($30.54). 543/C49 electric rear window defroster, not available with six-cylinder or electric rear window defogger ($63.19). 551/A31 power side windows, requires D55 ($115.85). 554/AU3 power door locks and seatback locks ($45.29). 572/D80 rear deck lid spoiler, Formula only, standard on Trans Am ($32.65). 582/C60 custom air conditioner, not available with six-cylinder ($407.59). 601/WU3 hood air inlet, with 455 H.O. V-8 only on Formula ($84.26). 652/W74 warning lamp group, includes warning lamps for low fuel, low washer fluid, seat belts and headlights, not available with 714, 718 and 722 ($42.13). 654/TP1 Delco X battery, with 455-cid V-8 only ($26.33). 664/Y92 convenience lamps ($11.59). 681/U05 dual horns in base Firebird, standard in others ($4.21). 684/N65 Space Saver spare tire ($15.80). 691/WU1 self-charging flashlight ($12.64). 692/UA1 heavy-duty battery, not available with air conditioner ($10.53). 701/V01 heavy-duty radiator ($21.06). 704/WT5 mountain performance option, with C60 ($10.53); without C60 ($31.60). 714/U30 Rally gauges, clock and instrument panel tachometer, not available with six-cylinder, 718, 722 or 652 ($94.79). 718/W63 Rally gauges and clock, not available with six-cylinder or 652; included with U35 ($47.39). 722/U35 electric clock, included with W74, U30 and W63 ($15.80). 731 Custom trim group, includes assist straps on door and above glove box, perforated headliner, molded vinyl trunk floor mat and body-color outside door handle inserts, standard Esprit, not available base on Firebird ($78.99). 734/V32 rear bumper guards ($15.80). SVT Cordova vinyl top on Base Firebird and Formula ($89.52); on Esprit ($73.72). HR/PL3 E78-14 white sidewall tires on Firebird and Esprit ($28.44 extra). GR/PX6 F78-14 white sidewall tires on Firebird and Esprit ($45.29 extra). ML/PL4 F70-14 raised white letter tires, on Firebird or Esprit ($76.88 extra); on Formula ($41.07 extra). MF/PY6 F70-14 black sidewall tires, on Firebird or Esprit ($35.81 extra).

HISTORICAL FOOTNOTES

Production of the 1971 models started Aug. 10, 1970. Model year production was 53,125 Firebirds. That included 46,655 cars with automatic transmission and 6,470 cars with manual transmission. Firebird sales were 49,078 for the model year and 55,462 for the calendar year. Firebird sales and production totals were pulled down by a United Auto workers strike that began Sept. 14, 1970, and lasted 67 days. A Trans Am-based racecar nicknamed the "Tirebird" was campaigned this year. Driven by John Cordts and sponsored by the B.F. Goodrich Tire Co., it took a third overall at Watkins Glen.

The Trans Am was still in production in 1972, but it was almost identical to the two previous years.

Nearly A Wrap

The Trans Am sported the familiar logo and blue-and-white paint scheme in 1972.

It was nearly a wrap for the Firebird in 1972. A 174-day-long U.A.W. strike at the Norwood, Ohio, factory created all kinds of problems. By the time it was over, federal laws had changed and the cars left sitting on the assembly line had to be trashed. GM seriously thought about killing the Firebird (and Camaro). This kept product changes minimal. A honeycomb grille, new interiors and restyled hubcaps and wheel covers were among the few alterations.

Standard equipment in base models included front bucket seats, rear bucket-style seats, vinyl trim, carpets, an Endura nose and a small full-width front air dam. The base engine was a Chevy inline six-banger. Prices ranged upwards from $2,838. Pontiac reported making 12,000 base coupes.

The Esprit had name scripts on its roof pillars, custom cloth-and-Morrokide trim, distinctive door panels, a perforated headliner and other slightly upscale trim features for about $300 additional. Pontiac made 11,415 of this model and most of them probably had the base two-barrel 350-cid V-8 and optional Turbo-Hydra-Matic.

The Formula retained a street-performance car image with a twin air scoops on its fiberglass hood, a thick front stabilizer, firm shocks, fat tires and dual exhausts with chrome tips. A four-barrel 350-cid V-8 was standard, but 400-cid and 455 H.O. V-8s could also be ordered. Model year output was 5,250 cars.

Trans Ams had a street-racer look with a Formula steering wheel, engine-turned dash, rally gauges, air dams, flares and spoilers. They included fast-rate power steering, fat stabilizers, high-rate springs, a Safe-T-Track axle and a 300-hp 455 H.O. V-8 with cold-air induction and a four-speed close-ratio gear box with floor shift. Turbo-Hydra-Matic was a no-cost option. Only 1,286 were built.

The 1972 Trans Am with a four-speed manual transmission could do the quarter mile in 14.3 seconds at 98 mph. *High Performance Cars* magazine tested the same 455 H.O. in two different states of tune in its September and October issues. The car had a four-speed gearbox and 3.42:1 rear axle. In stock trim it turned the quarter mile in 14.58 seconds at 98 mph. For the later test it was tuned by Nunzi's Automotive, a Brooklyn, New York, Pontiac specialty shop. This upgrade resulted in a 14.04-second quarter mile at 103.22 mph.

I.D. NUMBERS

The vehicle identification number (VIN) was stamped on a plate on the upper left-hand side of the instrument panel and visible through the windshield. The first symbol was the GM divisional code, 2=Pontiac. The second symbol indicated series: (S) for Base Firebird, (T) for Firebird Esprit, (U) for Formula Firebird, (V) for Trans Am. The third and fourth symbols indicated the body style: 87=sport coupe. The fifth symbol indicated engine: D=250-cid inline six; M=350-cid two-barrel V-8 with single exhaust system, N=350-cid two-barrel V-8 with dual exhaust system, R=400-cid four-barrel V-8 with single exhaust system, T=400-cid four-barrel V-8 with dual exhaust system,

X=455-cid four-barrel H.O. V-8 with dual exhaust system and P=400-cid two-barrel V-8 with dual exhaust system. The sixth symbol indicated model year: 2=1972. The seventh symbol indicated the assembly plant: L=Van Nuys, Calif.; N=Norwood, Ohio. The remaining symbols were sequential unit production number at factory, starting with 100001. The Body by Fisher plate on the engine side of the cowl contained the Fisher style number, which took the form 72-22887. The prefix 72=1972, the first symbol 2=Pontiac, the second and third symbols 28=Firebird Trans Am and the last two symbols 87=sport coupe. This plate also indicated interior trim, seat type, body color and build date. Six-cylinder engine code stamped on distributor mounting on right side of block. V-8 engine code on front of block below right cylinder head. Engine production codes for 1972 were: [250-cid, 110-nhp six] CBA-CBG-CBJ-CBC. [350-cid, 160-nhp V-8] WR-YJ-YU-YR. [400-cid, 175-nhp V-8] YX-ZX. [400-cid, 250-nhp] WK-YS-ZS-WS. [455-cid/300-nhp] WD-WM-YB-YE. (Note: Horsepower ratings expressed in net horsepower or "nhp" terms).

COLORS

11=Cameo White; 14=Revere Silver; 24=Adriatic Blue; 26=Lucerne Blue; 36=Julep Green; 43=Springfield Green; 48=Wilderness Green; 50=Brittany Beige; 53=Quezal Gold; 55=Shadow Gold; 56=Monarch Yellow; 57=Brasilia Gold; 63=Anaconda Gold; 65=Sundance Orange; 75=Cardinal Red.

BASE FIREBIRD - (SIX/V-8) SERIES 2S

There was a new honeycomb mesh grille insert, new interior trims, redesigned hubcaps and restyled wheel covers. Standard equipment in the basic model included front bucket seats, rear bucket type seats, all-vinyl seat trim, solid foam seat cushions with integral springs, loop-pile carpet, a deluxe steering wheel, an upper-level ventilation system, woodgrained dashboard accents, an ashtray light, an Endura front bumper, a small full-width front air dam, hubcaps, a windshield radio antenna, bright moldings on the windshield, rear window and grille, thin body sill moldings, front disc/rear drum brakes, a three-speed manual transmission with column-mounted gearshift lever on six-cylinder cars (floor-mounted gearshift lever on cars with V-8s) and E78-14 black sidewall tires.

Model Number	Body/Style Number	Body Type & Seating	Factory Price	Shipping Weight	Production Total
BASE FIREBIRD - 2S SERIES - (SIX)					
2S	87	2d sport coupe-4P	$2,838	3,357 lbs.	Note 1
BASE FIREBIRD - 2S SERIES - (V-8)					
2S	87	2d sport coupe-4P	$2,956	3,359 lbs.	Note 1

Note 1: Total production of the base Firebird was 12,001 units.
Note 2: 1,263 Firebirds had manual transmission and 10,738 had automatic transmission.
Note 3: 1,096 base Firebirds had six-cylinder engines and 10,905 had a 350-cid V-8.

FIREBIRD ESPRIT - (V-8) - SERIES 2T

The Esprit had model signature script moldings on the roof pillars. Standard equipment was the same as in basic Firebirds, plus custom cloth and Morrokide interior trim, distinctive door trim panels, a perforated vinyl headliner, added sound insulation, a custom cushion steering wheel, rear armrest ashtrays, a molded trunk mat, a dashboard assist grip, wheel trim rings, body-color sport style outside rearview mirrors (left-hand remote-controlled), body-color door handle inserts, concealed windshield wipers, bright roof rail trim, window sill moldings, rear hood edge accents, wheel opening moldings and wide rocker panel accent strips. A three-speed manual transmission with floor-mounted gearshift lever was also included.

Model Number	Body/Style Number	Body Type & Seating	Factory Price	Shipping Weight	Production Total
2T	87	2d sport coupe-4P	$3,194	3,359 lbs.	11,415

Note 4: 504 Firebird Esprits had manual transmission and 10,911 had automatic transmission.

FIREBIRD FORMULA - (V-8) SERIES 2U

Formula Firebirds had the same equipment features as the base Firebird, plus a fiberglass hood with forward-mounted twin air scoops, a custom cushion steering wheel, body-color outside rearview mirrors, special Formula identification, a 1-1/8-in. front stabilizer bar, firm control shock absorbers, a dual exhaust system with chrome tailpipe extensions, a 1-1/8-in. front stabilizer bar, a 5/8-in. rear stabilizer bar and F70-14 tires. A power-flex fan was standard with the 400- and 455-cid engines.

Model Number	Body/Style Number	Body Type & Seating	Factory Price	Shipping Weight	Production Total
2U	87	2d sport coupe-4P	$3,221	3,424 lbs.	5,249

Note 5: 1,082 Formula Firebirds had manual transmission and 4,167 had automatic transmission.
Note 6: The 455 H.O. V-8 was installed in 276 Formula Firebirds.

FIREBIRD TRANS AM - (V-8) SERIES 2V

The Trans Am had the same standard features as the Firebird, plus a 455 H.O. V-8, a Formula steering wheel, engine-turned dashboard trim, a Rally gauge cluster with clock and tachometer, a front air dam, front and rear wheel opening flares, a full-width rear deck spoiler, engine air extractors, a shaker hood, 15-in. Rally II wheel rims with trim rings, black-textured grille inserts, fast-rate power steering, power brakes with front discs and rear drums, a 1 1/4-in. front stabilizer bar, a 7/8-in. rear stabilizer bar, special high-rate rear springs, a Safe-T-Track differential, an air cleaner with rear-facing cold air induction system, a power-flex cooling fan, performance dual exhausts with chrome extensions, four-speed close-ratio manual transmission with floor-mounted gearshift (or Turbo-Hydra-Matic) and F60-15 white lettered tires. The Trans Am again came only in "Cameo White" with blue racing stripes or "Lucerne Blue" finish with white racing stripes.

Model Number	Body/Style Number	Body Type & Seating	Factory Price	Shipping Weight	Production Total
2V	87	2d sport coupe-4P	$4,256	3,564 lbs.	1,286

Note 7: 458 Trans Ams had manual transmission and 828 had automatic transmission.

ENGINES

Inline six-cylinder [UPC L22]: Overhead valves. Cast-iron block. Displacement: 250 cid. Bore & stroke: 3.875 x 3.531 in. Compression ratio: 8.5:1. Brake horsepower: 110 (net) at 4200 rpm. Torque: 235 ft. lbs. at 1600 rpm. Hydraulic valve lifters. Carburetor: One-barrel. Single exhaust system. Engine code: CBA, CBG, CBJ, CBC.

350 V-8 [UPC L30]: Overhead valves. Cast-iron block. Displacement: 350 cid. Bore & stroke: 3.875 x 3.75 in. Compression ratio: 8.0:1. Brake horsepower: 160 (net) at 4400 rpm. Torque: 270 ft. lbs. at 2000 rpm. Hydraulic valve lifters. Carburetor: Two-barrel. Single exhaust system. Engine code: WR, YV, YR.

350 V-8 [UPC L30]: Overhead valves. Cast-iron block. Displacement: 350 cid. Bore & stroke: 3.875 x 3.75 in. Compression ratio: 8.0:1. Brake horsepower: 175 (net) at 4400 rpm. Torque: 275 ft. lbs. at 2000 rpm. Hydraulic valve lifters. Carburetor: Two-barrel. Dual exhaust system. Engine code: YV.

400 V-8 [UPC L65]: Overhead valves. Cast-iron block. Displacement: 400 cid. Bore & stroke: 4.125 x 3.75 in. Compression ratio: 8.2:1. Brake horsepower: 175 (net) at 4000 rpm. Torque: 310 ft. lbs. at 2400 rpm. Five main bearings. Hydraulic valve lifters. Carburetor: Two-barrel. Single exhaust system. Engine code: YX, ZX.

400 V-8 [UPC L78]: Overhead valves. Cast-iron block. Displacement: 400 cid. Bore & stroke: 4.125 x 3.75 in. Compression ratio: 8.2:1. Brake horsepower: 250 at 4400 rpm. Torque: 325 ft.-lbs. at 3200 rpm. Five main bearings. Hydraulic valve lifters. Carburetor: Four-barrel. Dual exhaust system. Engine code: WK, YS, WS.

400 H.O. V-8 [UPC LS5]: Overhead valves. Cast-iron block. Displacement: 455 cid. Bore & stroke: 4.15 x 4.21 in. Compression ratio: 8.4:1. Brake horsepower: 300 at 4000 rpm. Torque: 415 ft. lbs. at 3200 rpm. Five main bearings. Hydraulic valve lifters. Carburetor: Rochester four-barrel. Dual exhaust system. Engine code: (with breaker point ignition) WD, YE; (with unitized breakerless ignition) WM, YB.

CHASSIS

Base V-8, Esprit, Formula: Wheelbase: 108.0 in. Overall Length: 191.6 in. Overall width: 73.4 in. Overall height: 50.4 in. Front tread: 61.6 in. with 7-inch rims. Rear tread: 60.3 in. with 7-inch rims.

Trans Am: Wheelbase: 108.0 in. Overall length: 191.6 in. Overall width: 73.4 in. Overall height: 50.4 in. Front tread: 61.7 in. Rear tread: 60.4 in.

TECHNICAL

Base/Esprit: Body and frame: Integral body and frame with separate bolted-on sub-frame for engine and front suspension. Front suspension: Independent with upper and lower control arms, coil springs, tubular shocks and .940-in. diameter stabilizer bar. Rear suspension: Hotchkiss solid axle, multi-leaf rear springs and tubular shocks. Steering: Optional power assist coaxial re-circulating ball bearing.

Formula: Body and frame: Integral body and frame with separate ladder-type front frame section. Front suspension: Independent with upper and lower control arms, heavy-duty coil springs, heavy-duty tubular shocks and 1.125-in. diameter stabilizer bar. Rear suspension: Hotchkiss solid axle, multi-leaf rear springs and tubular shocks. Steering: Optional power assist coaxial re-circulating ball bearing. Fuel tank: 17 gal.

Trans Am: Body and frame: Integral body and frame with separate ladder-type front frame section. Front suspension: Independent with upper and lower control arms, heavy-duty coil springs, heavy-duty tubular shocks and 1.250-in. diameter stabilizer bar. Rear suspension: Hotchkiss solid axle, multi-leaf rear springs, .875-in. stabilizer bar and tubular shocks. Steering: Saginaw variable-ratio steering with power assist. Fuel tank: 17 gal.

OPTIONS

321/Y88 basic group includes AM radio with windshield antenna, Turbo-Hydra-Matic transmission, standard size white sidewall tires, custom wheel trim rings and power steering, standard on Trans Am; on

Pontiac built 29,951 Firebirds in model year 1972, and only 1,286 were Trans Ams.

2387 six ($447); on 2387 V-8 ($458); on 2487 V-8 ($432); on 2687 with 350-cid V-8 ($470); on 2687 with optional V-8s ($490). 321/Y88 basic group includes AM/FM radio with windshield antenna, Turbo-Hydra-Matic transmission, standard size white sidewall tires, custom wheel trim rings and power steering, on Trans Am only ($66). 331/Y96 Handling package, on Formula, includes P05. Package consists of honeycomb wheels, F60-15 white letter tires, heavy-duty front and rear stabilizer bars and heavy-duty front and rear springs. ($200). 34H/L30 350-cid two-barrel V-8, base Firebird ($118). 34R/L30 350-cid two-barrel V-8, base Firebird, California, requires THM ($118). 34R/L65 400-cid two-barrel V-8 in Esprit with THM ($51). 34S/L78 400-cid four-barrel V-8 in Formula ($97). 34U/LS5 455-cid H.O. four-barrel V-8 in Formula, requires 601. 634, with THM ($231). 35B/M02 three-speed manual transmission with floor shift in base Firebird with 34D six-cylinder engine ($10). 35E/M20 four-speed manual transmission with floor shift, requires 34H 350-cid two-barrel V-8 or 34S 400-cid four-barrel V-8 and not available with six-cylinder or Trans Am ($200). 35G/M22 close-ratio four-speed manual transmission with floor shift in Formula Firebird, 400-cid four-barrel V-8 or 35X 455-cid four-barrel H.O. V-8 required ($231). 35J/M35 two-speed automatic transmission in base Firebird, except California cars, with six-cylinder engine ($174). 35J/M35 two-speed automatic transmission in base Firebird and Esprit, except California cars, without 34D six-cylinder engine ($185). 35K/M38 three-speed Turbo-Hydra-Matic transmission in Firebirds, except Trans Am, without 34D six-cylinder engine ($215). 35K/M38 three-speed Turbo-Hydra-Matic transmission in base Firebird with 34D six-cylinder engine ($205). 35L/M40 three-speed Turbo-Hydra-Matic transmission in Esprit and Formula Firebird ($236). 361/G80 Safe-T-Track rear axle, standard with Trans Am ($45). 368/G92 performance axle ($10). 401/U63 AM push-button radio with windshield antenna ($65). 403/U69 AM/FM radio and windshield antenna ($135). 405/U58 AM/FM stereo radio and windshield antenna, not available with rear seat speaker ($233). 411/U80 rear speaker ($18). 412/U57 stereo eight-track tape player ($130). 414/U55 cassette tape player, not available with U80 or U57 ($130). 423/K45 heavy-duty air cleaner, except Trans Am ($9). 424/D58 rear console ($26). 431/D55 front console, with floor shift only ($57). 432 recessed windshield wipers on 22387 and 22687 ($18). 434/D35 dual body-colored sport-type outside rearview mirrors, left-hand remote-controlled, on base Firebird ($26). 441/D34 right-hand visor vanity mirror ($3). 442/D31 non-glare rearview mirror, included with 734 ($6). 444/D33 left-hand outside rearview mirror, remote-control type ($12). 451/AK1 custom seat belts ($15). 461/N30 custom cushion steering wheel ($15). 462/N31 custom sport steering wheel, included with 332 ($56). 464/Nk3 Formula steering wheel, Esprit and Formula ($41); base with 501 only ($56). 471/P06 wheel trim rings, included with 474 and 332 ($26). 472/P02 custom finned wheel covers for Formula without 332, 474 and 478 ($50);

for Esprit ($24). 474/N98 Rally II wheels ($87). 476/P01 Deluxe wheel covers on base Firebird and Formula, not available with 332 ($31); on Esprit ($5). 478/P05 honeycomb wheels, on Firebird and Formula ($123); on Esprit ($97). 481/B80 roof drip moldings, standard on Esprit ($15). 484/B85 belt reveal moldings, except Trans Am, required with 582 and 534 ($15). 491/B96 front and rear wheel opening moldings, base Firebird and Formula only ($21). 492/B93 door edge guards ($6). 494/B84 vinyl body side moldings, black, not available with Trans Am ($31). 501/N41 variable-ratio power steering, standard in Trans Am, required with 582 and 534 ($113). 502 front disc brakes, standard in Trans Am ($46). 504 tilt steering wheel, requires 501, not available with 35J, 35K or 35L without 431 ($46). 521/B32 front floor mats, pair ($7). 522/B33 rear floor mats, pair ($6). 524 fitted trunk floor mats, included in 724 ($8). 531/A01 Soft-Ray tinted glass, all windows ($37). 532/A02 Soft-Ray tinted glass, windshield only ($30). 534/C49 electric rear window defroster, not available with six-cylinder or electric rear window defogger ($62). 541/C50 rear window defogger, not available with electric rear window defroster ($31). 551/A31 power side windows, required with 431 ($113). 554/AU3 power door locks ($44). 582/C60 manual air conditioning ($397). 591/VJ9 California emission test requirements ($15). 601/WU3 hood air inlet, requires 34X ($56). 611/D80 rear air spoiler, Formula only ($32). 614/D98 vinyl tape stripes, not available with 494 or Trans Am ($41). 634/K65 unitized ignition, required with 34X in Formula ($77). 664/Y92 convenience lamps ($11). 681/U05 dual horns in base Firebird, standard in others ($4). 684/N65 Space Saver spare tire, without 474 or 478 ($13). 692/UA1 heavy-duty battery, not available with air conditioner ($10). 701/V01 heavy-duty radiator ($21). 714/U30 Rally gauges, clock and instrument panel tachometer, not available with six-cylinder, 718 or 722 ($92). 718/W63 Rally gauges and clock, not available with six-cylinder or 722 ($46). 722/U35 electric clock ($15). 731 Custom trim group, includes assist straps on door and above glove box, perforated headliner, molded vinyl trunk floor mat and body-color outside door handle inserts, standard Esprit, not available on base Firebird ($77). 731/V30 rear bumper guards ($25). SPS/W51 solid special paint, with vinyl top except Trans Am ($97). SPS/W51 solid special paint, without vinyl top except Trans Am ($113). SVT Cordova vinyl top on base Firebird and Formula ($87); on Espirit ($72). TNL/YH99 Formula handling package ($87). THR/PL3 E78-14 white sidewall tires on Firebird and Esprit ($28 extra). TGR/PX6 F78-14 white sidewall tires on Firebird and Esprit ($44 extra). TML/PL4 F70-14 raised white letter tires, on Firebird or Esprit ($75 extra); on Formula ($40 extra). TMF/PY6 F70-14 black sidewall tires, on Firebird or Esprit ($35 extra).

HISTORICAL FOOTNOTES

Production of the 1972 models started Aug. 12, 1971. Firebird sales were 31,204 for the model year and 22,865 for the calendar year.

Jerry Heasley photo

The 1973 Trans Am SD 455 coupe clocked a 13.54-second quarter mile in one magazine test.

1973

Super Duty

Jerry Heasley photo

The '73 was nicely appointed inside.

This was the year to add performance, but the appearance of the Firebird changed only modestly. There was a new grille with rows of boxes you could store eggs in. GM also had to work out some affordable changes to the Endura nose to make it meet government crash standards. Prices rose modestly and production climbed to 14,096.

Firebird Esprits could be identified by the chrome model "signatures" on their roof pillars. Standard equipment included a custom interior, concealed wipers, twin body-color mirrors and African crossfire mahogany interior accents. A 150-hp version of the 350-cid V-8 with a two-barrel carburetor was standard. This model gained additional buyers in 1973 and 17,249 were made.

Formula Firebirds could again be identified by the special twin-scoop hoods. Other features included a custom cushion steering wheel, heavy-duty suspension, black-textured grille, 175-hp Formula 350 V-8 with dual exhausts, and F70-14 tires. Engine options up to 310 hp were offered. The popularity of the Formula nearly doubled as its model year production rose to 10,166.

The most significant 1973 Trans Am changes were the addition of stylized Firebird graphics on the hood and the release of a "Super-Duty" 455-cid V-8, which

was also available in Formulas. Stylist John Schinella created the so-called "chicken" hood decal, a modernized rendition of the legendary Indian symbol.

The SD-455 V-8 evolved from the Trans-Am racing program of the early 1970s. It represented a low-compression, extra-horsepower option made available in limited quantities. It featured a special block with reinforced webbing, large forged-steel connecting rods, special aluminum pistons, a heavy-duty oiling system with dry sump pump provision, a high-lift camshaft, four-bolt main bearing caps, special valve train components, dual exhausts and a special intake manifold. The SD-455 heads were a variation on Pontiac's Ram Air IV heads. They had 1.77-in. exhaust valves and 2.11-in. intake valves with special cupped heads and swirl-polish finish. The SD-455's free-flowing, cast-iron, round-port headers were designed for performance, too. An SD-455 Trans Am was capable of 0 to 60 mph in 7.3 seconds and did the quarter mile in 15 seconds.

Standard Trans Am equipment was the same as 1972, plus the new "chicken" hood graphics. For the model year, a total of 4,802 Trans Ams were built. Production of SD-455 Trans Ams totaled 252, of which 180 had automatic and 72 had stick shift. Fifty Formula Firebirds also had the SD-455 V-8.

I.D. NUMBERS

The vehicle identification number (VIN) was stamped on a plate on the upper left-hand side of the instrument panel and visible through the windshield. The first symbol was the GM divisional code, 2=Pontiac. The second symbol indicated series: S=Base Firebird, T=Firebird Esprit, U=Formula Firebird, V=Trans Am. The third and fourth symbols indicated the body style: 87=sport coupe. The fifth symbol indicated engine: D=250-cid inline six; M=350-cid two-barrel V-8 with single exhaust system; N=350-cid two-barrel V-8 with dual exhaust system; P=400-cid two-barrel V-8 with dual exhausts; R=400-cid two-barrel V-8 with single exhaust system; S=400-cid four-barrel V-8 with single exhausts; T=400-cid four-barrel V-8 with dual exhaust system; X=455-cid four-barrel Super-Duty V-8 with dual exhaust system; and Y=455-cid four-barrel V-8 with dual exhaust system. The sixth symbol indicated model year: 3=1973. The seventh symbol indicated the assembly plant: N=Norwood, Ohio. The remaining symbols were sequential unit production number at factory, starting with 100001. The Body by Fisher plate on the engine side of the cowl contained the Fisher style number, which took the form 73-2FT87. The prefix 73=1973, the first symbol 2=Pontiac, the second symbol F=Firebird, the third symbol T=Esprit and the last two symbols 87=sport coupe. This plate also indicated interior trim, seat type, body color and build date. Six-cylinder engine code stamped on distributor mounting on right side of block. V-8 engine code on front of block below right cylinder head. Engine production codes for 1973 were: [250-cid one-barrel 100-nhp six with single exhaust] CCA-CCB-CCC-CCD. [350-cid two-barrel 150-nhp V-8 with single exhaust] ZR-ZT-YR-YL. [350-cid two-barrel 175-nhp V-8 with dual exhausts] XR-ZB, [400-cid two-barrel 170-nhp V-8 with single exhaust] YZ-ZX-ZK. [400-cid two-barrel 185-nhp V-8 with dual exhausts] X4-X3-W5. [400-cid four-barrel 230-nhp V-8 with dual exhausts] Y6-YG-XN-XX-WK-WP-WS-Y3-YS-XK. [455-cid four-barrel 250-nhp V-8 with dual exhausts] YK-X7-XM-XL-XE-ZE-ZZ-WW-WT. [455-cid four-barrel 290-nhp SD-455 V-8 with dual exhausts only] ZJ-XD. (Note: Horsepower ratings expressed in net horsepower or "nhp" terms).

COLORS

11=Cameo White, 24=Porcelain Blue, 26=Regatta Blue, 29=Admiralty Blue, 42=Verdant Green, 44=Slate Green, 46=Golden Olive, 48=Brewster Green, 51=Sunlight Yellow, 56=Desert Sand, 60=Valencia Gold, 64=Ascot Silver, 68=Burma Brown, 74=Florentine Red, 75=Buccaneer Red, 97=Navajo Orange.

BASE FIREBIRD - (SIX/V-8) SERIES 2FS

Standard equipment in the basic model included front bucket seats, rear bucket type seats, all-vinyl seat trim, solid foam seat cushions with integral springs, loop-pile carpet, a deluxe steering wheel, an upper-level ventilation system, woodgrain dashboard accents, an ashtray light, an Endura front bumper, a small full-width front air dam, hubcaps, a windshield radio antenna, bright moldings on the windshield, rear window and grille, thin body sill moldings, front disc/rear drum brakes, a three-speed manual transmission with floor shift and E78-14 black sidewall tires.

Model Number	Body/Style Number	Body Type & Seating	Factory Price	Shipping Weight	Production Total
BASE FIREBIRD - SERIES 2FS - (SIX)					
2FS	87	2d sport coupe-4P	$2,895	3,159 lbs.	1,370
BASE FIREBIRD - SERIES 2FS - (V-8)					
2FS	87	2d sport coupe-4P	$3,013	3,380 lbs.	12,726

The Buccaneer Red T/A made a bold statement.

Jerry Heasley photo

Cosmetic difference between the Trans Am (left) and Formula included different hood scoops and spoiler treatments.

FIREBIRD ESPRIT - (V-8) - SERIES 2FT

The Firebird Esprit could be most easily identified by the model signature scripts on the roof pillars. Also considered standard equipment were a custom interior, concealed windshield wipers, twin body-color outside rearview mirrors (left-hand remote-control), dual horns, deluxe wheel covers, all-vinyl or cloth-and-vinyl custom interior trim, African crossfire mahogany dash and console accent panels, a 350-cid 150-nhp two-barrel V-8 and a three-speed manual transmission.

Model Number	Body/Style Number	Body Type & Seating	Factory Price	Shipping Weight	Production Total
2FT	87	2d sport coupe-4P	$3,249	3,309 lbs.	17,299

Note 1: A total of 15,550 Esprits had a 350-cid V-8 and 1,749 had a 400-cid V-8.

FIREBIRD FORMULA - (V-8) SERIES 2FU

Formula Firebirds could again be identified by the special twin-scoop hoods. Other features included a custom cushion steering wheel, heavy-duty suspension, black-textured grille, dual exhausts and F70-14 tires, plus all items included on lower-priced lines. This year Formula Firebird owners initially had a choice of three V-8 engines, the 350 cid, the 400 cid and the 455 cid. Late in the year, the Super-Duty version of the 455-cid V-8 was also offered to Formula buyers. See the Trans Am section for information about this engine. The "SD-455" was used in only 43 Formula Firebirds in 1973.

Model Number	Body/Style Number	Body Type & Seating	Factory Price	Shipping Weight	Production Total
FIREBIRD FORMULA 350 - SERIES 2FU - (V-8)					
2FU	87	2d sport coupe-4P	$3,276	3,318 lbs.	4,771
FIREBIRD FORMULA 400 - SERIES 2FU - (V-8)					
2FU	87	2d sport coupe-4P	$3,373	3,318 lbs.	4,622
FIREBIRD FORMULA 455 - SERIES 2FU - (V-8)					
2FU	87	2d sport coupe-4P	$3,430	3,318 lbs.	730
FIREBIRD FORMULA SD-455 - SERIES 2FU - (V-8)					
2FU	87	2d sport coupe-4P	$3,951	3,318 lbs.	43

Note 2: Total production of Formula Firebirds was 10,166.

FIREBIRD TRANS AM - (V-8) - SERIES 2FV

The most significant change to the Firebird Trans Am this season was the addition of the optional, but very popular, "chicken" or "big bird" graphics treatment for the hood. Stylist John Schinella created this modernized rendition of the legendary Indian symbol. Standard equipment included a Formula steering wheel, a Rally gauge cluster with clock and tachometer, a full-width rear deck spoiler, power steering, power front disc/rear drum brakes, a Safe-T-Track differential, wheel opening flares, front fender air extractors, dual exhausts with chrome extensions, heavy-duty underpinnings, Rally II wheels with trim rings, dual body-color outside rearview mirrors (left-hand remote-controlled), F60-15 white-lettered tires and a choice of Turbo-Hydra-Matic or four-speed manual transmission. The Super-Duty 455 V-8 engine was an option that evolved from Pontiac's Trans Am racing program of the early 1970s. It represented a low-compression, extra-horsepower option made available in extremely limited quantities. The "SD-455" featured a special block with reinforced webbing, large forged-steel connecting rods, special aluminum pistons, a heavy-duty oiling system (with dry sump pump provisions), a high-performance camshaft, special round port cylinder heads, four-bolt main bearing caps, a special intake manifold, a special dual exhausts system and high-performance valve train components. The SD-455 Trans Am could do the quarter mile in 13.54 seconds at 104.29 mph. A pre-production version of the SD-455 had a 310-hp motor, but all SD-455s sold to the public had 290 hp. The SD-455 was available in cars with only three colors: Brewster Green, Cameo White and Buccaneer Red.

Model Number	Body/Style Number	Body Type & Seating	Factory Price	Shipping Weight	Production Total
FIREBIRD TRANS AM - SERIES 2FV - (L75 V-8)					
2FV	87	2d sport coupe-4P	$4,204	3,504 lbs.	4,550
FIREBIRD TRANS AM SD-455 - SERIES 2FV - (LS2 V-8)					
2FV	87	2d sport coupe-4P	$4,204	3,504 lbs.	252

Note 3: SD-455 engines were installed in 72 cars with manual transmission and 180 cars with Turbo-Hydra-Matic transmission.

ENGINES

Inline six-cylinder [UPC L22]: Overhead valves. Cast-iron block. Displacement: 250 cid. Bore & stroke: 3.875 x 3.531 in. Compression ratio: 8.5:1. Brake horsepower: 110 at 3800 rpm. Torque: 185 ft. lbs. at 1600 rpm. Hydraulic valve lifters. Carburetor: One-barrel. VIN Code: D.

350 V-8 [UPC L30]: Cast-iron block. Displacement: 350 cid. Bore & stroke: 3.875 x 3.75 in. Compression ratio: 7.6:1. Brake horsepower: 150 at 4000 rpm. Torque: 270 ft. lbs. at 2000 rpm. Hydraulic valve lifters. Carburetor: Two-barrel. Single exhaust. VIN Code: M.

350 V-8 [UPC L30]: Overhead valves. Cast-iron block. Displacement: 350 cid. Bore & stroke: 3.875 x 3.75 in. Compression ratio: 7.6:1. Brake horsepower: 175 at 4400 rpm. Torque: 280 ft. lbs. at 2400 rpm. Hydraulic valve lifters. Carburetor: Two-barrel. Dual exhausts. VIN Code: N.

400 V-8 [UPC L65]: Overhead valves. Cast-iron block. Displacement: 400 cid. Bore & stroke: 4.125 x 3.75 in. Compression ratio: 8.0:1. Brake horsepower: 170 at 3600 rpm. Torque: 320 ft. lbs. at 2000 rpm. Five main bearings. Hydraulic valve lifters. Carburetor: Two-barrel. Single exhaust. VIN code: R.

400 V-8 [UPC L65]: Overhead valves. Cast-iron block. Displacement: 400 cid. Bore & stroke: 4.125 x 3.75 in. Compression ratio: 8.0:1. Brake horsepower: 185 at 4000 rpm. Torque: 320 ft. lbs. at 2400 rpm. Five main bearings. Hydraulic valve lifters. Carburetor: Two-barrel. Dual exhausts. VIN code: P.

400 V-8 [UPC L78]: Overhead valves. Cast-iron block. Displacement: 400 cid. Bore & stroke: 4.125 x 3.75 in. Compression ratio: 8.0:1. Brake horsepower: 230 at 4400 rpm. Torque: 325 ft. lbs. at 3200 rpm. Five main bearings. Hydraulic valve lifters. Carburetor: Four-barrel. Dual exhausts. VIN code: T.

455 V-8 [UPC L75]: Overhead valves. Cast-iron block. Displacement: 455 cid. Bore & stroke: 4.15 x 4.21 in. Compression ratio: 8.0:1. Brake horsepower: 250 at 4000 rpm. Torque: 370 ft. lbs. at 2800 rpm. Five main bearings. Hydraulic valve lifters. Carburetor: Four-barrel. Dual exhausts. VIN code: Y.

455 Super-Duty V-8 [UPC LS2]: Overhead valves. Cast-iron block. Displacement: 455 cid. Bore & stroke: 4.15 x 4.21 in. Compression ratio: 8.0:1. Brake horsepower 290 at 4000 rpm Torque: 390 ft. lbs. at 3600 rpm. Five main bearings. Hydraulic valve lifters. Carburetor: Rochester four-barrel. VIN code: X.

CHASSIS

Base V-8, Esprit, Formula: Wheelbase: 108.0 in. Overall length: 191.6 in. Overall width: 73.4 in. Overall height: 50.4 in. Front tread: 61.3 in. with 6-inch rims; 61.6 in. with 7-inch rims. Rear tread: 60 in. with 6-inch rims; 60.3 in. with 7-inch rims.

Trans Am: Wheelbase: 108.0 in. Overall Length: 191.6 in. Overall width: 73.4 in. Overall height: 50.4 in. Front tread: 61.7 in. Rear tread: 60.4 in.

TECHNICAL

Base/Esprit: Body and frame: Integral body and frame with separate bolted-on sub-frame for engine and front suspension. Front suspension: Independent with upper and lower control arms, coil springs, tubular shocks and .940-in. diameter stabilizer bar. Rear suspension: Hotchkiss solid axle, multi-leaf rear springs and tubular shocks. Steering: Optional power assist coaxial re-circulating ball bearing. Fuel tank: 18 gal.

Formula: Body and frame: Integral body and frame with separate ladder-type front frame section. Front suspension: Independent with upper and lower control arms, heavy-duty coil springs, heavy-duty tubular shocks and 1.125-in. diameter stabilizer bar. Rear suspension: Hotchkiss solid axle, multi-leaf rear springs, .620-in. stabilizer bar and tubular shocks. Steering: Optional power assist coaxial re-circulating ball bearing. Fuel tank: 18 gal.

Trans Am: Body and frame: Integral body and frame with separate ladder-type front frame section. Front suspension: Independent with upper and lower control arms, heavy-duty coil springs, heavy-duty tubular shocks and 1.250-in. diameter stabilizer bar. Rear suspension: Hotchkiss solid axle, multi-leaf rear springs, .875-in. stabilizer bar and tubular shocks. Steering: Saginaw variable-ratio steering with power assist. Fuel tank: 18 gal.

A base 1973 Firebird coupe with a six-cylinder engine could be had new for about $2,900.

OPTIONS

331/Y88 basic group includes AM radio with windshield antenna, Turbo-Hydra-Matic transmission, standard-size white sidewall tires (or white letter tires on Formula), deluxe wheel covers on Esprit, custom wheel trim rings on Formula and power steering, standard on Trans Am; on 2387 six ($441); on 2387 V-8 ($451); on 2487 V-8 ($421); on 2687 with 350-cid V-8 ($459); on 2687 with optional V-8s ($480); on Trans Am ($65). 334/Y95 body protection group, includes door edge guards, vinyl body side moldings and rear bumper guards, except Trans Am ($52). 342/Y99 Formula Handling package, for Formula only, includes F60-15 white letter tires or G70-15 white sidewall radial tires, heavy-duty rear springs, heavy-duty shock absorbers, heavy-duty front and rear stabilizer bars and 15 x 7-in. wheel rims, with F60 tires and 684 ($72.60); with F60 tires without 684 ($87); with G70 tires without 684 ($157); with G70 tires with 684 ($150.60). 344/Y92 Lamp group. Includes luggage compartment lamp, glove box lamp and interior courtesy panel lamp ($10). 724/Y90 custom trim group, includes deluxe front bucket seats, assist straps on door and glove box, roof insulator pads, formed vinyl trunk mat, body color outside door handles and rear quarter ashtray, standard in Esprit; available in Formula and Trans Am ($77). 35D standard six-cylinder engine, not available with air conditioning (no cost). 35M/L30 350-cid two-barrel V-8, Turbo-Hydra-Matic transmission required in California ($118). 35R/L65 400-cid two-barrel V-8, requires Turbo-Hydra-Matic at extra cost ($51). 35S/L78 400-cid four-barrel V-8 in Formula, requires Turbo-Hydra-Matic or four-speed manual transmission ($97). 35W/L75 455-cid four-barrel V-8 in requires Turbo-Hydra-Matic or four-speed manual transmission in Formula; standard in Trans Am ($155). 35X/LS2 455-cid four-barrel SD-455 V-8 in requires Turbo-Hydra-Matic or four-speed manual transmission and air inlet hood in Formula ($675); in Trans Am ($521). 36B/M12 three-speed manual transmission with floor shift, standard in base six and Esprit 350 (no cost). 36E/M20 four-speed manual transmission with floor shift, standard Trans Am; not available with two-barrel V-8s ($200). 36H/M21 close-ratio four-speed manual transmission with floor shift, in Formula two-barrel and all 400/455 four-barrel ($200). 36L/M38 three-speed Turbo-Hydra-Matic transmission with six-cylinder engine ($205); with 350-cid V-8 ($215). 371/G80 Safe-T-Track rear axle, standard with Trans Am ($45). 378/G92 performance axle ($10). 411/U63 AM push-button radio with windshield antenna ($65). 413/U69 AM/FM radio and windshield antenna ($135). 415/U58 AM/FM stereo radio and windshield antenna, not available with rear seat speaker ($233). 421/U80 rear speaker ($18). 422/U57 stereo eight-track tape player ($130). 424/D58 rear console ($26). 431/D55 front console, with floor shift only ($57). 432 recessed windshield wipers on 22387 and 22687 ($18). 434/D35 dual body-colored sport-type outside rearview mirrors, left-hand remote-controlled, on base Firebird ($26). 441/D34 right-hand visor vanity mirror ($3). 451/AK1 custom seat belts ($15). 461/N30 custom cushion steering wheel on base Fire-

The Esprit was the best-selling Firebird in 1973.

bird only ($15). 464/NK3 Formula steering wheel, Esprit and Formula ($41); base with 501 only ($56). 421/P06 wheel trim rings, included with 474 and 332 ($26). 422/P02 custom finned wheel covers, not available with 342, on Formula ($50); on Esprit ($24). 474/N98 Rally II wheels on Firebird/Formula with GR70 tires without 684 ($87); with 684 ($74.80); on Esprit ($61). 476/P01 Deluxe wheel covers on base Firebird and Formula with 342 ($26). 478/P05 honeycomb wheels, on Firebird and Formula without 684 with GR70 tires ($123); with 684 and GR70 tires (($103.60); on Esprit ($97). 481/B80 roof drip moldings, standard on Esprit ($31). 484/B85 window and rear hood moldings, standard with Esprit ($21). 491/B96 front and rear wheel opening moldings, base Firebird and Formula only ($15). 492/B93 door edge guards ($6). 502/JL2 power front disc brakes, standard in Trans Am ($46). 504 tilt steering wheel, requires 501, not available with 35J, 35K or 35L without 431 ($44). 512/WW7 Trans Am hood decal, Trans Am only ($55). 621/B32 front floor mats, pair ($7). 622/B33 rear floor mats, pair ($6). 604/B42 fitted trunk floor mats, included in Esprit and with Custom trims ($8). 531/A09 Soft-Ray tinted glass, all windows ($37). 532/A02 Soft-Ray tinted glass, windshield only ($30). 534/AU3 electric door locks ($44). 534/C49 electric rear window defroster, not available with six-cylinder or electric rear window defogger ($62). 541/C50 rear window defogger, not available with electric rear window defroster ($31). 542/K45 heavy-duty air cleaner, not available with Trans Am SD-455 ($9). 551/A31 power side windows, with front console only ($75). 554/AV6 power door locks ($44). 582/C60 custom air conditioning ($397). 631/D98 vinyl tape stripes, not available for Trans Am ($41). 611/75F Red carpet with trims 521, 361, 421, 461 (no cost). 612/97F orange carpet, with trims 321, 421 (no cost). 614/24F bright blue carpet with trims 321, 421 (no cost). 632/D80 rear air spoiler, standard with Trans Am ($113). 634/K65 unitized ignition, required with 34X in Formula ($77). 634/WU3 Ram Air hood, with Formula 400/455 ($56). 681/U05 dual horns in base Firebird, standard in others ($4). 684/N65 Space Saver spare tire, without 474 or 478 ($15). 691/TP1 Delco X battery ($26). 692/UA1 heavy-duty battery, not available with air conditioner ($10). 694/K65 unitized ignition with 400-cid four-barrel V-8 and

455-cid four-barrel V-8 in Formula and Trans Am ($77). 701/V01 heavy-duty radiator ($21). 711/U35 electric clock with rally gauges, standard in Trans Am ($15). 714/WW8 Rally gauges with instrument panel tachometer, not available with six-cylinder, 712; standard in Trans Am ($92). 712/W63 Rally gauges and clock, not available with six-cylinder or 722 ($46). 732/V32 rear bumper guards ($15). SVT Cordova vinyl top on base Firebird and Formula ($87); on Esprit ($72). THR/PL3 E78-14 white sidewall tires on Firebird and Esprit without 684 ($28 extra); with 684 ($22.40 extra). TGF/PX5 E78-14 black sidewall tires on Firebird and Esprit without 582/684 ($14 extra); without 582 with 684 ($11.20 extra). TGR/PX6 F78-14 white sidewall tires on Firebird and Esprit with 582/684 ($24); with 582 without 684 ($30); without 582/684 ($44 extra). TMF/PY6 F70-14 black sidewall tires on Firebird and Esprit with 582/684 ($16.80); with 582 without 684 ($21); without 582/684 ($28 extra); without 582 with 684 ($35 extra). TML/PL4 F70-14 raised white letter tires, on Firebird and Esprit with 582/684 ($48.80); with 582 without 684 ($51); without 582/684 ($60 extra); without 582 with 684 ($75 extra); on Formula without 342 with 684 ($32); on Formula without 342 with 684 ($40). TVJ/P85 GR70-14 white sidewall steel-belted radial tires, on Trans Am without 684 ($70); with 684 ($56).

HISTORICAL FOOTNOTES

Model year production of all Firebirds was 46,313. Model year sales were 43,869 units and calendar year sales stood at 52,219 units. A "Buccaneer Red" pre-production version of the SD-455 with the 308/320 "K" camshaft and 310 hp, TH400 transmission and 3.42:1 gears was tested by *Hot Rod* magazine in June 1973. It did 0 to 60 mph in 7.3 seconds and the quarter mile in 13.54 seconds at 104.29 mph. At midyear, the Environmental Protection Agency issued an order to remove a time-delay emissions system from Pontiac engines. All engines built after March 15 with serial numbers above 532727 were so modified, along with 700 earlier engines. Power plants having this change were painted a darker-than-normal shade of blue. They also had two thermal valves tapped into the intake manifold and no exhaust gas re-circulation (EGR) system solenoid.

Jerry Heasley photo

This ultra-rare 1974 Trans Am SD-455 shared the year's new front-end styling

1974

Quicker Than A 'Vette

By 1974, it was time to give the Firebird a "facial." The new front end had shovel-nose styling and twin-slot grilles with vertical fins. At the rear, the taillights took the form of long, horizontal slots. Stylists lowered the rear fender line. The new image was not warmly embraced by the car-buying public and only 26,372 Firebirds rolled out of the factory in Ohio.

As usual, model badges decorated the Esprit's roof. Standard on this line were trim and convenience-feature upgrades. Production was up to 22,583 units.

In addition to equipment standard in Esprits, Formulas featured hubcaps, dual-scoop fiberglass hoods, special heavy-duty suspension, black-textured grilles, dual exhausts and F70-14 tires. Available model options included Formula 350, Formula 400, and Formula 455. Production was 14,519 cars.

Standard equipment on Trans Ams included a formula steering wheel, Rally gauges with clock and tachometer, swirl-grain dash trim, full-width rear deck lid spoiler, power steering and front disc brakes, limited-slip differential, wheel opening air flares, front fender air extractors, dual exhausts with chrome extensions, Rally II wheels with trim rings, special heavy-duty suspension, four-speed manual transmission (or M40 Turbo-Hydra-Matic), dual outside racing mirrors and F60-15 white-lettered tires. Production climbed to 10,255.

The SD-455 V-8 went into 212 Firebirds, most of which were Trans Ams. Despite this low number, PMD did great publicizing the SD-455's outstanding performance. Several car magazines reported that Firebirds with this option were faster and quicker than a Corvette. Publicity like that enhanced PMD's performance image and attracted many Firebird buyers to Pontiac showrooms.

I.D. NUMBERS

The vehicle identification number (VIN) was stamped on a plate on the upper left-hand side of the instrument panel and was visible through the windshield. The first symbol was the GM divisional code, 2=Pontiac. The second symbol indicated series: S=Base Firebird, T=Firebird Esprit, U=Formula Firebird, V=Trans Am. The third and fourth symbols indicated the body style: 87=sport coupe. The fifth symbol indicated engine: D=250-cid inline six; M=350-cid two-barrel V-8 with single exhaust system, N=350-cid two-barrel V-8 with dual exhaust system, P=400-cid two-barrel V-8 with dual exhausts, R=400-cid two-barrel V-8 with single exhaust system, S=400-cid four-barrel V-8 with single exhausts. T=400-cid four-barrel V-8 with dual exhaust system, X=455-cid four-barrel Super-Duty V-8 with dual exhaust system and Y=455-cid four-barrel V-8 with dual exhaust system. The sixth symbol indicated model year: 4=1974. The seventh symbol indicated the assembly plant: N=Norwood, Ohio. The remaining symbols were sequential unit production number at the factory, starting with 100001. The Body by Fisher plate on the engine side of the cowl contained the Fisher style number, which took the form 74-2FU87. The prefix 74=1974, the first symbol 2=Pontiac, the second symbol F=Firebird, the third symbol U=Formula and the last two symbols

87=sport coupe. This plate also indicated interior trim, seat type, body color and build date. Engine production codes for 1974 were: [250-cid one-barrel 100-nhp six with single exhaust and manual transmission] CCR. [250-cid one-barrel 100-nhp six with single exhaust and automatic transmission] CCX-CCW. [350-cid two-barrel 155/170-nhp V-8 with manual transmission WA. [350-cid two-barrel 155/170-nhp V-8 with automatic transmission] YA-ZA-AA. [400-cid two-barrel 175/190-nhp V-8 with automatic transmission] YF-YH-AD-AH-ZJ-ZK. [400-cid four-barrel 225-nhp V-8 with manual transmission] Y3-WT-WR. [400-cid four-barrel 225-nhp V-8 with automatic] YL-YM-A3-YT-AT-ZT-YZ-ZS. [455-cid four-barrel 215/250-nhp V-8 with automatic transmission] Y9-A4-Z4-YY-AU-ZU-YW-ZW. [SD-455 four-barrel 290-nhp V-8 manual transmission] W8. [SD-455-cid four-barrel 290-nhp V-8 with automatic transmission] Y8.

COLORS

11=Cameo White, 26=Regatta Blue, 29=Admiralty Blue, 36=Gulfmist Aqua, 40=Fernmist Green, 46=Limefire Green, 49=Pinehurst Green, 50=Caramel Beige, 51=Sunstorm Yellow, 53=Denver Gold, 55=Colonial Gold, 59=Crestwood Brown, 64=Ascot Silver, 66=Fire Coral Bronze, 74=Honduras Maroon, 75=Buccaneer Red. Six-cylinder engine code stamped on distributor mounting on right side of block. V-8 engine code on front of block below right cylinder head.

BASE FIREBIRD - (SIX/V-8) SERIES - 2FS

New Firebird styling changes included a shovel-nosed Endura front end, a horizontal slotted taillight treatment, a lowered rear fender line and twin horizontal rectangular grille inserts with vertical blades. All Firebird models had ashtrays, lamps, nylon carpeting, high/low ventilation, Endura styling and a windshield radio antenna. The basic Firebird also featured a deluxe two-spoke steering wheel, a single-buckle seat and shoulder belt arrangement, narrow rocker panel moldings and E78-14 tires. A reduced compression ratio gave the base six-cylinder engine 10 less horsepower. A 350-cid V-8 with a two-barrel carburetor was optional. Cars with this engine got "350" engine call-outs on the front fenders. Firebird interiors were carried over from 1973, except for new color schemes. Buyers could order multi-color combinations such as white seats with red door panels, dashboard and carpeting. Also, the fabric formerly known as Bravo bolster cloth was renamed Bravado bolster cloth.

Model Number	Body/Style Number	Body Type & Seating	Factory Price	Shipping Weight	Production Total
FIREBIRD - SERIES 2FS - (SIX)					
2FS	87	2d sport coupe-4P	$3,175	3,283 lbs.	7,063
FIREBIRD - SERIES 2FS - (V-8)					
2FS	87	2d sport coupe-4P	$3,305	3,504 lbs.	18,769

FIREBIRD ESPRIT - (V-8) - SERIES 2FT

As usual, the model name in chrome script on the rear roof pillar was a trait of the Firebird Esprit. Standard extras on this line included a custom cushion steering wheel, a custom interior package, body-color door handle inserts, concealed wipers with articulated left arm, deluxe wheel covers, dual horns, body-colored dual outside rearview sport mirrors (left-hand remote-controlled), roof drip and wheel opening moldings, wide body sill moldings, window sill and rear hood edge moldings, a three-speed manual floor shift (with base engine only), a safety belt warning system and E78-14 tires. A 350-cid V-8 with a two-barrel carburetor and single exhaust was the standard engine. A 400-cid V-8 with a two-barrel carburetor and automatic transmission attachment was optional.

Model Number	Body/Style Number	Body Type & Seating	Factory Price	Shipping Weight	Production Total
2FT	87	2d sport coupe-4	$3,527	3,540 lbs.	22,583

FORMULA FIREBIRD - (V-8) SERIES 2FU

In addition to equipment standard in the base Firebird, the Formula featured hubcaps, a dual-scoop fiberglass hood, a special heavy-duty suspension, black-textured grilles, a dual exhaust system, a custom cushion steering wheel and F70-14 tires. Available model options included Formula 350, Formula 400 and Formula 455, as well as the rare Formula SD-455.

Model Number	Body/Style Number	Body Type & Seating	Factory Price	Shipping Weight	Production Total
FORMULA 350 FIREBIRD - SERIES 2FU - (V-8)					
2FU	87	2d sport coupe-4P	$3,614	3,548 lbs.	Note 1
FORMULA 400 FIREBIRD - SERIES 2FU - (V-8)					
2FU	87	2d sport coupe-4P	$3,711	3,548 lbs.	Note 1
FORMULA 455 FIREBIRD - SERIES 2FU - (V-8)					
2FU	87	2d sport coupe-4P	$3,768	3,548 lbs.	Note 1
FORMULA SD 455 FIREBIRD - SERIES 2FU - (V-8)					
2FU	87	2d sport coupe-4P	$4,289	3,548 lbs.	58

Note 1: Total production of non SD-455 Formulas was 14,461 units.

FIREBIRD Trans Am - (V-8) SERIES 2FV

Standard equipment on Trans Am included a formula steering wheel, a Rally gauge cluster with clock and dash panel tachometer, swirl grain dashboard trim, a full-width rear deck lid spoiler, power steering, power front disc/rear drum brakes, a limited-slip differential, wheel opening air deflectors (flares), front fender air extractors, dual exhausts with chrome extensions, Rally II wheels with trim rings, a special heavy-duty suspension, a four-speed manual transmission (or M40 Turbo-Hydra-Matic), dual outside racing mirrors and F60-15 white-lettered tires. The standard engine was a 400-cid 225-nhp V-8 with a four-barrel carburetor. The 455-cid 250-nhp L75 engine was optional. A rare option was the SD-455 engine.

Model Number	Body/Style Number	Body Type & Seating	Factory Price	Shipping Weight	Production Total
FIREBIRD TRANS AM 400 - SERIES 2FV - (V-8)					
2FV	87	2d sport coupe-4P	$4,351	3,655 lbs.	4,664
FIREBIRD TRANS AM 455 - SERIES 2FV - (V-8)					
2FV	87	2d sport coupe-4P	$4,408	3,655 lbs.	4,648
FIREBIRD TRANS AM SD-455 - SERIES 2FV - (V-8)					
2FV	87	2d sport coupe-4P	$4,929	3,655 lbs.	943

Note 2: Of the 4,664 Trans Ams with a 400-cid V-8, 1,750 had manual transmission and 2,914 had Turbo-Hydra-Matic transmission.
Note 3: Of the 4,648 Trans Ams with a 455-cid V-8, all had Turbo-Hydra-Matic transmission.
Note 4: Of the 943 SD-455 Trans Ams, 212 had manual transmission and 731 had Turbo-Hydra-Matic transmission.

ENGINES

Inline six-cylinder [UPC L22]: Overhead valves. Cast-iron block. Displacement: 250 cid. Bore & stroke: 3.875 x 3.531 in. Compression ratio: 8.2:1. Brake horsepower: 100 at 3600 rpm. Torque: 175 ft. lbs. at 1600 rpm. Hydraulic valve lifters. Carburetor: One-barrel. VIN Code: D.

350 V-8 [UPC L30]: Overhead valves. Cast-iron block. Displacement: 350 cid. Bore & stroke: 3.875 x 3.75 in. Compression ratio: 7.6:1. Brake horsepower: 155 at 3600 rpm. Torque: 275 ft. lbs. at 2400 rpm. Hydraulic valve lifters. Carburetion: Two-barrel. Single exhaust. VIN Code: M.

350 V-8 [UPC L30]: Overhead valves. Cast-iron block. Displacement: 350 cid. Bore & stroke: 3.875 x 3.75 in. Compression ratio: 7.6:1. Brake horsepower: 170 at 4000 rpm. Torque: 290 ft. lbs. at 2400 rpm. Hydraulic valve lifters. Carburetion: Two-barrel. Dual exhausts. VIN Code: N.

400 V-8 [UPC L65]: Overhead valves. Cast-iron block. Displacement: 400 cid. Bore & stroke: 4.125 x 3.75 in. Compression ratio: 8.0:1. Brake horsepower: 190 at 4000 rpm. Torque: 330 ft. lbs. at 2400 rpm. Five main bearings. Hydraulic valve lifters. Carburetor: Two-barrel. Dual exhausts. VIN code: P.

400 V-8 [UPC L78]: Overhead valves. Cast-iron block. Displacement: 400 cid. Bore & stroke: 4.125 x 3.75 in. Compression ratio: 8.0:1. Brake horsepower: 200. Five main bearings. Hydraulic valve lifters. Carburetor: Four-barrel. Single exhausts. VIN code: S.

400 V-8 [UPC L78]: Overhead valves. Cast-iron block. Displacement: 400 cid. Bore & stroke: 4.125 x 3.75 in. Compression ratio: 8.0:1. Brake horsepower: 225 at 4000 rpm. Torque: 330 ft. lbs. at 2400 rpm. Five main bearings. Hydraulic valve lifters. Carburetor: Four-barrel. Dual exhausts. VIN code: T.

455 V-8 [UPC L75]: Overhead valves. Cast-iron block. Displacement: 455 cid. Bore & stroke: 4.15 x 4.21 in. Compression ratio: 8.0:1. Brake horsepower: 250 at 4000 rpm. Torque: 380 ft. lbs. at 2800 rpm. Five main bearings. Hydraulic valve lifters. Carburetor: Four-barrel. Dual exhausts. Turbo-Hydra-Matic transmission only. VIN code: Y.

455 Super-Duty V-8 [UPC LS2]: V-8. Overhead valves. Cast-iron block. Displacement: 455 cid. Bore & stroke: 4.15 x 4.21 in. Compression ratio: 8.0:1. Brake horsepower: 290 at 4000 rpm. Torque: 395 ft. lbs. at 3200 rpm. Five main bearings. Hydraulic valve lifters. Carburetor: Rochester four-barrel. VIN code: X.

CHASSIS

Base V-8, Esprit, Formula: Wheelbase: 108.0 in. Overall length: 196 in. Overall width: 73 in. Overall height: 49.2 in. Front tread: Base, Esprit 61.3 in.; Formula 61.6 in. Rear tread: Base, Esprit 60 in.; Formula 60.3 in.

Trans Am: Wheelbase: 108.0 in. Overall length: 191.6 in. Overall width: 73.4 in. Overall height: 50.4 in. Front tread: 61.7 in. Rear tread: 60.4 in.

TECHNICAL

Base/Esprit: Body and frame: Integral body and frame with separate bolted-on sub-frame for engine and front suspension. Front suspension: Independent with upper and lower control arms, coil springs, tubular shocks and .938-in. diameter stabilizer bar (1.00-in. diameter with RTS). Rear suspension: Hotchkiss solid axle, multi-leaf rear springs and tubular shocks (and .625-in. rear stabilizer bar with RTS). Steering: Optional power assist coaxial re-circulating ball bearing. Fuel tank: 20.2 gal.

Formula: Body and frame: Integral body and frame with separate ladder-type front frame section. Front suspension: Independent with upper and lower control arms, heavy-duty coil springs, heavy-duty tubular shocks and 1.00-in. diameter stabilizer bar. Rear suspension: Hotchkiss solid axle, multi-leaf rear springs, .625-in. stabilizer bar and tubular shocks. Steering: Optional power assist coaxial re-circulating ball bearing. Fuel tank: 20.2 gal.

Trans Am: Body and frame: Integral body and frame with separate ladder-type front frame section. Front suspension: Independent with upper and lower control arms, heavy-duty coil springs, heavy-duty tubular shocks and 1.250-in. diameter stabilizer bar. Rear suspension: Hotchkiss solid axle, multi-leaf rear springs, .812-in. stabilizer bar and tubular shocks. Steering: Saginaw variable-ratio steering with power assist. Fuel tank: 20.2 gal.

The '74 T/A was not lacking in bells and whistles. The exterior goodies included hood scoop, flared wheel wells, dual exhaust and sport mirrors.

OPTIONS

604 heavy-duty dual-stage air cleaner, not available with Trans Am with 35X ($9). 582 custom air conditioning (not available with 35D ($446). 378 performance axle required with 682 with manual transmission ($10). 371 Safe-T-Track axle, standard with Trans Am ($45). 574 Maintenance-free battery, not available with 591 ($26). 591 heavy-duty battery, not available with 574 ($10). 502 power front disc brakes, required with 35X ($46). 711 electric clock, included with Trans Am and 712 and 714 ($15). 431 front console, not available with 36A ($58). 424 rear console ($26). 594 rear window defogger, not available with 592 ($33). 592 electric rear window defroster, not available with 35D engine or 594 ($64). 682 dual exhaust, not available with 35D engine; standard with Formula and Trans Am ($45). 571 Soft-Ray glass, all windows ($38). 572 Soft-Ray glass, windshield only ($31). 492 door edge guards ($6). 601 engine block heater, not available with 35D engine ($10). 512 Trans Am hood decal ($35). 694 dual horns, base Firebird only; standard with other Firebirds ($4). 602 unitized ignition with 35S and 35W engines only, not available with base Firebird or Esprit ($77). 654 lamp package with luggage compartment, glove box and instrument panel courtesy lamps ($10). 554 electric door locks ($46). 622 front floor mats ($7). 624 rear floor mats ($6). 614 trunk mat, standard with custom bucket seats and Esprit, ($8). 441 right-hand visory-vanity mirror, ($3). 434 dual sport mirrors, standard with Esprit, Formula and Trans Am ($26). 494 black vinyl body side moldings, not available with Trans Am ($31). 481 roof drip moldings, standard with Esprit ($15). 491 wheel opening moldings, standard with Esprit; not available with Trans Am ($15). 484 window sill and rear hood edge moldings, standard with Esprit ($21). 511 custom pedal trim plates, standard with Esprit ($5). 411 AM push-button radio ($65). 413 AM/FM radio ($135). 415 AM/FM stereo ($233). 712 Rally gauges and clock, not available with 714 or 711 or Trans Am ($46). 714 Rally gauges with clock and tachometer, not available with 711 or 712; standard with Trans Am ($92). 514 Ram Air hood, for Formula with 35S engine only; included with 35X engine and standard on Trans Am ($56). 691 custom front and rear seat and shoulder belts ($15). 421 rear seat speaker, not available with 415 or 422; 411 or 413 required ($21). 681 rear air spoiler, standard with Trans Am; not available with Esprit ($32). 461 custom cushion steering wheel, standard with Esprit, Formula; not available with Trans Am ($15). 464 Formula steering wheel, standard with Trans Am; 501 required ($41 in Esprit and Formula; $56 in base Firebird). 504 tilt steering wheel, not available with column-shift automatic transmission, ($45). 638 vinyl tape stripes, not available with Trans Am ($41). 422 stereo eight-track player, 431 with 411, 413 and 415 required ($130). 684 space saver spare tire ($15). 472 custom finned wheel covers, not available on Trans Am (for Esprit $24; for base Firebird and Formula $50). 476 deluxe wheel covers, standard with Esprit; not available with Trans Am ($26). 471 wheel trim rings, standard with Trans Am; not available with Esprit ($26).

The Trans Am again came with multiple engine options for 1974, including an S-D 445 version.

474 Rally II wheel rims (on base Firebird and Formula without 684 $87; on Formula with 684 $74.80; on Esprit $97). 478 honeycomb wheel rims (on base Firebird and Formula without 684 $123; on Formula with 684 $103; on Esprit $61). 551 power windows, with 431 only ($78). 432 concealed wipers, standard with Esprit, Trans Am ($18). 541 California emissions test, required on cars sold in California ($20). SVT vinyl top (on Esprit $72; on base Firebird, Formula and Trans Am $87). 734 impact protection bumper ($5). 722 heavy-duty radiator, not available with 582 ($21). 804 kilometer speedometer ($20). 35D inline 250-cid six-cylinder engine, in base Firebird (standard). 35M V-8 350-cid two-barrel engine, standard with Esprit and Formula; not available with Trans Am ($118). 35R V-8 400-cid two-barrel engine, not available with base Firebird or Trans Am; with 36L only ($51). 35S V-8 400-cid four-barrel engine, with 36L or 36E only; not available with base Firebird or Esprit ($97). 35W V-8 455-cid four-barrel engine (in Formula with 36L required $134; in Trans Am $57). 35X SD-455 V-8, 455-cid four-barrel engine (in Formula with 36E and 36L required $785; in Trans Am with 36E and 36L required $578). 36B three-speed manual transmission with floor shift; with 35D, 35M only (no cost). 36L M-40 Turbo-Hydra-Matic transmission, not available with 587; standard with Trans Am ($242). 36E four-speed manual transmission, not available with 35D, 35R or 35W ($207). 36K M-38 Turbo-Hydra-Matic transmission (with base six-cylinder Firebird $221; with Esprit or Formula $211). 308 custom trim package ($77). TGJ Radial Tuned Suspension package, includes FR78-14 steel-belted radial white sidewall tires, a rear stabilizer bar, special springs, firm shocks and RTS identification on Esprit without 582 and 684 ($145 extra). TGJ Radial Tuned Suspension package, includes FR78-14 steel-belted radial white sidewall tires, a rear stabilizer bar, special springs, firm shocks and RTS identification on Esprit with 582 without 684 ($119 extra Radial Tuned Suspension package, includes FR78-14 steel-belted radial white sidewall tires, a rear stabilizer bar, special spring). TGJ, firm shocks and RTS identification on Esprit without 582 with 684 ($131 extra). TGJ Radial

Tuned Suspension package, includes FR78-14 steel-belted radial white sidewall tires, a rear stabilizer bar, special springs, firm shocks and RTS identification on Esprit with 582 and 684 ($108 extra). TGJ Radial Tuned Suspension package, includes FR78-14 steel-belted radial white sidewall tires, a rear stabilizer bar, special springs, firm shocks and RTS identification on Formula without 684 ($30 extra). TGJ Radial Tuned Suspension package, includes FR78-14 steel-belted radial white sidewall tires, a rear stabilizer bar, special springs, firm shocks and RTS identification on Formula with 684 ($24 extra). TGK Radial Tuned Suspension package, includes FR78-14 steel-belted radial raised white letter tires, a rear stabilizer bar, special springs, firm shocks and RTS identification on base Firebird or Esprit without 582 and 684 ($155 extra). TGK Radial Tuned Suspension package, includes FR78-14 steel-belted radial raised white letter tires, a rear stabilizer bar, special springs, firm shocks and RTS identification on base Firebird or Esprit without 582 with 684 ($127 extra). TGK Radial Tuned Suspension package, includes FR78-14 steel-belted radial raised white letter tires, a rear stabilizer bar, special springs, firm shocks and RTS identification on base Firebird or Esprit with 582 without 684 ($141 extra). TGK Radial Tuned Suspension package, includes FR78-14 steel-belted radial raised white letter tires, a rear stabilizer bar, special springs, firm shocks and RTS identification on base Firebird or Esprit with 582 and 684 ($116 extra). TGR FR78-14 fiberglass-belted white sidewall tires on base Firebird or Esprit without 582 and 684 ($44 extra). TGR FR78-14 fiberglass-belted white sidewall tires on base Firebird or Esprit with 582, without 684 ($35 extra). TGR FR78-14 fiberglass-belted white sidewall tires on base Firebird or Esprit without 582 with 684 ($30 extra). TGR FR78-14 fiberglass-belted white sidewall tires on base Firebird or Esprit with 582 and 684 ($24 extra). TGF FR78-14 fiberglass-belted black sidewall tires on base Firebird or Esprit without 582 and 684 ($14 extra). TGF FR78-14 fiberglass-belted black sidewall tires on base Firebird or Esprit without 582 and 684 ($11 extra). THB E78-14 fiberglass-belted white letter tires on base Firebird or Esprit without 582 and 684 ($28 extra). THB E78-14 fiberglass-belted white letter tires on base Firebird or Esprit with 684 ($22 extra). TML F70-14 black sidewall tires with white lettering on base Firebird or Esprit without 582 and 684 ($75 extra). TML F70-14 black sidewall tires with white lettering on base Firebird or Esprit with 582 without 684 ($61 extra). TML F70-14 black sidewall tires with white lettering on base Firebird or Esprit without 582 with 684 ($60 extra). TML F70-14 black sidewall tires with white lettering on base Firebird or Esprit with 582 and 684 ($49 extra). TVH GR-70x15 steel-belted radial tires on Formula with 684 ($40). base Firebird or Esprit with 582 and 684 ($49 extra). TVH GR-70x15 steel-belted radial tires on Formula without 684 ($50). TVK GR-70x15 steel-belted radial tires with raised white lettering on base Firebird and Esprit without 684 ($92). TVK GR-70x15 steel-belted radial tires with raised white lettering on base Firebird or Esprit with 684 ($74 extra). TVK GR-70x15 steel-belted radial tires with raised white lettering on Trans Am without 684 ($42). TVK GR-70x15 steel-belted radial tires with raised white lettering on Trans Am with 684 ($34).

HISTORICAL FOOTNOTES

The 1974 Pontiacs were introduced on Sept. 20, 1973. Model year production of Firebirds rose to 73,729 vehicles of which 66,126 had V-8 engines. A total of 1,008 Trans Ams were built with LS2 SD-455 engines. Sales came in at 66,350 units for the model year and 67,391 for the calendar year. *Motor Trend* nominated the Firebird for its "Car of the Year" award and described the car as the "best combination available of pure performance and handling in the U.S. Grand Touring market." In one survey, *Motor Trend* asked 1,500 Japanese car enthusiasts to pick the best car in the world. The Firebird came out ahead of the Mustang by a slight margin and well ahead of the Corvette. *Super Stock* magazine (June 1974) put an SD-455 Trans Am through its paces. This car had the TH-400 transmission and 3.08:1 rear axle. It did the quarter mile in 14.25 seconds at 100.93 mph.

Pontiac sold more than 10,000 1974 Trans Ams.

Jerry Heasley photo

Flared wheel wells, hood scoop and spoiler made the T/A easily recognizable.

Business Picks Up

Firebird sales picked up in 1975, although the cars continued to look much the same as before. The biggest update was a new rear window that wrapped around the corners of the roof to give the driver improved vision. GM's HEI electronic ignition system was added to the equipment list along with a radial tuned suspension system. The base Firebirds were the plainest-looking and had visible windshield wipers. Esprits had concealed wipers, dressy moldings, body-color door handle inserts and chrome "Esprit" signatures on the roof. Formulas featured were ready for some street action with their heavy-duty underpinnings and dual hood scoops. The Trans Am was ready to go sports-car racing with its bolt-on flares, spoilers, engine air extractors, shaker hood scoop and "chicken" decals.

There were some technical changes. The Espirit's base engine became the Chevy-built six instead of the 350-cid two-barrel V-8. At the start of the year, the biggest Trans Am engine was the 400-cid V-8. At midyear, the 455-cid V-8 was reinstated, but with single exhausts and a catalytic converter. Due to decreased horsepower, the M38 Turbo-Hydra-Matic was the only automatic used. All Firebirds certified for sale in California were required to use this transmission.

Model-year production included 22,293 Firebirds, 20,826 Esprits, 13,670 Formula Firebirds and 27,274 Trans Ams. Only 8,314 Firebirds were built with the in-line six-cylinder engine. Most (26,417) Trans Ams had the 400-cid 185-hp L78 four-barrel V-8. Only 857 Trans Ams were built with the 455-cid 200-hp L75 four-barrel V-8. Road testers found the 1975 Trans Am with the L78 drive train capable of 0 to 60 mph in 9.8 seconds and the quarter mile in 16.8 seconds.

I.D. NUMBERS

The vehicle identification number (VIN) was stamped on a plate on the upper left-hand side of the instrument panel and visible through the windshield. The first symbol was the GM divisional code, 2=Pontiac. The second symbol indicated series: S=Base Firebird, T=Firebird Esprit, U=Formula Firebird, V=Trans Am. The third and fourth symbols indicated the body style: 87=sport coupe. The fifth symbol indicated engine: D=250-cid inline six, M=350-cid two-barrel V-8 with single exhaust system, H=350-cid four-barrel V-8 with single exhaust system, S=400-cid four-barrel V-8 with single exhaust system and W=455 H.O. four-barrel V-8 with dual "splitter" exhaust system. The sixth symbol indicated model year: 5=1975. The seventh symbol indicated the assembly plant: N=Norwood, Ohio. The remaining symbols were sequential unit production number at factory, starting with 100001. The Body by Fisher plate on the engine side of the cowl contained the Fisher style number, which took the form 75-2FV87. The prefix 75=1975, the first symbol 2=Pontiac, the second symbol F=Firebird, the third symbol V=Trans Am and the last two symbols 87=sport coupe. This plate also indicated interior trim, seat type, body color and build date. Six-cylinder engine code stamped on distributor mounting on right side of block. V-8 engine code on front of block below right cylinder head. Engine production codes for 1975 were: [250-cid, 105-nhp six-cylinder] JU-JT-JL, [350-cid, 155 hp V-8] YA-YB, [350-cid, 175-nhp V-8] WN-YN-ZP, [400-cid/185-nhp V-8] YS-WT-YM-YT-ZT, [455-cid, 200-nhp V-8] WX.

COLORS

11=Cameo White, 13=Sterling Silver, 15=Graystone, 24=Arctic Blue, 26=Bimini Blue, 29-Stellar Blue, 44=Lakemist Green, 49=Alpine Green, 50=Caramel Beige, 51=Sunstorm Yellow, 55=Sandstone, 58=Ginger Brown, 63=Copper Mist, 64=Persimmon, 74=Honduras Maroon and 75=Buccaneer Red.

BASE FIREBIRD - (SIX/V-8) SERIES 2FS

This was the year that GM added performance-robbing catalytic converters to all of its cars, including the Firebird. Firebirds continued to look much the same as in 1974, except for a new roofline with a 10 percent larger wraparound backlight. The grille had new rectangular running lamps and turn signal lamps. High Energy Ignition and Radial Tuned Suspension systems were added to the equipment list. As usual, base models had conventional wipers, "baby moon" hubcaps, a deluxe two-spoke steering wheel and minimal bright work. Inside the standard Madrid Morrokide bucket seat interior came in black, white or saddle regular combinations. Options included black or saddle interiors with white seats or four special combinations. The standard 250-cid overhead valve in-line six was up to 105 hp. Three-speed manual transmission was standard in 49 states and a Turbo-Hydra-Matic 350 (THM-350) transmission was standard in cars sold in California. A four-speed manual transmission was optional. The 350-cid two-barrel V-8 was $130 extra and required installation of Turbo-

Hydra-Matic transmission as a separate $237 option.

Model Number	Body/Style Number	Body Type & Seating	Factory Price	Shipping Weight	Production Total
FIREBIRD - SERIES 2FS - (SIX)					
2FS	87	2d sport coupe-4P	$3,713	3,386 lbs.	Notes 1, 2
FIREBIRD - SERIES 2FS - (V-8)					
2FS	87	2d sport coupe-4P	$4,080	3,653 lbs.	Note 2

Note 1: Combined production of base Firebirds and Esprits with the six-cylinder engine was 8,314 cars.
Note 2: Total production of base Firebirds was 22,293, including cars with both six-cylinder and V-8 engines.

FIREBIRD ESPRIT - (SIX/V-8) SERIES 2FT

Esprits had all of the same standard features as the base Firebird, plus concealed windshield wipers, a custom interior, decor moldings, colored vinyl door handle inserts, wide rocker moldings, deluxe wheel covers, dual horns, "Esprit" roof pillar signature scripts and an "Esprit" script on the right-hand corner of the rear deck lid. The base power plant in Esprit was now the Chevy-built six. The 350-cid two-barrel V-8 was available at the same price as in base Firebirds and the Turbo-Hydra-Matic 350 was the only transmission available

Model Number	Body/Style Number	Body Type & Seating	Factory Price	Shipping Weight	Production Total
FIREBIRD ESPRIT - SERIES 2FT - (SIX)					
2FT	87	2d sport coupe-4P	$3,958	3,431 lbs.	Notes 3,4
FIREBIRD ESPRIT - SERIES 2FT - (V-8)					
2FT	87	2d sport coupe-4P	$4,455	3,655 lbs.	Note 4

Note 3: Combined production of Base Firebirds and Esprits with the six-cylinder engine was 8,314 cars.
Note 4: Total production of Esprits was 20,826 including cars with both six-cylinder and V-8 engines.

FORMULA FIREBIRD - (V-8) SERIES 2FU

Formula Firebirds featured heavy-duty chassis components, wider front and rear tracks and a distinctive twin scoop hood. The base engine was a 350-cid V-8 with a four-barrel carburetor and dual outlet "splitter" exhausts. The standard transmission was

The read deck lid spoiler and dual splitter exhaust helped give the rear of the Trans Am a sports car image.

either a four-speed manual with a floor-mounted gearshift or Turbo-Hydra-Matic, also with a floor-mounted gearshift. The THM-350 was required for cars sold in California.

Model Number	Body/Style Number	Body Type & Seating	Factory Price	Shipping Weight	Production Total
FORMULA 350 FIREBIRD - SERIES 2FU - (V-8)					
2FU	U87	2d sport coupe-4P	$4,349	3,631 lbs.	Note 5
FORMULA 400 FIREBIRD - SERIES 2FU - (V-8)					
2FU	U87	2d sport coupe-4P	$4,405	3,631 lbs.	Note 5

Note 5: Total production of Formula Firebirds with both engines was 13,670.

TRANS AM - (V-8) - SERIES 2FV

The Trans Am had flares, front and rear air dams, extractors, shaker hood scoop, Firebird decals, a rear deck lid spoiler, rally gauges, rally wheel rims and a shaker hood scoop. There were some changes in a technical sense. At the beginning of the year, the biggest engine for the 1975 Trans Am was a 400-cid, 185-hp V-8 that included a four-barrel carburetor and a dual outlet "splitter" exhaust system. At midyear, a 455-cid, 200-hp four-barrel V-8 was reinstated. Labeled the 455 H.O., it included a tuned exhaust setup with pipes that branched into dual "splitters" behind the catalytic converter. The 445 H.O. option also included a 3.23:1 performance rear axle and semi-metallic disc brakes. Trans Am colors were Sterling Silver, Stellar Blue, Buccaneer Red and Cameo White.

Model Number	Body/Style Number	Body Type & Seating	Factory Price	Shipping Weight	Production Total
TRANS AM 400 - SERIES 2FV - (V-8)					
2FV	87	2d sport coupe-4P	$4,740	3,716 lbs.	26,417
TRANS AM 455 H.O. - SERIES 2FV - (V-8)					
2FV	87	2d sport coupe-4P	$4,740	3,716 lbs.	857

NOTE 6: 20,277 Trans Am 400s had Turbo-Hydra-Matic transmission and 6,140 had manual transmission.
NOTE 7: All Trans Ams with the 455 H.O. V-8 had manual transmission.

ENGINE

Inline six-cylinder [UPC L22]: Overhead valves. Cast-iron block. Displacement: 250 cid. Bore & stroke: 3.875 x 3.531 in. Compression ratio: 8.25:1. Brake horsepower: 105 at 3800 rpm. Torque: 185 ft.

The 400 engine was much more common than the 455 H.O. in the 1975 Trans Am.

Jerry Heasley photo

lbs. at 1200 rpm. Hydraulic valve lifters. Carburetor: One-barrel. VIN Code: D.

350 V-8 [UPC L30]: Overhead valves. Cast iron block. Displacement: 350 cid. Bore & stroke: 3.875 x 3.75 in. Compression ratio: 7.6:1. Brake horsepower: 155 at 3600 rpm. Torque: 280 ft. lbs. at 2000 rpm. Hydraulic valve lifters. Carburetion: Two-barrel. Single exhaust. VIN Code: M.

350 V-8 [UPC L76]: Overhead valves. Cast-iron block. Displacement: 350 cid. Bore & stroke: 3.875 x 3.75 in. Compression ratio: 7.6:1. Brake horsepower: 175 at 4000 rpm. Torque: 280 ft. lbs. at 2000 rpm. Hydraulic valve lifters. Carburetion: Four-barrel. Dual outlet "splitter" exhausts. VIN Code: H.

400 V-8 [UPC L78]: Overhead valves. Cast-iron block. Displacement: 400 cid. Bore & stroke: 4.125 x 3.75 in. Compression ratio: 7.6:1. Brake horsepower: 185 at 3600 rpm. Torque: 310 ft. lbs. at 1600 rpm. Five main bearings. Hydraulic valve lifters. Carburetor: Four-barrel. VIN code: R, S.

455 H.O. V-8 [UPC L75]: Overhead valves. Cast-iron block. Displacement: 455 cid. Bore & stroke: 4.15 x 4.21 in. Compression ratio: 7.6:1. Brake horsepower: 200 at 3500 rpm. Torque: 330 ft. lbs. at 2000 rpm. Five main bearings. Hydraulic valve lifters. Carburetor: Four-barrel. Tuned exhaust with splitters. VIN code: W.

CHASSIS

Base V-8, Esprit, Formula: Wheelbase: 108.1 in. Overall Length: 196 in. Overall width: 73 in. Overall height: 49.1 in. Front tread: [Base, Esprit] 60.9 in.; [Formula] 61.3 in. Rear tread: [Base, Esprit] 60 in.; [Formula] 60.4 in.

Trans Am: Wheelbase: 108.1 in. Overall length: 196 in. Overall width: 73 in. Overall height: 49.1 in. Front tread: 61.2 in. Rear tread: 60.3 in.

TECHNICAL:

Base/Esprit: Body and frame: Integral body and frame with separate bolted-on sub-frame for engine and front suspension. Front suspension: Independent with upper and lower control arms, coil springs, tubular shocks and 1.00-in. diameter stabilizer bar. Rear suspension: Hotchkiss solid axle, multi-leaf rear springs and tubular shocks. Steering: Optional power assist coaxial re-circulating ball bearing. Fuel tank: 20.2 gal.

Formula: Body and frame: Integral body and frame with separate ladder-type front frame section. Front suspension: Independent with upper and lower control arms, heavy-duty coil springs, heavy-duty tubular shocks and 1.125-in. diameter stabilizer bar. Rear suspension: Hotchkiss solid axle, multi-leaf rear springs, 0.562-in. stabilizer bar and tubular shocks. Steering: Optional power assist coaxial re-circulating ball bearing. Fuel tank: 20.2 gal.

Trans Am: Body and frame: Integral body and frame with separate ladder-type front frame section. Front suspension: Independent with upper and lower control arms, heavy-duty coil springs, heavy-duty tubular shocks and 1.250-in. diameter stabilizer bar. Rear suspension: Hotchkiss solid axle, multi-leaf rear

Jerry Heasley photo

The familiar Trans Am cockpit setup with Formula steering wheel, bucket seats, and Rally gauges returned for 1975.

springs, .812-in. stabilizer bar and tubular shocks. Steering: Saginaw variable-ratio steering with power assist. Fuel tank: 20.2 gal.

OPTIONS

36D/L22 inline 250-cd six-cylinder engine in base Firebird and Esprit (no cost). 36M/L30 V-8 350-cid two-barrel engine, in base Firebird and Esprit ($130). 36E/L76 V-8 350-cid four-barrel engine, standard in Formula; in base Firebird and Esprit ($180). 36S/L78 V-8 400-cid four-barrel engine, standard in Trans Am; in Formula ($56). 36W/L75 V-8 455-cid four-barrel engine, in Trans Am only ($150). 37L/M38 Turbo-Hydra-Matic transmission, standard in Formula and Trans Am (in base Firebird and Esprit $237). 37B/Ml5 three-speed manual transmission with floor shift, in base Firebird and Esprit (no cost). 37E/M20 four-speed manual transmission, standard no-cost option in Formula and Trans Am, in base Firebird and Esprit ($219). 37F/M21 close-ratio four-speed manual transmission, in Formula and Trans Am (no cost option). 602/K45 heavy-duty air cleaner, standard with Trans Am ($11). 582/C60 custom air conditioning ($435). 381/G80 Safe-T-Track axle and differential, standard in Trans Am; in base Firebird, Esprit and Formula ($49). 591/UA1 heavy-duty battery ($11). 441/AK1 custom seat belts and soft-tone warning ($19). 541/VJ California emissions equipment and test ($45). 711/U35 electric clock without Rally gauges or speedometer ($16). 711/U35 electric clock with Rally gauges or speedometer (no cost). 431/D55 front seat console ($68). 424/D58 rear seat console ($41).

594/C50 rear window defogger ($41). 592/C49 electric rear window defroster ($70). 601/K05 engine block heater ($11). 704/URI fuel economy vacuum gauge, except Trans Am ($22.50). 712/W63 Rally gauges and clock in base Firebird, Esprit or Formula ($50). 714/WW8 Rally gauge cluster, clock and tachometer, standard in Trans Am; in other Firebirds ($99). 571/AQ1 Soft-Ray glass, all windows ($43). 572/AQ2 Soft-Ray glass, windshield only ($34). 492/B93 door edge guards ($7). 444/T63 headlamp warning buzzer ($6). 512/WW7 Trans Am hood decal, on Trans Am only. ($55) 584/BS1 added acoustical insulation, standard in Esprit ($20). 654/Y92 lamp group including glove box lamp, instrument panel courtesy and luggage lamp ($11.50). 622/B32 front floor mats ($8). 624/B33 rear floor mats ($7). 422/D35 sport mirrors; left-hand remote control, right-hand fixed (on base Firebird $27; on Esprit, Formula and Trans Am no cost). 432/D34 right-hand visor vanity mirror ($3). 494/B84 body side moldings, except Trans Am ($35). 481/B80 roof drip moldings standard on Esprit; on other Firebirds without Cordova vinyl top ($15); with Cordova vinyl top (no cost). 491/B96 wheel lip moldings, not available on Trans Am; standard on Esprit; on base Firebird and Formula ($16). 484/B85 window sill and rear hood edge molding, standard with Esprit; on other Firebirds ($21). 502/JL2 front power disc brakes, standard on Formula and Trans Am; on other Firebirds ($55). 554/AU3 power door locks ($56). 551/A31 power windows ($91). 401/U63 AM radio ($69). 403/U69 AM/FM radio ($135). 405/U58 AM/FM stereo radio ($233). 684/N65

Space Saver spare (no cost). 804/Ul8 speedometer with kilometers and clock ($21). 411/U80 rear seat speaker ($19). 681/D80 rear air spoiler, not available on Esprit; standard with Trans Am; on other Firebirds ($45). 461/DBO custom cushion steering wheel, base Firebird only ($16). 464/NK3 formula steering wheel, standard in Trans Am; in base Firebird ($57); in Formula and Esprit ($41). 504/N33 tilt steering wheel ($49). 412/U57 stereo 8-track player ($130). 638/D98 accent stripes, except Trans Am ($43). PVT/C09 Cordova vinyl top ($99). 32W/Y90 custom trim group standard in Esprit; in Formula and Trans Am ($81). 511/JL1 pedal trim package, standard with Esprit and with Y90 option; otherwise ($5). 472/P02 custom finned wheel covers, on Esprit ($24); on base Firebird and Formula ($54) 476/P0l deluxe wheel covers, no cost on Esprit; on base Firebird and Formula ($30). 478/P05 Honeycomb wheels, standard on Trans Am; on base Firebird and Formula without 684 ($127); on base Firebird and Formula with 684 ($107.60); on Esprit without 684 ($97); on Esprit with 684 ($77.60). 474/N98 Rally II wheels and trim rings, no cost on Trans Am; on base Firebird and Formula without 684 ($91); on base Firebird and Formula with 684 ($78.80); on Esprit without 684 ($61); on Esprit with 684 ($48.80). 471/P06 wheel trim rings, on base Firebird and Formula without 474 ($30). 414/C24 recessed windshield wipers, on base Firebird and Formula ($18). 39A/QBU FR78 x l5 black sidewall steel-belted radial tires, on base Firebird, Esprit and Formula (no cost). 39B/QBX GR70 x 15 black sidewall steel-belted radial tires on Formula without space saver spare ($40 extra); on Formula with Space Saver spare ($32 extra); on Trans Am (no cost). 39L/QBP FR78 x 15 white letter steel-belted radial tires, on base Firebird, Esprit and Formula without Space Saver spare ($43 extra); on base Firebird, Esprit and Formula with Space Saver spare ($34.40 extra). 39M/QCY GR70x15 white-letter steel-belted radial tires, on Formula without Space Saver spare ($85 extra); on Formula with Space Saver spare ($68 extra); Trans Am without Space Saver spare ($45 extra); Trans Am with Space Saver spare ($36 extra). 39L/QBW FR78 x 15 white sidewall steel-belted radial tires, on Firebird, Esprit and Formula without Space Saver spare ($33 extra); on Firebird, Esprit and Formula with Space Saver spare ($26.40 extra). 39Y/QFM F78 x 14 white sidewall fiberglass tires on Firebird and Esprit without Space Saver spare ($73 credit); on Firebird and Esprit with Space Saver spare ($60.40 credit). 39Z/QFL F78 x 14 black sidewall fiberglass tires on Firebird and Esprit without Space Saver spare ($106.00 credit); on Firebird and Esprit with Space Saver spare ($86.80 credit).

HISTORICAL FOOTNOTES

The 1975 Firebirds appeared in showrooms on Sept. 27, 1974. Model year output was 84,063 cars. Sales came out as 75,565 in the model year and 82,652 in the calendar year. Road testers found the 1975 Trans Am with the 185-nhp V-8 capable of 0 to 60 mph in 9.8 seconds and the quarter mile in 16.8 seconds. *Car and Driver* magazine (September 1975) tested a Trans Am with the 455-cid V-8, four-speed manual transmission and 3.23:1 gears. It did the quarter mile in 16.1 seconds at 88.8 mph. In March of 1975 *Road Test* magazine put a Trans Am with a 400-cid V-8, a THM-350 and 2.56:1 gears through its paces and recorded quarter-mile performance of 17.99 seconds at 79.36 mph.

1975 Pontiac Firebird Formula (left) and Trans Am sport coupes.

The '76 Limited Edition Trans Am came only in Starlight Black.

Limited Edition

The "chrome-bumper" Firebird had disappeared! This year all four Pontiac F-cars wore body-colored urethane bumpers front and rear. For a little bit extra, buyers could add a new canopy-style vinyl top. Other product innovations included a Formula appearance package and a fuel economy indicator. Stylists recessed the square, single headlamps into the front fenders and topped things off with a traditional Pontiac split grille. It had a mesh pattern insert.

Firebird/Esprit equipment included the 250-cid six with three-speed manual gearbox, power steering and radial-tuned suspension. Esprits added sport mirrors and deluxe wheel covers. Formula had a 350-cid two-barrel V-8, a choice of four-speed manual or Turbo-Hydra-Matic transmission and a full-length console. Trans Am added an air dam, a rear spoiler, a shaker hood, Rally II wheels, Rally gauges, fat GR70 x 15 tires and a 400-cid four-barrel V-8.

A special Trans Am that created excitement and sales was introduced at the 1976 Chicago Auto Show. This "Limited Edition" model featured Starlight black finish with gold striping, gold interior accents, gold honeycomb wheels and a super-sized version of the "chicken" hood decal. This original Limited Edition

T/A commemorated PMD's 50th anniversary and was actually modified with a T-top conversion installed by Hurst. A total of 2,590 were made.

The overall popularity of Firebird and Esprit models remained much the same as the previous year with 21,209 base models and 22,252 Espirits leaving the factory in 1976. However, the Formula was becoming a hotter product with 20,613 assemblies and the Trans Am was on fire with 46,701 built. That was a production increase of 51 percent for Formulas and 71 percent for Trans Ams!

I.D. NUMBERS

The vehicle identification number (VIN) was stamped on a plate on the upper left-hand side of the instrument panel and was visible through the windshield. The first symbol was the GM divisional code, 2=Pontiac. The second symbol indicated series: S=Base Firebird, T=Firebird Esprit, U=Formula Firebird, W=Trans Am. The third and fourth symbols indicated the body style: 87=sport coupe. The fifth symbol indicated engine: D=250-cid inline six; M=350-cid two-barrel V-8 with single exhaust system, P=350-cid four-barrel V-8 with single exhaust system, Z=400-cid four-barrel V-8 with dual splitter exhaust system and W=455 H.O. four-barrel V-8 with dual splitter exhaust system. The sixth symbol indicated model year:

6=1976. The seventh symbol indicated the assembly plant: N=Norwood, Ohio. The remaining symbols were sequential unit production number at factory, starting with 100001. The Body by Fisher plate on the engine side of the cowl contained the Fisher style number, which took the form 76-2FS87. The prefix 76=1976, the first symbol 2=Pontiac, the second symbol F=Firebird, the third symbol S=base Firebird and the last two symbols 87=sport coupe. This plate also indicated interior trim, seat type, body color and build date. Six-cylinder engine code stamped on distributor mounting on right side of block. V-8 engine code on front of block below right cylinder head. Engine production codes for 1976 were: [250-cid six-cylinder] CC-CD-CF-CH-CJ-CL, [350-cid two-barrel V-8] YR-YB-XR, [350-cid four-barrel V-8] ZX-ZF, [400-cid four-barrel V-8] WU-XY-XS-YZ-YS-WT-ZK-ZJ-X9-Y9, [455-cid four-barrel V-8] WX. Engine production code note: According to *Pontiac Technical Service Bulletin* No. 76-I-33 dated Feb. 2, 1976, most automatic-equipped 350- and 400-cid V-8s received a "damper" in place of the traditional harmonic balancer. In most cases, the first letter in the engine production code, which was usually a "Y," was replaced by an "X."

COLORS

Paint codes for 1976 were: 11=Cameo White, 13=Sterling Silver, 19=Starlight Black, 28=Athena Blue, 35=Polaris Blue, 36=Firethorn Red, 37=Cordovan Maroon, 40=Metalime Green, 49=Alpine Green, 50=Bavarian Cream, 51=Goldenrod Yellow, 65=Buckskin Tan, 67=Durango Bronze and 78=Carousel Red

FIREBIRD - (SIX/V-8) - SERIES 2FS

The 1976 Firebird again had a twin-section grille with a mesh pattern insert set into a sloping front panel. The single round headlamps were recessed into square bezels. The parking and signal lamps were located at each end of a wide, slot-like opening below the bumper strip. Another styling change was that all Firebirds featured body-colored urethane bumpers at both ends. New-for-1976 options included a canopy-style vinyl half-top, a new appearance package for Formula models and a fuel economy indicator. Brake systems on all Firebirds were refined to meet federal standards, axle ratios were lowered to promote better fuel economy and V-8 engines idled slower for the same reason. There were improvements to the cooling and air-conditioning system. Seat patterning in the standard interior was changed to vertical ribbing, with the seat backs having three distinct sections. The door panels had twin, vertical-ribbed sections similar to, but not identical to, the 1975 design. A rosewood instrument panel appliqué replaced the crossfire mahogany insert. All Firebirds had a new brake fluid level sensor and Turbo-Hydra-Matic transmission was required on all cars sold in California. Standard Firebird equipment included all federally mandated safety, anti-theft, convenience and emissions control features, a Chevrolet-built 250-cid inline six with a three-speed manual transmission, power steering, front disc/rear drum brakes, a heater, a defroster, carpeting, dual horns, FR78-15 black sidewall tires and a Radial Tuned Suspension.

The '76 Formula received a new all-steel, twin-scoop hood.

Model Number	Body/Style Number	Body Type & Seating	Factory Price	Shipping Weight	Production Total
FIREBIRD - SERIES 2FS - (SIX)					
2FS	87	2d sport coupe-4P	$3,906	3,383 lbs.	Notes 1, 2
FIREBIRD - SERIES 2FS - (V-8)					
2FS	87	2d sport coupe-4P	$4,046	3,563 lbs.	Note 2

Note 1: Combined production of base Firebirds and Esprits with the six-cylinder engine was 9,405 cars.
Note 2: Total production of base Firebirds was 21,209, including cars with both six-cylinder and V-8 engines.

FIREBIRD ESPRIT - (SIX/V-8) SERIES 2FT

Standard Firebird Esprit equipment included all federally mandated safety, anti-theft, convenience and emissions control features, a Chevrolet-built 250-cid inline six with a three-speed manual transmission, power steering, front disc/rear drum brakes, a heater, a defroster, custom interior trim, rocker panel moldings, roof drip moldings, wheel opening moldings, window moldings, carpeting, dual sport mirrors (left-hand remote controlled), extra acoustical insulation, dual horns, deluxe wheel covers, FR78-15 black sidewall tires and a Radial Tuned Suspension. The custom interior that was standard in the Esprit featured wider vertical ribs than the standard interior. On the seatbacks the ribs were bordered by a "horse collar" and on the seat cushions they ran right down to the floor. Custom door panels were the same as the 1975 design.

Model Number	Body/Style Number	Body Type & Seating	Factory Price	Shipping Weight	Production Total
FIREBIRD ESPRIT - SERIES 2FT - (SIX)					
2FT	87	2d sport coupe-4P	$4,162	3,431 lbs.	Notes 3, 4
FIREBIRD ESPRIT - SERIES 2FT - (V-8)					
2FT	87	2d sport coupe-4P	$4,302	3,611 lbs.	Note 4

Note 3: Combined production of base Firebirds and Esprits with the six-cylinder engine was 9,405 cars.
Note 4: Total production of Firebird Esprits was 22,252, including cars with both six-cylinder and V-8 engines.

FORMULA FIREBIRD - (V-8) SERIES 2FU

Standard Formula Firebird equipment included all federally mandated safety, anti-theft, convenience and emissions control features, a 350-cid (5.7-liter) V-8 engine, a Turbo-Hydra-Matic or close-ratio four-speed manual (code M-21 Borg-Warner Super T-10) transmission, a new all-steel duct-type dual scoop hood, power steering, a front seat console, front disc/rear drum brakes, a heater, a defroster, carpeting, rocker panel moldings, windshield moldings, a luxury steering wheel, dual sport mirrors with left-hand remote controlled, dual horns, a rear deck lid spoiler, chrome side-splitter tailpipe extensions, FR78-15 black sidewall tires and a radial-tuned suspension. The two-barrel 350-cid V-8 (available only with the THM-350 transmission) was not legal in California and buyers there had to order the four-barrel version as a mandatory option. It came only with Turbo-Hydra-Matic drive. The 400-cid V-8 was available nationwide for $118 extra. The new W50 Formula Appearance package was an option that included contrasting finish on the lower body perimeter and air scoops and "Formula" graphics on the lower body sides. At first the W50 package came only with a yellow main body and black body side and scoop finish,

but it was later available in four color combinations C, N, T and V. Over 85 percent of Formula customers ordered this option. The 455-cid V-8 wasn't offered in the Formula.

Model Number	Body/Style Number	Body Type & Seating	Factory Price	Shipping Weight	Production Total
FORMULA 350 FIREBIRD - SERIES 2FU - (V-8)					
2FU	87	2d sport coupe-4P	$4,566	3,625 lbs.	Note 5
FORMULA 400 FIREBIRD - SERIES 2FU - (V-8)					
2FU	87	2d sport coupe-4P	$4,684	3,625 lbs.	Note 5

Note 5: Total production of Formula Firebirds with both engines was 20,613.

FIREBIRD TRANS AM - (V-8) SERIES 2FW

Standard Trans Am equipment included all federally mandated safety, anti-theft, convenience and emissions control features, a 400-cid (6.6-litre) V-8 engine, an M-21 close-ratio four-speed manual transmission (Turbo-Hydra-Matic was optional), a shaker hood scoop and air cleaner, a front air dam, concealed windshield wipers, front fender air extractors, rear wheel opening air deflectors, power steering, Rally gauges with a clock and tachometer, front disc/rear drum brakes, a heater, a defroster, carpeting, windshield moldings, a formula steering wheel, dual sport mirrors with left-hand remote controlled, dual horns, a rear deck lid spoiler, chrome side-splitter tailpipe extensions, Rally II wheels with trim rings, GR70-15 raised white letter tires and a Radial Tuned Suspension. Trans Am color choices for 1976 were: Firethorn Red, Sterling Silver, Starlight Black, Carousel Red, Goldenrod Yellow and Cameo White.

FIREBIRD TRANS AM LIMITED EDITION - (V-8) SERIES 2W/Y81/Y82

In February 1976, at the Chicago Automobile Show, Pontiac introduced the Limited Edition Trans Am. This package featured Starlight Black exterior body finish, gold pin striping, gold interior accents (including gold anodized instrument panel appliqués and gold steering wheel spokes), gold grilles, gold headlight liners, gold honeycomb wheel rims and a host of other special distinctions. The car was promoted as a commemorative edition for Pontiac Motor Division's 50th anniversary. The 1976 Limited Edition models were inspired by a 1974 show car that took its theme from the black-and-gold John Player racing cars. The package was designed by John Schinella and featured a gold version of his trademark "screaming chicken" decal on the hood. Pontiac built the entire car and then sent it to Hurst Corp. for modifications such as having "T-tops" installed. Hurst Hatch T-top roofs were installed on 643 cars. This T-top design was originally devised for the 50th Anniversary Grand Prix and there were problems adapting it to the Firebird body. Production did not start until April of 1976 and Hurst Hatch roofs were used on only about 25 percent of the Limited Editions made that year.

Model Number	Body/Style Number	Body Type & Seating	Factory Price	Shipping Weight	Production Total
TRANS AM 400 - SERIES 2FW - (V-8)					
2FV	87	2d sport coupe-4P	$4,987	3,640 lbs.	37,015

Pontiac sold more than 20,000 Formula versions of its Firebird in 1976.

TRANS AM 455 H.O. - SERIES 2FW - (V-8)

2FV	87	2d sport coupe-4P	$5,112	3,716 lbs.		7,099

TRANS AM 400 LIMITED EDITION - SERIES 2FW/Y81 - (V-8)

2FV	87	2d sport coupe-4P	$5,553	—		1,628

TRANS AM 455 LIMITED EDITION - SERIES 2FW/Y81 - (V-8)

2FV	87	2d sport coupe-4P	$5,678	—		319

TRANS AM 400 LIMITED EDITION - SERIES 2FW/Y82 - (V-8)

2FV	87	2d T-top coupe-4P	$6,130	—		533

TRANS AM 455 LIMITED EDITION - SERIES 2FW/Y82 - (V-8)

2FV	87	2d T-top coupe-4P	$6,255	—		110

NOTE 6: 33,752 Trans Am 400s had Turbo-Hydra-Matic transmission and 5,424 had manual transmission.

NOTE 7: All 7,528 Trans Ams with the 455 H.O. V-8 had manual transmission.

ENGINE

Inline six-cylinder [UPC L22]: Overhead valves. Cast-iron block. Displacement: 250 cid. Bore & stroke: 3.875 x 3.531 in. Compression ratio: 8.3:1. Brake horsepower: 110 at 3600 rpm. Torque: 185 ft. lbs. at 1200 rpm. Hydraulic valve lifters. Carburetor: One-barrel. VIN Code: D.

350 V-8 [UPC L30]: Overhead valves. Cast-iron block. Displacement: 350 cid. Bore & stroke: 3.875 x 3.75 in. Compression ratio: 7.6:1. Brake horsepower: 160 at 4000 rpm. Torque: 280 ft. lbs. at 2000 rpm. Hydraulic valve lifters. Carburetion: Two-barrel. Single exhaust. VIN Code: M.

350 V-8 [UPC L76]: Overhead valves. Cast-iron block. Displacement: 350 cid. Bore & stroke: 3.875 x 3.75 in. Compression ratio: 7.6:1. Brake horsepower: 165 at 4000 rpm. Torque: 260 ft. lbs. at 2400 rpm. Hydraulic valve lifters. Carburetion: Four-barrel. Single exhausts. VIN Code: P.

400 V-8 [UPC L78]: Overhead valves. Cast-iron block. Displacement: 400 cid. Bore & stroke: 4.125 x 3.75 in. Compression ratio: 7.6:1. Brake horsepower: 185 at 3600 rpm. Torque: 310 ft. lbs. at 1600 rpm. Five main bearings. Hydraulic valve lifters. Carburetor: Four-barrel. Splitter exhausts. VIN code: Z.

455 V-8 [UPC L75]: Overhead valves. Cast-iron block. Displacement: 455 cid. Bore & stroke: 4.15 x 4.21 in. Compression ratio: 7.6:1. Brake horsepower: 200 at 3500 rpm. Torque: 330 ft. lbs. at 2000 rpm. Five main bearings. Hydraulic valve lifters. Carburetor: Four-barrel. Tuned exhaust with splitters. VIN code: W. (Note: Due to criticism over using the H.O. designation on cars with lowered performance capabilities, the L75 V-8 was no longer called the 455 H.O.)

CHASSIS

Base V-8, Esprit, Formula: Wheelbase: 108.1 in. Overall length: 196.8 in. Overall width: 73 in. Overall height: 49.1 in. Front tread: [Base, Esprit] 60.9 in.; [Formula] 61.3 in. Rear tread: [Base, Esprit] 60 in.; [Formula] 60.4 in.

Trans Am: Wheelbase: 108.1 in. Overall length: 196.8 in. Overall width: 73 in. Overall height: 49.1 in. Front tread: 61.2 in. Rear tread: 60.3 in.

TECHNICAL

Base/Esprit: Body and frame: Integral body and frame with separate bolted-on sub-frame for engine and front suspension. Front suspension: Independent with upper and lower control arms, coil springs, tubular shocks and 1.00-in. diameter stabilizer bar. Rear suspension: Hotchkiss solid axle, multi-leaf rear springs and tubular shocks. Steering: Optional power assist coaxial re-circulating ball bearing. Fuel tank: 20.2 gal.

Formula: Body and frame: Integral body and frame with separate ladder-type front frame section. Front suspension: Independent with upper and lower control arms, heavy-duty coil springs, heavy-duty tubular shocks and 1.125-in. diameter stabilizer bar. Rear suspension: Hotchkiss solid axle, multi-leaf rear springs, .562-in. stabilizer bar and tubular shocks. Steering: Optional power assist coaxial re-circulating ball bearing. Fuel tank: 20.2 gal.

Trans Am: Body and frame: Integral body and frame with separate ladder-type front frame section. Front suspension: Independent with upper and lower control arms, heavy-duty coil springs, heavy-duty tubular shocks and 1.250-in. diameter stabilizer bar.

R. Boone photo

Firethorn Red with a black interior was a nice color combination for the 1976 Trans Am. This was one of about 5,400 400 four-speeds built that year.

Rear suspension: Hotchkiss solid axle, multi-leaf rear springs, .812-in. stabilizer bar and tubular shocks. Steering: Saginaw variable-ratio steering with power assist. Fuel tank: Fuel tank: 20.2 gal.

OPTIONS

37D/L22 inline 250-cid six-cylinder engine, base Firebird and Esprit (no cost). 37M/L30 V-8 350-cid two-barrel engine in base Firebird and Esprit; not available in California; standard with Formula; Turbo-Hydra-Matic required ($140). 37E/L76 V-8 350-cid four-barrel engine in base Firebird and Esprit; California only; Turbo-Hydra-Matic required ($195). 37E/L76 V-8 350-cid four-barrel engine in Formula; California only; Turbo Hydra-Matic required ($55). 37S/L78 V-8 400-cid four-barrel in base Firebird and Esprit; not available in California; Turbo-Hydra-Matic required ($258). 37S/L78 V-8 400-cid four-barrel in Formula; not available in California, Turbo-Hydra-Matic required ($118). 37S/L78 V-8 400-cid four-barrel in Trans Am (standard). 37W/L75 V-8 455-cid four-barrel engine, Trans Am only; not available in California; Turbo-Hydra-Matic required ($125). 38B/Ml5 three-speed manual transmission, including floor shift; with six-cylinder engine only (no cost). 38F/M21 close-ratio four-speed manual transmission; with 400- and 455-cid V-8 only; not available in California ($242). 38F/M21 close-ratio four-speed manual transmission in Trans Am; not available California (no cost). 38L/M40 Turbo-Hydra-Matic transmission in base Firebird and Esprit; standard in Formula and Trans Am ($262). 492/C60 custom air conditioning ($452). 674/K97 heavy-duty alternator available for V-8s only; without C50 and C50 with C60 ($42); with C50 and C60 (no cost). 582/W50 Formula Appearance package, colors C, N, T, V only ($100). 391/G80 Safe-T-Track axle, standard in Trans Am; in base Firebird, Esprit and Formula ($51). 681/UA1 heavy-duty battery ($16). 524/AK1 custom front and rear seat belts and front shoulder belts ($20). 721/VJ9 Califor-

nia emissions equipment and test ($50). 474/U35 electric clock (no charge with W63 or WW8; otherwise $18). 581/D55 front console, standard in Formula; required with Turbo-Hydra-Matic ($71). 572/D58 rear seat console ($43). 462/C50 rear window defogger ($48). 461/C49 electric rear window defroster, V-8s only ($77). 684/K05 engine block heater ($12). 481/UR1 vacuum gauge, in base Firebird, Esprit and Formula with W63 only ($25). 502/W63 Rally gauge cluster and clock, in base Firebird, Esprit and Formula; required with UR1 and six-cylinder engine ($54). 504/WW8 Rally gauge cluster with clock and tachometer, in base Firebird, Esprit and Formula with V-8s only ($106). 442/A0l Soft-Ray tinted glass, all windows ($46). 612/B93 door edge guards ($8). 664/WW7 hood decal, Trans Am only ($58). 521/BS1 added acoustical insulation; standard in Esprit; in other models ($25). 631/Y92 lamp group, includes glove box lamp, instrument panel courtesy lamp and luggage compartment lamp ($14). 601/B32 front floor mats ($8). 602/B33 rear floor mats ($7). 642/D35 dual sport mirrors, left-hand remote control, standard with Esprit, Formula and Trans Am; on base Firebird ($29). 652/D34 visor vanity mirror ($4). 611/B84 color-keyed vinyl body moldings, on base Firebird, Esprit and Formula ($38). 584/B80 roof drip moldings, standard on Esprit and Trans Am; on base Firebird and Formula without C87 ($16). 614/B96 wheel lip moldings, standard Esprit; not available on Trans Am ($17). 591/885 window and rear hood moldings, base Firebird, Formula and Trans Am; standard with Esprit ($22). 452/JL2 power front disc brakes, required with V-8; standard with Formula and Trans Am ($58). 434/AU3 power door locks ($62). 431/A31 power windows, with D55 only ($99). 682/VQ2 supercooling radiator, without C60 ($49); with C60 ($37). 411/U63 AM radio ($75). 413/U69 AM/FM radio ($137). 415/U58 AM/FM stereo radio ($233). 802/UN9 radio accommodation package, no charge with optional radios; otherwise ($22). 441/N65 stowaway spare, standard with Trans Am; with base Firebird, Esprit and Formula ($1.22). 421/U80 rear seat speaker, optional only with U63 and U69 ($20). 562/D80 rear spoiler, standard with Trans Am; on base Firebird, Esprit, Formula ($48). 541/N30 custom cushion steering wheel, standard in esprit and Formula; in base Firebird ($17). 544/N K3 Formula steering wheel, standard in trans Am; in base Firebird ($60); in Esprit and Formula ($43). 444/N33 tilt steering wheel ($52). 422/U57 stereo 8-track player; required with D55 and radio ($134). 358/D98 vinyl accent stripes on base Firebird, Esprit and Formula ($46). CVT/CB7 canopy top, not available on Trans Am; on base Firebird, Esprit and Formula ($96). 32N/Y90 custom trim group. standard in Esprit, not available base Firebird; in Formula and Trans Am ($81). 561/JL1 pedal trim package, standard in Esprit; base Firebird, Formula and Trans Am without Y90 ($6). 556/POI deluxe wheel covers, standard on Esprit; not available on Trans Am; on base Firebird, Formula ($6). 558/P05 four honeycomb wheels with radial tires on base Firebird and Formula ($135 extra). 558/P05 four Honeycomb wheels with radial tires, no cost on Trans Am; on Formula ($103 extra). 554/N98 Argent Silver Rally II wheels and trim rings, with fiberglass tires without N65 on base Firebird (five wheels $113 extra); with fiberglass tires with N65 on base Firebird (four wheels $97 extra); without fiberglass tires on base Firebird (four wheels $97 extra); with fiberglass tires without N65 on Esprit (five wheels $81 extra); with fiberglass tires with N65 on Esprit (four wheels $65 extra); without fiberglass tires on Esprit (four wheels) $65 extra; without fiberglass tires on Formula (four wheels $97 extra); without fiberglass tires on Trans Am (four wheels, no charge). 559/N67 body-color Rally II wheels and trim rings, with fiberglass tires without N65 on base Firebird (five wheels $113 extra); with fiberglass tires with N65 on base Firebird (four wheels $97 extra); without fiberglass tires on base Firebird (four wheels $97 extra); with fiberglass tires without N65 on Esprit (five wheels $81 extra); with fiberglass tires with N65 on Esprit (four wheels $65 extra); without fiberglass tires on Esprit (four wheels) $65 extra; without fiberglass tires on Formula (four wheels $97 extra); without fiberglass tires on Trans Am (four wheels, no charge).

574/C24 recessed windshield wipers, standard on Formula and Trans Am; on base Firebird and Esprit ($22). 40B/QBU FR78 x 15 black sidewall radial tires on base Firebird, Esprit and Formula (no cost). 40W/0BW FR78 x 15 steel-belted white sidewall radial tires; without N65; except Trans Am ($35 extra); with N65, except Trans Am ($28 extra). 40L/QBP FR78 x 15 steel-belted raised white letter radial tires, except Trans Am; without N65 ($46 extra); except Trans Am with N65 ($36.80 extra). 40G/QBX GR79 x 15 black sidewall steel-belted radial tires, standard on Trans Am; on Formula ($34.44 extra). 40F/QCY GR70 x 15 white-letter steel-belted radial tires, on Formula with N65 required ($72.84 extra); on Trans Am with N65 required ($38.40 extra). 40D/QFM F78 x 14 white sidewall fiberglass radial tires, on base Firebird and Esprit without N65 ($62.45 extra); on base Firebird and Esprit with N65 ($49.96 extra). 40C/QFL F78 x 14 black sidewall fiberglass radial tires, on base Firebird and Esprit without N65 ($97.45 extra); on base Firebird and Esprit with N65 ($77.96 extra)

HISTORICAL FOOTNOTES

Introduced September 25, 1975. Model-year production of Firebirds was 110,775, an all-time record and the first six-figure year since 1968. Sales totals stood at 98,405 Firebirds for the model year and 108,348 Firebirds for the calendar year, both of which were records for the nameplate. *CARS* magazine named the 1976 Trans Am "Top Performance Car of the Year." Editor Joe Oldham said it was the "best looking" of all the Trans Ams. In April 1976, *Car and Driver* did an article on America's fastest car. The 455 Trans Am finished in second place behind the L82 Corvette. The Trans Am had a top speed of 117.6 mph. It did 0 to 60 mph in 7 seconds and covered the standing-start quarter mile in 15.6 seconds at 90.3 mph. *High Performance Cars* magazine tested two Trans Ams during 1976. The first (February) had a 455-cid V-8, four-speed manual gearbox and 3.23:1 gears. It did the quarter mile in 15.62 seconds at 91 mph. In September the magazine tried out a Limited Edition T-top coupe with a 400-cid V-8, four-speed manual transmission and 3.08:1 gears. It recorded a 16.64-second quarter-mile trip at 85 mph.

The 1977 Espirit came with three engine choices: V-6, 301 V-8 and 350 V-8.

1977

Sky's the Limit

By the late '70s the wisdom of keeping the Firebird in the Pontiac line was becoming evident with sales numbers zooming and profit levels rising thanks to the second-generation F-car's longevity. For 1977, the designers favored a front end with four rectangular headlights and "honeycomb" grille texture. The grille insert was recessed and it jutted out at the bottom, in the center, to give the vertical center divider a more aggressive V shape.

Four models were offered: base, Esprit, and performance Formula and Trans Am. Formula's had a new hood with simulated air scoops and a rear-deck-lid spoiler. Engine choices ranged from a Buick-built 231-cid (3.8-liter) V-6 to an Oldsmobile-built 403-cid (6.6-liter) V-8. Esprit buyers could order a new blue "Sky Bird" appearance package with blue velour seating, a subtle two-tone blue body finish and blue cast-aluminum wheels. A new 301-cid (5.0-liter) two-barrel V-8 was standard in Formulas, which also had black-out trim and large "Formula" graphics on the lower part of the doors. Trans Ams had a new shaker hood and came with a standard 400- or 403-cid V-8. Also available was an optional "T/A 6.6" version of the Pontiac-built 400-cid power plant with an 8.0:1 compression ratio and 200 hp. Cars so-equipped could do 0 to 60 in 9.3 seconds and had a top speed approaching 110 mph.

The Trans Am could again be ordered with an extra-cost package, which was called the Special Edition rather than Limited Edition. It was available in Y81 coupe and Y82 Hurst Hatch (or T-top) models. Custom gold decals and gold snowflake wheels really set off this well-integrated appearance option. PMD records indicate that 15,567 Special Edition Trans Ams were built in 1977.

While performance may have been down somewhat from earlier years, the Trans Am still had a hot, sexy sports-racing-car image that drove the Firebird's popularity higher. Model year production totals included 30,642 base Firebirds, 34,548 Esprits, 21,801 Formulas and 68,745 high-profit-margin Trans Ams. To put the Firebird's success in perspective, remember that less than 30,000 were made just five years earlier, when the model's future seemed dim.

I.D. NUMBERS

The vehicle identification number (VIN) was stamped on a plate on the upper left-hand side of the instrument panel and visible through the windshield. The first symbol was the GM divisional code, 2=Pontiac. The second symbol indicated series: S=Base Firebird, T=Firebird Esprit, U=Formula Firebird, W=Trans Am. The third and fourth symbols indicated the body style: 87=sport coupe. The fifth symbol indicated engine: C=231-cid Buick-built two-barrel V-6; Y=301-cid Pontiac-built two-barrel V-8, L=350-cid Chevrolet-built four-barrel V-8, R=350-cid Oldsmobile-built four-barrel V-8, Z=400-cid Pontiac-built four-barrel V-8 and K=403-cid Oldsmobile-built four-barrel V-8. The sixth symbol indicated model year: 7=1977. The seventh symbol indicated the assembly plant: N=Norwood, Ohio. The remaining symbols were sequential unit production number at factory, starting with 100001. The Body by Fisher plate on the engine side of the cowl contained the Fisher style number, which took the form ST 77 2FS87 for all models. The prefix ST=Style, the symbols 77=1977, the symbol 2=Pontiac, the symbol F=Firebird, the symbol S=base Firebird and the last two symbols 87=sport coupe. On the fourth line the designation W66=Formula and the designation WS4=Trans Am. This plate also indicated interior trim, seat type, body color and build date. Six-cylinder (now V-6) engine code stamped on distributor mounting on right side of block. V-8 engine code on front of block below right cylinder head. Engine production codes for 1977 were: [231-cid V-6] SG-SI-SK-SM-SU-ST, [301-cid V-8] WB-YH-YK, [305-cid Chevrolet-built four-barrel V-8] CPY, [350-cid four-barrel Oldsmobile-built V-8] Q8-Q9-TX-TY, [350-cid Pontiac-built four-barrel V-8] Y9, [400-cid V-8] XA, [400-cid Pontiac-built T/A four-barrel V-8] Y6-WA and [403-cid Oldsmobile-built four-barrel V-8] U2-U3-VA-VB.

COLORS

11=Cameo White, 13=Sterling Silver, 19=Starlight Black, 21=Lombard Blue; 22=Glacier Blue; 29=Nautilus Blue; 36=Firethorn Red, 44=Bahia Green; 51=Goldenrod Yellow, 55=Gold Metallic, 58=Bright Blue, 61=Mohave Tan; 63=Buckskin; 69=Brentwood Brown; 75=Buccaneer Red and 78=Mandarin Orange.

FIREBIRD - (V-6/V-8) - SERIES 2FS

New front-end styling for the Firebird coupe featured quad rectangular headlamps and an "aggressive" grille. The wheelbase was 108 in. and engine choices ranged from a 231-cid two-barrel (3.8-liter) V-6 to the 350-cid four-barrel (5.7-liter) V-8. Firebird's new grille was deeply recessed, directly in line with the quad rectangular headlamps. Its simple pattern consisted of a series of round-like (hexagonal) holes that resembled fencing more than a customary grille. A "Pontiac" nameplate went on the driver's side of the grille. Crossbar-trimmed amber parking and signal lamps were also recessed, but into the outer ends of twin air intake slots positioned in the bumper valance panel, on either side of a solid and "veed" center section. The "nose" of the Firebird protruded forward to a slight point and held a V-shaped Pontiac

The black Special Edition Trans Am was star of the Firebird line for the second straight year in 1977.

The quad-headlight look was back for the 1977 Firebird.

emblem in the center, but the sides were more sharply angled than the prior version. Standard engine in the base Firebird was now the 231-cid (3.8-liter) V-6 with a two-barrel carburetor. A Chevrolet-built 301-cid (5.0-liter) two-barrel V-8 was a new engine for the base Firebird and Esprit that became available about Feb. 1, 1977. Other engine options for these models — in all regions of the country — included the 350-cid (5.7-liter) four-barrel V-8. A three-speed manual transmission was used with the base engine. Standard equipment included a new grille and new hood styling with integral body-colored bumpers, hubcaps with the Pontiac crest, new rectangular headlamps, bright windshield and rear window moldings, Firebird emblems on the sail panel and rear deck lid, dual horns, front bucket seats, bucket-type rear seats, all Morrokide seat trim, solid foam front seat cushions with integral springs, a new deluxe cushion steering wheel in matching interior colors, nylon blend cut-pile carpeting, a simulated rosewood appliqué on the instrument panel, a speedometer graduated in kilometers as well as miles per hour, single-buckle seat and shoulder belts, a fluid-on-demand windshield wiper washer system, an ashtray lamp, high-low level ventilation, a trunk floor mat, front disc/rear drum brakes, variable-ratio power steering, a coil spring front suspension, a leaf spring rear suspension, a High Energy Electronic (HEI) ignition system, a catalytic converter and a Radial Tuned Suspension including FR78-15 steel-belted radial tires, firm shock absorbers, jounce restrictors, computer-selected springs and a front stabilizer bar.

Model Number	Body/Style Number	Body Type & Seating	Factory Price	Shipping Weight	Production Total
FIREBIRD - SERIES 2FS - (V-6)					
2FS	87	2d sport coupe-4P	$4,269	3,264 lbs.	Notes 1, 2
FIREBIRD - SERIES 2FS - (301-cid V-8)					
2FS	87	2d sport coupe-4P	$4,334	3,349 lbs.	Note 2
FIREBIRD - SERIES 2FS - (350-cid V-8)					
2FS	87	2d sport coupe-4P	$4,424	—	Note 2

Note 1: Combined production of base Firebirds and Esprits with the six-cylinder engine was 15,080 cars.
Note 2: Total production of base Firebirds was 30,642, including cars with both six-cylinder and V-8 engines.

FIREBIRD ESPRIT - (V-6/V-8) SERIES 2FT

The Esprit could have a new blue "Skybird" appearance package with blue velour seating, two-tone blue body, a dark blue rear panel, dark blue grille panels, accent stripes, special identification and blue cast-aluminum wheels. Esprit engine choices were the same as those for the base Firebird. A three-speed manual transmission was used with the base engine. Standard Esprit equipment included a new black-out grille and new hood styling with integral body-colored bumpers, new deluxe wheel covers, new rectangular headlamps, bright windshield and rear window moldings, bright roof moldings, bright windowsill moldings, bright rear window moldings, bright grille moldings, Firebird emblems on the sail panel and rear deck lid, recessed windshield wipers, dual horns, front bucket seats, bucket-type rear seats, custom all-Morrokide bucket seats with lateral support design, solid foam front seat cushions with integral springs, a new luxury cushion steering wheel in matching interior colors, custom pedal trim plates, door and instrument panel assist straps, distinctive door trim panels, rear ash-trays, added acoustical insulations, nylon blend cut-pile carpeting, a simulated rosewood appliqué on the instrument panel, a speedometer graduated in kilometers as well as miles per hour, single-buckle seat and shoulder belts, dual body-colored sport mirrors (left-hand remote controlled), body-color door handle inserts, a fluid-on-demand windshield wiper washer system, an ashtray lamp, high-low level ventilation, a trunk floor mat, front disc/rear drum brakes, variable-ratio power steering, a coil spring front suspension, a leaf spring rear suspension, a High Energy Ignition (HEI) system, a catalytic converter and a Radial Tuned Suspension with FR78-15 steel-belted radial tires, firm shock absorbers, jounce restrictors, computer-selected springs and a front stabilizer bar.

Model Number	Body/Style Number	Body Type & Seating	Factory Price	Shipping Weight	Production Total
FIREBIRD ESPRIT- SERIES 2FT - (V-6)					
2FT	87	2d sport coupe-4P	$4,550	3,312 lbs.	Notes 3,4
FIREBIRD ESPRIT - SERIES 2FT - (301-cid V-8)					
2FT	87	2d sport coupe-4P	$4,615	3,397 lbs.	Note 4
FIREBIRD ESPRIT - SERIES 2FT - (350-cid V-8)					
2FT	87	2d sport coupe-4P	$4,705	—	Note 4

Note 3: Combined production of base Firebirds and Esprits with the six-cylinder engine was 15,080 cars.
Note 4: Total production of Esprits was 34,548, including cars with both six-cylinder and V-8 engines.

FORMULA FIREBIRD - (V-8) SERIES 2FU

Standard engine in the Formula in 49 states was a 301-cid (5.0-liter) two-barrel V-8 made by Pontiac. In California and "high-altitude" counties a 350-cid (5.7-liter) four-barrel V-8 was standard. Other options included the 5.7-liter four-barrel V-8 in "federal" areas, two versions of a 400-cid Pontiac four-barrel V-8 and a 403-cid Oldsmobile four-barrel V-8. Some engines were not available in California and others were available only in California. A power-flex radiator fan was used with 6.6-liter V-8s. A four-speed manual transmission was available with the 301-cid (5.0-liter) V-8 and the T/A 6.6-liter (400-cid) engines. Turbo-Hydra-Matic transmission was optional. Standard Formula equipment included the new black-out grille, a new steel hood with twin simulated air scoops, integral body-colored bumpers, new rectangular headlamps, bright windshield and rear window moldings, bright grille moldings, Firebird emblems on the sail panel and rear deck lid, a rear deck lid spoiler, dual horns, front bucket seats, bucket-type rear seats, all-Morrokide bucket seats, a full-length front console, a new luxury cushion steering wheel in matching interior colors, nylon blend cut-pile carpeting, a simulated rosewood appliqué on the instrument panel, a speedometer graduated in kilometers as well as miles per hour, single-buckle seat and shoulder belts, dual body-colored sport mirrors (left-hand remote controlled), a fluid-on-demand windshield wiper washer system, high-low level ventilation, a trunk floor mat, front disc/rear drum brakes, variable-ratio power steering, a coil spring front suspension, a leaf spring rear suspension, a High Energy Ignition (HEI) system, dual chrome "splitter" tailpipe exten-

sions, a catalytic converter and a Radial Tuned Suspension including FR78-15 steel-belted radial tires, firm shock absorbers, jounce restrictors, computer-selected springs and front and rear stabilizer bars. Buyers who ordered the optional Formula Appearance package got a blacked-out lower body and hood scoops, multi-color stripes and large "Formula" super graphics on the body sides. This year the package came in six color combinations: Cameo White with black lower body perimeter and blue striping; Sterling Silver with charcoal and light red; Starlight Black and gold; Goldenrod Yellow with gold, orange and black; Glacier Blue with medium blue and black; and Buccaneer Red with a black perimeter and light and dark red stripes.

Model Number	Body/Style Number	Body Type & Seating	Factory Price	Shipping Weight	Production Total
FORMULA FIREBIRD 5.0-LITER - SERIES 2FU - (PONTIAC 301-CID V-8)					
2FU	87	2d sport coupe-4P	$4,977	3,411 lbs.	Note 5
FORMULA FIREBIRD 5.0-LITER - SERIES 2FU - (CHEVY 305-CID V-8)					
2FU	87	2d sport coupe-4P	$4,977	3,411 lbs.	Note 5
FORMULA FIREBIRD 5.7-LITER - SERIES 2FU - (PONTIAC 350-CID V-8)					
2FU	87	2d sport coupe-4P	$5,067	3,526 lbs.	Note 5
FORMULA FIREBIRD 5.7-LITER - SERIES 2FU - (OLDS 350-CID V-8)					
2FU	87	2d sport coupe-4P	$5,067	3,526 lbs.	Note 5
FORMULA FIREBIRD 6.6-LITER - SERIES 2FU – (PONTIAC 400-CID V-8)					
2FU	87	2d sport coupe-4P	$5,132	-	Note 5
FORMULA FIREBIRD T/A 6.6-LITER - SERIES 2FU - (PONTIAC 400-CID V-8)					
2FU	87	2d sport coupe-4P	$5,182	-	Note 5
FORMULA FIREBIRD T/A 6.6-LITER - SERIES 2FU - (OLDS 403-CID V-8)					
2FU	87	2d sport coupe-4P	$5,456	-	Note 5

Note 5: Total production of Formula Firebirds with both engines was 21,801.

FIREBIRD TRANS AM - (V-8) SERIES 2FW

The Trans Am equipment list started off with all federally mandated safety, anti-theft, convenience and emissions control features. A 400-cid (6.6-liter) V-8 engine was standard in 49 states and a 403-cid (6.6-liter) V-8 was standard in California or high-altitude counties. The T/A 6.6-liter (400-cid) V-8 was optional. Other standard equipment included a Turbo-Hydra-Matic transmission (or four-speed manual transmission with the optional T/A 6.6-liter V-8), a Trans Am front fender decal, a blacked-out grille, a Trans Am grille panel decal, a Trans Am wraparound rear deck spoiler decal, a front center air dam, rear wheel opening air deflectors, a shaker hood scoop and air cleaner, concealed windshield wipers, front fender air extractors, power steering, a Power-Flex radiator fan, Rally gauges with a clock and tachometer, a front seat console, power front disc/rear drum brakes, a heater, a defroster, carpeting, windshield moldings, an aluminum machine-turned instrument panel trim plate, a formula steering wheel, dual sport mirrors with left-hand remote controlled, dual horns, a rear deck lid spoiler, dual chrome splitter tailpipe extensions, 15 x 7-in. Rally II wheels with trim rings, a Safe-T-Track limited-slip differential, GR70-15 black sidewall steel-belted radial tires and a Radial Tuned Suspension with larger front and rear stabilizer bars.

FIREBIRD TRANS AM BLACK SPECIAL EDITION - (V-8) - SERIES FW/Y81/Y82

The 1977 Special Edition package was similar to

More than 34,000 F-Car buyers chose the Esprit in model year 1977.

Henry Maher photo

the 1976 Limited Edition package. Its standard equipment started off with all federally mandated safety, anti-theft, convenience and emissions control features. The 400-cid (6.6-liter) V-8 was standard in 49 states and the 403-cid (6.6-liter) V-8 was standard in California or high-altitude counties. The T/A 6.6-liter (400-cid) V-8 was optional. Other standard equipment included a Turbo-Hydra-Matic transmission (or four-speed manual transmission with the optional T/A 6.6-liter V-8), a Trans Am front fender decal, a black-out grille, a Trans Am grille panel decal, a Trans Am wraparound rear deck spoiler decal, a front center air dam, rear wheel opening air deflectors, a shaker hood scoop and air cleaner, concealed windshield wipers, front fender air extractors, power steering, a Power-Flex radiator fan, Rally gauges with a clock and tachometer, a front seat console, power front disc/rear drum brakes, a heater, a defroster, carpeting, windshield moldings, an aluminum machine-turned instrument panel trim plate, a formula steering wheel, dual sport mirrors with left-hand remote controlled, dual horns, a rear deck lid spoiler, dual chrome splitter tailpipe extensions, 15 x 7-in. Rally II wheels with trim rings, a Saf-T-Track limited-slip differential, GR70-15 black sidewall steel-belted radial tires, a Radial Tuned Suspension with larger front and rear stabilizer bars, Starlight Black exterior body finish, gold body striping, gold interior and exterior accents, gold aluminum wheels and an available removable hatch roof.

Model Number	Body/Style Number	Body Type & Seating	Factory Price	Shipping Weight	Production Total
TRANS AM 6.6-LITER - SERIES 2FW - (400-CID PONTIAC L78 V-8)					
2FW	87	2d sport coupe-4P	$5,456	3,640 lbs.	29,313
TRANS AM 6.6-LITER - SERIES 2FW - (403-CID OLDS L80 V-8)					
2FW	87	2d sport coupe-4P	$5,456	3,716 lbs.	5,079
TRANS AM T/A 6.6-LITER - SERIES 2FW - (400-CID PONTIAC L78/W72 V-8)					
2FW	87	2d sport coupe-4P	$5,506	3,730 lbs.	18,785
TRANS AM 6.6-LITER SPECIAL EDITION - SERIES 2FW/Y81 - (400-CID PONTIAC L78 V-8)					
2FW/Y81	87	2d sport coupe-4P	$6,012	3,740 lbs.	748
TRANS AM 6.6-LITER SPECIAL EDITION - SERIES 2FW/Y81 - (403-CID OLDS L80 V-8)					
2FW/Y81	87	2d sport coupe-4P	$6,012	3,745 lbs.	180
T/A 6.6-LITER SPECIAL EDITION - SERIES 2FW/Y81 - (400-CID PONTIAC L78/W72 V-8)					
2FW/Y81	87	2d sport coupe-4P	$6,062	3,750 lbs.	933
TRANS AM 6.6-LITER SPECIAL EDITION - SERIES 2FW/Y82 - (400-CID PONTIAC L78 V-8)					
2FW/Y82	87	2d T-top coupe-4P	$6,599	3,840 lbs.	6,030
TRANS AM 6.6-LITER SPECIAL EDITION - SERIES 2FW/Y82 - (403-CID OLDS L80 V-8)					
2FW/Y82	87	2d T-top coupe-4P	$6,599	3,845 lbs.	1,217
TRANS AM T/A 6.6-LITER SPECIAL EDITION - SERIES 2FW/Y82 - (403-CID OLDS L78/W72 V-8)					
2FW/Y82	87	2d T-top coupe-4P	$6,649	3,850 lbs.	6,459

Note 6: A total of 11,402 Trans Ams built this year had the four-speed manual transmission. All had the L78/W72 engine. The total included 8,319 regular 2FW models, 384 2FW/Y81 Special Edition coupes and 2,699 2FW/Y82 Special Edition T-top coupes.

Note 7: Turbo-Hydra-Matic transmission (THM) was used in 57,342. In regular 2FW coupes the use of THM by engine was: [L78] 29,313; [L78/W72] 10,466; [L80] 5,079. In 2FW/Y81 Special Edition coupes the use of THM by engine was: [L78] 748; [L78/W72] 549; [L80] 180. In 2FW/Y82 Special Edition T-top coupes the use of THM by engine was: [L78] 6,030; [L78/W72] 3,760; [L80] 1,217.

ENGINE

Buick V-6 [UPC LD7]: Overhead valves. Cast-iron block. Displacement: 231 cid. Bore & stroke: 3.80 x 3.40 in. Compression ratio: 8.0:1. Brake horsepower: 105 at 3200 rpm. Torque: 185 ft. lbs. at 2000 rpm. Hydraulic valve lifters. Carburetor: Two-barrel. VIN Code: C.

301 Pontiac V-8 [UPC L27]: Overhead valves. Cast-iron block. Displacement: 301 cid. Bore & stroke: 4.00 x 3.00 in. Compression ratio: 8.2:1. Brake horsepower: 135 at 4000 rpm. Torque: 235 ft. lbs. at 2000 rpm. Hydraulic valve lifters. Carburetion: Two-barrel. Single exhaust or "splitter" exhaust on Formula. VIN Code: Y.

305 Chevrolet V-8 [UPC LG3]: Overhead valves. Cast-iron block. Displacement: 305 cid. Bore & stroke: 3.74 x 3.48 in. Compression ratio: 8.4:1. Brake horsepower: 145 at 3800 rpm. Torque: 245 ft. lbs. at

2400 rpm. Hydraulic valve lifters. Carburetion: Two-barrel. Single exhaust. VIN Code: U.

350 Pontiac V-8 [UPC L76]: Overhead valves. Cast-iron block. Displacement: 350 cid. Bore & stroke: 3.875 x 3.75 in. Compression ratio: 7.6:1. Brake horsepower: 170 at 4000 rpm. Torque: 280 ft. lbs. at 1800 rpm. Hydraulic valve lifters. Carburetion: Four-barrel. Single exhaust or "splitter" exhaust on Formula. VIN Code: L.

350 Oldsmobile V-8 [UPC L-34]: Overhead valves. Cast-iron block. Displacement: 350 cid. Bore & stroke: 4.06 x 3.39 in. Compression ratio: 8.0:1. Brake horsepower: 170 at 3800 rpm. Torque: 275 ft. lbs. at 20000 rpm. Hydraulic valve lifters. Carburetion: Four-barrel. Single exhausts. Optional Firebird, Esprit and Formula sold in California. VIN Code: R.

400 Pontiac V-8 [UPC L78]: Overhead valves. Cast-iron block. Displacement: 400 cid. Bore & stroke: 4.121 x 3.750 in. Compression ratio: 7.6:1. Brake horsepower: 180 at 3600 rpm. Torque: 325 ft. lbs. at 1600 rpm. Five main bearings. Hydraulic valve lifters. Carburetor: Four-barrel. Splitter exhausts. VIN code: Z.

Pontiac T/A 6.6 V-8 [UPC L78/W72]: Overhead valves. Cast-iron block. Displacement: 400 cid. Bore & stroke: 4.121 x 3.750. Compression ratio: 8.0:1. Brake horsepower: 200 at 3600 rpm. Torque: 325 ft. lbs. at 2400 rpm with four-speed manual transmission; 325 at 2200 rpm with Turbo-Hydra-Matic. Five main bearings. Hydraulic valve lifters. Carburetor: Four-barrel. Splitter exhausts. VIN code: Z.

403 Oldsmobile V-8 [UPC L80]: Overhead valves. Cast-iron block. Displacement: 403 cid. Bore & stroke: 4.35 x 3.385 in. Compression ratio: 8.0:1. Brake horsepower: 185 at 3600 rpm. Torque: 320 ft. lbs. at 2200 rpm. Five main bearings. Hydraulic valve lifters. Carburetor: Four-barrel. Mandatory standard equipment in Trans Ams sold in California and high-altitude counties; optional equipment in Formulas sold in California and high-altitude counties. VIN code: K.

CHASSIS

Base V-8, Esprit: Wheelbase: 108.1 in. Overall length: 196.8 in. Overall width: 73 in. Overall height: 49.1 in. Front tread: 60.9 in. Rear tread: 60 in. Front headroom: 37.5 in. Rear headroom: 35.9 in. Front

Standard equipment for the Esprit included body-color bumpers. The "snowflake" wheels were optional.

legroom: 43.9 in. Rear legroom: 28.4 in. Front shoulder room: 57.4 in. Rear shoulder room: 54.4 in. Front hip room: 52.4 in. Rear hip room: 45.8 in.

Formula: Wheelbase: 108.1 in. Overall length: 196.8 in. Overall width: 73 in. Overall height: 49.1 in. Front tread: 61.3 in. Rear tread: 60.4 in. Front headroom: 37.5 in. Rear headroom: 35.9 in. Front legroom: 43.9 in. Rear legroom: 28.4 in. Front shoulder room: 57.4 in. Rear shoulder room: 54.4 in. Front hip room: 52.4 in. Rear hip room: 45.8 in.

Trans Am: Wheelbase: 108.1 in. Overall length: 196.8 in. Overall width: 73 in. Overall height: 49.1 in. Front tread: 61.2 in. Rear tread: 60.3 in. Front headroom: 37.5 in. Rear headroom: 35.9 in. Front legroom: 43.9 in. Rear legroom: 28.4 in. Front shoulder room: 57.4 in. Rear shoulder room: 54.4 in. Front hip room: 52.4 in. Rear hip room: 45.8 in.

TECHNICAL

Base/Esprit: Body and frame: Integral body and frame with separate bolted-on sub-frame for engine and front suspension. Front suspension: Independent with upper and lower control arms, coil springs, tubular shocks and 1.125-in. diameter stabilizer bar. Rear suspension: Hotchkiss solid axle, multi-leaf rear springs and tubular shocks. Steering: Optional power assist coaxial re-circulating ball bearing. Fuel tank: 20.2 gal.

Formula: Body and frame: Integral body and frame with separate ladder-type front frame section. Front suspension: Independent with upper and lower control arms, heavy-duty coil springs, heavy-duty tubular shocks and 1.125-in. diameter stabilizer bar. Rear suspension: Hotchkiss solid axle, multi-leaf rear springs, .560-in. stabilizer bar and tubular shocks. Steering: Optional power assist coaxial re-circulating ball bearing. Fuel tank: 20.2 gal.

Trans Am: Body and frame: Integral body and frame with separate ladder-type front frame section. Front suspension: Independent with upper and lower control arms, heavy-duty coil springs, heavy-duty tubular shocks and 1.250-in. diameter stabilizer bar. Rear suspension: Hotchkiss solid axle, multi-leaf rear springs, .625-in. stabilizer bar and tubular shocks. Steering: Saginaw variable-ratio steering with power assist. Fuel tank: Fuel tank: 20.2 gal.

OPTIONS

LD 231-cid V-6 two-barrel in base Firebird or Esprit (no cost). L27 301-cid V-8 two-barrel, M20 or M40 transmission required, in base Firebird or Esprit ($65). L34 350-cid V-8 four-barrel in base Firebird or Esprit ($155); in Formula ($90). L76 350-cid V-8 four-barrel used in California cars only, in base Firebird or Esprit ($155); in Formula ($90). L78 400-cid V-8 four-barrel, M40 transmission required, in Formula ($155). W72 400-cid V-8 four-barrel, M20 or M40 transmission required, in Formula ($205); in Trans Am ($50). L80 403-cid V-8 four-barrel, standard in trans Ams sold in California, optional in Formulas sold in California ($155). M20 four-speed manual transmission with L27/W72 V-8 only, no cost in Formula and Trans Am, optional in base Firebird and

Esprit ($257). M40 Turbo-Hydra-Matic transmission, standard in Formula and Trans Am, in base Firebird and Esprit ($282). C60 air conditioning ($478). W50 Formula Appearance package, Formula only ($127). W60 Blue Skybird Appearance package for Esprit with Lombardy cloth trim ($342); for Esprit with doeskin vinyl trim ($315). Y82 Trans Am Special Edition package with T-tops ($1,143). Y81 Trans Am Special Edition package without T-top ($556). G80 Safe-T-Track differential, standard with Trans Am ($54). UA1 heavy-duty battery, maintenance-free ($31). AK1 custom safety belts, standard in Esprit with W60 ($21). JL2 power brakes, required with all V-8s; optional in base Firebird and Esprit ($61). U35 electric clock, no cost with Rally gauge package; otherwise ($21). D55 full-length front console, M40 transmission required in base Firebird and Esprit ($75). D58 rear console ($46). K30 cruise control ($80). A90 remote-control deck lid release ($18). C49 electric rear window defroster ($82). AU3 power door locks ($68). VJ9 California emissions equipment ($70). NA6 high-altitude performance option ($22). K05 engine block heater ($13). Y96 firm-ride suspension package, included with V81; otherwise ($11). URI economy and vacuum gauges, together with W63 only; except Trans Am ($27). W63 Rally gauges and clock, standard Trans Am, URI required with V-6 ($60). WW8 Rally gauges, clock and tachometer, standard in Trans Am, in other Firebirds with V-8 only ($116). A01 tinted glass, all windows ($50). QBX rally RTS handling package, Formula only, N65 required ($70). QCY Rally RTS handling package, on Formula ($116); on Trans Am ($46). WW7 Trans Am hood decal, Trans Am only ($62). BS1 additional acoustical insulation, standard in Esprit; in other Firebirds ($27). C95 dome reading lamp ($16). Y92 lamp group package ($16). B37 color-keyed front and rear floor mats ($18). D35 outside dual sport mirrors, left-hand remote control ($31). D34 visor vanity mirror ($4). D64 illuminated visor vanity mirror ($32). B84 vinyl body side moldings ($40). B93 door edge guard moldings ($9). B80 roof drip moldings, standard with Esprit; base Firebird and Formula without CB7; otherwise ($17). B96 wheel opening moldings on base Firebird ($18); on Formula without W50 ($18). B85 windowsill and rear hood moldings, standard on Esprit; on other Firebirds ($24). V02 super cooling radiator without C60 or V81 ($53); with C60 without V81 ($29); with V81 (no cost). U63 AM radio ($79). U69 AM/FM radio ($137). U58 AM/FM stereo ($233). UN8 citizen's band (CB) radio, 23-channel, D55 and UN9 required ($195). U57 8-track stereo player, D55 and an optional radio required ($134). UN9 radio accommodation package ($23 but no cost with optional radios). U80 rear speaker with AM or AM/FM radio only ($23). D80 rear spoiler, standard on Formula and Trans Am, on base Firebird and Esprit ($51). NK3 Formula steering wheel in base Firebird ($61); in Esprit or Formula ($43). N30 luxury cushion steering wheel in base Firebird ($18). N33 tilt steering wheel ($57). D98 vinyl accent strips for all models except Trans Am ($49). CC1 dual hatch glass sunroof without Y82 ($587). CB7 canopy top, not available on Trans Am;

The Esprits got some subtle improvements inside for 1977, including an upgraded padded steering wheel.

on other Firebirds ($105). V81 light trailer group without C60 ($64); with C60 ($40). Y90 custom vinyl doeskin trim in Formula or Trans Am ($91). Y90 custom Lombardy cloth trim in Formula or Trans Am ($118). Y90 custom regular vinyl trim in Esprit without W60 ($27). JL1 pedal trim package, available in Firebird, Formula and Trans Am without Y90 ($6). PO1 deluxe wheel covers, standard on Esprit; on base Firebird or Formula ($34). N95 wire wheel covers, Esprit ($100); on base Firebird or Formula ($134). YJ8 cast aluminum wheels, on base Firebird ($227); on Esprit without W60 ($193); on Formula ($227); on Trans Am without Y82 ($121). N98 Argent Silver Rally II wheels and trim rings, on base Firebird and Formula ($106); on Esprit ($72). N67 body color Rally II wheels and trim rings, on base Firebird and Formula ($106); on Esprit ($72). A31 power windows, D55 front console required ($108). N65 stowaway spare tire (no charge). QKM FR78 x 15 black sidewall fiberglass-belted radial tires, on base Firebird or Esprit without stowaway spare ($45 credit); on base Firebird or Esprit with stowaway spare ($36 credit). QKN FR78 x 15 white sidewall fiberglass-belted radial tires, on base Firebird or Esprit without stowaway spare ($4 credit); on base Firebird or Esprit with stowaway spare ($3 credit). QBW FR78 x 15 white sidewall steel-belted radial tires, standard on Trans Am; on other Firebirds without stowaway spare ($41 extra). QBP FR78 x 15 raised white letter steel-belted radial tires, standard on Trans Am; on other Firebirds without stowaway spare ($55 extra). QBP FR78 x 15 raised white letter steel-belted radial tires, on all except Trans Am with stowaway spare ($44 extra).

HISTORICAL FOOTNOTES

Motor Trend road tested a 1977 Firebird Formula with the base 301-cid V-8 and four-speed manual transmission and concluded "Detroit's putting some of the fun back." The car did 0 to 60 mph in 12 seconds and covered the quarter mile in 17.9 seconds at 75.2 mph while providing 20.9 mpg fuel economy. Total model-year production of Firebirds rose to a record 155,736 units. Sales stood at 133,154 for the model year and 137,807 for the calendar year.

There were few major changes in the Trans Am (above) and Firebird lineup for 1978.

Another Good Year

With Pontiac dealers struggling to accommodate hoards of Firebird buyers, GM saw no reason to make any sweeping changes in the 1978 models. Small changes were seen, including a couple of new engine options, redesigned seats and an expanded list of extra-cost items with some midyear additions.

Base engine was the 3.8-liter V-6 with three-speed shift. Formulas had a new 305-cid (5.0-liter) V-8, while the Trans Am included a 400-cid (6.6-liter) four-barrel V-8. Firebirds had Endura bumpers, small hubcaps and bucket seats were standard. Esprits added wheel covers, sport mirrors, bright hood and wheel opening moldings and custom pedal trim. Esprit buyers were offered a new "Red Bird" package that was similar to the Sky Bird option, except in red. The blue Sky Bird option also returned. Formulas again had black-out trim and large "Formula" graphics on the lower doors. Trans Am included a front air dam, black grille, rear spoiler, sport mirrors, rear wheel air deflectors, Rally II wheels, a "shaker" hood and air cleaner and rally instrument panel with tachometer. Automatic transmission was standard on Formulas and Trans Ams, but Formula could have a four-speed manual at no extra cost.

It was another good year for Firebirds, with production of 32,672 base Firebirds, 36,926 Esprits, 24,346 Formulas and 93,341 Trans Ams. Pontiac's calendar-year sales of 896,980 cars were the highest in its history up to the point and the booming popularity of the F-car was a big reason for this achievement.

I.D. NUMBERS

The vehicle identification number (VIN) was stamped on a plate on the upper left-hand side of the instrument panel and visible through the windshield. The first symbol was the GM divisional code, 2=Pontiac. The second symbol indicated series: S=Base Firebird, T=Firebird Esprit, U=Formula Firebird, W=Trans Am. The third and fourth symbols indicated the body style: 87=sport coupe. The fifth symbol indicated engine: A=231-cid Buick-built two-barrel V-6; U=305-cid Chevrolet-built two-barrel V-8, L=350-cid Chevrolet-built four-barrel V-8, Z=400-cid Pontiac-built four-barrel V-8, K=403-cid Oldsmobile-built four-barrel V-8. The sixth symbol indicated model year: 8=1978. The seventh symbol indicated the assembly plant: N=Norwood, Ohio, L=Van Nuys, California. The remaining symbols were sequential unit production number at factory, starting with 100001. The Body by Fisher plate on the engine side of the cowl contained the Fisher style number, which took the form ST 78 2FS87 for all models. The prefix ST=Style, the symbols 78=1978, the symbol 2=Pontiac, the symbol F=Firebird, the symbol S=base Firebird and the last two symbols 87=sport coupe. On the fourth line the designation W66=Formula and the designation WS4=Trans Am. This plate also indicated interior trim, seat type, body color and build date. V-6 engine code stamped on distributor mounting on right side of block. V-8 engine code on front of block below right cylinder head. Engine production codes for 1978 were: [231-cid V-6] EA-EC-EE, [305-cid V-8] TH-TJ-TK-3N, [350-cid Chevrolet-built four-barrel V-8] HF-HJ-HL-HR-3T, [400-cid four-barrel V-8] YA-X7-WC, [403-cid four-barrel V-8] VA-VB-U2.

COLORS

11=Cameo White, 15=Platinum Metallic, 19=Starlight Black, 22=Glacier Blue Metallic, 24=Martinique Blue Metallic, 30=Lombard Blue, 42=Redbird Red, 48=Berkshire Green Metallic, 50=Special Edition

Gold, 51=Sundance Yellow, 55=Gold Metallic accent color, 58=Blue accent color, 63=Laredo Brown Metallic, 67=Ember Mist Metallic, 69=Chesterfield Brown Metallic, 75=Mayan Red and 77=Carmine Metallic.

FIREBIRD - (V-6/V-8) - SERIES 2FS

The appearance of the 1978 Firebird was similar to 1977, with rectangular quad headlamps and a dark grille. The wide three-row taillights had back-up lights at the inner ends, close to the license plate. Taillight ribs filled most of the back panel. The base Firebird engine was a 3.8-liter (231-cid) V-6 with a two-barrel carburetor. The new 5.0-liter V-8 with 305 cid replaced the 301-cid V-8 used last year. It cost $117 extra in base Firebirds and Turbo-Hydra-Matic transmission was standard with any V-8. A four-speed manual gearbox was optional. The 5.7-liter (350-cid) V-8 was also available for $265. A three-speed manual transmission was used with the base V-6. Standard equipment included all standard safety, anti-theft, convenience and emissions control equipment, power steering, manual front disc/rear drum brakes, body-color Endura bumpers, hubcaps, dual horns, concealed windshield wipers, dual rectangular headlamps, bright windshield moldings, bright rear window moldings, bright grille moldings, Firebird emblems on sail panel and rear deck lid, a deluxe cushion steering wheel in matching interior colors, front bucket seats, rear bucket-type seats, solid foam seat cushions with integral springs, a heater and defroster, a flow-through ventilation system, nylon-blend cut-pile carpeting, a simulated rosewood instrument panel appliqué, a speedometer graduated in miles and kilometers, a single-buckle safety belt system, a fluid-on-demand windshield washer, an ashtray lamp, high-low level body ventilation, a thick trunk floor mat, a coil spring front suspension, a leaf-spring rear suspension, a GM HEI ignition system and a Radial Tuned Suspension with computer-selected springs, a front stabilizer bar and FR78 x 15 steel-belted radial tires.

Model Number	Body/Style Number	Body Type & Seating	Factory Price	Shipping Weight	Production Total
FIREBIRD - SERIES 2FS - (V-6)					
2FS	87	2d sport coupe-4P	$4,593	3,254 lbs.	Notes 1, 2
FIREBIRD - SERIES 2FS - (305-cid V-8)					
2FS	87	2d sport coupe-4P	$4,710	3,377 lbs.	Note 2
FIREBIRD - SERIES 2FS - (350-cid V-8)					
2FS	87	2d sport coupe-4P	$4,858	—	Note 2

Note 1: Combined production of base Firebirds and Esprits with the six-cylinder engine was 13,595 cars.
Note 2: Total production of base Firebirds was 32,671, including cars with both six-cylinder and V-8 engines.

FIREBIRD ESPRIT - (V-6/V-8) SERIES 2FT

In the early part of the 1978 model year Esprit buyers could still order the blue "Sky Bird" appearance package with a choice of code 30 Lombard Blue cloth upholstery with 24N1 Blue Doeskin trim or 24B1 Blue Lombardy trim, a two-tone blue body, a dark blue rear panel, dark blue grille panels, accent stripes, special identification and blue cast aluminum wheels. At midyear, the Sky Bird was replaced by a new "Red Bird" package that included two-tone Red paint, Carmine Red custom interior trim, a red Formula steering wheel, red grille liners and taillight bezels and red-trimmed snowflake aluminum wheel rims. There were also special "Red Bird" decals for the sail panels, but these were gold, as were the lower-body-perimeter pinstripes. Standard engine in the Esprit was the 3.8-liter (231-cid) V-6 with a two-barrel carburetor. The new 305-cid 5.0-liter V-8 was optional for $117 with a Turbo-Hydra-Matic transmis-

The Esprit had an optional "Sky Bird" package.

The optional Formula Appearance Package featured "Formula Super Graphics."

sion or a four-speed manual gearbox in Federal areas only. The 5.7-liter (350-cid) V-8 was also available for $265 with a Turbo-Hydra-Matic transmission or a four-speed manual gearbox in Federal areas only. The three-speed manual transmission was used with the base engine. Standard Esprit equipment included a new blacked-out grille and new hood styling with integral body-colored bumpers, new deluxe wheel covers, new rectangular headlamps, bright windshield and rear window moldings, bright roof moldings, bright window sill moldings, bright rear window moldings, bright grille moldings, Firebird emblems on the sail panel and rear deck lid, recessed windshield wipers, dual horns, front bucket seats, bucket-type rear seats, custom all-Morrokide bucket seats with lateral support design, solid foam front seat cushions with integral springs, a new luxury cushion steering wheel in matching interior colors, custom pedal trim plates, door and instrument panel assist straps, distinctive door trim panels, rear ash trays, added acoustical insulations, nylon blend cut-pile carpeting, a simulated rosewood appliqué on the instrument panel, a speedometer graduated in kilometers as well as miles per hour, single-buckle seat and shoulder belts, dual body-color sport mirrors (left-hand remote controlled), body-color door handle inserts, a fluid-on-demand windshield wiper washer system, an ashtray lamp, high-low level ventilation, a trunk floor mat, front disc/rear drum brakes, variable-ratio power steering, a coil spring front suspension, a leaf spring rear suspension, a GM HEI ignition system, a catalytic converter and a Radial Tuned Suspension including FR78-15 steel-belted radial tires, firm shock absorbers, jounce restrictors, computer-selected springs and a front stabilizer bar.

Model Number	Body/Style Number	Body Type & Seating	Factory Price	Shipping Weight	Production Total
FIREBIRD ESPRIT- SERIES 2FT - (V-6)					
2FT	87	2d sport coupe-4P	$4,897	3,285 lbs.	Notes 3, 4
FIREBIRD ESPRIT - SERIES 2FT - (305-cid V-8)					
2FT	87	2d sport coupe-4P	$5,014	3,408 lbs.	Note 4
FIREBIRD ESPRIT - SERIES 2FT - (350-cid V-8)					
2FT	87	2d sport coupe-4P	$5,162	—	Note 4

Note 3: Combined production of base Firebirds and Esprits with the six-cylinder engine was 13,595 cars.
Note 4: Total production of Esprits was 36,926, including cars with both six-cylinder and V-8 engines.

FORMULA FIREBIRD - (V-8) SERIES 2FU

Standard engine in the Formula was the Chevrolet 5.0-liter (305-cid) V-8 with a two-barrel carburetor. Other engine options included a 5.7-liter (350-cid) four-barrel V-8 in "federal" areas, two 6.6-liter (400-cid) Pontiac V-8s and a 403-cid Oldsmobile four-barrel V-8. Some engines were not available in California and others were available only in California. A Power-Flex radiator fan was used with 6.6-liter V-8s. A four-speed manual transmission was available with the base engine and Turbo-Hydra-Matic was optional. Standard Formula equipment included a black-out grille, a hood with two simulated air scoops, integral body-colored bumpers, rectangular headlamps, bright windshield and rear window moldings, bright grille moldings, Firebird emblems on the sail panel and rear deck lid, a rear deck lid spoiler, dual horns, front bucket seats, bucket-type rear seats, all-Morrokide bucket seats, a full-length front console, a new luxury cushion steering wheel in matching interior colors, nylon blend cut-pile carpeting, a simulated rosewood appliqué on the instrument panel, a speedometer graduated in kilometers as well as miles per hour, single-buckle seat and shoulder belts, dual body-color sport mirrors (left-hand remote controlled), a fluid-on-demand windshield wiper washer system, high-low level ventilation, a trunk floor mat, front disc/rear drum brakes, variable-ratio power steering, a coil spring front suspension, a leaf spring rear suspension, a High Energy Electronic (HEI) ignition system, dual chrome "splitter" tailpipe extensions, a catalytic converter, Rally II wheels with trim rings and a Radial Tuned Suspension including GR70-15 steel-belted radial tires, firm shock absorbers, jounce restrictors, computer-selected springs and front and rear stabilizer bars. The optional Formula Appearance package included a blacked-out lower body and hood scoops, multi-color stripes and large "Formula" super graphics on the body sides.

Model Number	Body/Style Number	Body Type & Seating	Factory Price	Shipping Weight	Production Total
FORMULA FIREBIRD 5.0-LITER - SERIES 2FU - (CHEVY 305-CID V-8)					
2FU	87	2d sport coupe-4P	$5,533	3,411 lbs.	Note 5
FORMULA FIREBIRD 5.7-LITER - SERIES 2FU - (CHEVY 350-CID V-8)					
2FU	87	2d sport coupe-4P	$5,648	3,411 lbs.	Note 5
FORMULA FIREBIRD 6.6-LITER - SERIES 2FU - (PONTIAC 400-CID V-8)					
2FU	87	2d sport coupe-4P	$5,738	3,411 lbs.	Note 5
FORMULA FIREBIRD T/A 6.6-LITER - SERIES 2FU - (PONTIAC 400-CID V-8)					
2FU	87	2d sport coupe-4P	$5,813	3,411 lbs.	Note 5
FORMULA FIREBIRD 6.6-LITER - SERIES 2FU - (OLDS 403-CID V-8)					
2FU	87	2d sport coupe-4P	$5,738	3,411 lbs.	Note 5

Note 5: Total production of Formula Firebirds with all engines was 24,346.

FIREBIRD TRANS AM - (V-8) SERIES 2FW

Standard Trans Am equipment included all federally mandated safety, anti-theft, convenience and emissions control features, a 400- or 403-cid (both called "6.6-liter") V-8, a Turbo-Hydra-Matic transmission, a Trans Am front fender decal, a black-out grille, a Trans Am wraparound rear deck spoiler decal, a front center air dam, rear wheel opening air deflectors, a shaker hood scoop and air cleaner, concealed windshield wipers, front fender air extractors, power steering, a Power-Flex radiator fan, Rally gauges with a clock and tachometer, a front seat console, power front disc/rear drum brakes, a heater, a defroster, car-

The Special Edition Trans Am came in gold in 1978.

peting, windshield moldings, an aluminum machine-turned instrument panel trim plate, a formula steering wheel, dual sport mirrors with left-hand remote controlled, dual horns, a rear deck lid spoiler, dual chrome splitter tailpipe extensions, 15 x 7-in. Rally II wheels with trim rings, a Safe-T-Track limited-slip differential, GR70-15 black sidewall steel-belted radial tires and a radial-tuned suspension with heavy front and rear stabilizer bars. Trans Ams were available in only seven colors, Cameo White, Platinum, Starlight Black, Martinique Blue, Solar Gold, Chesterfield Brown, Mayan Red and (early in the year) a Sundance Yellow. During early 1978 production, Trans Ams with the WS6 Special Performance package included the UPC W72 "T/A 6.6-Liter" V-8, so early 1978 Trans Ams with the W72 engine also had the WS6 package and a combined package price of $324. Later in the model year, the W72 engine could be ordered in Trans Ams without the WS6 package for $75 extra.

FIREBIRD TRANS AM BLACK SPECIAL EDITION - (V-8) SERIES 2FW/Y82/Y84

The original 1978 Black Special Edition package was similar to the 1977 Special Edition package. Standard Trans Am Black Special Edition equipment included all federally mandated safety, anti-theft, convenience and emissions control features, a 400-cid (6.6-liter) V-8 or 403-cid (6.6-liter V-8), a Turbo-Hydra-Matic transmission, a Trans Am front fender decal, a gold-trimmed grille, a Trans Am grille panel decal, a Trans Am wraparound rear deck spoiler decal, a front center air dam, rear wheel opening air deflectors, a shaker hood scoop and air cleaner, concealed windshield wipers, front fender air extractors, power steering, a Power-Flex radiator fan, Rally gauges with a clock and tachometer, a front seat console, power front disc/rear drum brakes, a heater, a defroster, carpeting, windshield moldings, an aluminum machine-turned instrument panel trim plate, a gold-spoke formula steering wheel, dual sport mirrors with left-hand remote controlled, dual horns, a rear deck lid spoiler, dual chrome splitter tailpipe extensions, 15 x 7-in. gold cast-aluminum wheels with trim rings, a Safe-T-Track limited-slip differential, GR70-15 black sidewall steel-belted radial tires, a Radial-Tuned Suspension with larger front and rear stabilizer bars, Starlight Black exterior body finish, gold body striping, gold interior and exterior accents, gold aluminum wheels and a removable hatch roof made by Hurst or GM's Fisher Body Div. During early 1978 production Trans Ams with the WS6 Special Performance package included the UPC W72 "T/A 6.6-Liter" V-8, so early 1978 Trans Ams with the W72 engine also had the WS6 package and a combined package price of $324. Later in the model year, the W72 engine could be ordered in Trans Ams without the WS6 package for $75 extra.

FIREBIRD TRANS AM GOLD SPECIAL EDITION - (V-8) - SERIES 2FW/Y88

The 1978 Gold Special Edition package was released at midyear. It came only with the new Fisher

T-top roof. Standard Trans Am Gold Special Edition equipment included all federally mandated safety, anti-theft, convenience and emissions control features, a 400-cid (6.6-liter) V-8 or 403-cid (6.6-liter V-8), a Turbo-Hydra-Matic transmission, a Trans Am front fender decal, a gold-trimmed grille, a Trans Am wraparound rear deck spoiler decal, a front center air dam, rear wheel opening air deflectors, a shaker hood scoop and air cleaner, concealed windshield wipers, front fender air extractors, power steering, a Power-Flex radiator fan, Rally gauges with a clock and tachometer, a front seat console, power front disc/rear drum brakes, a heater, a defroster, carpeting, windshield moldings, an aluminum machine-turned instrument panel trim plate, a formula steering wheel, dual sport mirrors with left-hand remote controlled, dual horns, a rear deck lid spoiler, dual chrome splitter tailpipe extensions, 15 x 7-in. gold cast-aluminum wheels with trim rings, a Saf-T-Track limited-slip differential, GR70-15 black sidewall steel-belted radial tires, a radial-tuned suspension with larger front and rear stabilizer bars, Solar Gold exterior body finish, dark gold body striping, a dark gold and bronze "big bird" hood decal, a Camel Tan interior, gold snowflake aluminum wheels and the removable hatch roof. Late in the model year, when the Gold Special Edition cars were offered, the W72 engine could be ordered in Trans Ams without the WS6 package for $75 extra.

Model Number	Body/Style Number	Body Type & Seating	Factory Price	Shipping Weight	Production Total
TRANS AM 6.6-LITER - SERIES 2FW - (400-CID PONTIAC L78 V-8)					
2FW	87	2d sport coupe-4P	$5,899	3,640 lbs.	63,812
TRANS AM 6.6-LITER - SERIES 2FW - (403-CID OLDS L80 V-8)					
2FW	87	2d sport coupe-4P	$5,899	3,716 lbs.	8,969
TRANS AM "T/A 6.6-LITER" - SERIES 2FW - (400-CID PONTIAC L78/W72 V-8)					
2FW	87	2d sport coupe-4P	$5,964	3,730 lbs.	8,251
TRANS AM 6.6-LITER BLACK SPECIAL EDITION - SERIES 2FW/Y82 - (400-CID PONTIAC L78 V-8)					
2FW/Y82	87	2d sport coupe-4P	$7,158	3,740 lbs.	3,345
TRANS AM 6.6-LITER BLACK SPECIAL EDITION - SERIES 2FW/Y84 - (400-CID PONTIAC L78 V-8)					
2FW/Y84	87	2d sport coupe-4P	$7,158	3,740 lbs.	88
TRANS AM 6.6-LITER BLACK SPECIAL EDITION - SERIES 2FW/Y84 - (403-CID OLDS L80 V-8)					
2FW/Y84	87	2d sport coupe-4P	$7,158	3,740 lbs.	210
TRANS AM 6.6-LITER GOLD SPECIAL EDITION - SERIES 2FW/Y88 - (400-CID PONTIAC L78 V-8)					
2FW/Y88	87	2d sport coupe-4P	$7,162	3,740 lbs.	7,786
TRANS AM 6.6-LITER GOLD SPECIAL EDITION - SERIES 2FW/Y88 - (403-CID OLDS L80 V-8)					
2FW/Y88	87	2d sport coupe-4P	$7,162	3,740 lbs.	880
TRANS AM 6.6-LITER - SERIES 2FW/Y82/Y84 - (400-CID PONTIAC W72 V-8)					
2FW/Y82/Y84	87	2d sport coupe-4P	$7,233	—	—
TRANS AM 6.6-LITER - SERIES Y88 - (400-CID PONTIAC W72 V-8)					
2FW/Y88	87	2d sport coupe-4P	$7,237	—	—

Note 6: A total of 12,665 Trans Ams built this year had a four-speed manual transmission. The total included 10,889 regular Trans Ams with the "T/A 6.6-liter" (W72) V-8; 489 Trans Am Y82 Black Special Edition coupes with the "T/A 6.6-liter" (W72) V-8; 20 Trans Am Y84 Black Special edition coupes with the "T/A 6.6-liter" (W72) V-8 and 1,267 Trans Am Y88 Gold Special Edition coupes with the "T/A 6.6-liter" V-8. Note: According to John Witzke, Historian and Pontiac Oakland club International (POCI) Technical Advisor for the 1977-1979 W72 Performance Package, Pontiac Historic Services, of Sterling Heights, Mich., has confirmed that all 12,665 Trans Ams built with four-speed transmissions this year had the optional W72 T/A 6.6-liter V-8.

Note 7: A total of 80,676 Trans Ams built this year had Turbo-Hydra-Matic transmission. The total included 57,035 regular Trans Ams with the 6.6-liter (L78) V-8; 8,969 regular Trans Ams with the 6.6-liter (L80) V-8; 2,856 Trans Am Y82 Black Special Edition coupes with the 6.6-liter (L78) V-8; 68 Trans Am Y84 Black Special edition coupes with the 6.6-liter (L78) V-8; 210 Trans Am Y84 Black Special edition coupes with the 6.6-liter (L80) V-8; 6,519 Trans Am Y88 Gold Special edition coupes with the 6.6-liter (L78) V-8 and 880 Trans Am Y88 Gold Special Edition coupes with the 6.6-liter L80 engine. According to John Witzke, no one knows the actual number of 1978 Trans Ams built with the W72 V-8 and Turbo-Hydra-Matic transmission.

Witzke says production of 4,139 such cars has been recorded, but adds that some estimates suggest that additional units may have been accidentally included with the figure for cars having the standard L78 V-8.

Note 8: All of the Y82 Black Special Edition Trans Ams with Hurst Hatch T-tops were built at Norwood, Ohio. It is believed that the Norwood assembly plant installed only Pontiac-built 400-cid V-8s, but John Witzke notes that this has not been verified. The Hurst Hatch T-top roof was phased out of production and replaced by the improved Fisher T-Top.

Note 9: All of the Y84 Black Special Edition Trans Ams were built at Van Nuys, California. And all had the new Fisher T-top. The California plant made 210 cars with the Oldsmobile-built 403-cid V-8 used in Trans Ams sold in California. John Witzke says that both Y82 and Y84 cars were phased out of production by February 1978.

Note 10: The Y88 Gold Special Edition Trans Ams were built at both assembly plants. All Y88s had the improved Fisher T-Top. The Solar Gold paint used on California units was a water-based paint formulated to meet the state's stricter air quality laws. It was not as lustrous or glossy and many of the California-built Y88s had paint flaws or bodies that did not match the color of the Endura bumpers. Dealers had to touch up or repaint many cars under warranty.

Jerry Heasley photo

The 1978 Trans Am was hard to beat when it came to muscle and style.

ENGINE

Buick V-6 [UPC LD5]: Overhead valves. Cast-iron block. Displacement: 231 cid. Bore & stroke: 3.80 x 3.40 in. Compression ratio: 8.0:1. Brake horsepower: 105 at 3400 rpm. Torque: 185 ft. lbs. at 2000 rpm. Hydraulic valve lifters. Carburetor: Two-barrel. VIN Code: A.

Chevrolet 305 V-8 [UPC LG3]: Overhead valves. Cast-iron block. Displacement: 305 cid. Bore & stroke: 3.736 x 3.48 in. Compression ratio: 8.4:1. Brake horsepower: 145 at 3800 rpm. Torque: 245 ft. lbs. at 2500 rpm. Hydraulic valve lifters. Carburetion: Two-barrel. Four-speed manual transmission. VIN Code: U. Federal engine.

Chevrolet 305 V-8 [UPC LG3]: Overhead valves. Cast-iron block. Displacement: 305 cid. Bore & stroke: 3.736 x 3.48 in. Compression ratio: 8.4:1. Brake horsepower: 135 at 3800 rpm. Torque: 240 ft. lbs. at 2000 rpm. Hydraulic valve lifters. Carburetion: Two-barrel. Turbo-Hydra-Matic transmission. VIN Code: U. California and high-altitude county engine.

Chevrolet 305 V-8 [UPC LM1]: Overhead valves. Cast-iron block. Displacement: 350 cid. Bore & stroke: 4.00 x 3.48 in. Compression ratio: 8.2:1. Brake horsepower: 170 at 4800 rpm. Torque: 270 ft. lbs. at 2400 rpm. Hydraulic valve lifters. Carburetion: Four-barrel. Four-speed manual transmission. VIN Code: L. Federal engine.

Chevrolet 305 V-8 [UPC LM1]: Chevrolet V-8. Overhead valves. Cast-iron block. Displacement: 350 cid. Bore & stroke: 4.00 x 3.48 in. Compression ratio: 8.2:1. Brake horsepower: 160 at 3800 rpm. Torque: 260 ft. lbs. at 2400 rpm. Hydraulic valve lifters. Carburetion: Four-barrel. Turbo-Hydra-Matic transmission. VIN Code: L. California and high-altitude county engine.

Pontiac 400 V-8 [UPC L78]: Pontiac V-8. Overhead valves. Cast-iron block. Displacement: 400 cid. Bore & stroke: 4.121 x 3.750 in. Compression ratio: 7.7:1. Brake horsepower: 180 at 3600 rpm. Torque: 325 ft.-lbs. at 1600 rpm. Five main bearings. Hydraulic valve lifters. Carburetor: Four-barrel. Turbo-Hydra-Matic transmission. Splitter exhausts. VIN code: Z. Federal engine.

Pontiac T/A 6.6 V-8 [UPC L78/W72]: Overhead valves. Cast-iron block. Displacement: 400 cid. Bore & stroke: 4.121 x 3.750 in. Compression ratio: 8.1:1. Brake horsepower: 200 at 4000 rpm. Torque: 320 ft. lbs. at 2800 rpm. Five main bearings. Hydraulic valve lifters. Carburetor: Four-barrel. Splitter exhausts. VIN code: Z. Federal engine.

Oldsmobile 350 V-8 [UPC L80]: Overhead valves. Cast-iron block. Displacement: 403 cid. Bore & stroke: 4.35 x 3.385 in. Compression ratio: 8.0:1. Brake horsepower: 185 at 3600 rpm. Torque: 320 ft. lbs. at 2000 rpm. Five main bearings. Hydraulic valve lifters. Carburetor: Four-barrel. Mandatory standard equipment in Trans Ams sold in California and high-altitude counties optional equipment in Formulas sold in California and high-altitude counties. VIN code: K. California and high-altitude county engine.

CHASSIS

Base V-8, Esprit: Wheelbase: 108.1 in. Overall length: 196.8 in. Overall width: 73.4 in. Overall height: 49.3 in. Front tread: 60.9 in. Rear tread: 60 in. Front headroom: 37.2 in. Rear headroom: 36 in. Front legroom: 43.9 in. Rear legroom: 28.4 in. Front shoulder room: 56.7 in. Rear shoulder room: 54.4 in.

Formula: Wheelbase: 108.1 in. Overall length: 196.8 in. Overall width: 73.4 in. Overall height: 49.3 in. Front tread: 61.3 in. Rear tread: 60.4 in. Front headroom: 37.2 in. Rear headroom: 36 in. Front legroom: 43.9 in. Rear legroom: 28.4 in. Front shoulder room: 56.7 in. Rear shoulder room: 54.4 in.

Trans Am: Wheelbase: 108.1 in. Overall length: 196.8 in. Overall width: 73 in. Overall height: 49.3 in. Front tread: 61.2 in. Rear tread: 60.3 in. Front headroom: 37.2 in. Rear headroom: 36 in. Front legroom: 43.9 in. Rear legroom: 28.4 in. Front shoulder room: 56.7 in. Rear shoulder room: 54.4 in.

TECHNICAL

Base/Esprit: Body and frame: Integral body and frame with separate bolted-on sub-frame for engine and front suspension. Front suspension: Independent with upper and lower control arms, coil springs, tubular shocks and stabilizer bar. Rear suspension: Hotchkiss solid axle, multi-leaf rear springs and tubular shocks. Steering: Optional power assist coaxial re-circulating ball bearing. Fuel tank: 21 gal.

Formula: Body and frame: Integral body and frame with separate ladder-type front frame section. Front suspension: Independent with upper and lower control arms, heavy-duty coil springs, heavy-duty tubular shocks and stabilizer bar. Rear suspension: Hotchkiss solid axle, multi-leaf rear springs, .560-in. stabilizer bar and tubular shocks. Steering: Optional power

assist coaxial re-circulating ball bearing. Fuel tank: 21 gal.

Trans Am: Body and frame: Integral body and frame with separate ladder-type front frame section. Front suspension: Independent with upper and lower control arms, heavy-duty coil springs, heavy-duty tubular shocks and stabilizer bar. Rear suspension: Hotchkiss solid axle, multi-leaf rear springs, .625-in. stabilizer bar and tubular shocks. Steering: Saginaw variable-ratio steering with power assist. Fuel tank: Fuel tank: 21 gal.

Trans Am WS6: Body and frame: Integral body and frame with separate ladder-type front frame section. Front suspension: Independent with upper and lower control arms, heavy-duty coil springs, heavy-duty tubular shocks and 1.250-in. stabilizer bar. Rear suspension: Hotchkiss solid axle, multi-leaf rear springs, .750-in. stabilizer bar and tubular shocks. Steering: Saginaw variable-ratio steering with power assist. Fuel tank: 21 gal.

OPTIONS

LD5 3.8-liter two-barrel V-6 in base Firebird and Esprit; not available with NA6 (standard). LG3 5.0-liter two-barrel V-8, standard in Formula; in base Firebird and Esprit ($117). LM1 5.7-liter four-barrel V-8 in Formula ($115); in base Firebird and Esprit ($265). L78 6.6-liter four-barrel Pontiac 400-cid V-8, not available with NA6 or VJ9 and automatic transmission required: in Formula ($205); in Trans Am (no cost). W72 T/A 6.6-liter four-barrel Pontiac 400-cid V-8, not available with NA6 or VJ9, available with automatic transmission or M21 four-speed manual transmission: in Formula ($280); in Trans Am ($75). L80 6.6-liter Oldsmobile 403-cid V-8-four-barrel with NA6 or VJ9 only and automatic transmission required: in Formula ($205); in Trans Am (no cost). MM3 three-speed manual transmission with floor shift, with V-6 only (no cost). MM4 four-speed manual transmission with LG3 or LM1 engines; not available with NA6 or VJ9: in Formula ($182); in base Firebird or Esprit ($125). M21 close-ratio four-speed manual transmission, with T/A 6.6 V-8 only and not available with NA6 or VJ9: in Formula (no cost); in Trans Am (no cost). MX1 three-speed automatic transmission, D55 required: in base Firebird or Esprit ($307); in Formula or Trans Am (no cost). C60 custom air conditioning ($508). K76 heavy-duty 61-amp. alternator with LG3 or LM1 engines without C49, C60 ($31); with C49 or C60 (no cost). K81 heavy-duty 63-amp. alternator with LD5, L78, W72 or L80 engines without C49, C60 ($31); with C49, C60 (no cost). W50 Formula appearance package for Formula only ($137). W60 Sky Bird appearance package for Esprit with velour Lombardy cloth ($461); for Esprit with vinyl doeskin trim ($426). W68 Red Bird appearance package, for Esprit with velour Lombardy cloth ($465); for Esprit with vinyl doeskin trim ($430). Y82 Trans Am Black Special Edition package, Norwood cars only ($1,259). Y84 Trans Am Black Special Edition package, Van Nuys cars only ($1,259). Y88 Trans Am Gold Special Edition package ($1,263). G80 Safe-T-Track rear axle on base Firebird, Esprit and Formula ($60). UA1 heavy-duty battery ($20). AK1 custom belts, in all except Sky Bird or Red Bird ($20); in Sky Bird or Red Bird (no cost). U35 electric clock (not available with Rally gauges ($22). D55 front console, required with automatic transmission in base Firebird or Esprit ($80); in Formula or Trans Am (no cost). K30 cruise control with LG3, LM1, L78, W72 V-8s, automatic transmission required ($90). A90 remote-control deck lid release ($21). C49 electric rear window defroster ($92). VJ9 California emissions system ($75). NA6 high-altitude emissions system ($33). K05 engine block heater ($14). W63 Rally cluster and clock, except Trans Am ($63). WW8 Rally cluster with clock and tachometer, except Trans Am ($123); Trans Am (no cost). A01 tinted glass, all windows ($56). CC1 Fisher hatch roof without Y84 or Y88 ($625); with Y84 or Y88 (standard). WY9 Hurst Hatch roof without Y82 ($625); with Y82 (standard). WW7 Trans Am hood decal, standard with Y82, Y84 or Y88; otherwise ($66). BS1 added acoustical insulation, included with Esprit ($29). C95 dome reading lamps ($18). Y92l lamp group ($18). B37 color-keyed front and rear mats ($21). D35 mirror group on base Firebird ($34). D34 visor vanity mirror ($5). B84 roof drip moldings, not available with WY9, CC1; without CB7: with base Firebird and Formula ($20); with Trans Am ($20); with Esprit (no cost). B96 wheel opening moldings, not available on Trans Am; for base Firebird or Formula without W50 ($21); for Formula with W50 and Esprit (no cost). B85 windowsill and rear hood moldings, standard on Esprit; on other Firebirds ($25). JL2 power brakes, required with V-8 or V-6 with C60; on base Firebird and Esprit ($69); on Formula and Trans Am (no cost). AU3 power door locks ($80) A31 power windows, required with D55 ($124). V02 super cooling radiator with C60 ($31); without C60 ($56). U63 AM radio ($83). UM1 AM radio with eight-track player ($233). U69 AM/FM radio ($154). UP5 AM/FM radio with 40-band CB, required with U80 ($436). U58 AM/FM stereo radio ($236). UN3 AM/FM radio with cassette ($351). UY8 AM/FM stereo with digital clock, not available in Trans Am with electric clock; otherwise ($392). UP6 AM/FM stereo radio with 40-channel CB ($518). UM2 AM/FM stereo radio with eight-track player ($341). UN9 radio accommodation package, no cost with optional radios; otherwise ($27). U80 rear seat speaker with UP5, U63 or U69 ($24). D80 rear deck spoiler, on base Firebird or Esprit ($55); on Formula or Trans Am (no cost). NK3 Formula steering wheel on base Firebird ($65); on Esprit without W60 ($46); on Esprit with W60 and Trans Am (no cost); on Formula ($46). N30 luxury steering wheel, standard in base Firebird; no cost option in Esprit or Formula; not available in Trans Am. N33 tilt steering ($72). D98 vinyl accent stripes with W50 or W60; not available on Trans Am ($52). C87 canopy top, not available on Trans Am; includes B80 ($111). WS6 Trans Am special performance package with T/A 6.6 V-8 ($324); with L80 ($249). Y90 custom trim group with doeskin vinyl trim in Formula or Trans Am ($99); with Lombardy cloth trim in Formula or Trans Am ($134); with Lombardy cloth trim in Esprit without W60 ($35); with Lombardy

cloth trim in Esprit with W60 (no cost). P0l deluxe wheel covers on base Firebird ($38). N95 wire wheel covers on base Firebird ($146); on Esprit ($108). YJ8 four painted cast aluminum wheels on base Firebird ($290); on Esprit without W60 ($252). N98 four Argent Silver Rally II wheels with trim rings, on base Firebird without N65 ($136); on Esprit with N65 ($79); on Esprit without N65 ($98); on Formula and Trans Am (no cost). N67 four body-color Rally II wheels with trim rings, on base Firebird without N65 ($136); on base Firebird with N65 ($117); on Esprit with N65 ($79); on Esprit without N65 ($98); on Formula and Trans Am (no cost). CD4 controlled-cycle windshield wipers ($32). N65 stowaway spare tire (no cost). QBU FR78-15 black sidewall steel-belted radial tires on base Firebird and Esprit (no cost). QBW FR78-15 white sidewall steel-belted radial tires on base Firebird or Esprit with N65 ($37 extra); on base Firebird or Esprit without N65 ($46 extra). QBP FR78-15 white letter steel-belted radial tires, on base Firebird or Esprit with N65 ($49 extra); on base Firebird or Esprit without N65 ($61 extras). QBX GR70-15 black sidewall steel-belted radial tires (no cost). QCY GR70-15 white letter steel-belted radial tires on Formula or Trans Am ($51 extra).

HISTORICAL FOOTNOTES

Car and Driver road tested a 1978 Firebird Trans Am with the 400-cid 200-nhp V-8 and Turbo-Hydra-Matic transmission and concluded it was "very sophisticated and impeccably well mannered." The car was fitted with non-stock 2.56:1 gears to produce a 130-mph top speed. It did 0 to 110 mph in 34.8 seconds. A better representation of stock Trans Am performance is found in the spring 1978 issue of *Road Test* magazine. This publication put a Trans Am with the W72 "T/A 6.6-liter" V-8 and a four-speed manual gearbox through its paces. The testers recorded a 7.2 second 0-to-60 performance and a 15.2-second quarter mile at 93 mph. Total model-year production of Firebirds rose to another new record of 187,285 units. Sales stood at 175,607 for the model year and 209,536 for the calendar year.

A Formula steering wheel and Rally gauges highlighted the '78 Trans Am interior.

Formula Firebirds like this one shared a new front-end look with the base Firebirds and Trans Ams in 1979.

Racing and Pacing

Sales were racing and Firebirds were pacing some leading races this year. A special model to celebrate a milestone in Trans Am history didn't hurt the excitement level one bit. The frontal appearance got a nice facelift with square headlights set into individually recessed housings on each side of a wider center panel. Horizontal ribbing was in vogue this year and the stylists used it for grilles below each set of headlights and across the rear end panel. The standard equipment list and model-option offerings were similar to those in 1977.

The Red Bird package was back and the new front-end look seemed to enhance its sophisticated image. A dressy new Custom cloth trim was offered to Esprit buyers. You could get the 1979 Formula without a rear spoiler and with a new Formula steering wheel, instead of the previous Custom Cushion style. A Rally gauge cluster with a clock and a Trans Am-style instrument panel trim plate became standard. Bringing "brawn to the surface," according to Pontiac copywriters, was a revived Formula Appearance package with lower door graphics.

While regular Trans Ams had few alterations, an exciting 10th Anniversary option was new. It included a large "bird" on the hood, silver finish, charcoal gray roof and special 10th anniversary decals. One of these $11,000 cars paced the Daytona 500. The gold-and-black Special Edition package was offered again.

By 1979, the price of a base V-6 Firebird was $4,825 and 38,642 were built. Esprit prices began at $5,193 and 30,853 were produced. Now costing just over $6,000, the Formula had a production run of 24,851 units. Really amazing was the Trans Am, which listed for about $300 more than a Formula and still had 117,108 total assemblies. This added up to more than 211,000 Firebirds built

I.D. NUMBERS

The vehicle identification number (VIN) was stamped on a plate on the upper left-hand side of the instrument panel and was visible through the windshield. The first symbol was the GM divisional code, 2=Pontiac. The second symbol indicated series: S=Base Firebird, T=Firebird Esprit, U=Formula Firebird, W=Trans Am, X=10th Anniversary Trans Am. The third and fourth symbols indicated the body style: 87=sport coupe. The fifth symbol indicated engine: A=231-cid two-barrel V-6; W=301-cid four-barrel V-8, Y=301-cid two-barrel V-8, G=305-cid two-barrel V-8, L=350-cid four-barrel V-8, Z=400-cid four-barrel V-8, K=403-cid Oldsmobile-built four-barrel V-8; R=350-cid four-barrel V-8. The sixth symbol indicated model year: 9=1979. The seventh symbol indicated the assembly plant: N=Norwood, Ohio, L=Van Nuys, California. The remaining symbols were sequential unit production number at factory, starting with 100001. The Body by Fisher plate on the engine side of the cowl contained the Fisher style number, which took the form ST79-2FS87. The prefix ST=style, 79=1979, the symbol 2=Pontiac, the symbol F=Firebird, the symbol S=base Firebird and the last two symbols 87=sport coupe. On the fourth line the designation W66=Formula and the designation WS4=Trans Am. This plate also indicated interior trim, seat type, body color and build date. V-6 engine code stamped on distributor mounting on right side of block. V-8 engine code on front of block below right cylinder head. Engine production codes for 1979 were: [231-cid V-6] NL-RX-RY, [301-cid two-barrel V-8] XP-XR-NA, [301-cid four-barrel V-8 X4-X6, [305-cid two-barrel V-8] DNF-DNJ-DNK-DNZ, [350-cid four-barrel V-8] DRY-DRJ, [400-cid four-barrel V-8] WH, [403-cid four-barrel V-8] Q6-QE-QJ-QK-QL-TD-TE.

COLORS

11=White, 15=Platinum, 16=Dark Charcoal (two-tone only), 24=Atlantic Blue, 29=Nocturne Blue, 50=Solar Gold (special order), 51=Sundance Yellow, 63=Sierra Copper, 69=Heritage Brown, 75=Mayan Red, 77=Carmine, 80=(special order) Red Bird Red (special order), 19=Starlight Black

FIREBIRD - (V-6/V-8) - SERIES 2FS

The third and last facelift for the second-generation Firebird came in 1979. Pontiac literature described the new grilleless look as "a broad new forefront cast in durable urethane." The treatment was used on all Firebird models. It featured a more gently contoured, slanted front nose panel with twin, rectangular-shaped headlights set into squarish ports at either end. The center of the panel came to a V-shaped peak. Below this was another bumper panel with a large license plate recess in its center and two long, thin, horizontal openings on either side. The openings were filled with six grille louvers and white-lensed parking lights. Base Firebirds and Esprits had full-width taillights with dark-finished bezels, but they lacked the black, opaque covers over the red lenses to create a "blacked-out" look. Exterior color choices were reduced from 18 to 13, but the Trans Am gained one and now had nine. The base Firebird came with all standard safety, anti-theft, convenience and emission control equipment, a 231-cid two-barrel V-6 engine, a three-speed manual transmission, power steering, manual front disc/rear drum brakes, Endura

front and rear bumpers, dual horns, concealed windshield wipers, dual rectangular headlamps, hubcaps, a heater and defroster unit, a flow-through ventilation system, a deluxe steering wheel, carpeting, front bucket seats and FR78-15 black sidewall steel-belted radial tires. The V-6 was not available in high-altitude counties. Instead, a 350-cid four-barrel V-8 was a required extra-cost option, adding $428 to the car's price and requiring a Turbo-Hydra-Matic transmission attachment at additional cost. Other changes on all 1979 Firebirds included steering-column-mounted headlight dimmer levers, the use of convex glass in right-hand outside rearview mirrors and the installation of a tri-band power antenna on cars with the optional Citizens Band (CB) radio.

Model Number	Body/Style Number	Body Type & Seating	Factory Price	Shipping Weight	Production Total
FIREBIRD - SERIES 2FS - (V-6)					
2FS	87	2d sport coupe-4P	$5,260	3,257 lbs.	Note 1, 2
FIREBIRD - SERIES 2FS - (5.0-LITER/301-CID LG3 V-8)					
2FS	87	2d sport coupe-4P	$5,530	3,330 lbs.	Note 2
FIREBIRD - SERIES 2FS - (5.0-LITER/305-CID L27 V-8)					
2FS	87	2d sport coupe-4P	$5,530	—	Note 2
FIREBIRD - SERIES 2FS - (4.9-LITER/301-CID L37 V-8)					
2FS	87	2d sport coupe-4P	$5,615	—	Note 2
FIREBIRD - SERIES 2FS - (5.7-LITER/350-CID LM1 V-8)					
2FS	87	2d sport coupe-4P	$5,685	—	Note 2

Note 1: Combined production of base Firebirds and Esprits with the six-cylinder engine was 12,687 cars.
Note 2: Total production of base Firebirds was 38,642, including cars with both six-cylinder and V-8 engines.

FIREBIRD ESPRIT - (V-6/V-8) SERIES 2FT

The styling changes seen on the base Firebird were also characteristic of the 1979 Esprit. This year the two-tone blue Sky Bird package was not available, but the UPC W68 Red Bird package was back with the Hobnail velour cloth trim version priced at $491 and the doeskin vinyl trim version priced at $449. The Esprit came with all standard safety, anti-theft, convenience and emission control equipment, a 231-cid

White was again a staple base color for the Trans Am in 1979.

two-barrel V-6 engine, a three-speed manual transmission, power steering, manual front disc/rear drum brakes, Endura front and rear bumpers, dual horns, concealed windshield wipers, dual rectangular headlamps, hubcaps, a heater and defroster unit, a flow-through ventilation system, a deluxe steering wheel, carpeting, front bucket seats and FR78-15 black sidewall steel-belted radial tires, plus deluxe wheel covers, dual sport-style outside rearview mirrors (left-hand mirror remote controlled), window sill moldings, a hood rear edge molding, wheel opening moldings, roof drip moldings, a luxury steering wheel, extra acoustical insulation and custom interior trim. The deluxe wheel covers that were standard on the Esprit were redesigned. The also-standard custom cloth interior was plusher than ever before, featuring hobnail cloth seat cushions and seatback inserts. It came in black, blue, tan or red. As was the case with the base Firebird, the V-6 was not available in Esprits sold in designated high-altitude counties. Instead, the 350-cid four-barrel V-8 was a required extra-cost option, adding $428 to the car's price and requiring Turbo-Hydra-Matic transmission attachment at additional extra cost.

Model Number	Body/Style Number	Body Type & Seating	Factory Price	Shipping Weight	Production Total
FIREBIRD ESPRIT- SERIES 2FT - (V-6)					
2FT	87	2d sport coupe-4P	$5,638	3,287 lbs.	Notes 3,4
FIREBIRD ESPRIT - SERIES 2FT - (5.0-LITER/301-CID LG3 V-8)					
2FT	87	2d sport coupe-4P	$5,908	3,360 lbs.	Note 4
FIREBIRD ESPRIT - SERIES 2FT - (5.0-LITER/305-CID L27 V-8)					
2FS	87	2d sport coupe-4P	$5,908	—	Note 4
FIREBIRD ESPRIT - SERIES 2FT - (4.9-LITER/301-CID L37 V-8)					
2FS	87	2d sport coupe-4P	$5,993	—	Note 4
FIREBIRD ESPRIT - SERIES 2FT - (5.7-LITER/350-CID LM1 V-8)					
2FS	87	2d sport coupe-4P	$6,063	—	Note 4

Note 3: Combined production of base Firebirds and Esprits with the six-cylinder engine was 12,687 cars.
Note 4: Total production of Esprits was 30,853, including cars with both six-cylinder and V-8 engines.

FORMULA FIREBIRD - (V-8) SERIES 2FU

The styling changes seen on the base Firebird were also characteristic of the 1979 Formula Firebird. The Formula came with all standard safety, anti-theft, convenience and emission control equipment, a 4.9-liter (301-cid) two-barrel V-8, a Turbo-Hydra-Matic transmission, power steering, power front disc/rear drum brakes, Endura front and rear bumpers, dual horns, concealed windshield wipers, dual rectangular headlamps, hubcaps, a heater and defroster unit, a flow-through ventilation system, carpeting, front bucket seats, a black-accented grille, a simulated dual air scoop hood design, sport-type outside rearview mirrors (left-hand remote controlled), dual chrome splitter tailpipe extensions, Rally II wheel rims with trim rings, a Formula steering wheel, Rally gauges with a tachometer and clock, a front console, black-out style taillights, a simulated engine-turned instrument panel trim plate and 225/70R-15 black sidewall steel-belted radial tires. Four-wheel disc brakes were a new Formula option. A 5.0-liter (305-cid) V-8 was a required option in California cars and a 5.7-liter (350-cid) V-8 was the required option in designated high-altitude counties. Sales catalogs said that the W50 Formula Appearance package "brought the brawn to the surface." It included contrasting lower-body perimeter finish with the color break line accentuated with a broad stripe of a third color, which was repeated along the bottom of the taillight panel. Only with this option was a rear deck lid spoiler standard on 1979 Formula Firebirds.

Model Number	Body/Style Number	Body Type & Seating	Factory Price	Shipping Weight	Production Total
FORMULA FIREBIRD 4.9-LITER - SERIES 2FU - (301-CID TWO-BARREL V-8)					
2FU	87	2d sport coupe-4P	$6,564	3,411 lbs.	Note 5
FORMULA FIREBIRD 4.9-LITER - SERIES 2FU - (301-CID FOUR-BARREL V-8)					
2FU	87	2d sport coupe-4P	$6,649	3,411 lbs.	Note 5
FORMULA FIREBIRD 5.0-LITER - SERIES 2FU - (305-cid TWO-BARREL V-8; WITH CALIFORNIA EMISSIONS)					
2FU	87	2d sport coupe-4P	$6,564	3,411 lbs.	Note 5
FORMULA FIREBIRD 5.7-LITER - SERIES 2FU - (350-CID FOUR-BARREL V-8; WITH HIGH-ALTITUDE EMISSIONS)					
2FU	87	2d sport coupe-4P	$6,719	3,411 lbs.	Note 5
FORMULA FIREBIRD "T/A 6.6-LITER" - SERIES 2FU/WS6 - (400-CID FOUR-BARREL V-8)					
2FU	87	2d sport coupe-4P	$7,431	3,411 lbs.	Notes 5, 6

The popular Trans Am helped Pontiac sell more than 211,000 F-Cars for the 1979 model year.

This 10th Anniversary '79 Trans Am was decked out in Platinum.

FORMULA FIREBIRD 6.6-LITER - SERIES 2FU - (403-CID FOUR-BARREL V-8)

2FU	87	2d sport coupe-4P	$6,934	3,411 lbs.	Note 5

Note 5: Total production of Formula Firebirds with all engines was 24,850.
Note 6: Formulas with the "T/A 6.6-liter" V-8 required the WS6 Special Performance package and the G80 rear axle.

FIREBIRD TRANS AM - (V-8) SERIES 2FW

The styling changes seen on the base Firebird were also characteristic of the 1979 Trans Am. Standard Trans Am equipment included all federally mandated safety, anti-theft, convenience and emissions control features, a 403-cid (6.6-liter) V-8 engine, a Turbo-Hydra-Matic or four-speed manual transmission, a Trans Am front fender decal, a blacked-out grille, blacked-out taillights, a Trans Am grille panel decal, a Trans Am wraparound rear deck spoiler decal, a front center air dam, rear wheel opening air deflectors, a shaker hood scoop and air cleaner, concealed windshield wipers, front fender air extractors, power steering, a Power-Flex radiator fan, Rally gauges with a clock and tachometer, front bucket seats, front seat console, power front disc/rear drum brakes, heater, defroster, carpeting, windshield moldings, aluminum machine-turned instrument panel trim plate, Formula steering wheel, dual sport mirrors with left-hand remote controlled, dual horns, rear deck lid spoiler, dual chrome splitter tailpipe extensions, 15 x 7-in. Rally II wheels with trim rings, Safe-T-Track limited-slip differential, 225/70R15 black sidewall steel-belted radial tires and a radial-tuned suspension with heavy front and rear stabilizer bars. Trans Ams were available in nine colors. Four-wheel disc brakes were also a new Trans Am option. In a return to the past, but a change from 1978, raised white letter tires could be ordered as a separate option without ordering the WS6 package. Engine options included the 4.9-liter four-barrel V-8 for a credit and the higher-performance T/A 6.6-liter four-barrel V-8 as a $90 option.

FIREBIRD TRANS AM BLACK SPECIAL EDITION - (V-8) - SERIES 2FW/Y84

The Y84 Black Special Edition package with gold graphics and accents was available for $674 without hatch roof panels or for $1,329 with the Fisher Hatch Roof. Standard Trans Am Black Special Edition equipment included all federally mandated safety, anti-theft, convenience and emissions control features, a 403-cid (6.6-liter) V-8 engine, a Turbo-Hydra-Matic or four-speed manual transmission, a Trans Am front fender decal, a blacked-out grille, blacked-out taillights, a Trans Am grille panel decal, a Trans Am wraparound rear deck spoiler decal, a front center air dam, rear wheel opening air deflectors, a shaker hood scoop and air cleaner and "big bird" hood decal, concealed windshield wipers, front fender air extractors, power steering, a Power-Flex radiator fan, Rally gauges with a clock and tachometer, front bucket seats, a front seat console, power front disc/rear drum brakes, a heater, a defroster, carpeting, windshield moldings, a gold aluminum machine-turned instrument panel trim plate, a formula steering wheel, dual sport mirrors with left-hand remote controlled, dual horns, a rear deck lid spoiler, dual chrome splitter tailpipe extensions, 15 x 7-in. Rally II wheels with trim rings, a Safe-T-Track limited-slip differential, 225/70R15 black sidewall steel-belted radial tires, a radial-tuned suspension with larger front and rear stabilizer bars, Starlight Black exterior body finish, gold body striping, gold interior and exterior accents, gold aluminum wheels and a removable hatch roof made by GM's Fisher Body Division.

FIREBIRD TRANS AM 10th ANNIVERSARY - (V-8) - SERIES 2FX

The first Trans Am was a 1969 1/2 model, so 1979 was the model's 10th anniversary. A special 10th Anniversary model was announced on Jan. 26, 1979, and made its initial public appearance at the Chicago Automobile Show on Feb. 24. The car was displayed there with four special concept cars and a Trans Am with a rear-mounted jet engine that was used in the movie "Hooper." The package included all standard Trans Am features, plus a host of special appearance and performance extras as regular equipment. Since this was an all-inclusive deal, the 10th Anniversary Trans Am was considered a separate model, rather than an option package. You took all the equipment and laid out $10,619 for the privilege (if you bought at full sticker price). The standard goodies included a larger-than-normal "super bird" hood decal, a front air dam with bolder styling, special cast-aluminum turbo-air-flow wheel rims with finned perimeter openings and knock-off style hubs and a complete complement of convenience features, including air conditioning, power windows, power door locks, an electronically tuned digital display AM/FM stereo radio with seek-and-scan feature and eight-track tape player, Rally gauges with a tachometer, a special leather-wrapped steering wheel and cruise control. The special interior trimmings featured silver leather bucket seats with vinyl side facings, silver door panel trim and exclusive instrument lighting similar to that used in aircraft cockpits. These cars came only in Platinum Silver with a silver hatch roof and charcoal accents on the shaker-style hood scoop, the bumper panel, the windowsills, the rear window surround and portions of the roof. Red, white and charcoal pinstripes accented numerous body panels. Behind the front wheel openings were red Trans Am lettering and 10th Anniversary Limited Edition decals. Most 10th Anniversary Trans Ams had the base L80 (403-cid) V-8 with Turbo-Hydra-Matic attachment. A few were produced with the T/A 6.6 V-8 linked to a four-speed manual transmission.

FIREBIRD TRANS AM 10th ANNIVERSARY DAYTONA PACE CAR (V-8) SERIES 2FX

Some historical sources indicate that a limited number of 10th Anniversary Trans Ams were turned out as Official Pace Car Replicas patterned after the car that paced the Daytona 500 stock car race on Feb. 18, 1979. According to John Witzke, Historian and Pontiac Oakland Club International (POCI) Technical Advisor for the 1977-1979 W72 Performance Package, this information has not been confirmed. Firebird expert Dave Doern confirms that Daytona 500 decals were made available through the Pontiac parts department as a dealer-installed decal package.

Model Number	Body/Style Number	Body Type & Seating	Factory Price	Shipping Weight	Production Total
TRANS AM COUPE 4.9-LITER - SERIES 2FW - (301-CID PONTIAC L37 V-8)					
2FW	87	2d sport coupe-4P	$6,688	3,716 lbs.	8,605
TRANS AM COUPE 6.6-LITER - SERIES 2FW - (403-CID OLDS L80 V-8)					
2FW	87	2d sport coupe-4P	$6,883	3,716 lbs.	48,488
TRANS AM COUPE T/A 6.6-LITER - SERIES 2FW - (400-CID PONTIAC L78/W72 V-8)					
2FW	87	2d sport coupe-4P	$7,407	3,730 lbs.	2,485
TRANS AM T-TOP 4.9-LITER - SERIES 2FW - (301-CID PONTIAC L37 V-8)					
2FW	87	2d sport coupe-4P	$7,343	3,716 lbs.	4,831
TRANS AM T-TOP 6.6-LITER - SERIES 2FW - (403-CID OLDS L80 V-8)					
2FW	87	2d sport coupe-4P	$7,548	3,716 lbs.	30,728
TRANS AM T-TOP T/A 6.6-LITER - SERIES 2FW - (400-CID PONTIAC L78/W72 V-8)					
2FW	87	2d sport coupe-4P	$8,062	3,730 lbs.	2,917
TRANS AM T-TOP 4.9-LITER BLACK SPECIAL ED. - SERIES 2FW/Y84 - (301-CID PONTIAC L37 V-8)					
2FW/Y82	87	2d sport coupe-4P	$8,017	3,740 lbs.	573
TRANS AM T-TOP 6.6-LITER BLACK SPECIAL ED. - SERIES 2FW/Y84 - (403-CID OLDS L80 V-8)					
2FW/Y84	87	2d sport coupe-4P	$8,212	3,740 lbs.	9,874
TRANS AM T-TOP T/A 6.6-LITER BLACK SP. ED. - SERIES 2FW/Y84 - (400-CID PONTIAC L78 V-8)					
2FW/Y84	87	2d sport coupe-4P	$8,552	3,740 lbs.	1,107
TRANS AM T-TOP 6.6-LITER 10th ANNIVERSARY - SERIES 2FX - (403-CID OLDS L80 V-8)					
2FW/Y84	87	2d sport coupe-4P	$10,620	3,740 lbs.	5,683
TRANS AM T-TOP T/A 6.6-LITER 10th ANNIVERSARY - SERIES 2FX - (400-CID PONTIAC L78 V-8)					
2FW/Y84	87	2d sport coupe-4P	$10,607	3,740 lbs.	1,817
TRANS AM T-TOP 6.6-LITER 10th ANN. DAYTONA PACE CAR - SERIES 2FX - (403-CID OLDS L80 V-8)					
2FW/Y84	87	2d sport coupe-4P	$10,620	—	—
TRANS AM T-TOP T/A 6.6-LITER 10th ANN. DAYTONA PACE CAR - SERIES 2FX - (400-CID PONTIAC L78 V-8)					
2FW/Y84	87	2d sport coupe-4P	$10,607	—	—

Note 7: The WS6 package was mandatory with the L78 400-cid V-8 and cost $250 with the Y84 S.E. package.

Note 8: All cars with the base 6.6-liter (403-cid) V-8 had Turbo-Hydra-Matic transmission. All cars with the T/A 6.6-liter (400-cid) V-8 had four-speed manual transmission. The 4.9-liter (301-cid) V-8 was the only engine available with both transmissions and four-speed manual attachments were rarer; they included 1,590 Trans Am coupes, 1,530 Trans Am T-Tops and 213 Black Special Editions Trans Ams with T-Tops. The 4.9-liter V-8 with Turbo-Hydra-Matic attachments was used in 7,015 Trans Am coupes, 3,301 Trans Am T-Tops and 360 Trans Am Black Special Editions with T-Tops.

The L80 and L78 V-8s gave the Trans Am two 6.6-liter engine options

ENGINES

Buick V-6 [UPC LD5]: Overhead valves. Cast-iron block. Displacement: 231 cid. Bore & stroke: 3.80 x 3.40 in. Compression ratio: 8.0:1. Brake horsepower: 105 at 3400 rpm. Torque: 185 ft. lbs. at 2000 rpm. Hydraulic valve lifters. Carburetor: Two-barrel. VIN Code: A.

Pontiac 301 V-8 [UPC L27]: Overhead valves. Cast-iron block. Displacement: 301 cid. Bore & stroke: 4.00 x 3.00 in. Compression ratio: 8.1:1. Brake horsepower: 140 at 3600 rpm. Torque: 235 ft. lbs. at 2000 rpm. Hydraulic valve lifters. Carburetion: Two-barrel. VIN Code: Y.

Pontiac 301 V-8 [UPC L37]: Overhead valves. Cast-iron block. Displacement: 301 cid. Bore & stroke: 4.00 x 3.00 in. Compression ratio: 8.1:1. Brake horsepower: 150 at 4000 rpm. Torque: 240 ft. lbs. at 2000 rpm. Hydraulic valve lifters. Carburetion: Four-barrel. VIN Code: W.

Chevrolet 305 V-8 [UPC LG3]: Overhead valves. Cast-iron block. Displacement: 305 cid. Bore & stroke: 3.736 x 3.48 in. Compression ratio: 8.4:1. Brake horsepower: 133 at 4000 rpm. Torque: 244 ft. lbs. at 2000 rpm. Hydraulic valve lifters. Carburetion: Two-barrel. Four-speed manual transmission. VIN Code: G.

Chevrolet 350 V-8 [UPC LM1]: Overhead valves.

Cast-iron block. Displacement: 350 cid. Bore & stroke: 4.00 x 3.48 in. Compression ratio: 8.2:1. Brake horsepower: 160 at 3800 rpm. Torque: 260 ft. lbs. at 2400 rpm. Hydraulic valve lifters. Carburetion: Four-barrel. Four-speed manual transmission. VIN Code: R.

Pontiac 6.6-liter V-8 [UPC L78]: Overhead valves. Cast-iron block. Displacement: 400 cid. Bore & stroke: 4.121 x 3.750 in. Compression ratio: 8.1:1. Brake horsepower: 220 at 4000 rpm. Torque: 320 ft. lbs. at 2800 rpm. Five main bearings. Hydraulic valve lifters. Carburetor: Four-barrel. Splitter exhausts. VIN code: Z.

Oldsmobile 403 V-8 [UPC L80]: Overhead valves. Cast-iron block. Displacement: 403 cid. Bore & stroke: 4.35 x 3.385 in. Compression ratio: 7.9:1. Brake horsepower: 185 at 3600 rpm. Torque: 320 ft. lbs. at 2200 rpm. Five main bearings. Hydraulic valve lifters. Carburetor: Four-barrel. Mandatory standard equipment in Trans Ams sold in California and high-altitude counties; optional equipment in Formulas sold in California and high-altitude counties. VIN code: K.

CHASSIS

Base V-8, Esprit: Wheelbase: 108.1 in. Overall length: 198.1 in. Overall width: 73.4 in. Overall height: 49.3 in. Front tread: 61.3 in. Rear tread: 60 in. Front headroom: 37.2 in. Rear headroom: 36 in. Front legroom: 43.9 in. Rear legroom: 28.4 in. Front shoulder room: 56.7 in. Rear shoulder room: 54.4 in.

Formula: Wheelbase: 108.1 in. Overall length: 198.1 in. Overall width: 73.4 in. Overall height: 49.3 in. Front tread: 61.3 in. Rear tread: 60 in. Front headroom: 37.2 in. Rear headroom: 36 in. Front legroom: 43.9 in. Rear legroom: 28.4 in. Front shoulder room: 56.7 in. Rear shoulder room: 54.4 in.

Trans Am: Wheelbase: 108.1 in. Overall length: 198.1 in. Overall width: 73.4 in. Overall height: 49.3 in. Front tread: 61.3 in. Rear tread: 60 in. Front headroom: 37.2 in. Rear headroom: 36 in. Front legroom: 43.9 in. Rear legroom: 28.4 in. Front shoulder room: 56.7 in. Rear shoulder room: 54.4 in.

TECHNICAL:

Base/Esprit: Body and frame: Integral body and frame with separate bolted-on sub-frame for engine and front suspension. Front suspension: Independent with upper and lower control arms, coil springs, tubular shocks and stabilizer bar. Rear suspension: Hotchkiss solid axle, multi-leaf rear springs and tubular shocks. Steering: Optional power assist coaxial re-circulating ball bearing. Fuel tank: 21 gal.

Formula: Body and frame: Integral body and frame with separate ladder-type front frame section. Front suspension: Independent with upper and lower control arms, heavy-duty coil springs, heavy-duty tubular shocks and stabilizer bar. Rear suspension: Hotchkiss solid axle, multi-leaf rear springs, .560-in. stabilizer bar and tubular shocks. Steering: Optional power assist coaxial re-circulating ball bearing. Fuel tank: 21 gal.

Trans Am: Body and frame: Integral body and frame with separate ladder-type front frame section.

Front suspension: Independent with upper and lower control arms, heavy-duty coil springs, heavy-duty tubular shocks and stabilizer bar. Rear suspension: Hotchkiss solid axle, multi-leaf rear springs, .625-in. stabilizer bar and tubular shocks. Steering: Saginaw variable-ratio steering with power assist. Fuel tank: Fuel tank: 21 gal.

Trans Am WS6: Body and frame: Integral body and frame with separate ladder-type front frame section. Front suspension: Independent with upper and lower control arms, heavy-duty coil springs, heavy-duty tubular shocks and 1.250-in. stabilizer bar. Rear suspension: Hotchkiss solid axle, multi-leaf rear springs, .750-in. stabilizer bar and tubular shocks. Steering: Saginaw variable-ratio steering with power assist. Fuel tank: Fuel tank: 21 gal.

The "shaker" scoop protruded though an opening in the hood

OPTIONS

LD5 3.8-liter four-barrel V-6 in base Firebird and Esprit, not available with NA6 (no cost). L27 4.9-liter V-8 two-barrel in base Firebird and Esprit, federal only, with automatic transmission required ($270). L27 4.9-liter V-8 two-barrel in Formula, federal only, with automatic transmission required (no cost). L37 4.9-liter V-8 four-barrel in base Firebird and Esprit, federal only ($355). L37 4.9-liter V-8 four-barrel in Formula, federal only ($85). L37 4.9-liter V-8 four-barrel in Trans Am, federal only ($195 credit). LG3 5.0-liter V-8 two-barrel in base Firebird and Esprit, with VJ9 automatic transmission required ($270). LG3 5.0-liter V-8 two-barrel in Formula with VJ9 automatic transmission required (no cost). LM1 5.7-liter V-8 four-barrel in base Firebird and Esprit with NA6 automatic transmission required ($425). LM1 5.7-liter V-8 four-barrel in Formula with NA6 automatic transmission required ($155). L78 T/A 6.6-liter V-8 four-barrel in Formula, federal only with M21 and WS6 required ($370). L78 T/A 6.6-liter V-8 four-barrel in Trans Am, 10th Anniversary Trans Am, federal only with M21, WS6 required ($90). MM3 three-speed manual transmission, required with V-6, not available with VJ9 (no charge). M21 close-ratio four-speed manual transmission in base Firebird and Esprit with L37 engine required ($325). M21 close-ratio four-speed manual transmission in Formula, Trans Am and 10th Anniversary Trans Am with L78 or L37 V-8 (no cost). MX1 Turbo-Hydra-Matic automatic transmission in base Firebird or Esprit, with D55 required, not available with L78. MX1Turbo-Hydra-Matic automatic transmission in Formula, Trans Am or 10th Anniversary Trans Am, with D55 required, not available with L78 (no cost). C60 custom air conditioning ($529). K81 63-amp. Heavy-duty alternator without C60 or C49 ($32). K81 heavy-duty 63-amp. alternator with C60 or C49 (no cost). W50 Formula Appearance package for Formula only ($92). W68 Red Bird appearance package for Esprit with hobnail cloth trim ($491). W68 Red Bird appearance package for Esprit with doeskin vinyl trim ($449). Y84 Black Special Edition appearance package for Trans Am without CC1 hatch roof ($674). Y84 Black Special Edition package for Trans Am, includes CC1 hatch roof ($1,329). G80 Limited slip differential on base Firebird, Esprit and Formula ($63); standard on Trans Am and 10th Anniversary Trans Am. UA1 heavy-duty battery ($21). AK1 custom seat belts (no cost). U35 electric clock without W63 ($24); standard with W63. D55 front console, required with automatic transmission in base Firebird and Esprit ($80); standard in Formula and Trans Am. K30 cruise control, MX1 transmission required and not available with L78 engine ($103). A90 remote-control rear deck lid release ($24). C49 electric rear window defroster ($99). VJ9 California emissions equipment ($83). NA6 high-altitude emissions equipment ($35). K05 engine block heater ($15). W63 Rally gauge cluster with clock in base Firebird or Esprit with V-8 ($67). U17 Rally gauges with tachometer and clock in base Firebird or Esprit ($130); with Formula, Trans Am and 10th Anniversary Trans Am ($63). A01 tinted glass ($64). CC1 hatch roof with removable panels for Trans Am without Y84 ($655). D53 Trans Am hood bird decal, not available with Y84 ($95). BS1 added acoustical insulation in base Firebird, Formula and Trans Am; standard with Esprit ($31). C95 dome reading lamp ($19). B37 color-keyed front and rear floor mats ($25). D35 dual sport mirrors for base Firebird, left-hand remote control ($43). D34 right-hand visor vanity mirror ($6). B84 vinyl body side moldings ($43). B93 door edge guards ($13). B83 rocker panel moldings, not available with Formula or Trans Am; standard with Esprit ($18). B80 roof drip moldings for all models without a canopy top except Esprit ($24). B96 wheel opening moldings, base Firebird only ($22). B85 windowsill and rear hood moldings for all Firebirds except the Esprit and the Trans Am with the Y84 Special Edition Appearance package ($26). JL2 power brakes, required with V-6, V-8 or C60 ($76); standard on Formula and Trans Am at no cost. J65 four-wheel disc power brakes on Formula or Trans Am without Special Edition package ($150). AU3 power door locks ($86). A31 power windows, required with D55 ($132). V02 super cooling radiator with C60; not available with L80 or WS6 or NA6 ($59); with C60 only ($32). U75 power antenna without optional radio; not available with UP5 or UP6 ($66). U75 power antenna with optional radio ($47). U83 power AM/FM tri-band antenna, without optional radio ($87); with UP5 or UP6 radio (no cost); with

other optional radios ($68). U63 AM radio ($86). UM1 AM radio with integral eight-track stereo player ($248). U69 AM/FM radio ($163). UP5 AM/FM with CB, includes U83 ($492). U58 AM/FM stereo radio ($236). UN3 AM/FM radio with stereo cassette ($351). UY8 AM/FM stereo radio with digital clock ($402). UP6 AM/FM stereo radio with integral 40-channel CB, includes U83 ($574). UM2 AM/FM stereo radio with integral eight-track player ($345). UN9 radio accommodation package without U83 or optional radio ($29). UN9 radio accommodation package with U83, but without optional radio ($10). U80 rear seat speaker only with UP5, U63 or U69 ($25). UP8 dual rear speakers, with UP5, U63 or U69 ($38); standard with all others ($38). WS6 Special Performance package on Formula and Trans Am only, requires L37, L78 or L80 V-8 ($434). WS6 Special Performance package on Trans Am with Y84 ($250). D80 rear deck spoiler on base Firebird, Esprit and Formula without W50 ($57). NK3 Formula steering wheel on base Firebird ($68); on Esprit without W68 ($48). N30 luxury steering wheel in base Firebird ($20). D98 vinyl accent stripes on base Firebird or Esprit ($54). CB7 canopy top ($115); not available on Trans Am or 10th Anniversary Trans Am; on Esprit with W68 ($116). B18 custom trim group in base Firebird and Trans Am with vinyl doeskin trim ($108); in Formula and Trans Am with hobnail velour cloth trim ($150); in Esprit with W68, hobnail velour cloth trim ($42). P01 new design deluxe wheel cover on base Firebird ($42). N95 wire wheel covers on base Firebird ($157); on Esprit ($115). N90 cast-aluminum wheels on base Firebird ($310). N90 cast-aluminum wheels on Esprit without W68 ($268); on Esprit with W68 ($184). N98 Argent Silver Rally II rims on base Firebird with N65 ($126); on base Firebird without N65 ($146); on Esprit with N65 ($84); on Esprit without N65 ($104). N67 body-color Rally II wheel rims on base Firebird with N65 ($126); on base Firebird without N65 ($146); on Esprit with N65 ($84); on Esprit without N65 ($104). CD4 controlled-cycle windshield wipers ($38). N65 stowaway spare tire (no cost). QBU FR78-15 black sidewall steel-belted radial tires on (base Firebird and Esprit (no extra cost). QBW FR78-15 white sidewall steel-belted radial tires on base Firebird and Esprit ($48 extra); on base Firebird and Esprit with N65 ($39 extra). QBP FR78-15 white-letter steel-belted radial tires on base Firebird and Esprit without N65 ($64 extra); on base Firebird and Esprit with N65 ($52). QGQ 225/70R-15 black sidewall steel-belted radial tires on Formula, Trans Am and 10th Anniversary Trans Am (no charge). QGR 225/70R-15 white-letter steel-belted tires on Formula or Trans Am with WS6 ($53).

HISTORICAL FOOTNOTES

Car and Driver road tested a 1979 Firebird with the "T/A 6.6-liter" V-8 in a January 1979. The car did 0 to 60 mph in 6.7 seconds and traveled down the quarter mile in 15.3 seconds at 96.6 mph. Total model-year production of Firebirds rose to another new record of 211,454 cars.

The Indy Pace Car Trans Am featured the 4.9-liter turbo engine.

Drastic Drop

New options and engineering refinements were the big changes in 1980 Firebirds. A drastic dip in production was seen for the first time in eight years. The output of Firebirds, Esprits, Formulas and Trans Ams was almost half what it had been the previous season.

Up front, a center console was now standard in all models. A dozen new body colors were offered, plus a new upholstery selection — dark blue. Dual exhaust systems made of lightweight alloys were introduced. Optional new four-speaker ETR sound systems were introduced. Tungsten halogen headlamps were optional.

A new Yellow Bird package with gold accent striping replaced the Red Bird for Esprits. On Oct. 16 1979, Pontiac announced that the Trans Am had been selected to pace the 64th Indianapolis 500 race the next May. To commemorate this, a Trans Am Indy Pace Car replica was issued as a separate model.

The Indy Pace Car replicas came only with a 4.9-liter 210-hp turbo V-8. They were two-toned with white upper bodies and charcoal gray bottoms set off by tri-color stripes. Oyster-colored vinyl bucket seats with matching hobnail cloth inserts were standard. These $11,200-and-up cars came basically fully loaded and 5,700 were built. Turbo graphics were on the hood and spoiler. PMD said the Indy Pacer was the first domestic car to have a *standard* turbo engine.

The turbocharger was made by AiResearch Corporation. It was exclusive to Trans Ams, but not pace cars. It could be added to *any* model. All Turbo Trans Ams included a unique hood and special bird hood decals. Road testers registered a 0-to-60 time of 8.2 seconds and a top speed of 116 mph for the turbo. The quarter mile took 16.7 seconds at 86 mph.

Trans Am buyers could again get a black-painted Special Edition package, either with or without a hatch roof. It could be had with conventional 4.9- and 5.0-liter V-8s as well as with the 4.9-liter turbo. New color combinations for regular Trans Ams included bronze/burgundy and a revised red/gold combination.

Model-year production included 29,811 Firebirds, 17,277 Esprits, 9,356 Formulas and 50,896 Trans Ams. Some Firebirds were rare. For instance, only 12 Special Edition Trans Ams were made with the 5.0-liter LG4 V-8.

I.D. NUMBERS

The vehicle identification number (VIN) was stamped on a plate on the upper left-hand side of the instrument panel and visible through the windshield. The first symbol was the GM divisional code, 2=Pontiac. The second symbol indicated series: S=Base Firebird, T=Firebird Esprit, V=Formula Firebird, W=Trans Am, X=Turbo 6.6 Indy Pace Car. The third and fourth symbols indicated the body style: 87=sport coupe. The fifth symbol indicated engine: A=231-cid two-barrel V-6, W=301-cid four-barrel V-8, T=301-cid four-barrel turbocharged V-8, H=305-cid four-barrel V-8, S=265-cid two-barrel V-8. The sixth symbol indicated model year: A=1980. The seventh symbol indicated the assembly plant: N=Norwood, Ohio, L=Van Nuys, California. The remaining symbols were sequential unit production number at factory, starting with 100001. The Body by Fisher plate on the engine side of the cowl contained the Fisher style number, which took the form 80-2T87. The prefix 80=1980, the first symbol 2=Pontiac, the second symbol T=Esprit and the last two symbols 87=sport coupe. This plate also indicated interior trim, seat type, body color and build date. V-6 engine code stamped on distributor mounting on right side of block. V-8 engine code on front of block below right cylinder head. Engine production codes for 1980 were: [231-cid V-6] MS-MX-OJ-OK-OL-OM-ON-OZ, [301-cid four-barrel V-8] XC-XM-XN-YN-YZ, [305-cid four-barrel V-8] CEL-CEM, [265-cid two-barrel V-8] XR.

COLORS

11=White, 15=Platinum Silver, 24=Bright Blue Irid, 29=Dark Blue Irid, 37=Accent Yellow, 51=Yellowbird Yellow, 57=Gold Poly, 67=Dark Brown, 71=Francisco Red, 72=Red, 76=Dark Claret, 79=Red Orange, 80=Rust, 84=Charcoal, 19=Black.

FIREBIRD - (V-6/V-8) - SERIES 2FS

For 1980, engineering improvements and new options headlined the changes in Firebird land. The technical upgrades included a lightweight dual exhaust system, the use of low-friction ball joints, revised engine offerings and the deletion of a four-speed manual gear box. The bucket seats had smooth—rather than pleated—headrests and could be had in a new dark blue trim combination. A front console was added to the standard equipment list. Twelve new exterior paint colors were offered. New options included dual front radio speakers, extended-range dual rear speakers and an electronically controlled radio with seek/scan feature. During the year a wheel cover locking package and audio power booster were added to the options list. The electric clock now had a quartz mechanism and after Nov. 20, 1979, a roof rack was available for the Firebird as a dealer-installed option. The base Firebird came with all standard safety, anti-theft, convenience and emission control equipment, a 231-cid two-barrel V-6 engine (305-cid two-barrel V-8 at extra cost in California), a three-speed manual transmission (Turbo-Hydra-Matic at extra cost in California), power steering, manual front disc/rear drum brakes, a body-color one-piece resilient Endura front-end panel and front bumper with recessed grilles and dual rectangular headlights,

an Endura rear bumper, dual horns, concealed windshield wipers, hubcaps with the Pontiac crest, a heater and defroster unit, a flow-through ventilation system, a rosewood instrument panel appliqué on the instrument panel trim plate, a deluxe cushion steering wheel, a column-mounted headlight dimmer switch, nylon-blend cut-pile carpeting, front vinyl bucket seats, fully-upholstered door trim panels, a front console, high/low ventilation, a luggage compartment mat, a Radial Tuned Suspension and 205/75R-15 black sidewall steel-belted radial tires.

Model Number	Body/Style Number	Body Type & Seating	Factory Price	Shipping Weight	Production Total
FIREBIRD - SERIES 2FS - (V-6)					
2FS	87	2d sport coupe-4P	$5,604	3,269 lbs.	Notes 1, 2
FIREBIRD - SERIES 2FS - (V-8)					
2FS	87	2d sport coupe-4P	$5,784	3,342 lbs.	Note 2

Note 1: Combined production of base Firebirds and Esprits with the six-cylinder engine was 30,270 cars, a large increase.
Note 2: Total production of base Firebirds was 29,811, including cars with both six-cylinder and V-8 engines.

FIREBIRD ESPRIT - (V-6/V-8) SERIES 2FT

The changes for the base Firebird were the same for the Esprit. A new Esprit feature was the addition of wide rocker panel moldings to the standard equipment list. The Esprit came with all standard safety, anti-theft, convenience and emission control equipment, a 231-cid two-barrel V-6 engine (305-cid two-barrel V-8 at extra cost in California), a three-speed manual transmission (Turbo-Hydra-Matic at extra cost in California), power steering, manual front disc/rear drum brakes, a body-color one-piece resilient Endura front end panel and front bumper with recessed grilles and dual rectangular headlights, an Endura rear bumper, body-color door handle inserts, dual horns, concealed windshield wipers, outside sport mirrors (left-hand remote controlled), Esprit identification, bright window sill and hood rear edge moldings, wheel opening moldings, roof drip

The 1980 Formula came with either standard 4.9-liter four-barrel or 4.9-liter turbo power plants.

The name of the Yellow Bird package appeared on the rear panel.

moldings, deluxe wheel covers, a heater and defroster unit, a flow-through ventilation system, a rosewood instrument panel appliqué on the instrument panel trim plate, a luxury cushion steering wheel, added acoustical insulation, a column-mounted headlight dimmer switch, nylon-blend cut-pile carpeting, front vinyl bucket seats with custom interior trim, fully-upholstered door trim panels with integral assist straps, custom pedal trim plates, a front console, high/low ventilation, a luggage compartment mat, a Radial Tuned Suspension and 205/75R-15 black sidewall steel-belted radial tires. A new Yellow Bird option package replaced the Red Bird package. It added basically the same features in a different color scheme, but black-out style taillights were added.

Model Number	Body/Style Number	Body Type & Seating	Factory Price	Shipping Weight	Production Total
FIREBIRD ESPRIT - SERIES 2FT - (V-6)					
2FT	87	2d sport coupe-4P	$5,967	3,304 lbs.	Notes 3, 4
FIREBIRD ESPRIT - SERIES 2FT - (V-8)					
2FT	87	2d sport coupe-4P	$6,147	3,377 lbs.	Note 4

Note 3: Combined production of base Firebirds and Esprits with the six-cylinder engine was 30,270 cars, a large increase.
Note 4: Total production of Esprits was 17,277, including cars with both six-cylinder and V-8 engines.

FORMULA FIREBIRD - (V-8) SERIES 2FV

The changes seen on the base Firebird were also characteristic of the 1980 Formula Firebird. The Formula came with all standard safety, anti-theft, convenience and emission control equipment, a 4.9-liter (301-cid) four-barrel V-8 engine, Turbo-Hydra-Matic transmission, power steering, power front disc/rear drum brakes, Endura front and rear bumpers, dual horns, concealed windshield wipers, dual rectangular headlamps, hubcaps, a heater and defroster unit, a flow-through ventilation system, carpeting, front bucket seats, a black-accented grille, a lower body accent color with striping, a simulated dual air scoop hood design, outside sport mirrors (left-hand remote controlled/right-hand manual convex), Formula iden-

tification, Rally II wheel rims with trim rings, a Formula steering wheel, Rally gauges with a quartz clock, a front console, black-out style taillights, a splitter exhaust system, a machine-turned instrument panel trim plate and 225/70R-15 black sidewall steel-belted radial tires. A 5.0-liter (305-cid) four-barrel V-8 was a required option in California cars. A new option in Formula Firebirds was a turbocharged 301-cid V-8.

FIREBIRD FORMULA TURBO 4.9 (V-8) - SERIES 2FW/LU8

The Turbo 4.9 Formula Firebird came with all standard safety, anti-theft, convenience and emission control equipment, a 301-cid (4.9-liter) V-8 engine with a TBO305 AiResearch Corp. turbocharger, a Turbo-Hydra-Matic transmission, power steering, power front disc/rear drum brakes, Endura front and rear bumpers, dual horns, concealed windshield wipers, dual rectangular headlamps, hubcaps, a heater and defroster unit, a flow-through ventilation system, carpeting, front bucket seats, a black-accented grille, a lower-body accent color with striping, a specific hood with an off-center power bulge designed to accommodate the turbocharger (with "Turbo 4.9 lettering on the left-hand side), outside sport mirrors (left-hand remote controlled/right-hand manual convex), Formula identification, Rally II wheel rims with trim rings, a Formula steering wheel, Rally gauges with a quartz clock, a front console, black-out style taillights, a splitter exhaust system, a machine-turned instrument panel trim plate and 225/70R-15 black sidewall steel-belted radial tires.

Model Number	Body/Style Number	Body Type & Seating	Factory Price	Shipping Weight	Production Total
FORMULA FIREBIRD 4.9-LITER - SERIES 2FV - (301-CID FOUR-BARREL V-8)					
2FV	87	2d sport coupe-4P	$6,955	3,411 lbs.	Note 5
FORMULA FIREBIRD 4.9-LITER E/C - SERIES 2FV - (301-CID FOUR-BARREL E/C V-8)					
2FV	87	2d sport coupe-4P	$7,135	—	Note 5
FORMULA FIREBIRD 4.9-LITER TURBO - SERIES 2FV - (301-CID FOUR-BARREL TURBO V-8)					

The Esprit "Yellow Bird" option replaced the Red Bird.

2FV	87	2d sport coupe-4P	$7,485	—	Note 5

FORMULA FIREBIRD 5.0-LITER - SERIES 2FV - (305-CID FOUR-BARREL V-8)

2FV	87	2d sport coupe-4P	$6,955	—	Note 5

Note 5: Total production of Formula Firebirds with all engines was 9,356.

FIREBIRD TRANS AM - (V-8) SERIES 2FW

The styling changes seen on the base Firebird were also characteristic of the 1980 Trans Am. Standard Trans Am equipment included all federally mandated safety, anti-theft, convenience and emissions control features, a 4.9-liter E/C (301-cid) four-barrel V-8 engine, a Turbo-Hydra-Matic transmission, a Trans Am front fender decal, a blacked-out grille, blacked-out taillights, a Trans Am grille panel decal, a Trans Am wraparound rear deck spoiler decal, a front center air dam, front and rear wheel opening air deflectors, a shaker hood scoop and air cleaner, concealed windshield wipers, front fender air extractors, power steering, a Power-Flex radiator fan, Rally gauges with a quartz clock and tachometer, front vinyl bucket seats, a front seat console, power front disc/rear drum brakes, a heater, a defroster, carpeting, windshield moldings, an aluminum machine-turned instrument panel trim plate, a formula steering wheel, dual sport mirrors with left-hand remote controlled/right-hand manual convex, dual horns, a rear deck lid spoiler, dual resonator tailpipes with chrome splitter tailpipe extensions, 15 x 7-in. Rally II wheels with trim rings, a Safe-T-Track limited-slip differential, 225/70R-15 black sidewall steel-belted radial tires and a Radial Tuned Suspension with heavy front and rear stabilizer bars. Engine options included the Formula's base L37 4.9-liter four-barrel V-8 for a $180 credit (and no dual resonator tailpipes), the 5.0-liter V-8 in California cars and the 4.9-liter Turbo V-8.

FIREBIRD TRANS AM BLACK SPECIAL EDITION - (V-8) - SERIES 2FW/Y84

The Y84 Black Special Edition package returned with slightly gaudier gold graphics and accents. It was available for $748 without hatch roof panels or for $1,443 with the Fisher Hatch Roof. Standard Trans Am Black Special Edition equipment included all federally mandated safety, anti-theft, convenience and emissions control features, a 301-cid (4.9-liter) V-8 engine, a Turbo-Hydra-Matic transmission, a Trans Am front fender decal, a blacked-out grille, blacked-out taillights, a Trans Am grille panel decal, a Trans Am wraparound rear deck spoiler decal, a front center air dam, front and rear wheel opening air deflectors, a shaker hood scoop and air cleaner and "big bird" hood decal, concealed windshield wipers, front fender air extractors, power steering, a Power-Flex radiator fan, Rally gauges with a clock and tachometer, front vinyl bucket seats with custom interior trim, a front seat console, power front disc/rear drum brakes, a heater, a defroster, carpeting, windshield moldings, an aluminum machine-turned instrument panel trim plate, a formula steering wheel, dual sport mirrors with left-hand remote controlled, dual horns, a rear deck lid spoiler, dual chrome splitter tailpipe extensions, 15 x 7-in. Rally II wheels with trim rings, a Safe-T-Track limited-slip differential, GR70-15 raised white letter steel-belted radial tires, a Radial Tuned Suspension with larger front and rear stabilizer bars, Starlight Black exterior body finish, gold body striping, gold interior and exterior accents, gold aluminum wheels and a removable hatch roof made by GM's Fisher Body Division.

FIREBIRD TRANS AM TURBO 4.9 (V-8) - SERIES 2FW/LU8

Trans Am Turbo 4.9 equipment included all federally mandated safety, anti-theft, convenience and emissions control features, a 301-cid (4.9-liter) V-8 engine with a TBO305 AiResearch Corp. turbocharger, a Turbo-Hydra-Matic transmission, a Trans Am front fender decal, a blacked-out grille, blacked-out taillights, a Trans Am grille panel decal, a Trans Am wraparound rear deck spoiler decal, a front center air dam, front and rear wheel opening air deflectors, a specific hood with an off-center power bulge designed to accommodate the turbocharger (with "Turbo 4.9 lettering on the left-hand side), concealed windshield wipers, front fender air extractors, power steering, a power-flex radiator fan, Rally gauges with a clock and tachometer, front vinyl bucket seats with custom interior trim, a front seat console, power front disc/rear drum brakes, a heater, a defroster, carpeting, windshield moldings, an aluminum machine-turned instrument panel trim plate, a formula steering wheel, dual sport mirrors with left-hand remote controlled, dual horns, a rear deck lid spoiler, dual chrome splitter tailpipe extensions, 15 x 7-in. Rally II wheels with trim rings, a Safe-T-Track limited-slip differential, GR70-15 raised white letter steel-belted radial tires and a Radial Tuned Suspension with larger front and rear stabilizer bars. (Not available in California).

FIREBIRD TRANS AM TURBO 4.9 INDY PACE CAR - (V-8) SERIES 2FW/LU8

Trans Am Turbo 4.9 equipment included all federally mandated safety, anti-theft, convenience and emissions control features, a 301-cid (4.9-liter) V-8 engine with a TBO305 AiResearch Corp. turbocharger, a Turbo-Hydra-Matic transmission, two-tone finish with gray upper body and white lower body, tri-color body accent stripes, Trans Am front fender decal, blacked-out grille, blacked-out taillights, Trans Am grille panel decal, optional Indy 500 Pace Car door graphics, Trans Am wraparound rear deck spoiler decal, a front center air dam, front and rear wheel opening air deflectors, specific hood with an off-center power bulge designed to accommodate the turbocharger (with "Turbo 4.9" lettering on the left-hand side), specific hood bird decal, halogen headlights with white headlight bezels, concealed windshield wipers, front fender air extractors, power steering, Power-Flex radiator fan, Rally gauges with a clock and tachometer, oyster-colored front vinyl bucket seats with oyster-colored hobnail cloth inserts, special interior trim with Firebirds embroidered into the door pads and the center of the rear seat, a front seat console, power four-wheel front disc brakes, 63-amp. alternator, electronically tuned AM/FM stereo cassette with seek-and-scan feature and digital display, audio

power booster, heater, defroster, air conditioning, power windows, carpeting, windshield moldings, aluminum machine-turned instrument panel trim plate, red instrument panel lighting, tinted glass, a leather-wrapped formula steering wheel, dual sport mirrors with left-hand remote controlled, dual horns, rear deck lid spoiler, dual chrome splitter tailpipe extensions, 15 x 8 white turbo-cast aluminum wheels, 3.08:1 rear axle ratio, a Safe-T-Track limited-slip differential, GR70-15 raised white letter steel-belted radial tires, Radial Tuned Suspension with larger front and rear stabilizer bars and silver-tinted hatch roof panels. In addition, 14 separate options could be added. (Not available in California.)

FIREBIRD TRANS AM TURBO 4.9 DAYTONA PACE CAR - (V-8) SERIES 2FW/LU8

Trans Am Turbo 4.9 equipment included all federally mandated safety, anti-theft, convenience and emissions control features, a 301-cid (4.9-liter) V-8 engine with a TBO305 AiResearch Corp. turbocharger, a Turbo-Hydra-Matic transmission, two-tone finish, accent stripes, Trans Am front fender decal, a blacked-out grille, blacked-out taillights, Trans Am grille panel decal, optional Daytona 500 Pace Car door graphics, Trans Am wraparound rear deck spoiler decal, front center air dam, front and rear wheel opening air deflectors, specific hood with an off-center power bulge designed to accommodate the turbocharger (with "Turbo 4.9 lettering on the left-hand side), specific hood bird decal, halogen headlights, concealed windshield wipers, front fender air extractors, power steering, Power-Flex radiator fan, Rally gauges with a clock and tachometer, front vinyl bucket seats with inserts, special interior trim, front seat console, power four-wheel front disc brakes, a 63-amp. alternator, electronically tuned AM/FM stereo cassette with seek-and-scan feature and digital display, audio power booster, a heater, a defroster, air conditioning, power windows, carpeting, windshield moldings, aluminum machine-turned instrument panel trim plate, tinted glass, formula steering wheel, dual sport mirrors with left-hand remote controlled, dual horns, rear deck lid spoiler, dual chrome splitter

The Turbo Trans Am featured a 4.9-liter V-8.

Pontiac produced more than 17,000 Esprits for 1980.

tailpipe extensions, 15 x 8 white turbo-cast aluminum wheels, 3.08:1 rear axle ratio, a Safe-T-Track limited-slip differential, GR70-15 raised white letter steel-belted radial tires, Radial Tuned Suspension with larger front and rear stabilizer bars and hatch roof panels.

Model Number	Body/Style Number	Body Type & Seating	Factory Price	Shipping Weight	Production Total
TRANS AM COUPE 4.9-LITER - SERIES 2FW - (301-CID PONTIAC L37 V-8)					
2FW	87	2d sport coupe-4P	$7,179	3,410 lbs.	14,866
TRANS AM COUPE 4.9-LITER TURBO - SERIES 2FW/LU8 - (301-CID PONTIAC LU8 TURBO V-8)					
2FW	87	2d sport coupe-4P	$7,529	—	5,753
TRANS AM COUPE 5.0-LITER - SERIES 2FW - (305-CID CHEVROLET LG4 V-8)					
2FW	87	2d sport coupe-4P	$6,789	—	1,635
TRANS AM T-TOP 4.9-LITER - SERIES 2FW - (301-CID PONTIAC L37 V-8)					
2FW	87	2d sport coupe-4P	$7,874	3,410 lbs.	8,692
TRANS AM T-TOP 4.9-LITER TURBO - SERIES 2FW/LU8 - (301-CID PONTIAC LU8 TURBO V-8)					
2FW	87	2d sport coupe-4P	$8,224	—	7,176
TRANS AM T-TOP 5.0-LITER - SERIES 2FW - (305-CID CHEVROLET LG4 V-8)					
2FW	87	2d sport coupe-4P	$7,484	—	896
TRANS AM BLACK SPECIAL ED. COUPE 4.9-LITER - SERIES 2FW - (301-CID PONTIAC L37 V-8)					
2FW/Y84	87	2d sport coupe-4P	$7,927	—	72
TRANS AM BLACK SPECIAL ED. COUPE 4.9-LITER TURBO - SERIES 2FW/LU8 - (301-CID PONTIAC LU8 TURBO V-8)					
2FW/Y84	87	2d sport coupe-4P	$8,277	—	103
TRANS AM BLACK SPECIAL ED. COUPE 5.0-LITER - SERIES 2FW - (305-CID CHEVROLET LG4 V-8)					
2FW/Y84	87	2d sport coupe-4P	$7,747	—	12
TRANS AM BLACK SPECIAL ED. T-TOP 4.9-LITER - SERIES 2FW - (301-CID PONTIAC L37 V-8)					
2FW/Y84	87	2d sport coupe-4P	$8,622	—	2,084
TRANS AM BLACK SPECIAL ED. T-TOP 4.9-LITER TURBO - SERIES 2FW/LU8 - (301-CID PONTIAC LU8 TURBO V-8)					
2FW/Y84	87	2d sport coupe-4P	$8,972	—	3,444
TRANS AM BLACK SPECIAL ED. T-TOP 5.0-LITER - SERIES 2FW - (305-CID CHEVROLET LG4 V-8)					
2FW/Y84	87	2d sport coupe-4P	$8,442	—	463
FIREBIRD TRANS AM TURBO 4.9 INDY PACE CAR - (V-8) - SERIES 2FW/LU8 – (301-CID PONTIAC LU8 TURBO V-8)					
2FX	87	2d sport coupe-4P	$11,195	—	5,700
FIREBIRD TRANS AM TURBO 4.9 DAYTONA PACE CAR - (V-8) - SERIES 2FW/LU8 – (301-CID PONTIAC LU8 TURBO V-8)					
2FX	87	2d sport coupe-4P	—	—	—

Note 6: All Trans Ams had Turbo-Hydra-Matic transmission.

ENGINE

Buick V-6 [UPC LD5]: Overhead valves. Cast-iron block. Displacement: 231 cid. Bore & stroke: 3.80 x 3.40 in. Compression ratio: 8.0:1. Brake horsepower: 115 at 3800 rpm. Torque: 188 ft. lbs. at 2000 rpm.

Hydraulic valve lifters. Carburetor: Two-barrel. VIN Code: A.

Pontiac 265 V-8 [UPC LS57]: Overhead valves. Cast-iron block. Displacement: 265 cid. Bore & stroke: 3.75 x 3.00 in. Compression ratio: 8.3:1. Brake horsepower: 120 at 3600 rpm. Torque: 210 ft. lbs. at 1600 rpm. Hydraulic valve lifters. Carburetion: Two-barrel. VIN Code: S.

Pontiac 301 V-8 [UPC L37]: Overhead valves. Cast-iron block. Displacement: 301 cid. Bore & stroke: 4.00 x 3.00 in. Compression ratio: 8.1:1. Brake horsepower: 140 at 4000 rpm. Torque: 240 ft. lbs. at 1800 rpm. Hydraulic valve lifters. Carburetion: Four-barrel. VIN Code: W.

Chevrolet 305 V-8 [UPC LG4]: Overhead valves. Cast-iron block. Displacement: 305 cid. Bore & stroke: 3.74 x 3.48 in. Compression ratio: 8.4:1. Brake horsepower: 150 at 3800 rpm. Torque: 230 ft. lbs. at 2400 rpm. Hydraulic valve lifters. Carburetion: Two-barrel. Four-speed manual transmission. VIN Code: H.

Pontiac 301 E/C V-8 [UPC L37 & W72]: Overhead valves. Cast-iron block. Displacement: 301 cid. Bore & stroke: 4.00 x 3.00 in. Compression ratio: 8.1:1. Brake horsepower: 155 at 4400 rpm. Torque: 240 ft.-lbs. at 2200 rpm. Hydraulic valve lifters. Carburetion: Four-barrel. Four-speed manual transmission. VIN Code: W.

Pontiac 4.9 Turbo V-8 [UPC LU8]: Overhead valves. Cast-iron block. Displacement: 301 cid. Bore & stroke: 4.00 x 3.00 in. Compression ratio: 7.6:1. Brake horsepower: 210 at 4000 rpm. Torque: 345 ft. lbs. at 2000 rpm. Five main bearings. Hydraulic valve lifters. Carburetor: Four-barrel. Splitter exhausts. VIN code: S.

CHASSIS

Base V-8, Esprit: Wheelbase: 108.2 in. Overall length: 196.8 in. Overall width: 73 in. Overall height: 49.3 in. Front tread: 61.3 in. Rear tread: 60.9 in. Front headroom: 36.9 in. Rear headroom: 35.7 in. Front legroom: 43.9 in. Rear leg room: 28.4 in. Front shoulder room: 57.4 in. Rear shoulder room: 54.4 in. Front hip room: 52.4 in. Rear hip room: 46.8 in. Trunk capacity: 7.1 cu. ft.

Formula: Wheelbase: 108.2 in. Overall Length:

196.8 in. Overall width: 73 in. Overall height: 49.3 in. Front tread: 61.3 in. Rear tread: 60.9 in. Front headroom: 36.9 in. Rear headroom: 35.7 in. Front legroom: 43.9 in. Rear legroom: 28.4 in. Front shoulder room: 57.4 in. Rear shoulder room: 54.4 in. Front hip room: 52.4 in. Rear hip room: 46.8 in. Trunk capacity: 7.1 cu. ft.

Trans Am: Wheelbase: 108.2 in. Overall Length: 196.8 in. Overall width: 73 in. Overall height: 49.3 in. Front tread: 61.3 in. Rear tread: 60.9 in. Front headroom: 36.9 in. Rear headroom: 35.7 in. Front legroom: 43.9 in. Rear legroom: 28.4 in. Front shoulder room: 57.4 in. Rear shoulder room: 54.4 in. Front hip room: 52.4 in. Rear hip room: 46.8 in. Trunk capacity: 7.1 cu. ft.

TECHNICAL

Base/Esprit: Body and frame: Integral body and frame with separate bolted-on sub-frame for engine and front suspension. Front suspension: Independent with upper and lower control arms, coil springs, tubular shocks and stabilizer bar. Rear suspension: Hotchkiss solid axle, multi-leaf rear springs and tubular shocks. Steering: Optional power assist coaxial re-circulating ball bearing. Fuel tank: 20.8 gal.

Formula: Body and frame: Integral body and frame with separate ladder-type front frame section. Front suspension: Independent with upper and lower control arms, heavy-duty coil springs, heavy-duty tubular shocks and stabilizer bar. Rear suspension: Hotchkiss solid axle, multi-leaf rear springs, stabilizer bar and tubular shocks. Steering: Optional power assist coaxial re-circulating ball bearing. Fuel tank: 20.8 gal.

Trans Am: Body and frame: Integral body and frame with separate ladder-type front frame section. Front suspension: Independent with upper and lower control arms, heavy-duty coil springs, heavy-duty tubular shocks and stabilizer bar. Rear suspension: Hotchkiss solid axle, multi-leaf rear springs, stabilizer bar and tubular shocks. Steering: Saginaw variable-ratio steering with power assist. Fuel tank: Fuel tank: 20.8 gal.

OPTIONS

LD5 3.8 liter V-6 in base Firebird and Esprit; not available with California emissions (no cost). L37* 4.9-liter V-8 including chrome exhaust splitters, in base Firebird and Esprit, not available with California emissions ($180). L37* 4.9 liter V-8 including chrome exhaust splitter in Formula, not available with California emissions (no cost). L37* 4.9-liter V-8 including chrome exhaust splitter in Trans Am, not available with California emissions and deletes dual resonators ($180 credit). W72 4.9-liter E/C V-8 on Trans Am, not available with California emissions (no cost). W72 4.9-liter E/C V-8 on Formula, includes dual resonators and tailpipes ($180). LU8 4.9-liter Turbo in Formula, not available with California emissions, includes dual resonators and tailpipes ($530). LU8 4.9-liter Turbo in Trans Am, not available with California emissions, includes dual resonators and tailpipes ($350). LG4 5.0-liter V-8 required with California emissions and air conditioning in base Firebird or Esprit ($195).

LG4 5.0-liter V-8 and dual resonators exhaust (dual splitters deleted), required with California emissions and air conditioning in Formula (no cost). LG4 5.0-liter V-8 required with California emissions and air conditioning in Trans Am, deletes dual resonator exhaust ($180 credit). LS5 4.3-liter/265-cid V-8 base Firebird and Esprit, not available with California emissions ($180). MX1 automatic transmission in base Firebird and Esprit ($358). C60 air conditioning ($566). K81** heavy-duty 63-amp. alternator without C49 or C60 ($36); with C49 or C60 (no cost). W73 Yellow Bird, for Esprit only; with velour hobnail trim ($550). W73 Yellow Bird, for Esprit only; with doeskin vinyl trim ($505). W50 Formula appearance package, Formula only ($100). Y84 Trans Am Black Special Edition package, Trans Am only; without hatch roof ($748). Y84 Trans Am Black Special Edition package, Trans Am only; with hatch roof ($1,443). G80 limited-slip differential for all except Trans Am ($68). UA1 heavy-duty battery ($23). AK1 custom seat belts, except Esprit without B18 ($25). U35 electric quartz clock, without Rally gauges ($30). K30 cruise control, requires MXI transmission with V-8 or JL2 with V-6 ($112). A90 remote-control deck lid release ($26). C49 electric rear window defroster ($107). VJ9 California emissions ($250). K05 engine block heater ($16). W63 Rally gauges with clock in base Firebird or Esprit; requires V-8 ($91); in Formula (no cost). U17 Rally gauges with clock and tachometer, in base Firebird or Esprit, requires V-8 ($159); in Formula ($68); in Trans Am (no cost). A01 tinted glass ($68). CC1 hatch roof without Y84 Black Special Edition Trans Am package ($695). TT5 halogen high-beam headlights ($27). D53 hood decal without Y84 Black Special Edition Trans Am package ($120). BS1 added acoustical insulation, except standard with Esprit ($34). C95 dome reading lamp ($21). TR9 lamp group ($22). B37 front and rear color-keyed floor mats ($27). D35 Sport OSRV mirrors with left-hand remote control in base Firebird ($47). D34 visor vanity mirror ($7). B84 color-keyed body side moldings ($46). B93 door edge guards ($14). B83 rocker panel molding on base Firebird only, standard on Esprit; and not available with other Firebirds ($20). B80 scalp moldings, standard with Esprit and Trans Am with Y84 ($26). B96 wheel opening moldings, standard with Esprit, not available with others ($24). B85 window sill and rear hood edge moldings, standard with Esprit and Trans Am with Y84 ($28). JL2 power front disc/rear drum brakes in base Firebird; and Esprit; standard with others ($81). J65 four-wheel power disc brakes in Formula or Trans Am with G80, without WS6 ($162); in Formula and Trans Am with G80 and WS6 (no cost). AU3 power door locks ($93). A31 power windows ($143). V02 super-cooling radiator with air conditioning, not available with LU8 ($35). V02 super-cooling radiator without air conditioning, not available with LU8 engine ($64). U75 power antenna without optional radios; not available with UP6 radio ($70). U75 power antenna with optional radios; not available with UP6 radio ($51). U83 power AM/FM/CB tri-band antenna, without optional radio ($93); with optional radio ($74). U63 AM radio ($97).

UM1 AM radio with integral 8-track stereo tape player ($249). U69 AM/FM radio ($153). UM7 AM/FM ETR radio with seek/scan, includes digital clock ($375). U58 AM/FM stereo radio ($192). UN3 AM/FM stereo radio with cassette stereo tape player ($285). UM2 AM/FM stereo radio with integral 8-track stereo tape player ($272). UP6 AM/FM stereo with 40-channel CB, includes U83 ($525). UN9 radio accommodation package, standard with optional radios. UN9 radio accommodation package without U75/U83 power antenna or optional radios ($29). UN9 radio accommodation package with U75/U83 power antennas, but without optional radios ($10). U80 rear seat speaker with U63 or U69 only ($20). UX6 dual front speakers, with U63 or U69 only ($14). UP8 dual front and rear speakers, with U63 or U69 only ($43). U01 dual rear extended range speakers with U63 or U69 ($68). U01 dual rear extended range speakers with UM1, U58, UN3, UM2 or UP6 ($25). U01 dual rear extended range speakers with UM7 ETR radio (no cost). WS6 Special Performance package for Formula with L37, LG4, LU8 or W72 engines ($481). WS6 Special Performance package for regular Trans Am with L37, LG4, LU8 or W72 engines ($481). WS6 Special Performance package for Black Special Edition Trans Am with L37, LG4, LU8 or W72 engines ($281). D80 rear deck spoiler on base Firebird, Esprit and Formula without W50 ($62). D80 rear deck spoiler on Formula with W50 or W87 (no cost). NK3 Formula steering wheel on base Firebird ($74); on Esprit without W73 ($52); on Esprit with W73 and Formula or Trans Am (no cost). N30 luxury cushion steering wheel on base Firebird ($22). N33 tilt steering wheel ($81). D98 vinyl tape stripes on base Firebird and Esprit without W50 or W73 only ($58). B18 custom trim group for Formula/Trans Am with vinyl doeskin trim ($142); for Formula/Trans Am with hobnail cloth trim ($187); for Esprit with hobnail cloth trim without W73 ($45). P01 deluxe wheel covers for base Firebird ($45). N95 wire wheel covers for base Firebird ($171); for Esprit ($126). N18 wheel cover locking package, with N95 only ($35). N90 four cast aluminum wheels on base Firebird ($336); on Esprit without W73 ($291). N98

Rally II wheels and four trim rings, on base Firebird with N65 ($136); on base Firebird without N65 ($158); on Esprit with N65 ($91); on Esprit without N65 ($113); on Formula or Trans Am (no cost). N67 body-color Rally II wheels and four trim rings, on base Firebird with N65 ($136); on base Firebird without N65 ($158); on Esprit with N65 ($91); on Esprit without N65 ($113); on Formula or Trans Am (no cost). Code unknown†, Turbo-Cast aluminum wheels, requires WS6 and Turbo V-8 (price not available). UR4 turbo boost gauge, required with LU8 turbo V-8 ($40). CD4 controlled-cycle windshield wipers ($41). N65 stowaway spare (no cost). QJU 205/75R15 black sidewall steel-belted radial tires on base Firebird and Esprit (no cost). QJW 205/75R15 white sidewall steel-belted radial tires on base Firebird and Esprit without N65 ($62 extra); on base Firebird or Esprit with N65 ($50 extra). QMC 205/75R15 white letter steel-belted radial tires on base Firebird or Esprit without N65 ($80 extra); on base Firebird or Esprit with N65 ($64 extra). QGR 205/75Rl5 white letter steel-belted radials tires with Rally Tuned Suspension on Formula or Trans Am without WS6 ($68 extra.

*L37 engine for (base Firebird) Firebird and Esprit increased to $225 around April 1980.

**70-amp. alternator was released in April at following prices: without C49 or C60 ($51); with C49 or with C60 ($15); with both C49 and C60 (no charge). The 70-amp alternator was not available with the LD5 or LG4 engines.

†No price was listed for the Turbo-Cast aluminum wheels. They could be installed in place of Rally II wheels when teamed with specific other options.

HISTORICAL FOOTNOTES

The gas crunch put the crunch on the Firebird line in 1980. Total model-year production of Firebirds was only 107,340 units. Sales were even worse and stood at 81,592 for the calendar year. The Turbo Trans Am could do 0 to 60 mph in 8.2 seconds and cover the quarter mile in 16.7 seconds at 86 mph. Top speed was 116 mph.

The 1980 Special Edition Trans Am was even bolder than previous years.

The 1981 Trans Am had T-tops and a familiar racy look.

Last Pontiac V-8

A shuffle of powertrains highlighted Pontiac Firebird changes for 1981. A new Trans Am option was a two-color hood decal in five combinations. Two-tone paint became optional on the Formula and several new cloth bucket seat options were made available, including a silver doeskin vinyl interior in place of the oyster vinyl offering.

Standard in Formulas was a Pontiac-made 4.3-liter V-8, also optional on Firebirds and Esprits. Trans Ams used a Pontiac-built 4.9-liter four-barrel V-8 with Electronic Spark Control. Trans Ams and Formulas offered a turbocharged 4.9-liter, which was now available in California. Base transmission for the Esprit was the automatic, while the standard Firebird stuck with a three-speed manual gearbox. A four-speed manual gearbox was again available in Formulas and Trans Ams with the four-barrel 5.0-liter V-8.

A famous publicity photo showed a 1967 Firebird convertible on the lower ramp of a transporter and a 1981 Trans Am coupe above it. They represented the first and last Firebirds assembled with Pontiac-built V-8s. Starting in 1982, the only V-8 would be a 5.0-liter made by Chevrolet or GM of Canada.

Among other 1981 improvements was a Computer Command Control engine-management system, a quick-take-up brake master cylinder, an early fuel-evaporation system and a new lightweight Delco Freedom battery with side terminals. The standard power brakes now included a low-drag front caliper.

Burt Reynolds's cult film *Smokey and the Bandit* had given national exposure to a Turbo Trans Am and Pontiac tried to capitalize on its popularity by featuring the actor, in his "Bandit" attire, in the centerfold of the 1981 Pontiac sales catalog. It did not do much to help the Firebird's sagging model-year production, which came in at 20,541 base Firebirds, 10,938 Esprits, 5,927 Formulas and 33,493 Trans Ams. The high price tag on the black-and-gold Special Edition may have been another thing driving sales down 34 percent.

The summer 1981 release of a sequel movie *Smokey and the Bandit II* prompted a New Jersey company to release a $30,000 Trans Am Bandit model that had its aftermarket upgrades, like a 380-hp 462-cid V-8, Doug Nash five-speed manual gearbox, Recaro seats, a Blaupunkt sound system and Goodyear Eagle GT tires. There was also a midyear, factory-issued $12,244 Daytona 500 Pace Car package built in a limited run of 2,000 copies. It is known to enthusiasts as the "NASCAR Turbo Pace Car" and was similar to the 1980 Indy Pace Car with black accents replacing the Indy car's charcoal accents.

I.D. NUMBERS

The vehicle identification number (VIN) was stamped on a plate on the upper left-hand side of the instrument panel and visible through the windshield. The first symbol indicated country of origin: 1=United States, 2=Canada. The second symbol indicated the manufacturer: 2=General Motors. The third symbol indicated make: 2=Pontiac. The fourth symbol indicated the type of restraint system: A=non-passive restraints (manual seat belts); B=passive restraints (automatic seat belts); C=passive restraints (front airbags) series with A used in all Firebirds. The fifth symbol indicated car line or series: S=Base Firebird, T=Firebird Esprit, V=Formula Firebird, W=Trans Am, X=Turbo and Special Edition. Sixth and seventh symbols indicated the body style: 87=two-door, plainback special coupe. The eighth symbol indicated engine: A=231-cid two-barrel Buick V-6, W=301-cid four-barrel Pontiac V-8, T=301-cid four-barrel turbocharged Pontiac V-8, H=305-cid four-barrel Chevrolet V-8, S=265-cid two-barrel Pontiac V-8. The ninth symbol indicated model year: B=1981. The 10th symbol indicated the assembly plant: N=Norwood, Ohio, L=Van Nuys, California. The remaining symbols were sequential unit production number at factory, starting with 100001. The Body by Fisher plate on the engine side of the cowl contained the Fisher style number, which took the form 2V87. The first symbol 2=Pontiac, the second symbol V=Formula and the last two symbols 87= two-door, plainback special coupe. This plate also indicated interior trim, seat type, body color and build date. V-6 engine code stamped on distributor mounting on right side of block. V-8 engine code on front of block below right cylinder head. Engine production codes for 1981 were: [231-cid V-6] LZ-NA-NB-NC-ND-NF-NJ-NK-NL-NZ-RA-RB-RC-RD-RK-RL, [301-cid four-barrel V-8] BD-BJ-BO-CJ, [305-cid four-barrel V-8] D6B-D6C-D6D-DHA-DHB-DHC-DHD-DHF-DHH-DHJ-DHK-DHU-DHZ-DJ-DKB-DND, [265-cid two-barrel V-8] AU-AW-AZ-BA-DB-DC-DH.

COLORS

11=White, 16=Stardust Silver, 19=Starlight Black, 20=Vibrant Blue, 21=Baniff Blue, 29=Nightwatch Blue Irid, 51=Tahitian Yellow, 54=Dorado Gold, 56=Yellow, 57=Navajo Orange, 67=Barclay Brown, 75=Spectra Red, 77=Autumn Maroon and 84=Ontario Gray.

FIREBIRD - (V-6/V-8) - SERIES 2FS

Small external differences identified 1981 Firebirds. A white bird emblem was placed on the fuel filler door between the taillights. New up front was a black-finished grille with Argent Silver accents. There

were new exterior colors. Engineering upgrades included low-drag front disc brakes, a quick-take-up brake master cylinder, early fuel evaporation system, new lightweight side terminal Delco Freedom battery and General Motors' Computer Command Control (CCC) system. Standard equipment for the base Firebird included a 3.8-liter (231-cid) two-barrel V-8 engine, three-speed manual transmission, floor shift, front console, power steering, power front disc/rear drum brakes, 205/75R15 steel-belted black sidewall tires, compact spare tire, coolant recovery system, maintenance-free battery, concealed two-speed electric windshield wipers, body-color one-piece resilient Endura front end panel and front bumper, dual rectangular headlamps, black-finished grille with Argent Silver accents, bright windshield molding, bright rear window molding, an Endura rear bumper, hubcaps with the Pontiac crest, vinyl front bucket seats, a deluxe cushion steering wheel, a day/night inside rearview mirror, dual horns, cut-pile carpeting, a simulated rosewood appliqué on the instrument panel trim plate, a cigar lighter, a luggage compartment mat and acoustical insulation.

Model Number	Body/Style Number	Body Type & Seating	Factory Price	Shipping Weight	Production Total
FIREBIRD - SERIES 2FS - (V-6)					
2FS	87	2d sport coupe-4P	$7,155	3,275 lbs.	Notes 1,2
FIREBIRD - SERIES 2FS - (V-8)					
2FS	87	2d sport coupe-4P	$7,205	3,350 lbs.	Note 2

Note 1: Combined production of base Firebirds and Esprits with the six-cylinder engine was 23,468 cars.
Note 2: Total production of base Firebirds was 20,541, including cars with both six-cylinder and V-8 engines.
Note 3: All 1981 Firebird prices are those that applied after April 13, 1981, when prices rose 6.5 percent.

FIREBIRD ESPRIT - (V-6/V-8) SERIES 2FT

In addition to changes outlined for base Firebirds, the custom interiors used in the Esprit featured a new combination featuring Pimlico cloth bucket seats with Durand cloth bolsters in a new beige color choice. Standard equipment for the Esprit included the 3.8-liter (231-cid) two-barrel V-8 engine, Turbo-Hydra-Matic transmission, floor shift, a front console, body-color door handle inserts, body-color sport mirrors (left-hand remote controlled), power steering, power front disc/rear drum brakes, 205/75R15 steel-belted black sidewall tires, compact spare tire, coolant recovery system, maintenance-free battery, concealed two-speed electric windshield wipers, body-color one-piece resilient Endura front end panel and front bumper, dual rectangular headlamps, a black-finished grille with Argent Silver accents, bright windshield molding, bright rear window molding, bright windowsill moldings, hood rear edge molding, wheel opening moldings, roof drip moldings, wide rocker panel moldings, Endura rear bumper, deluxe wheel covers, front bucket seats with custom interior trim, deluxe door trim with integral assist grips and carpeting on lower portion, rear quarter ashtrays, instrument panel assist strap, custom pedal trim plates, custom color-keyed safety belts, luxury cushion steering wheel, day/night inside rearview mirror, dual horns, cut-pile carpeting, a simulated rosewood appliqué on the instrument panel trim plate, a cigar lighter, a luggage compartment mat and additional acoustical insulation.

Model Number	Body/Style Number	Body Type & Seating	Factory Price	Shipping Weight	Production Total
FIREBIRD ESPRIT- SERIES 2FT - (V-6)					
2FT	87	2d sport coupe-4P	$8,021	3,312 lbs.	Notes 4, 5
FIREBIRD ESPRIT - SERIES 2FT - (V-8)					
2FT	87	2d sport coupe-4P	$8,071	3,387 lbs.	Note 5

Note 4: Combined production of base Firebirds and Esprits with the six-cylinder engine was 23,468 cars.
Note 5: Total production of Esprits was 10,938, including cars with both six-cylinder and V-8 engines.

FORMULA FIREBIRD - (V-8) SERIES 2FV

The changes seen on the base Firebird were also characteristic of the 1981 Formula Firebird. Standard equipment for the Formula Firebird included a 4.3-liter (265-cid) two-barrel V-8 engine, Turbo-Hydra-Matic transmission, dual air scoop hood design, floor shift, front console, power steering, power front disc/rear drum brakes, 225/70R15 steel-belted black sidewall tires, compact spare tire, coolant recovery system, maintenance-free battery, concealed two-speed electric windshield wipers, body-color one-piece resilient Endura front end panel and front bumper, dual rectangular headlamps, dual body-color outside sport mirrors (left-hand remote controlled), black-finished grille with Argent Silver accents, black-finished windshield molding, black-finished rear window molding, Endura rear bumper, black-out taillights, rear deck lid spoiler, Rally II wheel rims with trim rings, vinyl front bucket seats, a formula steering wheel, rally gauges with a clock, day/night inside rearview mirror, dual horns, cut-pile carpeting, a simulated engine turned insert the instrument panel trim plate, cigar lighter, luggage compartment mat and acoustical insulation.

FORMULA FIREBIRD TURBO 4.9 (V-8) SERIES 2FW/LU8

The changes seen on the base Firebird were also characteristic of the 1981 Formula Firebird. The 1981 Turbo 4.9 Formula Firebird came with all standard safety, anti-theft, convenience and emission control equipment, a 301-cid (4.9-liter) V-8 engine with a TBO305 AiResearch Corp. turbocharger, Turbo-Hydra-Matic transmission, a floor shift, a front console, power steering, power front disc/rear drum brakes, 225/70R15 steel-belted black sidewall tires, compact spare tire, coolant recovery system, maintenance-free battery, concealed two-speed electric windshield wipers, body-color one-piece resilient Endura front end panel and front bumper, dual rectangular headlamps, lower body accent color with striping, specific hood with an off-center power bulge designed to accommodate the turbocharger (with "Turbo 4.9" lettering on the left-hand side), dual body-color outside sport mirrors (left-hand remote controlled), black-finished grille with Argent Silver accents, black-finished windshield molding, black-finished rear window molding, Endura rear bumper, black-out taillights, rear deck lid spoiler, Rally II wheel rims with trim rings, vinyl front bucket seats,

formula steering wheel, rally gauges with a clock, day/night inside rearview mirror, dual horns, cut-pile carpeting, simulated engine turned insert the instrument panel trim plate, cigar lighter, luggage compartment mat and acoustical insulation.

Model Number	Body/Style Number	Body Type & Seating	Factory Price	Shipping Weight	Production Total
FORMULA FIREBIRD 4.3-LITER - SERIES 2FV - (265-CID FOUR-BARREL V-8)					
2FV	87	2d sport coupe-4P	$8,143	3,297 lbs.	Note 6
FORMULA FIREBIRD 5.0-LITER - SERIES 2FV - (305-CID FOUR-BARREL V-8)					
2FV	87	2d sport coupe-4P	$8,218	3,350 lbs.	Note 6
FORMULA FIREBIRD 4.9-LITER E/C - SERIES 2FV - (301-CID FOUR-BARREL V-8)					
2FV	87	2d sport coupe-4P	$8,358	—	Note 6
FORMULA FIREBIRD 4.9-LITER TURBO - SERIES 2FV - (301-CID FOUR-BARREL TURBO V-8)					
2FV	8	2d sport coupe-4P	$8,795	—	Note 6

Note 6: Total production of Formula Firebirds with all engines was 5,927.

FIREBIRD TRANS AM - (V-8) SERIES 2FW

Pontiac had no big surprises in store for 1981 Trans Am buyers. The base engine was the 4.9-liter E/C V-8, also known as the Trans Am 4.9-liter. When the 5.0-liter V-8 was ordered, as a delete option, it came with dual resonators and pipes instead of chrome exhaust splitters. The Turbo 4.9-liter V-8 came with a special hood with an off-center power blister and a turbo-boost gauge. The styling changes seen on the base Firebird were also characteristic of the 1981 Trans Am. Standard equipment for the Trans Am also included a Turbo-Hydra-Matic transmission, floor shift, a front console, Rally gauges with a clock and a tachometer, power steering, power front disc/rear drum brakes, 225/70R15 steel-belted black sidewall tires, Radial Tuned Suspension, compact spare tire, coolant recovery system, maintenance-free battery, concealed two-speed electric windshield wipers, body-color one-piece resilient Endura front end panel and front bumper, front center air dam, shaker hood and air cleaner, black-accented dual rectangular headlamps, black-finished grille, black-finished windshield molding, black-finished rear window molding, Endura rear bumper, rear deck lid spoiler, front fender air extractors, front and rear wheel opening air deflectors, 15 x 7-in. Rally II wheels with trim rings, vinyl front bucket seats, Formula steering wheel, a day/night inside rearview mirror, dual outside sport mirrors (left-hand remote controlled), dual horns, cut-pile carpeting, simulated engine-turned instrument panel trim plate, chrome side splitter exhaust extensions, a cigar lighter, a luggage compartment mat and acoustical insulation.

FIREBIRD TRANS AM BLACK SPECIAL EDITION - (V-8) - SERIES 2FW/Y84

The Y84 Black Special Edition package returned with slightly gaudier gold graphics and accents. It was available for $735 without hatch roof panels or for $1,430 with the hatch roof. Standard Trans Am Black Special Edition equipment included all federally mandated safety, anti-theft, convenience and emissions control features, a 4.9-liter E/C (301-cid) V-8 engine, Turbo-Hydra-Matic transmission, Trans Am front fender decal, a blacked-out grille, blacked-out taillights, a Trans Am grille panel decal, Trans Am wraparound rear deck spoiler decal, a front center air dam, front and rear wheel opening air deflectors, shaker hood scoop and air cleaner and "big bird" hood decal, concealed windshield wipers, front fender air extractors, power steering, Power-Flex radiator fan, Rally gauges with a clock and tachometer, front vinyl bucket seats with custom interior trim, front seat console, power front disc/rear drum brakes, heater, defroster, carpeting, black-finished windshield moldings, black-finished rear window moldings, aluminum machine-turned instrument panel trim plate, a formula steering wheel, dual sport mirrors with left-hand remote controlled, dual horns, rear deck lid spoiler, dual chrome splitter tailpipe extensions, 15 x 7-in. Rally II wheels with trim rings, a Safe-T-Track limited-slip differential, GR70-15 raised white letter steel-belted radial tires, Radial Tuned Suspension with larger front and rear stabilizer bars, Starlight Black exterior body finish, gold body striping, gold interior and exterior accents, gold aluminum wheels and removable hatch roof made by GM's Fisher Body Division.

FIREBIRD TURBO TRANS AM BLACK SPECIAL EDITION - (V-8) SERIES 2FW/Y84

The Y84 Black Special Edition package could be combined with the turbocharged V-8. Standard features included all federally mandated safety, anti-theft, convenience and emissions control features, a 301-cid (4.9-liter) V-8 engine with a TBO305 AiResearch Corp. turbocharger, Turbo-Hydra-Matic transmission, Trans Am front fender decal, blacked-out grille, blacked-out taillights, Trans Am grille panel decal, Trans Am wraparound rear deck spoiler decal, front center air dam, front and rear wheel opening air deflectors, specific hood with an off-center power bulge designed to accommodate the turbocharger (with "Turbo 4.9" lettering on the left-hand side), special "big bird" hood decal, concealed windshield wipers, front fender air extractors, power steering, a Power-Flex radiator fan, Rally gauges with a clock and tachometer, front bucket seats, custom interior trim, hatch roof, electronically tuned AM/FM stereo radio with cassette, a front seat console, power front disc/rear drum brakes, heater, defroster, carpeting, black-finished windshield moldings, black-finished rear window moldings, aluminum machine-turned instrument panel trim plate, formula steering wheel, dual sport mirrors with left-hand remote controlled, dual horns, rear deck lid spoiler, dual chrome splitter tailpipe extensions, gold Turbo-Cast aluminum wheels, a Safe-T-Track limited-slip differential, the WS6 Special Performance package, GR70-15 raised white letter steel-belted radial tires, Radial Tuned Suspension with larger front and rear stabilizer bars, Starlight Black exterior body finish, gold body striping, gold interior and exterior accents and a removable hatch roof made by GM's Fisher Body Division.

FIREBIRD TRANS AM TURBO 4.9 (V-8) - SERIES 2FW/LU8

Trans Am Turbo 4.9 equipment included all feder-ally mandated safety, anti-theft, convenience and emissions control features, a 301-cid (4.9-liter) V-8 engine with a TBO305 AiResearch Corp. turbocharger, a Turbo-Hydra-Matic transmission, a Trans Am front fender decal, a blacked-out grille, blacked-out taillights, a Trans Am grille panel decal, a Trans Am wraparound rear deck spoiler decal, a front center air dam, front and rear wheel opening air deflectors, a specific hood with an off-center power bulge designed to accommodate the turbocharger (with "Turbo 4.9" lettering on the left-hand side), concealed windshield wipers, front fender air extractors, power steering, a Power-Flex radiator fan, Rally gauges with a clock and tachometer, front vinyl bucket seats with custom interior trim, a front seat console, power front disc/rear drum brakes, a heater, a defroster, carpeting, windshield moldings, an aluminum machine-turned instrument panel trim plate, a formula steering wheel, dual sport mirrors with left-hand remote controlled, dual horns, a rear deck lid spoiler, dual chrome splitter tailpipe extensions, 15 x 7-in. Rally II wheels with trim rings, a Safe-T-Track limited-slip differential, GR70-15 raised white letter steel-belted radial tires and a Radial Tuned Suspension with larger front and rear stabilizer bars. (Not available in California).

Y87 FIREBIRD TRANS AM TURBO 4.9 DAYTONA PACE CAR - (V-8) SERIES 2FW/LU8

Turbo 4.9 Daytona Pace Car equipment included all federally mandated safety, anti-theft, convenience and emissions control features, a 301-cid (4.9-liter) V-8 engine with a TBO305 AiResearch Corp. turbocharger, a Turbo-Hydra-Matic transmission, two-tone finish with white upper body and black lower body, body accent stripes, a Trans Am front fender decal, a blacked-out grille, blacked-out taillights, a Trans Am grille panel decal, optional pace car graphics, a Trans Am wraparound rear deck spoiler decal, a front center air dam, front and rear wheel opening air deflectors, a specific hood with an off-center power bulge designed to accommodate the turbocharger (with "Turbo 4.9" lettering on the left-hand side), a specific hood bird decal, halogen headlights with white headlight bezels, concealed windshield wipers, front fender air extractors, power steering, a Power-Flex radiator fan, Rally gauges with a clock and tachometer, Recaro front bucket seats with (black with red inserts), special interior trim with Firebirds embroidered into the door pads and the center of the rear seat, a front seat console, power four-wheel front disc brakes, a 63-amp alternator, an electronically tuned AM/FM stereo cassette with seek/scan feature and digital display, an audio power booster, a heater, a defroster, air conditioning, power windows, carpeting, windshield moldings, an aluminum machine-turned instrument panel trim plate, red instrument panel lighting, tinted glass, a leather-wrapped formula steering wheel, dual sport mirrors with left-hand remote controlled, dual horns, a rear deck lid spoiler, dual chrome splitter tailpipe extensions, 15 x 8 white turbo cast-aluminum wheels, a 3.08:1 rear axle ratio, a Safe-T-Track limited-slip differential, GR70-15 raised white letter steel-belted radial tires, a Radial Tuned Suspension with larger front and rear stabilizer bars and silver-tinted hatch roof panels. In addition, 14 separate options could be added. (Not available in California).

Model Number	Body/Style Number	Body Type & Seating	Factory Price	Shipping Weight	Production Total
TRANS AM COUPE 4.9-LITER E/C - SERIES 2FW - (301-CID PONTIAC L37 V-8)					
2FW	87	2d sport coupe-4P	$8,322	3,419 lbs.	5,087
TRANS AM COUPE 4.9-LITER TURBO - SERIES 2FW/LU8 - (301-CID PONTIAC LU8 TURBO V-8)					
2FW	87	2d sport coupe-4P	$8,759	3,475 lbs.	3,851
TRANS AM COUPE 5.0-LITER - SERIES 2FW - (305-CID CHEVROLET LG4 V-8)					
2FW	87	2d sport coupe-4P	$8,182	—	2,866
TRANS AM T-TOP 4.9-LITER E/C - SERIES 2FW - (301-CID PONTIAC L37 V-8)					
2FW	87	2d sport coupe-4P	$9,017	3,450 lbs.	4,589
TRANS AM T-TOP 4.9-LITER TURBO - SERIES 2FW/LU8 - (301-CID PONTIAC LU8 TURBO V-8)					
2FW	87	2d sport coupe-4P	$8,919	—	6,612
TRANS AM T-TOP 5.0-LITER - SERIES 2FW - (305-CID CHEVROLET LG4 V-8)					
2FW	87	2d sport coupe-4P	$8,877	—	3,225
TRANS AM BLACK SPECIAL EDITION COUPE 4.9-LITER E/C - SERIES 2FW - (301-CID PONTIAC L37 V-8)					
2FW/Y84	87	2d sport coupe-4P	$8,662	—	41
TRANS AM BLACK SPECIAL EDITION COUPE 4.9-LITER TURBO - SERIES 2FW/LU8 - (301-CID PONTIAC LU8 TURBO V-8)					
2FW/Y84	87	2d sport coupe-4P	$9,012	—	65
TRANS AM BLACK SPECIAL EDITION COUPE 5.0-LITER - SERIES 2FW - (305-CID CHEVROLET LG4 V-8)					
2FW/Y84	87	2d sport coupe-4P	$8,182	—	15
TRANS AM BLACK SPECIAL EDITION T-TOP 4.9-LITER E/C - SERIES 2FW - (301-CID PONTIAC L37 V-8)					
2FW/Y84	87	2d sport coupe-4P	$10,052	—	1,160
TRANS AM BLACK SPECIAL EDITION T-TOP 4.9-LITER TURBO - SERIES 2FW/LU8 - (301-CID PONTIAC LU8 TURBO V-8)					
2FW/Y84	87	2d sport coupe-4P	$10,402	—	3,050
TRANS AM BLACK SPECIAL EDITION T-TOP 5.0-LITER - SERIES 2FW - (305-CID CHEVROLET LG4 V-8)					
2FW/Y84	87	2d sport coupe-4P	$9,872	—	932
FIREBIRD TRANS AM TURBO 4.9 NASCAR PACE CAR - (V-8) - SERIES 2FW/LU8 – (301-CID PONTIAC LU8 TURBO V-8)					
2FX	87	2d sport coupe-4P	$12,244	—	2,000

Note 6: All Trans Ams with the 5.0-liter had manual transmission.

ENGINE

Buick V-6 [UPC LD5]: Overhead valves. Cast-iron block. Displacement: 231 cid. Bore & stroke: 3.80 x 3.40 in. Compression ratio: 8.0:1. Brake horsepower: 110 at 3800 rpm. Torque: 190 ft. lbs. at 1600 rpm. Hydraulic valve lifters. Carburetor: Two-barrel. VIN Code: A.

Pontiac 265 V-8 [UPC LS4]: Overhead valves. Cast-iron block. Displacement: 265 cid. Bore & stroke: 3.75 x 3.00 in. Compression ratio: 8.3:1. Brake horsepower: 120 at 4000 rpm. Torque: 205 ft. lbs. at 2000 rpm. Hydraulic valve lifters. Carburetion: Two-barrel. VIN Code: S.

Pontiac 301 V-8 [UPC L37]: Overhead valves. Cast-iron block. Displacement: 301 cid. Bore & stroke: 4.00 x 3.00 in. Compression ratio: 8.1:1. Brake horsepower: 150 at 4000 rpm. Torque: 245 ft. lbs. at 2000 rpm. Hydraulic valve lifters. Carburetion: Four-barrel. VIN Code: W.

Pontiac 4.9 Turbo V-8 [UPC LU8]: Overhead valves. Cast-iron block. Displacement: 301 cid. Bore & stroke: 4.00 x 3.00 in. Compression ratio: 7.5:1. Brake horsepower: 200 at 4000 rpm. Torque: 340 ft. lbs. at 2000 rpm. Five main bearings. Hydraulic valve lifters. Carburetor: Four-barrel. Splitter exhausts. VIN code: T.

Chevrolet 305 V-8 [UPC LG4]: Overhead valves. Cast-iron block. Displacement: 305 cid. Bore & stroke: 3.74 x 3.48 in. Compression ratio: 8.6:1. Brake horsepower: 145 at 4000 rpm. Torque: 230 ft. lbs. at 2400 rpm. Hydraulic valve lifters. Carburetion: Four-barrel. Four-speed manual transmission required. VIN Code: H.

CHASSIS

Base V-8, Esprit: Wheelbase: 108.2 in. Overall length: 196.8 in. Overall width: 73 in. Overall height: 50.3 in. Front tread: 61.3 in. Rear tread: 60.9 in. Front headroom: 36.9 in. Rear headroom: 35.7 in. Front legroom: 43.9 in. Rear legroom: 28.4 in. Front shoulder room: 57.4 in. Rear shoulder room: 54.4 in. Front hip room: 52.4 in. Rear hip room: 46.8 in. Trunk capacity: 7.1 cu. ft.

Formula: Wheelbase: 108.2 in. Overall length: 196.8 in. Overall width: 73 in. Overall height: 50.3 in. Front tread: 61.3 in. Rear tread: 60.9 in. Front headroom: 36.9 in. Rear headroom: 35.7 in. Front legroom: 43.9 in. Rear legroom: 28.4 in. Front shoulder room: 57.4 in. Rear shoulder room: 54.4 in. Front hip room: 52.4 in. Rear hip room: 46.8 in. Trunk capacity: 7.1 cu. ft.

Trans Am: Wheelbase: 108.2 in. Overall length: 196.8 in. Overall width: 73 in. Overall height: 50.3 in. Front tread: 61.3 in. Rear tread: 60.9 in. Front headroom: 36.9 in. Rear headroom: 35.7 in. Front legroom: 43.9 in. Rear legroom: 28.4 in. Front shoulder room: 57.4 in. Rear shoulder room: 54.4 in. Front hip room: 52.4 in. Rear hip room: 46.8 in. Trunk capacity: 7.1 cu. ft.

TECHNICAL

Base/Esprit: Body and frame: Integral body and frame with separate bolted-on sub-frame for engine and front suspension. Front suspension: Independent with upper and lower control arms, coil springs, tubular shocks and stabilizer bar. Rear suspension: Hotchkiss solid axle, multi-leaf rear springs and tubular shocks. Steering: Optional power assist coaxial re-circulating ball bearing. Fuel tank: 21 gal.

Formula: Body and frame: Integral body and frame with separate ladder-type front frame section. Front suspension: Independent with upper and lower control arms, heavy-duty coil springs, heavy-duty tubular shocks and stabilizer bar. Rear suspension: Hotchkiss solid axle, multi-leaf rear springs, stabilizer bar and tubular shocks. Steering: Optional power assist coaxial re-circulating ball bearing. Fuel tank: 21 gal.

Trans Am: Body and frame: Integral body and frame with separate ladder-type front frame section. Front suspension: Independent with upper and lower control arms, heavy-duty coil springs, heavy-duty tubular shocks and stabilizer bar. Rear suspension: Hotchkiss solid axle, multi-leaf rear springs, stabilizer bar and tubular shocks. Steering: Saginaw variable-ratio steering with power assist. Fuel tank: Fuel tank: 21 gal.

OPTIONS

LD5 3.8-liter V-6 in base Firebird and Esprit (no

The '81 Formula came standard with a 4.3-liter V-8.

cost). LS5 4.3-liter two-barrel V-8, requires automatic transmission; in base Firebird and Esprit ($50); in Formula (no cost). L37 4.9-liter E/C V-8 including chrome exhaust splitters and requires automatic transmission, in base Firebird, Esprit and Formula ($215). L37 4.9-liter E/C V-8 in Trans Am (no cost). LU8 4.9 liter Turbo in Trans Am, requires air conditioning and automatic transmission, includes dual resonators and tailpipes ($437). LU8 4.9-liter Turbo in Formula, requires air conditioning and automatic transmission, includes chrome exhaust splitters ($652). LG4 5.0-liter V-8 in Formula, requires four-speed manual transmission and includes dual resonator tailpipes ($75). LG4 5.0-liter V-8 in Trans Am, requires California emissions and air conditioning, deletes dual resonator tailpipes and adds chrome splitter exhaust ($180 credit). MX3 three-speed manual transmission with floor shift with V-6 only (no charge). MX4 four-speed manual transmission with floor shift and LG4 V-8 in Formula or Trans Am (no cost). MX1 automatic transmission in base Firebird and Esprit ($349). C60 custom air conditioning ($560). K73 heavy-duty 70-amp. alternator with C49 or Turbo V-8 (no cost); without C49 or Turbo V-8 ($51). W50 Formula appearance package, Formula only ($200). Y84 Trans Am Black Special Edition package, Trans Am only; without hatch roof ($735). Y84 Trans Am Black Special Edition package, Trans Am only; with hatch roof ($1,430). G80 limited-slip differential for all except Trans Am, with WS6 Special Performance package (no cost); without WS6 Special Performance package ($67). UA1 heavy-duty battery ($22). AK1 custom seat belts, with Esprit (no cost); with B18 Custom trim group (no cost); without B18 Custom trim group ($24). U35 electric quartz clock, with Rally gauges (no cost); without Rally gauges ($28). K35 cruise control with resume feature, requires MXI automatic transmission ($132). A90

remote-control deck lid release ($27). C49 electric rear window defroster ($107). VJ9 California emissions ($46). K05 engine block heater ($16). W63 Rally gauges with clock in Formula (no cost); in base Firebird or Esprit; requires V-8 ($89). U17 Rally gauges with clock and tachometer, in Trans Am (no cost); in base Firebird or Esprit, requires V-8 ($156); in Formula ($67). A01 tinted glass ($75). CC1 hatch roof without Y84 Black Special Edition Trans Am package ($695). TT5 tungsten quartz halogen high-beam headlights ($27). D53 hood decal without Y84 Black Special Edition Trans Am package ($118). BS1 added acoustical insulation, except standard with Esprit and not available with three-speed manual transmission ($34). C95 dome reading lamp ($20). TR9 lamp group ($33). B37 front and rear color-keyed floor mats, not available with three-speed manual transmission, in Esprit (no cost); in other Firebirds ($34). D35 Sport OSRV mirrors with left-hand remote control in base Firebird ($47). D34 right-hand visor vanity mirror ($7). B84 color-keyed vinyl body side moldings ($44). B93 door edge guards ($13). B83 rocker panel molding on base Firebird without three-speed manual transmission only, standard on Esprit and not available with other Firebirds ($22). B80 roof drip moldings, standard with Esprit and Trans Am with Y84 Special Edition package ($28). B96 wheel opening moldings on base Firebird, standard with Esprit, not available with others ($25). B85 windowsill and rear hood edge moldings, standard with Esprit and Trans Am with Y84 Special Edition package ($25). J65 power front disc/rear disc brakes without WS6 Special performance package, which includes them ($158). AU3 power door locks ($93). A31 power windows ($140). V02 super-cooling radiator without air conditioning ($63); with air conditioning ($34); LU8 Turbo V-8 (no cost). U75 power antenna without optional radios; not available with UP6 radio ($65). U75 power antenna with optional radios; not available with UP6 radio ($47). U83 power AM/FM/CB tri-band antenna, without optional radio ($86); with optional radio except for UP6 ($68); with UP6 radio (no cost). U63 AM radio ($90). UM1 AM radio with integral 8-track stereo tape player ($231). U69 AM/FM radio ($142). UM7 AM/FM ETR radio with seek/scan, includes digital clock, four speaker sound system and extended range feature ($347). U58 AM/FM stereo radio ($178). UN3 AM/FM stereo radio with cassette stereo tape player including dual rear speakers with extended range feature ($267). UM6 ETR AM/FM stereo radio with cassette, includes digital readouts, clock and four speakers with dual rear extended-range speakers ($475). UM2 AM/FM stereo radio with integral 8-track stereo tape player ($252). UP6 AM/FM stereo with 40-channel CB, includes U83 power antenna ($486). UN9 radio accommodation package, standard with optional radios. UN9 radio accommodation package without U75/U83 power antenna or optional radios ($27). UN9 radio accommodation package with U75/U83 power antennas, but without optional radios ($9). U80 rear seat speaker, requires U63 or U69 radios ($19). UX6 dual front speakers, requires U63 or U69 radio ($19). UP8 dual front and rear speakers, with U63 or U69 radios only ($40). UQ1 dual rear extended-range speakers with U63 or U69 ($63). U01 dual rear extended range speakers with UM1, U58, UN3, UM2 or UP6 ($23). U01 dual rear extended-range speakers with UM7 ETR radio (no cost). UQ3 audio power booster, except with UM6/UM7 or UN3 radio ($10); with UM6, UM7 or UN3 radios (no charge). A51 bucket seats, with vinyl oxen trim in Firebird, Formula and Trans Am (no cost); with cloth Sparta trim in Firebird, Formula or Trans Am ($23). WS6 Special Performance package for Formula with L37, LG4 or LU8 engine on Formula ($546); on Trans Am without Y84 Special Edition package ($546); on Trans Am with Y84 Special Edition package ($350). D80 rear deck spoiler on base Firebird or Esprit without three-speed manual transmission ($60). NK3 For-

mula steering wheel on base Firebird ($74); on Esprit ($52). N30 luxury cushion steering wheel on base Firebird ($22). N33 tilt steering wheel ($81). D98 vinyl tape stripes, not available on Trans Am or Formula with W50 Formula appearance package ($58). B18 custom trim group for Formula/Trans Am with vinyl doeskin trim ($139); for Formula/Trans Am with velour Pimlico cloth trim with Durand bolsters ($184); for Esprit with vinyl doeskin trim (no cost); for Esprit with velour Pimlico cloth trim with Durand bolsters ($45). P01 deluxe wheel covers for base Firebird ($46). N95 wire wheel covers for base Firebird ($169); for Esprit ($123). N18 wheel cover locking package, with N95 wire wheels only ($34). N90 four cast aluminum wheels on base Firebird ($331); on Esprit ($285); on Formula or Trans Am without WS6 or Y84 ($196); on Formula or Trans Am with WS6 or Y84 (no cost). N98 Rally II wheels and four trim rings, on base Firebird with automatic transmission ($135); on Esprit ($89); on Formula or Trans Am (no cost). N67 body-color Rally II wheels and four trim rings, on base Firebird ($135); on Esprit ($89). CD4 controlled-cycle windshield wipers ($41). QJU 205/75R15 black sidewall steel-belted radial tires on base Firebird and Esprit (no cost). QJW 205/75R15 white sidewall steel-belted radial tires on base Firebird and Esprit without N65 ($63 extra). QMC 205/75R15 white-letter steel belted radial tires on base Firebird or Esprit without N65 ($70 extra). QGQ 225/70R15 steel-belted black sidewall radial tires, included in RTS Handling package on Formula and Trans Am (no cost). QGR 205/75Rl5 white letter steel-belted radials tires with Rally Tuned Suspension on Formula or Trans Am without WS6 ($72); with WS6 (no cost).

HISTORICAL FOOTNOTES

Total model-year production of Firebirds was 70,899. Sales stood at 61,460 for the model year and 52,188 for the calendar year. The Turbo Trans Am could do 0 to 60 mph in 8.7 seconds and cover the quarter mile in 16 seconds at 86 mph.

The 1982 Trans Am showed off the F-Car's dramatically different front end.

Now the Excitement Really Begins

"The excitement began 15 years ago when those electrifying 'Birds' came rolling like thunder to capture the hearts of enthusiasts everywhere and a legend was born," said a 1982 Pontiac advertisement. "Now comes the road machine that will fire-up a new generation."

From its saber-like nose to its rakish tail, the new Firebird was a brilliant orchestration of aerodynamic function. All Firebirds rode on a 101-inch wheelbase and had a 189.8-in. overall length and a height of only 49.8 inches. The F-Car's .34 drag co-efficient was the best of any production car that GM had ever tested. The front tapered to a low nose with split grilles housed inside twin air slots below electrically powered hidden headlights. The windshield had a 62-degree slant. Taillights were in a full-width back panel. Reclining front bucket seats were standard.

The revised F-Cars came in base, luxury S/E and Trans Am models. Each one had its own suspension and tires. The base engine was a fuel-injected 151-cid (2.5-liter) four hooked to four-speed manual gearbox. S/Es carried a standard 173-cid (2.8-liter) two-barrel V-6, also with four-speed. The Trans Am had the 5.0-liter four-barrel V-8 with a four-speed. Trans Am buyers could also step up to a dual throttle-body (crossfire) fuel injection V-8 with fresh-air hood induction.

Standard Firebird equipment included a front air dam, power brakes and steering, front stabilizer bar and black-finished instrument panel. S/Es added full-width black taillights, body-color body side moldings, lower accent paint (with striping) and turbo cast-aluminum wheels. Trans Ams added hood and sail panel bird decals, front fender air extractors, front/rear wheel opening flares and a spoiler.

Despite a late, midyear release, the all-new Firebirds proved very popular and assemblies picked back up again, rising above 100,000 for the abbreviated model year. Pontiac's total output of the three Firebird models was: 41,683 base Firebirds, 21,719 Firebird S/Es and 52,960 Trans Ams.

I.D. NUMBERS

The vehicle identification number (VIN) was stamped on a plate on the upper left-hand side of the instrument panel and visible through the windshield. The first symbol indicated country of origin: 1=United States, 2=Canada. The second symbol indicated the manufacturer: 2=General Motors. The third symbol indicated make: 2=Pontiac. The fourth symbol indicated the type of restraint system: A=non-passive restraints (manual seat belts); B=passive restraints (automatic seat belts); C=passive restraints (front airbags) series with A used in all Firebirds. The fifth symbol indicated car line or series: S=Base Firebird, W=Firebird Trans Am, X=Firebird Special Edition. The sixth and seventh symbols indicated the body style: 87=two-door special hatchback. The eighth symbol indicated engine: 2=2.5-liter (151-cid) TBI I-4, 1=2.8-liter (173-cid) four-barrel Chevrolet V-6, H=5.0-liter (305-cid) four-barrel Chevrolet V-8, 7=5.0-liter (305-cid) EFI Chevrolet V-8. The ninth symbol indicated model year: C=1982. The 10th symbol indicated the assembly plant: N=Norwood, Ohio, L=Van Nuys, California. The remaining symbols were sequential unit production number at factory, starting with 100001. The Body by Fisher plate on the engine side of the cowl contained the Fisher style number, which took the form 2FW87. The first symbol 2=Pontiac, the second symbol FW=Firebird Trans Am and the last two symbols 87=two-door, plain-back special coupe. This plate also indicated interior trim, seat type, body color and build date. Four-cylinder engine code on left front of engine below water pump. V-6 engine code on right side of block near water pump. V-8 engine code on pad on front of block below right cylinder head. Engine production codes for 1982 were: [2.5-liter I-4] 5A-5F-5H-X3A-X3C-X3F-X3H-X5A-X5F-X5H. [2.8-liter V-6] CKB-CJB-CKA-C7A-C7B-C7C-C7D-CBT-CBU-CBW-CBX-CBZ, [5.0-liter V-8 four-barrel] C2R-C2S-C2T-C2U-C2W-C2X-CFR-CFT-CFW-CFY-CFZ-CRA, [5.0-liter EFI V-8] CFJ-CFK-CFM-CFN.

COLORS

11=White, 16=Silver Metallic, 19=Black, 21=Dark Blue Metallic, 45=Light Jadestone Metallic, 49=Dark Jadestone Metallic, 55=Goldwing Metallic, 74=Autumn Maple, 75=Spectra Red, 78=Dark Claret Metallic and 84=Charcoal Metallic.

FIREBIRD - (I-4/V-6/V-8) - SERIES 2FS

The all-new third-generation Firebird arrived in January 1982. The only body style was a wedge-shaped hatchback coupe available in "first-level" Firebird, Firebird S/E and Trans Am models. It was shorter, narrower and lower than the previous Firebird and more than 500 lbs. lighter in weight. The front tapered to an ultra-low nose with split grilles inside twin air slots. The parking lights were in slots above the grilles and below were electrically operated hidden headlamps with rectangular halogen bulbs. The windshield had a rakish 62-degree slant and the hatch consisted almost entirely of a piece of "frameless," contoured glass. The rear seats folded to provide 30.9 cu. ft. of cargo area with two-passenger seating. Standard equipment for the first-level Firebird included a 2.5-liter four-cylinder engine with electronic fuel injection, a four-speed manual transmission, dual black-finished grilles, a body-color one-piece resilient Endura front panel and front bumper, concealed rectangular quartz halogen headlights, electrically operated hide-away headlight housings, an Endura rear bumper, power steering, power front disc/rear drum brakes, dual outside mirrors (left-hand manual and right-hand manual convex), hidden headlights, a formula steering wheel, 195/75R14 glass-belted black sidewall tires, a compact spare tire, hubcaps, a wraparound glass hatch with strut supports, a black-finished instrument panel, cargo area carpeting, a cigar lighter, a cloth headliner with foam backing, cut-pile carpeting, a day/night inside rearview mirror, a folding rear seat, a full-length front center console with

integral instrument panel, an inside hood release, a lockable storage compartment in the left-hand interior quarter panel, a multi-function control lever, reclining front bucket seats, side window defoggers, a Delco Freedom battery, fluidic windshield washers with dual nozzles, GM Computer Command Control, rear wheel drive, a front stabilizer bar and a torque arm/track bar rear suspension.

Model Number	Body/Style Number	Body Type & Seating	Factory Price	Shipping Weight	Production Total
FIREBIRD - SERIES 2FS - (I-4)					
2FS	87	2d hatchback-4P	$7,996	2,750 lbs.	Notes 1, 2
FIREBIRD - SERIES 2FS - (V-6)					
2FS	87	2d hatchback-4P	$8,121	2,843 lbs.	Notes 1, 2
FIREBIRD - SERIES 2FS - (V-8)					
2FS	87	2d hatchback-4P	$8,290	3,023 lbs.	Note 2

Note 1: Combined production of base Firebirds with the four-cylinder engine was 17,804 cars.
Note 2: Combined production of base Firebirds and S/E models with the six-cylinder engine was 34,444 cars.
Note 3: Total production of base Firebirds was 41,683, including cars with all engines.

FIREBIRD SPECIAL EDITION (S/E) (V-6/V-8) - SERIES 2FX

The new S/E was priced slightly lower than the Trans Am. It actually had more standard equipment upgrades than the Trans Am, but the S/E engine was a V-6 instead of the Trans Am's base V-8. When the V-8 was added, the price was higher than that for a base Trans Am. Standard equipment for the Firebird S/E included a 2.8-liter V-6 engine with two-barrel carburetor, a four-speed manual transmission, dual black-finished grilles, a body-color one-piece resilient Endura front panel and front bumper, concealed rectangular quartz halogen headlights, electrically operated hide-away headlight housings, an Endura rear bumper, lower-body accent paint with striping, power steering, power front disc/rear drum brakes, body-color outside mirrors (left-hand remote and right-hand manual convex), body-color side moldings, body-color door handle tape inserts, a lockable fuel filler door, a rear hatch wiper/washer, hidden headlights, a formula steering wheel, 205/70R14 steel-belted black sidewall tires, a compact spare tire, Turbo cast-aluminum wheels with body-color center caps, a wraparound glass hatch with strut supports, black full-width taillights, a black-finished instrument panel with full gauges (clock not included with tachometer), cargo area carpeting, a cigar lighter, a cloth headliner with foam backing, cut-pile carpeting, added acoustical insulation, custom pedal trim, custom color-keyed

Goldwing Metallic was one of 11 color choices for 1982.

The F-Cars for 1982 had front ends that featured dual black-finished grilles, a body-color one-piece resilient Endura front panel and front bumper, and concealed rectangular quartz halogen headlights.

seat and shoulder belts, a day/night inside rearview mirror, an electric-operated hatch release, a leather map pocket mounted on the instrument panel, a folding rear seat, a full-length front center console with integral instrument panel, an inside hood release, a lockable storage compartment in the left-hand interior quarter panel, a multi-function control lever, reclining front bucket seats with Viscount cloth trim, side window defoggers, a Delco Freedom battery, fluidic windshield washers with dual nozzles, GM Computer Command Control, rear wheel drive, front and rear stabilizer bars and a torque arm/track bar rear suspension.

Model Number	Body/Style Number	Body Type & Seating	Factory Price	Shipping Weight	Production Total
FIREBIRD S/E- SERIES 2FX - (V-6)					
2FX	87	2d Hatchback-4P	$9,624	2,805 lbs.	Notes 4,5
FIREBIRD S/E - SERIES 2FX - (FOUR-BARREL V-8)					
2FX	87	2d Hatchback-4P	$9,794	2,985 lbs.	Note 5

Note 4: Combined production of base Firebirds and S/E models with the V-6 was 34,444 cars.
Note 5: Total production of Firebird S/E models was 21,719, including cars with all engines.

FIREBIRD TRANS AM - (V-8) SERIES 2FW

Standard equipment for the first-level Trans Am included a 5.0-liter four-barrel V-8 engine with dual resonator exhaust and dual tailpipes, a four-speed manual transmission, dual black-finished grilles, a body-color one-piece resilient Endura front panel and front bumper, concealed rectangular quartz halogen headlights, electrically operated hide-away headlight housings, an Endura rear bumper, front fender air extractors, front and rear wheel opening flares, lower-body accent paint with striping, power steering, power front disc/rear drum brakes, dual black-finished outside mirrors (left-hand remote and right-hand manual convex), black-finished door handles and key lock cylinders, hidden headlights, a formula steering wheel, 205/70R14 steel-belted black sidewall tires, a compact spare tire, Turbo cast-aluminum wheels with black-finished center caps, a wraparound

This immaculate 1982 T/A came in Silver Metallic with black trim.

glass hatch with strut supports, black full-width taillights, a black-finished rear deck aero wing spoiler, a black-finished instrument panel with full gauges (clock not included with tachometer), cargo area carpeting, a cigar lighter, a cloth headliner with foam backing, cut-pile carpeting, a day/night inside rearview mirror, a folding rear seat, a full-length front center console with integral instrument panel, an inside hood release, a lockable storage compartment in the left-hand interior quarter panel, a multi-function control lever, reclining front bucket seats, side window defoggers, a Delco Freedom battery, fluidic windshield washers with dual nozzles, GM Computer Command Control, rear wheel drive, front and rear stabilizer bars and a torque arm/track bar rear suspension. The Crossfire fuel-injected (EFI) V-8 was an $899 option for 1982 Trans Am without the UPC Y84 Recaro Trans Am option package.

FIREBIRD RECARO TRANS AM - (V-8) SERIES 2FW/Y84

The UPC Y84 Recaro Trans Am package was only available on Black Trans Am with gold accents. While it was basically an interior trim option, the Recaro package included styling and suspension upgrades and was available with either engine. If you ordered the Recaro package with the four-barrel V-8, the package was $2,486 and the base four-speed manual transmission was required. If you ordered the Recaro option with the EFI V-8, the engine was considered part of the package, but the price was $2,968 and automatic transmission was required at $72 additional cost. The Recaro Trans Am option included Recaro front bucket seats, a rear luxury seat, Parella cloth seat trim, luxury door trim panels, map pockets, custom seat belts, 215/65R15 steel-belted black sidewall tires, a special handling package, a limited-slip differential, a sport hood, four-wheel disc brakes, removable hatch roof panels and gold-finished Turbo cast-aluminum wheels.

Model Number	Body/Style Number	Body Type & Seating	Factory Price	Shipping Weight	Production Total
TRANS AM - SERIES 2FW - (5.0-LITER FOUR-BARREL V-8)					
2FW	87	2d hatchback-4P	$9,658	3,419 lbs.	Note 6
TRANS AM - SERIES 2FW - (5.0-LITER EFI V-8 WITHOUT RECARO PACKAGE)					
2FW	87	2d hatchback-4P	$10,557	—	Note 6
TRANS AM - SERIES 2FW - (5.0-LITER FOUR-BAREL V-8 WITH RECARO PACKAGE)					
2FW	87	2d hatchback-4P	$12,144	—	Note 7
TRANS AM - SERIES 2FW - (5.0-LITER EFI V-8 WITH RECARO PACKAGE)					
2FW	87	2d hatchback-4P	$12,698	—	Note 7

Note 6: Total production of Trans Ams was 52,960.
Note 7: About 2,000 cars had the Recaro Trans Am package; they are included in the production total given in Note 6.

ENGINES

Pontiac I-4 [UPC LQ9]: Overhead valves. Cast-iron block. Displacement: 151 cid. (2.5 liter). Bore & stroke: 4.00 x 3.00 in. Compression ratio: 8.2:1. Brake horsepower: 90 at 4000 rpm. Torque: 134 ft. lbs. at 2400 rpm. Hydraulic valve lifters. Induction: Throttle-body fuel injected. VIN Code: 2.

Chevrolet V-6 [UPC LC1]: Overhead valves. Cast-iron block. Displacement: 173 cid. Bore & stroke: 3.50 x 3.00 in. Compression ratio: 8.5:1. Brake horsepower: 105 at 4800 rpm. Torque: 142 ft. lbs. at 2400 rpm. Hydraulic valve lifters. Carburetion: Two-barrel. VIN Code: S.

Chevrolet 305 V-8 [UPC LG4]: Overhead valves. Cast-iron block. Displacement: 305 cid. Bore & stroke: 3.74 x 3.48 in. Compression ratio: 8.6:1. Brake horsepower: 145 at 4000 rpm. Torque: 240 ft. lbs. at 2000 rpm. Hydraulic valve lifters. Carburetion: four-barrel. VIN Code: H.

Chevrolet 305 V-8 [UPC LU5]: Overhead valves. Cast-iron block. Displacement: 305 cid. Bore & stroke: 3.74 x 3.48 in. Compression ratio: 9.5:1. Brake horsepower: 165 at 4200 rpm. Torque: 240 ft. lbs. at 2400 rpm. Hydraulic valve lifters. Induction: Crossfire fuel injection (EFI). VIN Code: 7.

CHASSIS

Firebird: Wheelbase: 101 in. Overall length: 189.8 in. Overall width: 72 in. Overall height: 49.8 in. Front tread: 60.7 in. Rear tread: 60.6 in.

Firebird S/E: Wheelbase: 101 in. Overall length: 189.8 in. Overall width: 72 in. Overall height: 49.8 in. Front tread: 60.7 in. Rear tread: 60.6 in.

Trans Am: Wheelbase: 101 in. Overall length: 189.8 in. Overall width: 72 in. Overall height: 49.8 in. Front tread: 60.7 in. Rear tread: 60.6 in.

TECHNICAL

Base: Body and frame: Integral body and frame with separate bolted-on sub-frame for engine and front suspension. Front suspension: Modified MacPherson struts with coil springs between lower control arm and X-member and front stabilizer bar. Rear suspension: Torque arm/track bar with coil springs. Brakes: front disc/rear drum. Steering: Power assist coaxial re-circulating ball bearing. Fuel tank: 16 gal.

S/E: Body and frame: Integral body and frame with separate bolted-on sub-frame for engine and front suspension. Front suspension: Modified MacPherson struts with coil springs between lower control arm and X-member and front stabilizer bar. Rear suspension: Torque arm/track bar with coil springs and rear stabilizer bar. Brakes: front disc/rear drum. Steering: Power assist coaxial re-circulating ball bearing. Fuel tank: 16 gal.

Trans Am: Body and frame: Integral body and frame with separate bolted-on sub-frame for engine and front suspension. Front suspension: Modified MacPherson struts with coil springs between lower control arm and X-member and front stabilizer bar. Rear suspension: Torque arm/track bar with coil springs and rear stabilizer bar. Brakes: front disc/rear drum. Steering: Power assist coaxial re-circulating ball bearing. Fuel tank: 16 gal.

OPTIONS

LQ9 2.5-liter EFI I-4, in first-level Firebird (no cost); in Firebird S/E without WS6 ($125 credit). LC1 2.8-liter two-barrel V-6, in first-level Firebird ($125.08); in Firebird S/E (no cost); in Trans Am (not available). LG4 5.0-liter four-barrel V-8 with single exhaust in first-level Firebird with four-speed manual transmission ($295). LG4 5.0-liter four-barrel V-8 with single exhaust in Firebird S/E with MX1 automatic transmission without WS6 Special Performance package ($170). LG4 5.0-liter four-barrel V-8 with dual exhausts in Firebird S/E with MM4 four-speed manual transmission or WS6 Special Performance package ($195). LG4 5.0-liter four-barrel V-8 with dual exhausts in Trans Am (no cost). LU5 Dual EFI engine package for Trans Am only; includes 5.0-liter dual EFI Crossfire-Injection V-8, 215/65Rl5 black sidewall steel-belted radial tires, Special Handling package, limited-slip differential, sport hood, front and rear power disc brakes and dual exhaust system, without Y84 ($899); with Y84 (no cost). MM4 four-speed manual transmission in first-level Firebird 5.0-liter V-8 (no cost). MXI automatic transmission, in Firebird and Firebird S/E ($396); in Trans Am ($72). C60 custom air conditioning, requires A01 Soft-Ray tinted glass ($675). G80 limited-slip differential axle, without J65 four-wheel disc brakes ($76.45); with J65 four-wheel disc brakes (.45). UA1 heavy-duty battery ($25). AK1 custom color-keyed front and rear safety belts in Firebird and Trans Am with B20 Luxury Trim group (no cost); in Firebird and Trans Am without B20 Luxury Trim group ($26); in Firebird S/E (no cost). D42 Cargo security screen ($64). UE8 digital quartz clock, option required only with U63 Delco AM

The 1982 Trans Ams got new looks and a new standard 5.0-liter engine.

radio ($60). K35 cruise control with resume feature, teamed with MX1 automatic transmission ($155); teamed with MM4 four-speed manual transmission ($165). A90 remote control deck lid release in first-level Firebird and Trans Am ($32); in Firebird S/E (no cost). C49 electric rear window defogger ($125). VJ9 California emission requirements ($65). K05 engine block heater, available with LQ9 only ($18). B57 custom exterior group with left-hand remote mirror, roof drip molding and belt reveal molding without CC1 ($134). B57 custom exterior group with left-hand remote mirror with CC1 ($73). N09 locking fuel filler door on first-level Firebird and Trans Am ($11); on Firebird S/E (no cost). U21 Rally gauges including trip odometer and instrument panel tachometer in first-level Firebird ($149); in Trans Am and Firebird S/E (no cost). K81 63-amp heavy-duty alternator with LQ9 and LC1 and C49 (no cost); with LQ9 and LC1 without C49 ($51). K73 70-amp heavy-duty alternator on LG4 V-8 without air conditioning, with C49 (no cost); without C49 ($51). K99 85-amp heavy-duty alternator teamed with LG4 V-8 ($15). K99 85-amp heavy-duty alternator teamed with LG4 four-cylinder engine or LU5 V-8 engine without C49 electric rear window defogger ($15); with C49 electric rear window defogger (no cost). A01 Soft-Ray tinted glass in all windows, required with C60 air conditioning ($88). CC1 hatch roof, with removable glass panels and no roof drip moldings, with Y84 Recaro package (no cost); without Y84 Recaro package ($790). BS1 additional acoustical insulation in Firebird and Trans Am ($39); in Firebird S/E (no cost). C95 dome reading lamp ($22). TR9 lamp group ($45). B48 luggage compartment trim ($123). B34 carpeted front floor mats ($20). B35 carpeted rear floor mats ($15). D35 sport outside rearview mirrors, left-hand remote controlled and right-hand convex manual on first-level Firebird without B57 custom exterior group ($48); with B57 custom exterior group (no cost). D35 sport outside rearview mirrors, left-hand remote controlled and right-hand convex manual on Firebird S/E and Trans Am (no cost). DG7 sport outside rearview mirrors, left-hand power, right-hand convex power, on first-level Firebird without B57 custom exterior group ($137). DG7 sport outside rearview mirrors, left-hand power, right-hand convex power, on first-level Firebird with B57 custom exterior group ($89). DG7 sport outside rearview mirrors, left-hand power, right-hand

The F-Car had a black rear spoiler.

convex power, on Firebird S/E and Trans Am ($89). D34 right-hand visor-vanity mirror ($7). B84 black vinyl body side moldings on Firebird and Trans Am (no cost). B84 color-keyed vinyl body side moldings on Firebird S/E (no cost). B93 bright door edge guards on first-level Firebird ($15). B91 black door edge guards on first-level Firebird S/E and Trans Am ($55). B80 bright roof drip moldings and belt reveal moldings for cars without CC1 hatch roof option, on Firebird without B57 custom exterior group ($61); with B57 custom exterior group (no cost). BX5 black roof drip moldings on Firebird S/E and Trans without CC1 hatch roof option ($29). J65 front and rear power disc brakes, including limited-slip rear axle on first-level Firebird (not available); on Firebird S/E or Trans Am without WS6 Special Performance package ($255); with WS6 Special Performance package (no cost). AU3 power door locks ($106). AC3 six-way power driver's seat, not available with Y84 Recaro package ($197). A31 power windows ($175). V08 heavy-duty radiator ($40). U75 power antenna without optional radios ($85); with optional radios ($55). U63 Delco AM radio system ($102). U69 Delco AM/FM radio system ($232). U58 Delco AM/FM stereo radio system ($317). UN3 Delco AM/FM stereo cassette system ($411). UM6 Delco AM/FM ETR cassette system ($606). UM7 Delco AM/FM ETR stereo system ($438). UN9 radio accommodation package with optional radios (no cost). UN9 radio accommodation package without U75 power antenna and without optional radios ($39). UN9 radio accommodation package with U75 without optional radios ($9). UP8 dual front and rear radio speakers, with U63 or U69 monaural radios only; includes rear speakers with extended range ($79). Y99 Rally tuned suspension for first-level Firebird only and QYA or QYC radial tires required at extra cost ($408). Y84 Recaro Trans Am option in Trans Am with LU5 V-8, also requires MX1 automatic transmission ($2,968). Y84 Recaro Trans Am option in Trans Am with LG4 V-8, also requires MX4 four-speed manual transmission ($2,486). AR9 bucket seats in Firebird or Trans Am, with vinyl Derma trim (no cost); with Pompey cloth trim ($28). WS6 Special Performance package, includes 215/65R15 black side-wall steel-belted radial tires, Special Handling package, limited-slip differential and four-wheel disc brakes, on Trans Am with LU5 Crossfire-injected V-8 and Y84 Recaro package, including Sport hood and black wheel covers (no cost). WS6 Special Performance package includes 215/65R15 black sidewall steel-belted radial tires, Special Handling package, limited-slip differential and four-wheel disc brakes, on Trans Am without LU5 Crossfire-injected V-8 with Y84 Recaro package ($417). WS6 Special Performance package, includes 215/65R15 black sidewall steel-belted radial tires, Special Handling package, limited-slip differential and four-wheel disc brakes, on Firebird S/E with P20 bright aluminum wheel hubcaps ($387). WS7 Special Performance package, includes 215/65R15 black sidewall steel-belted radial tires, Special Handling package, and limited-slip differential on Trans Am with LU5 Crossfire-injected V-8 and Y84 Recaro package, including Sport hood and black wheel covers (no cost). WS7 Special Performance package, includes 215/65R15 black sidewall steel-belted radial tires, Special Handling package and limited-slip differential, on Trans Am without LU5 Crossfire-injected V-8 with Y84 Recaro package ($238). WS7 Special Performance package, includes 215/65R15 black sidewall steel-belted radial tires, Special Handling package and limited-slip differential, on Firebird S/E with P20 bright aluminum wheel hubcaps ($208). D80 rear deck spoiler on Firebird S/E ($69); on Trans Am (no cost). N33 tilt steering wheel ($95). B20 Luxury trim group, includes luxury front and rear seats, luxury interior door trim, custom seat belts and map pocket for first-level Firebird with doeskin vinyl or Parella cloth upholstery ($299). B20 Luxury trim group, includes luxury front and rear seats, luxury interior door trim, custom seat belts and map pocket for first-level Firebird with leather upholstery ($844). B20 Luxury trim group, includes luxury front and rear seats, luxury interior door trim, custom seat belts and map pocket for Trans Am without Y84 Recaro option and doeskin vinyl or Parella cloth trim ($299). B20 Luxury trim group, includes luxury front and rear seats, luxury interior door trim, custom seat belts and map pocket for Trans Am with Y84 Recaro

option and doeskin vinyl or Parella cloth trim (no cost). B20 Luxury trim group, includes luxury front and rear seats, luxury interior door trim, custom seat belts and map pocket for Trans Am with leather upholstery ($844). B20 Luxury trim group, includes luxury front and rear seats, luxury interior door trim, custom seat belts and map pocket for Firebird S/E with doeskin vinyl or Parella cloth trim (no cost). B20 Luxury trim group, includes luxury front and rear seats, luxury interior door trim, custom seat belts and map pocket for Firebird S/E with leather upholstery ($545). P06 wheel trim rings, for first-level Firebird only ($37). PE5 Rally V wheel covers, with base Firebird only ($144). N91 wire wheel covers with locking package, base Firebird only ($229). N90 silver or gold cast-aluminum wheels, except base Firebird ($375). N24 15 x 7 in. finned turbo-cast aluminum wheels with WS6 or WS7 Special Performance packages only (no cost). P20 bright aluminum wheel hubcaps, available with Firebird S/E and Trans Am only and includes WS6 or WS7 on Firebird S/E (no cost). PB4 wheel locking package, with base wheel on Firebird S/E or Trans Am or with N90 cast-aluminum wheels on first-level Firebird ($16). C25 rear window wiper/washer system on Firebird and Trans Am ($117). CD4 controlled-cycle windshield wiper system ($47). QYF195/75R14 black sidewall wall fiberglass-belted radial tires on first-level Firebird (no cost). QYG 195/75R14 whitewall fiberglass-belted radial tires on first-level Firebird ($62 extra). QXV 195/75R14 black sidewall steel-belted radial tires on first-level Firebird ($64.60 extra). QVJ 195/75R14 white sidewall steel-belted radial tires on first-level Firebird ($126.60 extra). QXQ 195/75R14 white-letter steel-belted radial tires on first-level Firebird ($148.60 extra). QYA 205/70Rl4 black sidewall steel-belted radial tires on Firebird with Y99 and without WS6 ($123.76 extra); on Firebird S/E and Trans Am with Y99 and without WS6 (no cost). QYC 205/70Rl4 white letter steel-belted radial tires on Firebird with Y99 and without WS6 ($211.76 extra); on Firebird S/E and Trans Am ($88 extra). QYZ 215/65Rl5 black sidewall steel-belted radial tires with WS6 only, on Firebird S/E and Trans Am (no cost). QYH 215/65Rl 5 white letter steel-belted radial tires with WS6 only on Firebird S/E or Trans Am ($92).

HISTORICAL FOOTNOTES

Model-year production of Firebirds increased from just 70,899 in 1981 to 116,364 in 1982. The Firebird's share of the overall U.S. market rose from 1.06 percent the previous year to 2.26 percent in 1982. Trans Am Specialties of Cherry Hill, N.J., produced a "Bandit" model based on the Firebird used in the Burt Reynolds's film *Smokey and the Bandit*.

The 1983 Trans Am came in Recaro and 25th Anniversary Limited Editions, but the base Trans Am wasn't bad, either.

Special Editions

The sleek, aerodynamic Firebird unveiled in 1982 featured upgraded power options for 1983. In addition to the base 2.5-liter fuel-injected four-cylinder engine, there was a 2.8-liter V-6 High Output engine and a 5.0-liter V-8 with a four-barrel carburetor. Then, on June 6, 1983, Pontiac announced the release of a 190-hp 5.0 H.O. V-8 for the Trans Am with high-performance hardware and cold-air-induction system. A limited Daytona edition Trans Am featured two-tone paint and pigskin Recaro bucket seats. Prices started at $10,810.

Base models featured a fuel-injected 2.5-liter four with four-speed manual shift. S/Es had new cloth seats and a split-folding back seat (also available with Custom trim). Lear Siegler articulated front bucket seats became optional. The Trans Am again had a standard 5.0-liter V-8, but with the five-speed and a 3.73:1 axle. Standard T/A equipment included power brakes and steering, reclining front bucket seats, a rear spoiler, wheel-opening flares and P195/75R14 glass-belted radial tires. The S/E added P205/70R14 SBR tires on turbo cast-aluminum wheels, a beefy suspension, a five-speed gearbox, sport mirrors, color-keyed body side moldings and lower accent paint with striping.

There were two special 1983 Firebirds. The 25th Anniversary Daytona 500 Limited Edition model commemorated Pontiac's 25th season as pace car for the Florida stock-car race. It had white upper and Midnight Sand Gray Metallic lower body finish. An aero package was included along with many options and special identification features. This model was priced around $18,000 and 2,500 production units were scheduled.

Another special model was the Special Edition Recaro Trans Am, which included a $3,200 package with black-and-gold finish, special gold trim, gold turbo-cast wheels, a gold sport hood appliqué, a hatch roof and Recaro seats. Mecum Racing, then located in Spokane, Washington, also released a Motor Sports Edition or MSE Trans Am with suspension upgrades, special interior features and a killer Motorola sound system.

PMD was actively involved in motorsports following race driver Elliott Forbes-Robinson's successful 1982 season driving the yellow-and-blue No. 1 "STP Sun of a Gun" Trans Am built by Huffaker Engineering. The author attended several exciting Trans Am Territories at Elkhart Lake, Wisconsin, in this period and watched the down-sized Firebirds compete.

The base four-cylinder Firebird now had an $8,399 base price and model year production of 32,020. The S/E was about $2,000 pricier and 10,934 were built. Trans Am prices started at $10,396 and 31,930 were built.

I.D. NUMBERS

The vehicle identification number (VIN) was stamped on a plate on the upper left-hand side of the instrument panel and visible through the windshield. The first symbol indicated country of origin: 1=United States. The second symbol indicated the manufacturer: 2=General Motors. The third symbol indicated make: 2=Pontiac. The fourth symbol indicated the type of restraint system: A=non-passive restraints (manual seat belts). The fifth symbol indicated car line or series: S=Base Firebird, W=Firebird Trans Am, X=Firebird S/E. The sixth and seventh symbols indicated the body style: 87=two-door special hatchback. The eighth symbol indicated engine: F or 2=2.5-liter (151-cid) TBI I-4, 1=2.8-liter (173-cid) Chevrolet TBI V-6, L=2.8-liter (173-cid) Chevrolet TBI V-6, H=5.0-liter (305-cid) four-barrel Chevrolet V-8, S=5.0-liter (305-cid) EFI Chevrolet V-8. The ninth symbol indicated model year: D=1983. The 10th symbol indicated the assembly plant: N=Norwood, Ohio, L=Van Nuys, California. The remaining symbols were sequential unit production number at factory, starting with 100001. The Body by Fisher plate on the engine side of the cowl contained the Fisher style number, which took the form 2FX87. The first symbol 2=Pontiac, the second and third symbols FX=Firebird S/E and the last two symbols 87=two-door hatchback special coupe. This plate also indicated interior trim, seat type, body color and build date. Four-cylinder engine code on left front of engine below water pump. V-6 engine code on right side of block near water pump. V-8 engine code on pad on front of block below right cylinder head. Engine production codes for 1983 were: [2.5-liter I-4] YZZ-YBS-YMM-YMT [2.8-liter V-6] D6A-D6B-D6C-D6D-DAA-DAB-DAC-DAD-DAF-DAJ-DAK, [5.0-liter V-8 four-barrel] D5B-D5C-D5F-D5H-DDB-DDC-DDD-DDF-DDH-DDJ-DDK-DDN, [5.0-liter EFI V-8] DDA-DUA.

COLORS

11=White, 15=Silver Sand Irid, 19=Black, 22=Light Royal Blue Irid, 27=Medium Dark Royal Blue, 55=Gold Metallic, 62=Light Briar Brown Irid, 67=Dark Briar Brown Irid, 75=Spectra Red and 82=Dark Sand Gray Metallic.

FIREBIRD - (I-4/V-6/V-8) - SERIES 2FS

For 1983, Firebirds had some new engines and transmissions, suspension refinements, slight interior revisions and minor equipment changes including 13 new and five revised options. A 25th anniversary Daytona 500 Limited Edition Trans Am and Special Edition Recaro Trans Am were new, along with a midyear H.O. V-8 engine. The first-level Firebird had no changes in exterior appearance, but included a new wide-ratio four-speed manual transmission with an integral rail shifter. Also new was a set of redesigned Rally wheel rims with exposed black lug nuts. Another upgrade was an improved dual-retractor seat belt system. A front stabilizer bar was no longer included at base price. Standard equipment for the first-level Firebird included a 2.5-liter four-cylinder engine with electronic fuel injection, a four-speed manual trans-

mission, dual black-finished grilles, a body-color one-piece resilient Endura front panel and front bumper, concealed rectangular quartz halogen headlights, electrically operated hide-away headlight housings, an Endura rear bumper, a front air dam, power steering, power front disc/rear drum brakes, dual outside mirrors (left-hand manual and right-hand manual convex), a formula steering wheel, 195/75R14 glass-belted black sidewall tires, a compact spare tire, 14 x 6-in. Rally wheels with black caps and exposed black lug nuts, a wraparound liftback glass with strut supports, a black-finished instrument panel, cargo area carpeting, a cigar lighter, a cloth headliner with foam backing, cut-pile carpeting, a day/night inside rearview mirror, a folding rear seat, a full-length front center console with integral instrument panel, an inside hood release, a lockable storage compartment in the left-hand interior quarter panel, a multi-function control lever, reclining front bucket seats, side window defoggers, a Delco-GM Freedom II battery, fluidic windshield washers with dual nozzles, GM Computer Command Control, MacPherson strut front suspension, rear wheel drive and a torque arm/track bar rear suspension.

Model Number	Body/Style Number	Body Type & Seating	Factory Price	Shipping Weight	Production Total
FIREBIRD - SERIES 2FS - (I-4)					
2FS	87	2d hatchback-4P	$8,399	2,866 lbs.	Notes 1, 2
FIREBIRD - SERIES 2FS - (V-6)					
2FS	87	2d hatchback-4P	$8,549	2,948 lbs.	Notes 1, 2
FIREBIRD - SERIES 2FS - (V-8/AUTOMATIC)					
2FS	87	2d hatchback-4P	$8,749	3,050 lbs.	Note 2
FIREBIRD - SERIES 2FS - (V-8/5-SPEED MANUAL)					
2FS	87	2d hatchback-4P	$8,774	3,050 lbs.	Note 2

Note 1: Combined production of base Firebirds with the four-cylinder engine was 7,640 cars.
Note 2: Combined production of base Firebirds and S/E models with six-cylinder engines was 27,337 cars.
Note 3: Total production of base Firebirds was 32,020, including cars with all engines.

FIREBIRD SPECIAL EDITION (S/E) (V-6/V-8) - SERIES 2FX

The 1983 Firebird S/E had a few minor equipment deletions, including the rear hatch washer/wiper and custom pedal trim, but a split-folding seatback was new. A new option was a handling suspension that included 205/70R14 tires, 14 x 7-in. Turbo cast-aluminum wheels and rear stabilizer bars. Standard equipment for the Firebird S/E included a 2.8-liter H.O. V-6 with electronic fuel injection, a five-speed manual transmission, dual black-finished grilles, a body-color one-piece resilient Endura front panel and front bumper, body-color body side moldings, body-color door handle tape inserts, a lockable fuel filler door, concealed rectangular quartz halogen headlights, electrically-operated hide-away headlight housings, an Endura rear bumper, a front air dam, power steering, power front disc/rear drum brakes, dual body-color outside mirrors (left-hand manual and right-hand manual convex), a formula steering wheel, 195/75R14 glass-belted black sidewall tires, a compact spare tire, Turbo cast-aluminum wheels with body-colored center caps, a wraparound liftback glass hatch with strut supports, a black-finished instrument panel, cargo area carpeting, a cigar lighter, cloth seat

The hatch roof was an $825 option.

trim, a cloth headliner with foam backing, cut-pile carpeting, a day/night inside rearview mirror, a full-length front center console with integral instrument panel, added acoustical insulation, custom color-keyed seat and shoulder belts, a folding split-back rear seat, an instrument panel-mounted leather map pocket, an inside hood release, a lockable storage compartment in the left-hand interior quarter panel, a multi-function control lever, reclining front bucket seats, side window defoggers, a Delco-GM Freedom II battery, fluidic windshield washers with dual nozzles, GM Computer Command Control, MacPherson strut front suspension, rear wheel drive and a torque arm/track bar rear suspension.

Model Number	Body/Style Number	Body Type & Seating	Factory Price	Shipping Weight	Production Total
FIREBIRD S/E- SERIES 2FX - (H.O. V-6)					
2FX	87	2d hatchback-4P	$10,322	2,965 lbs.	Notes 4, 5
FIREBIRD S/E - SERIES 2FX - (FOUR-BARREL V-8/AUTOMATIC)					
2FX	87	2d hatchback-4P	$10,377	3,145 lbs.	Note 5
FIREBIRD S/E - SERIES 2FX - (FOUR-BARREL V-8/5-SPEED MANUAL)					
2FX	87	2d hatchback-4P	$10,399	3,145 lbs.	Note 5

Note 4: Combined production of base Firebirds and S/E models with six-cylinder engines was 27,337 cars.
Note 3: Total production of Firebird S/E models was 10,934, including cars with all engines.

FIREBIRD TRANS AM - (V-8) SERIES 2FW

The Trans Am also saw minor changes. The equipment list now specified Firebird decals, but no longer specified black mirrors or a black airfoil. A new standard transmission was also specified. Standard equipment for the first-level Trans Am included a 5.0-liter four-barrel V-8 engine with dual resonator exhaust and dual tailpipes, a five-speed manual transmission, dual black-finished grilles, a body-color one-piece resilient Endura front panel and front bumper, Firebird decals on the hood and sail panels, concealed rectangular quartz halogen headlights, electrically operated hide-away headlight housings, an Endura rear bumper, front fender air extractors, front and

rear wheel opening flares, lower-body accent paint with striping, power steering, power front disc/rear drum brakes, dual outside sport mirrors (left-hand remote and right-hand manual convex), black-finished door handles and key lock cylinders, hidden headlights, a formula steering wheel, 205/70R14 steel-belted black sidewall tires, a compact spare tire, Turbo cast-aluminum wheels with black-finished center caps, a MacPherson front suspension, a wrap-around glass hatch with strut supports, black full-width taillights, a rear deck aero wing spoiler, a black-finished instrument panel with full gauges (clock not included with tachometer), cargo area carpeting, a cigar lighter, a cloth headliner with foam backing, cut-pile carpeting, a day/night inside rearview mirror, a folding rear seat, a full-length front center console with integral instrument panel, an inside hood release, a lockable storage compartment in the left-hand interior quarter panel, a multi-function control lever, reclining front bucket seats, side window defoggers, a Delco Freedom battery, fluidic windshield washers with dual nozzles, GM Computer Command Control, rear wheel drive, front and rear stabilizer bars and a torque arm/track bar rear suspension.

FIREBIRD SPECIAL EDITION RECARO TRANS AM - (V-8) - SERIES 2FW/Y84

The UPC Y84 package was now called the Special Edition Recaro Trans Am option. It was only available on Black Trans Ams and included gold lower body accents, gold letter Recaro tape door handle inserts, cloisonné gold-and-black Firebird emblems on the sail panels, a gold hood appliqué and gold Turbo finned cast-aluminum wheels. Also featured in the package were leather-trimmed Recaro front luxury seats with adjustable thigh and lumbar supports, rear luxury seats, luxury doors, a split-folding rear seat, 215/65R15 black sidewall steel-belted tires, the Special Handling package, a limited-slip differential, a space saver spare tire (in place of a compact spare tire), an ETR AM/FM stereo radio (with cassette, seek/scan function, graphic equalizer and clock), four-wheel disc brakes and removable hatch roof panels. The price was $3,160 with the four-barrel V-8 and five-speed manual transmission or $3,610 with the Crossfire-injected V-8 and automatic transmission.

FIREBIRD 25th ANNIVERSARY DAYTONA 500 LIMITED EDITION TRANS AM - (V-8) - SERIES 2FW

The Firebird 25th Anniversary Daytona 500 Limited Edition Trans Am was announced to the public on Nov. 1, 1982. The official press release said that production of 2,500 replicas was planned. This model-option was design specifically to mark Pontiac Motor Division's 25th season as pace car for the Daytona 500 stock car race. The car featured special mid-body two-tone paint with white upper finish and Midnight Sand Gray Metallic lower finish. It included a special aero package consisting of rocker panel extensions, an air dam, rocker fences, grille pads and special covers on its 15 x 7-in. Turbo-aero aluminum wheels. Also included was a sport hood appliqué, a locking fuel filler door, tinted glass all around, a power antenna and special Daytona 500 graphics. The interior sported Light Sand Gray Recaro front bucket seats with leather bolsters and headrests and Medium Sand Gray pigskin leather seat inserts. The sides and backs of the seats were upholstered in Pallex cloth and matching door panel inserts were Light Sand Gray with Pallex cloth inserts. On the standard equipment list were red instrument panel lighting, an AM/FM stereo cassette sound system with a graphic equalizer, air conditioning, cruise control, a remote deck lid release, an electric rear window defogger, added acoustical insulation, a lamp group and dome reading lamp, luggage compartment trim, special Daytona 500 floor mats, power mirrors, power windows, power door locks, a tilt steering wheel, controlled-cycle windshield wipers and a leather-wrapped steering wheel. In California, the 25th Anniversary Daytona 500 Limited Edition Trans Am came only with the 5.0-liter four-barrel V-8 attached to the automatic transmission. In other regions you could get it with the four-barrel V-8 and five-speed manual gearbox or with the Crossfire-injected V-8 and automatic transmission.

Model Number	Body/Style Number	Body Type & Seating	Factory Price	Shipping Weight	Production Total
TRANS AM - SERIES 2FW - (5.0-LITER FOUR-BARRELV-8)					
2FW	87	2d hatchback-4P	$10,396	3,419 lbs.	Note 6
TRANS AM - SERIES 2FW - (5.0-LITER CROSSFIRE V-8)					
2FW	87	2d hatchback-4P	$11,254	—	Note 6
SPECIAL EDITION RECARO TRANS AM - SERIES 2FW - (5.0-LITER FOUR-BARREL V-8/5-SPEED MANUAL)					
2FW	87	2d hatchback-4P	$13,556	—	Note 7
SPECIAL EDITION RECARO TRANS AM - SERIES 2FW - (5.0-LITER CROSSFIRE V-8/AUTOMATIC)					
2FW	87	2d hatchback-4P	$14,006	—	Note 7
25th ANN. DAYTONA 500 LIMITED EDITION TRANS AM - SERIES 2FW - (5.0-LITER 4-BARREL V-8/AUTOMATIC)					
2FW	87	2d hatchback-4P	$18,000	—	Note 8
25th ANN. DAYTONA 500 LIMITED EDITION TRANS AM - SERIES 2FW - (5.0-LITER 4-BARREL V-8/5-SPEED MANUAL)					
2FW	87	2d hatchback-4P	$18,000	—	Note 8
25th ANN. DAYTONA 500 LIMITED EDITION TRANS AM - SERIES 2FW - (5.0-LITER CROSSFIRE V-8/AUTOMATIC)					
2FW	87	2d hatchback-4P	$18,858	—	Note 8

Note 6: Total production of Trans Ams was 31,930.
Note 7: Recaro Trans Am production not available.
Note 8: About 2,500 cars had the Daytona Pace Car Trans Am package; they are included in the production in Note 6.
Note 9: Prices for the Daytona Pace Car models are estimates.

ENGINES

Pontiac I-4 [UPC LQ9]: Pontiac I-4. Overhead valves. Cast-iron block. Displacement: 151 cid. (2.5 liter). Bore & stroke: 4.00 x 3.00 in. Compression ratio: 8.2:1. Brake horsepower: 90-94 at 4000 rpm. Torque: 132-135 ft. lbs. at 2400 rpm. Hydraulic valve lifters. Induction: Throttle-body fuel injected. VIN Code: R or 2.

Chevrolet V-6 [UPC LC1]: Overhead valves. Cast-iron block. Displacement: 173 cid. Bore & stroke: 3.50 x 3.00 in. Compression ratio: 8.5:1. Brake horsepower: 107 at 4800 rpm. Torque: 145 ft. lbs. at 2100 rpm. Hydraulic valve lifters. Carburetion: Two-barrel Rochester E2SE. VIN Code: X or 1.

Chevrolet H.O. V-6 [UPC LL1]: Overhead valves. Cast-iron block. Displacement: 173 cid. Bore & stroke: 3.50 x 3.00 in. Compression ratio: 8.9:1. Brake

horsepower: 125 at 5400 rpm. Torque: 145 ft. lbs. at 2400 rpm. Hydraulic valve lifters. Carburetion: Two-barrel Rochester E2SE. VIN Code: Z.

Chevrolet 305 V-8 [UPC LG4]: Overhead valves. Cast-iron block. Displacement: 305 cid. Bore & stroke: 3.74 x 3.48 in. Compression ratio: 8.6:1. Brake horsepower: 150 at 4000 rpm. Torque: 240 ft. lb. at 2400 rpm. Hydraulic valve lifters. Carburetion: Four-barrel Rochester E4ME. (EFI). VIN Code: H.

Chevrolet 305 V-8 [UPC LU5]: Overhead valves. Cast-iron block. Displacement: 305 cid. Bore & stroke: 3.74 x 3.48 in. Compression ratio: 9.5:1. Brake horsepower: 175 at 4200 rpm. Torque: 250 ft. lbs. at 2800 rpm. Hydraulic valve lifters. Induction: Crossfire fuel injection (EFI). VIN Code: 7.

CHASSIS

Firebird: Wheelbase: 101 in. Overall length: 189.8 in. Overall width: 79 in. Overall height: 50.7 in. Front tread: 60.7 in. Rear tread: 61.6 in. Front headroom: 37 in. Front legroom: 43 in. Front shoulder room: 57.7 in. Front hip room: 56.3 in. Rear headroom: 35.6 in. Rear legroom: 28.6 in. Rear shoulder room: 56.1 in. Rear hip room: 42.8 in.

Firebird S/E: Wheelbase: 101 in. Overall length: 189.8 in. Overall width: 79 in. Overall height: 50.7 in. Front tread: 60.7 in. Rear tread: 61.6 in. Front headroom: 37 in. Front legroom: 43 in. Front shoulder room: 57.7 in. Front hip room: 56.3 in. Rear headroom: 35.6 in. Rear legroom: 28.6 in. Rear shoulder room: 56.1 in. Rear hip room: 42.8 in.

Trans Am: Wheelbase: 101 in. Overall length: 189.8 in. Overall width: 79 in. Overall height: 50.7 in. Front tread: 60.7 in. Rear tread: 61.6 in. Front headroom: 37 in. Front legroom: 43 in. Front shoulder room: 57.7 in. Front hip room: 56.3 in. Rear headroom: 35.6 in. Rear legroom: 28.6 in. Rear shoulder room: 56.1 in. Rear hip room: 42.8 in.

TECHNICAL

Base: Body and frame: Integral body and frame with separate bolted-on sub-frame for engine and front suspension. Front suspension: Modified MacPherson struts with coil springs between lower control arm and X-member. Rear suspension: Torque arm/track bar with coil springs. Brakes: Front disc/rear drum. Steering: Power assist coaxial re-circulating ball bearing. Fuel tank: 16 gal.

S/E: Body and frame: Integral body and frame with separate bolted-on sub-frame for engine and front suspension. Front suspension: Modified MacPherson struts with coil springs between lower control arm and X-member. Rear suspension: Torque arm/track bar with coil springs. Brakes: Front disc/rear drum. Steering: Power assist coaxial re-circulating ball bearing. Fuel tank: 16 gal.

Trans Am: Body and frame: Integral body and frame with separate bolted-on sub-frame for engine and front suspension. Front suspension: Modified MacPherson struts with coil springs between lower control arm and X-member. Rear suspension: Torque arm/track bar with coil springs. Brakes: Front disc/rear drum. Steering: Power assist coaxial re-cir-

The 1983 Pontiac Firebird Trans Am hatchback.

culating ball bearing. Fuel tank: 16 gal.

OPTIONS

LQ9 2.5-liter EFI I-4, in first-level Firebird (no cost); in Firebird S/E without WS6 ($300 credit). LC1 2.8-liter two-barrel V-6, in first-level Firebird ($150). LL1 2.8-liter H.O. V-6, requires MX0 four-speed automatic transmission teamed with VJ9 California emissions in Firebird S/E (no charge). LG4 5.0-liter four-barrel V-8 in first-level Firebird with MX0 four-speed automatic transmission and single exhaust ($350). LG4 5.0-liter four-barrel V-8 in first-level Firebird with MM5 five-speed manual transmission and single exhaust ($375). LG4 5.0-liter four-barrel V-8 with single exhaust in Firebird S/E with MX0 four-speed automatic transmission without WS6 Special Performance package ($50). LG4 5.0-liter four-barrel V-8 with dual exhausts in Firebird S/E with MM5 five-speed manual transmission or WS6 Special Performance package ($75). LG4 5.0-liter four-barrel V-8 with dual exhausts in Trans Am (no cost). LU5 5.0-liter V-8 Crossfire EFI engine package for Trans Am only, includes 5.0-liter dual EFI Crossfire-injection V-8, 215/65R15 black sidewall steel-belted radial tires, Special Handling package, limited-slip differential, front and rear power disc brakes and dual exhaust system, without Y84 ($858); with Y84 (no cost). MM4 four-speed manual transmission in first-level Firebird 5.0-liter V-8 (no cost). MM5 five-speed manual transmission teamed with LU5 V-8 in first-level Firebird ($125); in Trans Am and Firebird S/E (no charge). MX1 three-speed automatic transmission, in first-level Firebird teamed with LQ9 four-cylinder or LC1 V-6 engine ($425). MXI three-speed automatic transmission in Firebird S/E teamed with LL1 V-6 or LG4

V-8 engines ($1925). MX0 four-speed automatic transmission in first-level Firebird teamed with LG4 V-8 only ($525). MX0 four-speed automatic transmission in Firebird S/E teamed with LL1 V-6 or LG4 V-8 only ($295). MX0 four-speed automatic transmission in Trans Am ($295). C60 custom air conditioning, requires A01 Soft-Ray tinted glass ($725). G80 limited-slip differential axle, includes Space Saver spare tire in place of compact spare tire, without J65 four-wheel disc brakes ($95.43); with J65 four-wheel disc brakes (.43). UA1 heavy-duty battery ($25). AK1 custom color-keyed front and rear safety belts in Firebird and Trans Am with B20 Luxury Trim group (no cost). AK1 custom color-keyed front and rear safety belts in Firebird and Trans Am without B20 Luxury Trim group ($26). AK1 custom color-keyed front and rear safety belts in Firebird S/E (no cost). D42 Cargo area security screen ($64). UE8 digital quartz clock, option required only with U63 Delco AM radio ($60). K35 cruise control with resume feature ($170). A90 remote control deck lid release in first-level Firebird and Trans Am ($40); in Firebird S/E (no cost). C49 electric rear window defogger ($135). VJ9 California emission requirements ($75). K05 engine block heater ($18). B57 custom exterior group with dual sport mirrors (left-hand remote controlled), door handle ornamentation, roof drip molding and belt reveal molding without CC1 hatch roof ($112). B57 custom exterior group with dual sport mirrors (left-hand remote controlled) and door handle ornamentation with CC1 hatch roof ($51). D53 hood bird decal, Trans Am only, replaces standard smaller bird decal (no charge). DX1 hood appliqué for raised portion of Sport hood, without Y84 Special Edition Recaro Trans Am option ($38). DX1 hood appliqué for raised portion of Sport hood, with Y84 Special Edition Recaro Trans Am option (no charge). N09 locking fuel filler door on first-level Firebird and Trans Am ($11). N09 locking fuel filler door on Firebird S/E (no cost). U21 Rally gauges, including trip odometer and instrument panel tachometer, in first-level Firebird ($150). U21 Rally gauges, including trip odometer and instrument panel tachometer, in Trans Am and Firebird S/E (no cost). K81 66-amp heavy-duty alternator with LC1 or LL1 V-6 engines and C49 rear window defogger (no cost). K81 66-amp heavy-duty alternator with LC1 or LL1 V-6 engines without C49 rear window defogger ($51). K64 78-amp heavy-duty alternator with LG4 engine without air conditioning, with C49 electric rear window defogger (no cost). K64 78-amp heavy-duty alternator with LQ9 engine without air conditioning, with C49 electric rear window defogger ($25). K64 78-amp heavy-duty alternator with LQ9 engine without air conditioning, without C49 electric rear window defogger ($51). K99 85-amp heavy-duty alternator teamed with LU5 V-8, air conditioning and C49 rear window defogger (no cost). K99 85-amp heavy-duty alternator teamed with LG4 four-cylinder engine or LU5 V-8 engine in all applications except previous one ($25). A01 Soft-Ray tinted glass in all windows, required with C60 air conditioning ($105). Y99 Rally Tuned Suspension Handling package for first-level Firebird [requires QYA or QYC tires and includes special front stabilizer bar, special rear stabilizer bar, special steering gear and special suspension] without N90 cast-aluminum wheels or N91 wire wheels ($50). CC1 hatch roof, with removable glass panels and no roof drip moldings, with Y84 Recaro package (no cost). CC1 hatch roof, with removable glass panels and no roof drip moldings, without Y84 Recaro package ($825). BS1 additional acoustical insulation in Firebird and Trans Am ($40). BS1 additional acoustical insulation in Firebird S/E (no cost). C95 dome reading lamp ($23). TR9 lamp group consisting of instrument panel courtesy lamp, luggage compartment lamp, headlamp-on warning and chime tone generator ($34). B48 luggage compartment trim, consisting of lockable load floor, deluxe carpeting and sound barrier ($123). B34 carpeted front floor mats ($20). B35 carpeted rear floor mats ($15). D35 sport outside rearview mirrors, left-hand remote controlled and right-hand convex manual on first-level Firebird without B57 custom exterior group ($51). D35 sport outside rearview mirrors, left-hand remote controlled and right-hand convex manual on first-level Firebird with B57 custom exterior group (no cost). D35 electric sport outside rearview mirrors, left-hand remote controlled and right-hand convex manual on Firebird S/E and Trans Am (no cost). DG7 sport outside rearview mirrors, left-hand power, right-hand convex power, on first-level Firebird without B57 custom exterior group ($140). DG7 sport outside rearview mirrors, left-hand power, right-hand convex power, on first-level Firebird with B57 custom exterior group ($89). DG7 sport outside rearview mirrors, left-hand power, right-hand convex power, on Firebird S/E and Trans Am ($89). D34 right-hand visor-vanity mirror ($7). B84 black vinyl body side moldings on Firebird

and Trans Am ($55). B84 color-keyed vinyl body side moldings on Firebird S/E (no cost). B93 bright door edge guards on first-level Firebird ($15). B91 black door edge guards on first-level Firebird S/E and Trans Am ($15). B80 bright roof drip moldings and belt reveal moldings for cars without CC1 hatch roof option, on Firebird without B57 custom exterior group ($61). B80 bright roof drip moldings and belt reveal moldings for cars without CC1 hatch roof option, on Firebird with B57 custom exterior group (no cost). BX5 black roof drip moldings on Firebird S/E and Trans Am without CC1 hatch roof option ($29). J65 front and rear power disc brakes, including limited-slip rear axle on first-level Firebird (not available); on Firebird S/E or Trans Am without WS6 Special Performance package ($274); with WS6 Special Performance package (no cost). AU3 power door locks ($120). AC3 six-way power driver's seat, not available with Y84 Recaro package ($210). A31 power windows ($180). U63 AM radio system including Delco AM radio, dual front speakers and fixed mast antenna ($112). UL6 AM radio system with clock, including Delco AM radio, integral digital clock, dual front speakers and fixed mast antenna ($151). UU9 AM/FM ETR radio system, including Delco AM/FM ETR stereo radio, dual front and rear acoustically matched response speakers and fixed mast antenna ($248). UL1 AM/FM ETR stereo radio system with clock, including Delco AM/FM ETR stereo radio, dual front and rear acoustically matched response speakers, integral digital clock and fixed mast antenna ($287). UU7 AM/FM ETR stereo radio system with cassette and clock, including Delco AM/FM ETR stereo radio and cassette, dual front and rear acoustically matched response speakers, integral digital clock and fixed mast antenna ($387). UU6 AM/FM ETR cassette system with seek/scan feature, graphic equalizer and clock without Y84 Special Edition Recaro Trans Am package ($590). UU6 AM/FM ETR cassette system with seek/scan feature, graphic equalizer and clock with Y84 Special Edition Recaro Trans Am package (no cost). UN9 radio accommodation package with optional radios (no cost). UN9 radio accommodation package without U75 power antenna and without optional radios ($39). UN9 radio accommodation package with U75 without optional radios ($9). UP8 dual front and rear radio speakers with monaural radio only ($40). U75 power antenna without optional radios ($90). U75 power antenna teamed with optional radios ($60). Y84 Recaro Trans Am option in Trans Am with LU5 V-8, also requires MXO automatic transmission ($3,610). Y84 Recaro Trans Am option in Trans Am with LG4 V-8, also requires MM5 five-speed manual transmission ($3,160). WS6 Special Performance package, includes 215/65R15 black sidewall steel-belted radial tires, Special Handling package, limited-slip differential and four-wheel disc brakes, on Trans Am with LU5 Crossfire-injected V-8 or Y84 Recaro package, including Sport hood and black wheel covers (no cost). WS6 Special Performance package includes 215/65R15 black sidewall steel-belted radial tires, Special Handling package, limited-slip differential and four-wheel disc brakes, on

Trans Am without LU5 Crossfire-injected V-8 or Y84 Recaro package ($408). WS6 Special Performance package, includes 215/65R15 black sidewall steel-belted radial tires, Special Handling package, limited-slip differential and four-wheel disc brakes, on Firebird S/E ($408). AR9 bucket seats in Firebird or Trans Am, with oxen vinyl trim (no cost); with Pompey cloth trim ($30). D80 rear deck lid spoiler on first-level Firebird or Firebird S/E ($70). D80 rear deck lid spoiler on Trans Am (no cost). NP5 leather-wrapped formula steering wheel ($40). N33 tilt steering wheel ($105). D98 vinyl sport stripes on first-level Firebird only ($75). DE1 hinge-mounted louvered rear window sunshield, not available teamed with C25 rear window washer/wiper ($210). B20 Luxury trim group, includes luxury front and rear seats, luxury interior door trim, custom color-keyed seat belts, carpeted cowl kick panel, split-folding rear seat and map pocket for first-level Firebird with Pallex cloth upholstery ($349). B20 Luxury trim group, includes luxury front and rear seats, luxury interior door trim, custom color-keyed seat belts, carpeted cowl kick panel, split-folding rear seat and map pocket for Trans Am with Pallex cloth upholstery ($349). B20 Luxury trim group, includes luxury front and rear seats, luxury interior door trim, custom color-keyed seat belts, carpeted cowl kick panel, split-folding rear seat and map pocket for Firebird S/E with Pallex cloth upholstery (no cost). B20 Luxury trim group, includes luxury Lear Siegler adjustable front seat, luxury rear seat, luxury interior door trim, custom color-keyed seat belts, carpeted cowl kick panel, split-folding rear seat and map pocket for first-level Firebird with Pallex cloth upholstery ($749). B20 Luxury trim group, includes luxury Lear Siegler adjustable front seat, luxury rear seat, custom color-keyed seat belts, carpeted cowl kick panel, split-folding rear seat and map pocket for Trans Am with Pallex cloth upholstery ($749). B20 Luxury trim group, includes luxury Lear Siegler adjustable front seat, luxury rear seat, luxury interior door trim, custom color-keyed seat belts, carpeted cowl kick panel, split-folding rear seat and map pocket for Firebird S/E with Pallex cloth upholstery ($400). B20 Luxury trim group, includes luxury Lear Siegler adjustable front seat, luxury rear seat, luxury interior door trim, custom color-keyed seat belts, carpeted cowl kick panel, split-folding rear seat and map pocket for first-level Firebird with leather trim upholstery ($1,294). B20 Luxury trim group, includes luxury Lear Siegler adjustable front seat, luxury rear seat, custom color-keyed seat belts, carpeted cowl kick panel, split-folding rear seat and map pocket for Trans Am with leather trim upholstery ($1,294). B20 Luxury trim group, includes luxury Lear Siegler adjustable front seat, luxury rear seat, luxury interior door trim, custom color-keyed seat belts, carpeted cowl kick panel, split-folding rear seat and map pocket for Firebird S/E with leather trim upholstery ($945). P06 wheel trim rings, for first-level Firebird only ($38). PE5 Rally V wheel covers, with base Firebird only ($95). N91 wire wheel covers with locking package, base Firebird without Y99 only ($185). N90 silver cast-aluminum wheels for base Firebird with Y99 ($185). N24 finned turbo-cast aluminum wheels for first-level Firebird with Y99 ($325). N24 finned turbo-cast aluminum wheels for Trans Am or Firebird S/E, replacing standard Turbo cast-aluminum wheels (no cost). PB4 wheel locking package, with base wheel on Firebird S/E or Trans Am or with N24 or N90 cast-aluminum wheels on first-level Firebird ($16). C25 rear window wiper/washer system on Firebird and Trans Am ($120). CD4 controlled-cycle windshield wiper system ($49). QYF 195/75R14 black sidewall fiberglass-belted radial tires on first-level Firebird (no cost). QYG 195/75R14 whitewall fiberglass-belted radial tires on first-level Firebird ($62 extra). QXV 195/75R14 black sidewall steel-belted radial tires on first-level Firebird ($64.48 extra). QVJ 195/75R14 white sidewall steel-belted radial tires on first-level Firebird ($126.48 extra). QXQ 195/75R14 white letter steel-belted radial tires on first-level Firebird ($148.48 extra). QYA 205/70Rl4 black sidewall steel-belted radial tires on Firebird with Y99 and without WS6 ($122.68 extra); on Firebird S/E and Trans Am with Y99 and without WS6 (no cost). QYC 205/70Rl4 white letter steel-belted radial tires on Firebird with Y99 and without WS6 ($210.68 extra); on Firebird S/E and Trans Am ($88 extra). QYZ 215/65Rl5 black sidewall steel-belted radial tires with WS6 only, on Firebird S/E and Trans Am ($1.40 extra). QYH 215/65Rl 5 white letter steel-belted radial tires with WS6 only on Firebird S/E or Trans Am ($93.40).

HISTORICAL FOOTNOTES

Model-year production of Firebirds dropped back to 74,897 units in 1983. Of that total, 22 percent had four-wheel disc brakes, 80 percent had automatic transmission, 18.6 percent had a five-speed manual transmission, 80.2 percent had steel-belted radial tires, 56.4 percent had power windows, 36.1 percent had power door locks, 7.8 percent had a power seat, 0.3 percent had a stereo radio and cassette system, 25.3 percent had a limited-slip differential and 39.8 percent had removable roof hatches. The Firebird's share of the overall U.S. market was 1.32 percent in 1983. Mecum Racing of Arizona offered a Mecum Motor Sports Edition (MSE) Trans Am.

Firebirds and Trans Ams both came with optional two-tone paint schemes for 1984.

The Bird is the Word

A higher-output 5.0-liter engine replaced the Cross-Fire Injected engine as standard equipment in the 1984 Trans Am. Pontiac claimed 7.5-second 0 to 60-mph performance for the car with this power plant. A small hood bird emblem became standard on all Firebirds.

Other engines available in Firebirds included a 2.5-liter inline four-cylinder, a 2.8-liter V-6 and a more powerful 5.0-liter V-8. Prices started at $8,763.

Trans Am buyers could add an optional Aero package with new front and rear fascias, a larger air dam, door and rocker panel extensions and wide lower body graphics. Also available: a Recaro package with gold strobe graphics and gold deep-dish turbo wheels.

Model-year production was 62,621 Firebirds, 10,309 S/Es and 55,374 Trans Ams. This was an 86 percent increase and base models were selling best.

I.D. NUMBERS

The vehicle identification number (VIN) was stamped on a plate on the upper left-hand side of the instrument panel and visible through the windshield. The first symbol indicated country of origin: 1=United States. The second symbol indicated the manufacturer: 2=General Motors. The third symbol indicated make: 2=Pontiac. The fourth symbol indicated the type of restraint system: A=non-passive restraints (manual seat belts). The fifth symbol indicated car line or series: S=Base Firebird, W=Firebird Trans Am, X=Firebird S/E. The sixth and seventh symbols indicated the body style: 87=two-door plainback special. The eighth symbol indicated engine: 2=2.5-liter (151-cid) TBI I-4, 1=2.8-liter (173-cid) Chevrolet TBI V-6, L=2.8-liter (173-cid) Chevrolet TBI High-Output V-6, H=5.0-liter (305-cid) four-barrel Chevrolet V-8, G=5.0-liter (305-cid) H.O. Chevrolet V-8. The ninth symbol indicated model year: E=1984. The 10th symbol indicated the assembly plant: N=Norwood, Ohio, L=Van Nuys, California. The remaining symbols were

sequential unit production number at the factory, starting with 100001. The Body by Fisher plate on the engine side of the cowl contained the Fisher style number, which took the form 2FW87. The first symbol 2=Pontiac, the second and third symbols FW=Firebird Trans Am and the last two symbols 87=two-door plainback special. This plate also indicated interior trim, seat type, body color and build date. Engine production codes for 1984 were: [2.5-liter I-4] Y5F-Z3F-Z3H, [2.8-liter V-6] C3A-C3B-C3C-C3D-SAC-SAD-SAN-SAR, [5.0-liter V-8 four-barrel] C4A-C4B-C4C-C4D-C4W-SDA-SDH-SDN-SDR-SDS-SDJ-SDU, [5.0-liter EFI V-8] SUF-SUH-SUJ-SXA. Four-cylinder engine code on left front of engine below water pump.

COLORS

11=White (3967), 19=Black (848), 22=Light Royal Blue (8238), 27=Medium Dark Royal Blue (7686), 59=Cream Beige (8509), 62=Light Briar Brown Metallic (8240), 67=Dark Briar Brown Metallic (7688), 75=Spectra Red (7211), 65E/65W=Dark Goldwing Metallic (8652/8653), 82E/82W=Midnight Sand Gray Metallic (8322/7714), 15E/15W=Silver Sand Gray Metallic (8310/8311), 22E/22W=Light Royal Blue Metallic (8312/8313), 27E/27W=Medium Dark Royal Blue Metallic (8314/8315), 62E/62W=Light Briar Brown Metallic (8318/8319) and 67E/67W=Dark Briar Brown Metallic (8320/8321).

Note: the exterior color numbers in parenthesis are those used in a new body identification labeling system introduced in mid-1984.

FIREBIRD - (I-4/V-6/V-8) - SERIES 2FS

For 1984, there were no drastic styling changes for Firebirds. The base 2.5-liter four-cylinder engine had new swirl-port cylinder heads and higher compression. New features found on the first-level Firebird included a black-finished mast-type radio antenna, fourth-generation all-weather radial tires and a tinted rear hatch glass. Dual horns were another new standard equipment item, along with an upshift indicator light when manual transmission was ordered. New options included two-tone paint and a rear deck lid spoiler. Standard equipment for the first-level Firebird included a Pontiac-built 2.5-liter, overhead-valve, four-cylinder engine with electronic fuel injection, a four-speed manual transmission, a black-finished fixed-mast antenna, dual black-finished grilles, a body-color one-piece resilient Endura front panel and front bumper, concealed rectangular quartz halogen headlights, electrically operated hide-away headlight housings, bright door handles and lock cylinders, an Endura rear bumper, a front air dam, power steering, power front disc/rear drum brakes, dual outside mirrors (left-hand manual and right-hand manual convex), fourth-generation all-season 195/75R14 steel-belted black sidewall tires, a compact spare tire, 14 x 6-in. Rally wheels with black caps and lug nuts, a wraparound Soft-Ray tinted liftback glass with strut supports, a black-finished instrument panel, cargo area carpeting, a cigar lighter, a cloth headliner with foam backing, cut-pile carpeting, a day/night inside rearview mirror, dual horns, a folding rear seat, a full-length front center console with integral instrument panel, an inside hood release, a lockable storage compartment in the left-hand interior quarter panel, a multi-function control lever, reclining front bucket seats, side window defoggers, a formula steering wheel, a Delco-GM Freedom II battery, a hidden windshield washers system, GM Computer Command Control, MacPherson strut front suspension, rear wheel drive and a torque arm/track bar rear suspension.

Model Number	Body/Style Number	Body Type & Seating	Factory Price	Shipping Weight	Production Total
FIREBIRD - SERIES 2FS - (I-4)					
2FS	87	2d hatchback-4P	$8,753	2,866 lbs.	Notes 1, 2
FIREBIRD - SERIES 2FS - (V-6)					
2FS	87	2d hatchback-4P	$9,003	2,948 lbs.	Notes 1, 2
FIREBIRD - SERIES 2FS - (V-8/AUTOMATIC)					
2FS	87	2d hatchback-4P	$9,828	—	Note 2
FIREBIRD - SERIES 2FS - (V-8/5-SPEED MANUAL)					
2FS	87	2d hatchback-4P	$9,945	—	Note 2

Note 1: Combined production of base Firebirds with the four-cylinder engine was 7,570 cars.
Note 2: Combined production of base Firebirds and S/E models with six-cylinder engines was 47,986 cars.
Note 3: Total production of base Firebirds was 62,621, including cars with all engines.

FIREBIRD SPECIAL EDITION (S/E) (V-6/V-8) - SERIES 2FX

The 1984 Firebird S/E had a new steering wheel. It was a color-keyed version of the leather-wrapped Formula design. The headrests on the bucket seats were also redesigned and the base H.O. V-6 got 15 additional horsepower. Standard equipment for the Firebird S/E included the Chevrolet-built (this was actually specified on the sales sheet this year) 2.8-liter H.O. V-6 with electronic fuel injection hooked to the five-speed manual transmission. Also standard were the black-finished mast antenna, dual black-finished grilles, a body-color one-piece resilient Endura front panel and front bumper, black full-width taillights, front fender air extractors, a rear deck lid spoiler, body-color body side moldings, body-color door handle tape inserts, a lockable fuel filler door, concealed rectangular quartz halogen headlights, electrically-operated hide-away headlight housings, an Endura

rear bumper, a front air dam, power steering, power front disc/rear drum brakes, dual sport mirrors (left-hand manual and right-hand manual convex), a leather-wrapped Formula steering wheel and shift knob and parking brake handle, a Rally-tuned suspension with 205/70R14 steel-belted black sidewall tires and front and rear stabilizer bars, a compact spare tire, Turbo cast-aluminum wheels with body-colored center caps, rear wheel opening flares, an electric-operated wraparound liftback glass with strut supports, a black-finished instrument panel, cargo area carpeting, a cigar lighter, cloth seat trim, a cloth headliner with foam backing, cut-pile carpeting, a day/night inside rearview mirror, a folding rear seat, a full-length front center console with integral instrument panel, full gauges including a tachometer and trip odometer, added acoustical insulation, custom color-keyed seat and shoulder belts, a folding split-back rear seat, an instrument panel-mounted leather map pocket, an inside hood release, a lockable storage compartment in the left-hand interior quarter panel, a multi-function control lever, reclining front bucket seats, side window defoggers, a Delco-GM Freedom II battery, fluidic windshield washers with dual nozzles, GM Computer Command Control, MacPherson strut front suspension, rear wheel drive and a torque arm/track bar rear suspension.

Model Number	Body/Style Number	Body Type & Seating	Factory Price	Shipping Weight	Production Total
FIREBIRD S/E- SERIES 2FX - (H.O. V-6)					
2FX	87	2d hatchback-4P	$11,053	2,965 lbs.	Notes 4, 5
FIREBIRD S/E - SERIES 2FX - (FOUR-BARREL V-8/AUTOMATIC)					
2FX	87	2d hatchback-4P	$11,548	3,145 lbs.	Note 5
FIREBIRD S/E - SERIES 2FX - (FOUR-BARREL V-8/5-SPEED MANUAL)					
2FX	87	2d hatchback-4P	$11,770	—	Note 5

Note 4: Combined production of base Firebirds and S/E models with six-cylinder engines was 47,986 cars.
Note 5: Total production of Firebird S/E models was 10,309, including cars with all engines.

FIREBIRD TRANS AM - (V-8) SERIES 2FW

The 1984 Trans Am also saw minor changes, but there were several option packages that could perk the interest of collectors. One was a slick-looking new Aero package consisting of front and rear fascia extensions, rocker panel extensions and fade-away lower body graphics. There was also a 15th Anniversary Trans Am package. Standard equipment for the Trans Am included a Chevrolet-built 5.0-liter four-barrel V-8 engine with dual resonator exhaust and dual tailpipes, a five-speed manual transmission (with upshift indicator lamp), a black-finished mast antenna, dual black-finished grilles, a body-color one-piece resilient Endura front panel and front bumper, bird decals on hood and sail panels, concealed rectangular quartz halogen headlights, electrically operated hide-away headlight housings, an Endura rear bumper, a front air dam, front fender air extractors, rear wheel opening flares, lower-body accent paint with striping, power steering, power front disc/rear drum brakes, dual outside sport mirrors (left-hand remote and right-hand manual convex), black-finished door handles and key lock cylinders, hidden headlights, a formula steering wheel, 205/70R14 steel-belted black sidewall tires, a compact spare tire, Turbo cast-aluminum wheels with black-finished center caps, a MacPherson front suspension, a wraparound glass hatch with strut supports, black full-width taillights, a rear deck aero wing spoiler, a black-finished instrument panel with full gauges (with tachometer and trip odometer), cargo area carpeting, a cigar lighter, a cloth headliner with foam backing, cut-pile carpeting, a day/night inside rearview mirror, a folding rear seat, a full-length front center console with integral instrument panel, an inside hood release, a lockable storage compartment in the left-hand interior quarter panel, a multi-function control lever, reclining front bucket seats, side window defoggers, a Delco Freedom battery, a hidden windshield washer system, GM Computer Command Control, rear wheel drive, front and rear stabilizer bars and a torque arm/track bar rear suspension.

FIREBIRD SPECIAL EDITION RECARO TRANS AM - (V-8) - SERIES 2FW/Y84

The UPC Y84 package was again called the Special Edition Recaro Trans Am option. It now included the Aero package components with front and rear fascia extensions, rocker panel extensions and fade-away lower body graphics, plus a leather-wrapped formula steering wheel, a leather-wrapped shift knob, a leather-wrapped parking brake handle, a gold hood appliqué, gold 15 x 7-in. Turbo finned cast-aluminum wheels, leather-trimmed Recaro front luxury seats with adjustable thigh and lumbar supports, rear luxury seats, luxury doors, a split-folding rear seat and an instrument panel map pocket. If that sounds like considerably less standard equipment than last year, it was. As a result the price of the Y84 package was only $1,621, about half as much as the previous year.

FIREBIRD 15th ANNIVERSARY TRANS AM - (V-8) - SERIES 2FW

The Firebird 15th Anniversary Trans Am was announced to the public early in the 1984 model year. This special model-option was finished in white with medium blue trim. The package included white aero skirting, white grille slot covers, 16-in. white aluminum high-tech wheels and a white rear deck lid spoiler. The interior had white Recaro bucket seats with blue inserts lettered with the Trans Am name. The Formula steering wheel was wrapped in white leather with a blue shield-shaped badge reading "Trans Am 15" in the center of its hub. The same special badge appeared on the sail panels and the Trans Am name, lettered in blue, adorned the lower body sides. A hatch roof with dark-colored glass panels set the roof off against the white body and multiple blue pinstripes traced around the perimeter of the body. On the hood was a blue "venetian blind" decal with a white outlined hood bird and 5.0-liter H.O. lettering. The 15th Anniversary model featured a 190-hp 5.0-liter V-8 under its hood. The engine came linked to the five-speed manual transmission. The package sold for $3,499 over the price of a base Trans Am. Pontiac said that it planned to build 1,500 of the $17,500-plus cars.

Model Number	Body/Style Number	Body Type & Seating	Factory Price	Shipping Weight	Production Total
TRANS AM - SERIES 2FW - (5.0-LITER FOUR-BARREL V-8)					
2FW	87	2d hatchback-4P	$11,103	3,419 lbs.	Note 6
TRANS AM - SERIES 2FW - (5.0-LITER H.O. V-8)					
2FW	87	2d hatchback-4P	$11,946	—	Note 6
SPECIAL EDITION RECARO TRANS AM - SERIES 2FW - (5.0-LITER FOUR-BARREL V-8)					
2FW	87	2d hatchback-4P	$12,724	—	Note 7
15th ANNIVERSARY TRANS AM - SERIES 2FW - (5.0-LITER 4-BARREL H.O. V-8 w/ 5-SPEED MANUAL)					
2FW	87	2d hatchback-4P	$17,500	—	Note 8

Note 6: Total production of Trans Ams was 55,374.
Note 7: Recaro Trans Am production not available.
Note 8: About 1,500 cars had the 15th Anniversary Trans Am package; they are included in the production in Note 6.
Note 9: The price for the 15th Anniversary Trans Am model-option is an estimate.

ENGINES

Pontiac I-4 [UPC LQ9]: Overhead valves. Cast-iron block. Displacement: 151 cid. (2.5 liter). Bore & stroke: 4.00 x 3.00 in. Compression ratio: 9.0:1. Brake horsepower: 92 at 4000-4400 rpm. Torque: 132-134 ft. lbs. at 2800 rpm. Hydraulic valve lifters. Induction: Throttle-body fuel injected. VIN Code: 2.

Chevrolet V-6 [UPC LC1]: Overhead valves. Cast-iron block. Displacement: 173 cid. Bore & stroke: 3.50 x 3.00 in. Compression ratio: 8.5:1. Brake horsepower: 107 at 4800 rpm. Torque: 145 ft. lbs. at 2100 rpm. Hydraulic valve lifters. Carburetion: Two-barrel Rochester E2SE. VIN Code: 1.

Chevrolet H.O. V-6 [UPC LL1]: Overhead valves. Cast-iron block. Displacement: 173 cid. Bore & stroke: 3.50 x 3.00 in. Compression ratio: 8.9:1. Brake horsepower: 125 at 5400 rpm. Torque: 145 ft. lbs. at 2400 rpm. Hydraulic valve lifters. Carburetion: Two-barrel Rochester E2SE. VIN Code: L.

Chevrolet 305 V-8 [UPC LG4]: Chevrolet V-8. Overhead valves. Cast-iron block. Displacement: 305 cid. Bore & stroke: 3.74 x 3.48 in. Compression ratio: 8.6:1. Brake horsepower: 150 at 4000 rpm. Torque: 240 ft. lbs. at 2400 rpm. Hydraulic valve lifters. Carburetion: four-barrel Rochester E4ME. (EFI). VIN Code: H.

Chevrolet 305 V-8 [UPC L69]: Overhead valves. Cast-iron block. Displacement: 305 cid. Bore & stroke: 3.74 x 3.48 in. Compression ratio: 9.5:1. Brake horsepower: 190 at 4800 rpm. Torque: 240 ft. lbs. at 3200 rpm. Hydraulic valve lifters. Carburetion: Four-barrel. VIN Code: G.

CHASSIS

Firebird: Wheelbase: 101 in. Overall length: 189.9 in. Overall width: 72.4 in. Overall height: 49.7 in. Front tread: 60.7 in. Rear tread: 61.6 in. Front headroom: 37 in. Front legroom: 43 in. Front shoulder room: 57.7 in. Front hip room: 56.3 in. Rear headroom: 35.6 in. Rear legroom: 29.8 in. Rear shoulder room: 56.3 in. Rear hip room: 42.8 in.

Firebird S/E: Wheelbase: 101 in. Overall length: 189.9 in. Overall width: 72.4 in. Overall height: 49.7 in. Front tread: 60.7 in. Rear tread: 61.6 in. Front headroom: 37 in. Front legroom: 43 in. Front shoulder room: 57.7 in. Front hip room: 56.3 in. Rear headroom: 35.6 in. Rear legroom: 29.8 in. Rear shoulder room: 56.3 in. Rear hip room: 42.8 in.

Trans Am: Wheelbase: 101 in. Overall length:

189.9 in. Overall width: 72.4 in. Overall height: 49.7 in. Front tread: 60.7 in. Rear tread: 61.6 in. Front headroom: 37 in. Front legroom: 43 in. Front shoulder room: 57.7 in. Front hip room: 56.3 in. Rear headroom: 35.6 in. Rear legroom: 29.8 in. Rear shoulder room: 56.3 in. Rear hip room: 42.8 in.

TECHNICAL

Base: Body and frame: Integral body and frame with separate bolted-on sub-frame for engine and front suspension. Front suspension: Modified MacPherson struts with coil springs between lower control arm and X-member and front stabilizer bar. Rear suspension: Torque arm/track bar with coil springs. Brakes: front disc/rear drum. Steering: Power assist coaxial re-circulating ball bearing. Fuel tank: 16.1 gal.

S/E: Body and frame: Integral body and frame with separate bolted-on sub-frame for engine and front suspension. Rally tuned suspension. Front suspension: Modified MacPherson struts with coil springs between lower control arm and X-member and larger front stabilizer bar. Rear suspension: Torque arm/track bar with coil springs and added rear stabilizer bar. Brakes: front disc/rear drum. Steering: Power assist coaxial re-circulating ball bearing. Fuel tank: 16.1 gal.

Trans Am: Body and frame: Integral body and frame with separate bolted-on sub-frame for engine and front suspension. Rally tuned suspension. Front suspension: Modified MacPherson struts with coil springs between lower control arm and X-member and larger front stabilizer bar. Rear suspension: Torque arm/track bar with coil springs and larger rear stabilizer bar. Brakes: front disc/rear drum. Steering: Power assist coaxial re-circulating ball bearing. Fuel tank: 16.1 gal.

The 1984 Pontiac Firebird Trans Am received few changes, but there were several notable option packages that year.

OPTIONS

LQ9 2.5-liter EFI I-4, in first-level Firebird (no cost); in Firebird S/E without special performance packages ($350 credit). LC1 2.8-liter two-barrel V-6, in first-level Firebird without four-speed manual transmission ($250). LL1 2.8-liter H.O. V-6 in Firebird S/E, requires MX0 four-speed automatic transmission and teamed with VJ9 emissions requirements for California (no cost). LG4 5.0-liter four-barrel V-8 in first-level Firebird, requires special performance package when teamed with five-speed manual trans-

mission; also available with four-speed automatic transmission and single exhaust ($550). LG4 5.0-liter four-barrel V-8 in Firebird S/E, requires special performance package when teamed with five-speed manual transmission; also available with four-speed automatic transmission and single exhaust ($200). LG4 5.0-liter four-barrel V-8 in Trans Am, requires special performance package when teamed with five-speed manual transmission; also available with four-speed automatic transmission and single exhaust (no cost). L69 5.0-liter H.O. four-barrel V-8 for Trans Am only, requires WS6 or WY6 special performance package and mandatory with Y84 Special Edition Recaro Trans Am package ($530). MM4 four-speed manual transmission in first-level Firebird with 2.5-liter four-cylinder engine only and not available in Firebird S/E (no cost). MM5 five-speed manual transmission in first-level Firebird ($125); in Trans Am and Firebird S/E (no charge). MX0 four-speed automatic transmission in first-level Firebird ($525). MX0 four-speed automatic transmission in Firebird S/E and Trans Am ($295). C60 custom air conditioning, requires A01 Soft-Ray tinted glass ($730). G80 limited-slip differential axle, includes Space Saver spare tire in place of compact spare tire, without special performance packages ($95). G80 limited-slip differential axle, includes Space Saver spare tire in place of compact spare tire, with special performance packages (no cost). UA1 heavy-duty battery ($26). AK1 custom color-keyed front and rear safety belts in Firebird and Trans Am with B20 Luxury Trim group (no cost). AK1 custom color-keyed front and rear safety belts in Firebird and Trans Am without B20 Luxury Trim group ($26). AK1 custom color-keyed front and rear safety belts in Firebird S/E (no cost). D42 cargo area security screen ($69). V08 heavy-duty cooling system on cars without L69 H.O. V-8 and without air conditioning ($70). V08 heavy-duty cooling system on cars without L69 H.O. V-8 and with air conditioning ($40). K34 cruise control with resume and accelerate features ($175). A90 remote control deck lid release in first-level Firebird and Trans Am ($40); in Firebird S/E (no cost). C49 electric rear window defogger ($140). VJ9 California emission requirements ($99). K05 engine block heater ($18). W62 Trans Am Aero package, includes front and rear fascia extensions, rocker panel extensions and lower accent stripe without Y84 Special Edition Recaro Trans Am option ($199). W62 Trans Am Aero package, includes front and rear fascia extensions, rocker panel extensions and lower accent stripe with Y84 Special Edition Recaro Trans Am option (no cost). W51 first-level Firebird Black Appearance group, without B57 Custom Exterior group, includes black rear deck spoiler, black manual right-hand sport mirror, black remote controlled left-hand sport mirror, black door handle tape and key locks and black roof drip moldings on cars without hatch roof only ($152). W51 first-level Firebird Black Appearance group, without B57 Custom Exterior group, includes black rear deck spoiler, black manual right-hand sport mirror, black remote-controlled left-hand sport mirror, black door handle tape and black key lock cylinders on cars with hatch

The Pontiac Firebird S/E hatchback was again available with a V-6 or V-8 in 1984.

roof ($123). B57 first-level Firebird Custom Exterior group, includes manual right-hand sport mirror, remote controlled left-hand sport mirror, door handle ornamentation, roof drip molding and belt reveal molding without CC1 hatch roof ($112). B57 custom exterior group with dual sport mirrors (left-hand remote controlled) and door handle ornamentation with CC1 hatch roof ($51). DX1 hood appliqué for raised portion of Sport hood, without Y84 Special Edition Recaro Trans Am option ($38). DX1 hood appliqué for raised portion of Sport hood, with Y84 Special Edition Recaro Trans Am option (no charge). N09 locking fuel filler door on first-level Firebird and Trans Am ($11). N09 locking fuel filler door on Firebird S/E (no cost). U21 Rally gauges including trip odometer and instrument panel tachometer in first-level Firebird ($150). U21 Rally gauges including trip odometer and instrument panel tachometer in Trans Am and Firebird S/E (no cost). K81 66-amp heavy-duty alternator with LC1 or LL1 V-6 engines and C49 rear window defogger (no cost). K81 66-amp heavy-duty alternator with LC1 or LL1 V-6 engines without C49 rear window defogger ($51). K64 78-amp heavy-duty alternator with LQ9 or LG4 engines without air conditioning, with C49 electric rear window defogger (no cost). K64 78-amp heavy-duty alternator with LQ9 engine without air conditioning, with C49 electric rear window defogger ($25). K64 78-amp heavy-duty alternator with LQ9 engine without air conditioning, without C49 electric rear window defogger ($51). K99 85-amp heavy-duty alternator teamed with LG4 V-8, air conditioning and C49 rear window defogger (no cost). K99 85-amp heavy-duty alternator teamed with L69 V-8, air conditioning and C49 rear window defogger (no cost). K99 85-amp heavy-duty alternator teamed with LQ9 four-cylinder engine or LG4 V-8 engine in all applications except previous one ($25). A01 Soft-Ray tinted glass in all windows, required with C60 air conditioning ($110). CC1 hatch roof, with removable glass panels and no roof drip moldings ($850). BS1 additional acoustical insulation in Firebird and Trans Am ($40). BS1 additional acoustical insulation in Firebird S/E (no cost). C95 dome reading lamp ($23). TR9 lamp group consisting of instrument panel courtesy lamp, luggage compart-

ment lamp, headlamp-on warning lamp, console lamp and chime tone generator ($34). B48 luggage compartment trim, consisting of lockable load floor, deluxe carpeting and sound barrier ($123). B34 carpeted front floor mats ($20). B35 carpeted rear floor mats ($15). D35 sport outside rearview mirrors, left-hand remote controlled and right-hand convex manual on first-level Firebird without B57 custom exterior group ($53). D35 sport outside rearview mirrors, left-hand remote controlled and right-hand convex manual on first-level Firebird with B57 custom exterior group (no cost). D35 electric sport outside rearview mirrors, left-hand remote controlled and right-hand convex manual on Firebird S/E and Trans Am (no cost). DG7 sport outside rearview mirrors, left-hand power, right-hand convex power, on first-level Firebird without B57 custom exterior group ($140). DG7 sport outside rearview mirrors, left-hand power, right-hand convex power, on first-level Firebird with B57 or W51 custom exterior group ($91). DG7 sport outside rearview mirrors, left-hand power, right-hand convex power, on Firebird S/E and Trans Am ($91). D34 right-hand visor-vanity mirror ($7). B84 black vinyl body side moldings on Firebird without W51 ($15). B84 color-keyed vinyl body side moldings on Firebird S/E (no cost). B93 bright door edge guards on first-level Firebird without W51($15). B91 black door edge guards on first-level Firebird with W51 ($15). B91 black door edge guards on first-level Firebird S/E and Trans Am ($15). B80 bright roof drip moldings and belt reveal moldings for cars without CC1 hatch roof option, on Firebird without B57 or W51 custom exterior group ($61). B80 bright roof drip moldings and belt reveal moldings for cars without CC1 hatch roof option, on Firebird with B57 custom exterior group (no cost). BX5 black roof drip moldings on Firebird S/E and Trans Am ($29). D84 two-tone paint on base Firebird ($205). J65 front and rear power disc brakes for S/E or Trans Am without LC1 V-6 with five-speed manual transmission, without WS6 or WY6 Special Performance package ($179). J65 front and rear power disc brakes for S/E or Trans Am without LC1 V-6 with five-speed manual transmission, with WS6 or WY6 Special Performance package (no cost). AU3 power door locks ($125). AC3 six-way power driver's seat ($215). A31 power windows without B20 Luxury Trim group ($185). A31 power windows with B20 Luxury Trim group, includes door map pockets ($215). A31 power windows with Firebird S/E, includes door map pockets ($215). U63 AM radio system, including Delco AM radio, dual front speakers and fixed mast antenna ($112). UL6 AM radio system with clock, including Delco AM radio, integral digital clock, dual front speakers and fixed mast antenna ($151). UU9 AM/FM ETR radio system, including Delco AM/FM ETR stereo radio, dual front and rear acoustically matched response speakers and fixed mast antenna ($248). UL1 AM/FM ETR stereo radio system with clock, including Delco AM/FM ETR stereo radio, dual front and rear acoustically matched response speakers, integral digital clock and fixed mast antenna ($287). UU7 AM/FM ETR stereo radio system with cassette and clock, including Delco AM/FM ETR stereo radio and cassette, dual front and rear acoustically matched response speakers, integral digital clock and fixed mast antenna ($387). UU6 AM/FM ETR cassette system with seek/scan feature, graphic equalizer and clock without Y84 Special Edition Recaro Trans Am package ($590). UU6 AM/FM ETR cassette system with seek/scan feature, graphic equalizer and clock with Y84 Special Edition Recaro Trans Am package (no cost). UP8 dual front and rear radio speakers with monaural radio only ($40). UQ7 subwoofer speaker system for cars with UL1, UU6, UU7 and UU9 radios only, includes dual front and rear coaxial speakers and dual rear low-frequency subwoofer speakers plus subwoofer amplifier ($60). U75 power antenna ($60). AR9 bucket seats with Sierra vinyl trim in first-level Firebird and Trans Am (no cost). AR9 bucket seats with Pompey cloth trim in Firebird or Trans Am ($30). Y84 Recaro Trans Am option in Trans Am, includes Aero package, leather-wrapped Formula steering wheel, leather-wrapped shift knob, leather-wrapped parking brake handle, Recaro leather trim luxury front seats, rear luxury seats, luxury door panels, a split-folding rear seat, an instrument panel map pocket, color-keyed seat belts, 15 x 7-in. gold High-Tech Turbo wheels and a gold hood appliqué ($1,621). WS6 Special Performance package includes 215/65R15 black sidewall steel-belted radial tires and Special Handling package teamed with limited-slip differential with four-wheel disc brakes on Firebird S/E and Trans Am ($408). WS7 Special Performance package includes 215/65R15 black sidewall steel-belted radial tires and Special Handling package teamed with limited-slip differential without four-wheel disc brakes on first-level Firebird ($612). WS7 Special Performance package includes 215/65R15 black sidewall steel-belted radial tires and Special Handling package teamed with limited-slip differential without four-wheel disc brakes on Firebird S/E and Trans Am ($229). WY6 Special Performance package includes 215/65R15 black sidewall steel-belted radial tires and Special Handling package without limited-slip differential teamed with four-wheel disc brakes on Firebird S/E or Trans Am only ($313). WY5 Special Performance package includes 215/65R15 black sidewall steel-belted radial tires and

Special Handling package, without limited-slip differential or four-wheel disc brakes on first-level Firebird ($517). WY5 Special Performance package includes 215/65R15 black sidewall steel-belted radial tires and Special Handling package, without limited-slip differential or four-wheel disc brakes on Firebird S/E or Trans Am ($134). NP5 leather appointment group including leather-wrapped shift knob and parking brake handle on first-level Firebird, black only ($75). NP5 color-keyed leather appointment group including leather-wrapped shift knob and parking brake handle on Firebird S/E and Y84 Special Edition Recaro Trans Am (no charge). N33 tilt steering wheel ($110). D98 vinyl Sport stripes, available only on first-level Firebird without two-tone paint ($75). DE1 hinge-mounted louvered rear window sunshield, not available teamed with C25 rear window washer/wiper ($210). Y99 Rally Tuned Suspension group, includes special front stabilizer bar, special rear stabilizer bar, special steering gear and special suspension, for first-level Firebird with QYA or QYC steel-belted radial tires and without N91 wire wheel covers ($50). Y99 Rally Tuned Suspension group, includes special front stabilizer bar, special rear stabilizer bar, special steering gear and special suspension, for first Firebird S/E and Trans Am with QYA or QYC steel-belted radial tires and without N91 wire wheel covers (no cost). B20 Luxury trim group, includes luxury front and rear seats, luxury interior door trim, custom color-keyed seat belts, carpeted cowl kick panel, split-folding rear seat and map pocket for first-level Firebird with Pallex cloth upholstery ($349). B20 Luxury trim group, includes luxury front and rear seats, luxury interior door trim, custom color-keyed seat belts, carpeted cowl kick panel, split-folding rear seat, map pocket and left-hand knee pad for Trans Am with Pallex cloth upholstery ($359). B20 Luxury trim group, includes luxury front and rear seats, luxury interior door trim, custom color-keyed seat belts, carpeted cowl kick panel, split-folding rear seat and map pocket for Firebird S/E with Pallex cloth upholstery (no cost). B20 Luxury trim group, includes luxury Lear Siegler adjustable front seat, luxury rear seat, luxury interior door trim, custom color-keyed seat belts, carpeted cowl kick panel, split-folding rear seat and map pocket for first-level Firebird with Pallex cloth upholstery ($749). B20 Luxury trim group, includes luxury Lear Siegler adjustable front seat, luxury rear seat, custom color-keyed seat belts, carpeted cowl kick panel, split-folding rear seat, map pocket and left-hand knee pad for Trans Am with Pallex cloth upholstery ($749). B20 Luxury trim group, includes luxury Lear Siegler adjustable front seat, luxury rear seat, luxury interior door trim, custom color-keyed seat belts, carpeted cowl kick panel, split-folding rear seat and map pocket for Firebird S/E with Pallex cloth upholstery ($400). B20 Luxury trim group, includes luxury Lear Siegler adjustable front seat, luxury rear seat, luxury interior door trim, custom color-keyed seat belts, carpeted cowl kick panel, split-folding rear seat and map pocket for first-level Firebird with leather trim upholstery ($1,294). B20 Luxury trim group, includes luxury Lear Siegler adjustable front seat, luxury rear seat, custom color-keyed seat belts, carpeted cowl kick panel, split-folding rear seat, map pocket and left-hand knee pad for Trans Am with leather trim upholstery ($1,294). B20 Luxury trim group, includes luxury Lear Siegler adjustable front seat, luxury rear seat, luxury interior door trim, custom color-keyed seat belts, carpeted cowl kick panel, split-folding rear seat and map pocket for Firebird S/E with leather trim upholstery ($945). P06 wheel trim rings, for first-level Firebird only ($38). P02 five-port wheel covers for first-level Firebird ($38). N91 wire wheel covers with locking package, base Firebird without Y99 only ($185). N89 Turbo Aero cast-aluminum wheels on Firebird S/E or Trans Am ($185). N24 finned turbo-cast aluminum wheels for first-level Firebird without special performance packages ($325). N24 finned turbo cast-aluminum wheels for Trans Am or Firebird S/E and base Firebird with special performance package (no cost). PB4 wheel locking package with N24, N78 or N89 cast-aluminum wheels ($16). C25 rear window wiper/washer system on Firebird and Trans Am without sun shield ($120). CD4 controlled-cycle windshield wiper system ($50). QMW 195/75R14 black sidewall steel-belted radial tires, on first-level Firebird (no cost). QMX 195/75R14 white sidewall steel-belted radial tires for first-level Firebird ($62 extra). QYA 205/70Rl4 black sidewall steel-belted radial tires on first-level Firebird teamed with Y99 and without special performance packages ($58 extra). QYA 205/70Rl4 black sidewall steel-belted radial tires on Firebird S/E or Trans Am without special performance packages (no cost). QYC 205/70Rl4 white letter steel-belted radial tires on first-level Firebird with Y99 and without special performance package ($146 extra). QYC 205/70Rl4 white letter steel-belted radial tires on Firebird S/E or Trans Am without special performance package ($88 extra). QYZ 215/65Rl5 black sidewall steel-belted radial tires with special performance packages only (no cost). QYH 215/65Rl5 white letter steel-belted radial tires with special performance packages only and not with L69 H.O. V-8 engine ($92). Excitement Plus option package WS1 for first-level Firebird, includes U21 Rally gauges with tachometer, W51 exterior appearance package, P02 custom wheel covers, N33 tilt steering wheel and A01 tinted glass for discount price of $410. Excitement Plus option package WS3 for first-level Firebird, includes D35 sport mirrors, UL1 ETR AM/FM stereo with clock, P02 custom wheel covers, U21 Rally gauges with tachometer and N33 tilt steering wheel for discount price of $463. Excitement Plus option package WS5 for first-level Firebird, includes D84 two-tone paint, D35 sport mirrors, UL1 ETR AM/FM stereo with clock, P02 custom wheel covers and B20 trim group with luxury bucket seats for discount price of $732. Excitement Plus option package

WS1 for Trans Am includes N33 tilt steering wheel, UL1 ETR AM/FM stereo with clock, DX1 hood appliqué and B20 trim group with luxury bucket seats for discount price of $619. Excitement Plus option package WS3 for Trans Am includes N33 tilt steering wheel, AU3 power door locks, A31 power windows, D42 cargo security screen and CC1 hatch roof for discount price of $1,114. Excitement Plus option package WS5 for Trans Am, includes W62 Aero package, L69 H.O. V-8 engine with WY6 special performance package and DX1 hood appliqué for discount price of $880. Excitement Plus option package WS1 for Firebird S/E includes N33 tilt steering wheel, AU3 power door locks, A31 power windows, UU7 ETR AM/FM stereo with cassette and D80 rear deck spoiler for discount price of $677. Excitement Plus option package WS3 for Firebird S/E includes N33 tilt steering wheel, AU3 power door locks, A31 power windows, CC1 hatch roof and D80 rear deck spoiler for discount price of $1,090. Excitement Plus option package WS5 for Firebird S/E includes N33 tilt steering wheel, UU7 ETR AM/FM stereo with cassette, AU3 power door locks, A31 power windows and B20 Custom Lear Siegler bucket seats for discount price of $982.

HISTORICAL FOOTNOTES

J. Michael Losh was the general manager of Pontiac Motor Division in 1984. The division celebrated the 75th anniversary of the founding of Oakland Motor Car Co., the firm that brought out the first Pontiac in 1926. During the year General Motors reorganized its domestic car divisions into two car groups called BOC (Buick, Oldsmobile and Cadillac) and CPC (Chevrolet, Pontiac and GM of Canada). Many Pontiac engineers were merged into a consolidated CPC engineering unit and many were relocated. Pontiac Engineering became smaller and controlled the integration of the total car. Model-year production of Firebirds climbed to 128,304 units in 1984. Of that total, 18.8 percent had a five-speed manual transmission, 1.5 percent had a four-speed manual transmission, 26.8 percent had four-wheel disc brakes, 58.2 percent had styled aluminum wheel, 88.4 percent had air conditioning, 100 percent had steel-belted radial tires, 57.1 percent had power windows, 38.8 percent had power door locks, 10.2 percent had power seats, 36 percent had an AM/FM stereo, 39.7 percent had a stereo cassette player, 15.2 percent had a graphic equalizer, 80.5 percent had a tilt steering wheel, 48.1 percent had cruise control, 5.1 percent had a rear window wiper and 41.2 percent had hatch roof panels. The Firebird's share of the overall U.S. market was 1.57 percent in 1984. Mecum Racing of Arizona again offered a Mecum Motor Sports Edition (MSE) Trans Am.

The 1985 Firebirds, including the SE, received some new interior features and a standard Rally Tuned Suspension.

Power-Packed

The base Firebird and the Firebird LE model received new front and rear fascias for 1985, while the Trans Am's taillights, hood and striping graphics were revised. The high-performance model sported a new 5.0-liter V-8 with multiport fuel injection. An aero-wing rear deck lid spoiler was also available at extra cost. The Firebird's base four-cylinder engine was refined by adding roller lifters, a low-inertia clutch disc and improved engine control software. Prices started at $9,177.

A new exterior appearance package was available for base models. It included black door handles, sport mirrors, a spoiler and "bird" roof decals. Also available at extra cost were a two-tone paint treatment in 13 color combinations.

A refined Firebird S/E added details and features to improve its competitive position against the sophisticated and sporty imported cars. It had a new louvered hood, new taillights (shared with Trans Ams) and the same rear-end revisions as the base model. The Firebird's new optional overhead console was standard in the S/E, which also got the new optional electronic instrument panel as standard equipment. New diamond-spoke aluminum wheels were seen.

The Trans Am got a louvered hood with air extractors, new front and rear fascias and fender extractors. The integral aero package was revised to include a "whale-tail" spoiler. The Trans Am also had new integrated fog lamps and 16-inch aluminum wheels with 245/50R16 tires. A new heavy-duty, limited-slip axle was used with V-8s.

Although PMD was obviously trying to pump up sales of the hot-selling base Firebird, its model year production dropped to 46,644. PMD also assembled 5,208 S/Es and 44,028 T/As. Not only did production drop, but also the Trans Am nearly caught up to the base Firebird model in total popularity.

I.D. NUMBERS

The vehicle identification number (VIN) was stamped on a plate on the upper left-hand side of the instrument panel and visible through the windshield. The first symbol indicated country of origin: 1=United States. The second symbol indicated the manufacturer: G=General Motors. The third symbol indicated make: 2=Pontiac. The fourth symbol indicated car line and the fifth symbol indicated series: FS=Base Firebird, FW=Firebird Trans Am, FX=Firebird S/E. The sixth and seventh symbols indicated the body style and type of restraint system: 87=two-door plain-back special with non-passive restraints (manual seat belts). The eighth symbol indicated engine: 2=2.5-liter (151-cid) TBI I-4, S=2.8-liter (173-cid) Chevrolet MFI V-6, H=5.0-liter (305-cid) four-barrel Chevrolet V-8, G=5.0-liter (305-cid) Chevrolet four-barrel H.O. V-8 with manual transmission, F=5.0-liter (305-cid) Chevrolet MFI V-8 with automatic transmission. The ninth symbol indicated the check digit. The 10th symbol indicated the model year: F=1985. The 11th symbol indicated the assembly plant: N=Norwood, Ohio, L=Van Nuys, California. The remaining symbols were sequential unit production number at factory, starting with 100001. The Body by Fisher plate on the engine side of the cowl contained the Fisher style number, which took the form 2FW87. The first symbol 2=Pontiac, the second and third symbols FW=Firebird Trans Am and the last two symbols 87=two-door plain-back special. This plate also indicated interior trim, seat type, body color and build date. Four-cylinder engine code was on left front of engine below water pump. V-6 engine code was on right side of block near water pump. V-8 engine code was on pad on front of block below right cylinder head. Engine production codes for 1985 were: [2.5-liter I-4] AAM-AAP, [2.8-liter V-6] CAD-CAF, [5.0-liter V-8 four-barrel] CAP-CAR-CTA-CTB-CDD-CDF-CDH-CDJ-CDL-CKA, [5.0-liter H.O. four-barrel V-8] CDK-CDM, [5.0-liter EFI V-8] CDN-CDR-CFA-CFB.

COLORS

11=White (3967), 12=Silver Metallic (8535), 15=Medium Gray Metallic (8573), 19=Black (848), 26=Dark Blue (8596), 30E=Bright Blue Metallic (8587), 30W=Bright Blue Metallic (8604), 50=Yellow Gold (8740), 54=Yellow Beige (8525), 60E=Light Chestnut Metallic (8590), 60W=Light Chestnut Metallic (8606), 69E=Russet Metallic (8591), 69W=Russet Metallic (8607), 75=Blaze Red (8537) and 78=Dark Red (8524).

Note: Exterior color numbers in brackets are those used on the body identification label introduced in mid-1984.

FIREBIRD - (I-4/V-6/V-8) SERIES 2FS

For 1985, the rally-tuned suspension became available on the base Firebird. In addition, the instrument panel and console were redesigned for a softer and more rounded look. The console was split into two parts and covered with a new soft vinyl material. A pod containing the radio was attached to the instrument panel. New standard features included Firebird decals on the hood and sail panel, black taillight bezels and black-finished front fascia pads. There was a new W51 exterior package available for the 1985 base Firebird. It included black door handles, sport mirrors, a rear deck lid spoiler and Firebird decals on the sail panels. Also available at extra cost was a D84 two-tone paint treatment that was offered in 13 different color combinations. The standard equipment list for the first-level Firebird included a Pontiac-built 2.5-liter overhead-valve four-cylinder engine with electronic fuel injection, a UPC MM5 five-speed manual transmission, a black-finished stationary mast antenna, dual black-finished fascia pads, a body-color one-piece resilient Endura front panel and front bumper, concealed rectangular quartz halogen headlights, electrically operated hide-away headlight housings, a Firebird decal on the hood, Firebird decals on the sail panels, bright door handles and door lock cylinders, an Endura rear bumper, a front air dam, power steering, power front disc/rear drum brakes, dual outside mirrors (left-hand manual and right-hand manual convex), UPC QMW black sidewall P195/75R14 steel-belted radial tires on 14 x 6-in.

Rally wheels with black caps and lug nuts, a T125/70D15 compact spare tire, a wraparound Soft-Ray tinted liftback glass with strut supports, a graphite-finished instrument panel, cargo area carpeting, a cigar lighter, a cloth headliner with foam backing, cut-pile carpeting, a day/night inside rearview mirror, a Delco-GM AM radio with dual front speakers (could be deleted for credit), dual horns, a folding rear seat, a full-length front center console integral with instrument panel, an UPC C41 heater, an inside hood release, a lockable storage compartment in the left-hand interior quarter panel, a multi-function control lever, reclining front bucket seats, side window defoggers, a formula steering wheel, a Delco-GM Freedom II battery, a hidden windshield wiper system with washers, GM Computer Command Control, modified MacPherson strut front suspension, rear wheel drive and a torque arm/track bar rear suspension. Buyers ordering the new UPC Y99 rally-tuned suspension got P215/65R15 steel-belted black sidewall tires on 15 x 7-in. wheels with a larger front stabilizer bar and an added rear stabilizer bar.

Model Number	Body/Style Number	Body Type & Seating	Factory Price	Shipping Weight	Production Total
FIREBIRD - SERIES 2FS - (I-4)					
2FS	87	2d hatchback-4P	$9,623	2,866 lbs.	Notes 1,2
FIREBIRD - SERIES 2FS - (V-6)					
2FS	87	2d hatchback-4P	$9,973	2,948 lbs.	Notes 1,2
FIREBIRD - SERIES 2FS - (V-8/AUTOMATIC)					
2FS	87	2d hatchback-4P	$10,698	—	Note 3
FIREBIRD - SERIES 2FS - (V-8/5-SPEED MANUAL)					
2FS	87	2d hatchback-4P	$10,273	—	Note 3

Note 1: Combined production of base Firebirds with the four-cylinder engine was 3,068 cars.
Note 2: Combined production of base Firebirds and S/E models with six-cylinder engines was 38,544 cars.
Note 3: Total production of base Firebirds was 46,644, including cars with all engines.

FIREBIRD SPECIAL EDITION (S/E) (V-6/V-8) - SERIES 2FX

Changes to the 1985 Firebird S/E were characterized by new front and rear fascia designs. Up front, black-finished bumper pads replaced the regular grille. They provided better aerodynamics and gave the S/E a more sophisticated look. The sail panel carried new Firebird decals and Firebird S/E lettering was on the lower front edge of the doors and new

The F-Cars had were again long on good looks and could be packed with power.

accent striping was seen. Other standard exterior features included neutral-density taillight lenses with a smooth contour look and 14 x 7-in. diamond spoke aluminum wheels with a Light Chestnut or Charcoal finish. A revised interior featured high-contour firm-foam bucket seats upholstered in Pallex cloth, an interior roof console, Custom seat trim and Custom door panels. Recaro seats were available as a separate option. Standard equipment for the Firebird S/E included a new Chevrolet built 2.8-liter EFI V-6 with multi-port fuel injection and an electric cooling fan hooked to the UPC MM5 five-speed manual transmission. Also standard were the black-finished mast antenna, dual black-finished fascia pads, a body-color one-piece resilient Endura front panel and front bumper, neutral-density full-width taillights with a smooth contour appearance, hood air louvers, body-color body side moldings, black-finished door handles and key lock cylinders, a UPC N09 locking fuel filler door, lower accent paint with striping, concealed rectangular quartz halogen headlights, electrically operated hide-away headlight housings, an Endura rear bumper, a front air dam, power steering, power front disc/rear drum brakes, dual sport mirrors (left-hand remote control and right-hand manual convex), a leather-wrapped three-spoke formula steering wheel and shift knob and parking brake handle, UPC QHX P205/70R14 steel-belted black sidewall tires, 14 x 7 diamond spoke aluminum wheels, a compact spare tire, Turbo cast-aluminum wheels with body-colored center caps, rear wheel opening flares, an electric-operated wraparound liftback glass with strut supports, a black-finished instrument panel, cargo area carpeting, a cigar lighter, cloth seat trim, a cloth headliner with foam backing, cut-pile carpeting, a day/night inside rearview mirror, a folding rear seat, a full-length front center console with integral instrument panel, full gauges, including a tachometer and trip odometer, added acoustical insulation, an interior roof console, custom color-keyed seat and shoulder belts, a folding split-back rear seat, an instrument panel-mounted leather map pocket, an inside hood release, a lockable storage compartment in the left-hand interior quarter panel, a multi-function control lever, reclining front bucket seats, side window defoggers, a Delco-GM Freedom II battery, fluidic windshield washers with dual nozzles, GM Computer Command Control, a MacPherson strut front suspension, rear wheel drive and a torque arm/track bar rear suspension.

FIREBIRD TRANS AM - (V-8) SERIES 2FW

The 1985 Trans Am came standard with an enhanced version of the 1984 Aero package. It was fully integrated into the front and rear fascias and new front fog lights were included. The new hood had louvers and engine air extractors. Also new was a better-integrated rear deck lid spoiler. The Trans Am served as the Daytona 500 Pace Car for the fifth year in a row. However, the factory did not issue a limited edition pace car package. Standard equipment for the Trans Am included a Chevrolet-built 5.0-liter four-barrel V-8 engine with dual resonator exhaust and dual tailpipes, a five-speed manual transmission (with upshift indicator lamp), a black-finished mast antenna, a body-color one-piece resilient Endura front panel and front bumper, an Aero package with specific front and rear fascias and rocker panel and quarter panel extensions, hood air extractors, hood air louvers, front fender air extractors, Firebird decals on hood and sail panels, a rear deck lid spoiler, concealed rectangular quartz halogen headlights, electrically operated hide-away headlight housings, rear wheel opening flares, black-finished door handles and lock cylinders, power steering, power front disc/rear drum brakes, dual outside sport mirrors (left-hand remote and right-hand manual convex), black-finished door handles and key lock cylinders, hidden headlights, a leather-wrapped three-spoke formula steering wheel, a rally-tuned suspension with P215/65R15 steel-belted black sidewall tires, 15 x 7-in. diamond spoke wheels, a larger front stabilizer bar, an added rear stabilizer bar, a compact spare tire, a MacPherson front suspension, a wraparound glass hatch with strut supports, black full-width taillights, a black-finished instrument panel with full gauges (with tachometer and trip odometer), cargo area carpeting, a cigar lighter, a cloth headliner with foam backing, cut-pile carpeting, a day/night inside rearview mirror, a folding rear seat, a full-length front center console with integral instrument panel, an inside hood release, a lockable storage compartment in the left-hand interior quarter panel, a multi-function control lever, reclining front bucket seats, side window defoggers, a Delco Freedom battery, a hidden windshield washer system, GM Computer Command Control, rear wheel drive, front and rear stabilizer bars and a torque arm/track bar rear suspension.

Model Number	Body/Style Number	Body Type & Seating	Factory Price	Shipping Weight	Production Total
FIREBIRD S/E- SERIES 2FX - (EFI V-6)					
2FX	87	2d hatchback-4P	$11,709	2,965 lbs.	Notes 4, 5
FIREBIRD S/E - SERIES 2FX - (FOUR-BARREL V-8/AUTOMATIC)					
2FX	87	2d hatchback-4P	$12,434	3,145 lbs.	Note 5
FIREBIRD S/E - SERIES 2FX - (FOUR-BARREL V-8/5-SPEED MANUAL)					
2FX	87	2d hatchback-4P	$12,009	—	Note 5

Note 4: Combined production of base Firebirds and S/E models with six-cylinder engines was 38,544 cars.
Note 5: Total production of Firebird S/E models was 5,208, including cars with all engines.

Model Number	Body/Style Number	Body Type & Seating	Factory Price	Shipping Weight	Production Total
TRANS AM - SERIES 2FW - (5.0-LITER FOUR-BARREL V-8)					
2FW	87	2d hatchback-4P	$11,709	3,419 lbs.	Note 6
TRANS AM - SERIES 2FW - (5.0-LITER H.O. V-8; 5-SPEED ONLY)					
2FW	87	2d hatchback-4P	$12,404	—	Note 6
TRANS AM - SERIES 2FW - (5.0-LITER EFI V-8)					
2FW	87	2d hatchback-4P	$12,404	—	Note 6

Note 6: Total production of Trans Ams was 44,028.

ENGINES

Pontiac I-4 [UPC LQ9]: Overhead valves. Cast-iron block. Displacement: 151 cid. (2.5 liter). Bore & stroke: 4.00 x 3.00 in. Compression ratio: 9.0:1. Brake horsepower: 88 at 4400 rpm. Torque: 132-134 ft. lbs. at 2800 rpm. Hydraulic valve lifters. Induction: Throttle-body fuel injected. VIN Code: 2.

Chevrolet EFI V-6 [UPC LB8]: Overhead valves.

The Trans Am received a few exterior tweaks for 1985.

Cast-iron block. Displacement: 173 cid. Bore & stroke: 3.50 x 3.00 in. Compression ratio: 8.5:1. Brake horsepower: 135 at 5100 rpm. Torque: 160-165 ft. lbs. at 3600 rpm. Hydraulic valve lifters. Electronic fuel injection. VIN Code: S.

Chevrolet 305 V-8 [UPC LG4]: Overhead valves. Cast-iron block. Displacement: 305 cid. Bore & stroke: 3.74 x 3.48 in. Compression ratio: 9.5:1. Brake horsepower: 160 at 4200 rpm. Torque: 250 ft. lbs. at 2400 rpm. Hydraulic valve lifters. Carburetion: four-barrel Rochester E4ME. VIN Code: H.

Chevrolet H.O. V-8 [UPC L69]: Overhead valves. Cast-iron block. Displacement: 305 cid. Bore & stroke: 3.74 x 3.48 in. Compression ratio: 9.5:1. Brake horsepower: 190 at 4800 rpm. Torque: 240 ft. lbs. at 3200 rpm. Hydraulic valve lifters. Carburetor: Four-barrel. VIN Code: G.

Chevrolet V-8 [UPC LB9]: Overhead valves. Cast-iron block. Displacement: 305 cid. Bore & stroke: 3.74 x 3.48 in. Compression ratio: 9.5:1. Brake horsepower: 205 at 4400 rpm. Torque: 275 ft. lbs. at 3200 rpm. Hydraulic valve lifters. Electronic tuned port fuel injection. VIN Code: F.

CHASSIS

Firebird: Wheelbase: 101 in. Overall length: 189.9 in. Overall width: 72.4 in. Overall height: 49.7 in. Front tread: 60.7 in. Rear tread: 61.6 in. Front headroom: 37 in. Front legroom: 43 in. Front shoulder room: 57.7 in. Front hip room: 56.3 in. Rear headroom: 35.6 in. Rear legroom: 29.8 in. Rear shoulder room: 56.3 in. Rear hip room: 42.8 in.

Firebird S/E: Wheelbase: 101 in. Overall length: 189.9 in. Overall width: 72.4 in. Overall height: 49.7 in. Front tread: 60.7 in. Rear tread: 61.6 in. Front headroom: 37 in. Front legroom: 43 in. Front shoulder room: 57.7 in. Front hip room: 56.3 in. Rear headroom: 35.6 in. Rear legroom: 29.8 in. Rear shoulder room: 56.3 in. Rear hip room: 42.8 in.

Trans Am: Wheelbase: 101 in. Overall length: 191.6 in. Overall width: 72.4 in. Overall height: 49.7 in. Front tread: 60.7 in. Rear tread: 61.6 in. Front headroom: 37 in. Front legroom: 43 in. Front shoulder room: 57.7 in. Front hip room: 56.3 in. Rear headroom: 35.6 in. Rear legroom: 29.8 in. Rear shoulder room: 56.3 in. Rear hip room: 42.8 in.

TECHNICAL

Base: Body and frame: Integral body and frame with separate bolted-on sub-frame for engine and front suspension. Front suspension: Modified MacPherson struts with coil springs between lower control arm and X-member. Rear suspension: Torque arm/track bar with coil springs. Brakes: front disc/rear drum. Steering: Power assist coaxial re-circulating ball bearing. Fuel tank: 15.5 gal.

S/E: Body and frame: Integral body and frame with separate bolted-on sub-frame for engine and front suspension. Rally tuned suspension. Front suspension: Modified MacPherson struts with coil springs between lower control arm and X-member and larger front stabilizer bar. Rear suspension: Torque arm/track bar with coil springs and added rear stabilizer bar. Brakes: front disc/rear drum. Steering: Power assist re-circulating ball bearing. Fuel tank: 15.5 gal.

Trans Am: Body and frame: Integral body and frame with separate bolted-on sub-frame for engine and front suspension. Rally tuned suspension. Front suspension: Modified MacPherson struts with coil springs between lower control arm and X-member and larger front stabilizer bar. Rear suspension: Torque arm/track bar with coil springs and larger rear stabilizer bar. Brakes: front disc/rear drum. Steering: Power assist coaxial re-circulating ball bearing. Fuel tank: 15.5 gal.

OPTIONS

LQ9 2.5-liter EFI four-cylinder engine in base Firebird (no cost). LB8 2.8-liter EFI V-6 in Firebird S/E (no cost). LB8 2.8-liter EFI V-6 in base Firebird ($350). LG4 5.0-liter four-barrel V-8, requires five-speed manual transmission and Y99 rally tuned suspension in Trans Am (no cost). LG4 5.0-liter four-barrel V-8, requires five-speed manual transmission and Y99 rally tuned suspension in Firebird S/E ($300). LG4 5.0-liter four-barrel V-8, requires five-speed manual transmission and Y99 rally tuned suspension in base Firebird ($650). L69 5.0-liter H.O. four-barrel V-8 in Trans Am with five-speed only, requires G80 with AC or QDZ ($695). LB9 5.0-liter EFI V-8 for Trans Am only, requires automatic transmission with/QAC or QDZ ($695). MM5 five-speed manual transmission, not available with LB9 V-8 (no cost). MX0 four-speed automatic transmission, not available with L69 V-8 ($425). C60 air conditioning, required with A01 ($750). G80 limited-slip differential axle, without WS6 ($100). G80 limited-slip differential axle with WS6 (no cost). UA1 heavy-duty battery, not available with LQ9 four-cylinder engine ($26). AK1 color-keyed seat belts in base Firebird and Trans Am without B20 ($26). AK1 color-keyed seat belts in base Firebird and Trans Am with B20 (no cost). AK1 color-keyed seat belts in Firebird S/E (no cost). D42 cargo security screen ($69). V08 heavy-duty cooling system, not available with L69 V-8, without C60 ($70). V08 heavy-duty cooling system, not available with L69 V-8, with C60 ($40). DK6 interior roof console in base Firebird or Trans Am ($50). DK6 interior roof console in Firebird S/E (no cost). K34 cruise control with resume and accelerate features ($175). DX1 hood appliqué decal, with Trans Am only ($95). A90 remote control deck lid release on base Firebird or Trans Am ($40). A90 remote control deck lid release on Firebird S/E (no cost). C49 electric rear window defogger ($145). VJ9 emission requirements for Cali-

The 1985 Trans Am came standard with a new aero package that included fog lights and redesigned facias.

fornia ($99). K05 engine block heater ($18). W51 base Firebird black appearance group, without B57 custom exterior group and without CC1 hatch roof; includes black roof drip moldings ($152). W51 base Firebird black appearance group, without B57 custom exterior group and with CC1 hatch roof; not including black roof drip moldings ($123). B57 Custom exterior group including left-hand remote sport mirror, right-hand manual sport mirror, roof drip molding and belt reveal molding, without hatch roof ($112). B57 Custom exterior group including left-hand remote sport mirror, right-hand manual sport mirror with hatch roof ($51). N09 Locking fuel filler door on base Firebird or Trans Am ($11). N09 locking fuel filler door on Firebird S/E (no cost). U21 Rally gauge cluster with tachometer and trip odometer in base Firebird ($150). U21 Rally gauge cluster with tachometer and trip odometer in Firebird S/E and Trans Am (no cost). K64 78-amp heavy-duty generator with LQ9, LB8 and LG4 engines without air conditioning and without electric rear window defogger ($25). K64 78-amp heavy-duty generator with LQ9, LB8 and LG4 engines without air conditioning, but with electric rear window defogger (no cost). K22 94-amp heavy-duty generator with L69 engines and air conditioning (no cost). K22 94-amp heavy-duty generator with LQ9 or LG4 engines and air conditioning ($25). A01 Soft-Ray glass, all windows, required with C60 air conditioning ($115). CC1 locking hatch roof, not available with BX5 or B80 ($875). BS1 additional acoustical insulation in base Firebird or Trans Am ($40). BS1 additional acoustical insulation in Firebird S/E (no cost). C95 dome reading lamp, not available with DK6 ($23). TR9 lamp group ($34). D27 luggage compartment lockable load floor ($75). B48 luggage compartment trim ($48). B34 carpeted front floor mats ($20). B35 carpeted rear floor mats ($15). D35 dual Sport OSRV mirrors, left-hand remote, right-hand manual, on base Firebird without B57 or W51 ($53). D35 dual Sport OSRV mirrors, left-hand remote, right-hand manual, on base Firebird with B57 or W51 (no cost). D35 dual Sport OSRV mirrors, left-hand remote, right-hand manual, on Firebird S/E or Trans Am (no cost). DG7 dual Sport electric OSRV mirrors on Firebird without B57 or W51 ($139). DG7 dual Sport electric OSRV mirrors on Firebird with B57 or W51 ($91). DG7 dual Sport electric OSRV mirrors on Firebird S/E or Trans Am ($91). D34 right-hand visor vanity mirror ($7). B84 black vinyl body side moldings, not available with D84, on base Firebird and Trans Am ($55). B84 body-color vinyl body side moldings, not available with D84, on Firebird S/E (no cost). B93 bright door edge guards, on base Firebird without W51 black appearance group ($15). B91 black door edge guards, on base Firebird with W51 black appearance package ($15). B91 black door edge guards, on Firebird S/E or Trans Am ($15). B80 bright roof drip moldings on base Firebird without hatch roof, without B57 or W51 ($61). B80 black roof drip moldings on base Firebird without hatch roof, with B57 or W51 (no cost). B80 black roof drip moldings on Firebird S/E or Trans Am without hatch roof ($29). D84 two-tone paint on base Firebird only ($205). J65 four-wheel power disc brakes on Firebird S/E or Trans Am without WS6 special performance package ($179). J65 four-wheel power disc brakes on Firebird S/E or Trans Am with WS6 special performance package (no cost). AU3 power door locks ($130). AC3 six-way power driver seat ($225). A31 power windows in base Firebird and Trans Am without B20 ($195). A31 power windows in base Firebird and Trans Am with B20, including door map pockets ($225). A31 power windows in Firebird S/E, including door map pockets ($225). UK4 AM/FM ETR stereo radio with seek/scan ($168). UM7 AM/FM ETR stereo radio with seek/scan feature and clock ($207). UM6 AM/FM ETR stereo radio system with cassette, seek/scan feature and clock ($329). UX1 AM stereo/FM stereo ETR radio system with cassette, seek-and-scan, graphic equalizer and clock ($479). UT4 AM/FM stereo ETR radio system with cassette, seek/scan, graphic equalizer, clock and touch control ($519). UL5 AM radio, delete for credit ($56 credit). UQ7 subwoofer speaker system, available with optional radios only ($150). U75 power antenna ($65). AR9 bucket seats in base Firebird or Trans Am with Sierra vinyl trim (no cost). AR9 bucket seats in base Firebird or Trans Am with Genor cloth trim ($30). WS6 Special Performance package, with Trans Am only ($664). D80 rear deck spoiler on base Firebird or Firebird S/E ($70). D80 rear deck spoiler with Trans Am or with W51 black appearance package (no cost). D81 aero wing rear deck spoiler with Trans Am only ($199). NP5 leather-wrapped Formula steering wheel in base Firebird or Trans Am ($75). NP5 leather-wrapped formula steering wheel in Firebird S/E (no cost). N33 tilt steering wheel ($115). D98 vinyl sport stripes, base Firebird without D84 two-tone paint only ($75). DE1 hinge-mounted louvered rear window sunshield without C25 ($210). Y99 Rally tuned suspension, required with QYZ or QYH and with PE1, N24 or N90 on base Firebird ($30). Y99 Rally Tuned Suspension, required with QYZ or QYH on Firebird S/E ($30). Y99 Rally Tuned Suspension on Trans Am (no cost). B20 luxury trim group including luxury front and rear seats, luxury doors, color-keyed seat belts, split folding rear seat, map pockets, carpeted cowl kick panel and luxury reclining bucket seats with Pallex cloth trim in Base Firebird ($349). B20 luxury trim group including luxury front and rear seats, luxury doors, color-keyed seat belts, split folding rear seat, map pockets, carpeted cowl kick panel and luxury reclining bucket seats with Pallex cloth trim in Trans Am ($359). B20 luxury trim group including luxury front and rear seats, luxury doors, color-keyed seat belts, split folding rear seat, map pockets, carpeted cowl kick panel and luxury reclining bucket seats with Pallex cloth trim in Firebird S/E (no cost). B20 luxury trim group including luxury front and rear seats, luxury doors, color-keyed seat belts, split folding rear seat, map pockets, carpeted cowl kick panel and adjustable Lear Siegler bucket seats with Pallex cloth trim in base Firebird ($749). B20 luxury trim group including luxury front and rear seats, luxury doors, color-keyed seat belts, split folding rear seat, map pockets, carpeted cowl kick panel and adjustable Lear Siegler bucket seats with Pallex cloth trim in Trans Am ($759). B20 luxury trim group including luxury front and rear seats, luxury doors, color-keyed seat belts, split folding rear seat, map pockets, carpeted cowl kick panel and adjustable Lear Siegler bucket seats with Pallex cloth trim in Firebird S/E ($400). B20 luxury trim group including luxury front and rear seats, luxury doors, color-keyed seat belts, split folding rear seat, map pockets, carpeted cowl kick panel and adjustable Lear Siegler bucket seats with Pallex-and-leather cloth trim in base Firebird ($1,294). B20 luxury trim group including luxury front and rear seats, luxury doors, color-keyed seat belts, split folding rear seat, map pockets, carpeted cowl kick panel and adjustable Lear Siegler bucket seats with Pallex-and-leather cloth trim in Trans Am ($1,304). B20 luxury trim group with luxury front and rear seats, luxury doors, color-keyed seat belts, split folding rear seat, map pockets, carpeted cowl kick panel and adjustable Lear Siegler bucket seats with Pallex-and-leather cloth trim in Firebird S/E ($945). B20 luxury trim group including luxury front and rear seats, luxury doors, color-keyed seat belts, split folding rear seat, map pockets, carpeted cowl kick panel and adjustable Recaro bucket seats with Pallex cloth trim in base Firebird ($985). B20 luxury trim group including luxury front and rear seats, luxury doors, color-keyed seat belts, split folding rear seat, map pockets, carpeted cowl kick panel and adjustable Recaro bucket seats with Pallex cloth trim in Trans Am ($995). B20 luxury trim group with luxury front and rear seats, luxury doors, color-keyed seat belts, split folding rear seat, map pockets, carpeted cowl kick panel and adjustable Recaro bucket seats with Pallex cloth trim in Firebird S/E ($636). P06 wheel

The sleek T/A had three available V-8 engines for 1985.

trim rings on base Firebird ($39). P02 five-port wheel covers on base Firebird ($39). N91 wire wheel covers with locking package on base Firebird without Y99 ($199). PE1 14-in. cast-aluminum diamond-spoke wheels on base Firebird ($325). PE1 14-in. cast-aluminum diamond-spoke wheels on Firebird S/E (no cost). N90 15-in. cast-aluminum diamond-spoke wheels, required with Y99 and QYZ or QYH on base Firebird ($325). N90 15-in. cast-aluminum diamond-spoke wheels, requires Y99 and QYZ or QYH on Firebird S/E or Trans Am (no cost). N24 15 in. cast-aluminum deep-dish High-Tech turbo wheels, requires Y99 and QYZ or QYH on base Firebird ($325). N24 15 in. cast-aluminum deep-dish High-Tech turbo wheels, requires Y99 and QYZ or QYH on Firebird S/E (no cost) N96 16-in. cast-aluminum High-Tech turbo wheels, requires WS6 special performance package on Trans Am (no cost). PB4 wheel locking package, available with PE1, N24 or N90 ($16). C25 rear window wiper/washer system, not available with Trans Am ($125). CD4 controlled-cycle windshield wiper system ($50). QMW195/75R14 black sidewall steel-belted radial tires on base Firebird (no cost). QMX 195/75R14 white sidewall steel-belted radial tires on base Firebird ($62). QMY 195/75Rl4 white letter steel-belted radial tires on Firebird ($84). QHX 205/70Rl4 black sidewall steel-belted radial tires on base Firebird without Y99 ($58). QHX 205/70Rl4 black sidewall steel-belted radial tires on Firebird S/E (no cost). QHW205/70R14 white letter steel-belted radial tires on base Firebird without Y99 ($146). QHW 205/70R14 white letter steel-belted radial tires on Firebird S/E without Y99 ($88). QYZ 215/65R15 black sidewall steel-belted radial tires with LB8 and LG4 engines only on base Firebird with Y99 only ($132). QYZ 215/65R15 black sidewall steel-belted radial tires with LB8 and LG4 engines only on Firebird S/E with Y99 only ($132). QYZ 215/65R15 black sidewall steel-belted radial tires with LB8 and LG4 engines only on base Trans Am (no cost). QYH 215/65R15 white letter steel-belted radial tires with LB8 and LG4 engines on base Firebird with Y99 only ($224). QYH 215/65R15 white letter steel-belted radial tires with LB8 and LG4 engines on Firebird S/E with Y99 only ($166). QYH 215/65R15 white letter steel-belted radial tires with LB8 and LG4 engines on Trans Am (no cost). QAC 235/60VR15 black sidewall steel-belted radial tires on Trans Am with L69 or LB9 engines only ($177). QDZ 245/50VR16 black sidewall steel-belted radial tires on T/As with WS6 (no cost).

HISTORICAL FOOTNOTES

The 1985 Firebird line was introduced on Nov. 11, 1984, five weeks and two days later than the rest of the new Pontiacs. *Motor Trend* gave the new tune-port-injected EFI Trans Am a workout and wrote up the results in its October, 1984 issue. The magazine disliked the return of the "chicken" hood decal, but liked the WS6 suspension that was mandatory with the 205-hp V-8. The editors also liked the all-new digital electronic instrument panel. The test car moved from 0 to 60 mph in 7.79 seconds and did the quarter mile with an 84.5-mph terminal speed.

The F-Cars came in 12 different color choices for 1986.

Performance Tuned

All 1986 Firebirds ordered with a V-6 or V-8 received performance suspensions and 15-inch wheels with P215/65R15 tires. Up front the stylists concocted a new center panel to facelift the new model and there were revisions to the taillights to add a more distinct look. The lower body was accented with contrasting paint colors and sports striping was standard. A restyled bird decal decorated the hood. All models featured a power pull-down hatch. A programmable inside rearview mirror that was adjustable for daytime or nighttime driving was optional. Prices started at $9,693.

Base and SE Firebirds with V-6s or V-8s now had the Rally Tuned Suspension. New lightweight pistons went into the base 2.5-liter "Tech IV" engine. S/Es included an MFI V-6. A 5.0-liter four-barrel V-8 was optional. Trans Ams had a standard 155-hp version of the 5.0-liter V-8. The 190-hp TPI version was an option. Five-speed manual shift was standard and a four-speed overdrive automatic transmission was

required with the TPI engine.

The Trans Ams WS6 suspension included four-wheel disc brakes, a limited-slip axle, larger stabilizer bars and Gatorback tires. A new backlit instrument cluster used a 140-mph electric speedometer in Firebirds equipped with a TPI V-8. Pontiac made 59,334 Firebirds, 2,259 S/Es and 48,870 Trans Ams.

I.D. NUMBERS

The vehicle identification number (VIN) was stamped on a plate on the upper left-hand side of the instrument panel and visible through the windshield. The first symbol indicated country of origin: 1=United States. The second symbol indicated the manufacturer: G=General Motors. The third symbol indicated make: 2=Pontiac. The fourth symbol indicated car line and the fifth symbol indicated series: FS=Base Firebird, FW=Firebird Trans Am, FX=Firebird S/E. The sixth and seventh symbols indicated the body style and type of restraint system: 87=two-door plainback special with non-passive restraints (manual seat belts). The eighth symbol indicated engine: 2=2.5-

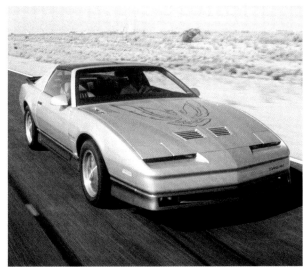

The hatch roof on this Trans Am was an $875 option.

liter (151-cid) TBI I-4, S=2.8-liter (173-cid) Chevrolet MFI V-6, H=5.0-liter (305-cid) four-barrel Chevrolet V-8, G=5.0-liter (305-cid) Chevrolet four-barrel H.O. V-8 with manual transmission, F=5.0-liter (305-cid) Chevrolet MFI V-8 with automatic transmission. The ninth symbol indicated the check digit. The 10th symbol indicated the model year: G=1986. The 11th symbol indicated the assembly plant: N=Norwood, Ohio, L=Van Nuys, California. The remaining symbols were sequential unit production numbers at factory, starting with 100001. The GM Service Parts identification label on the console door contained the complete VIN number, the option codes, the paint type, paint code and interior trim code. Four-cylinder engine code on left front of engine below water pump. V-6 engine code on right side of block near water pump. V-8 engine code on pad on front of block below right cylinder head. Engine production codes for 1986 were: [2.5-liter I-4] B3L-B3P-BBP, [2.8-liter V-6] DAD-DAX-DBC-DBB, [5.0-liter V-8 four-barrel] DDY-DFU-DDC-DDD-C7D-C7H-DFT, [5.0-liter H.O. four-barrel V-8] DFR-DFS, [5.0-liter EFI V-8] DDX-DDS-DDA-DDT-DDH-D4K-D4C.

COLORS

13S=Silver Metallic [9021], 23=Bright Blue Metallic [8751], 28=Black Sapphire Metallic [8743], 40=White [8554], 41=Black [8555], 51=Yellow Gold [8929], 60=Champagne Gold Metallic [8753], 66=Russet Metallic [8754], 68=Medium Russet Metallic [8757], 74=Flame Red Metallic [8748], 81=Bright Red [8774], 84=Gunmetal Metallic [7782]. The exterior color numbers in brackets are those used on the GM Service Parts label.

FIREBIRD - (I-4/V-6/V-8) - SERIES 2FS

For 1986, the first-level Firebird featured an all-new taillight design that was distinctive from that of the other Firebird models. The standard equipment list was expanded to include RTS, Rally wheels, a spoiler, new mirrors, new tires and new paint treatments. Several new paint colors were offered. The

seats were redesigned and a high-mounted stoplight was added. The standard equipment list for the first-level Firebird included concealed rectangular quartz halogen headlamps, body-color sport mirrors (left-hand remote control, right-hand manual), two-tone paint treatment with lower accent color, lower accent color striping, body-color rear deck lid spoilers, a one-piece multi-colored taillight lens with amber turn signal lamps, P215/65R15 steel-belted radial black sidewall tires, Rally II wheel rims, cut-pile carpet, a full-length console integrated with the instrument panel, a Delco-GM monaural push-button radio, reclining front bucket seats, a folding rear seatback, a graphite-color three-spoke formula steering wheel, a Delco-GM Freedom II battery, power front disc/rear drum brakes, GM Computer Command Control engine management system, power steering, a rally-tuned modified MacPherson strut front suspension (RTS), a 2.5-liter inline four-cylinder Tech IV engine with throttle-body fuel injection and a five-speed manual transmission.

Model Number	Body/Style Number	Body Type & Seating	Factory Price	Shipping Weight	Production Total
FIREBIRD - SERIES 2FS - (I-4)					
2FS	87	2d hatchback-4P	$9,279	2,789 lbs.	Note 1
FIREBIRD - SERIES 2FS - (V-6)					
2FS	87	2d hatchback-4P	$9,629	2,909 lbs.	Note 1
FIREBIRD - SERIES 2FS - (V-8)					
2FS	87	2d hatchback-4P	$10,029	2,955 lbs.	Note 1

Note 1: Total production of base Firebirds was 59,334, including cars with all engines.

FIREBIRD SPECIAL EDITION (S/E) (V-6/V-8) - SERIES 2FX

In addition to sharing some new features with the base Firebird, the 1986 Firebird S/E featured a new backlit instrument cluster as standard equipment, along with an electric remote-control deck lid release. The air conditioning condenser was redesigned to reduce vehicle weight and the base engine was now offered with a choice of two transmissions, the five-speed manual or a newly recalibrated four-speed automatic. The complete standard equipment list for the Firebird S/E included concealed rectangular quartz halogen headlamps, hood air louvers, body-color sport mirrors (left-hand remote control, right-hand manual), a lower accent color with striping, neutral-density taillights, P215/65R15 steel-belted radial black sidewall tires, diamond-spoke aluminum wheel rims, cut-pile carpet, a full-length console integrated with the instrument panel, an interior roof console, full gauge instrumentation with a tachometer and trip odometer, added acoustical insulation, a Delco-GM monaural push-button radio, Custom color-keyed seat and shoulder safety belts, reclining front bucket seats, luxury trim group upholstery, a folding rear seat back, a color-coordinated leather-wrapped three-spoke Formula steering wheel, color-keyed body side moldings, a Delco-GM Freedom II battery, power front disc/rear drum brakes, GM Computer Command Control engine management system, power steering, a rally-tuned modified MacPherson strut front suspension (RTS), a 2.8-liter V-6 engine with electronic multi-port fuel injection and a five-speed manual transmission.

Model Number	Body/Style Number	Body Type & Seating	Factory Price	Shipping Weight	Production Total
FIREBIRD S/E- SERIES 2FX - (EFI V-6)					
2FX	87	2d hatchback-4P	$11,995	2,909 lbs.	Note 2
FIREBIRD S/E- SERIES 2FX - (5.0-LITER V-8)					
2FX	87	2d hatchback-4P	$12,395	2,965 lbs.	Note 2

Note 2: Total production of Firebird S/E models was 2,259, including cars with all engines.

FIREBIRD TRANS AM SERIES 2FW - V-8

A revised hood bird decal, a backlit instrument panel, redesigned door map pockets and an improved rally-tuned suspension with 34-mm front and 23-mm rear stabilizer bars were among changes in the 1986 Trans Am. A 140-mph speedometer was added with optional engines and various option packages were upgraded. For example, the WS6 Special Performance package now featured 36-mm front and 24-mm rear stabilizer bars, Gatorback tires and four-wheel disc brakes. The standard equipment list for the Trans Am included an Aero body package, fog lamps integrated into the front fascia, front fender air extractors, concealed rectangular quartz halogen headlamps, hood air extractors, hood air louvers, an aero wing rear spoiler, body-color sport mirrors (left-hand remote control, right-hand manual), lower accent striping, neutral-density taillights, P215/65R15 steel-belted radial black sidewall tires, gold and silver 15 x 7-in. High-Tech turbo cast-aluminum wheels, cut-pile carpet, a full-length console integrated with the instrument panel, full gauge instrumentation with a tachometer and trip odometer, a Delco-GM monaural push-button radio, reclining front bucket seats, a folding rear seatback, a graphite-color three-spoke formula steering wheel, a Delco-GM Freedom II battery, power front disc/rear drum brakes, GM Computer Command Control engine management system, power steering, a Rally-Tuned modified MacPherson strut front suspension (RTS), a 5.0-liter four-barrel V-8 engine and a five-speed manual transmission.

Model Number	Body/Style Number	Body Type & Seating	Factory Price	Shipping Weight	Production Total
TRANS AM - SERIES 2FW - (5.0-LITER FOUR-BARREL V-8)					
2FW	87	2d hatchback-4P	$12,395	3,132 lbs.	48,870

ENGINES

Pontiac I-4 [UPC LQ9]: Overhead valves. Cast-iron block. Displacement: 151 cid. (2.5 liter). Bore & stroke: 4.00 x 3.00 in. Compression ratio: 9.0:1. Brake horsepower: 88 at 4400 rpm. Torque: 132-134 ft.-lbs. at 2800 rpm. Hydraulic valve lifters. Induction: Throttle-body fuel injected. VIN Code: 2. Standard in base Firebird and available only in base Firebird.

Chevrolet EFI V-6 [UPC LB8]: Overhead valves. Cast-iron block. Displacement: 173 cid. Bore & stroke: 3.50 x 3.00 in. Compression ratio: 8.9:1. Brake horsepower: 135 at 5100 rpm. Torque: 160-165 ft. lbs. at 3600 rpm. Hydraulic valve lifters. Electronic fuel injection. VIN Code: S. Standard in Firebird S/E. Optional in base Firebird. Not available in Trans Am.

Chevrolet 305 V-8 [UPC LG4]: Overhead valves.

Pontiac sold nearly 49,000 Trans Ams in 1986.

Cast-iron block. Displacement: 305 cid. Bore & stroke: 3.74 x 3.48 in. Compression ratio: 9.5:1. Brake horsepower: 155 at 4000 rpm. Torque: 235-245 ft. lbs. at 2000-2400 rpm. Hydraulic valve lifters. Carburetion: Four-barrel Rochester E4ME. VIN Code: H. Standard in Trans Am. Optional in base Firebird and Firebird S/E.

Chevrolet 305 H.O. V-8 [UPC L69]: Overhead valves. Cast-iron block. Displacement: 305 cid. Bore & stroke: 3.74 x 3.48 in. Compression ratio: 9.5:1. Brake horsepower: 190 at 4800 rpm. Torque: 240 ft. lbs. at 3200 rpm. Hydraulic valve lifters. Carburetor: Four-barrel. VIN Code: G. Optional in Trans Am only.

Chevrolet 305 V-8 [UPC LB9]: Overhead valves. Cast-iron block. Displacement: 305 cid. Bore & stroke: 3.74 x 3.48 in. Compression ratio: 9.5:1. Brake horsepower: 205 at 4400 rpm. Torque: 275 ft. lbs. at 3200 rpm. Hydraulic valve lifters. Induction: Electronic fuel injection. VIN Code: F. Optional in Trans Am only.

CHASSIS

Firebird: Wheelbase: 101 in. Overall length: 188.1 in. Overall width: 72.4 in. Overall height: 50 in. Front tread: 60.7 in. Rear tread: 61.6 in. Front headroom: 37 in. Front legroom: 43 in. Front shoulder room: 57.7 in. Front hip room: 56.3 in. Rear headroom: 35.6 in. Rear legroom: 29.8 in. Rear shoulder room: 56.3 in. Rear hip room: 42.8 in.

Firebird S/E: Wheelbase: 101 in. Overall length: 188.1 in. Overall width: 72.4 in. Overall height: 50 in. Front tread: 60.7 in. Rear tread: 61.6 in. Front headroom: 37 in. Front legroom: 43 in. Front shoulder room: 57.7 in. Front hip room: 56.3 in. Rear headroom: 35.6 in. Rear legroom: 29.8 in. Rear shoulder room: 56.3 in. Rear hip room: 42.8 in.

Trans Am: Wheelbase: 101 in. Overall length: 191.6 in. Overall width: 72.4 in. Overall height: 50 in. Front tread: 60.7 in. Rear tread: 61.6 in. Front headroom: 37 in. Front legroom: 43 in. Front shoulder room: 57.7 in. Front hip room: 56.3 in. Rear headroom: 35.6 in. Rear legroom: 29.8 in. Rear shoulder room: 56.3 in. Rear hip room: 42.8 in.

TECHNICAL

Base: Body and frame: Integral body and frame with separate bolted-on sub-frame for engine and front suspension. Front suspension: Modified MacPherson struts with coil springs between lower control arm and X-member. Rear suspension: Torque arm/track bar with coil springs. Brakes: front disc/rear drum. Steering: Power assist coaxial re-circulating ball bearing. Fuel tank: 15.5 gal.

S/E: Body and frame: Integral body and frame with separate bolted-on sub-frame for engine and front suspension. Rally Tuned Suspension. Front suspension: Modified MacPherson struts with coil springs between lower control arm and X-member and larger front stabilizer bar. Rear suspension: Torque arm/track bar with coil springs and added rear stabilizer bar. Brakes: front disc/rear drum. Steering: Power assist coaxial re-circulating ball bearing. Fuel tank: 15.5 gal.

Trans Am: Body and frame: Integral body and frame with separate bolted-on sub-frame for engine and front suspension. Rally Tuned Suspension. Front suspension: Modified MacPherson struts with coil springs between lower control arm and X-member and larger front stabilizer bar. Rear suspension: Torque arm/track bar with coil springs and larger rear stabilizer bar. Brakes: front disc/rear drum. Steering: Power assist coaxial re-circulating ball bearing. Fuel tank: 15.5 gal.

OPTIONS

LQ9 2.5-liter EFI four-cylinder engine in base Firebird (no cost). LB8 2.8-liter EFI V-6 in Firebird S/E (no cost). LB8 2.8-liter EFI V-6 in base Firebird ($350). LG4 5.0-liter four-barrel V-8, requires five-speed manual transmission and Y99 Rally Tuned Suspension in Trans Am (no cost). LG4 5.0-liter four-barrel V-8, requires five-speed manual transmission and Y99 Rally Tuned Suspension in Firebird S/E ($300). LG4 5.0-liter four-barrel V-8, requires five-speed manual transmission and Y99 Rally Tuned Suspension in base Firebird ($650). L69 5.0-liter H.O. four-barrel V-8 in Trans Am with five-speed only, requires G80 with AC or QDZ ($695). LB9 5.0-liter EFI V-8 for

Trans Am only, requires automatic transmission with QAC or QDZ ($695). MM5 five-speed manual transmission, not available with LB9 V-8 (no cost). MX0 four-speed automatic transmission, not available with L69 V-8 ($425). C60 air conditioning, required with A01 ($750). G80 limited-slip differential axle, without WS6 ($100). G80 limited-slip differential axle with WS6 (no cost). UA1 heavy-duty battery, not available with LQ9 four-cylinder engine ($26). AK1 color-keyed seat belts in base Firebird and Trans Am without B20 ($26). AK1 color-keyed seat belts in base Firebird and Trans Am with B20 (no cost). AK1 color-keyed seat belts in Firebird S/E (no cost). D42 cargo security screen ($69). V08 heavy-duty cooling system, not available with L69 V-8, without C60 ($70). V08 heavy-duty cooling system, not available with L69 V-8, with C60 ($40). DK6 interior roof console in base Firebird or Trans Am ($50). DK6 interior roof console in Firebird S/E (no cost). K34 cruise control with resume and accelerate features ($175). DX1 hood appliqué decal, with Trans Am only ($95). A90 remote control deck lid release on base Firebird or Trans Am ($40). A90 remote control deck lid release on Firebird S/E (no cost). C49 electric rear window defogger ($145). VJ9 emission requirements for California ($99). K05 engine block heater ($18). W51 base Firebird black appearance group, without B57 custom exterior group and without CC1 hatch roof; includes black roof drip moldings ($152). W51 base Firebird black appearance group, without B57 custom exterior group and with CC1 hatch roof; not including black roof drip moldings ($123). B57 Custom exterior group including left-hand remote sport mirror, right-hand manual sport mirror, roof drip molding and belt reveal molding, without hatch roof ($112). B57 Custom exterior group with left-hand remote sport mirror, right-hand manual sport mirror and hatch roof

Even Richard Petty had to smile over the prospect of jumping into an '86 Trans Am.

Jerry Heasley photo

The 1986 Pontiac Firebirds and Firebird SE's got new taillight designs.

($51). N09 Locking fuel filler door on base Firebird or Trans Am ($11). N09 locking fuel filler door on Firebird S/E (no cost). U21 Rally gauge cluster with tachometer and trip odometer in base Firebird ($150). U21 Rally gauge cluster with tachometer and trip odometer in Firebird S/E and Trans Am (no cost). K64 78-amp heavy-duty generator with LQ9, LB8 and LG4 engines without air conditioning and without electric rear window defogger ($25). K64 78-amp heavy-duty generator with LQ9, LB8 and LG4 engines without air conditioning, but with electric rear window defogger (no cost). K22 94-amp heavy-duty generator with L69 engines and air conditioning (no cost). K22 94-amp heavy-duty generator with LQ9 or LG4 engines and air conditioning ($25). A01 Soft-Ray glass, all windows, required with C60 air conditioning ($115). CC1 locking hatch roof, not available with BX5 or B80 ($875). BS1 additional acoustical insulation in base Firebird or Trans Am ($40). BS1 additional acoustical insulation in Firebird S/E (no cost). C95 dome reading lamp, not available with DK6 ($23). TR9 lamp group ($34). D27 luggage compartment lockable load floor ($75). B48 luggage compartment trim ($48). B34 carpeted front floor mats ($20). B35 carpeted rear floor mats ($15). D35 dual Sport outside rearview mirror mirrors, left-hand remote, right-hand manual, on base Firebird without B57 or W51 ($53). D35 dual Sport outside rearview mirror mirrors, left-hand remote, right-hand manual, on base Firebird with B57 or W51 (no cost). D35 dual Sport outside rearview mirror mirrors, left-hand remote, right-hand manual, on Firebird S/E or Trans Am (no cost). DG7 dual Sport electric outside rearview mirror mirrors on Firebird without B57 or W51 ($139). DG7 dual Sport electric outside rearview mirror mirrors on Firebird with B57 or W51 ($91). DG7 dual Sport electric outside rearview mirror mirrors on Firebird S/E or Trans Am ($91). D34 right-hand visor vanity mirror ($7). B84 black vinyl body side moldings, not available with D84, on base Firebird and Trans Am ($55). B84 body-color vinyl body side moldings, not

available with D84, on Firebird S/E (no cost). B93 bright door edge guards, on base Firebird without W51 black appearance group ($15). B91 black door edge guards, on base Firebird with W51black appearance package ($15). B91 black door edge guards, on Firebird S/E or Trans Am ($15). B80 bright roof drip moldings on base Firebird without hatch roof, without B57 or W51 ($61). B80 black roof drip moldings on base Firebird without hatch roof, with B57 or W51 (no cost). B80 black roof drip moldings on Firebird S/E or Trans Am without hatch roof ($29). D84 two-tone paint on base Firebird only ($205). J65 four-wheel power disc brakes on Firebird S/E or Trans Am without WS6 special performance package ($179). J65 four-wheel power disc brakes on Firebird S/E or Trans Am with WS6 special performance package (no cost). AU3 power door locks ($130). AC3 six-way power driver seat ($225). A31 power windows in base Firebird and Trans Am without B20 ($195). A31 power windows in base Firebird and Trans Am with B20, including door map pockets ($225). A31 power windows in Firebird S/E, including door map pockets ($225). UK4 AM/FM ETR stereo radio with seek/scan ($168). UM7AM/FM ETR stereo radio with seek/scan feature and clock ($207). UM6 AM/FM ETR stereo radio system with cassette, seek/scan feature and clock ($329). UX1 AM stereo/FM stereo ETR radio system with cassette, seek/scan, graphic equalizer and clock ($479). UT4AM/FM stereo ETR radio system with cassette, seek/scan, graphic equalizer, clock and touch control ($519). UL5 AM radio, delete for credit ($56 credit). UQ7 subwoofer speaker system, available with optional radios only ($150). U75 power antenna($65). AR9 bucket seats in base Firebird or Trans Am with Sierra vinyl trim (no cost). AR9 bucket seats in base Firebird or Trans Am with Genor cloth trim ($30). WS6 special performance package, with Trans Am only ($664). D80 rear deck spoiler on base Firebird or Firebird S/E ($70). D80 rear deck spoiler with Trans Am or with W51 black appearance package (no cost). D81 aero wing rear deck spoiler with Trans Am only ($199). NP5 leather-wrapped Formula steering wheel in base Firebird or Trans Am ($75). NP5 leather-wrapped Formula steering wheel in Firebird S/E (no cost). N33 tilt steering wheel ($115). D98 vinyl sport stripes, base Firebird without D84 two-tone paint only ($75). DE1 hinge-mounted louvered rear window sunshield without C25 ($210). Y99 Rally Tuned Suspension, required with QYZ or QYH and with PE1, N24 or N90 on base Firebird ($30). Y99 Rally Tuned Suspension, required with QYZ or QYH on Firebird S/E ($30). Y99 Rally Tuned Suspension on Trans Am (no cost). B20 luxury trim group including luxury front and rear seats, luxury doors, color-keyed seat belts, split-folding rear seat, map pockets, carpeted cowl kick panel and luxury reclining bucket seats with Pallex cloth trim in Base Firebird ($349). B20 luxury trim group including luxury front and rear seats, luxury doors, color-keyed seat belts, split-folding rear seat, map pockets, carpeted cowl kick panel and luxury reclining bucket seats with Pallex cloth trim in Trans Am ($359). B20 luxury trim group with luxury front and rear seats, luxury doors, color-keyed seat belts, split-folding rear seat, map pockets, carpeted cowl kick panel and luxury reclining bucket seats with Pallex cloth trim in Firebird S/E (no cost). B20 luxury trim group with luxury front and rear seats, luxury doors, color-keyed seat belts, split-folding rear seat, map pockets, carpeted cowl kick panel and adjustable Lear Siegler bucket seats with Pallex cloth trim in base Firebird ($749). B20 luxury trim group with luxury front and rear seats, color-keyed seat belts, split-folding rear seat, map pockets, carpeted cowl kick panel and adjustable Lear Siegler bucket seats with Pallex cloth trim in Trans Am ($759). B20 luxury trim group including luxury front and rear seats, luxury doors, color-keyed seat belts, split-folding rear seat, map pockets, carpeted cowl kick panel and adjustable Lear Siegler bucket seats with Pallex cloth trim in Firebird S/E ($400). B20 luxury trim group with luxury front and rear seats, luxury doors, color-keyed seat belts, split-folding rear seat, map pockets, carpeted cowl kick panel and adjustable Lear Siegler bucket seats with Pallex-and-leather cloth trim in base Firebird ($1,294). B20 luxury trim group with luxury front and rear seats, luxury doors, color-keyed seat belts, split-folding rear seat, map pockets, carpeted cowl kick panel and adjustable Lear Siegler bucket seats with Pallex-and-leather cloth trim in Trans Am ($1,304). B20 luxury trim group with luxury front and rear seats, luxury doors, color-keyed seat belts, split-folding rear seat, map pockets, carpeted cowl kick panel and adjustable Lear Siegler bucket seats with Pallex-and-leather cloth trim in Firebird S/E ($945). B20 luxury trim group including luxury front and rear seats, luxury doors, color-keyed seat belts, split-folding rear seat, map pockets, carpeted cowl kick panel and adjustable Recaro bucket seats with Pallex cloth trim in base Firebird ($985). B20 luxury trim group with luxury front and rear seats, luxury doors, color-keyed seat belts, split-folding rear seat, map pockets, carpeted cowl kick panel and adjustable Recaro bucket seats with Pallex cloth trim in Trans Am ($995). B20 luxury trim group with luxury front and rear seats, luxury doors, color-keyed seat belts, split-folding rear seat, map pockets, carpeted cowl kick panel and adjustable Recaro bucket seats with Pallex cloth trim in Firebird S/E ($636). P06 wheel trim rings on base Firebird ($39). P02 five-port wheel covers on base Firebird ($39). N91 wire wheel covers with locking package on base Firebird without Y99 ($199). PE1 14-in. cast aluminum diamond-spoke wheels on base Firebird ($325). PE114-in. cast-aluminum diamond-spoke wheels on Firebird S/E (no cost). N90 15-in. cast-aluminum diamond-spoke wheels, required with Y99 and QYZ or QYH on base Firebird ($325). N90 15-in. cast-aluminum diamond-spoke wheels, requires Y99 and QYZ or QYH on Firebird S/E or Trans Am (no cost). N24 15 in. cast-aluminum deep-dish High-Tech turbo wheels, requires Y99 and QYZ or QYH on base Firebird ($325). N24 15 in. cast aluminum deep-dish High-Tech turbo wheels, requires Y99 and QYZ or QYH on Firebird S/E (no cost). N96 16-in. cast-aluminum High-Tech turbo wheels, requires WS6 special performance package on

Trans Am (no cost). PB4 wheel locking package, available with PE1, N24 or N90 ($16). C25 rear window wiper/washer system, not available with Trans Am ($125). CD4 controlled-cycle windshield wiper system ($50). QMW195/75R14 black sidewall steel-belted radial tires on base Firebird (no cost). QMX 195/75R14 white sidewall steel-belted radial tires on base Firebird ($62). QMY 195/75Rl4 white-letter steel-belted radial tires on Firebird ($84). QHX 205/70Rl4 black sidewall steel-belted radial tires on base Firebird without Y99 ($58). QHX 205/70Rl4 black sidewall steel-belted radial tires on Firebird S/E (no cost). QHW205/70R14 white-letter steel-belted radial tires on base Firebird without Y99 ($146). QHW 205/70R14 white-letter steel-belted radial tires on Firebird S/E without Y99 ($88). QYZ 215/65R15 black sidewall steel-belted radial tires with LB8 and LG4 engines only on base Firebird with Y99 only ($132). QYZ 215/65R15 black sidewall steel-belted radial tires with LB8 and LG4 engines only on Firebird S/E with Y99 only ($132). QYZ 215/65R15 black sidewall steel-belted radial tires with LB8 and LG4 engines only on base Trans Am (no cost). QYH 215/65R15 white letter steel-belted radial tires with LB8 and LG4 engines on base Firebird with Y99 only ($224). QYH 215/65R15 white letter steel-belted radial tires with LB8 and LG4 engines on Firebird S/E with Y99 only ($166). QYH 215/65R15 white letter steel-belted radial tires with LB8 and LG4 engines on Trans Am (no cost). QAC 235/60VR15 black sidewall steel-belted radial tires on Trans Am with L69 or LB9 engines only ($177). QDZ 245/50VR16 black sidewall steel-belted radial tires with Trans Am with WS6 (no cost).

HISTORICAL FOOTNOTES

On Sept. 12, 1985, Pontiac Motor Division General Manager J. Michael Losh held a press conference during Pontiac's national press preview at Waterford Hills Race Course. Losh stated that Pontiac expected to build 900,000 cars during model-year 1986 and set an all-time record for sales. Losh pointed out that "image" cars like the Firebird would lead the way towards increased sales in 1986. It was fitting that the conference was held at the Michigan racetrack, since Pontiac was emphasizing racing involvements in 1986. In fact, Pontiac's Motorsports Engineering Dept. turned out a *Performance Plus* book that gave enthusiasts information on Firebird drag racing vehicle construction with Super Duty parts. Among Super Duty items available were parts to turn the 2.5-liter four into a 3.0-liter 300-hp engine! A Super Duty V-8 block (part No. 10049804) and Super Duty aluminum heads for V-8s were also offered. A number of aftermarket companies were offering special Firebird conversion packages. Cars & Concepts, of Brighton, Michigan, offered a Skylite T-Roof treatment (kit no 4720051 AOO) for the 1986 Firebird. Chattanooga Custom Center, Inc., of Chattanooga, Tennessee, offered the Pontiac Pro/Am II Firebird. Coca-Cola gave away three 1986 Pontiac Trans Ams in a $50 million Gold Rush contest that ended on Oct. 4, 1986.

The Formula Firebird came with signature graphics and decals along with
color-keyed body side moldings.

Brenda Rose photo

Little GTA

A high-mounted stoplight set into a body-color spoiler was one of the biggest changes for the little-altered 1987 Firebird. Pontiac took the Firebird S/E off the model roster and added a Formula package to the options list. When Firebird buyers tested the new ripple cloth seats they found they could now adjust the headrest up or down. A 5.7-liter V-8 was available (with four-speed automatic transmission only) in the new-for-1987 GTA model. The base Firebird engine was the 2.8-liter V-6 and prices for V-6 models started at $10,773.

The Formula featured an aero-style spoiler, analog instruments, a domed hood, 16 x 8-inch Hi-Tech aluminum wheels and a performance suspension. Trans Ams added an aero body skirting package, hood and front fender air extractors, hood air louvers, fog lamps, soft ray tinted glass and a rally-tuned suspension. Trans Am buyers had a choice between the 5.0-liter four-barrel V-8 or the 5.0-liter MFI V-8. The injected version got a five-speed manual transmission option for the first time.

The new GTA version of the Trans Am added articulating front bucket seats, a limited-slip rear axle, a special aero package, a special performance suspension, a leather-wrapped steering wheel and lightweight 16 x 8-inch diamond-spoke gold wheels.

New options included body-color exterior moldings, molded door panel trim (except in GTAs) and a performance suspension for base models. A 5.7-liter

MPI V-8 performance engine was optional in Formulas and standard in GTAs. Firebird production hit 42,558 Firebirds, 13,164 Formulas and 32,890 Trans Ams.

In August 1987, General Motors boarded up the F-Car plant in Norwood, Ohio, and all Firebirds (and Camaros) through 1991 were made in the Van Nuys, California, factory. Also ended was the GM80 program that had been launched to develop a plastic-bodied, front-wheel-drive replacement for F-cars.

I.D. NUMBERS

The vehicle identification number (VIN) was stamped on a plate on the upper left-hand side of the instrument panel and visible through the windshield. The first symbol indicated country of origin: 1=United States. The second symbol indicated the manufacturer: G=General Motors. The third symbol indicated make: 2=Pontiac. The fourth symbol indicated car line and the fifth symbol indicated series: FS=Base Firebird, FW=Firebird Trans Am. The sixth symbol indicated the body style: 2=two-door hatchback. The seventh symbol indicated type of restraint system: 1=non-passive restraints (manual seat belts) for all Firebirds. The eighth symbol indicated engine: S=2.8-liter (173-cid) Chevrolet-built MFI V-6, H=5.0-liter (305-cid) four-barrel Chevrolet-built V-8, F=5.0-liter (305-cid) Chevrolet-built MFI V-8 with automatic transmission, 8=5.7-liter (350-cid) Chevrolet-built MFI V-8. The ninth symbol indicated the check digit. The 10th symbol indicated the model year: H=1987. The 11th symbol indicated the assembly plant:

N=Norwood, Ohio, L=Van Nuys, California. The remaining symbols were sequential unit production numbers at factory, starting with 100001. The GM Service Parts identification label on the console door contained the complete VIN number, the option codes, the paint type, paint code and interior trim code. V-6 engine code on right side of block near water pump. V-8 engine code on pad on front of block below right cylinder head. Engine production codes for 1987 were: [2.8-liter V-6] SCC-SCD-DBP-DBR, [5.0-liter V-8 four-barrel] C7L-C7M-SDB-DFL, [5.0-liter EFI V-8] SFD-SFS-SDK-SDD-D3Y-SRL-D4W, [350-cid EFI V-8] SNA-SNB.

COLORS

13=Silver Metallic [7781], 23=Bright Blue Metallic [8751], 28=Black Sapphire Metallic [8743], 40=White [8554], 41=Black [8555], 51=Yellow Gold [8929], 60=Champagne Gold Metallic [8753], 68=Medium Russet Metallic [8757], 74=Flame Red Metallic [8748], 81=Bright Red [8774], 84=Gunmetal Metallic [7782]. The exterior color numbers in brackets are those used on the GM Service Parts label.

FIREBIRD - (V-6/V-8) - SERIES 2FS

Technically, the base Firebird was one of only two Firebird series that returned for 1987 — along with the Trans Am. However, a new Formula option package was offered, along with a new Trans Am GTA model-option. That gives collectors four 1987 Firebird "models" to chose from. Engine changes were the big news, as Pontiac prepared to go head to head in the sporty car sales battle with Ford's 5.0-liter Mustang. The slow-selling four-cylinder engine was discontinued. A multi-port fuel-injected 2.8-liter V-6 was standard in the first-level Firebird. The Firebird coupe also had a more integrated appearance that was achieved by relocating its center high-mounted stoplight in the body-color rear deck lid spoiler. Inside were new ripple cloth reclining bucket seats with separately adjusted headrests and custom door trim pads. Other new features included body-colored side moldings and a softer re-tuned suspension. A partial list of standard equipment in the base Firebird included the 2.8-liter V-6 with multiport fuel-injection

(MFI), a five-speed manual transmission, a center high-mounted stoplight, a full-length console with instrument panel, side window defoggers, a front air dam, the GM Computer Command Control engine management system, a hatch "pull-down" feature, concealed rectangular quartz halogen headlamps, a MacPherson front suspension, power brakes, a U63 Delco AM radio, reclining front bucket seats with ripple cloth upholstery, a split-folding rear seat with ripple cloth upholstery, a formula three-spoke steering wheel, a lockable storage compartment, "wet-arm" windshield wipers, front disc/rear drum brakes and P215/65R15 black sidewall steel-belted radial tires.

Model Number	Body/Style Number	Body Type & Seating	Factory Price	Shipping Weight	Production Total
FIREBIRD - SERIES 2FS - (V-6)					
2FS	87	2d hatchback-4P	$10,773	2,885 lbs.	Note 1/Note 2
FIREBIRD - SERIES 2FS - (V-8)					
2FS	87	2d hatchback-4P	$11,173	2,985 lbs.	Note 1/Note 2

Note 1: Total production of base Firebirds was 42,552.
Note 2: Approximately 30,969 cars – all base Firebirds – came with the V-6.

FORMULA FIREBIRD - (V-6/V-8) SERIES 2FS

The Formula name returned to the Firebird line in 1987. The Formula option was available in two content levels. The W61 version retailed for $1,273. The W63 version included more power options and retailed for $1,842. Both cars had a "street machine" image and a V-8 was part of both packages. The standard equipment list for the Formula Firebird included concealed rectangular quartz halogen headlamps, a domed hood, body-color sport mirrors (left-hand remote control, right-hand manual), a body-colored aero wing spoiler, a lower accent color with striping, Formula graphics and decals, neutral-density taillights, P245/50VR16 Goodyear Eagle black sidewall tires, 16 x 8-in. High-Tech aluminum wheels, cut-pile carpet, a full-length console integrated with the instrument panel, an interior roof console, Rally gauges with analog instruments and a tachometer, added acoustical insulation, a Delco-GM monaural push-button radio, Custom color-keyed seat and shoulder safety belts, reclining front bucket seats, luxury trim group upholstery, a folding rear seatback, a color-coordinated leather-wrapped three-spoke for-

The 1987 Pontiac Firebird Trans Am GTA received a new tuned port injection (TPI) engine that promised an increase to 210 hp.

mula steering wheel, color-keyed body side moldings, a Delco-GM Freedom II battery, power front disc/rear drum brakes, quick-ratio power steering, the GM Computer Command Control engine management system, power steering, a WS6 Special Performance type modified MacPherson strut front suspension, a 5.0-liter four-barrel V-8 and a five-speed manual transmission.

Model Number	Body/Style Number	Body Type & Seating	Factory Price	Shipping Weight	Production Total
FORMULA FIREBIRD - SERIES 2FS - (FOUR-BARREL V-8)					
2FS/W61	87	2d hatchback-4P	$12,046	3,002 lbs.	Note 3
FORMULA FIREBIRD - SERIES 2FS - (FOUR-BARREL V-8)					
2FS/W63	87	2d hatchback-4P	$12,615	3,102 lbs.	Note 3

Note 3: Total production of all Formula Firebird models was 13,160.

FIREBIRD TRANS AM - (V-8) SERIES 2FW

The regular 1987 Trans Am was promoted as a "driving excitement" car. The complete standard equipment list for the Trans Am included an Aero body package, fog lamps integrated into the front fascia, front fender air extractors, concealed rectangular quartz halogen headlamps, hood air extractors, hood air louvers, a body-color aero rear deck spoiler, body-color sport mirrors (left-hand remote control, right-hand manual), lower accent striping, neutral-density taillights, P215/65R15 steel-belted radial black sidewall tires, gold and silver 15 x 7-in. deep-dish High-Tech turbo cast-aluminum wheels, cut-pile carpet, a full-length console integrated with the instrument panel, full Rally gauge instrumentation with a tachometer and trip odometer, a Delco-GM monaural push-button radio, Soft-Ray tinted glass, reclining front bucket seats, a folding rear seatback, a graphite-color three-spoke formula steering wheel, a Delco-GM Freedom II battery, power front disc/rear drum brakes, GM Computer Command Control engine management system, power steering, a Rally-Tuned modified MacPherson strut front suspension (RTS), a 5.0-liter four-barrel V-8 engine and a five-speed manual transmission.

Model Number	Body/Style Number	Body Type & Seating	Factory Price	Shipping Weight	Production Total
TRANS AM - SERIES 2FW - (5.0-LITER FOUR-BARREL V-8)					
2FW	87	2d hatchback-4P	$13,673	3,227 lbs.	21,779

FIREBIRD TRANS AM GTA - (V-8) SERIES 2FW

The first GTA was an option package for the regular Trans Am. It gave the hot Firebird a sleek, aerodynamic and powerful look. Pontiac described it as "the ultimate Trans Am." It was referred to as "210 hp of precision driving excitement ready to exert its influence over the road of your choice." The standard equipment list for the Trans Am GTA included a special Aero body package, fog lamps integrated into the front fascia, front fender air extractors, concealed rectangular quartz halogen headlamps, hood air extractors, hood air louvers, a body-color aero rear deck spoiler, dual power-paddle-type outside rearview mirrors (on first 100 cars produced), lower accent striping, neutral-density taillights, P245/50VR15 Goodyear steel-belted radial black sidewall tires, gold and silver 16 x 8-in. diamond spoke aluminum wheels, cut-pile carpeting, a full-length console integrated with the instrument panel, full Rally gauge instrumentation with a tachometer and trip odometer, a Delco-GM monaural push-button radio, Soft-Ray tinted glass, articulating front bucket seats, a folding rear seatback, a leather-wrapped steering wheel, a Delco-GM Freedom II battery, power four-wheel disc brakes, a limited-slip rear axle, the GM Computer Command Control engine management system, power steering, a WS6 Special Performance type modified MacPherson strut front suspension, a 5.7-liter TPI (tuned port injected) V-8 engine and a four-speed automatic transmission. Since the 5.7-liter TPI engine was available in limited quantities, the 1987 Pontiac sales catalog noted "limited availability — may be deleted."

Model Number	Body/Style Number	Body Type & Seating	Factory Price	Shipping Weight	Production Total
TRANS AM GTA - SERIES 2FW/W61 - (5.7-LITER TPI V-8)					
2FW	87	2d hatchback-4P	$15,374	3,327 lbs.	Note 6
TRANS AM GTA - SERIES 2FW - (5.7-LITER TPI V-8)					
2FW	87	2d hatchback-4P	$15,631	3,327 lbs.	Note 6

Note 4: Total production of all Trans Am GTA models was 11,096.

ENGINES

Chevrolet EFI V-6 [UPC LB8]: Overhead valves. Cast-iron block. Displacement: 173 cid. Bore & stroke: 3.50 x 3.00 in. Compression ratio: 8.9:1. Brake horsepower: 135 at 5100 rpm. Torque: 160-165 ft. lbs. at 3600 rpm. Hydraulic valve lifters. Electronic multi

The Formula was back in the Firebird line for 1987 and came in two equipment levels, both with a base 5.0-liter four-barrel V-8.

The GTA again stood out.

port fuel injection. VIN Code: S. Standard with five-speed manual transmission in base Firebird. Available with four-speed automatic transmission in base Firebird.

Chevrolet 305 V-8 [UPC LG4]: Overhead valves. Cast-iron block. Displacement: 305 cid. Bore & stroke: 3.74 x 3.48 in. Compression ratio: 9.5:1. Brake horsepower: 155 at 4200 rpm. Torque: 235-245 ft. lbs. at 2000-2400 rpm. Hydraulic valve lifters. Carburetion: four-barrel Rochester E4ME. VIN Code: H. Standard with five-speed manual transmission in base Firebird V-8, Formula and Trans Am.

Chevrolet 305 V-8 [UPC LB9]: Overhead valves. Cast-iron block. Displacement: 305 cid. Bore & stroke: 3.74 x 3.48 in. Compression ratio: 9.5:1. Brake horsepower: 165 at 4400 rpm. Torque: 235 ft. lbs. at 2000 rpm. Hydraulic valve lifters. Multi-port fuel injection. VIN Code: 8. Available with five-speed manual transmission in Formula or Trans Am. Available as a delete option in the Trans Am GTA.

Chevrolet 350 V-8 [UPC L98]: Overhead valves. Cast-iron block. Displacement: 350 cid. Bore & stroke: 4.00 x 3.48 in. Compression ratio: 9.5:1. Brake horsepower: 210 at 4000 rpm. Torque: 315 ft. lbs. at 3200 rpm. Hydraulic valve lifters. Induction: Tuned port fuel injection. VIN Code: F. Includes roller valve lifters, a hardened steel camshaft, fast-burn combustion chambers, a remote-mounted coil, dual cooling fans, a low-profile air-induction system with aluminum plenum and individual tuned runners, an extruded dual fuel rail assembly with computer-controlled fuel injectors and a special low-restriction exhaust system. Limited-interimavailability as base engine in the Trans Am GTA; optional in Formula Firebird and regular Trans Am.

CHASSIS

Firebird: Wheelbase: 101 in. Overall length: 188 in. Overall width: 72 in. Overall height: 49.7 in. Front tread: 60.7 in. Rear tread: 61.6 in. Front headroom: 37 in. Front legroom: 43 in. Front shoulder room: 57.7 in. Front hip room: 56.3 in. Rear headroom: 35.6 in. Rear legroom: 29.8 in. Rear shoulder room: 56.3 in. Rear hip room: 42.8 in.

Formula Firebird: Wheelbase: 101 in. Overall length: 188 in. Overall width: 72 in. Overall height: 49.7 in. Front tread: 60.7 in. Rear tread: 61.6 in. Front headroom: 37 in. Front legroom: 43 in. Front shoulder room: 57.7 in. Front hip room: 56.3 in. Rear headroom: 35.6 in. Rear legroom: 29.8 in. Rear shoulder room: 56.3 in. Rear hip room: 42.8 in.

Trans Am: Wheelbase: 101 in. Overall length: 191.6 in. Overall width: 72 in. Overall height: 49.7 in. Front tread: 60.7 in. Rear tread: 61.6 in. Front headroom: 37 in. Front legroom: 43 in. Front shoulder room: 57.7 in. Front hip room: 56.3 in. Rear headroom: 35.6 in. Rear legroom: 29.8 in. Rear shoulder room: 56.3 in. Rear hip room: 42.8 in.

Trans Am GTA: Wheelbase: 101 in. Overall length: 191.6 in. Overall width: 72 in. Overall height: 49.7 in. Front tread: 60.7 in. Rear tread: 61.6 in. Front headroom: 37 in. Front legroom: 43 in. Front shoulder room: 57.7 in. Front hip room: 56.3 in. Rear headroom: 35.6 in. Rear legroom: 29.8 in. Rear shoulder room: 56.3 in. Rear hip room: 42.8 in.

TECHNICAL

Base: Body and frame: Integral body and frame with separate bolted-on sub-frame for engine and front suspension. Front suspension: Modified MacPherson struts with coil springs between lower control arm and X-member. Rear suspension: Torque arm/track bar with live axle and coil springs. Brakes: front disc/rear drum. Steering: Power assist coaxial re-circulating ball bearing. Fuel tank: 15.5 gal. with V-6 or TPI V-8; 16.2 gal. with four-barrel V-8.

Formula: Body and frame: Integral body and frame with separate bolted-on sub-frame for engine and front suspension. Front suspension: Modified MacPherson struts with coil springs between lower control arm and X-member and larger front stabilizer bar. Rear suspension: Torque arm/track bar with live axle and coil springs and added rear stabilizer bar. WS6 Special Performance package including P245/50VR16 steel-belted black sidewall tires, 16 x 8-in High-Tech turbo or diamond-spoke aluminum wheels, specific springs, gas-filled shock absorbers, special front and rear stabilizer bars and quick-ratio steering. Brakes: Front disc/rear drum. Steering: Power assist coaxial re-circulating ball bearing. Fuel tank: 15.5 gal. with V-6 or TPI V-8; 16.2 gal. with four-barrel V-8.

Trans Am: Body and frame: Integral body and frame with separate bolted-on sub-frame for engine

Trans Ams accounted for about 33,000 cars for the 1987 model year.

and front suspension. Rally tuned suspension. Front suspension: Modified MacPherson struts with coil springs between lower control arm and X-member and larger front stabilizer bar. Rear suspension: Torque arm/track bar with live axle and coil springs and larger rear stabilizer bar. Brakes: Front disc/rear drum. Steering: Power assist coaxial re-circulating ball bearing. Fuel tank: Fuel tank: 15.5 gal. with V-6 or TPI V-8; 16.2 gal. with four-barrel V-8.

Trans Am GTA: Body and frame: Integral body and frame with separate bolted-on sub-frame for engine and front suspension. Front suspension: Modified MacPherson struts with coil springs between lower control arm and X-member and larger front stabilizer bar. Rear suspension: Torque arm/track bar with live axle and coil springs and larger rear stabilizer bar. WS6 Special Performance package with P245/50VR16 steel-belted black sidewall tires, 16 x 8-in High-Tech turbo or diamond-spoke aluminum wheels, specific springs, gas-filled shock absorbers, special front and rear stabilizer bars and quick-ratio steering. Brakes: Four-wheel disc. Steering: Power assist coaxial re-circulating ball bearing. Fuel tank: 15.5 gal. with V-6 or TPI V-8; 16.2 gal. with four-barrel V-8.

FIREBIRD OPTIONS

W61 Firebird coupe option group No. 1 ($1,273). W63 Firebird coupe option group No. 2 ($1,792). W61 Firebird Formula option group No. 1 ($1,273). W63 Firebird Formula option group No. 2 ($1,842). W61 Firebird Trans Am coupe option group No. 1 ($1,697). W63 Firebird Trans Am coupe option group No. 2 ($1,949). W61 Firebird GTA coupe option group No. 1 ($1,701). W63 Firebird GTA coupe option group No. 2 ($1,958). WS1 base Firebird performance value package No. 1 ($265). WS3 base Firebird performance value package No. 2 ($709). WS1 Trans Am performance value package No. 1 ($839). W66 Formula option for base Firebird, includes LG4 5.0-liter V-8, QDZ tires, N96 High-Tech Turbo wheels, WS6 performance package, U21 gauge cluster, rear aero wing spoiler and Formula exterior ornamentation ($1,070). Y84 GTA option for Trans Am consists of L98 5.7-liter V-8, QDZ tires, PW7 gold diamond spoke wheels, WS6 performance package, KC4 oil cooler, J65 four-wheel disc

brakes, G80 limited-slip axle, articulating seats with custom trim, DD9 power paddle-type mirrors (on approximately the first 100 cars produced), NP5 leather appointment group, B34 front and rear mats and GTA exterior ornamentation ($2,700). LG4 5.0-liter V-8 ($400). LB9 5.0-liter TPI V-8, except in GTA ($745). LB9 5.0-liter TPI V-8 in GTA ($300 credit). L98 5.7L V-8 in Formula or Trans Am, requires MXO automatic transmission, KC4 oil cooler, WS6 performance package, J65 four-wheel disc brakes and G80 limited-slip axle ($1,045). MXO four-speed automatic transmission ($490). MM5 five-speed manual transmission in GTA ($490 credit). C60 custom air conditioning ($825). G80 limited-slip differential axle ($100). UA1 heavy-duty battery ($26). DX1 Trans Am large hood bird decal ($95). C49 electric rear window defogger ($145). NB2 California emissions ($99). KC4 engine oil cooler ($110). U21 rally gauge cluster with tachometer, trip odometer in base Firebird ($150). U52 electronic instrument cluster ($275). CC1 locking hatch roof with removable glass panels ($920). B34 front and rear floor mats ($35). DG7 dual remote-control power sport mirrors ($91). WX1 two-tone lower accent paint delete, base Firebird and Formula ($150 credit). J65 four-wheel power disc brakes ($179). UM7 seek/scan stereo radio equipment ($217). UM6 seek/scan stereo radio equipment with cassette ($339). UX1 seek/scan ETR radio with graphic equalizer and cassette ($489). UT4 seek/scan stereo radio equipment with cassette, graphic equalizer, "touch control" and more ($529). UQ7 sub-woofer speaker system ($150). UL5 AM radio delete ($56 credit). U75 power antenna ($70). D42 cargo security screen ($69). AH3 four-way manual seat adjuster ($35). AC3 six-way power driver's seat. B20 luxury trim group with custom seat belts, deluxe split folding rear seat, custom front reclining bucket seats and Pallex cloth trim, deluxe door trim, a dash-mounted map pocket and door map pockets with power windows ($319-$349). B20 custom interior with reclining bucket seats and Pallex cloth and leather trim ($619-$649). B20 custom interior with articulating bucket seats and Pallex cloth trim ($619-$649). Y99 Rally Tuned Suspension ($59). WS6 special performance package including QDZ tires and performance suspension components on Trans Am ($385). Optional tires ($68-$318) depending upon model. [Note: QDZ tires are P245/50VR16.] N24 15-in. High-Tech color-coordinated turbo wheels with locks ($215). N90 15-in. diamond-spoke color-coordinated wheels with lock ($215). AK3 custom seat and shoulder safety belts. AQ9 adjustable custom bucket seats. AU3 power door locks. A01 all tinted windows. A31 power windows. A90 power deck lid release. BS1 added acoustical insulation. B48 luggage compartment trim package with deluxe carpeting, a storage well cover with lock and carpet inserts on side, carpeted rear panels and a spare tire cover. B84 vinyl body side moldings. CD4 controlled-cycle windshield wipers. DD8 electronic day/night rearview mirror. DK6 interior roof console. D34 right-hand visor-vanity mirror. D81 body-color rear aero spoiler. D83 Rally II wheel rims. K34 cruise control with resume feature. NK3 graphite-colored three-spoke formula steering wheel. NP5 leather-wrapped formula steering wheel. N24 15 x 7-in. deep-dish High-Tech turbo cast-aluminum wheels. N33 tilt steering wheel. N90 15 x 7-in. diamond spoke cast-aluminum wheels. N96 16-in. High-Tech turbo cast-aluminum wheels with WS6 special performance package. PW7 16-in. diamond spoke cast-aluminum wheels. QAC P235/60VR15 steel-belted black sidewall tires. QYH P215/65R15 steel-belted white lettered tires. TBD articulating performance seats. TR9 lamp group with instrument panel courtesy lamp. Luggage compartment lamp, tone generator warning, seat belt warning and keys warning. WS6 performance package includes P245/50VR16 steel-belted black sidewall tires or 16 x 8-in. High-Tech turbo cast-aluminum or diamond-spoke wheels, limited-slip differential, four-wheel disc brakes, a space saver spare tire, specific springs, specific shocks, specific suspension bushings, specific front and rear stabilizer bars and quick-ratio steering.

HISTORICAL FOOTNOTES

A low-production, but historically significant, change this year was the release of a TPI V-8, similar to that used in the Corvette, as a Trans Am option. This 210-hp engine promised 6.5-second 0 to 60-mph times and enhanced the Trans Am's image among youthful new-car buyers. Nevertheless, model-year new-car sales by U.S. dealers came to 77,635 Firebirds in 1987, a decline from 96,208 in 1986. As a result, production of the Firebird and Camaro was chopped down to one factory in Van Nuys, California, and the facility in Norwood, Ohio, was permanently closed in August 1987. General Motors also canceled its GM80 program, which had the goal of developing a plastic-bodied, front-wheel-drive car to replace the Firebird/Camaro F-car series. Total model-year production of Firebirds (for all markets) stood at 88,623 cars compared to 110,483 in 1986. Based on an output of 80,439 Firebirds produced for the U.S. market only, 38.5 percent had the V-6, 30.3 percent had a carbureted V-8 and 31.2 percent had a fuel-injected V-8. Automatic transmission was used in 88.1 percent of those cars and 11.9 percent had the five-speed manual gearbox. Of the 80,439 cars, 14.8 percent had four-wheel disc brakes, 34.3 percent had a limited-slip differential, 20.8 percent had styled steel wheels, 72.6 percent aluminum wheels, 6.7 percent had automatic air conditioning and 91 percent had manual air conditioning, 67.3 percent had power windows, 56.2 percent had power door locks, 27.9 percent had an AM/FM stereo, 46.1 percent had an AM/FM cassette stereo and 24.5 percent had a premium sound system. Based on the same "universe" of 80,439 cars, 96.8 percent had an adjustable steering column, 72.7 percent had cruise control and 39 percent had the hatch roof option.

The GTA received four-wheel disc brake, more power equipment, and 225-hp TPI engine for 1998.

1988

Higher-tech

For 1988, the Firebird was available in base, Formula, Trans Am and GTA iterations. A 2.8-liter V-6 teamed with a five-speed manual transmission was the base power train. The Formula and Trans Am came standard with a 5.0-liter V-8, while the 5.7-liter GTA V-8 was optional. Prices started at $11,413.

Seventeen major product changes were promoted. An improved TPI system for V-8s was even available on base models, which also gained serpentine drive belts, 15 x 7 in. deep-dish High-Tech Turbo or diamond-spoke aluminum wheels, a redesigned four-spoke steering wheel, an AM/FM stereo with seek-and-scan and clock, Pallex cloth interior trim, a new Camel-colored interior, monotone paint treatments and a choice of two new exterior hues, Silver Blue Metallic or Orange Metallic.

Formulas had new 16 x 8-inch High-Tech Turbo cast-aluminum wheels and a new 5.0-liter TPI V-8 that was also standard in Trans Ams. All 5.0- and 5.7-liter TPI V-8s now came with new analog full-gauge clusters and a 140-mph speedometer. New standard features for Trans Am GTAs included a remote deck-lid release, a power antenna, a right-hand visor vanity mirror, power windows and door locks, side moldings, air conditioning, tinted glass, lamps, a PASS-Key theft-deterrent system, controlled-cycle wipers, a rear window defogger, cruise control, tilt steering, AM/FM stereo with cassette and graphic equalizer, redundant radio controls, integral rear headrests and Metrix cloth trim.

Firebird model year production totaled 42,448 base Firebirds and 20,007 Trans Ams. The Formula

and GTA models were considered option packages.

I.D. NUMBERS

Pontiac's 17-symbol Vehicle Identification Number (VIN) was on the upper left surface of the instrument panel, visible through the windshield. The first symbol indicates country of origin: 1=U.S. The second symbol indicates manufacturer: G=General Motors. The third symbol indicates make: 2=Pontiac division. The fourth and fifth symbols indicate body type and series: F/S=Firebird; F/W=Firebird Trans Am. The sixth symbol denotes body type: 2=two-door hatchback style 87. Symbol seven indicates restraint code: 1=manual belts; 3=manual belts with driver's airbag; 4=automatic belts. Symbol eight is an engine code: S=2.8-liter Mexico-built EFI/TBI V-6; E=5.0-liter U.S.-built EFI/TBI V-8; F=5.0-liter U.S.-built 5.0-liter EFI/TPI H.O. V-8; 8=5.7-liter U.S.-built EFI/TPI V-8. The 11th symbol indicates the GM assembly plant: L=Van Nuys, California. The remaining symbols were sequential unit production number at factory, starting with 100001. The GM Service Parts identification label on the console door contained the complete VIN number, the option codes, the paint type, paint code and interior trim code. V-6 engine code on right side of block near water pump. V-8 engine code on pad on front of block below right cylinder head. Engine production codes for 1988 were: [2.8-liter EFI/TBI V-6] CFA-CFB-CBL-CBM, [5.0-liter EFI/TBI V-8] CJB-CJC, [5.0-liter EFI/TPI V-8] CHA-CHB-CHP, [5.7-liter 230-hp EFI/TPI V-8] CUA.

COLORS

11=White [3967], 12=Silver Metallic [8535],

13S=Silver Metallic [9021], 15=Medium Gray Metallic [8573], 19=Black [848], 23=Medium Maui Blue Metallic [9184], 40=White [8554], 41=Black [8555], 51=Yellow Gold [8929], 63=Medium Orange Metallic [9188], 74=Flame Red Metallic [8748], 81=Bright Red [8774], 87=Gunmetal Metallic [9243]. The exterior color numbers in brackets are those used on the GM Service Parts label.

FIREBIRD - SERIES 2F - V-6/V-8

Base models shared an improved Tuned Port Induction (TPI) system on V-8 engines, which also had new serpentine accessory belt drives. Base models now came with standard 15 x 7 in. deep-dish High-Tech Turbo cast-aluminum or diamond-spoke aluminum wheels, a redesigned four-spoke steering wheel, a UM7 Delco ETR AM/FM stereo with seek/scan and clock, Pallex cloth interior trim, a new Camel colored interior, monotone paint treatments and a choice of two new exterior colors (Silver Blue Metallic or Orange Metallic). Base Firebirds also featured a 2.8-liter MFI V-6, a center high-mounted stop lamp, complete analog instrumentation, a full-length console with instrument panel, side window defoggers, a front air dam, the GM Computer Command Control system, a hatch "pull-down" feature, rectangular-shaped concealed quartz halogen headlights, cloth reclining front bucket seats, a folding rear seat, a lockable storage compartment, P215/65R15 BSW tires, a five-speed manual transmission, and "wet-arm" windshield wipers.

Model Number	Body/Style Number	Body Type & Seating	Factory Price	Shipping Weight	Production Total
FIREBIRD SERIES F/S (V-6)					
2F	FS2	2d hatchback-5P	$10,999	3,083 lbs.	Note 1
FIREBIRD SERIES F/S (V-8)					
2F	FS2	2d hatchback-5P	$11,399	3,102 lbs.	Note 1

Note 1: Base Firebird series production totaled 28,973.

FORMULA FIREBIRD - SERIES F/S (V-8)

Formulas had new 16 x 8 in. High-Tech Turbo cast-aluminum wheels and a new 5.0-liter EFI/TBI V-8 engine that was also standard in the Trans Am. The high-output 5.0-liter EFI/TPI V-8 was available at extra cost along with the 5.7-liter EFI/TPI V-8 and all cars with TPI engines now came with full-gauge analog clusters and a 140-mph speedometer. Formula

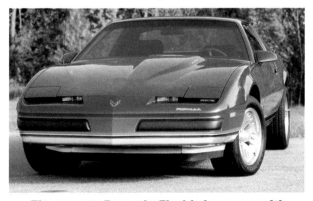

The sporty Formula Firebirds came with domed hoods and some different body graphics.

Firebirds also featured a body-color aero rear deck lid spoiler, a dome hood, Formula graphics, a center high-mounted stop lamp, a full-length console with instrument panel, side window defoggers, a front air dam, the GM Computer Command Control system, a hatch "pull-down" feature, rectangular-shaped concealed quartz halogen headlights, a UM7 Delco ETR AM/FM stereo, cloth reclining front bucket seats, a folding rear seat, a four-spoke steering wheel, a lockable storage compartment, 16 x 8-in. High-Tech aluminum wheels, the WS6 special performance suspension with MacPherson strut front suspension, P245/50VR16 Goodyear Eagle black sidewall tires, a five-speed manual transmission, "wet-arm" windshield wipers and two-tone paint and striping.

Model Number	Body/Style Number	Body Type & Seating	Factory Price	Shipping Weight	Production Total
2F	FS2	2d hatchback-5P	$11,999	3,296 lbs.	13,475

FIREBIRD TRANS AM - SERIES F/W (V-8)

Firebird Trans Ams featured a body Aero package, hood and front fender air extractors, hood air louvers, a body-color aero rear deck lid spoiler, fog lamps, Soft-Ray tinted glass, a 5.0-liter throttle-body-injection (EFI/TBI) V-8, a center high-mounted stop lamp, complete analog instrumentation, a full-length console with instrument panel, side window defoggers, a front air dam, the GM Computer Command Control system, a hatch "pull-down" feature, rectangular-shaped concealed quartz halogen headlights, monochromatic paint, a UM7 Delco ETR AM/FM stereo, cloth reclining front bucket seats, a folding rear seat, a four-spoke steering wheel, a lockable storage compartment, a five-speed manual transmission, 15 x 7 in. deep-dish High-Tech turbo cast-aluminum or diamond-spoke aluminum wheels as a no-cost option, "wet-arm" windshield wipers and the Y99 Rally Tuned Suspension with P215/65R15 Goodyear Eagle GT black sidewall tires, a 32-mm front stabilizer bar a 23-mm rear stabilizer bar and 12.7:1 quick-ratio steering.

Model Number	Body/Style Number	Body Type & Seating	Factory Price	Shipping Weight	Production Total
FIREBIRD TRANS AM SERIES F/W (V-8)					
2F	FW2	2d hatchback-5P	$13,999	3,355 lbs.	8,793

FIREBIRD TRANS AM GTA - SERIES F/W - (V-8)

New features for GTA models included a power antenna, a right-hand visor-vanity mirror, power windows, power door locks, body side moldings, tinted glass, a lamp group, the PASS-Key theft deterrent system, controlled-cycle wipers, a rear window defogger, cruise control, tilt steering, an AM/FM stereo with cassette and graphic equalizer, steering wheel mounted radio controls, integral rear seat headrests and Metrix cloth interior trim (optional for the Trans Am). In addition, leather-trimmed articulating front bucket seats were a new GTA model option. To the standard Trans Am features GTAs also added four-wheel disc brakes, air conditioning, dual power mirrors, power articulating cloth front bucket seats, a power deck lid release, power door locks, a Delco UT4 ETR "touch control" AM/FM stereo with cassette and anti-theft feature, a WS6 Special Performance package, a leather-wrapped steering wheel, P245/50VR16 Goodyear Eagle tires, a four-speed automatic transmission and 16 x 8-in. gold-colored lightweight diamond-spoke aluminum wheels. The 5.7-liter 225-hp Tune Port Injected (EFI/TPI) V-8 was standard with four-speed automatic transmission in the GTA. (It was also optional in Formula and Trans Am models).

A total of 13,475 Formula Firebirds rolled off the assembly lines for 1988.

Model Number	Body/Style Number	Body Type & Seating	Factory Price	Shipping Weight	Production Total
2F	FW2	2d hatchback-5P	$19,299	3,406 lbs.	11,214

ENGINES

Base V-6 [UPC LB8]: Overhead valve. Cast-iron block and head. Aluminum intake manifold. Displacement: 173 cid. (2.8 liter). Bore & stroke: 3.50 x 2.99 in. Compression ratio: 8.5:1. Brake horsepower: 135 at 4900 rpm. Torque: 160 ft. lbs. at 3900 rpm. Fuel system: EFI/TBI. Standard in base Firebird. Produced in U.S., Canada, or Mexico. [VIN code S].

Base 5.0-liter V-8 [UPC LO3]: Overhead valve. Cast-iron block and head. Aluminum intake manifold. Displacement: 305 cid. Bore & stroke: 3.74 x 3.48 in. Brake horsepower: 170 at 4000 rpm. Torque: 225 ft. lbs.. at 2400 rpm. Compression ratio: 9.3:1. Fuel system: EFI/TBI. Produced in U.S. or Canada. Standard Formula and Trans Am. Available in base Firebird. [VIN code E].

5.0-liter H.O. V-8 [UPC LB9]: Overhead valve. Cast-iron block and head. Aluminum intake manifold. Displacement: 305 cid. Bore & stroke: 3.74 x 3.48 in. Brake horsepower: 190 at 4000 rpm (automatic). Torque: 295 ft. lbs. at 2800 rpm (automatic). Compression ratio: 9.3:1. Fuel system: TPI. Available with four-speed automatic in Formula and Trans Am (delete option in GTA). [VIN code F].

5.0-liter H.O. V-8 [UPC LB9]: Overhead valve. Cast-iron block and head. Aluminum intake manifold. Displacement: 305 cid. Bore & stroke: 3.74 x 3.48 in. Brake horsepower: 215 at 4400 rpm (manual). Torque: 285 ft. lbs. at 3200 rpm (manual). Compression ratio: 9.3:1. Fuel system: TPI. UPC Code: LB9. Available with five-speed manual in Formula and Trans Am (delete option in GTA). [VIN code F].

5.7-liter GTA V-8 [UPC B2L]: Overhead valve. Cast-iron block and head. Aluminum intake manifold. Displacement: 350 cid. Bore & stroke: 4.00 x 3.48 in. Brake horsepower: 225 at 4400 rpm. Torque: 330 ft. lbs. at 3200 rpm. Compression ratio: 9.3:1. Fuel system: EFI/TPI. UPC Standard with four-speed automatic in GTA (optional in Formula and Trans Am). Includes low-profile air induction system with aluminum plenum and individual aluminum tuned runners, an extruded dual fuel rail assembly with computer controlled fuel injectors and a special low-restriction single exhaust system. [VIN code 8].

CHASSIS

Firebird: Wheelbase: 101 in. Overall length: 188 in. Overall width: 72.4 in. Overall height: 50 in. Front

tread: 60.7 in. Rear tread: 61.6 in. Front headroom: 37 in. Front legroom: 43 in. Front shoulder room: 57.7 in. Front hip room: 56.3 in. Rear headroom: 35.6 in. Rear legroom: 29.8 in. Rear shoulder room: 56.3 in. Rear hip room: 42.8 in.

Formula Firebird: Wheelbase: 101 in. Overall length: 188 in. Overall width: 72.4 in. Overall height: 50 in. Front tread: 60.7 in. Rear tread: 61.6 in. Front headroom: 37 in. Front legroom: 43 in. Front shoulder room: 57.7 in. Front hip room: 56.3 in. Rear headroom: 35.6 in. Rear legroom: 29.8 in. Rear shoulder room: 56.3 in. Rear hip room: 42.8 in.

Trans Am: Wheelbase: 101 in. Overall length: 191.6 in. Overall width: 72.4 in. Overall height: 50 in. Front tread: 60.7 in. Rear tread: 61.6 in. Front headroom: 37 in. Front legroom: 43 in. Front shoulder room: 57.7 in. Front hip room: 56.3 in. Rear headroom: 35.6 in. Rear legroom: 29.8 in. Rear shoulder room: 56.3 in. Rear hip room: 42.8 in.

Trans Am GTA: Wheelbase: 101 in. Overall length: 191.6 in. Overall width: 72.4 in. Overall height: 50 in. Front tread: 60.7 in. Rear tread: 61.6 in. Front headroom: 37 in. Front legroom: 43 in. Front shoulder room: 57.7 in. Front hip room: 56.3 in. Rear headroom: 35.6 in. Rear legroom: 29.8 in. Rear shoulder room: 56.3 in. Rear hip room: 42.8 in.

TECHNICAL

Base Firebird: Body and frame: Integral body and frame with separate bolted-on sub-frame for engine and front suspension. Chassis: Front engine/rear drive. Base transmission: Five-speed manual with overdrive. Optional transmission: Four-speed automatic. Axle ratio: 3.08:1 (with 5.0-liter TBI V-8 and manual transmission). Axle ratio: 2.73:1 (with 5.0-liter TBI V-8 and four-speed automatic transmission). Front suspension: MacPherson struts with coil springs. Rear suspension: Live axle with coil springs and torque arm. Front brakes: Power-assisted vented discs. Rear brakes: Power-assisted drums. Brake system total swept area: 389.9 sq. in. Steering: Power assist coaxial re-circulating ball bearing. Fuel tank: 15.5.

Formula Firebird: Body and frame: Integral body and frame with separate bolted-on sub-frame for engine and front suspension. Chassis: Front engine/rear drive. Base transmission: Five-speed manual with overdrive. Optional transmission: Four-speed automatic. Axle ratio: 3.08:1 (with 5.0-liter TBI V-8 and manual transmission). Axle ratio: 2.73:1 (with 5.0-liter TBI V-8 and four-speed automatic transmission). Axle ratio: 3.45:1 (with 5.0-liter TPI V-8 and five-speed manual transmission). Axle ratio: 3.23:1 (with 5.0-liter TPI V-8 and four-speed automatic transmission). Axle ratio: 3.27:1 (with 5.7-liter V-8 and four-speed automatic transmission and with 5.0-liter TPI V-8 and four-speed automatic transmission). Front suspension: MacPherson struts with coil springs, torque bar and 36-mm stabilizer bar. Rear suspension: Live axle with coil springs, torque arm and 24-mm rear stabilizer bar. Front brakes: Power-assisted vented discs. Rear brakes: Power-assisted drums. Brake system total swept area: 389.9 sq. in. Steering: Power assist 12.7:1 quick-ratio. Fuel tank: 15.5.

Trans Am: Body and frame: Integral body and frame with separate bolted-on sub-frame for engine and front suspension. Chassis: Front engine/rear drive. Base transmission: Five-speed manual with overdrive. Optional transmission: Four-speed automatic. Axle ratio: 3.08:1 (with 5.0-liter TBI V-8 and manual transmission). Axle ratio: 2.73:1 (with 5.0-liter TBI V-8 and four-speed automatic transmission). Axle ratio: 3.45:1 (with 5.0-liter TPI V-8 and five-speed manual transmission). Axle ratio: 3.23:1 (with 5.0-liter TPI V-8 and four-speed automatic transmission). Axle ratio: 3.27:1 (with 5.7-liter V-8 and four-speed automatic transmission and with 5.0-liter TPI V-8 and four-speed automatic transmission). Front suspension: MacPherson struts with coil springs and 32-mm front stabilizer bar. Rear suspension: Live axle with coil springs, torque arm and 23-mm rear stabilizer bar. Special springs and bushings and 12.7:1 quick-ratio steering. Front brakes: Power-assisted vented discs. Rear brakes: Power-assisted drums. Brake system total swept area: 389.9 sq. in. Steering: Power assist coaxial re-circulating ball bearing. Fuel tank: 15.5.

Trans Am GTA: Body and frame: Integral body and frame with separate bolted-on sub-frame for engine and front suspension. Chassis: Front engine/rear drive. Base transmission: Four-speed automatic. Axle ratio: 2.73:1 (with 5.0-liter TBI V-8 and four-speed automatic transmission). Axle ratio: 3.45:1 (with 5.0-liter TPI V-8 and five-speed manual transmission). Axle ratio: 3.23:1 (with 5.0-liter TPI V-8 and four-speed automatic transmission). Axle ratio: 3.27:1

The hot 225-hp 5.7-liter engine and gold diamond-spoke wheels were standard on the GTA.

(with 5.7-liter V-8 and four-speed automatic transmission and with 5.0-liter TPI V-8 and four-speed automatic transmission). Front suspension: MacPherson struts with coil springs, torque bar and 36-mm stabilizer bar. Rear suspension: Live axle with coil springs, torque arm and 24-mm rear stabilizer bar. Brakes: Power-assisted four-wheel vented discs 307 sq. in. total swept area. Steering: Power assist 12.7:1 quick-ratio. Fuel tank: 15.5.

OPTIONS

Air conditioning with Soft-Ray tinted glass. Limited-slip axle. Four-wheel disc brakes. Electric rear window defogger. 5.0-liter EFI V-8. 5.0-liter TPI high-output V-8. 5.7-liter TPI high-output V-8. Gauge package, requires electronic air conditioning controls. Hatch roof with removable glass panels. Luxury trim group. Power antenna. Power door locks. Power windows. UM6 Delco ETR AM/FM stereo. UX1 Delco ETR AM/FM stereo. Subwoofer six-speaker system. Articulating bucket seats with inflatable lumbar and back-wing bolsters. Leather seat trim. Four-speed automatic transmission. Deep-dish High-Tech 15-in. Turbo cast-aluminum wheels with locking package (no-charge option). 15-in. diamond-spoke cast-aluminum wheels. 16-in. diamond-spoke cast-aluminum wheels. 16-in. High-Tech Turbo cast-aluminum wheels, available with WS6 suspension only. Base Firebird option group No. 1 includes air conditioning with Soft-Ray

The 1988 Pontiac Formula received new cast-aluminum wheels and a new 5.0-liter engine.

tinted glass, tilt steering, custom-colored safety belts, body side moldings, controlled-cycle windshield wipers and passenger visor-vanity mirror. Base Firebird option group No. 2 includes air conditioning with Soft-Ray tinted glass, tilt steering, custom-colored safety belts, body side moldings, controlled-cycle windshield wipers, passenger visor-vanity mirror, lamp group, cruise control, remote deck lid release and four-way manual driver's seat adjuster. Base Firebird option group No. 3 includes air conditioning with Soft-Ray tinted glass, tilt steering, custom-colored safety belts, body side moldings, controlled-cycle windshield wipers, passenger visor-vanity mirror, lamp group, cruise control, remote deck lid release, four-way manual driver's seat adjuster, power windows and power door locks. Firebird Formula option group No. 1 includes air conditioning with Soft-Ray tinted glass, tilt steering, custom-colored safety belts, body side moldings, controlled-cycle windshield wipers and passenger visor-vanity mirror. Firebird Formula option group No. 2 includes air conditioning with Soft-Ray tinted glass, tilt steering, custom-colored safety belts, body side moldings, controlled-cycle windshield wipers, passenger visor-vanity mirror, lamp group, cruise control, remote deck lid release and four-way manual driver's seat adjuster. Firebird Formula option group No. 3 includes air conditioning with Soft-Ray tinted glass, tilt steering, custom-colored safety belts, body side moldings, controlled-cycle windshield wipers, passenger visor-vanity mirror, lamp group, cruise control, remote deck lid release, four-way manual driver's seat adjuster, power windows and power door locks. Firebird Trans Am option group No. 1 includes air conditioning with Soft-Ray tinted glass, tilt steering, custom-colored safety belts, body side moldings, controlled-cycle windshield wipers, passenger visor-vanity mirror, lamp group, cruise control, remote deck lid release and standard Trans Am extras. Firebird Trans Am option group No. 3 includes air conditioning with Soft-Ray tinted glass,

tilt steering, custom-colored safety belts, body side moldings, controlled-cycle windshield wipers, passenger visor-vanity mirror, lamp group, cruise control, remote deck lid release, power windows, power door locks, leather appointments group and power sport mirrors, plus standard Trans Am extras.

HISTORICAL FOOTNOTES

Michael J. Losh continued as Pontiac Motor Division general manager in 1988, with E. M. Schlesinger heading up sales and service responsibilities. Bill O'Neill once again handled public relations. John Sawruk from Engineering was also the official Pontiac historian. All 1988 Firebirds were built in Van Nuys, California. Model-year production of Firebirds was 62,467 units. Model year U.S. dealer sales were 59,459 Firebirds. The fuel-injected V-6 was used in 35.3 percent of all Firebirds built and 64.7 percent were fitted with a fuel-injected V-8. The four-speed automatic transmission was used in 85.2 percent of production, while 14.8 percent had the five-speed manual gearbox. All Firebirds had power steering and power brakes, 24.8 percent had four-wheel disc brakes, 100 percent had steel-belted radial tires and aluminum wheel rims, 12.3 percent had automatic air conditioning and 81.4 percent had manual air conditioning, 98.3 percent had Solar-Ray tinted glass, 70.9 percent had power windows, 62.5 percent had power door locks, 26.3 percent had power seats, 94.3 percent had an adjustable steering column, 67.6 percent had cruise control, 94.3 percent had windshield wipers with a delay feature, 98.9 percent had a digital clock, 72.4 percent had a rear window defogger, 100 percent had a remote-control left-hand rearview mirror and 29.7 percent had a similar right-hand rearview mirror. The hatch roof option was installed on 42.2 percent of all 1988 Firebirds, 12.2 percent had an AM/FM stereo, 56.5 percent had a stereo-cassette system, 30.2 percent had a premium sound system and 10.2 percent had premium radio speakers.

The 1988 Firebird featured many changes inside and out.

The hot 20th Anniversary GTA boasted a turbo V-6 power plant.

The Trans Am Turns 20

To commemorate the first Trans Am, 1,500 copies of a special 20th Anniversary model were built in 1989. They had a 250-hp turbocharged V-6 was coupled to a four-speed automatic and limited-slip axle. All 20th Anniversary cars were white with a camel interior. The GTA nose emblem was changed to a cloisonné 20th Anniversary insignia with a similar emblem on the sail panels. Turbo Trans Am emblems were on the front fenders. This model featured a competition-type 18-gallon fuel tank, four-wheel power disc brakes, gold 16-in. diamond-spoke aluminum wheels, stainless steel exhaust splitters, analog gauges with a turbo boost gauge, contoured rear seats and Official Indy 500 Pace Car decals that could be installed by Pontiac dealers at the buyer's request.

All Firebirds had new basecoat/clearcoat paint for a glossy, long-lasting finish. A new color was Bright Blue Metallic. Door-glass seals were improved to allow less wind noise. The self-adjusting rear disc brakes were completely revised with a new caliper-and-rotor design. Standard equipment across the entire 1989 Firebird lineup included three-point lap and shoulder belts for rear-seat occupants. PASS-Key anti-theft protection, previously standard on GTAs, was now standard on all models. An electronic resistor embedded in the ignition key activated a control module in the ignition lock to determine when the anti-theft system was activated. GM said that the system had reduced Corvette thefts by 40 percent and suggested that it should be helpful in reducing insurance costs.

The lowest-priced Firebird was the base model with a standard 2.8-liter V-6 and five-speed manual transmission. All V-6s now had the FE1 suspension package with 30mm front/18mm rear anti-roll bars.

Added standard equipment for V-8 models included a Trans Am-style F41 suspension and air conditioning. Base Firebirds carried the same exterior striping package as Formulas.

The Formula was aimed at buyers interested in high-performance "street machines." It provided maximum "oomph" for a minimum price. This package's "Trans Am engine" had 10 additional horsepower thanks to a new dual catalytic converter low-back-pressure exhaust system. Pontiac claimed this equated to a two- to three-second cut in 0 to 60-mph times. Also standard was a WS6 suspension, air conditioning and revised exterior graphics with narrower stripes.

The Trans Am used a 5.0-liter TBI 170-hp V-8, five-speed manual transmission, limited-slip differential, F41 suspension, Firestone Firehawk GTX tires, 15 x 7-in. cast-aluminum wheels and air conditioning.

Described as the "ultimate Firebird," the Trans Am GTA had a 5.7-liter 235-hp TPI V-8 borrowed from the Corvette and a long list of upgraded technical or upscale cosmetic features, including cross-laced aluminum wheels, cloth articulating bucket seats and redundant radio controls on the steering wheel hub. The GTA notchback also had 45/55 split folding rear seats with integral headrests. Special leather-upholstered bucket seats were optional.

Firebird model year production included 49,048 base Firebirds and 15,358 Trans Ams. Production of Formula and GTA model options was not broken out.

I.D. NUMBERS

Pontiac's 17-symbol vehicle identification number (VIN) was on the upper left surface of the instrument panel, visible through the windshield. The first symbol indicates country of origin: 1=U.S. The second symbol indicates manufacturer: G=General Motors. The third symbol indicates make: 2=Pontiac division. The fourth and fifth symbols indicate body type and series: F/S=Firebird, F/W=Firebird Trans Am. The sixth symbol denotes body type: 2=two-door hatchback style 87. The seventh symbol indicates restraint system: 1=manual belts, 3=manual belts with driver's airbag. Symbol eight is an engine code: E=5.0-liter U.S./Canada-built fuel-injected V-8; F=5.0-liter U.S.-built fuel-injected V-8; S=2.8-liter Mexico-built fuel-injected V-6; 7=Turbocharged 3.8-liter U.S.-built fuel-injected V-6 and 8=5.7-liter U.S.-built fuel-injected V-8. Next is a check digit. The tenth symbol denotes model year (K=1989). The 11th symbol indicates the GM assembly plant L=Van Nuys, California. The last six symbols are the consecutive unit number at the factory. The GM Service Parts identification label on the console door contained the complete VIN number, the option codes, the paint type, paint code and interior trim code. V-6 engine code on right side of block near water pump. V-8 engine code on pad on front of block below right cylinder head. Engine production codes for 1989 were: [2.8-liter EFI/TBI V-6] AAH-AAJ-ACM-AAK, [3.8-liter Turbocharged EFI/TBI V-6] NDA, [5.0-liter EFI/TBI V-8] AKH-AKJ, [5.0-liter EFI/TPI V-8] ATA-ATB-ATF-ATM, [5.7-liter EFI/TPI V-8] AWA-AWK.

COLORS

19=Black [848], 23=Medium Maui Blue Metallic [9537], 40=White [8554], 41=Black [8555], 74=Flame Red Metallic [9535], 81=Bright Red [8774], 82=Medium Rosewood Metallic [8990], 87=Gunmetal Metallic [9243], 87=Gunmetal Metallic [9536] and 98=Bright Blue Metallic [9591]. The exterior color numbers in brackets are those used on the GM Service Parts label.

FIREBIRD - SERIES 2F - V-6/V-8

For 1989, Pontiac's premium performer continued its more-than-two-decades heritage of high-powered excitement. From performance machine enthusiasts to sporty car buyers looking for trademark styling, the Firebird offered a complete range of power and price. Again there were four regular models: Firebird, Formula, Trans Am and Trans Am GTA. There was also a special limited edition 25th Anniversary "Indy Pace Car" version of the GTA with a high-output V-6 pirated from the Buick GNX. All Firebirds came with V-8s and the base model also came with a V-6 for entry-level sports car buyers. Multi-tec fuel injectors were added to 1989 engines for more reliability and less susceptibility to fuel fouling. The self-adjusting rear disc brakes were completely revised with a new caliper and rotor design. PASS-Key anti-theft protection, previously standard only on the GTA, became standard on all Firebirds. An electronically coded resistor embedded in the ignition key activated a control module in the ignition lock, which determined when the anti-theft vehicle start-up system should be activated. GM noted that the system had been successful in reducing Corvette thefts by 40 percent and said that it should be helpful in holding down Firebird owners' insurance premiums. Door glass seals were improved for better sealing and less wind noise. The entire Firebird line also got clearcoat paint over the

base color for a long-lasting high-gloss finish. New in the color lineup was Bright Blue Metallic. Standard equipment across the entire 1989 Firebird lineup included three-point lap and shoulder belts for rear seat occupants. Available options now offered across the F-car line included removable T-tops, a variety of radios and an all-new compact digital disc player with the Delco II theft deterrent system that rendered the unit inoperative if power was interrupted. The lowest-priced Firebird was the base model with a standard 2.8-liter V-6 and five-speed manual transmission. For 1989, V-6s received the FE1 suspension package with 30mm front and 18mm rear anti-roll bars. Added standard equipment for V-8 models included a Trans Am-style F41 suspension and air conditioning. The base Firebird carried the same exterior striping package as the Formula. Standard equipment for the base Firebird included the V-6, power brakes, a center high-mounted stoplight, a full-length console with integral instrument panel, a front air dam, a Rally gauge cluster (including a coolant temperature gauge, an oil pressure gauge, a water temperature gauge, a voltmeter and a tachometer), GM's Computer Command Control system, a hatch "pull-down" feature, concealed rectangular quartz halogen headlights, monochromatic paint themes, a UM7 Delco ETR AM/FM stereo, safety belts, cloth-upholstered reclining front bucket seats, side window defoggers, Soft-Ray tinted glass, a four-spoke steering wheel, a lockable storage compartment, P215/65R15 steel-belted black sidewall radial tires, a five-speed manual transmission, "wet-arm" windshield wipers and High-Tech Turbo cast-aluminum wheel rims.

Model Number	Body/Style Number	Body Type & Seating	Factory Price	Shipping Weight	Production Total
FIREBIRD SERIES F/S (V-6)					
F/S	87	2d hatchback-5P	$11,999	3,083 lbs.	Note 1
FIREBIRD SERIES F/S (V-8)					
F/S	87	2d hatchback-5P	$12,399	3,300 lbs.	Note 1

Note 1: Base Firebird series production totaled 32,376.

FORMULA FIREBIRD - SERIES 2F/S V-6/V-8

For 1989, the Formula Firebird carried the same exterior striping package as the base model. The Formula Firebird was aimed at buyers interested in high-performance "street machines" and was designed to provide maximum "oomph" for a minimum price. This package provided the Trans Am engine, which had a 10-hp boost in power due to the use of a new dual catalytic converter low-back-pressure exhaust system. Pontiac claimed this equated to a .2 to .3-second cut in 0 to 60-mph acceleration times. Also standard on Formulas was the WS6 package and revised exterior graphics with narrower body side stripes. As on the base Firebird, the Formula's standard equipment included a center high-mounted stoplight, a full-length console with integral instrument panel, a front air dam, a Rally gauge cluster (including a coolant temperature gauge, an oil pressure gauge, a water temperature gauge, a voltmeter and a tachometer), GM's Computer Command Control system, a hatch "pull-down" feature, concealed rectangular quartz halogen headlights, monochromatic paint themes, a

UM7 Delco ETR AM/FM stereo, safety belts, cloth-upholstered reclining front bucket seats, side window defoggers, Soft-Ray tinted glass, a four-spoke steering wheel, a lockable storage compartment, a five-speed manual transmission, "wet-arm" windshield wipers and High-Tech Turbo cast-aluminum wheel rims. The Formula also added a 5.0-liter EFI V-8, air conditioning, a body-color aero rear deck lid spoilers, a dome hood, "Formula" body graphics, two-tone paint and striping, High-Tech Turbo deep-dish cast-aluminum wheels and a special Level III performance suspension with P245/50ZR16 Goodyear Eagle steel-belted black sidewall tires.

Model Number	Body/Style Number	Body Type & Seating	Factory Price	Shipping Weight	Production Total
FORMULA FIREBIRD SERIES FS (V-8)					
F/S	87	2d hatchback-5P	$13,949	3,334 lbs.	16,670

FIREBIRD TRANS AM SERIES 2F/W V-8

The 1989 Trans Am had a standard 5.0-liter TBI V-8 engine, five-speed manual transmission and limited-slip differential. Also included were F41 underpinnings with 34-mm front and 23-mm rear anti-roll bars and recalibrated springs and shocks, Firestone Firehawk GTX tires, 15 x 7-in. High-Tech Turbo cast-aluminum wheels and air conditioning. As on the base Firebird, the Tran Am standard equipment included a center high-mounted stoplight, a full-length console with integral instrument panel, a front air dam, a Rally gauge cluster (including a coolant temperature gauge, an oil pressure gauge, a water temperature gauge, a voltmeter and a tachometer), GM's Computer Command Control system, a hatch "pull-down" feature, concealed rectangular quartz halogen headlights, monochromatic paint themes, a UM7 Delco ETR AM/FM stereo, safety belts, cloth-upholstered reclining front bucket seats, side window defoggers, Soft-Ray tinted glass, a four-spoke steering wheel, a

lockable storage compartment, P215/65R15 steel-belted black sidewall radial tires, a five-speed manual transmission, "wet-arm" windshield wipers and High-Tech Turbo cast-aluminum wheel rims. The Trans Am also added the 170-hp engine, an Aero body package, hood air louvers, a body-color Aero rear deck lid spoiler, integral fog lamps, a leather appointments group and a Level II suspension.

Model Number	Body/Style Number	Body Type & Seating	Factory Price	Shipping Weight	Production Total
F/W	87	2d hatchback-5P	$15,999	3,298 lbs.	9,631

FIREBIRD TRANS AM GTA - SERIES F/W - V-8

The Trans Am GTA was described as the "ultimate Firebird" (even though the Indy Pace Car version really was the ultimate Firebird). The regular Trans Am GTA had a 5.7-liter TPI V-8 borrowed from the Corvette, plus four-speed automatic transmission, a limited-slip differential, the special level III WS6 performance suspension with Goodyear P245/50ZR16 steel-belted black sidewall tires, 36-mm front and 24-mm rear anti-roll bars, deflected-disc gas-filled shocks and struts, 16-in. lightweight cross-laced aluminum wheels, cloth articulating bucket seats, air conditioning, cruise control, power windows, power door locks, a power antenna, a Delco ETR "touch control" AM/FM cassette radio with graphic equalizer and redundant radio controls on the steering wheel hub and Delco-lock anti-theft feature. Also included on the GTA notchback (a $700 option that replaced the rear glass hatch with a coupe-like rear window treatment and full rear deck lid) was a 45/55 split-folding rear seats with integral headrests. Leather bucket seats with increased thigh support and inflatable lumbar and side bolsters were optional. As on the base Firebird, the Tran Am standard equipment included a center high-mounted stoplight, a full-length console with integral instrument panel, a front air dam, a Rally

This car is one of two special 1989 turbo V-6 convertibles created by PAS, Inc.

gauge cluster (including a coolant temperature gauge, an oil pressure gauge, a water temperature gauge, a voltmeter and a tachometer), GM's Computer Command Control system, a hatch "pull-down" feature, concealed rectangular quartz halogen headlights, monochromatic paint themes, safety belts, side window defoggers, Soft-Ray tinted glass, a lockable storage compartment, "wet-arm" windshield wipers and High-Tech Turbo aluminum wheel rims. To this the GTA also added the features listed above, plus a power deck lid release, dual power-operated Sport-style outside rearview mirrors, a cargo screen (except GTA notchback), an electric rear window defogger and a leather-wrapped steering wheel.

Model Number	Body/Style Number	Body Type & Seating	Factory Price	Shipping Weight	Production Total
F/W	87	2d hatchback-5P	$20,339	3,519 lbs.	Note 2
F/W	87	2d notchback-5P	$21,039	3,486 lbs.	Note 2

Note 2: Trans Am GTA series production totaled 11,214.

FIREBIRD 20th ANNIVERSARY TRANS AM GTA INDY PACE CAR - SERIES F/W – TURBOCHARGED V-6

To commemorate the 20th anniversary of the first Firebird Trans Am, a special series of 1,500 20th Anniversary Trans Ams was produced. These cars were above the level of the GTA model and were really the "ultimate" Trans Ams of this year. Power was provided by a 3.8-liter V-6 with a Garrett T3 turbocharger and air-to-air intercooler that developed 250 hp. It was coupled to a four-speed automatic transmission and limited-slip rear axle. All 20th Anniversary Trans Ams were painted white and had camel-colored interiors. Externally, the GTA emblem on the nose was changed to a special "20th Anniversary" insignia. A similar cloisonné emblem could be found on the sail panels. "Turbo Trans Am" emblems on the front fenders replaced the standard GTA script in the same location. Also included with this model was a larger, baffled, competition-type 18-gal. fuel tank, four-wheel power disc brakes, 16-in. gold-finished lightweight diamond-spoke aluminum wheels, stainless steel exhaust splitters, analog gauges with turbo boost gauge, unique contoured rear seats. Each of these cars came with a complete set of Official Indianapolis 500 Pace Car decals for the doors and windshield. These could be owner or dealer installed.

Model Number	Body/Style Number	Body Type & Seating	Factory Price	Shipping Weight	Production Total
F/W	87	2d hatchback-5P	$32,000	3,346 lbs.	Note 3

Note 3: Pontiac originally announced that it would build 1,500 20th Anniversary Pace Cars as part of the total run of Firebirds. Actually, 1,550 turbo V-6 models were made, including two convertibles created by PAS, Inc. (the firm that built all of the pace cars) by utilizing Camaro parts. T-tops were used on 1,515 of the cars and 1,350 had leather interiors. These totals are imbedded in the figures above.

ENGINES

Base V-6 [UPC LB8]: V-block. Overhead valve. Cast-iron block and head. Aluminum intake manifold. Displacement: 173 cid. (2.8 liters). Bore & stroke: 3.50 x 2.99 in. Compression ratio: 8.5:1. Brake horsepower: 135 at 4900 rpm. Torque: 160 ft. lbs. at 3900 rpm. Fuel system: EFI/TBI. Standard in base Firebird. Produced in U.S., Canada, or Mexico. VIN code W, S,

The 1989 20th Anniversary Trans Am GT Indy Pace car was equipped with a special 3.8-liter turbo V-6 that kicked out 250 HP.

Jerry Heasley photo

or 9.

305 V-8 [UPC L03]: Overhead valve. Eight-cylinder. Cast-iron block and head. Aluminum intake manifold. Displacement: 305 cid. (5.0-liter). Bore & stroke: 3.74 x 3.48 in. Brake horsepower: 170 at 4000 rpm. Torque: 255 ft. lbs. at 2400 rpm. Compression ratio: 9.3:1. Fuel system: EFI/TBI. UPC Code: L03. Produced in U.S. or Canada. Standard Formula and Trans Am. Available in base Firebird. VIN code E or F.

5.0-liter V-8 [UPC LB9]: Cast-iron block and head. Aluminum intake manifold. Displacement: 305 cid. (5.0-liter). Bore & stroke: 3.74 x 3.48 in. Brake horsepower: 190 at 4000 rpm (automatic) or 225 at 4400 rpm (manual/dual exhausts). Torque: 295 ft. lbs. at 2800 rpm (automatic) or 285 ft. lbs. at 3200 rpm (manual). Compression ratio: 9.3:1. Fuel system: TPI. UPC Code: LB9. Available with five-speed manual in Formula and Trans Am (delete option in GTA). Available with four-speed automatic in same applications. VIN code E or F.

GTA 5.7-liter V-8 [UPC B2L]: Overhead valve. Cast-iron block and head. Aluminum intake manifold. Displacement: 350 cid. (5.7-liter). Bore & stroke: 4.00 x 3.48 in. Brake horsepower: 235 at 4400 rpm. Torque: 330 ft. lbs. at 3200 rpm. Compression ratio: 9.3:1. Fuel system: EFI/TPI. Standard with four-speed automatic in GTA (optional in Formula and Trans Am). Includes low-profile air induction system with aluminum plenum and individual aluminum tuned runners, an extruded dual fuel rail assembly with computer controlled fuel injectors and a special low-restriction single exhaust system. VIN code 8.

Indy Pace Car Turbo V-6 [UPC LG3]: Garrett T3 turbocharger. Overhead valve. Cast-iron block and head. Aluminum intake manifold. Displacement: 231 cid. (3.8-liter). Bore & stroke: 3.80 x 3.40 in. Brake horsepower: 250 at 4000 rpm. Torque: 340 ft. lbs. at 2800 rpm. Compression ratio: 8.0:1. Fuel system: EFI/SFI. Standard in 20th Anniversary Trans Am Indy Pace Car. VIN code W, S, or 9.

CHASSIS

Firebird: Wheelbase: 101 in. Overall length: 188 in. Overall width: 72.4 in. Overall height: 50 in. Front tread: 60.7 in. Rear tread: 61.6 in. Front headroom:

37 in. Front legroom: 43 in. Front shoulder room: 57.7 in. Front hip room: 56.3 in. Rear headroom: 35.6 in. Rear legroom: 29.8 in. Rear shoulder room: 56.3 in. Rear hip room: 42.8 in.

Formula Firebird: Wheelbase: 101 in. Overall length: 188 in. Overall width: 72.4 in. Overall height: 50 in. Front tread: 60.7 in. Rear tread: 61.6 in. Front headroom: 37 in. Front legroom: 43 in. Front shoulder room: 57.7 in. Front hip room: 56.3 in. Rear headroom: 35.6 in. Rear legroom: 29.8 in. Rear shoulder room: 56.3 in. Rear hip room: 42.8 in.

Trans Am: Wheelbase: 101 in. Overall length: 191.6 in. Overall width: 72.4 in. Overall height: 50 in. Front tread: 60.7 in. Rear tread: 61.6 in. Front headroom: 37 in. Front legroom: 43 in. Front shoulder room: 57.7 in. Front hip room: 56.3 in. Rear headroom: 35.6 in. Rear legroom: 29.8 in. Rear shoulder room: 56.3 in. Rear hip room: 42.8 in.

Trans Am GTA: Wheelbase: 101 in. Overall length: 191.6 in. Overall width: 72.4 in. Overall height: 50 in. Front tread: 60.7 in. Rear tread: 61.6 in. Front headroom: 37 in. Front legroom: 43 in. Front shoulder room: 57.7 in. Front hip room: 56.3 in. Rear headroom: 35.6 in. Rear legroom: 29.8 in. Rear shoulder room: 56.3 in. Rear hip room: 42.8 in.

TECHNICAL

Base Firebird: Body and frame: Integral body and frame with separate bolted-on sub-frame for engine and front suspension. Chassis: Front engine/rear drive. Base transmission: Five-speed manual with overdrive. Optional transmission: Four-speed automatic. Axle ratio: 3.08:1 (with 5.0-liter TBI and manual). Axle ratio: 2.73:1 (with 5.0-liter TBI and four-speed automatic). Front suspension: MacPherson struts with coil springs. Rear suspension: Live axle with coil springs and torque arm. Front brakes: Power-assisted vented discs. Rear brakes: Power-assisted drums. Brake system total swept area: 389.9 sq. in. Steering: Power assist coaxial re-circulating ball bearing. Fuel tank: 15.5.

Formula Firebird: Body and frame: Integral body and frame with separate bolted-on sub-frame for engine and front suspension. Chassis: Front engine/rear drive. Base transmission: Five-speed manual with overdrive. Optional transmission: Four-speed automatic. Axle ratio: 3.08:1 (with 5.0-liter TBI and manual). Axle ratio: 2.73:1 (with 5.0-liter TBI and four-speed automatic). Axle ratio: 3.45:1 (with 5.0-liter TPI and five-speed manual). Axle ratio: 3.23:1 (with 5.0-liter TPI and four-speed automatic). Axle ratio: 3.27:1 (with 5.7-liter and four-speed automatic and with 5.0-liter TPI and four-speed automatic). Front suspension: MacPherson struts with coil springs, torque bar and 36-mm stabilizer bar. Rear suspension: Live axle with coil springs, torque arm and 24-mm rear stabilizer bar. Front brakes: Power-assisted vented discs. Rear brakes: Power-assisted drums. Brake system total swept area: 389.9 sq. in. Steering: Power assist 12.7:1 quick-ratio. Fuel tank: 15.5.

Trans Am: Body and frame: Integral body and frame with separate bolted-on sub-frame for engine and front suspension. Chassis: Front engine/rear drive. Base transmission: Five-speed manual with overdrive. Optional transmission: Four-speed automatic. Axle ratio: 3.08:1 (with 5.0-liter TBI and manual). Axle ratio: 2.73:1 (with 5.0-liter TBI and four-speed automatic). Axle ratio: 3.45:1 (with 5.0-liter TPI and five-speed manual). Axle ratio: 3.23:1 (with 5.0-liter TPI and four-speed automatic). Axle ratio: 3.27:1 (with 5.7-liter and four-speed automatic and with 5.0-liter TPI and four-speed automatic). Front suspension: MacPherson struts with coil springs and 32-mm front stabilizer bar. Rear suspension: Live axle with coil springs, torque arm and 23-mm rear stabilizer bar. Special springs and bushings and 12.7:1 quick-ratio steering. Front brakes: Power-assisted vented discs. Rear brakes: Power-assisted drums. Brake system total swept area: 389.9 sq. in. Steering: Power assist co-axial re-circulating ball bearing. Fuel tank: 15.5.

Trans Am GTA: Body and frame: Integral body and frame with separate bolted-on sub-frame for engine and front suspension. Chassis: Front engine/rear drive. Base transmission: Four-speed automatic. Axle ratio: 2.73:1 (with 5.0-liter TBI and four-speed automatic). Axle ratio: 3.23:1 (with 5.0-liter TPI and four-speed automatic). Axle ratio: 3.27:1 (with 5.7-liter and four-speed automatic). Front suspension: MacPherson struts with coil springs, torque bar and 36-mm stabilizer bar. Rear suspension: Live axle with coil springs, torque arm and 24-mm rear stabilizer bar. Brakes: Power-assisted four-wheel vented discs 307 sq. in. total swept area. Steering: Power assist 12.7:1 quick-ratio. Fuel tank: 15.5.

OPTIONS

1SA option package No. 1 for V-6 Firebird includes C60 air conditioning, B84 body side moldings, TR9 lamp group with instrument panel courtesy lamp, luggage compartment lamp, console lamp and tone generator warnings for seat belt, keys and headlamps (Total package $1,200; savings $311; net price $889). ISB option package No. 2 for V-6 Firebird includes option package No. 1, plus A31 power windows, AU3 power door locks and door map pockets, AH3 four-way manual driver seat adjustment, K34 cruise control, A90 remote deck lid release and DC4 inside rear view mirror with dual reading lamps (Total package $1,587; savings $1,400; net price $187). 1SA option package No. 1 for Firebird V-8, Formula and Trans Am, includes B84 body side moldings, TR9 lamp group A31 power windows and AU3 power door locks including door map pockets (Total package $1,200; savings $499; net price $701). 1SB option package No. 2 for Firebird V-8 and Formula includes option package No. 1, plus AH3 four-way manual driver seat adjustment, K34 cruise control, A90 remote deck lid release, DC4 inside rear view mirror with dual reading lamps and DG7 left- and right-hand power sport mirrors (Total package $883; savings $1,400; net price $517). 1SB option package No. 2 for Trans Am, Firebird V-8 and Formula, includes same as option package No.2 for Firebird, except no charge for AH3 power adjustable driver's seat (Total package $848;

The 1989 Trans Am GTA was equipped with a performance suspension and the base engine was a TPI V-8 borrowed from the Corvette.

savings $1,400; net price ($552). R6A Firebird and Formula Value Option package, includes CC1 T-top roof and UM6 AM/FM stereo with cassette (Total package $1,052; savings $250; net price $802). R6A Trans Am Value Option package includes CC1 T-top roof, B20 Custom interior trim, UM6 AM/FM stereo with cassette and D42 cargo area screen (Total package $1,414; savings $325; net price $1,089). R6A Trans Am GTA Value Option package includes CC1 T-top roof and AQ9 leather interior B20 (Total package $1,370; savings $350; net price $1,020). L88 MPFI V-6 engine in Firebird (no charge). L03 5.0-liter TBI V-8 (not available in GTA, no-cost option in Formulas and Trans Ams, in base Firebird $409). LB9 5.0-liter MPFI V-8 with G80 limited-slip differential (in Formula or Trans Am $745; in GTA $300 credit). B2L 5.7-liter MPFI V-8 requires automatic transmission, engine oil cooler, four-wheel disc brakes, limited-slip differential and QLC tires ($1,045 in Formula or Trans Am; no charge GTA). MM5 five-speed manual transmission, not available with 5.7-liter V-8 and requires four-wheel disc brakes with LB9 engine (Firebird, Formula and Trans Am no charge; GTA with LB9 $490). MXO four-speed automatic transmission ($515 in Firebird, Formula and Trans Am; standard: in GTA). C60 Custom air conditioning, required on Firebird with L03 V-8, standard on other models (in other Firebirds $795). G80 Limited-slip differential, available only and required with LB9 or B2L V-8s (standard in GTA; in Firebird, Formula or Trans Am $100). C49 Electric rear window defogger, included on GTA ($150). N10 Dual converter exhaust, required with LB9 V-8 with MM5 transmission on Firebird Formula and Trans Am GTA, required with B2L V-8 on Formula ($155). KC4 Engine oil cooler, required with B2L V-8, not available with other V-8s and standard on GTA ($110). NB2 required California emissions ($100). CC1 Locking hatch roof with removable glass panels, includes sunshades ($920). TR9 Lamp group with instrument panel courtesy lamp, luggage compartment lamp, console lamp and tone generator warnings (Standard: in GTA; in others ($34). D86 Deluxe two-tone paint, not available Trans Am or GTA; standard Formula; in base Firebird ($150). WX1 Lower-accent-style two-tone paint, as a delete option

for Formula only ($150 credit). J65 four-wheel power disc brakes, available only and required with B2L V-8 or LB9 V-8 with MM5 manual transmission; standard in GTA; in Formula ($79). AU3 Power door locks, available only with A31 power windows and standard with GTA (in other models $155). DG7 Dual power remote sport mirrors, standard on GTA ($91). A31 Power windows, only with power door locks and door map pockets, standard in GTA ($250). UM7 AM/FM ETR stereo and clock with Delco electronic seek/scan tuning, integral digital clock, co-axial front speakers and dual extended-range rear speakers, not available in GTA; in other Firebirds (no charge). UM6 Delco AM/FM ETR stereo and cassette with auto reverse, electronic seek/scan tuning, integral digital clock and dual front and rear co-axial speakers, not available in GTA; in other Firebirds ($132). UX1 AM/FM Delco AM stereo/FM ETR stereo radio and cassette with auto reverse and search-and-replay, electronic seek/scan tuning, integral five-band graphic equalizer, integral digital clock and dual front and rear co-axial speakers; not available GTA; in Firebird, Formula, Trans Am without value package R6A ($282). UX1 AM/FM Delco AM stereo/FM ETR stereo radio and cassette with auto reverse and search-and-replay, electronic seek/scan tuning, integral five-band graphic equalizer, integral digital clock and dual front and rear co-axial speakers; not available GTA; in Firebird, Formula, Trans Am with value package R6A ($150). UT4 Delco AM stereo/FM ETR stereo radio and cassette with auto reverse and search-and-replay, electronic seek/scan tuning, integral five-band graphic equalizer, integral digital clock, touch control for volume, tone, balance and fade, steering wheel controls and dual front and rear co-axial speakers (Not available in Firebird; standard in GTA; in Formula and Trans Am without value package R6A $447). UT4 Delco AM stereo/FM ETR stereo radio and cassette with auto reverse and search-and-replay, electronic seek/scan tuning, integral five-band graphic equalizer, integral digital clock, touch control for volume, tone, balance and fade, steering wheel controls and dual front and rear co-axial speakers (Not available Firebird; standard: in GTA; in Formula and Trans Am with value package R6A $315). UA1 Delco AM stereo/FM ETR stereo radio and compact disc player, electronic seek/scan tuning, integral five-band graphic equalizer, integral digital clock and dual front and rear co-axial speakers (not available in Firebird; standard in GTA; in Formula and Trans Am without value package R6A $528). UA1 Delco AM stereo/FM ETR stereo radio and compact disc player, electronic seek/scan tuning, integral five-band graphic equalizer, integral digital clock and dual front and rear co-axial speakers (not available in Firebird; standard in GTA; in Formula and Trans Am with value package R6A $394; in GTA $79). U75 Power antenna, standard: on GTA; on other Firebirds ($70). D42 Cargo security screen (standard with GTA hatchback; not available with GTA notchback; with other Firebirds ($59). AR9 Custom reclining bucket seats with Palex cloth trim, front-and-rear luxury seats, luxury door panels, a split-folding rear seat, a carpeted cowl kick panel and Matrix cloth trim (not available in GTA; no charge with B20 luxury interior trim; in Trans Am ($293). AQ9 Articulating luxury bucket seats (standard in GTA with Metrix cloth trim; optional only in GTA with Ventura leather trim $450). AQ9 notchback roof for GTA only ($700). QPH P215/65R15 black sidewall touring tires, Firebird only (no charge). QNS P215/65R15 black sidewall steel-belted radial on Trans Am only, not available with B2LV-8 (no cost). QLC High-performance P245/50ZRl6 black sidewall steel-belted radial tires, includes WS6 performance suspension and PW7 wheels (standard Formula and GTA; not available on Firebird; on Trans Am ($385). N24 15-in. deep-dish charcoal High-Tech Turbo aluminum wheels with locking package (not available for Formula or GTA (no charge other Firebirds). PEO 16-in. deep-dish High-Tech Turbo aluminum wheels with locking pack-age, Formula only (no charge). PW7 16-in. color-coordinated (black, silver or gold) diamond-spoke aluminum wheels with locking package (Trans Am and GTA only at no charge).

HISTORICAL FOOTNOTES

John Middlebrook was the general manager of Pontiac Motor Division. Firebird sales managed to stay about even with 1988, although Pontiac lost a bit of overall market share. Model-year production of Firebirds was 64,406 units. Of those cars, 2.4 percent had the turbocharged V-6, 38.8 percent had the regular V-6, 58.8 percent had a V-8, 85.9 percent had an automatic transmission and 14.1 percent had the five-speed manual transmission. A limited-slip differential was ordered for 32.7 percent of the total production, 9 percent had an AM/FM stereo radio, 64.8 percent had an AM/FM cassette radio, 25.6 percent had a premium sound system, 0.6 percent had a CD changer, 16.5 percent had premium radio speakers, 100 percent had reclining seats and an adjustable steering column, 71.5 percent had cruise control, 69.5 percent had a rear window defogger, 53.5 percent had dual remote-control outside rearview mirrors, 59.8 percent had a hatch roof, 25.3 percent had four-wheel disc brakes, 23.5 percent had styled steel wheels, 76.5 percent had styled aluminum wheels, 98.2 percent had manual air conditioning, 81.7 percent had power windows, 82.5 percent had power door locks, 30.9 percent had sequential fuel injection and 69.1 percent had multi-port fuel injection. *Road & Track* magazine road tested a Turbo Trans Am and recorded a 5.3-second 0-to-60 run. The car did the quarter mile in 13.91 seconds at about 90 mph.

Pontiac produced only 1,054 regular Trans Ams for model year 1990.

Last of its Generation

Vital to Pontiac's future plans in 1990 was GM's decision to replace the aging F-Car platform. Once again, there were rumors floating around the auto industry that perhaps no replacement at all would be forthcoming. But the corporation would soon snuff out the scuttlebutt by announcing a major decision to source both Firebirds and Camaros from a factory in Canada. As a result, a build out of the current model was scheduled for mid-December 1989 at the Van Nuys, California, factory where F-Cars were manufactured.

Firebirds grew larger in 1990 and were upgraded to a new 3.1-liter base V-6 engine. All TPI V-8s (standard in Trans Ams) had a speed-density-metering system. All Firebirds also got driver and passenger airbags, a new self-adjusting parking brake, dual body-color sport mirrors and new instrument panel switches for the rear defogger, rear hatch release and fog lamps. Brilliant Red Metallic was a new color for the year.

Base Firebirds had new seat and armrest trim, plus a different rear spoiler design. Standard features included a five-speed manual gearbox, FE1 suspension, P215/65R15 tires, front disc/rear drum brakes and AM/FM stereo with clock. The 15 x 7-in. High-Tech aluminum wheels were standard.

Formulas got more of a performance image with a new aero-style rear deck lid spoiler. Also standard were air conditioning, tinted glass, a WS6 sport suspension, P245/50ZR16 tires and a TBI V-8 engine. The Formula's 6-in. deep-dish, High-Tech wheels had machine-finished faces and silver metallic ports.

The Trans Am switched from the TBI V-8 to a hotter TPI V-8. It also had an F41 handling suspension, limited-slip differential, P215/65R15 Firehawk GTX

tires and 15-in. deep-dish, High-Tech, turbo cast-aluminum wheels with machined faces and charcoal metallic ports, plus a leather appointment group. The luxury version of the Trans Am was the fully loaded GTA with its 5.7-liter TPI V-8, dual catalytic converter exhaust system, four-speed automatic transmission, four-wheel disc brakes, P245/50ZR-16 Goodyear performance tires and 16 x 8-in. gold crosslace aluminum wheels. Also standard were a leather-wrapped steering wheel, articulating custom bucket seats with inflatable lumbar and lateral supports, a rear defogger, a cargo screen, a full-featured Delco ETR AM/FM stereo cassette with equalizer, a power antenna, power side view mirrors, power windows and power door locks.

Model-year production was 18,046 base Firebirds and 2,570 Trans Ams. That was a 68 percent reduction from 1989, caused by a recession that severely impacted automobile sales across the entire market spectrum.

I.D. NUMBERS

Pontiac's 17-symbol vehicle identification number (VIN) for passenger cars was on the upper left surface of the instrument panel, visible through the windshield. The first symbol indicates country of origin: 1=U.S. The second symbol indicates manufacturer: G=General Motors. The third symbol indicates make: 2=Pontiac division. The fourth and fifth symbols for passenger cars indicated body type and series: F/S=Firebird, F/W=Firebird Trans Am. The sixth symbol on passenger cars denoted body type: 2=two-door hatchback style 87. The seventh symbol on passenger cars indicated the type of restraint system: 3=manual belts with driver airbag. Symbol eight for passenger cars was an engine code: E=5.0-liter fuel-injected V-8,

F=5.0-liter fuel-injected V-8, T=3.1-liter fuel-injected V-6, 8=5.7-liter fuel-injected V-8. The ninth symbol for cars and trucks is a check digit. The tenth symbol for cars and trucks denotes model year (L=1990). The 11th symbol for cars and trucks indicates the GM assembly plant: L=Van Nuys, California. The last six symbols are the consecutive unit number at the factory. V-6 engine code on right side of block near water pump. V-8 engine code on pad on front of block below right cylinder head. Engine production codes for 1990 were: [2.8-liter EFI/TBI V-6] BSH-BTJ-CDC-CFD, [5.0-liter EFI/TBI V-8] BLC-BLD, [5.0-liter EFI/TPI V-8] BLF-BLH-BLJ, [5.7-liter EFI/TPI V-8] BMB-BMK.

COLORS

23=Medium Maui Blue Metallic [9537], 40=White [8554], 41=Black [848], 75=Brilliant Red Metallic [9540], 81=Bright Red Metallic [8774], 87=Medium Gray Metallic Gunmetal [9243] and 98=Ultra Blue Metallic [9591].

FIREBIRD - SERIES 2F/S - V-6/V-8

For 1990, Firebirds had a larger and more powerful base V-6. All TPI V-8s (standard in Trans Ams) had a speed-density metering system. All Firebirds also had an inflatable airbag restraint system, a new self-adjusting parking brake, dual body-color sport mirrors and new instrument panel switches for the rear defogger, rear hatch release and fog lamps. Brilliant Red Metallic was a new color replacing Flame Red. Base Firebirds had new seat and armrest trim, plus a different rear spoiler design. Standard features included a 3.1-liter V-6 with MFI, power brakes, a center high-mounted stoplight, a full-length console with integral instrument panel, a front air dam, a Rally gauge cluster (including coolant temperature gauge, oil pressure gauge, water temperature gauge, voltmeter and tachometer), the GM Computer Command Control engine management system, a hatch pull-down feature, concealed rectangular quartz halogen headlamps, a monochromatic paint theme, a PASS-Key theft-deterrent system, a Delco ETR stereo radio, safety belts (including manual lap and shoulder belts for driver and right front passenger and three-point rear seat belts in outboard positions only), reclining front bucket seats with cloth trim, a rear folding seat with cloth trim, side window defoggers, Soft-Ray tinted glass, a four-spoke tilt steering wheel with driver's side inflatable restraint system (airbag), a lockable storage compartment, P215/65R15 steel-belted black sidewall tires, a five-speed manual transmission and High-Tech Turbo cast-aluminum wheels with locks.

Model Number	Body/Style Number	Body Type & Seating	Factory Price	Shipping Weight	Production Total
FIREBIRD SERIES F/S (V-6)					
F/S	87	2d hatchback-5P	$11,320	3,210 lbs.	Note 1
FIREBIRD SERIES F/S (V-8)					
F/S	87	2d hatchback-5P	$11,670	3,266 lbs.	Note 1

Note 1: Total base Firebird production was 13,204.

FORMULA FIREBIRD - SERIES F/S V-8

The Formula package was actually an option for the base Firebird, but it was merchandised almost as if it was a separate model. For 1990, the Formula Firebird had more of a performance image. Its equipment list added an aero-style rear deck lid spoiler, air conditioning, tinted glass, the WS6 suspension and a TBI V-8 engine. The Formula's 6-in. deep-dish High-Tech wheels had machined-finished faces and silver metallic ports. Standard features included power brakes, a center high-mounted stoplight, a full-length console with integral instrument panel, a front air dam, a Rally gauge cluster (including coolant temperature gauge, oil pressure gauge, water temperature gauge, voltmeter and tachometer), the GM Computer Command Control engine management system, a hatch pull-down feature, concealed rectangular quartz halogen headlamps, a monochromatic paint theme, a PASS-Key theft-deterrent system, a Delco ETR stereo radio, safety belts (including manual lap and shoulder belts for driver and right front passenger and three-point rear seat belts in outboard positions only), reclining front bucket seats with cloth trim, a rear folding seat with cloth trim, side window defoggers, Soft-Ray tinted glass, a four-spoke tilt steering wheel with driver's side inflatable restraint system (airbag), a lockable storage compartment and a five-speed manual transmission. In addition the Formula also had a 5.0-liter V-8 engine with EFI, air conditioning, a body-color aero rear deck lid spoiler, a dome hood, Formula graphics, a special Level III performance suspension, P245/50ZR16 speed-rated Goodyear Eagle steel-belted black sidewall tires, two-tone paint and striping and deep-dish High-Tech Turbo cast-aluminum wheels with locks.

Model Number	Body/Style Number	Body Type & Seating	Factory Price	Shipping Weight	Production Total
F/S	87	2d hatchback-5P	$14,610	3,338 lbs.	4,832

TRANS AM - SERIES F/W - V-8

For 1990, the Trans Am had a more powerful engine, an F41 handling suspension, a limited-slip differential and 15-in. deep-dish High-Tech Turbo cast-aluminum wheels with machined faces and charcoal metallic ports. Standard features included power brakes, a center high-mounted stoplight, a full-length console with integral instrument panel, a front air dam, a Rally gauge cluster (including coolant temperature gauge, oil pressure gauge, water temperature gauge, voltmeter and tachometer), the GM Computer Command Control engine management system, a hatch pull-down feature, concealed rectangular quartz halogen headlamps, a monochromatic paint theme, a PASS-Key theft-deterrent system, a Delco ETR stereo radio, safety belts (including manual lap and shoulder belts for driver and right front passenger and three-point rear seat belts in outboard positions only), reclining front bucket seats with cloth trim, a rear folding seat with cloth trim, side window defoggers, Soft-Ray tinted glass, a four-spoke tilt steering wheel with driver's side inflatable restraint system (airbag), a lockable storage compartment and a five-speed manual transmission. In addition, the Trans Am added a 5.0-liter TPI V-8, an aero body package, hood air louvers and air extractors, a body-color aero rear deck lid spoiler, fender air extractors, fog lamps, a leather appointment group, a Level II suspension and P215/65R15 steel-belted black sidewall Firestone Firehawk GTX radial tires

Model Number	Body/Style Number	Body Type & Seating	Factory Price	Shipping Weight	Production Total
F/S	87	2d hatchback-5P	$16,510	3,338 lbs.	1,054

TRANS AM GTA - SERIES F/W - V-8

The GTA package was actually an option for the Trans Am, but it was merchandised almost as if it was a separate model. For 1990, this luxury version of the Trans Am had standard features including power brakes, a center high-mounted stoplight, a full-length console with integral instrument panel, a front air dam, a Rally gauge cluster (including coolant temperature gauge, oil pressure gauge, water temperature gauge, voltmeter and tachometer), the GM Computer Command Control engine management system, a hatch pull-down feature, concealed rectangular quartz halogen headlamps, a monochromatic paint theme, a PASS-Key theft-deterrent system, a Delco ETR stereo radio, safety belts (including manual lap and shoulder belts for driver and right front passenger and three-point rear seat belts in outboard positions only), reclining front bucket seats with cloth trim, a rear folding seat with cloth trim, side window defoggers, Soft-Ray tinted glass, a four-spoke tilt steering wheel with driver's side inflatable restraint system (airbag), a lockable storage compartment and a five-speed manual transmission. In addition the GTA had a 5.7-liter H.O. V-8 with TPI, an aero package, hood air louvers, hood air extractors, a limited-slip axle, a body-color aero rear deck lid spoiler, four-wheel power disc brakes, cruise control, fog lamps, a leather appointment group, dual power Sport outside rearview mirrors, power articulating front bucket seats, a power rear deck lid release, power door locks, power windows, a Delco ETR "touch control" AM/FM stereo with cassette and graphic equalizer and Delco-Lock anti-theft system, a special Level III performance suspension, a leather-wrapped steering wheel with supplemental restraint system and redundant radio controls, P245/50ZR16 Goodyear "Gatorback" steel-belted black sidewall radial tires, a four-speed automatic transmission and diamond-spoke aluminum wheels.

Model Number	Body/Style Number	Body Type & Seating	Factory Price	Shipping Weight	Production Total
F/W	87	2d hatchback-5P	$23,320	3,554 lbs.	1,442

ENGINES

Base V-6 [UPC L88]: Overhead valve. Cast-iron block and head. Low-restriction aluminum intake manifold. Fast burn combustion chambers. Electronic spark control. Displacement: 191 cid. (3.1-liter). Bore x stroke: 3.50 x 3.31 in. Compression ratio: 8.75:1. Brake horsepower: 140 at 4400 rpm. Torque: 180 ft. lbs. at 3600 rpm. Fuel system: EFI/MFI. Standard in base Firebird. Produced in U.S., Canada, or Mexico. VIN code T.

5-liter V-8 [UPC L03]: Overhead valve. Cast-iron block and head. Aluminum intake manifold. Fast burn combustion chambers. Electronic spark control. Roller valve lifters. Crank-triggered triple-coil ignition. Displacement: 305 cid. Bore x stroke: 3.74 x 3.48 in. Brake horsepower: 170 at 4400 rpm. Torque: 255 lb.-ft. at 2400 rpm. Compression ratio: 9.3:1. Fuel system: EFI/TBI. UPC Code: L03. Produced in U.S. or Canada. Standard Formula. Available in base Firebird. VIN code E or F.

5.0-liter H.O. V-8 [UPC LB9]: Optional in Formula or Trans Am with four-speed automatic transmission Overhead valve. Cast-iron block and head. Aluminum tuned runner intake manifold. Roller lifter hydraulic cam. Displacement: 305 cid. Bore x stroke: 3.74 x 3.48 in. Brake horsepower: 200 at 4400 rpm. Torque: 295 ft. lbs. at 3200 rpm. Compression ratio: 9.3:1. Fuel system: EFI/TPI. VIN code E or F.

5.0-liter H.O. V-8 [UPC LB9]: Optional H.O. V-8 in Formula and GTA with five-speed manual transmission. Overhead valve. Cast-iron block and head. Aluminum tuned runner intake manifold. Roller lifter hydraulic cam. Displacement: 305 cid. Bore x stroke: 3.74 x 3.48 in. Brake horsepower: 225 at 4600 rpm. Torque: 300 ft. lbs. at 3200 rpm. Compression ratio: 9.3:1. Fuel system: EFI/TPI. Available with five-speed manual in Formula and Trans Am (delete option in GTA). VIN code E or F.

GTA 5.7-liter V-8 [UPC B2L]: Overhead valve. Cast-iron block and head. Aluminum tuned runner intake manifold. Roller lifter hydraulic cam. Fast-burn combustion chambers. Displacement: 350 cid. (5.7-liter). Bore x stroke: 4.00 x 3.48 in. Brake horsepower: 235 at 4400 rpm. Torque: 340 ft. lbs. at 3200 rpm. Compression ratio: 9.3:1. Fuel system: EFI/TPI. Standard with four-speed automatic in GTA (optional in Formula and Trans Am). Includes low-profile air induction system with aluminum plenum and individual aluminum tuned runners, an extruded dual fuel rail assembly with computer controlled fuel injectors and a special low-restriction single exhaust system. VIN code 8.

CHASSIS

Base Firebird: Wheelbase: 101.0 in. (all). Overall length: 188.1 in. Width: 72.4 in. Height: 50.0 in. Front tread: 60.7 in. Rear tread: 61.6 in. Front headroom: 37 in. Rear headroom: 35.6 in. Front legroom: 43 in. Rear legroom: 29.8 in. Front shoulder room: 57.7 in. Rear shoulder room: 56.3 in. Front hip room: 56.3 in. Rear hip room: 42.8 in.

Formula Firebird: Wheelbase: 101.0 in. (all). Overall length: 188.1 in. Width: 72.4 in. Height: 50.0 in. Front tread: 60.7 in. Rear tread: 61.6 in. Front headroom: 37 in. Rear headroom: 35.6 in. Front legroom: 43 in. Rear legroom: 29.8 in. Front shoulder room: 57.7 in. Rear shoulder room: 56.3 in. Front hip room: 56.3 in. Rear hip room: 42.8 in.

Trans Am: Wheelbase: 101.0 in. (all). Overall length: 191.6 in. Width: 72.4 in. Height: 50.0 in. Front tread: 60.7 in. Rear tread: 61.6 in. Front headroom: 37 in. Rear headroom: 35.6 in. Front legroom: 43 in. Rear legroom: 29.8 in. Front shoulder room: 57.7 in. Rear shoulder room: 56.3 in. Front hip room: 56.3 in. Rear hip room: 42.8 in.

The 1990 GTA was loaded inside and usually featured the standard 5.7-liter H.O V-8.

Trans Am GTA: Wheelbase: 101.0 in. (all). Overall length: 191.6 in. Width: 72.4 in. Height: 50.0 in. Front tread: 60.7 in. Rear tread: 61.6 in. Front headroom: 37 in. Rear headroom: 35.6 in. Front legroom: 43 in. Rear legroom: 29.8 in. Front shoulder room: 57.7 in. Rear shoulder room: 56.3 in. Front hip room: 56.3 in. Rear hip room: 42.8 in.

TECHNICAL

Base Firebird: Chassis: Front engine/rear drive. Base transmission: Five-speed manual. Optional transmission: Four-speed automatic. Front suspension: Fully independent with modified MacPherson strut and low-friction ball bearing upper strut mount and 30mm anti-roll bar. Rear suspension: Live axle with coil springs, longitudinal lower control arm and torque arm, transverse track bar and 18mm anti-roll bar. Steering: Power re-circulating ball, 14.1:1 ratio. Turns lock to lock: 2.72. Turning circle: 39.1 ft. Brakes: Power vented 10.5-in. front disc/9.5-in. rear drum. Rear brakes: Power-assisted 7.87-in. drums. Fuel tank: 15.5 gal.

Formula: Front engine/rear drive. Base transmission: Five-speed manual. Optional transmission: Four-speed automatic. Front suspension: Fully independent with modified MacPherson strut and low-friction ball bearing upper strut mount and 36mm anti-roll bar. Rear suspension: Live axle with coil springs, longitudinal lower control arm and torque arm, transverse track bar and 24mm anti-roll bar. Steering: Power re-circulating ball, 12.7:1 quick-ratio with sport effort valving. Turns lock to lock: 2.26. Turning circle: 32.6 ft. (Levels II and III). Brakes: Power vented 10.5-in. front disc/9.5-in. rear drum on Formula with 5.0-liter EFI, power four-wheel vented disc 10.5-in. front and 11.7-in. rear with 5.7-liter V-8 or 5.0-liter V-8 with TPI and five-speed on Formula. Rear brakes: (with base Formula V-8) Power-assisted 7.87-in. drums. Fuel tank: 15.5 gal.

Trans Am: Front engine/rear drive. Base transmission: Five-speed manual. Optional transmission: Four-speed automatic. Front suspension: Fully inde-pendent with modified MacPherson strut and low-friction ball bearing upper strut mount and 34mm anti-roll bar. Rear suspension: Live axle with coil springs, longitudinal lower control arm and torque arm, transverse track bar and 23mm anti-roll bar. Steering: Power re-circulating ball, 12.7:1 quick-ratio with sport effort valving. Turns lock to lock: 2.47. Turning circle: 32.6 ft. Brakes: Power vented 10.5-in. front disc/9.5-in. rear drum. Rear brakes: Power-assisted 7.87-in. drums. Fuel tank: 15.5 gal.

Trans Am GTA: Chassis: Front engine/rear drive. Base transmission: Five-speed manual. Optional transmission: Four-speed automatic. Front suspension: Fully independent with modified MacPherson strut and low-friction ball bearing upper strut mount and 36mm anti-roll bar. Rear suspension: Live axle with coil springs, longitudinal lower control arm and torque arm, transverse track bar and 24mm anti-roll bar. Steering: Power re-circulating ball, 12.7:1 quick-ratio with sport effort valving. Turns lock to lock: 2.26. Turning circle: 32.6 ft. (Levels II and III). Brakes: Power four-wheel vented disc 10.5-in. front and 11.7-in. rear with 5.7-liter or 5.0-liter with TPI and five-speed. Fuel tank: 15.5 gal.

OPTIONS

1SB option package No. 1 for Firebird V-6 includ-ing C60 air conditioning and B84 body side moldings ($865). 1SC option package No. 2 for Firebird V-6 including option package No. 1 plus A31 power win-dows, AU3 power door locks and door map pockets, AH3 four-way manual driver seat adjustment, K34 cruise control, A90 remote deck lid release and DC4 inside rear view mirror with dual reading lamps ($1,603). 1SB option package No. 1 for Firebird V-8, Formula and Trans Am including B84 body side mold-ings, A31 power windows and AU3 power door locks and door map pockets ($495). 1SC option package No. 2 for Firebird V-8, and Formula including option package No. 1 plus AH3 four-way manual driver seat adjustment, K34 cruise control, A90 remote deck lid release, DC4 inside rearview mirror with dual reading lamps and DG7 left- and right-hand power Sport mirrors ($889). 1SC option package No. 2 for Trans Am, same as option package No. 2 for Firebird V-8 ($854). R6A Firebird/Formula Value Option package including CC1 T-top roof and UM6 AM/FM stereo with cassette; not available with B2L V-8 (Total package $1,070; savings $250; net price $820). R6A Trans Am Value Option package includes CC1 T-top roof, UM6 AM/FM stereo with cassette and D42 cargo area screen, not available with B2L V-8 (Total package $1,139; savings $250; net price $869). R6A Trans Am GTA Value Option package including CC1 T-top roof and AQ9 leather interior, not available with B2L V-8 (Total package $1,370; savings $350; net price $1,020). LHO 3.1-liter MPFI V-6 in Firebird (no charge). L03 5.0-liter TBI V-8, not available in Trans Am or GTA; requires C60 custom air conditioning in Formula ($350). LB9 5.0-liter MPFI V-8 requires G80 limited-slip differential; not available in Firebird; in Formula ($745); in Trans Am (no charge); in GTA in place of base V-8 ($300 credit). B2L 5.7-liter MPFI V-8, requires MX0 automatic transmission, KC4 engine oil cooler, J65 four-wheel disc brakes, G80 limited-slip differential and QLC tires; not available: in Firebird; in Formula ($1,045); in Trans Am ($300); in GTA (no charge). MM5 five-speed manual transmission, not available with 5.7-liter V-8; requires J65 four-wheel disc brakes with LB9 engine; in Firebird, Formula and Trans Am (no charge); in GTA with LB9 V-8 ($515). MX0 four-speed automatic transmission, in Firebird, Formula and Trans Am ($515); in GTA (standard equipment). C60 custom air conditioning; required on Firebird with L03 V-8; standard on other models ($805). G80 limited-slip differential, available only and required with LB9 or B2L V-8s; in Trans Am or GTA (standard); in Firebird or Formula ($100). C49 electric rear window defogger, included on GTA ($160). N10 dual converter exhaust, required with LB9 V-8 with MM5 transmission on Formula and Trans Am GTA, required with B2L V-8 on Formula ($155). NB2 required California emissions ($100). CC1 locking hatch roof with removable glass panels, includes sunshades, not available with B2L V-8, included in price of Value Option package, otherwise ($920). D86 deluxe two-tone paint, not available for Trans Am or GTA, standard on Formula, on Firebird ($150). WX1 lower-accent-style two-tone paint, as a delete option for Formula only ($150 credit). J65 four-wheel power disc brakes, available only with and required with B2L V-8, standard in GTA, in Formula and Trans Am ($179). AU3 power door locks, available only with A31 power windows, standard in GTA, in other models ($175). DG7 dual power remote Sport Mirrors, standard in GTA, in other Firebirds ($91). A31 power windows, available only with AU3 power door locks, includes door map pockets, standard in GTA, in other Firebirds ($260). U75 power antenna, standard in GTA, in other Firebirds ($70). UM7

AM/FM ETR stereo and clock with Delco electronic seek-and-scan tuning, integral digital clock, coaxial front speakers and dual extended-range rear speakers; not available in GTA and no charge in other Firebirds. UM6 Delco AM/FM ETR stereo with cassette with auto reverse, electronic seek-and-scan tuning, integral digital clock and dual front and rear coaxial speakers, not available: in GTA, in other Firebirds ($150). UX1 Delco AM/FM ETR stereo with stereo radio, cassette with auto reverse, search-and-replay, electronic seek/scan tuning, integral five-band graphic equalizer, integral digital clock and dual front and rear coaxial speakers, standard in GTA, in Firebird, Formula and Trans Am without value package R6A ($300); in Firebird, Formula and Trans Am with value package R6A ($150). U1A Delco AM/FM ETR stereo with compact disc player, electronic seek/scan tuning, integral five-band graphic equalizer, integral digital clock and dual front and rear coaxial speakers, not available in Firebird, standard in GTA; in Formula and Trans Am without value package R6A ($526); in Formula and Trans Am with value package R6A ($376). D42 cargo security screen, standard in GTA hatchback, not available in GTA notchback ($69). AR9 custom reclining bucket seats with Pallex cloth trim, not available GTA, no charge in other Firebirds. AQ9 articulating luxury bucket seats, standard in GTA with Metrix cloth trim, optional only in GTA with Ventura leather trim, included with Value Option package, without Value Option package ($450). QPH P215/65R15 black sidewall touring tires, on Firebird only (no charge). QNS P215/65R15 black sidewall steel-belted radial tires, not with B2L V-8, Trans Am only (no charge). QLC high-performance P245/50ZR16 black sidewall steel-belted radial tires; not available with Firebird, includes WS6 performance suspension and PW7 wheels, standard on Formula and GTA, optional on Trans Am only ($385).

HISTORICAL FOOTNOTES

Pontiac's model-year production was 49,657 Firebirds. That represented a mere .79 percent of all cars built in the U.S. The four-speed automatic transmission was used in 93.6 percent of the cars. The rest had the five-speed manual gearbox. Ed Lechtzin became Pontiac's director of public relations. Of the 46,760 cars made for sale in the U.S. (the balance were built here but sold in another nation), 21 percent had a limited-slip differential, 10.5 percent had four-wheel disc brakes, 9.3 percent had manual air conditioning, 79.1 percent had power door locks and windows, 64.6 percent had cruise control, 40.4 percent had dual power rearview mirrors, 57.2 percent had hatch roofs, 52.3 percent had an AM/FM stereo with cassette, 43.6 percent had a premium sound system and 1.8 percent had a CD player. Model-year sales of Firebirds hit just 39,781 cars.

The GTA was fast, but it wasn't the hottest Firebird around in 1991. Pontiac had some even faster birds racing in the SCCA Trans-Am series after a seven-year hiatus.

More Driving Fun

Although they seemed minor on the surface, 14 major changes were made on the 1991 Firebirds that bowed, early in 1990, as 1991 models. By the spring of 1990, these cars were hitting Pontiac dealerships. PMD called them "perpetual emotion machines." They had 14 major changes led by new styling that was backed up by a hot Street Legal Performance (SLP) option. A new Firebird convertible was a running addition to the model lineup.

The most visible change was a new exterior appearance. All models had restyled front and rear fascias. The front fascias — made of body-color resilient "Endura" thermoplastic — incorporated low-profile turn signals and integral air dams. At the rear, the GTA, Trans Am and Formula got a redesigned spoiler. New fascias on GTA and Trans Am models incorporated restyled taillights.

The base Firebird's Sport Appearance package included fog lights in the fascia and carried the aero look to the sides with distinctive lateral skirting. The headlights were more compact, with no sacrifice of light output. Available from dealers for all 5.0- and 5.7-liter TPI V-8s was the SLP kit, which boosted engine performance without engine modifications. It could be dealer installed or owner installed.

On all models the standard radio was upgraded to an AM/FM cassette stereo. The GTA included a cassette with five-band graphic equalizer. Acoustics were improved. New colors included Dark Green Metallic and Bright White.

Models and options were unchanged and equipment offerings were about the same. Pontiac's new general manager John G. Middlebrook announced, "Convertibles will be built on Firebird's fun-to-drive image" and a new ragtop — the first since 1969 — debuted. The Firebird version was $19,159 and the Trans Am convertible was $22,980. Both had a standard Sport Appearance package.

PMD teamed up with PAS — the firm that helped it make the 1989 20th Anniversary model's Turbo V-6 — to create a Firefox GTA with a 5.7-liter TPI V-8 in 1991. It was promoted as the prototype of a future production option. It produced 330 hp and had a ZF six-speed transmission. It could do 0-to-60 mph in 5.6 seconds and cover the quarter mile in 13.38 seconds at 103.5 mph.

Firebird model year output for 1991 went up a bit: 23,977 base models and 6,343 Trans Ams. Convertible production came to 2,000 units.

I.D. NUMBERS

Pontiac's 17-symbol Vehicle Identification Number (VIN) for passenger cars was on the upper left surface of the instrument panel, visible through the windshield. The first symbol indicates country of origin: 1=U.S. The second symbol indicates manufacturer: G=General Motors. The third symbol indicates make: 2=Pontiac Division. The fourth and fifth symbols indicated body type and series: F/S=Firebird, F/W=Firebird Trans Am. The sixth symbol on passenger cars denoted body type: 2=two-door hatchback style 87,

3=two-door convertible style 67. The seventh symbol indicated the type of restraint system: 3=manual belts with driver airbag. Symbol eight was an engine code: E=UPC L03 5.0-liter TBI V-8, F=UPC LB9 5.0-liter TPI V-8, T=UPC LH0 3.1-liter MFI V-6, 8=UPC L98 5.7-liter TPI V-8. The ninth symbol is a check digit. The tenth symbol denotes model year (M=1991). The 11th symbol indicates the GM assembly plant: L=Van Nuys, California. The last six symbols are the consecutive unit number at the factory. V-6 engine code on right side of block near water pump. V-8 engine code on pad on front of block below right cylinder head. Engine production codes for 1991 were: [2.8-liter EFI/TBI V-6] CDC-CFA-CFD, [5.0-liter EFI/TBI V-8] CLC-CLD, [5.0-liter EFI/TPI V-8] CLF-CLH-CLJ-CLW, [5.7-liter EFI/TPI V-8] CMB-CMP.

COLORS

10=White [9567], 23=Medium Maui Blue Metallic [9537], 41=Black [8555], 45=Medium Green Metallic [9539], 75=Brilliant Red Metallic [9540], 81=Bright Red Metallic [8774], 87=Medium Gray Metallic Gunmetal [9536] and 98=Ultra Blue Metallic [9591].

FIREBIRD - SERIES 2F/S - V-6/V-8

The new 1991 Firebirds were actually introduced in the spring of 1990. Their most visible change was a new exterior appearance. All models benefited from restyled front and rear fascias. The front fascia was made of body-color resilient "Endura" thermoplastic and incorporated low-profile turn signals and integral air dams. Pontiac General Manager John C. Middlebrook announced convertible versions of the base Firebird and the Trans Am on Jan. 3, 1990. All Firebirds had a driver's side airbag. All 1991 Firebirds were also protected by a PASS-Key theft deterrent system. The standard radio was upgraded to an AM/FM cassette stereo and the GTA included a cassette with five-band graphic equalizer. Acoustics were improved in all models. The Sport Appearance package on the base Firebird included fog lights in the fascia and carried the aero look to the sides with distinctive lateral skirting. The headlights were more compact, without sacrificing light output. Standard features included a 3.1-liter V-6 with MFI, power brakes, a center high-mounted stoplight, a full-length console with integral instrument panel, a front air dam, a Rally gauge cluster (including coolant temperature gauge, oil pressure gauge, water temperature

The Sport Appearance package gave base Firebirds a more aerodynamic look for 1991.

gauge, voltmeter and tachometer), the GM Computer Command Control engine management system, a hatch pull-down feature, concealed rectangular quartz halogen headlamps, a monochromatic paint theme, a PASS-Key theft-deterrent system, a Delco ETR stereo radio with cassette and clock, safety belts (including manual lap and shoulder belts for driver and right front passenger and three-point rear seat belts in outboard positions only), reclining front bucket seats with cloth trim, a rear folding seat with cloth trim, side window defoggers, Soft-Ray tinted glass, a four-spoke tilt steering wheel with driver's side inflatable restraint system (airbag), a lockable storage compartment, the FE1 suspension, P215/65R15 steel-belted black sidewall tires, a four-speed automatic transmission and 15 x 7-in. High-Tech cast-aluminum wheels with locks.

Model Number	Body/Style Number	Body Type & Seating	Factory Price	Shipping Weight	Production Total
FIREBIRD - SERIES F/S - (V-6)					
F/S	87	2d hatchback-5P	$12,690	3,121 lbs.	Note 1
F/S	67	2d convertible-5P	$19,159	—	Note 1
FIREBIRD - SERIES F/S - (V-8)					
F/S	87	2d hatchback -5P	$13,040	3,287 lbs.	Note 1
F/S	67	2d convertible-5P	$19,509	—	Note 1

Note 1: Total base Firebird production was 39,906.

FORMULA FIREBIRD - SERIES 2F/S V-8

The new 1991 Formula was fitted with a redesigned rear deck lid spoiler. New fascias on GTA and Trans Am models incorporated restyled taillights. Basic standard features included power brakes, a center high-mounted stoplight, a full-length console with integral instrument panel, a front air dam, a Rally gauge cluster (including coolant temperature gauge, oil pressure gauge, water temperature gauge, voltmeter and tachometer), the GM Computer Command Control engine management system, a hatch pull-down feature, concealed rectangular quartz halogen headlamps, a monochromatic paint theme, a PASS-Key theft-deterrent system, a Delco ETR stereo radio with cassette and clock, safety belts (including manual lap and shoulder belts for driver and right front passenger and three-point rear seat belts in outboard positions only), reclining front bucket seats with cloth trim, a rear folding seat with cloth trim, side window defoggers, Soft-Ray tinted glass, a four-spoke tilt steering wheel with driver's side inflatable restraint system (airbag) and a lockable storage compartment. The Formula added a 5.0-liter TBI V-8, a five-speed manual gearbox, the WS6 Sport Suspension, P245/50ZR16 tires, 16 x 8-in. deep-dish High-Tech Turbo cast-aluminum wheels, a limited-slip differential and air conditioning.

Model Number	Body/Style Number	Body Type & Seating	Factory Price	Shipping Weight	Production Total
F/S	87	2d hatchback-5P	$15,530	3,370 lbs.	5,549

FIREBIRD TRANS AM - SERIES 2F/W V-8

The new Trans Am also had a redesigned rear deck lid spoiler that included restyled taillights. Basic standard features included power brakes, a center high-mounted stoplight, a full-length console with integral instrument panel, a front air dam, a Rally gauge cluster (including coolant temperature gauge, oil pressure gauge, water temperature gauge, voltmeter and tachometer), the GM Computer Command Control engine management system, a hatch pull-down feature, concealed rectangular quartz halogen headlamps, a monochromatic paint theme, a PASS-Key theft-deterrent system, a Delco ETR stereo radio with cassette and clock, safety belts (including manual lap and shoulder belts for driver and right front passenger and three-point rear seat belts in outboard positions only), reclining front bucket seats with cloth trim, a rear folding seat with cloth trim, side window defoggers, Soft-Ray tinted glass, a four-spoke tilt steering wheel with driver's side inflatable restraint system (airbag) and a lockable storage compartment. The Trans Am added or substituted a 5.0-liter TPI V-8, the F41 Rally Tuned Suspension, 16 x 8-in. diamond spoke wheels, an aero package with special side treatment, a leather appointment group (including leather-wrapped steering wheel) and a four-way manual driver's seat adjuster.

Model Number	Body/Style Number	Body Type & Seating	Factory Price	Shipping Weight	Production Total
F/W	87	2d hatchback-5P	$17,530	3,343 lbs.	2,409
F/W	67	2d convertible-5P	$22,980	—	555

FIREBIRD TRANS AM GTA - SERIES F/W – (V-8)

At the rear, the 1991 GTA was fitted with a redesigned rear deck lid spoiler incorporating restyled taillights. Basic standard features included power brakes, a center high-mounted stoplight, a full-length console with integral instrument panel, a front air dam, a Rally gauge cluster (including coolant temperature gauge, oil pressure gauge, water temperature gauge, voltmeter and tachometer), the GM Computer Command Control engine management system, a hatch pull-down feature, concealed rectangular quartz halogen headlamps, a monochromatic paint theme, a PASS-Key theft-deterrent system, a Delco ETR stereo radio with cassette and clock, safety belts (including manual lap and shoulder belts for driver and right front passenger and three-point rear seat belts in outboard positions only), reclining front bucket seats, a rear folding seat, side window defoggers, Soft-Ray tinted glass, a four-spoke tilt steering wheel with driver's side inflatable restraint system (airbag) and a lockable storage compartment. The GTA also added the 5.7-liter TPI V-8, a four-speed automatic transmission, the WS6 Sport suspension, P245/50ZR16 tires, 16 x 8-in. diamond spoke wheels, a limited-slip differential, disc/drum brakes, a Performance Enhancement group (with engine oil cooler, dual converters and performance axle), new front/rear fascias, an aero package with side treatment, air conditioning, an upgraded sound system, a power antenna, the leather appointment group, a four-way manual driver's seat, power windows and power door locks, cruise control, a remote deck lid release and power outside mirrors.

Model Number	Body/Style Number	Body Type & Seating	Factory Price	Shipping Weight	Production Total
F/W	87	2d hatchback-5P	$24,530	3,456 lbs.	2,035

ENGINES

Base V-6 [UPC LHO]: Overhead valve. Cast-iron block and head. Aluminum intake manifold. Displacement: 191 cid. (3.1-liter). Bore & stroke: 3.50 x 3.31 in. Compression ratio: 8.5:1. Brake horsepower: 140 at 4400 rpm. Torque: 180 ft lbs. at 3600 rpm. Fuel system: EFI/MFI. Standard in base Firebird. VIN code T.

5.0-liter V-8 [UPC L03]: Overhead valve. Cast-iron block and head. Aluminum intake manifold. Displacement: 305 cid. (5.0-liter). Bore & stroke: 3.74 x 3.48 in. Brake horsepower: 170 at 4400 rpm. Torque: 255 ft. lbs. at 2400 rpm. Compression ratio: 9.3:1. Fuel system: EFI/TBI. Standard Formula. Available in base Firebird. VIN code E or F.

5.0-liter V-8 [UPC LB9]: Optional with automatic

The 1991 Formula had redesigned taillights and deck lid spoiler.

Pontiac produced 2,035 GTAs for model year 1991.

transmission. Overhead valve. Eight-cylinder. Cast-iron block and head. Aluminum intake manifold. Displacement: 305 cid. Bore & stroke: 3.74 x 3.48 in. Brake horsepower: 205 at 4200 rpm (Formula/Trans Am/GTA). Torque: 285 ft. lbs. at 3200 rpm (GTA/Formula/Trans Am). Compression ratio: 9.3:1. Fuel system: EFI/TPI. (Delete option in GTA). VIN code E or F.

5.0-liter V-8 [UPC LB9]: Optional with 5-speed manual transmission. Overhead valve. Cast-iron block and head. Aluminum intake manifold. Displacement: 305 cid. Bore & stroke: 3.74 x 3.48 in. Brake horsepower: 230 hp at 4400 rpm (GTA/Formula, optional Trans Am). Torque: 300 ft. lbs. at 3200 rpm (GTA and Formula, optional Trans Am.) Compression ratio: 9.3:1. Fuel system: EFI/TPI. (Delete option in GTA). VIN code E or F.

5.7-liter GTA V-8 [UPC B2L]: Overhead valve. Cast-iron block and head. Aluminum intake manifold. Displacement: 350 cid. Bore & stroke: 4.00 x 3.48 in. Brake horsepower: 240 at 4400 rpm. Torque: 340 ft. lbs. at 3200 rpm. Compression ratio: 9.3:1. Fuel system: EFI/TPI. Standard with four-speed automatic in GTA (optional in Formula and Trans Am.) Includes Performance Enhancement group with dual catalytic converter exhausts, engine oil cooler and performance axle ratio. VIN code 8.

CHASSIS

Base Firebird: Wheelbase: 101.0 in. Overall length: 195.1 in. Width: 72.4 in. Height: 50.0 in. Front tread: 60.7 in. Rear tread: 61.6 in. Front headroom: 37 in. Rear headroom: 35.6 in. Front legroom: 43 in. Rear legroom: 29.8 in. Front shoulder room: 57.7 in. Rear shoulder room: 56.3 in. Front hip room: 56.3 in. Rear hip room: 42.8 in.

Formula Firebird: Wheelbase: 101.0 in. Overall length: 195.1 in. Width: 72.4 in. Height: 50.0 in. Front tread: 60.7 in. Rear tread: 61.6 in. Front headroom: 37 in. Rear headroom: 35.6 in. Front legroom: 43 in. Rear legroom: 29.8 in. Front shoulder room: 57.7 in.

Rear shoulder room: 56.3 in. Front hip room: 56.3 in. Rear hip room: 42.8 in.

Trans Am: Wheelbase: 101.0 in. Overall length: 195.2 in. Width: 72.4 in. Height: 50.0 in. Front tread: 60.7 in. Rear tread: 61.6 in. Front headroom: 37 in. Rear headroom: 35.6 in. Front legroom: 43 in. Rear legroom: 29.8 in. Front shoulder room: 57.7 in. Rear shoulder room: 56.3 in. Front hip room: 56.3 in. Rear hip room: 42.8 in.

Trans Am GTA: Wheelbase: 101.0 in. Overall length: 195.2 in. Width: 72.4 in. Height: 50.0 in. Front tread: 60.7 in. Rear tread: 61.6 in. Front headroom: 37 in. Rear headroom: 35.6 in. Front legroom: 43 in. Rear legroom: 29.8 in. Front shoulder room: 57.7 in. Rear shoulder room: 56.3 in. Front hip room: 56.3 in. Rear hip room: 42.8 in.

TECHNICAL

Base Firebird: Chassis: Front engine/rear drive. Base transmission: Five-speed manual. Optional transmission: Four-speed automatic. Front suspension: Fully independent with modified MacPherson strut and low-friction ball bearing upper strut mount and 30mm anti-roll bar. Rear suspension: Live axle with coil springs, longitudinal lower control arm and torque arm, transverse track bar and 18mm anti-roll bar. Steering: Power re-circulating ball: 14.1:1 ratio. Turns lock-to-lock: 2.72. Turning circle: 39.1 ft. Brakes: Power vented 10.5-in. front disc/9.5-in. rear drum. Rear brakes: Power-assisted 7.87-in. drums. Fuel tank: 15.5 gal.

Formula: Chassis: Front engine/rear drive. Base transmission: Five-speed manual. Optional transmission: Four-speed automatic. Front suspension: Fully independent with modified MacPherson strut and low-friction ball bearing upper strut mount and 36mm anti-roll bar. Rear suspension: Live axle with coil springs, longitudinal lower control arm and torque arm, transverse track bar and 24mm anti-roll bar. Steering: Power re-circulating ball: 12.7:1 quick ratio with sport effort valving. Turns lock-to-lock: 2.26.

Turning circle: 32.6 ft. (Levels II and III). Brakes: Power vented 10.5-in. front disc/9.5-in. rear drum on Formula with 5.0-liter EFI, power four-wheel vented disc 10.5-in. front and 11.7-in. rear with 5.7-liter V-8 or 5.0-liter V-8 with TPI and five-speed on Formula. Rear brakes: (with base Formula V-8) Power-assisted 7.87-in. drums. Fuel tank: 15.5 gal.

Trans Am: Chassis: Front engine/rear drive. Base transmission: Five-speed manual. Optional transmission: Four-speed automatic. Front suspension: Fully independent with modified MacPherson strut and low-friction ball bearing upper strut mount and 34mm anti-roll bar. Rear suspension: Live axle with coil springs, longitudinal lower control arm and torque arm, transverse track bar and 23mm anti-roll bar. Steering: Power re-circulating ball: 12.7:1 quick ratio with sport effort valving. Turns lock-to-lock: 2.47. Turning circle: 32.6 ft. Front brakes: Power vented 10.5-in. front disc. Rear brakes with 5.0-liter 205-hp EFI/TPI V-8: Power-assisted 7.87-in. drums. Rear brakes with 5.0-liter 230-hp EFI/TPI V-8: 9.5-in. rear drum. Fuel tank: 15.5 gal.

Trans Am GTA: Chassis: Front engine/rear drive. Base transmission: Five-speed manual. Optional transmission: Four-speed automatic. Front suspension: Fully independent with modified MacPherson strut and low-friction ball bearing upper strut mount and 36mm anti-roll bar. Rear suspension: Live axle with coil springs, longitudinal lower control arm and torque arm, transverse track bar and 24mm anti-roll bar. Steering: Power re-circulating ball: 12.7:1 quick ratio with sport effort valving. Turns lock-to-lock: 2.26. Turning circle: 32.6 ft. (Levels II and III). Brakes: Power four-wheel vented disc 10.5-in. front and 11.7-in. rear with the 5.7- or 5.0-liter V-8s with TPI and the five-speed manual transmission. Fuel tank: 15.5 gal.

OPTIONS

1SB Firebird V-6 engine option package No. 1 includes C60 Custom air conditioning, B84 body side moldings, DC4 Inside rear view mirror with flood lamp, on base Firebird coupe ($913); on base Firebird convertible ($890). 1SC base Firebird V-6 engine option package No. 2 includes option package No. 1 plus A31 power windows, AU3 power door locks including door map pockets, A90 remote deck lid release and DG7 dual power convex Sport mirrors; in Firebird coupe (total package $1,554, savings $500, net price $1,054); in Firebird convertible (total package $1,471, savings $500, net price $971). 1SB base Firebird V-8 option package No. 1, includes B84 body side moldings, A31 power windows with door map pockets, AU3 power door locks and DC4 inside rear view mirror with flood lamps; in Firebird coupe (total package $573, savings $500, net price $73); in Firebird convertible (total package $550, savings $500, net price $50). 1SC base Firebird V-8 option package No. 2 includes same as 1SB option package No. 1 plus AH3 four-way manual adjustable driver's seat, K34 cruise control, A90 remote-control deck lid release and DG7 dual power convex Sport mirrors, in Firebird coupe (total package $984, savings $500, net price

$484); in Firebird convertible (total package $901, savings $500, net price $401). 1SB Formula and Trans Am option Package No.1 Includes B84 body side moldings, A31 power windows including door map pockets, AU3 power door locks and DC4 Inside rearview mirror with flood lamp in Formula or Trans Am coupe (total package $573, savings $350, net price $223); in Trans Am convertible (total package $550, savings $350, net price $200). 1SC Formula option package No. 2 includes same as 1SB option package No.1 plus AH3 four-way manual adjustable driver's seat, K34 cruise control, A90 remote-control deck lid release and DG7 dual power convex Sport mirrors, in Formula coupe (total package $984, savings $500, net price $484). 1SC Trans Am option package No. 2 includes same as 1SC option package No. 1 plus AH3 four-way manual adjustable driver's seat, K34 cruise control, A90 remote-control deck lid release and DG7 dual power convex Sport mirrors, in Trans Am coupe (total package $949, savings $500, net price $449); in Trans Am convertible (total package $866, savings $500, net price $366). R6A Firebird and Formula Value option package includes CC1 locking T-top roof, not available with B2L V-8 and UX1 AM/FM stereo with cassette and graphic equalizer (total package $1,070, savings $250, net price $820). R6B Firebird and Formula Value option package includes CC1 locking T-top roof, not available with B2L V-8, U75 power antenna and D42 cargo area security screen (total package $1,074, savings $250, net price $824). R6A Trans Am Value option package includes CC1 T-top roof, not available with B2L V-8, UX1 AM/FM stereo with cassette and graphic equalizer and D42 cargo area screen (total package $1,139, savings $250, net price $889). R6A Trans Am GTA Value option package, includes CC1 T-top roof, not available with B2L V-8 and AQ9 leather interior (total package $1,395, savings $350, net price $1,045). LHO 3.1-liter multi-port fuel-injected V-6 in Firebird (no charge). L03 5.0-liter TBI V-8, not available in Trans Am or GTA, requires C60 custom air conditioning in Formula ($350). LB9 5.0-liter MFI V-8 requires G80 limited-slip differential and R6P Performance Enhancement Group with MM5 manual transmission on GTA and Formula, not available in Firebird; in Formula ($745); in Trans Am (no charge); in GTA in place of base V-8 ($300 credit). B2L 5.7-liter MFI V-8 requires MX0 automatic transmission, KC4 engine oil cooler, J65 four-wheel disc brakes, G80 limited-slip differential and (QLC) tires, not available in base Firebird; in Formula ($1,045); in Trans Am ($300); in GTA (no charge). MM5 five-speed manual transmission, not available in Firebird with LHO 3.1-liter V-6 or 5.7-liter V-8, no charge in Formula and Trans Am; In Firebird with L03 V-8 and GTA ($515). MX0 four-speed automatic transmission, in base Firebird or GTA (no charge); in Formula and Trans Am ($515). C60 custom air conditioning, required on Firebird with L03 V-8, standard on all models except base Firebird ($830). G80 limited-slip differential, available only and required with LB9 or B2L V-8s, standard on Trans Am and GTA; on Formula ($100). C49 Electric rear window defogger, included on GTA; on other

Firebirds ($170). K34 cruise control, requires 1SB option package, included in 1SC option package; on Firebird, Formula and Trans Am ($225). A90 remote deck lid release, requires 1SB option on Firebird with L03 V-8, included in 1SC Formula and Trans Am option packages; standard in GTA; in other Firebirds ($60). NB2 required California emissions ($100). CC1 locking hatch roof with removable glass panels and sunshades, not available with B2L V-8, included in price of Value Option package; otherwise ($920). DG7 dual power remote Sport mirrors, standard on GTA; on other Firebirds ($91). R6P Performance Enhancement group, except Firebird; not available with LB9 V-8 with MX0 transmission, required with B2L V-8 with MX0 transmission on Formula and GTA, includes N10 dual converter exhausts, J41/J42 power front disc/rear drum brakes, KC4 engine oil cooler and GU6 performance axle with LB9 V-8, GU5 performance axle with B2L V-8 or performance axle ratio; in GTA with LB9 V-8 and MM5 transmission or B2L V-8 (no charge); in base Firebird (not available); in Formula or Trans Am ($265); in GTA with LB9 V-8 and MX0 transmission ($265 credit). AU3 power door locks, available only with and required with A31 power windows, standard with GTA; in other models ($210). A31 power windows, available only and required with AU3 power door locks, includes door map pockets; standard in GTA; in other models ($280). U75 power antenna, standard on GTA; on other Firebirds ($85). UM6 AM/FM ETR Delco AM/FM ETR stereo and cassette with auto reverse, electronic seek/scan tuning, integral digital clock and dual front and rear coaxial speakers, not available in GTA; in other Firebirds (no charge). UX1 Delco AM FM ETR stereo radio and cassette with auto reverse, search-and-replay, electronic seek/scan tuning, integral five-band graphic equalizer, integral digital clock and dual front and rear coaxial speakers, not available in Firebird, Formula and Trans Am; in GTA ($150). U1A Delco AM stereo/FM ETR stereo and CD player with electronic seek up/down tuning, next and previous CD controls, integral 5-band graphic equalizer, integral digital clock, and dual front and rear coaxial speakers; in Formula and Trans Am without value package R6A ($376); in Firebird, Formula and Trans Am with value package R6A ($226); in GTA ($226). AH3 four-way manual adjustable driver's seat, not available on Firebird with LHO V-6, available only with and included in 1SC option package on Firebird with L03 V-8, available with 1SB option on Formula and included in 1SC option on Formula on GTA (no charge); on Firebird and Formula with required equipment ($35). AR9 custom reclining bucket seats with Pallex cloth trim, not available GTA; on other Firebirds (no charge). AQ9 articulating luxury bucket seats, standard in GTA with Metrix cloth trim, optional only in GTA with Ventura leather trim and included with Value Option package; without Value Option package ($450). W68 Sport Appearance package for Firebird only, requires 1SB or 1SC option package with LHO engine; option includes Trans Am front and rear aero fascias, fog lamps and aero-style Trans Am body side moldings ($450). QPH P215/65Rl5 black sidewall touring tires with N24 wheels, Firebird only (no charge). QPEP215/60Rl6 black sidewall steel-belted radial touring tires including PW7 wheels, not available with B2L V-8; on Trans Am only (no charge). QLC high-performance P245/50ZR16 black sidewall steel-belted radial, not available with Firebird, includes WS6 performance suspension and PW7 wheels on Trans Am and GTA or PEO wheels with Formula; on Formula and GTA (no charge); on Trans Am only ($313). WDV tire warranty enhancement for New York ($65). N24 15-in. deep-dish charcoal High-Tech Turbo cast-aluminum wheels with locking package, not available for Formula or GTA; on other Firebirds (no charge). PEO 16-in. deep-dish High-Tech Turbo cast-aluminum wheels with locking package, on Formula only (no charge). PW7 16-in. color-coordinated diamond spoke cast-aluminum wheels with locking package, Charcoal colored on Trans Am and Gold on GTA (no charge).

HISTORICAL FOOTNOTES

Pontiac's model-year production in the United States included 50,247 Firebirds. That represented 0.87 percent of total U.S. auto production. The model year sales total was recorded as 24,601 Firebirds. Of the 30,323 cars made as 1991 models during the 1991 model year (some '91s were built in the 1990 model year and counted as 1990s), 92.9 percent had power door locks and windows, 60.7 percent had cruise control, 60.5 percent had a rear window defogger, 72.1 percent had dual power rearview mirrors, 54.6 percent had hatch roofs, 44 percent had an AM/FM stereo with cassette, 52.1 percent had a premium sound system and 3.9 percent had a CD player. Available in 1991 for Firebirds with 5.0- and 5.7-liter TPI V-8s was a new "Street Legal Performance" (SLP) package of GM high-performance hardware. The SLP kit, created by SLP Engineering, was available from GM dealers. It boosted engine performance without modifications to the power plants. The kit could be dealer installed or owner installed. The Trans Am returned to Sports Car Club of America Trans-Am series racing in 1991 after a seven-year hiatus. A car sponsored by Electronic Data Systems (EDS was a wholly owned subsidiary of GM) was constructed by Group 44 Racing of Winchester, Virginia. The chassis building company was owned by Bob Tullius of Pontiac racing fame. The competition engines were constructed by Ed Pink Racing Engines. The car made its initial appearance at the Dallas Grand Prix on June 2, 1991. It was piloted by Scott Lagasse, who had been a driver in the well-known Corvette Challenge series.

The hatchback GTA came with an $18,105 price tag.

25 Years and Counting

Pontiac made the base Firebird a little more afford-able in 1992. The range of prices started at $12,995, as opposed to $13,159 the year before. However, at the upper end of the spectrum the pricier models ran to $26,370 as opposed to a high of $24,999 for the '91 models. There were few alterations, though Pontiac promoted "structural enhancements" and new asbestos-free brake pads. New colors for the year included Yellow, Dark Jade Gray Metallic and Dark Aqua Metallic. The AM/FM cassette radio had revised graphics and a Beige interior was introduced. Strange-ly, there was no special package to celebrate the nameplate's 25th anniversary.

Engines for the Firebird, Firebird Formula, Trans Am and Trans Am GTA were carried over from 1991, except for the power plant used in a new Formula Firehawk model. This wasn't a factory-built car — it was a special creation that stemmed from a partner-ship between PMD and SLP Engineering, an aftermar-ket modifier. Firehawks were based on Formulas with the 5.0-liter TPI V-8 and came in "street" and "com-petition" versions. The $39,995 street version pro-duced 350 hp. The competition kit cost nearly $10,000 and provided even higher output.

SLP kits were available through GM Service Parts Organization's 1992 high-performance catalog. SLP Engineering installed only 25 kits. They went on 24 coupes and one convertible. Interestingly, these cars carried serial numbers between 1 and 27 because cars no. 18 and no. 25 were never built.

With the country in a recession, the Firebird series, with a production total of only 25,180 cars, was getting the same "evil eye" it had felt 10 years earlier. General manager John Middlebrook admitted to *Automotive News* that Firebird sales were down by 6 percent. A month later, GM announced huge layoffs and multiple plant closings. Industry observers then predicted doomsday for the F-Cars. However, an all-new Firebird due in the fall and released late in 1993 would turn things around and secure the future of the marque a second time.

I.D. NUMBERS

Pontiac's 17-symbol vehicle identification number (VIN) for passenger cars was on the upper left surface of the instrument panel, visible through the wind-shield. The first symbol indicates country of origin: 1=U.S. The second symbol indicates manufacturer: G=General Motors. The third symbol indicates make: 2=Pontiac division. The fourth and fifth symbols for passenger cars indicated body type and series: F/S=Firebird, F/V=Firebird Trans Am. The sixth sym-bol on passenger cars denoted body type: 2=two-door hatchback style 87, 3=two-door convertible style 67. The seventh symbol on passenger cars indicated the type of restraint system: 1=manual belts; 2=active manual belts with dual airbags; 3=active manual belts with driver airbag. Symbol eight for passenger cars was an engine code: E=UPC L03 5.0-liter fuel-injected (TBI) V-8; F=UPC LB9 5.0-liter fuel-injected (MFI) V-8; T=UPC LH0 3.1-liter fuel-injected (MFI) V-6 and

8=UPC L98 5.7-liter fuel-injected (MFI) V-8. The ninth symbol is a check digit. The tenth symbol denotes model year (N=1992). The 11th symbol indicates the GM assembly plant: L=Van Nuys, California. The last six symbols are the consecutive unit number at the factory. V-6 engine code on right side of block near water pump. V-8 engine code on pad on front of block below right cylinder head. Engine production codes for 1992 were: [2.8-liter EFI/TBI V-6] DKA-DMA, [5.0-liter EFI/TBI V-8] DBN-DBP-DBS, [5.0-liter EFI/TPI V-8] DBK-DBL, [5.7-liter EFI/TPI V-8] DJP.

COLORS

Bright White, Black, Dark Aqua Metallic, Yellow, Bright Blue Metallic, Bright Red, Brilliant Red Metallic, Dark Green Metallic and Dark Jade Gray Metallic.

FIREBIRD - SERIES F/S - V-6/V-8

Pontiac announced the first Firebird convertible in 21 years in 1991 and only 2,000 were built. The open model was continued in 1992. The full line consisted of Firebird, Firebird Formula, Trans Am and Trans Am GTA models. The convertible was available as a base Firebird or as a Trans Am. Other changes for 1992 included structural enhancements and non-asbestos brake pads. New Yellow, Dark Jade Gray Metallic and Dark Aqua Metallic exterior paint colors were also added. The interiors had revised AM/FM cassette radio graphics and new knobs and rings, plus a revised beige interior. Standard features of the base Firebird included a front air dam, a Delco Freedom II battery, power front disc/rear drum brakes, a body-color one-piece resilient Endura front panel and bumper, a rear Endura panel, a full-length front console, a multi-function control lever, corrosion protection (with a two-sided galvanized steel coating on hood, a one-sided galvanized steel coating on inner front doors, deck lid and panel and a Zincrometal coating on fenders and outer doors), courtesy lamps with rear compartment and console lamp-rearview mirror on convertibles, a side window defogger, a 3.1-liter V-6 engine with multi-port fuel injection, laminated safety glass with tinted Soft-Ray on liftback, the GM Computer Command Control engine management system, concealed quartz halogen headlamps, an inside hood release, a graphite-colored instrument panel, dual body-color Sport outside rearview mirrors (left-hand remote controlled), left- and right-hand visor-vanity mirrors (except T-top or convertible), the PASS-Key theft deterrent system, a Delco ETR AM/FM stereo cassette, a rear hatch/trunk pull-down feature, rear-wheel drive, reclining front bucket seats, a folding rear seat, a rear deck lid spoiler, a tilt adjustable steering wheel, a lockable storage compartment in left rear quarter panel (except convertible), a one-piece multi-colored taillight lens with amber turn signal, P215/65R15 steel-belted Touring tires, a Space Saver spare tire, a five-speed manual transmission, a tone-generator warning system with safety belts and head-lamp-on key-in warning feature, High-Tech Turbo aluminum wheel rims and a power vent system. Convertibles came with a choice of black or beige cloth tops that stowed away under a tonneau cover. Ragtops

also carried the aero package as standard equipment (including fog lights, brake cooling ducts in the front fascias and a distinctive body side treatment).

Model Number	Body/Style Number	Body Type & Seating	Factory Price	Shipping Weight	Production Total
FIREBIRD - SERIES F/S - (V-6)					
F/S	87	2d hatchback-5P	$12,505	3,121 lbs.	Note 1
F/S	67	2d convertible-5P	$19,375	3,280 lbs.	Note 2
FIREBIRD - SERIES F/S - (V-8)					
F/S	87	2d hatchback-5P	$12,874	3,281 lbs.	Note 1
F/S	67	2d convertible-5P	$19,744	3,440 lbs.	Note 2

Note 1: Total model year production of base Firebird coupes was 23,099.
Note 2: Total model year production of base Firebird convertibles was 1,265.

FORMULA FIREBIRD - SERIES F/S V-8

Basic standard Firebird features included a front air dam, a Delco Freedom II battery, power front disc/rear drum brakes, a body-color one-piece resilient Endura front panel and bumper, a rear Endura panel, a full-length front console, a multi-function control lever, corrosion protection (with a two-sided galvanized steel coating on hood, a one-sided galvanized steel coating on inner front doors, deck lid and panel and a Zincrometal coating on fenders and outer doors), courtesy lamps with rear compartment and console lamp-rearview mirror on convertibles, a side window defogger, laminated safety glass with tinted Soft-Ray on liftback, the GM Computer Command Control engine management system, concealed quartz halogen headlamps, an inside hood release, a graphite-colored instrument panel, dual body-color Sport outside rearview mirrors (left-hand remote controlled), left- and right-hand visor-vanity mirrors (except T-top coupe or convertible), the PASS-Key theft deterrent system, a Delco ETR AM/FM stereo cassette, a rear hatch/trunk pull-down feature, rear-wheel drive, reclining front bucket seats, a folding rear seat, a rear deck lid spoiler, a tilt adjustable steering wheel, a lockable storage compartment in left rear quarter panel (except convertible), a one-piece multi-colored taillight lens with amber turn signal, a Space Saver spare tire, a five-speed manual transmission, a tone-generator warning system with safety belts and headlamp-on key-in warning feature and a power vent system. The Firebird Formula added or substituted a 5.0-liter EFI V-8, the WS6 Sport suspension, P245/50ZR16 tires, 15 x 7-in. deep-dish High-Tech aluminum wheels, air conditioning and a leather appointment group with leather-wrapped steering wheel.

Model Number	Body/Style Number	Body Type & Seating	Factory Price	Shipping Weight	Production Total
2F	87	2d hatchback-5P	$16,205	3,370 lbs.	1,052

TRANS AM - SERIES F/V - V-8

Standard Firebird Trans Am features included an aero body package (with aerodynamic front and rear fascias, rocker panel extensions and quarter panel extensions), a front air dam, hood air extractors, a Delco Freedom II battery, power front disc/rear drum brakes, a body color one-piece resilient Endura front panel and bumper, a rear Endura panel, a full-length front console, a multi-function control lever, corrosion protection (with a two-sided galvanized steel coating on hood, a one-sided galvanized steel coating on inner front doors, deck lid and panel and a Zincrometal coating on fenders and outer doors), courtesy lamps including rear compartment and console lamp and rearview mirror on convertibles, a side window defogger, a 5.0-liter H.O. TPI V-8, laminated safety glass with tinted Soft-Ray on liftback, the GM Computer Command Control engine management system, concealed quartz halogen headlamps, an inside hood release, a graphite-colored instrument panel, a leather appointment group, hood louvers, dual body-color Sport outside rearview mirrors (left-hand remote control), left- and right-hand visor-vanity mirrors (except T-top or convertible), the PASS-Key theft deterrent system, a Delco ETR AM/FM stereo cassette, a rear hatch/trunk pull-down feature, rear-wheel drive, reclining front bucket seats, a folding rear seat, a rear deck lid spoiler, a tilt adjustable steering wheel, a lockable storage compartment in left rear quarter panel (except convertible), neutral-density taillight lenses with a smooth contour appearance, P215/60R16 touring tires, a Space Saver spare tire, a five-speed manual transmission, a tone-generator warning system with safety belts, headlamp-on and key-in warning feature and diamond spoke cast-aluminum wheel rims. The Trans Am convertible also came with a choice of black or beige cloth tops that stowed away neatly under a tonneau cover and leather-clad articulated bucket seats.

Model Number	Body/Style Number	Body Type & Seating	Factory Price	Shipping Weight	Production Total
F/W	87	2d hatchback-5P	$18,105	3,343 lbs.	980
F/W	67	2d convertible-5P	$23,875	3,441 lbs.	663

TRANS AM GTA - SERIES F/V - V-8

Standard Firebird Trans Am features included an aero body package (with aerodynamic front and rear fascias, rocker panel extensions and quarter panel extensions), a front air dam, hood air extractors, a Delco Freedom II battery, power front disc/rear drum brakes, a body color one-piece resilient Endura front panel and bumper, a rear Endura panel, a full-length front console, a multi-function control lever, corrosion protection (with a two-sided galvanized steel coating on hood, a one-sided galvanized steel coating on inner front doors, deck lid and panel and a Zincrometal coating on fenders and outer doors), courtesy lamps including rear compartment, console lamp and rearview mirror on convertibles, a side window defogger, laminated safety glass with tinted Soft-Ray on liftback, the GM Computer Command Control engine management system, concealed quartz halogen headlamps, an inside hood release, a graphite-colored instrument panel, a leather appointment group, hood louvers, dual body-color Sport outside rearview mirrors (left-hand remote controlled), the PASS-Key theft deterrent system, a rear hatch/trunk pull-down feature, rear-wheel drive, reclining front bucket seats, a folding rear seat, a rear deck lid spoiler, a tilt adjustable steering wheel, a lockable storage compart-

ment in left rear quarter panel (except convertible), neutral-density taillight lenses with a smooth contour appearance, a Space Saver spare tire, a tone-generator warning system with safety belts, headlamp-on and key-in warning feature and diamond-spoke cast-aluminum wheel rims. The Trans Am convertible also came with a choice of a black or beige cloth top that stowed away neatly under a tonneau cover and leather-clad articulated bucket seats. The GTA added or substituted the following over the Trans Am: 5.7-liter TPI V-8, a four-speed automatic transmission, the WS6 Sport suspension, P245/50ZR16 tires, dual catalytic converters, a performance axle, a Delco ETR AM/FM stereo with CD and five-band equalizer, a power antenna, the leather appointment group, a four-way manual driver's seat adjuster, power windows and door locks, cruise control, a remote deck lid release, a rear window defogger and power outside mirrors.

Model Number	Body/Style Number	Body Type & Seating	Factory Price	Shipping Weight	Production Total
F/W	87	2d hatchback-5P	$25,880	3,456 lbs.	508

The 1992 Formula featured a 5.0-liter EFI V-8 and upgraded Sport suspension.

ENGINES

Base V-6 [UPC LHO]: Overhead valve. Cast-iron block and head. Aluminum intake manifold. Displacement: 191 cid. (3.1 liter). Bore & stroke: 3.50 x 3.31 in. Compression ratio: 8.8:1. Brake horsepower: 140 at 4400 rpm. Torque: 185 ft. lbs. at 3200 rpm. Fuel system: EFI/MFI. Standard in base Firebird. VIN code T.

5.0-liter V-8 [UPC LO3]: Overhead valve. Cast-iron block and head. Aluminum intake manifold. Displacement: 305 cid. Bore & stroke: 3.74 x 3.48 in. Brake horsepower: 170 at 4000 rpm. Torque: 255 ft. lbs. at 2400 rpm. Compression ratio: 9.3:1. Fuel system: EFI/TBI. Standard in Formula. Available in base Firebird. VIN code E or F.

5.0-liter V-8 [UPC LB9]: Overhead valve. Cast-iron block and head. Aluminum intake manifold. Displacement: 305 cid. Bore & stroke: 3.74 x 3.48 in. Brake horsepower: 205 at 4200 rpm. Torque: 285 ft. lbs. at 3200 rpm. Compression ratio: 9.3:1. Fuel system: EFI/TPI. UPC Code: LB9. Available with five-speed manual in Formula and Trans Am (delete option in GTA.) VIN code E or F.

5.7-liter GTA V-8 [UPC B2L]: Overhead valve. Cast-iron block and head. Aluminum intake manifold. Displacement: 350 cid. Bore & stroke: 4.00 x 3.48 in. Brake horsepower: 240 at 4400 rpm. Torque: 340 ft. lbs. at 3200 rpm. Compression ratio: 9.3:1. Fuel system: EFI/TPI. Standard with four-speed automatic in GTA (optional in Formula and Trans Am). Includes Performance Enhancement group with dual catalytic converter exhausts, engine oil cooler and performance axle ratio. VIN code 8.

CHASSIS

Base Firebird: Wheelbase: 101.0 in. Overall length: 195.1 in. Width: 72.4 in. Height: 49.7 in. Front tread: 60.7 in. Rear tread: 61.6 in. Front headroom: 37 in. Rear headroom: 35.6 in. Front legroom: 43 in. Rear legroom: 28.9 in. Front shoulder room: 57.2 in. Rear shoulder room: 56.3 in. Front hip room: 55.6 in. Rear hip room: 42.8 in. Standard tires: P215/65R15.

Formula: Wheelbase: 101.0 in. Overall length: 195.1 in. Width: 72.4 in. Height: 49.7 in. Front tread: 60.7 in. Rear tread: 61.6 in. Front headroom: 37 in. Rear headroom: 35.6 in. Front legroom: 43 in. Rear legroom: 28.9 in. Front shoulder room: 57.2 in. Rear shoulder room: 56.3 in. Front hip room: 55.6 in. Rear hip room: 42.8 in. Standard tires: P245/50ZR16 Goodyear Eagle ZR50 "Gatorback."

Trans Am: Wheelbase: 101.0 in. Overall length: 195.2 in. Width: 72.4 in. Height: 49.7 in. Front tread: 60.7 in. Rear tread: 61.6 in. Front headroom: 37 in. Rear headroom: 35.6 in. Front legroom: 43 in. Rear legroom: 28.9 in. Front shoulder room: 57.2 in. Rear shoulder room: 56.3 in. Front hip room: 55.6 in. Rear hip room: 42.8 in. Standard tires: P215/60R16.

Trans Am GTA: Wheelbase: 101.0 in. Overall length: 195.2 in. Width: 72.4 in. Height: 49.7 in. Front tread: 60.7 in. Rear tread: 61.6 in. Front headroom: 37 in. Rear headroom: 35.6 in. Front legroom: 43 in. Rear legroom: 28.9 in. Front shoulder room: 57.2 in. Rear shoulder room: 56.3 in. Front hip room: 55.6 in. Rear hip room: 42.8 in. Standard tires: P245/50ZR16 Goodyear Eagle ZR50 "Gatorback."

TECHNICAL

Base Firebird: Chassis: Front engine/rear drive. Base transmission: Five-speed manual. Optional transmission: Four-speed automatic. Front suspension: Fully independent with modified MacPherson strut and low-friction ball-bearing upper strut mount and 30mm anti-roll bar. Rear suspension: Live axle with coil springs, longitudinal lower control arm and torque arm, transverse track bar and 24mm anti-roll bar. Steering: Power re-circulating ball 14.1:1 ratio. Turns lock-to-lock: 2.57. Turning circle: 38.5 ft. Brakes: Power vented 10.5-in. front disc/9.5 x 2.0-in. rear drum. Fuel tank: 15.5 gal.

Formula: Chassis: Front engine/rear drive. Base transmission: Five-speed manual. Optional transmission: Four-speed automatic. Front suspension: Fully independent with modified MacPherson strut and low-friction ball-bearing upper strut mount and 36mm anti-roll bar. Rear suspension: Live axle with coil springs, longitudinal lower control arm and torque arm, transverse track bar and 18mm anti-roll bar. Steering: Power re-circulating ball 12.7:1 quick ratio with sport effort valving. Turn lock to lock: 2.14. Turning circle: 38.5 ft. Brakes: Power vented 10.5-in. front disc/9.5 x 2.0-in. rear drum. Fuel tank: 15.5 gal.

Trans Am: Chassis: Front engine/rear drive. Base transmission: Five-speed manual. Optional transmission: Four-speed automatic. Front suspension: Fully independent with modified MacPherson strut and low-friction ball bearing upper strut mount and 34mm anti-roll bar. Rear suspension: Live axle with coil springs, longitudinal lower control arm and torque arm, transverse track bar and 23mm anti-roll bar. Steering: Power re-circulating ball 12.7:1 quick ratio with sport effort valving. Turns lock to lock: 2.14. Turning circle: 38.5 ft. Brakes: Power vented 10.5-in. front disc/9.5 x 2.0-in. rear drum. Fuel tank: 15.5 gal.

A total of 25,180 F-Cars were built for model year 1992.

Trans Am GTA: Chassis: Front engine/rear drive. Base transmission: Five-speed manual. Optional transmission: Four-speed automatic. Front suspension: Fully independent with modified MacPherson strut and low-friction ball bearing upper strut mount and 36mm anti-roll bar. Rear suspension: Live axle with coil springs, longitudinal lower control arm and torque arm, transverse track bar and 24mm anti-roll bar. Steering: Power re-circulating ball 12.7:1 quick ratio with sport effort valving. Turns lock to lock: 2.14. Turning circle: 38.5 ft. Brakes: Power vented 10.5-in. front disc/10.5-in. rear vented discs. Fuel tank: 15.5 gal.

OPTIONS

1SB Firebird V-6 option package No. 1 includes C60 Custom air conditioning, B84 body side moldings, DC4 Inside rearview mirror with flood lamp, on base Firebird coupe (Total price $913; savings $500=net price $413). 1SC base Firebird V-6 engine option package No. 2 includes option package No. 1 plus A31 power windows, AU3 power door locks including door map pockets, A90 remote deck lid release and DG7 dual power convex Sport mirrors; in base Firebird coupe (total package $1,554; savings $750=net price $804). 1SB base Firebird V-8 and Formula option package No. 1 includes B84 body side moldings, DC4 Inside rear view mirror with flood lamp, A31 power windows and door map pockets and AU3 power door locks on base Firebird V-8 or Formula coupe (Total price $573; savings $350=net price $223). 1SC base Firebird V-8 and Formula option package No. 2 includes option package No. 1 plus DG7 dual power convex Sport mirrors, A90 deck lid release, AH3 four-way manual seat adjuster and K34 cruise control in Firebird V-8 or Formula coupe (total package $984; savings $500=net price $484). 1SC Trans Am coupe option package No. 2 includes option package No. 1 plus DG7 dual power convex Sport mirrors, A90 deck lid release, AH3 four-way manual seat adjuster and K34 cruise control in Firebird coupe (total package $984; savings $500=net price $484). 1SB Firebird V-6 option package No. 1 includes C60 air conditioning, B84 body side moldings on base Firebird convertible (Total price $890; savings $500=net price $390). 1SC base Firebird V-6 engine option package No. 2 includes option package No. 1 plus A31 power windows, AU3 power door locks including door map pockets and DG7 dual power convex Sport mirrors; in base Firebird convertible (total package $1,471; savings $750=net price $721). 1SB Firebird V-8 option package No. 1 includes B84 body side moldings, A31 power windows and door map pockets and AU3 power door locks on base Firebird convertible (Total price $550; savings $325=net price $225). 1SC base Firebird V-8 engine option package No. 2 includes option package No. 1 plus DG7 dual power convex Sport mirrors, AH3 four-way manual seat adjuster and K34 cruise control; in base Firebird convertible (total package $901; savings $500=net price $401). 1SB Trans Am option package No. 1 includes B84 body side moldings, A31 power windows and door map pockets and AU3 power door locks on

Trans Am convertible (Total price $550; savings $325=net price $225). 1SC Trans Am option package No. 2 includes option package No. 1 plus DG7 dual power convex Sport mirrors, AH3 four-way manual seat adjuster and K34 cruise control; in Trans Am convertible (total package $866; savings $500=net price $366). R6A base Firebird and Formula value option package including CC1 locking hatch roof with sunshades, UX1 AM/FM stereo; total price $1,064; savings $250=net price $814). R6A Trans Am convertible value option package with articulating luxury bucket seats with Ventura leather trim and UX1 AM/FM stereo (total package $930; savings $250=net price $814). LHO 3.1-liter multi-port fuel-injected V-6 in Firebird (no charge). L03 5.0-liter TBI V-8, not available in Trans Am or GTA, requires C60 custom air conditioning in Formula ($369). LB9 5.0-liter MFI V-8 requires G80 limited-slip differential and R6P Performance Enhancement Group with MM5 manual transmission on GTA and Formula, not available in Firebird; in Formula ($745); in Trans Am (no charge); in GTA in place of base V-8 ($300 credit). B2L 5.7-liter MFI V-8 requires MX0 automatic transmission, KC4 engine oil cooler, J65 four-wheel disc brakes, G80 limited-slip differential and (QLC) tires, not available in base Firebird; in Formula ($1,045); in Trans Am ($300); in GTA (no charge). MM5 five-speed manual transmission, not available in Firebird with LHO 3.1 -liter V-6 or 5.7-liter V-8, no charge in Formula and Trans Am; in Firebird with L03 V-8 and GTA ($530). MX0 four-speed automatic transmission, in base Firebird or GTA (no charge); in Formula and Trans Am ($530). C60 custom air conditioning, required on Firebird with L03 V-8, standard on all models except base Firebird ($830). G80 limited-slip differential, available only and required with LB9 or B2L V-8s, standard on Trans Am and GTA; on Formula ($100). C49 electric rear window defogger, included on GTA; on other Firebirds ($170). K34 cruise control, requires 1SB option package, included in 1SC option package; on Firebird, Formula and Trans Am ($225). A90 remote deck lid release, requires 1SB option on Firebird with L03 V-8, included in 1SC Formula and Trans Am option packages; standard in GTA; in other Firebirds ($60). NB2 required California emissions ($100). CC1 locking hatch roof with removable glass panels and sunshades, not available with B2L V-8, included in price of Value Option package; otherwise ($914). DG7 dual power remote Sport mirrors, standard on GTA; on other Firebirds ($91). R6P Performance Enhancement group, except Firebird; not available with LB9 V-8 with MX0 transmission, required with B2L V-8 with MX0 transmission on Formula and GTA, includes N10 dual converter exhausts, J41/J42 power front disc/rear drum brakes, KC4 engine oil cooler and GU6 performance axle with LB9 V-8, GU5 performance axle with B2L V-8 or performance axle ratio; in GTA with LB9 V-8 and MM5 transmission or B2L V-8 (no charge); in base Firebird (not available); in Formula or Trans Am ($444); in GTA with LB9 V-8 and MX0 transmission ($444 credit). AU3 power door locks, available only with and required with A31 power windows, standard with

GTA; in other models ($210). A31 power windows, available only and required with AU3 power door locks, includes door map pockets; standard in GTA; in other models ($280). U75 power antenna, standard on GTA; on other Firebirds ($85). UM6 AM/FM ETR Delco AM/FM ETR stereo and cassette with auto reverse, electronic seek/scan tuning, integral digital clock and dual front and rear coaxial speakers, not available in GTA; in other Firebirds (no charge). UX1 Delco AM/FM ETR stereo radio and cassette with auto reverse, search-and-replay, electronic seek/scan tuning, integral five-band graphic equalizer, integral digital clock and dual front and rear coaxial speakers, not available in Firebird, Formula and Trans Am; in GTA ($150). U1A Delco AM stereo/FM ETR stereo and CD player with electronic seek up/down tuning, next and previous CD controls, integral 5-band graphic equalizer, integral digital clock, and dual front and rear coaxial speakers; in Formula and Trans Am without value package R6A ($376); in Firebird, Formula and Trans Am with value package R6A ($226); in GTA ($226). D42 cargo area screen in Firebird, Formula or Trans Am coupe ($69); in Trans Am GTA (no cost). AH3 four-way manual adjustable driver's seat, not available on Firebird with LHO V-6, available only with and included in 1SC option package on Firebird with L03 V-8, available with 1SB option on Formula and included in 1SC option on Formula on GTA (no charge); on Firebird and Formula with required equipment ($35). AR9 custom reclining bucket seats with Pallex cloth trim, not available GTA; on other Firebirds (no charge). AQ9 articulating luxury bucket seats in Trans Am convertible with Ventura leather trim; without R6A value option package ($780); with R6A value option package (no extra cost); in GTA with Pallex cloth trim (no cost); in GTA with Ventura leather trim ($475). W68 Sport Appearance package for Firebird only, requires 1SB or 1SC option package with LHO engine; option includes Trans Am front and rear aero fascias, fog lamps and aero-style Trans Am body side moldings ($450). QPH P215/65R15 black sidewall touring tires including N24 wheels, Firebird only (no charge). QPE P215/60Rl6 black sidewall steel-belted radial touring tires including PW7 wheels, not available with B2L V-8; on Trans Am only (no charge). QLC high-performance P245/50ZR16 black sidewall steel-belted radial, not available with Firebird, includes WS6 performance suspension and PW7 wheels on Trans Am and GTA or PEO wheels with Formula; on Formula and GTA (no charge); on Trans Am only ($313). WDV tire warranty enhancement for New York ($25). N24 15 x 7-in. deep-dish High-Tech Turbo cast-aluminum wheels with locking package, not available for Formula or GTA; on other Firebirds (no charge). PEO 16 x 8-in. deep-dish High-Tech Turbo cast-aluminum wheels with locking package, on Formula only (no charge). PW7 16-in. color-coordinated diamond spoke cast-aluminum wheels with locking package, charcoal-colored on Trans Am and Gold on GTA (no charge). 52P 16 x 8-in. gold diamond spoke cast-aluminum wheels, including gold decals on Trans Am; included with beige top on Trans Am convertible; standard GTA (not available on Firebird coupe or convertible or Formula coupe); on Trans Am coupe and convertible and GTA (no extra cost).

Only 508 GTAs were built in 1992.

HISTORICAL FOOTNOTES

John Middlebrook was Pontiac Motor Division's general manager in 1992. E.M. Schlesinger was in charge of general sales and service. E.S. Lechtzin was the company's director of public relations. Lynn C. Myers was the director of marketing and production planning. B. L. Warner was chief engineer. Total production in U.S. and Canada was 27,567 Firebirds. That represented 0.49 percent of total U.S. auto production. The model-year sales total was recorded as 23,401 Firebirds. Calendar year sales were 21,501 Firebirds. Of 25,180 cars built for the domestic market in model year 1992, 89.1 percent had the four-speed automatic transmission, 7 percent had a five-speed manual gearbox, 99.7 percent had a manual air conditioner, 93 percent had power door locks and windows, 67.9 percent had cruise control, 63.3 percent had a rear window defogger, 84.4 percent had dual power rearview mirrors, 53.4 percent had hatch roofs, 41.6 percent had an AM/FM stereo with cassette, 54.4 percent had a premium sound system and 4.0 percent had a CD player. SLP Engineering of Tom's River, New Jersey, offered a Formula Firehawk conversion this year, as well as a "Street Legal Performance" kit that was made available through the GM Service Parts Organization.

The 1993 Trans Am was again plenty sporty with fog lamps, tinted windows, T-tops and a rear spoiler.

Fourth Generation

Firebirds had all-new sheet metal for 1993, when the brand's fourth-generation Firebird arrived. The radically new F-car was 90 percent different than its predecessor. Firebird, Formula and Trans Am coupes were offered in the model line up. Driver and passenger-side front airbags was a standard safety feature.

All Firebirds had a 68-degree windshield, new aluminum wheels and tires, composite body panels that were resistant to minor impacts and rust, new instruments, new suspensions and a standard new 3.4-liter V-6. A new 5.7-liter V-8 was standard in Formula and Trans Am models, which also got a six-speed manual transmission. Advanced four-wheel anti-lock brakes were standard on all Firebird models with four-wheel disc brakes standard on Formulas and Trans Ams.

Standard on all Firebirds was a front air dam, tinted glass, sport mirrors, aero rear-deck spoiler, side-window defogger, four-spoke steering wheel with adjustable steering column, P215/60R16 steel-belted touring tires, rack-and-pinion steering and a five-speed manual transmission. The high-performance Formula added body-color sport mirrors, smoothly contoured taillights with neutral-density lenses and 16-inch aluminum wheels. Trans Am buyers also got specific front and rear fascia panels and a specific deck-lid spoiler, plus fog lamps, rocker-panel extensions and Goodyear Eagle GS-C performance tires.

Back and more popular was SLP Engineering's Formula Firehawk, described as, "The most aggressive profile this side of Madonna." With 300 hp, it went from 0 to 60 in 4.9 seconds and did the quarter mile in 13.53 seconds at 103.5 mph. The price came down to $24,244 and sales went up to 250 units.

Only 14,112 Firebirds were built in model year 1993, but that was mostly due to the late introduction. Production of the cars in a factory in Ste. Therese, Quebec, Canada, did not start until November 1992. They were first due out early in calendar 1993 and didn't appear in showrooms until even later than that.

I.D. NUMBERS

Pontiac's 17-symbol Vehicle Identification Number (VIN) for passenger cars was on the upper left surface of the instrument panel, visible through the windshield. The first symbol indicates country of origin: 1 or 4=U.S., 2=Canada. The second symbol indicates manufacturer: G=General Motors. The third symbol indicates make: 2=Pontiac division, 7=GM of Canada. The fourth and fifth symbols indicate body type and series: F/S=Firebird, F/V=Firebird Formula or Trans Am. The sixth symbol denotes body type: 2=two-door hatchback/liftback style 87. The seventh symbol indicated the type of restraint system: 1=manual belts; 2=active manual belts with dual airbags; 3=active manual belts with driver airbag; 4=passive automatic belts; 5=passive automatic belts with driver airbag. Symbol eight is an engine code: P=UPC LT1 5.7-liter fuel-injected (MFI) V-8; S=UPC L32 3.4-liter fuel-injected (MFI) V-6. The ninth symbol is a check digit. The tenth symbol denotes model year (P=1993). The 11th symbol indicates the GM assembly plant 2=Ste. Therese, Canada. The last six symbols are the consecutive unit number at the factory. V-6 engine code on right side of block near water pump. V-8 engine code on pad on front of block below right cylinder head. Engine production codes for 1993 were: [3.4-liter MFI V-6] MTA, [5.7-liter EFI/TPI V-8] DJB-SAP-SAW-DJC-SAS-SAX-SFB-SAU-SAY.

COLORS

Dark Green Metallic, Yellow, Bright Red, Medium Red Metallic, Bright Blue Metallic, Gray Purple Metallic, Bright White and Black.

FIREBIRD - SERIES F/S - V-6/V-8

Pontiac's fourth-generation Firebird arrived in 1993 with 90 percent new content. This radical revision found most every component of the Firebird completely new or extensively updated. The full line consisted of Firebird, Formula Firebird and Trans Am three-door hatchback coupes. Included among the many changes for 1993 were a 68-degree windshield angle, new aluminum wheels and tires, composite body panels that were resistant to minor impacts and rust, new instrumentation, a locking glove box and new front and rear suspensions. A new 3.4-liter V-6 was standard in the Firebird and a LT1 5.7-liter V-8 was standard in Formula and Trans Am models. A new six-speed manual transmission was also standard in Formulas and Trans Ams. Other new features included advanced four-wheel antilock brakes (standard on Firebirds with four-wheel disc brakes including all Formulas and Trans Ams) and dual front airbags. A keyless entry system was now available on all Firebirds and standard on Trans Ams. Standard equipment on the base Firebird included 5-mph front and rear bumpers, composite body panels (doors, fenders, fascias, roof, rear deck and spoiler), a front air dam, a Solar-Ray tinted glass liftback with strut supports, electrically operated concealed quartz halogen headlights, dual body-color Sport outside rearview mirrors (left-hand remote controlled and right-hand manual convex), basecoat/clearcoat exterior body finish, an aero-style rear deck lid spoiler, P215/60R16 steel-belted radial touring tires, a T125/70D15 high-pressure compact spare tire on a 15 x 4-in. steel spare wheel, 16 x 7 1/2-in. cast-aluminum wheels, driver and front passenger airbags (supplemental inflatable restraint system), a full-length console with its front adjoining to the instrument panel, a multi-function control lever including controlled-cycle windshield wipers, side window defoggers, front floor mats, a glove box with light and lock, a remote hatch release, dual horns, full-gauge instrumentation including tachometer and trip odometer, a day/night inside rearview mirror with reading lamps, dual visor vanity mirrors, a Delco UM6 ETR stereo with cassette and clock, three-point front drive and passenger safety belts, two-way manual front seat adjusters for driver and passenger seats, reclining front bucket seats, a folding rear seat, a four-spoke steering wheel with Tilt-Wheel adjustable steering column, the PASS-Key II theft-deterrent system, a Delco Freedom II battery, a parking brake with self-adjusting feature, power front disc/rear drum brakes with antilock braking system (ABS), a 3.4-liter V-6 with sequential-port fuel injec-

tion, a low oil level monitor and warning, rear-wheel drive, power rack-and-pinion steering, a short-and-long arm front suspension, a torque arm/track bar rear suspension, a Ride & Handling package, a five-speed manual transmission, a three-year/36,000-mile no-deductible warranty program and 24-hour Roadside Assistance program providing lock-out assistance, dead-battery assistance, out-of-fuel assistance, flat-tire assistance and courtesy transportation.

Model Number	Body/Style Number	Body Type & Seating	Factory Price	Shipping Weight	Production Total
F/S	87	2d hatchback-5P	$13,995	3,241 lbs.	5,006

Note 1: Pontiac's official production total for Firebird, Formula Firebird and Trans Am models is 15,475. The difference may be in export production and Firehawk production.

FORMULA FIREBIRD - SERIES 2F V-6/V-8

The 1993 Formula Firebird was promoted as "Pontiac's new and improved Formula for performance." The 275-hp LT1 5.7-liter V-8 was standard and linked to the new six-speed manual transmission. A more rigid body structure, an Opti-Spark ignition system, a gear-driven water pump, de Carbon monotube shock absorbers and Goodyear Eagle GT touring tires contributed to the Formula Firebird's high-performance image. Additional standard equipment on the Formula Firebird included 5-mph front and rear bumpers, composite body panels (doors, fenders, fascias, roof, rear deck and spoiler), a front air dam, a Solar-Ray tinted glass liftback with strut supports, electrically-operated concealed quartz halogen headlights, dual body-color Sport outside rearview mirrors (left-hand remote controlled and right-hand manual convex), basecoat/clearcoat exterior body finish, an aero-style rear deck lid spoiler, taillights with a neutral-density lens and smooth contour appearance, P235/55R16 steel-belted radial touring tires, a T125/70D15 high-pressure compact spare tire on a 15 x 4-in. steel spare wheel, bright silver 16 x 8-in. Sport cast-aluminum wheels, driver and front passenger airbags (supplemental inflatable restraint system), air conditioning, a full-length console with its front adjoining to the instrument panel, a multi-function control lever with controlled-cycle windshield wipers, side window defoggers, front floor mats, a glove box with light and lock, a remote hatch release, dual horns, full-gauge instrumentation including tachometer and trip odometer, a day/night inside rearview mirror with reading lamps, dual visor-vanity mirrors, a Delco UM6 ETR stereo with cassette and clock, three-point front driver and passenger safety belts, two-way manual front seat adjusters for driver and passenger seats, reclining front bucket seats, a folding rear seat, a four-spoke steering wheel with Tilt-Wheel adjustable steering column, the PASS-Key II theft-deterrent system, a Delco Freedom II battery, a parking brake with self-adjusting feature, power four-wheel disc brakes with antilock braking system (ABS), a low oil level monitor and warning, rear-wheel drive, power rack-and-pinion steering, a short/long arm front suspension, a torque arm/track bar rear suspension, a Performance Ride & Handling suspension, a three-year/36,000-mile no-deductible warranty program and 24-hour Roadside

Assistance program providing lock-out assistance, dead-battery assistance, out-of-fuel assistance, flat-tire assistance and courtesy transportation.

Model Number	Body/Style Number	Body Type & Seating	Factory Price	Shipping Weight	Production Total
F/S	87	2d hatchback-5P	$17,995	3,381 lbs.	3,985

Note 2: Pontiac's official production total for Firebird, Formula Firebird and Trans Am models is 15,475. The difference may be in export production and Firehawk production.

TRANS AM - SERIES F/V - V-8

The 1993 Trans Am was promoted as "legendary excitement reborn." Standard equipment on the Trans Am included 5-mph front and rear bumpers, composite body panels (doors, fenders, fascias, roof, rear deck and spoiler), fog lamps, a front air dam, a Solar-Ray tinted glass liftback with strut supports, electrically operated concealed quartz halogen headlights, dual body-color power Sport outside rearview mirrors (right-hand convex with blue glass), body-color body side moldings, basecoat/clearcoat exterior body finish, an aero-style rear deck lid spoiler, taillights with a neutral-density lens and smooth contour appearance, P45/50ZR16 high-performance steel-belted radial tires, a T125/70D15 high-pressure compact spare tire on a 15 x 4-in. steel spare wheel, bright silver 16 x 8-in. Sport cast-aluminum wheels, driver and front passenger airbags (supplemental inflatable restraint system), air conditioning, a full-length console with its front adjoining to the instrument panel, a multi-function control lever including controlled-cycle windshield wipers, cruise control, side window defoggers, a rear window defogger, automatic power door locks, front and rear floor mats, a glove box with light and lock, a remote hatch release, dual horns, full-gauge instrumentation including tachometer and trip odometer, keyless remote entry, a day/night inside rearview mirror with reading lamps, dual visor vanity mirrors, a Delco UX1 ETR AM/FM stereo (with auto-reverse cassette player, five-band equalizer, clock, seek up/down, scan, search-and-replay, steering wheel radio controls, Delco Loc II theft-deterrent system and high-performance 10-speaker system; requires power windows, power door locks and leather appointment group), three-point front driver and passenger safety belts, four-way manual front seat adjuster for driver's seat and two-way manual seat adjuster for front passenger's seat, reclining front bucket seats, a folding rear seat, a leather-wrapped four-spoke steering wheel with Tilt-Wheel adjustable steering column (includes leather-wrapped shift knob and parking brake handle), the PASS-Key II theft-deterrent system, power windows with express-down driver's side window, a Delco Freedom II battery, a parking brake with self-adjusting feature, power four-wheel disc brakes with antilock braking system (ABS), the 5.7-liter LT1 V-8 with sequential-port fuel injection, a low oil level monitor and warning, a performance rear axle with 3.23:1 axle ratio, an engine oil cooler, rear-wheel drive, power rack-and-pinion steering, a short-and-long arm front suspension, a torque arm/track bar rear suspension, a Performance Ride & Handling suspension, a six-speed manual transmission, a three-year/36,000-mile no-deductible warranty program and 24-hour Roadside Assistance program providing lock-out assistance, dead-battery assistance, out-of-fuel assistance, flat-tire assistance and courtesy transportation.

Model Number	Body/Style Number	Body Type & Seating	Factory Price	Shipping Weight	Production Total
2F	FV2	2d Coupe-5P	$21,395	3,452 lbs.	5,121

Note 4: Pontiac's official production total for Firebird, Formula Firebird and Trans Am models is 15,475. The difference may be in export production and Firehawk production.

ENGINES

Base V-6 [UPC L32]: Overhead valve. Cast-iron block and head. Aluminum intake manifold. Displacement: 207 cid. (3.4 liter). Bore & stroke: 3.62 x 3.31. Compression ratio: 9.0:1. Brake horsepower: 160 at 4600 rpm. Torque: 200 ft. lbs. at 3200 rpm. Fuel system: EFI. Standard in Firebird. Not available in Formula and Trans Am. VIN code S.

Base V-8 [UPC LT1]: Overhead valve. Cast-iron block and head. Aluminum intake manifold. Displacement: 350 cid. (5.7 liter). Bore & stroke: 4.00 x 3.48. Compression ratio: 10.5:1. Brake horsepower: 270 at 4800 rpm. Torque: 325 ft. lbs. at 2400 rpm. Fuel system: PFI. Standard in Formula and Trans Am. Not available in Firebird. VIN code P.

CHASSIS

Base Firebird: Wheelbase: 101.0 in. Overall length: 195.6 in. Width: 74.5 in. Height: 52 in. Front tread: 60.7 in. Rear tread: 60.6 in. Front headroom: 37.2 in. Rear headroom: 35.3 in. Front legroom: 43 in. Rear

The 275-hp LT1 5.7-liter V-8 was one of the Formula's biggest selling points.

legroom: 28.9 in. Front shoulder room: 57.4 in. Rear shoulder room: 55.8 in. Front hip room: 52.8 in. Rear hip room: 44.4 in. Standard tires: P215/60R16 steel-belted radial touring.

Formula Firebird: Wheelbase: 101.0 in. Overall length: 195.6 in. Width: 74.5 in. Height: 52 in. Front tread: 60.7 in. Rear tread: 60.6 in. Front headroom: 37.2 in. Rear headroom: 35.3 in. Front legroom: 43 in. Rear legroom: 28.9 in. Front shoulder room: 57.4 in. Rear shoulder room: 55.8 in. Front hip room: 52.8 in. Rear hip room: 44.4 in. Standard tires: P235/55R16 steel-belted radial touring tires.

Firebird Trans Am: Wheelbase: 101.0 in. Overall length: 197 in. Width: 74.5 in. Height: 51.7 in. Front tread: 60.7 in. Rear tread: 60.6 in. Front headroom: 37.2 in. Rear headroom: 35.3 in. Front legroom: 43 in. Rear legroom: 28.9 in. Front shoulder room: 57.4 in. Rear shoulder room: 55.8 in. Front hip room: 52.8 in. Rear hip room: 44.4 in. Standard tires: P45/50ZR16 high-performance steel-belted radial tires.

TECHNICAL

Base Firebird: Chassis: Front engine/rear drive. Base transmission: Five-speed manual. Optional transmission: Four-speed automatic. Performance Ride & Handling suspension. Front suspension: Short-and-long arm (SLA) design with gas-filled monotube shocks including front stabilizer bar. Rear suspension: Live axle with revised spring mass and rates with gas-filled monotube shocks. Steering: Power assist rack-and-pinion. Turning circle: 37.8 ft. Brakes: Advanced Delco-Moraine ABS VI four-wheel antilock front disc/rear drum brakes. Fuel tank: 15.5 gal.

Formula: Chassis: Front engine/rear drive. Base transmission: Six-speed manual. Optional transmission: Four-speed automatic. Performance Ride & Handling suspension. Front suspension: Short/long arm (SLA) design with gas-filled monotube shocks including front stabilizer bar. Rear suspension: Live axle with revised spring mass and rates with gas-filled monotube shocks. Steering: Power assist rack-and-pinion. Turning circle: 37.8 ft. Brakes: Advanced Delco-Moraine ABS VI four-wheel disc brakes with antilock braking. Fuel tank: 15.5 gal.

Trans Am: Chassis: Front engine/rear drive. Base transmission: Six-speed manual. Optional transmission: Four-speed automatic. Performance Ride & Handling suspension. Front suspension: Short/long arm (SLA) design with gas-filled monotube shocks including front stabilizer bar. Rear suspension: Live axle with revised spring mass and rates with gas-filled monotube shocks. Steering: Power assist rack-and-pinion. Turning circle: 37.8 ft. Brakes: Advanced Delco-Moraine ABS VI four-wheel disc brakes with antilock braking. Fuel tank: 15.5 gal.

OPTIONS

FE9 Federal emissions (no cost). YF5 California emissions ($100). NG1 New York emissions ($100). QPE P215/60R16 black sidewall steel-belted radial touring tires, standard on Firebird, not available on Formula, Trans Am or Trans Am GT (no cost). QMT P235/55R16 black sidewall touring tires, standard on Formula and Trans Am, not available on Trans Am GT ($132). QLC P245/50ZR16 steel-belted radial black sidewall tires, standard Trans Am GT, not available on base Firebird ($225). B9 bucket seats with Metrix cloth trim in base Firebird, Formula Firebird and Trans Am coupe (standard, no cost). AR9 articulating bucket seats with leather trim in base Firebird, Formula Firebird and Trans Am coupe ($780). B9 bucket seats with Metrix cloth trim in base Firebird and Formula Firebird convertible (standard, no cost). AQ9 articulating bucket seats with leather trim in base Firebird and Formula Firebird convertible ($805). D8 articulating bucket seats with Metrix cloth trim in Trans Am GT (standard, no cost). AQ9 articulating bucket seats with leather trim in Trans Am GT ($475). AQ9 articulating bucket seats with Metrix cloth trim in base Trans Am and Trans Am GT convertible (standard, no cost). AQ9 articulating bucket seats with leather trim in base Trans Am and Trans Am GT convertible ($475). 1SA option group for base Firebird coupe with standard equipment (no cost). 1SB option group for base Firebird coupe includes air conditioning, rear floor mats, body side moldings and four-way seat adjuster ($1,005). 1SC option group for base Firebird coupe includes contents of 1SB plus power windows, power door locks, cruise control, power mirrors, remote keyless entry, 10-speaker sound system with graphic equalizer and steering wheel controls and four-way seat adjuster ($2,421). 1SA option group for Formula Firebird coupe with standard equipment (no cost). 1SB option group for Formula Firebird coupe includes air conditioning, rear floor mats, body side moldings and four-way seat adjuster ($906). 1SC option group for Formula Firebird coupe includes contents of 1SB plus power windows, power door locks, cruise control, power mirrors, remote keyless entry, 10-speaker sound system with graphic equalizer and steering wheel controls and four-way seat adjuster ($1,491). 1SA option group for Firebird convertible with standard equipment (no cost). 1SB option group for Firebird convertible includes remote keyless entry, six-speaker sound system with graphic equalizer and steering wheel controls and leather appointment group ($485). 1SA option group for Formula Firebird convertible with standard equipment (no cost). 1SB option group for Formula Firebird convertible includes remote keyless entry, six-speaker sound system with graphic equalizer and steering wheel controls and leather appointment group ($485). 1SA option group for Trans Am convertible with standard equipment (no cost). Y82 Trans Am option (standard) Y83 Trans Am GT option (standard). Y84 Trans Am GT convertible option (standard). C60 air conditioning, standard Formula, Trans Am and Trans Am GT ($895). C41 non-air conditioning, standard base Firebird, not available Trans Am and Trans Am GT ($895 credit). B84 body-color body side moldings on coupes, standard on Trans Am GT ($60). K34 cruise control with "resume" feature on coupes, standard on Trans Am and Trans Am GT ($225). C49 rear window defogger in coupe, standard Trans Am GT ($170). CC1 hatch roof for coupes, with removable glass panels, locks and stowage ($895).

YK3 front license plate bracket (no cost). DE4 hatch roof sunshades ($25). B35 rear floor mats for coupe, standard in Trans Am GT ($15). DG7 dual power outside rearview mirrors with blue glass for coupes, standard on Trans Am and Trans Am GT ($96). AU3 power door locks on coupe, standard on Trans Am and Trans Am GT ($220). A31 power windows for coupes, standard on Trans Am and Trans Am GT ($290). UN6 ETR AM/FM stereo with auto-reverse cassette, not available in Trans Am GT (standard). U1C ETR AM/FM stereo with CD player, not available in Trans Am GT ($226). UT6 ETR AM/FM stereo with auto-reverse cassette, graphic equalizer in coupe, standard in Trans Am GT ($450). UT6 ETR AM/FM stereo with auto-reverse cassette, graphic equalizer in convertible, standard in Trans Am GT convertible ($350). UP3 ETR AM/FM stereo with CD player and graphic equalizer, in base Firebird and Formula coupe without 1SC ($676). UP3 ETR AM/FM stereo with CD player and graphic equalizer, in base Firebird and Formula coupe with 1SC ($226). UP3 ETR AM/FM stereo with CD player and graphic equalizer, in Trans Am coupe ($676). UP3 ETR AM/FM stereo with CD player and graphic equalizer, in Trans Am GT coupe ($226). UP3 ETR AM/FM stereo with CD player and graphic equalizer, in base Firebird and Formula convertible without 1SB ($576). UP3 ETR AM/FM stereo with CD player and graphic equalizer, in base Firebird and Formula convertible with 1SB ($226). ($576). UP3 ETR AM/FM stereo with CD player and graphic equalizer, in Trans Am GT convertible ($226). GU5 performance axle, not available in base Firebird, Trans Am or Trans Am GT ($175). AU0 remote keyless entry, standard Trans Am GT ($135). AH3 four-way manual driver's seat adjuster for coupes, not available in Formula or Trans Am, standard in Trans Am GT ($35). AC3 six-way power driver's seat, not available in Trans Am GT, in Firebird coupe without 1SB and 1SC ($305). AC3 six-way power driver's seat, not available in Trans Am GT, in Firebird coupe with 1SB and 1SC ($270). AC3 six-way power driver's seat, in Formula and Trans Am coupes ($305). AC3 six-way power driver's seat in convertible, not available in Trans Am GT ($270). MM5 five-speed manual transmission, standard in base Firebird, not available in others (standard). MN6 six-speed manual transmission, not available in base Firebird, standard in Formula, Trans Am and Trans Am GT (standard). MXO four-speed automatic transmission ($775). 40P white wheels, not available on base Firebird (no cost).

HISTORICAL FOOTNOTES

John Middlebrook was Pontiac Motor Division's general manager in 1992. Total production in U.S. and Canada included 15,475 Firebirds. The model-year sales total was recorded as 19,068 Firebirds. Of 14,112 Firebird cars built for the domestic market in model year 1993, 90 percent had the four-speed automatic transmission, 4 percent had a five-speed manual gearbox, 6 percent had the new six-speed manual transmission, 99.9 percent had a manual air conditioner, 95.9 percent had power door locks and 96.3 percent had power windows, 5.8 percent had power seats, 96.3 percent had cruise control, 87 percent had a rear window defogger, 96.3 percent had dual power rearview mirrors, 10.8 percent had hatch roofs, 34.3 percent had an AM/FM stereo with cassette, 43 percent had a premium sound system and 22.7 percent had a CD player. SLP Engineering of Tom's River, N.J. offered a Formula Firehawk conversion this year, as well as a "Street Legal Performance" kit that was made available through the GM Service Parts Organization. The fourth-generation Firebirds came out later than other 1993 Pontiacs. Production began in November 1992 at a General Motors assembly plant in Ste. Therese, Quebec, Canada. The first cars were scheduled to arrive in dealer showrooms early in calendar year 1993, but actually appeared even later in the year. SLP also produced a potent 300-hp "Firehawk" version of the 1993 Trans Am, of which 201 examples were made.

The base Firebird coupe could be had for about $14,000 in 1993.

The Firebird family (clockwise from left): Trans Am, base coupe, Formula and Trans Am GT.

The Convertible Comes Back

The big news in Firebird country for 1994 was the release of a new drop-top model. This could be had as a base Firebird or a Trans Am and buyers could add the Formula or GT option to the more expensive version. Traction control was made available on Firebirds with a V-8 engine and automatic transmission. Prices for the year ranged from $14,589 to $21,999.

Additional new Firebird features included a Dark Aqua Metallic color, flood-lit interior door switches, visor straps, a Delco 2001 Series radio, a compact disc player without equalizer, a 5.7-liter sequentially fuel-injected (SFI) V-8, a Mass Air Flow Control System, a four-speed electronically controlled automatic transmission, driver-selectable automatic transmission controls, a 1-4-gear-skip feature on six-speed-manual-transmission models and two-part basecoat/clearcoat finish.

The new Trans Am GT package included body-colored side moldings, an air-foil-styled spoiler, an elec-

tric rear-window defogger, a Remote-Keyless Entry system, rear carpet mats, a Delco 2001 sound system, a four-way manual driver's seat and leather-wrapped steering wheel, shift knob and brake handle.

On January 27, 1994, Pontiac announced a special model to honor the silver anniversary of the Trans Am. This 25th Anniversary Edition Trans Am included Bright White exterior finish, a Bright Blue center-line stripe, anniversary logos and door badges, light-weight 16-inch aluminum wheels painted Bright White and white Prado leather seats with blue 25th Anniversary embroidery. Buyers received a special 25th Anniversary portfolio when they picked up a car.

As a special nod to Trans Am history, PMD head-quarters announced that it would build a very limited number of 25th Anniversary Trans Am GT convertibles to honor the eight famous T/A ragtops made when the sports-performance model was first released in mid-1969.

SLP Engineering again made Formula Firehawks and 500 were assembled. Model year production was 45,922 Firebirds. Model year sales more than doubled from 19,068 in 1993 to 46,499 in 1984.

I.D. NUMBERS

Pontiac's 17-symbol vehicle identification number (VIN) for passenger cars was on the upper left surface of the instrument panel, visible through the windshield. The first symbol indicates country of origin: 1 or 4=U.S.; 2=Canada; 3=Mexico; J=Japan. The second symbol indicates manufacturer: G=General Motors; G=Suzuki; 8=Isuzu; Y=NUMMI; C=CAMI. The third symbol G indicates make: 2=Pontiac division; 5=Pontiac incomplete (1G5); 7=GM of Canada; M=Pontiac Multi-Purpose Vehicle. The fourth and fifth symbols for passenger cars indicated body type and series: F/S=Firebird; F/V=Firebird Formula or Trans Am. The sixth symbol denoted body type: 2=two-door hatchback/liftback style 87; 3=two-door convertible style 67. The seventh symbol indicated the type of restraint system: 1=manual belts; 2=active manual belts with dual airbags; 3=active manual belts with driver airbag; 4=passive automatic belts; 5=passive automatic belts with driver airbag; 6=passive automatic belts with dual airbags. Symbol eight was an engine code: P=UPC LT1 5.7-liter fuel-injected (MFI) V-8; S=UPC L32 3.4-liter fuel-injected (MFI) V-6 The ninth symbol is a check digit. The tenth symbol denotes model year (R=1994). The 11th symbol for cars and trucks indicates the GM assembly plant: 2=Ste. Therese, Canada. The last six symbols are the consecutive unit number at the factory. V-6 engine code on right side of block near water pump. V-8 engine code on pad on front of block below right cylinder head.

COLORS

Dark Green Metallic, Yellow, Bright Red, Medium Red Metallic, Bright Blue Metallic, Gray Purple Metallic, Dark Aqua Metallic, Bright White and Black.

FIREBIRD - SERIES 2F - V-6/V-8

Pontiac's theme for its Firebird 1994 lineup could have been the "return of the ragtop." Each of its series — Firebird, Formula and Trans Am — had its 1993 coupe-only offering bolstered with the addition of a convertible. The Trans Am convertible was part of its GT series, while the coupe version was offered both as a Trans Am and a GT. New features for the overall Firebird line included a new Dark Aqua Metallic exterior color, flood-lit interior door switches, visor straps, a Delco 2001 Series radio, a compact disc player (without graphic equalizer), a 5.7-liter SFI V-8, a Mass Air Flow Control System, a four-speed electronically-controlled automatic transmission, driver-selectable automatic transmission controls, a six-speed manual transmission with a 1-4 gear skip shift feature, a 3.42:1 axle ratio, a traction-control system (V-8 automatic only) and two-component clearcoat paint. Additional standard equipment on the base Firebird included a black fixed mast antenna, soft fascia-type front and rear bumpers, composite body panels (doors, fenders, fascias, roof, rear deck and spoiler), Solar-Ray tinted glass liftback with strut supports, electrically operated concealed quartz halogen headlights, dual body-color Sport outside rearview mirrors (left-hand remote controlled and right-hand manual convex), a rear deck lid spoiler, P215/60R16 steel-belted radial touring tires, a T125/70D15 high-pressure compact spare tire on a 15 x 4-in. steel spare wheel, 16 x 7 1/2-in. cast-aluminum wheels, controlled-cycle windshield wipers, extensive acoustical insulation, driver's and passenger side front airbags, three-point active safety belts, a full-length console

adjoining to the instrument panel, side window defoggers, Metrix cloth fabric, analog instrumentation (including a tachometer, a trip odometer, a coolant temperature gauge, an oil pressure indicator, a voltmeter and a speedometer), lights for ashtray and dome and glove box, fully carpeted luggage compartment trim, front carpet mat, a day/night inside rearview mirror with reading lamps, dual covered visor vanity mirrors, a remote hatch release, a Delco 2001 Series ETR AM/FM stereo with auto-reverse cassette and search-and-replay and clock with Delco theft lock, passive lap and shoulder safety belts for driver and front passenger, lap and shoulder belts for rear outboard positions, two-way manual front seat adjusters for driver and passenger seats, reclining front bucket seats, a folding rear seat, a four-spoke steering wheel with Tilt-Wheel adjustable steering column, the PASS-Key II theft-deterrent system, a Delco Freedom II battery, power front disc/rear drum brakes with antilock braking system (ABS), a brake/transmission shift interlock feature with automatic transmission, a 3.4-liter V-6 with sequential port fuel injection, a stainless steel exhaust system, extensive anti-corrosion protection, the GM Computer Command Control engine management system, a low oil level monitor and warning, rear-wheel drive, power rack-and-pinion steering, a short/long arm front suspension, a torque arm/track bar rear suspension, a Ride & Handling suspension package, a five-speed manual transmission, a 3-year/36,000-mile no-deductible warranty program and 24-hour Roadside Assistance program providing lock-out assistance, dead-battery assistance, out-of-fuel assistance, flat-tire assistance and courtesy transportation. Firebird convertibles also featured a power-operated top with a fully trimmed headliner, a glass rear window with electric defogger, front and rear floor mats, dual power sport mirrors and a three-piece tonneau cover.

Model Number	Body/Style Number	Body Type & Seating	Factory Price	Shipping Weight	Production Total
F/S	87	2d hatchback-5P	$13,995	3,232 lbs.	25,509
F/S	67	2d convertible-5P	$21,179	3,346 lbs.	174

Note 1: T-tops were used on 8,440 base Firebird hatchbacks.

FORMULA FIREBIRD - SERIES F/S V-8

The Formula series also gained a convertible in the middle of the 1994 model year. The Formula was promoted as a safe and high-performance sports car. It included a hot V-8, disc brakes at all corners, a standard six-speed manual gearbox (or optional four-

The Formula came in a convertible version for 1994, as did the base Firebird and the Trans Am.

The Trans Am GT had several styling differences from the other F-Cars, including the shape of the spoiler.

speed automatic with "normal" and "performance" driver-selectable shift calibrations) and suspension and steering upgrades. The rigid body featured two-sided galvanized steel panels, rustproof composite panels (used for the fenders, doors, hood and hatch) and front fenders that could even spring back from minor impacts. Additional standard equipment for all Formula Firebirds included a black fixed-mast antenna, soft fascia-type front and rear bumpers, composite body panels (doors, fenders, fascias, roof, rear deck and spoiler), Solar-Ray tinted glass liftback with strut supports, electrically operated concealed quartz halogen headlights, dual body-color Sport outside rearview mirrors (left-hand remote controlled and right-hand manual convex), a rear deck lid spoiler, P235/55R16 steel-belted radial touring tires, a T125/70D15 high-pressure compact spare tire on a 15 x 4-in. steel spare wheel, bright silver 16 x 8-in. Sport cast-aluminum wheels, controlled-cycle windshield wipers, extensive acoustical insulation, driver's and passenger side front airbags, three-point active safety belts, air conditioning, a full-length console adjoining to the instrument panel, side window defoggers, Metrix cloth fabric, analog instrumentation (including a tachometer, a trip odometer, a coolant temperature gauge, an oil pressure indicator, a voltmeter and a speedometer), lights for ashtray, dome and glove box, fully carpeted luggage compartment trim, front carpet mat, a day/night inside rearview mirror with reading lamps, dual covered visor-vanity mirrors, a remote hatch release, a Delco 2001 Series ETR AM/FM stereo with auto-reverse cassette and search-and-replay and clock with Delco theft lock, passive lap and shoulder safety belts for driver and front passenger, lap and shoulder belts for rear outboard positions, two-way manual front seat adjusters for driver and passenger seats, reclining front bucket seats, a folding rear seat, a four-spoke steering wheel with Tilt-Wheel adjustable steering column, the PASS-Key II theft-deterrent system, a Delco Freedom II battery, power four-wheel disc brakes with an antilock braking system (ABS), a brake/transmission shift interlock feature with automatic transmission, a 5.7-liter V-8 with sequential port fuel injection, a stainless steel exhaust system, extensive anti-corrosion protection, the GM Computer Command Control engine management system, a low oil level monitor and warning, rear-wheel drive, power rack-and-pinion steering, a short-and-long arm front suspension, a torque arm/track bar rear suspension, a six-speed manual transmission, a Performance Ride & Handling suspension package, a three-year/36,000-mile no-deductible warranty program and 24-hour Roadside Assistance program providing lock-out assistance, dead-battery assistance, out-of-fuel assistance, flat-tire assistance and courtesy transportation. Formula Firebird convertibles also featured a power-operated top with a fully trimmed headliner, a glass rear window with electric defogger, front and rear floor mats, dual power sport outside rearview mirrors and a three-piece tonneau cover.

Model Number	Body/Style Number	Body Type & Seating	Factory Price	Shipping Weight	Production Total
F/S	87	2d hatchback-5P	$17,995	3,369 lbs.	9,057
F/S	67	2d convertible-5P	$24,279	3,485 lbs.	168

Note 2: T-tops were used on 4,685 Formula Firebird hatchbacks.

TRANS AM - SERIES F/V - V-8

The 1994 Trans Am could be spotted by its unique front end, which had no grille and two round fog lamps. Traction Control became available on Trans Ams after midyear. There was no convertible in the first-level Trans Am model line up. Standard equipment for the Trans Am included a black fixed mast antenna, soft fascia type front and rear bumpers, composite body panels (doors, fenders, fascias, roof, rear deck and spoiler), Solar-Ray tinted glass liftback with strut supports, electrically operated concealed quartz halogen headlights, fog lamps, dual body-color power Sport outside rearview mirrors (with blue glass), a rear deck lid spoiler, P235/55R16 steel-belted radial touring tires, a T125/70D15 high-pressure compact spare tire on a 15 x 4-in. steel spare wheel, bright silver 16 x 8-in. Sport cast-aluminum wheels, controlled-cycle windshield wipers, extensive acoustical insulation, driver's and passenger side front airbags, three-point active safety belts, air conditioning, a full-length console adjoining to the instrument panel, cruise control, side window defoggers, automatic power door locks, Metrix cloth fabric, analog instrumentation (including a tachometer, a trip odometer, a coolant temperature gauge, an oil pressure indicator, a voltmeter and a speedometer), lights for ashtray and dome and glove box, fully carpeted luggage compartment trim, front carpet mat, a day/night inside rearview mirror with reading lamps, dual covered visor-vanity mirrors, power windows with an express-down feature, a remote hatch release, a Delco 2001 Series ETR AM/FM stereo with auto reverse cassette and search-and-replay and clock with Delco theft lock, passive lap and shoulder safety belts for driver and front passenger, lap and shoulder belts for rear outboard positions, two-way manual front seat adjusters for driver and passenger seats, reclining front bucket seats, a folding rear seat, a four-spoke steering wheel with Tilt-Wheel adjustable steering column, the PASS-Key II theft-deterrent system, a Delco Freedom II battery, power four-wheel disc brakes with an antilock braking system (ABS), a brake/transmission shift interlock feature with automatic transmission, a 5.7-liter V-8 with sequential port fuel injection, a stainless steel exhaust system, extensive anti-corrosion protection, the GM Computer Command Control engine management system, a low oil level monitor and warning, rear-wheel drive, power rack-and-pinion steering, a short-and-long arm front suspension, a torque arm/track bar rear suspension, a Performance Ride & Handling suspension package, a three-year/36,000-mile no-deductible warranty program and 24-hour Roadside Assistance program providing lock-out assistance, dead-battery assistance, out-of-fuel assistance, flat-tire assistance and courtesy transportation.

Model Number	Body/Style Number	Body Type & Seating	Factory Price	Shipping Weight	Production Total
2F	FV2	2d hatchback-5P	$19,895	3,461 lbs.	3,389
2F	FV3	2d convertible-5P	—	—	463

Note 3: T-tops were used on 1,957 Trans Am hatchbacks.

TRANS AM GT - SERIES F/V - V-8

The Trans Am GT had styling features that set it apart from the first-level Trans Am. The main difference was the design of the rear deck lid spoiler. It also had different tires, an upgraded sound system and other perks for buyers who wanted a top-of-the-line Firebird. Standard equipment for the Trans Am GT included a black fixed-mast antenna, soft fascia-type front and rear bumpers, composite body panels (doors, fenders, fascias, roof, rear deck and spoiler), Solar-Ray tinted glass liftback with strut supports, electrically operated concealed quartz halogen headlights, fog lamps, dual body-color power Sport outside rearview mirrors (with blue glass), body-color side moldings, a rear deck lid spoiler, P245/50ZR16 steel-belted high-performance tires, a T125/70D15 high-pressure compact spare tire on a 15 x 4-in. steel spare wheel, bright silver 16 x 8-in. Sport cast-aluminum wheels, controlled-cycle windshield wipers, extensive acoustical insulation, driver's and passenger side front airbags, three-point active safety belts, air conditioning, a full-length console adjoining to the instrument panel, cruise control, side window defoggers, an electric rear window defogger, automatic power door locks, Metrix cloth fabric, analog instrumentation (including a tachometer, a trip odometer, a coolant temperature gauge, an oil pressure indicator, a voltmeter and a speedometer), a keyless entry system, lights for ashtray, dome and glove box, fully carpeted luggage compartment trim, front carpet mat, a rear carpeted mat, a day/night inside rearview mirror with reading lamps, dual covered visor vanity mirrors, power windows with an express-down feature, a remote hatch release, a Delco 2001 Series ETR AM/FM stereo with auto-reverse cassette and seven-band graphic equalizer (that included search-and-replay, seek up/down, a clock, a leather-wrapped steering wheel with redundant radio controls, a leather appointment group, Delco theft lock, a high-performance 10-speaker sound system, HSS speakers and tweeters in doors, 6 1/2-in. subwoofers in sail panels, a subwoofer amplifier in rear quarters and 4-inch speakers and tweeters in rear quarters), passive lap and shoulder safety belts for driver and front passenger, lap and shoulder belts for rear outboard positions, a four-way manual front seat adjuster for the driver's seat, a two-way manual front seat adjuster for the passenger's seat, reclining front bucket seats, a folding rear seat, a leather-wrapped four-spoke steering wheel with Tilt-Wheel adjustable steering column, a leather-wrapped shift knob and parking brake handle, the PASS-Key II theft-deterrent system, a Delco

The 25th Anniversary Trans Am was clocked at 14.2 seconds for the quarter mile.

Freedom II battery, power four-wheel disc brakes with an antilock braking system (ABS), a brake/transmission shift interlock feature with automatic transmission, a 5.7-liter V-8 with sequential port fuel injection engine, a stainless steel exhaust system, extensive anti-corrosion protection, the GM Computer Command Control engine management system, a low oil level monitor and warning, a 3.23:1 performance ratio rear axle, an engine oil cooler, rear-wheel drive, power rack-and-pinion steering, a short/long arm front suspension, a torque arm/track bar rear suspension, a Performance Ride & Handling suspension package, a three-year/36,000-mile no-deductible warranty program and 24-hour Roadside Assistance program providing lock-out assistance, dead battery assistance, out-of-fuel assistance, flat-tire assistance and courtesy transportation. Trans Am GT convertibles also featured a power-operated top with a fully trimmed headliner, a glass rear window and a three-piece tonneau cover.

Jerry Heasley photo

The 5.7-liter V-8 was the only engine option for 1994 Trans Ams.

Model Number	Body/Style Number	Body Type & Seating	Factory Price	Shipping Weight	Production Total
2F	FV2	2d hatchback-5P	$21,395	3,478 lbs.	6,142
2F	FV3	2d convertible-5P	$26,479	—	215

Note 4: T-tops were used on 4,342 Trans Am GT hatchbacks.

25th ANNIVERSARY TRANS AM GT SERIES F/V - V-8

The 25th Anniversary Trans Am was introduced on Jan. 27, 1994. As a special nod to Trans Am history, Pontiac also announced that it would build a very limited number of 25th Anniversary convertibles to honor the eight Trans Am convertibles made in 1969. The 25th Anniversary model's standard Trans Am equipment included a black fixed mast antenna, soft fascia type front and rear bumpers, composite body panels (doors, fenders, fascias, roof, rear deck and spoiler), Solar-Ray tinted glass liftback with strut supports, electrically operated concealed quartz halogen headlights, fog lamps, dual body-color power Sport outside rearview mirrors (with blue glass), a rear deck lid spoiler, P245/50ZR16 high-performance tires, a T125/70D15 high-pressure compact spare tire on a 15 x 4-in. steel spare wheel, bright silver 16 x 8-in. Sport cast-aluminum wheels, controlled-cycle windshield wipers, extensive acoustical insulation, driver's and

passenger side front airbags, three-point active safety belts, air conditioning, a full-length console adjoining to the instrument panel, cruise control, side window defoggers, automatic power door locks, Metrix cloth fabric, analog instrumentation (including a tachometer, a trip odometer, a coolant temperature gauge, an oil pressure indicator, a voltmeter and a speedometer), lights for ashtray, dome and glove box, fully carpeted luggage compartment trim, front carpet mat, a day/night inside rearview mirror with reading lamps, dual covered visor-vanity mirrors, power windows with an express-down feature, a remote hatch release, passive lap and shoulder safety belts for driver and front passenger, lap and shoulder belts for rear outboard positions, two-way manual front seat adjusters for driver and passenger seats, reclining front bucket seats, a folding rear seat, the PASS-Key II theft-deterrent system, a Delco Freedom II battery, power four-wheel disc brakes with an antilock braking system (ABS), a brake/transmission shift interlock feature with automatic transmission, a 5.7-liter V-8 with sequential-port fuel injection, a stainless steel exhaust system, extensive anti-corrosion protection, the GM Computer Command Control engine management system, a low oil level monitor and warning, rear-wheel drive, power rack-and-pinion steering, a short-and-long arm front suspension, a torque arm/track bar rear suspension, a Performance Ride & Handling suspension package, a three-year/36,000-mile no-deductible warranty program and 24-hour Roadside Assistance program. In addition to these standard Trans Am features, the 25th Anniversary model also included the GT-type rear deck lid spoiler, the UT6 upgraded 10-speaker sound system, a leather-wrapped steering wheel with radio controls and a Tilt-Wheel adjustable steering column, Bright White exterior finish, a Bright Blue centerline stripe, Anniversary logos and door badges, Bright White 16-in. lightweight aluminum wheels, White Prado leather seating surfaces with blue embroidery and a special 25th Anniversary portfolio for owners, a 3.23:1 performance ratio rear axle, an engine oil cooler, rear-wheel drive, power rack-and-pinion steering, a short/long arm front suspension, a torque arm/track bar rear suspension, a Performance Ride & Handling suspension package, a three-year/36,000-mile no-deductible warranty program and 24-hour Roadside Assistance program providing lock-out assistance, dead-battery assistance, out-of-fuel assistance, flat-tire assistance and courtesy transportation. Trans Am GT convertibles also featured a power-operated top with a fully trimmed headliner, a glass rear window and a three-piece tonneau cover.

Model Number	Body/Style Number	Body Type & Seating	Factory Price	Shipping Weight	Production Total
2F	FV2	2d hatchback-5P	$21,395	3,478 lbs.	1,750
2F	FV3	2d convertible-5P	$26,479	—	250

Note 5: T-tops were used on 1,412 Trans Am 25th Anniversary hatchbacks.

ENGINES

Base V-6 [UPC L32]: Overhead valve. Cast-iron block and head. Aluminum intake manifold. Displacement: 207 cid. (3.4-liter). Bore & stroke: 3.62 x 3.31.

Compression ratio: 9.0:1. Brake horsepower: 160 at 4600 rpm. Torque: 200 ft. lbs. at 3200 rpm. Fuel system: EFI. Standard in Firebird. Not available in Formula, Trans Am and Trans Am GT. VIN code S.

5.7-liter V-8 [UPC LT1]: Overhead valve. Cast-iron block and head. Aluminum intake manifold. Displacement: 350 cid. (5.7-liter). Bore & stroke: 4.00 x 3.48. Compression ratio: 10.5:1. Brake horsepower: 270 at 4800 rpm. Torque: 325 ft. lbs. at 2400 rpm. Fuel system: PFI. Standard in Formula, Trans Am and Trans Am GT. Not available in Firebird. VIN code P.

CHASSIS

Base Firebird: Wheelbase: 101.0 in. Overall length: 195.6 in. Width: 74.5 in. Height: 52 in. Front tread: 60.7 in. Rear tread: 60.6 in. Front headroom: 37.2 in. Rear headroom: 35.3 in. Front legroom: 43 in. Rear legroom: 28.9 in. Front shoulder room: 57.4 in. Rear shoulder room: 55.8 in. Front hip room: 52.8 in. Rear hip room: 44.4 in. Standard tires: P215/60R16 steel-belted radial touring.

Formula: Wheelbase: 101.0 in. Overall length: 195.6 in. Width: 74.5 in. Height: 52 in. Front tread: 60.7 in. Rear tread: 60.6 in. Front headroom: 37.2 in. Rear headroom: 35.3 in. Front legroom: 43 in. Rear legroom: 28.9 in. Front shoulder room: 57.4 in. Rear shoulder room: 55.8 in. Front hip room: 52.8 in. Rear hip room: 44.4 in. Standard tires: P235/55R16 steel-belted radial touring tires.

Trans Am: Wheelbase: 101.0 in. Overall length: 197 in. Width: 74.5 in. Height: 51.7 in. Front tread: 60.7 in. Rear tread: 60.6 in. Front headroom: 37.2 in. Rear headroom: 35.3 in. Front legroom: 43 in. Rear legroom: 28.9 in. Front shoulder room: 57.4 in. Rear shoulder room: 55.8 in. Front hip room: 52.8 in. Rear hip room: 44.4 in. Standard tires: P45/50ZR16 high-performance steel-belted radial tires.

TECHNICAL

Base Firebird: Chassis: Front engine/rear drive. Base transmission: Five-speed manual. Optional transmission: Four-speed automatic. Ride & Handling suspension. Front suspension: Short/long arm (SLA) design with gas-filled monotube shocks including front stabilizer bar. Rear suspension: Live axle with revised spring mass and rates with gas-filled monotube shocks. Steering: Power assist rack-and-pinion. Turning circle: 37.8 ft. Brakes: Advanced Delco-Moraine ABS VI four-wheel antilock front disc/rear drum brakes. Fuel tank: 15.5 gal.

Formula: Chassis: Front engine/rear drive. Base transmission: Six-speed manual. Optional transmission: Four-speed automatic. Performance Ride & Handling suspension. Front suspension: Short/long arm (SLA) design with gas-filled monotube shocks including front stabilizer bar. Rear suspension: Live axle with revised spring mass and rates with gas-filled monotube shocks. Steering: Power assist rack-and-pinion. Turning circle: 37.8 ft. Brakes: Advanced Delco-Moraine ABS VI four-wheel disc brakes with antilock braking. Fuel tank: 15.5 gal.

Trans Am: Chassis: Front engine/rear drive. Base transmission: Six-speed manual. Optional transmis-

The base Firebird was not lacking in creature comforts.

sion: Four-speed automatic. Performance Ride & Handling suspension. Front suspension: Short/long arm (SLA) design with gas-filled monotube shocks including front stabilizer bar. Rear suspension: Live axle with revised spring mass and rates with gas-filled monotube shocks. Steering: Power assist rack-and-pinion. Turning circle: 37.8 ft. Brakes: Advanced Delco-Moraine ABS VI four-wheel disc brakes with antilock braking. Fuel tank: 15.5 gal.

OPTIONS

FE9 Federal emissions (no cost). YF5 California emissions ($100). NG1 New York emissions ($100). QPE P215/60R16 black sidewall steel-belted radial touring tires, standard on Firebird, not available Formula, Trans Am or Trans Am GT (no cost). QMT P235/55R16 black sidewall touring tires, standard Formula and Trans Am, not available Trans Am GT ($132). QLC P245/50ZR16 steel-belted radial black sidewall tires, standard Trans Am GT, not available on base Firebird ($225). B9 bucket seats with Metrix cloth trim in base Firebird, Formula Firebird and Trans Am coupe (standard, no cost). AR9 articulating bucket seats with leather trim in base Firebird, Formula Firebird and Trans Am coupe ($780). B9 bucket seats with Metrix cloth trim in base Firebird and Formula Firebird convertible (standard-no cost). AQ9 articulating bucket seats with leather trim in base Firebird and Formula Firebird convertible ($805). D8 articulating bucket seats with Metrix cloth trim in Trans Am GT (standard-no cost). AQ9 articulating bucket seats with leather trim in Trans Am GT ($475). AQ9 articulating bucket seats with Metrix cloth trim in base Trans Am and Trans Am GT convertible (standard-no cost). AQ9 articulating bucket seats with leather trim in base Trans Am and Trans Am GT convertible ($475). 1SA option group for base Firebird coupe with standard equipment (no cost). 1SB option group for base Firebird coupe includes air conditioning, rear floor mats, body side moldings and four-way seat adjuster ($1,005). 1SC option group for base Firebird coupe includes contents of 1SB plus power windows, power door locks, cruise control, power mirrors, remote keyless entry, 10-speaker sound system with graphic equalizer and steering wheel controls and four-way seat adjuster ($2,421). 1SA option group for Formula Firebird coupe with standard equipment (no cost). 1SB option group for

Formula Firebird coupe includes air conditioning, rear floor mats, body side moldings and four-way seat adjuster ($906). 1SC option group for Formula Firebird coupe includes contents of 1SB plus power windows, power door locks, cruise control, power mirrors, remote keyless entry, 10-speaker sound system with graphic equalizer and steering wheel controls and four-way seat adjuster ($1,491). 1SA option group for Firebird convertible with standard equipment (no cost). 1SB option group for Firebird convertible includes remote keyless entry, six-speaker sound system with graphic equalizer and steering wheel controls and leather appointment group ($485). 1SA option group for Formula Firebird convertible with standard equipment (no cost). 1SB option group for Formula Firebird convertible includes remote keyless entry, six-speaker sound system with graphic equalizer and steering wheel controls and leather appointment group ($485). 1SA option group for Trans Am convertible with standard equipment (no cost). Y82 Trans Am option (standard) Y83 Trans Am GT option (standard). Y84 Trans Am GT convertible option (standard). C60 air conditioning, standard Formula, Trans Am and Trans Am GT ($895). C41 non-air conditioning, standard base Firebird, not available Trans Am and Trans Am GT ($895 credit). B84 body-color body side moldings on coupes, standard on Trans Am GT ($60). K34 cruise control with "resume" feature on coupes, standard on Trans Am and Trans Am GT ($225). C49 rear window defogger in coupe, standard Trans Am GT ($170). CC1 hatch roof for coupes, with removable glass panels, locks and stowage ($895). YK3 front license plate bracket (no cost). DE4 hatch roof sunshades ($25). B35 rear floor mats for coupe, standard in Trans Am GT ($15). DG7 dual power outside rearview mirrors with blue glass for coupes, standard on Trans Am and Trans Am GT ($96). AU3 power door locks on coupe, standard on Trans Am and Trans Am GT ($220). A31 power windows for coupes, standard on Trans Am and Trans Am GT ($290). UN6 ETR AM/FM stereo with auto-reverse cassette, not available in Trans Am GT (standard). U1C ETR AM/FM stereo with CD player, not available in Trans Am GT ($226). UT6 ETR AM/FM stereo with auto-reverse cassette, graphic equalizer in coupe, standard in Trans Am GT ($450). UT6 ETR AM/FM stereo with auto-reverse cassette, graphic equalizer in convertible, standard in Trans Am GT convertible ($350). UP3 ETR AM/FM stereo with CD player and graphic equalizer, in base Firebird and Formula coupe without 1SC ($676). UP3 ETR AM/FM stereo with CD player and graphic equalizer, in base Firebird and Formula coupe with 1SC ($226). UP3 ETR AM/FM stereo with CD player and graphic equalizer, in Trans Am coupe ($676). UP3 ETR AM/FM stereo with CD player and graphic equalizer, in Trans Am GT coupe ($226). UP3 ETR AM/FM stereo with CD player and graphic equalizer, in base Firebird and Formula convertible without 1SB ($576). UP3 ETR AM/FM stereo with CD player and graphic equalizer, in base Firebird and Formula convertible with 1SB ($226). ($576). UP3 ETR AM/FM stereo with CD player and graphic equalizer, in Trans Am GT convertible ($226). GU5 perform-

The '94 Firebirds offered more interior goodies, including a CD player.

ance axle, not available in base Firebird, Trans Am or Trans Am GT ($175). AU0 remote keyless entry, standard in Trans Am GT ($135). AH3 four-way manual driver's seat adjuster for coupes, not available in Formula or Trans Am, standard in Trans Am GT ($35). AC3 six-way power driver's seat, not available in Trans Am GT, in Firebird coupe without 1SB and 1SC ($305). AC3 six-way power driver's seat, not available in Trans Am GT, in Firebird coupe with 1SB and 1SC ($270). AC3 six-way power driver's seat, in Formula and Trans Am coupes ($305). AC3 6-way power driver's seat in convertible, not available in Trans Am GT ($270). MM5 five-speed manual transmission, standard in base Firebird, not available in others. MN6 six-speed manual transmission, not available in base Firebird, standard in Formula, Trans Am and Trans Am GT (standard). MXO four-speed automatic transmission ($775). 40P white wheels, not available on base Firebird (no cost).

HISTORICAL FOOTNOTES

John Middlebrook was Pontiac Motor Division's general manager in 1994. Total production in Canada included 51,523 Firebirds. The model year sales total was recorded as 46,499 Firebirds for a 0.5 percent share of the total U.S. market. Of 45,922 Firebirds built for the domestic market in the model year, 80.4 percent had the four-speed automatic transmission, 11 percent had a five-speed manual gearbox, 8.6 percent had the six-speed manual transmission, 0.1 percent had traction control (introduced at midyear), 43.7 percent had a limited-slip differential, 99.7 percent had a manual air conditioner, 90 percent had power windows, 90.5 percent had power door locks, 9.5 percent had power seats, 88.9 percent had cruise control, 72.1 percent had a rear window defogger, 77.9 percent had dual power rearview mirrors, 42.3 percent had hatch roofs, 26 percent had an AM/FM stereo with cassette, 52.3 percent had a premium sound system and 21.7 percent had a CD player. The 25th Anniversary Trans Am did the quarter mile in 14.2 seconds at 99 mph, which compared to 14.6 seconds at 99 mph for the original 1969 1/2 Trans Am. It had an estimated top speed of 152 mph, compared to 135 mph for the first Trans Am. SLP Engineering also built 501 Formula Firehawks and 12 Firehawk T/As.

The Formula Firebird again shared a formidable 5.7-liter engine with the Trans Am.

1995

The Lone Rear Driver

Pontiac's lone rear-wheel-drive car, the Firebird, continued being built in a Canadian factory. For 1995 it was offered in Firebird, Formula and Trans Am models. Each came as a coupe or a convertible.

By 1995, even the base Firebird was a heavily contented car. It featured soft fascia-type bumpers and composite body panels on the doors, front fenders, roof, rear deck lid and rear spoiler. Electrically operated concealed quartz-halogen headlamps were standard, along with one-piece multi-color-lens taillamps and a center high-mounted stop lamp. Body-color body-side moldings were on convertibles. Dual power remote-control Sport mirrors with blue glass were fitted.

The cars were finished with a waterborne base coat and two-component clearcoat system. A black, fixed-mast antenna was mounted at the right rear of the body. Solar-Ray tinted glass was standard. Also new were 16-inch, five-spoke aluminum wheels, speed-rated tires, a power antenna, a four-spoke Sport steering wheel and a remote CD changer.

Features that were standard exclusively to convertibles included: cruise control; electric rear window defogger; power automatic door locks; remote keyless entry; four-way manual front driver seat/two-way manual front passenger seat; and power windows with "express-down" feature. All 1995 Firebirds also had new maintenance-free ball joints and lubed-for-life front-end components.

The Formula Firehawk was merchandised in 300- and 315-hp models and got new optional chrome rims and a Hurst six-speed shifter. The price of the kit was up about $500 to $6,495, but Firehawk sales rose to 750 units. After a 143 percent rise in 1994, the Firebird enjoyed an additional 13 percent increase in production during 1995. Total model year output was 50,986 cars.

I.D. NUMBERS

Pontiac's 17-symbol Vehicle Identification Number (VIN) for passenger cars was on the upper left surface of the instrument panel, visible through the windshield. The first symbol indicates country of origin: 2=Canada. The second symbol indicates manufacturer: G=General Motors. The third symbol indicates make: 2=Pontiac division, 7=GM of Canada. The fourth and fifth symbols for passenger cars indicated body type and series: F/S=Firebird and convertible, F/V=Firebird Formula or Trans Am and convertible. The sixth symbol denoted body type: 2=two-door hatchback/liftback style 87, 3=two-door convertible style 67. The seventh symbol indicated the type of restraint system: 1=manual belts; 2=active manual belts with dual airbags; 3=active manual belts with driver airbag. Symbol eight was an engine code: P=UPC LT1 5.7-liter fuel-injected (MFI) V-8, X=UPC LQ1 3.4-liter fuel-injected (MFI) V-6. The ninth symbol is a check digit. The tenth symbol denotes model year (S=1995). The 11th symbol indicates the GM assembly plant: 2=Ste. Therese, Canada. The last six symbols are the consecutive unit number at the factory.

COLORS

10=Bright White, 80=Bright Blue Metallic,

41=Black, 37=Dark Aqua Metallic, 81=Bright Red, 05=Medium Dark Purple Metallic, 48=Dark Green Metallic, 71=Medium Red Metallic, 13=Bright Silver Metallic and 79=Blue Green Chameleon.

FIREBIRD - SERIES F/S - V-6/V-8

Pontiac's lone rear-wheel drive vehicle was offered in 1995 in coupe and convertible versions in three series: Firebird, Formula and Trans Am. The Canadian-produced muscle machines had several changes. First, a Traction Control system was available for V-8-powered cars with either manual or automatic transmission. Blue Green Chameleon, Medium Dark Purple Metallic and Bright Silver Metallic were new exterior colors. New Bright Red (all) and Bright White (convertible only) leather interiors were seen. Also new were 16-in. five-spoke aluminum wheels on V-8-powered Firebirds, all-weather speed-rated P245/50Z16 tires, a power antenna, a four-spoke Sport steering wheel and a remote compact disc changer (as a dealer-installed option). Standard equipment on the base Firebird included a black fixed mast antenna, soft fascia type front and rear bumpers, composite body panels (doors, fenders, fascias, roof, rear deck and spoiler), Solar-Ray tinted glass liftback with strut supports, electrically-operated concealed quartz halogen headlights, license plate brackets (illuminated at rear), dual body-color Sport outside rearview mirrors (left-hand remote controlled and right-hand manual convex), waterborne basecoat/clearcoat paint, a rear deck lid spoiler with integrated center high-mounted stoplight, a one-piece multi-color taillight lens, P215/60R16 steel-belted black sidewall radial touring tires, a T125/70D15 high-pressure compact spare tire on a 15 x 4-in. steel spare wheel, 16 x 7 1/2-in. machine-faced cast-aluminum wheels with gray ports, controlled-cycle windshield wipers, extensive acoustical insulation, driver's and passenger side front airbags, three-point active safety belts, full cut-pile carpeting, cargo area carpeting, a full-length console adjoining to the instrument panel and including a cupholder and storage box, side window defoggers, Metrix cloth fabric, a locking glove box, analog instrumentation (including a tachometer, a trip odometer, a coolant temperature gauge, an oil pressure indicator, a voltmeter and a speedometer), lights for ashtray dome and glove box, a day/night inside rearview mirror with reading lamps, dual covered visor-vanity mirrors, a remote hatch release, a Delco 2001 Series ETR AM/FM stereo with auto-reverse cassette and search-and-replay and clock with Delco theft lock, passive lap-and-shoulder safety belts for driver and front passenger, lap-and-shoulder belts for rear outboard positions, two-way manual front seat adjusters for driver and passenger seats, reclining front bucket seats, a folding rear seat, a four-spoke steering wheel with Tilt-Wheel adjustable steering column, the PASS-Key II theft-deterrent system, a Delco Freedom II battery, a 105-amp alternator, power front disc/rear drum brakes with antilock braking system (ABS), a brake/transmission shift interlock feature with automatic transmission, a 3.4-liter V-6 with sequential port fuel injection, a stainless steel exhaust system,

Formulas had the same sleek, bumperless front end as the base Firebirds and T/As.

extensive anti-corrosion protection, the GM Computer Command Control engine management system, a low oil level monitor and warning, rear-wheel drive, power rack-and-pinion steering, a short/long arm front suspension, a torque arm/track bar rear suspension with de Carbon gas-charged monotube shock absorbers, a Ride & Handling suspension package, a five-speed manual transmission, a three-year/36,000-mile no-deductible warranty program and 24-hour Roadside Assistance program providing lock-out assistance, dead battery assistance, out-of-fuel assistance, flat-tire assistance and courtesy transportation. Firebird convertibles also featured a power-operated top with a fully trimmed headliner, a glass rear window with electric defogger, cruise control, power windows with a express-down feature, front and rear floor mats, dual power sport mirrors, body-color body side moldings and a three-piece tonneau cover.

Model Number	Body/Style Number	Body Type & Seating	Factory Price	Shipping Weight	Production Total
FIREBIRD SERIES - F/S - (V-6)					
F/S	87	2d hatchback-5P	$15,359	3,230 lbs.	26,230
F/S	67	2d convertible-5P	$22,439	3,346 lbs.	2,926

Note 1: T-tops were used on 13,548 base Firebird hatchbacks.

FORMULA FIREBIRD SERIES F/V - V-8

"Now you're playing with fire," said the 1995 Pontiac sales catalog about the new Formula Firebird. Its standard equipment included a black fixed-mast antenna, soft fascia-type front and rear bumpers, composite body panels (doors, fenders, fascias, roof, rear deck and spoiler), Solar-Ray tinted glass liftback with strut supports, electrically operated concealed quartz halogen headlights, license plate brackets (illuminated at rear), dual body-color Sport outside rearview mirrors (left-hand remote controlled and right-hand manual convex), waterborne basecoat/clearcoat paint, a rear deck lid spoiler with integrated center high-mounted stoplight, taillights with neutral-density lenses and a smooth contoured appearance, P235/55R16 steel-belted black sidewall radial touring tires, a T125/70D15 high-pressure compact spare tire on a 15 x 4-in. steel spare wheel, Bright Silver 16 x 8-in. Sport cast-aluminum wheels, air conditioning, controlled-cycle windshield wipers, extensive acoustical insulation, driver's and passenger side

This Trans Am received the Bright Silver Metallic paint job.

front airbags, three-point active safety belts, full cut-pile carpeting, cargo area carpeting, a full-length console adjoining to the instrument panel and including a cup holder and storage box, side window defoggers, Metrix cloth fabric, a locking glove box, analog instrumentation (including a tachometer, a trip odometer, a coolant temperature gauge, an oil pressure indicator, a voltmeter and a speedometer), lights for ashtray and dome and glove box, a day/night inside rearview mirror with reading lamps, dual covered visor-vanity mirrors, a remote hatch release, a Delco 2001 Series ETR AM/FM stereo with auto-reverse cassette and search-and-replay and clock with Delco theft lock, passive lap-and-shoulder safety belts for driver and front passenger, lap-and-shoulder belts for rear outboard positions, two-way manual front seat adjusters for driver and passenger seats, reclining front bucket seats, a folding rear seat, a four-spoke steering wheel with Tilt-Wheel adjustable steering column, the PASS-Key II theft-deterrent system, a Delco Freedom II battery, a 125-amp alternator, power four-wheel disc brakes with antilock braking system (ABS), a brake/transmission shift interlock feature with automatic transmission, a 5.7-liter V-8 with sequential port fuel injection, a stainless steel exhaust system, extensive anti-corrosion protection, the GM Computer Command Control engine management system, a low oil level monitor and warning, rear-wheel drive, power rack-and-pinion steering, a short-and-long arm front suspension, a torque arm/track bar rear suspension with de Carbon gas-charged monotube shock absorbers, a Performance Ride & Handling suspension package, a six-speed manual transmission, a 3.43:1 performance rear axle, a three-year/36,000-mile no-deductible warranty program and 24-hour Roadside Assistance program providing lock-out assistance, dead-battery assistance, out-of-fuel assistance, flat-tire assistance and courtesy transportation. Formula convertibles also featured a power-operated top with a fully trimmed headliner, a glass rear window with electric defogger, cruise control, power windows with a express-down feature, front and rear floor mats, dual power sport mirrors, body-color body side moldings and a three-piece tonneau cover.

Model Number	Body/Style Number	Body Type & Seating	Factory Price	Shipping Weight	Production Total
FORMULA FIREBIRD - SERIES F/V - (V-8)					
F/V	87	2d hatchback-5P	$19,599	3,373 lbs.	7,448
F/V	67	2d convertible-5P	$25,629	3,489 lbs.	1,038

Note 2: T-tops were used on 4,342 Formula Firebird hatchbacks.

TRANS AM - SERIES F/V - V-8

Buyers could also choose between Coupe and con-

vertible versions in the Trans Am series. The Trans Am's standard equipment included a black fixed-mast antenna, soft fascia-type front and rear bumpers, front fog lamps, composite body panels (doors, fenders, fascias, roof, rear deck and spoiler), body-colored body side moldings, Solar-Ray tinted glass liftback with strut supports, electrically operated concealed quartz halogen headlights, license plate brackets (illuminated at rear), dual body-color Sport outside rearview mirrors (left-hand remote controlled and right-hand manual convex), waterborne basecoat/clearcoat paint, a rear deck lid spoiler with integrated center high-mounted stoplight, taillights with neutral-density lenses and a smooth contoured appearance, P245/50ZR16 speed-rated all-weather tires, a T125/70D15 high-pressure compact spare tire on a 15 x 4-in. steel spare wheel, Bright Silver 16 x 8-in. Sport cast-aluminum wheels, air conditioning, controlled-cycle windshield wipers, extensive acoustical insulation, driver's and passenger side front airbags, three-point active safety belts, power door locks, full cut-pile carpeting, cargo area carpeting, a full-length console adjoining to the instrument panel and including a cup holder and storage box, cruise control, automatic power door locks, side window defoggers, Metrix cloth fabric, a locking glove box, analog instrumentation (including a tachometer, a trip odometer, a coolant temperature gauge, an oil pressure indicator, a voltmeter and a speedometer), lights for ashtray and dome and glove box, a day/night inside rearview mirror with reading lamps, dual covered visor-vanity mirrors, a remote hatch release, a Delco 2001 Series ETR AM/FM stereo with auto-reverse cassette and 7-band graphic equalizer (that included search-and-replay, seek up/down, a clock, a leather-wrapped steering wheel with redundant radio controls, a leather appointment group, Delco theft lock, a high-performance 10-speaker sound system, HSS speakers and tweeters in doors, 6 1/2-in. subwoofers in sail panels, a subwoofer amplifier in rear quarters and 4-in. speakers and tweeters in rear quarters), passive lap-and-shoulder safety belts for driver and front passenger, lap-and-shoulder belts for rear outboard positions, two-way manual front seat adjusters for driver and passenger seats, reclining front bucket seats, a folding rear seat, a four-spoke steering wheel with Tilt-Wheel adjustable steering column, the PASS-Key II theft-deterrent system, a Delco Freedom II battery, a 125-amp alternator, power four-wheel disc brakes with antilock braking system (ABS), a brake/transmission shift interlock feature with automatic transmission, a 5.7-liter V-8 with sequential port fuel injection, a stainless steel exhaust system, extensive anti-corrosion protection, the GM Computer Command Control engine management system, a low oil level monitor and warning, rear-wheel drive, power rack-and-pinion steering, a short/long arm front suspension, a torque arm/track bar rear suspension with deCarbon gas-charged monotube shock absorbers, a Performance Ride & Handling suspension package, a six-speed manual transmission, a 3.43:1 performance rear axle, a three-year/36,000-mile no-deductible warranty program and 24-hour Roadside Assistance program providing lock-out assistance, dead battery assistance, out-of-fuel assistance, flat-tire assistance and courtesy transportation. Rear seat courtesy lamps and a luggage compartment lamp were not included with the Trans Am. Trans Am convertibles also featured a power-operated top with a fully trimmed headliner, a glass rear window with electric defogger, power windows with an express-down feature, front and rear floor mats, dual power sport mirrors and a three-piece tonneau cover.

Model Number	Body/Style Number	Body Type & Seating	Factory Price	Shipping Weight	Production Total
F/V	87	2d hatchback-5P	$21,569	3,445 lbs.	10,943
F/V	67	2d convertible-5P	$27,639	3,610 lbs.	2,402

Note 3: T-tops were used on 8,680 Trans Am hatchbacks.

ENGINES

Base V-6 [UPC L32]: Overhead valve. Cast-iron block and heads. Aluminum intake manifold. Displacement: 207 cid. (3.4-liter). Bore & stroke: 3.62 x 3.31 in. Compression ratio: 9.0:1. Brake horsepower: 160 at 4600 rpm. Torque: 200 ft. lbs. at 3600 rpm. Fuel system: SPFI. Standard in Firebird. Not available in Formula and Trans Am.

Formula/Trans Am 5-7-liter V-8 [UPC LT1]: Overhead valve. Cast-iron block and aluminum heads. Aluminum intake manifold. Displacement: 350 cid. Bore & stroke: 4.00 x 3.48 in. Compression ratio: 10.5:1. Brake horsepower: 275 at 5000 rpm. Torque: 325 ft. lbs. at 2400 rpm. Fuel system: SPFI. Standard in Formula and Trans Am. Not available in Firebird.

CHASSIS

Firebird: Wheelbase: 101.1 in. Overall length: 195.6 in. Width: 74.5 in. Height: Hatchback 52.0 in., Convertible 52.7 in. Front tread: 60.7 in. Rear tread: 60.6 in. Standard tires: P215/60R16.

Formula Firebird: Wheelbase: 101.1 in. Overall length: 195.6 in. Width: 74.5 in. Height: Hatchback 52.0 in., Convertible 52.7 in. Front tread: 60.7 in. Rear tread: 60.6 in. Standard tires: P235/55R16.

Trans Am: Wheelbase: 101.1 in. Overall length: 197.0 in. Width: 74.5 in. Height: Hatchback 52.0 in., Convertible 52.7 in. Front tread: 60.7 in. Rear tread: 60.6 in. Standard tires: P245/50ZR16.

TECHNICAL

Firebird: Chassis: Front engine/rear drive. Base transmission: (M49) Five-speed manual. Optional transmission: (MD8) Four-speed automatic. Axle ratio: 3.23:1 (with M49 five-speed manual); 3.23:1 (with MD8 four-speed automatic and 3.4-liter V-6). Front suspension: Short/long arm (SLA)/coil over mono-tube gas-charged shocks, tubular stabilizer bar with links, 30mm stabilizer bar. Rear suspension: Salisbury axle with torque arm, trailing arm, track bar, coil springs, 17mm stabilizer bar. Steering: Power rack-and-pinion with 16.9:1 ratio. Turns lock to lock: 2.67. Turning circle: 37.9 ft. (left) 40.6 ft. (right). Front brakes: 10.7 in. vented disc. Rear brakes: 9.5 in. power assisted Duo-Servo drum. Fuel tank: 15.5 gal.

Formula: Chassis: Front engine/rear drive. Base transmission: (MM6) six-speed manual. Optional transmission: (MD8) Four-speed automatic. Axle ratio: 3.42:1 (with MM6 six-speed manual), 2.73:1 (with MD8 four-speed automatic and 5.7-liter V-8. Front suspension: SLA/coil over mono-tube gas-charged shocks, tubular stabilizer bar with links, 30mm stabilizer bar. Rear suspension: Salisbury axle with torque arm, trailing arm, track bar, coil springs, 19mm stabilizer bar. Steering: Power, rack-and-pinion with 14.4:1 ratio. Turns lock to lock: 2.28. Turning circle: 37.7 ft. (left) 40.1 ft. (right). Front brakes: 10.7 in. vented disc. Rear brakes: 11.4 in. power assisted vented disc. Fuel tank: 15.5 gal.

Trans Am: Chassis: Front engine/rear drive. Base transmission: (MM6) six-speed manual. Optional transmission: (MD8) Four-speed automatic. Axle ratio: 3.42:1 (with MM6 six-speed manual), 2.73:1 (with MD8 four-speed automatic and 5.7-liter V-8. Front suspension: SLA/coil over mono-tube gas-charged shocks, tubular stabilizer bar with links, 30mm stabilizer bar. Rear suspension: Salisbury axle with torque arm, trailing arm, track bar, coil springs, 19mm stabilizer bar. Steering: Power, rack-and-pinion with 14.4:1 ratio. Turns lock-to-lock: 2.28. Turning circle: 37.7 ft. (left) 40.1 ft. (right). Front brakes: 10.7 in. vented disc. Rear brakes: 11.4 in. power assisted vented disc. Fuel tank: 15.5 gal.

OPTIONS

L32 3.4-liter SFI V-6, standard base Firebird, not available in Formula and Trans Am (standard). LT1 5.7-liter SFI V-8, standard in Formula and Trans Am, not available in base Firebird (standard). L36 3.8-liter SFI V-6, not available in Formula or Trans Am; required MXO transmission and C60 air conditioning ($350). FE9 Federal emissions (no cost). YF5 California emissions ($100). NG1 New York emissions ($100). QPE P215/60R16 black sidewall steel-belted radial touring tires, standard Firebird, not available in Formula, Trans Am or Trans Am GT (no cost). QMT P235/55R16 black sidewall touring tires, standard in Formula and Trans Am, not available in Trans Am GT ($132). QLC P245/50ZR16 steel-belted radial black sidewall tires, standard in Trans Am GT, not available on base Firebird ($225). B9 bucket seats with Metrix cloth trim in base Firebird, Formula Firebird and Trans Am coupe (standard-no cost). AQ9 articulating bucket seats with Metrix cloth, Trans Am only ($330). AQ9 articulating bucket seats with leather trim in base Firebird, Formula Firebird coupe, requires 1SC and UT6 or UP3 radio ($804); in Trans Am coupe or convertibles ($829). 1SA option group for base Firebird coupe with standard equipment (no cost). 1SB option group for base Firebird coupe includes air conditioning, rear floor mats, body side moldings and four-way seat adjuster ($1,005). 1SC option group for base Firebird coupe includes contents of 1SB plus power windows, power door locks, cruise control, power mirrors, remote keyless entry, 10-speaker sound system with graphic equalizer and steering wheel controls, leather steering wheel and power antenna ($2,614). 1SA option group for Formula Firebird coupe with standard equipment (no cost). 1SB option group for Formula Firebird coupe includes rear floor mats, body side moldings, power windows, power door locks, cruise control, power mirrors and electric rear window defogger ($1,076). 1SC option group for Formula Firebird coupe includes contents of 1SB plus remote keyless entry, 10-speaker sound system with graphic equalizer and steering wheel controls, leather steering wheel and power antenna ($1,684). 1SA option group for Trans Am coupe with standard equipment (no cost). 1SA Firebird and Formula convertible with standard equipment (no cost). 1SB option group for Firebird and Formula convertible with remote keyless entry, six-speaker sound system with graphic equalizer and steering wheel controls, power antenna and leather appointment group ($508). 1SA option group for Trans Am convertible with standard equipment (no cost). Y82 Trans Am option (standard) Y83 Trans Am GT option (standard). Y84 Trans Am GT convertible option (standard). C60 air conditioning, standard Formula, Trans Am and Trans Am GT ($895). C41 non-air conditioning, standard base Firebird, not available in Trans Am and Trans Am GT ($895 credit). B84 body-color body side moldings on coupes, standard on Trans Am GT ($60). K34 cruise control with "resume" feature on coupes, standard on Trans Am and Trans Am GT ($225). C49 rear window defogger in coupe, standard Trans Am GT ($170). CC1 hatch roof for coupes, with removable glass panels, locks and stowage, not available teamed with 1SA on Firebird or Formula ($970). VK3 front license plate bracket (no cost). DE4 hatch roof sunshades ($25). B35 rear floor mats for coupe, standard in Trans Am GT ($15). DG7 dual power outside rearview mirrors with blue glass for coupes, standard on Trans Am and Trans Am GT ($96). AU3 power door locks on coupe, standard on Trans Am and Trans Am GT ($220). A31 power windows for coupes, standard on Trans Am and Trans Am GT ($290). UN6 ETR AM/FM stereo with auto-reverse cassette, not available in Trans Am GT (standard). U1C ETR AM/FM stereo with CD player, not available in Trans Am GT ($100). UT6 ETR AM/FM stereo with auto-reverse cassette, graphic equalizer in base Firebird and Formula Firebird coupe ($473). UT6 ETR AM/FM stereo with auto-reverse cassette, graphic equalizer in base Firebird and Formula Firebird convertible ($373). UT6 ETR AM/FM stereo with auto-reverse cassette, graphic equalizer in Trans Am coupe ($398). UP3 ETR AM/FM stereo with CD player and graphic equalizer, in base Firebird and Formula coupe without 1SC ($573). UP3 ETR AM/FM stereo with CD player and graphic equalizer, in base Firebird and Formula coupe with 1SC ($100). UP3 ETR AM/FM stereo with CD player and graphic equalizer, in Trans Am coupe ($498). UP3 ETR AM/FM stereo with CD player and graphic equalizer, in base Firebird and Formula Firebird convertible without 1SB ($473). UP3 ETR AM/FM stereo with CD player and graphic equalizer, in base Firebird and Formula Firebird convertible with 1SB ($100). UP3 ETR AM/FM stereo with CD

Base Firebird coupes received a new optional traction control system and came in several new colors for 1995.

player and graphic equalizer in Trans Am convertible ($100). GU5 performance axle, not available in base Firebird, Trans Am or Trans Am GT ($175). AUO remote keyless entry, standard Trans Am GT ($135). AH3 four-way manual driver's seat adjuster for coupes, not available in Formula or Trans Am, standard in Trans Am GT ($35). AG1 six-way power driver's seat in Firebird coupe with 1SA ($305). AG1 six-way power driver's seat in Firebird coupe with 1SB or 1SC ($270). AG1 six-way power driver's seat in Formula Firebird or Trans Am coupe ($305). AG1 six-way power driver's seat in convertibles ($270). NW9 Traction Control ($450). MM5 five-speed manual transmission, standard in base Firebird, not available in others (standard). MN6 six-speed manual transmission, not available in base Firebird, standard in Formula, Trans Am and Trans Am GT (standard). MX0 four-speed automatic transmission ($775). T43 up-level rear deck lid spoiler, Trans Am coupe only ($395).

HISTORICAL FOOTNOTES

John Middlebrook put in his last season as Pontiac Motor Division's general manager in 1995. Total production in Canada included 56,723 Firebirds. The model year sales total was recorded as 41,947 Firebirds for a 0.5 percent share of the total U.S. market. Of 50,986 Firebirds built for the domestic market in the model year, 75.3 percent had the four-speed automatic transmission, 10.9 percent had a five-speed manual gearbox, 13.8 percent had the six-speed manual transmission, 6.3 percent had traction control, 42.8 percent had a limited-slip differential, 99.8 percent had a manual air conditioner, 85.7 percent had power windows, 86.6 percent had power door locks, 10.6 percent had power seats, 87.8 percent had cruise control, 76.7 percent had a rear window defogger, 85.7 percent had dual power rearview mirrors, 52.1 percent had hatch roofs, 24.3 percent had an AM/FM stereo with cassette, 44.8 percent had a premium sound system, 30.9 percent had a CD player and 69 percent had keyless remote entry system. SLP Engineering's Formula Firehawk was merchandised in 300- and 315-hp models and sales rose to some 671 units, all of which were Formula Firehawks. Also produced were two Comp T/A coupes and 70 Comp T/A T-tops.

A 1996 Formula Firebird with the Ram Air V-8 and T-tops was an appealing combination.

Hotter Than Ever

The Pontiac Firebird roared into 1996 with more excitement and more powerful engines. There were several new high-performance packages for V-8 models. Trans Am coupes had a new WS6 Pontiac Ram Air performance-and-handling option that was instantly desirable and appealed to late-model muscle car collectors. The Ram Air-equipped Trans Ams were promoted almost as if they were separate models. Prices ranged from $16,119 to $27,869.

A 3800 Series II 200-hp V-6 was the new standard engine for 1996 Firebird coupes and convertibles. It was available with a 3800 Performance Package featuring four-wheel disc brakes, a limited-slip differential, an up-level steering wheel, dual exhausts and five-spoke aluminum wheels.

The optional WS6 Ram Air Performance & Handling Package was available on Formula and Trans Am coupes with the 5.7-liter V-8. It included a Ram Air induction system, functional air scoops, 17-inch five-spoke aluminum wheels, P275/40ZR17 speed-rated tires and dual exhausts.

Model-year production was 30,937 Firebirds of all types.

I.D. NUMBERS

The vehicle identification number (VIN) is located on the top left-hand surface of the instrument panel and is visible through the windshield. The VIN has 17 symbols. The first symbol indicates the country of manufacture (1 or 4=United States; 2=Canada). The second symbol indicates the manufacturer (G=General Motors). The third symbol indicates the make/division (2=Pontiac and 7=GM of Canada). The fourth and fifth symbols indicate the car line and series (F/S=Firebird and convertible; F/V=Formula-Trans Am and convertible). The sixth symbol indicates body style (2=two-door model 87; 3=two-door convertible model 67). The seventh symbol indicates the restraint system: 1=Active manual belts; 2=Active manual belts with driver and passenger inflatable restraints; 3=Active manual belts with driver inflatable restraint; 4=Passive (automatic) belts; 5=Passive (automatic) belts with driver inflatable restraint; 6=Passive (automatic) belts with driver and passenger inflatable restraints; 7=Active (manual) belt driver and passive (automatic) belt passenger with driver inflatable restraint. The eighth symbol indicates the engine type: P=UPC LT1 5.7-liter V-8; K=UPC L36 3.8-liter V-6. (Note: All Pontiac engines are MFI multiport fuel injected). The ninth symbol is a check digit. The 10th symbol indicates model year (T=1996). The 11th symbol indicates the GM assembly plant (2=Ste. Therese, Canada). The last six symbols are the consecutive unit number at the factory.

COLORS

05=Medium Dark Purple Metallic, 10=Bright White, 13=Bright Silver Metallic, 37=Dark Aqua Metallic, 41=Black, 48=Dark Green Metallic, 79=Blue-Green Chameleon, 80=Bright Blue Metallic, 81=Bright Red and 96=Red-Orange Metallic.

FIREBIRD – CARLINE/SERIES F/S V-6/V-8

The 1996 Firebirds were members of a dwindling breed: rear-wheel-drive American muscle cars. Standard equipment on the base Firebird included a black fixed-mast antenna, soft fascia-type bumpers, composite doors, fenders, fascias and roof (except convertible), a rear deck spoiler, Solar-Ray tinted glass, concealed quartz-halogen headlights, a front license plate bracket, a lighted rear license plate bracket, dual sport mirrors (left-hand mirror remote controlled) or left- and right-hand power remote mirrors with blue glass on convertible, two-coat-component waterborne basecoat/clearcoat paint, a rear deck lid spoiler with integrated center high-mounted stoplight, one-piece multi-color taillight lenses, P215/60R16 steel-belted radial black sidewall touring tires, a high-pressure T125/70D15 compact spare tire on a 15 x 4-in. steel wheel, bright silver 16 x 8-in. Sport cast-aluminum wheels, controlled-cycle windshield wipers, extensive acoustical insulation, driver and passenger airbags, air conditioning (convertible only), a full-length console with cupholder and storage box adjoining to instrument panel, cruise control (convertible only), a electric rear window defogger (convertible only), power side windows, automatic power door locks (convertible only), Metrix cloth seat fabric, a locking glove box, a hatch release (or rear deck lid release on convertibles), instrumentation (including analog speedometer, tachometer, coolant temperature gauge, oil pressure gauge, voltmeter and trip odometer), an ashtray lamp, a dome lamp (except convertible), a glove box lamp, a rear seat courtesy lamp (convertible only), a trunk lamp (convertible only), carpeted front floor mats, a day/night rearview mirror with reading lamps, left- and right-hand covered visor-vanity mirrors, a Delco 2001 series electronically tuned AM/FM stereo radio with cassette and seven-band equalizer, clock, touch control, seek up/down, search and replay, Delco theft lock and remote compact disc player pre-wiring, a four-speaker coaxial sound system (convertible only), a rear deck lid release, safety belts, two-way manual reclining front bucket seats, a folding rear seat, a four-spoke steering wheel, an adjustable tilt steering column, power window controls with driver side "express-down" feature for convertible only (requires power

The base Firebird was again available as a convertible for 1996.

mirrors and power door locks), a 105-amp. alternator, extensive anti-corrosion protection, a Delco Freedom II battery, a four-wheel antilock-braking system with front discs and rear drums, a brake/transmission interlock with automatic transmission, a stainless steel exhaust system (federal), General Motors Computer Command Control system, a low oil level monitor and warning, driver-selectable transmission controls (automatic transmission only), V-6 normal second gear start (coupe only), power rack-and-pinion steering, a short-and-long arm suspension with front and rear stabilizer bars and the F41 Ride & Handling package, the PASS-Key II theft-deterrent system, a 3.8-liter V-6 and a five-speed manual transmission.

Model Number	Body/Style Number	Body Type & Seating	Factory Price	Shipping Weight	Production Total
F/S	87	2d Hatchback-4P	$15,614	3,131 lbs.	17,773
F/S	67	2d Convertible-4P	$22,444	3,346 lbs.	976

Note 1: T-tops were used on 8,529 base Firebird hatchbacks.

FORMULA FIREBIRD CARLINE/SERIES F/V – V-8

The Formula Firebird was again the street performance model. Standard equipment included a black fixed-mast antenna, soft fascia type bumpers, composite doors, fenders, fascias and roof (except convertible), a rear deck spoiler, Solar-Ray tinted glass, concealed quartz-halogen headlights, a front license plate bracket, a lighted rear license plate bracket, dual sport mirrors (left-hand mirror remote controlled) or left- and right-hand power remote mirrors with blue glass on convertible, two-coat-component waterborne basecoat/clearcoat paint, a rear deck

Duane and Lynne Haars photo

This Formula Firebird was one of only 524 with the Ram Air engine option.

lid spoiler with integrated center high-mounted stop-light, neutral-density taillights with smooth-contour lenses, P235/55R16 steel-belted radial touring tires, a high-pressure T125/70D15 compact spare tire on a 15 x 4-in. steel wheel, bright silver 16 x 8-in. Sport cast-aluminum wheels, controlled-cycle windshield wipers, extensive acoustical insulation, driver and passenger airbags, air conditioning (coupe and convertible), a full-length console with cupholder and storage box adjoining to instrument panel, cruise control (convertible only), an electric rear window defogger (convertible only), power side windows, automatic power door locks (convertible only), Metrix cloth seat fabric, a locking glove box, a hatch release or rear deck lid release on convertibles, instrumentation (including an analog speedometer, a tachometer, a coolant temperature gauge, an oil pressure gauge, a voltmeter and trip odometer), an ashtray lamp, a dome lamp (except convertible), a glove box lamp, a rear seat courtesy lamp (convertible only), a trunk lamp (convertible only), carpeted front floor mats, a day/night rearview mirror with reading lamps, left- and right-hand covered visor vanity mirrors, a Delco 2001 series electronically tuned AM/FM stereo radio (with cassette and seven-band equalizer, clock, touch control, seek up/down, search and replay, Delco theft lock and remote compact disc player pre-wiring), a four-speaker coaxial sound system (convertible only), a rear deck lid release, safety belts, two-way manual reclining front bucket seats, a folding rear seat, a four-spoke steering wheel, an adjustable tilt steering column, power window controls with driver side "express-down" feature for convertible only (requires power mirrors and power door locks), 125-amp alternator, extensive anti-corrosion protection, electric rear window defogger (convertible only), power door locks (convertible only), rear seat courtesy lamps (convertible only), a trunk lamp (convertible only), a Delco Freedom II battery, four-wheel power disc brakes with antilock, a brake/transmission interlock with automatic transmission, a stainless steel exhaust system, the General Motors Computer Command Control system, a low oil level monitor and warning, driver-selectable transmission controls (automatic transmission only), power rack-and-pinion steering, a short-and-long arm suspension with front and rear stabilizer bars and the F41 Ride & Handling package, the PASS-Key II theft-deterrent system, a 5.7-liter V-8, a six-speed manual transmission and driver-selectable transmission control (with optional automatic transmission). A new option available for the 1996 Formula coupe was the WS6 Ram Air Performance and Handling package that included a Ram Air induction system, specific 17-in. five-spoke aluminum wheels, P275/40ZR17 tires, specific dual outlet exhaust and a tuned suspension.

A Trans Am with a Ram Air V-8 was the hottest thing in the Pontiac family in 1996.

TRANS AM – CARLINE/SERIES F/V V-8

The ultimate 1996 Firebird was the Trans Am. Its standard equipment included a black fixed-mast antenna (or a power antenna on convertible only), soft fascia-type bumpers, composite doors, fenders, fascias and roof (except convertible), a rear deck spoiler, fog lamps, body-color body side moldings, Solar-Ray tinted glass, concealed quartz-halogen headlights, a front license plate bracket, a lighted rear license plate bracket, left- and right-hand power remote mirrors with blue glass, cruise control, an electric rear window defogger, automatic power door locks, rear floor mats (convertible only), two-coat-component waterborne basecoat/clearcoat paint, a rear deck lid spoiler with integrated center high-mounted stoplight, one-piece multi-color taillight lenses, P245/50ZR16 speed-rated tires (all-weather tires type on convertible only), a high-pressure T125/70D15 compact spare tire on 15 x 4-in. steel wheel, bright silver 16 x 8-in. sport cast aluminum wheels, controlled-cycle windshield wipers, extensive acoustical insulation, driver and passenger airbags, air conditioning, a full-length console with cupholder and storage box adjoining to instrument panel, power side windows, Metrix cloth seat fabric, a locking glove box, a hatch release (or rear deck lid release on convertibles), instrumentation (including an analog speedometer, a tachometer, a coolant temperature gauge, an oil pressure gauge, a voltmeter and a trip odometer), an ashtray lamp, a dome lamp (except convertible), a glove box lamp, rear seat courtesy lamp (convertible only), trunk lamp (convertible only), carpeted front floor mats, day/night rearview mirror with reading lamps, left- and right-hand covered visor-vanity mirrors, a Delco 2001 series electronically tuned AM/FM stereo radio (with cassette and seven-band equalizer, a clock, touch control, seek up/down, search and replay, Delco theft lock and remote compact disc player pre-wiring), a four-speaker coaxial sound system, a rear deck lid release, safety belts, a four-way manual driver's seat and two-way manual front passenger seat, a folding rear seat, a leather-wrapped shift knob and parking brake handle (coupe only), a leather-wrapped steering wheel with radio controls, power window controls with driver side "express-down" feature (requires power mirrors and power door locks), an adjustable tilt steering column, a 105-amp alternator, extensive anti-corrosion protection, a Delco Freedom II battery, a four-wheel

Model Number	Body/Style Number	Body Type & Seating	Factory Price	Shipping Weight	Production Total
FORMULA FIREBIRD - CARLINE/SERIES F/V - (285-hp V-8)					
F/V	87	2d hatchback-4P	$19,464	3,373 lbs.	3,033
F/V	67	2d convertible-4P	$25,284	3,489 lbs.	302
FORMULA FIREBIRD - WS6 RAM AIR - CARLINE/SERIES F/V - (305-hp V-8)					
F/V	87	2d hatchback-4P	$22,459	3,373 lbs.	Note 3

Note 2: T-tops were used on 1,708 Formula Firebird hatchbacks.
Note 3: A total of 524 Formula hatchbacks had the WS6 option.

antilock-braking system with front discs and rear drums, a brake/transmission interlock with automatic transmission, a stainless steel exhaust system, the General Motors Computer Command Control system, low oil level monitor and warning, driver-selectable transmission controls (automatic transmission only), V-6 normal second gear start (coupe only), power rack-and-pinion steering, a short-and-long arm suspension with front and rear stabilizer bars and the F41 Ride & Handling package, the PASS-Key II theft-deterrent system, a 5.7-liter V-8 and a five-speed manual transmission. A new option available for the 1996 Trans Am coupe was the WS6 Ram Air Performance and Handling package that included a Ram Air induction system, specific 17-in. five-spoke aluminum wheels, P275/40ZR17 tires, specific dual outlet exhaust and a tuned suspension. The sales catalog said, "For 1996, Trans Am gives you a new perspective on performance, especially when outfitted with the WS6 Ram Air package. Like that fitted to the original 1969 1/2 Trans Am, the available package increases the Tran Am's V-8 horsepower from 285 to 305, while it enhances handling with special chassis components (shocks, bushings, springs and massive, speed-rated 17-in. tires)."

Model Number	Body/Style Number	Body Type & Seating	Factory Price	Shipping Weight	Production Total
TRANS AM - CARLINE/SERIES F/V - (285-hp V-8)					
F/V	87	2d hatchback-4P	$21,414	3,345 lbs.	7,981
F/V	67	2d convertible-4P	$27,364	3,610 lbs.	917
TRANS AM - WS6 RAM AIR - CARLINE/SERIES F/V - (305-hp V-8)					
F/V	87	2d hatchback-4P	$21,414	3,345 lbs.	Note 5

Note 4: T-tops were used on 6,735 Trans Am hatchbacks.
Note 5: A total of 2,051 Trans Am hatchbacks had the WS6 option.

The WS6 Ram Air V-8 became a new option for Formula Firebirds and Trans Ams in 1996.

ENGINES

Base V-6 [UPC L36]: Overhead valve. Cast-iron block and head. Aluminum intake manifold. Displacement: 231 cid. (3.8-liter). Bore & stroke: 3.80 x 3.40 in. Compression ratio: 9.0:1. Brake horsepower: 200 at 5200 rpm. Torque: 225 ft. lbs. at 4000 rpm. Fuel system: SFI. VIN Code: X.

5.7-liter V-8 [UPC LT1]: Overhead valve. Cast-iron block and head. Aluminum intake manifold. Displacement: 350 cid. Bore & stroke: 4.00 x 3.48 in. Brake horsepower: 285 at 5000 rpm. Torque: 325 ft. lbs. at 2400 rpm. Compression ratio: 10.5:1. Fuel sys-

tem: SFI. VIN Code: P.

5.7-liter Ram Air V-8 [UPC LT1]: Overhead valve. Cast-iron block and head. Aluminum intake manifold. Displacement: 350 cid. (5.7-liter). Bore & stroke: 4.00 x 3.48 in. Brake horsepower: 305 at 5000 rpm. Torque: 325 ft. lbs. at 2400 rpm. Compression ratio: 10.5:1. Fuel system: SFI. VIN Code: 5. With WS6 Ram Air Performance package.

CHASSIS

Firebird: Wheelbase: 101.0 in. Overall length: 195.6 in. Width: 74.5 in. Height: Coupe 52.0 in., Convertible 52.7 in. Front tread: 60.7 in. Rear tread: 61.6 in. Standard tires: steel-belted radial P215/60R15 black sidewall touring.

Formula: Wheelbase: 101.0 in. Overall length: 195.6 in. Width: 74.5 in. Height: Coupe 52.0 in.; Convertible 52.7 in. Front tread: 60.7 in. Rear tread: 61.6 in. Standard tires: steel-belted radial P235/55R16 touring.

Trans Am: Wheelbase: 101.0 in. Overall length: 197 in. Width: 74.5 in. Height: Coupe 51.7 in.; Convertible 52.4 in. Front tread: 60.7 in. Rear tread: 61.6 in. Standard tires: P245/50ZR16 speed-rated, all-weather.

TECHNICAL

Firebird: Chassis: Front engine/rear drive. Base transmission: Five-speed manual. Front suspension: Modified MacPherson strut with 30mm (FE1), 34mm (F41), or 36mm (WS6) anti-roll bar. Rear suspension: Live axle with coil springs, control arms, torque arm, track bar, and 18mm (FE1) or 23mm (F41 and WS6) anti-roll bar. Steering: Power re-circulating ball; 14.0:1 ratio. Turns lock-to-lock: 2.57. Turning circle: 38.5 ft. Brakes: Power vented 10.5-in. front disc/9.5 x 2.0-in. rear drum. Fuel tank: 15.5 gal.

Formula: Chassis: Front engine/rear drive. Base transmission: Six-speed manual. Front suspension: Modified MacPherson strut with 34mm anti-roll bar. Rear suspension: Live axle with coil springs, control arms, torque arm, track bar and 23mm anti-roll bar. Steering: Power re-circulating ball; 12.7:1 quick ratio with sport effort valving. Turns lock-to-lock: 2.14. Turning circle: 38.5 ft. Brakes: Four-wheel disc. Fuel tank: 15.5 gal.

Trans Am: Chassis: Front engine/rear drive. Base transmission: Six-speed manual. Front suspension: Modified MacPherson strut with 34mm anti-roll bar. Rear suspension: Live axle with coil springs, control arms, torque arm, track bar and 23mm anti-roll bar. Steering: Power re-circulating ball; 12.7:1 quick ratio with sport effort valving. Turns lock-to-lock: 2.14. Turning circle: 38.5 ft. Brakes: Four-wheel disc. Fuel tank: 15.5 gal.

OPTIONS

FE9 Federal emissions (no cost). YF5 50 California emissions (no cost). NG1 New York/Massachusetts. Emissions (no cost). NB8 California/New York/Massachusetts Emissions override, requires FE9 (no cost). NC7 Federal emissions override, requires YF5 or NG1 (no cost). QCB P235/55R16 black sidewall touring tires for Firebird, standard Formula and Trans Am; not available in Trans Am convertible ($132). QFZ P245/50ZR16 black sidewall steel-belted radial all-weather performance tires for Formula and Trans Am coupe ($225). QLC P245/50ZR16 black sidewall steel-belted radial performance tires for Formula and Trans Am ($225). QFK P275/40ZR17 speed-rated tires for Formula and Trans Am coupe with WS6 only (no cost). AR9 articulating bucket seats (Firebird and Formula coupe $804; convertible $829). AQ9 articulating bucket seats including articulating headrests (Trans Am with Metrix cloth trim $320; Trans Am with Prado leather trim $829). 1SA Firebird coupe option package, includes vehicle with standard equipment (no cost). 1SB Firebird option group ($1,078). 1SC Firebird option group ($2,499). 1SA Formula coupe option package, includes vehicle with standard equipment (no cost). 1SB Formula coupe option group ($1,184). 1SC Formula coupe option group ($1,604). 1SA Firebird and Formula convertible option package, includes vehicle with standard equipment (no cost). 1SB Firebird and Formula convertible group ($580). 1SA Trans Am coupe/convertible option package, includes vehicle with standard equipment (no cost). R6A Firebird and Formula value package ($820). R6B value package Firebird and Formula ($814). Y82 Trans Am coupe option (standard). Y84 Trans Am convertible option (standard). Y87 3800 performance package ($535). WS6 Ram Air performance and handling package, includes Ram Air induction system; functional air scoops; 17-in. five-spoke aluminum wheels; P275/40ZR17 speed-rated tires and dual oval exhaust outlets ($2,995). B84 body color side moldings ($60). UA6 content theft alarm ($90). K34 cruise control ($225). C49 electric rear window defogger ($170). CC1 hatch roof ($970). DE4 hatch roof sunshades ($25). VK3 front license plate bracket (no cost). B35 rear carpet floor mats, standard Trans Ams ($15). DG7 dual sport mirrors ($96). U75 power antenna, requires radio upgrade, standard on Trans Am convertible ($85). AU3 power door locks ($220). A31 power windows ($290). W52 ETR AM/FM stereo with auto-reverse, graphic equalizer, clock, seek up/down, remote CD pre-wire and four coaxial speakers ($73). W53 ETR AM/FM stereo with CD player, graphic equalizer, clock, seek up/down and four coaxial speakers ($173). W54 ETR AM/FM stereo with auto-reverse, graphic equalizer, clock, seek up/down, remote CD pre-wiring and 10-speaker sound system ($115). W55 ETR AM/FM stereo with CD player, graphic equalizer, clock, seek up/down and 10-speaker sound system ($115). W58 ETR AM/FM stereo with CD player, graphic equalizer, clock, seek up/down and four-speaker sound system ($100). W59 ETR AM/FM stereo with auto-reverse cassette, graphic equalizer, clock, seek up/down, remote CD pre-wiring and six-speaker sound system ($50). W73 ETR AM/FM stereo with CD player, graphic equalizer, clock, seek up/down and six-speaker sound system ($150). U1S

The base Firebird coupe was priced at $15,614 in 1996.

trunk-mounted remote 12-disc CD changer ($595). GU5 performance axle ($175). AUO remote keyless entry ($135). AH3 manual four-way-adjustable driver's seat ($35). AG1 six-way power driver's seat ($270-$305). UK3 steering wheel radio controls (Firebird/Formula $200; Trans Am $125). NW9 traction control ($450). MX0 four-speed automatic transmission ($790). T43 up-level rear deck lid spoiler, Trans Am only ($395). PO5 chrome aluminum wheels, not available with 1SA Firebird coupe ($500).

HISTORICAL FOOTNOTES

Roy S. Roberts became Pontiac Motor Division's general manager in 1996. Total production in Canada included 32,799 Firebirds. The calendar year sales total was recorded as 32,622 Firebirds, which represented 6.2 percent of total Pontiac calendar year sales. Of 30,937 Firebirds built for the domestic market in the model year, 72.2 percent had the four-speed automatic transmission, 12.9 percent had a five-speed manual gearbox, 14.9 percent had the six-speed manual transmission, 8.5 percent had traction control, 55.5 percent had a limited-slip differential, 99.8 percent had a manual air conditioner, 80.7 percent had power windows, 81.9 percent had power door locks, 9.2 percent had power seats, 30.7 percent had leather seats, 86.8 percent had cruise control, 79.2 percent had a rear window defogger, 80.7 percent had dual power rearview mirrors, 54.9 percent had hatch roofs, 0.6 percent had an AM/FM stereo with cassette, 56.4 percent had a premium sound system, 43 percent had a CD player, 68.2 percent had the keyless remote entry system and 24.6 percent had an alarm system. A special Firebird model offered in 1996 was called the Harley-Davidson Edition Trans Am. The Milwaukee, Wisconsin, motorcycle maker took a black Trans Am equipped with the WS6 Ram Air package (without the factory upholstery) and added leather-and-fabric seats with the Harley-Davidson logo embroidered on them. The Harley-Davidson Edition Trans Am also had Harley decals on the front quarter panels just behind the tires. Only 40 such cars are believed to have been produced. Most of them were sold in Southern California. Also produced in 1996 were 10 Comp T/A hardtops and 35 Comp T/A T-tops — all had the WS6 Ram Air package.

Jerry Heasley photo

The 1997 Trans Am with the Ram Air V-8 produced 305 hp.

Variety of Flavors

In 1997, you could get a Firebird in a variety of flavors, from affordable to expensive, from economical to guzzler, and from sports car to muscle car — but you couldn't get a Firebird that would please everyone.

The typical buyer of a V-6 Firebird coupe was a 36-year-old person making $55,000 a year. Just over half were married and just below half were male college graduates working in a professional field. At the other end of the Firebird spectrum, Trans Am buyer demographics indicated a median age of 40, average household income of $75,000 and that slightly over 50 percent of buyers were married males with a college degree and professional occupation.

Models and engine carried over from 1996, but new performance and appearance options were added. A Ram Air Performance and Handling Package was offered for convertibles. Ram Air ragtops featured a 5.7-liter V-8, twin scoops with Ram Air logos on each "nostril," high-polished dual exhaust tips and 17-in. aluminum rims. A new package, introduced in mid-1996, was a Sport and Appearance package for V-6 Firebirds with ground effects, fog lamps and dual exhausts with cast-aluminum extensions. New Firebird interior features included a console with an auxiliary power outlet for electronic devices, a pull-out cup holder and revised storage. Air conditioning became standard and all-leather power seats were now available. A four-way seat adjuster and daytime running lamps were added standard equipment. New options included a 500-watt Monsoon sound system. Pontiac built 30,754 Firebirds in the model year.

FIREBIRD – CARLINE F/S – V-6/V-8

"Either you get it or you don't!" That's what a perceptive copywriter said about '97 Firebirds. "The first rule of success is to equip yourself with the proper tools. This axiom not only applies to business, but to automobiles as well. Firebird provides drivers with what's needed for command of the road." Standard equipment included dual front airbags, air conditioning, power front disc/rear drum four-wheel antilock brakes, side window defoggers, a UPC L36 3800 Series II 200-hp SFI V-6 engine, Solar-Ray tinted glass, full instrumentation with a tachometer and trip odometer, sport exterior mirrors (left-hand remote controlled), a rear deck lid spoiler, the PASS-Key II theft-deterrent system, an AM/FM stereo ETR radio and cassette (with a seven-band graphic equalizer, touch control, search-and-replay, a Delco theft lock, a clock, seek up/down, remote CD pre-wiring and a four-speaker coaxial sound system), a fixed-mast antenna, reclining front bucket seats with Cartagena cloth trim, a full-length console, performance-style analog instrumentation (with speedometer, odometer, tachometer, coolant temperature gauge, oil pressure indicator, voltmeter and trip odometer), four-way dual manual front seat adjusters, carpeted front and rear floor mats, day/night rearview mirrors with reading lamps, a four-spoke tilt steering wheel, power rack-and-pinion steering, a rear two-passenger folding seat, a tilt steering column, a remote hatch release, a short-and-long arm front suspension, a torque arm/track bar rear suspension, P215/60R16 touring tires with a high-pressure compact spare, a UPC MM5 five-speed manual transmission, controlled-cycle windshield wipers, bright silver 16 x 8-in. cast-aluminum wheels and an extensive three-year/36,000-mile bumper-to-bumper limited warranty (with 24-hour roadside assistance including free lockout, dead battery, out-of-fuel, flat-tire, towing and transportation protection). Convertibles also included (in addition to or in place of the respective coupe features) cruise control, a rear window defogger, power door locks, remote keyless entry, dual blue-tinted power mirrors, a six-speaker sound system and power windows with express-down feature.

I.D. NUMBERS

The vehicle identification number (VIN) is located

on the top left-hand surface of the instrument panel and is visible through the windshield. The VIN has 17 symbols. The first symbol indicates the country of manufacture (1 or 4=United States; 2=Canada; 3=Mexico). The second symbol indicates the manufacturer (G=General Motors). The third symbol indicates the make/division (2=Pontiac; M=MPV and 7=GM of Canada). The fourth, fifth symbols indicate the car line and series (F/S=Firebird and convertible; F/V=Formula and Trans Am and Formula and Trans Am convertibles). The sixth symbol indicates body style (2=two-door model 87; 3=two-door convertible model 67). The seventh symbol indicates the restraint system: 2=Active manual belts with driver and passenger inflatable restraints, 4=Active manual belts front and side. The eighth symbol indicates the engine type: K=UPC L36 3.8-liter V-6, P=UPC LT1 5.7-liter V-8. (Note: All Firebird engines made in U.S. and all are MFI multi-point fuel-injected engines). The ninth symbol is a check digit. The 10th symbol indicates model year (V=1997). The 11th symbol indicates the GM assembly plant (2=Ste. Therese, Canada). The last six symbols are the consecutive unit number at the factory.

COLORS

10=Bright White, 13=Bright Silver Metallic, 31=Bright Green Metallic, 41=Black, 48=Dark Green Metallic, 79=Blue-Green Chameleon, 80=Bright Blue Metallic, 81=Bright Red, 88=Bright Purple Metallic (midyear availability) and 96=Red-Orange Metallic.

Model Number	Body/Style Number	Body Type & Seating	Factory Price	Shipping Weight	Production Total
F/S	87	2d hatchback-4P	$17,649	3,131 lbs.	16,394
F/S	67	2d convertible-4P	$23,559	3,346 lbs.	1,226

FORMULA FIREBIRD – CARLINE F/V V-8

The Formula Firebird also came in hatchback coupe and convertible models. The Formula came standard with a 5.7-liter 285-hp SFI V-8. A Ram Air Performance and Handling Package was offered for the Formula Firebird coupe. Ram Air Formulas featured twin scoops with Ram Air logos on each "nostril," a 305-hp rating, high-polished dual exhaust tips, 17-in. five-spoke aluminum rims, P275/40ZR17 tires, specific dual outlet exhaust and a tuned suspension. Standard equipment of the Formula coupe included a black fixed-mast antenna, left- and right-hand Sport-style outside rearview mirrors (left-hand remote controlled), body-color body side moldings, a rear deck lid spoiler, P235/55R16 touring tires, bright silver 16 x 8-in. five-spoke Sport cast-aluminum wheels, driver and front passenger airbags and safety belts, rear seat lap and shoulder belts in all positions, air conditioning, a full-length console, side window defoggers, Cartagena cloth upholstery, a remote hatch release, performance-style analog instrumentation (with speedometer, odometer, tachometer, coolant temperature gauge, oil pressure indicator, voltmeter and trip odometer), carpeted front and rear floor mats, day/night inside rearview mirrors with reading lamps, a Delco 2001 series ETR stereo (with cassette, seven-band graphic equalizer, clock, touch control, seek up/down, search and replay, Delco TheftLock, remote CD pre-wiring and four-speaker coaxial sound system), reclining front bucket seats, a split folding rear seat, a four-way manual driver's seat adjuster, a two-way manual front passenger's seat adjuster, a four-

The Trans Am convertible was a fairly rare bird in 1997, with only 1,390 produced.

Jerry Heasley photo

The Formula Firebirds were again characterized by the "twin-nostril" hood in 1997.

spoke tilt steering wheel, the PASS-Key II theft-deterrent system, power four-wheel disc brakes with antilock braking system (ABS), a brake/transmission shift interlock safety feature (with automatic transmission), the 5.7-liter V-8 with sequential-port fuel injection, power rack-and-pinion steering, a short-and-long arm front suspension, a torque arm/track bar rear suspension, a four-speed automatic transmission and an extensive three-year/36,000-mile bumper-to-bumper limited warranty (with 24-hour roadside assistance including free lock-out, dead battery, out-of-fuel, flat-tire, towing and transportation protection). Formula Convertibles also included (in addition to or in place of the respective coupe features) an audible content theft-deterrent system, cruise control, a rear window defogger, power door locks, remote keyless entry, dual blue-tinted power mirrors, a six-speaker sound system and power windows with express-down feature.

Model Number	Body/Style Number	Body Type & Seating	Factory Price	Shipping Weight	Production Total
FORMULA FIREBIRD - SERIES F/V - (V-8)					
F/V	87	2d hatchback-4P	$21,179	3,373 lbs.	2,766
F/V	67	2d convertible-4P	$26,949	3,489 lbs.	324
FORMULA FIREBIRD – WS6 RAM AIR - SERIES F/V - (RAM AIR V-8)					
F/V	87	2d hatchback-4P	$24,524	3,373 lbs.	Note 1

Note 1: No separate breakout available.

TRANS AM – CARLINE F/V – V-8

The Trans Am was again the ultimate Firebird in 1997. It also came as a hatchback coupe or a convertible. A Ram Air Performance and Handling Package was offered for the Trans Am coupe. Ram Air cars featured twin scoops with Ram Air logos on each "nostril," a 305-hp rating, high-polished dual exhaust tips, 17-in. five-spoke aluminum rims, P275/40ZR17 tires, specific dual outlet exhaust and a tuned suspension. Standard equipment on the Trans Am coupe included a black fixed-mast antenna, front fog lamps, left- and right-hand Sport-style outside rearview mirrors (left-hand remote controlled), body-color body side moldings, an uplevel rear deck lid spoiler, P235/55R16 touring tires, bright silver 16 x 8-in. five-spoke Sport cast-aluminum wheels, driver and front passenger airbags and safety belts, rear seat lap and shoulder belts in all positions, air conditioning, a full-length console, cruise control, automatic power door locks, an electric rear window defogger, side window defoggers, Cartagena cloth upholstery, a remote hatch release, performance-style analog instrumentation (with speedometer, odometer, tachometer, coolant temperature gauge, oil pressure indicator, voltmeter and trip odometer), carpeted front and rear floor mats, power windows with driver's side express down, day/night inside rearview mirrors with reading lamps, a Delco 2001 series ETR stereo (with cassette, senenband graphic equalizer, clock, touch control, seek up/down, search and replay, Delco TheftLock, remote CD pre-wiring and four-speaker coaxial sound system), reclining front bucket seats, a split folding rear seat, a four-way manual driver's seat adjuster, a two-way manual front passenger's seat adjuster, a four-spoke leather-wrapped tilt steering wheel, the PASS-Key II theft-deterrent system, power four-wheel disc brakes with antilock braking system (ABS), a brake/transmission shift interlock safety feature (with automatic transmission), the 5.7-liter V-8 with sequential-port fuel injection, power rack-and-pinion steering, a short-and-long arm front suspension, a torque arm/track bar rear suspension, a four-speed automatic transmission and an extensive three-year/36,000-mile bumper-to-bumper limited warranty (with 24-hour roadside assistance including free lockout, dead battery, out-of-fuel, flat-tire, towing and transportation protection). Trans Am convertibles also included (in addition to or in place of the respective coupe features) a power antenna, P245/50ZR16 all-weather speed-rated performance tires, remote keyless entry and a four-spoke leather-wrapped steering wheel with "redundant" radio controls. The convertible also had the Firebird/Formula type rear deck lid spoiler, rather than the uplevel style used on the Trans Am coupe.

Model Number	Body/Style Number	Body Type & Seating	Factory Price	Shipping Weight	Production Total
TRANS AM - SERIES F/V - (V-8)					
F/V	87	2d hatchback-4P	$23,339	3,345 lbs.	8,656
F/V	67	2d convertible-4P	$28,899	3,610 lbs.	1,390
TRANS AM – WS6 RAM AIR - SERIES F/V - (V-8)					
F/V	87	2d hatchback-4P	$26,684	3,345 lbs.	Note 2

Note 2: No separate breakout available.

ENGINES

Base V-6 [UPC L36]: Overhead valve. Cast-iron block and head. Aluminum intake manifold. Displacement: 231 cid. (3.8-liter). Bore & stroke: 3.80 x 3.40 in. Compression ratio: 9.4:1. Brake horsepower: 200 at 5200 rpm. Torque: 225 ft. lbs. at 4000 rpm. Fuel system: SFI. VIN Code: K.

5.7-liter V-8 [UPC LT1]: Overhead valve. Cast-iron block and head. Aluminum intake manifold. Displacement: 350 cid. (5.7-liter). Bore & stroke: 4.00 x 3.48 in. Brake horsepower: 285 at 5000 rpm. Torque: 325 ft. lbs. at 2400 rpm. Compression ratio: 10.5:1. Fuel system: SFI. VIN Code: 5.

5.7-liter Ram Air V-8 [UPC LT1]: Overhead valve. Cast-iron block and head. Aluminum intake manifold. Displacement: 350 cid. (5.7-liter). Bore & stroke: 4.00 x 3.48 in. Brake horsepower: 305 at 5000 rpm. Torque: 325 ft. lbs. at 2400 rpm. Compression ratio: 10.5:1. Fuel system: SFI. VIN Code: 5. With WS6 Ram Air Performance package.

CHASSIS

Firebird: Wheelbase: 101.1 in. Overall length: 195.6 in. Width: 74.5 in. Height: (hatchback) 52.0 in., (convertible) 51.7 in. Front tread: 60.7 in. Rear tread: 60.6 in. Standard tires: steel-belted radial P215/60R15 black sidewall touring.

Formula: Wheelbase: 101.1 in. Overall length: 195.6 in. Width: 74.5 in. Height: (hatchback) 52.0 in., (convertible) 52.7 in. Front tread: 60.7 in. Rear tread: 60.6 in. Standard tires: steel-belted radial P235/55R16 touring.

Trans Am: Wheelbase: 101.1 in. Overall length: 197 in. Width: 74.5 in. Height: (coupe) 51.7 in., (convertible) 52.4 in. Front tread: 60.7 in. Rear tread: 60.6 in. Standard tires: (hatchback) P235/55R16 touring; (convertible) P245/50ZR16 speed-rated, all-weather.

TECHNICAL

Firebird: Chassis: Front engine/rear drive. Base transmission: Five-speed manual. Front suspension: Modified MacPherson strut with anti-roll bar. Rear suspension: Live axle with coil springs, control arms, torque arm, track bar and anti-roll bar. Steering: Power re-circulating ball. Brakes: Front disc/rear drum with ABS. Front headroom: 37.2 in. Rear headroom: 35.3 in. Front legroom: 43 in. Rear legroom: 28.9 in. Front shoulder room: 57.4 in. Rear shoulder room: 55.8 in. Front hip room: 52.8 in. Rear hip room: 44.4 in. Cargo room with rear seat up: 12.9 cu. ft. Cargo room with rear seat down: 33.7 cu. ft.

Formula: Chassis: Front engine/rear drive. Base transmission: Four-speed automatic. Front suspension: Modified MacPherson strut with anti-roll bar. Rear suspension: Live axle with coil springs, control arms, torque arm, track bar and anti-roll bar. Steering: Power re-circulating ball. Brakes: Power four-wheel discs with ABS. Front headroom: 37.2 in. Rear headroom: 35.3 in. Front legroom: 43 in. Rear legroom: 28.9 in. Front shoulder room: 57.4 in. Rear shoulder room: 55.8 in. Front hip room: 52.8 in. Rear hip room: 44.4 in. Cargo room with rear seat up: 12.9 cu. ft. Cargo room with rear seat down: 33.7 cu. ft.

Trans Am: Chassis: Front engine/rear drive. Base transmission: Four-speed automatic. Front suspension: Modified MacPherson strut with anti-roll bar. Rear suspension: Live axle with coil springs, control arms, torque arm, track bar and anti-roll bar. Steering: Power re-circulating ball. Brakes: Power four-wheel discs with ABS. Front headroom: 37.2 in. Rear headroom: 35.3 in. Front legroom: 43 in. Rear legroom: 28.9 in. Front shoulder room: 57.4 in. Rear shoulder room: 55.8 in. Front hip room: 52.8 in. Rear hip room: 44.4 in. Cargo room with rear seat up: 12.9 cu. ft. Cargo room with rear seat down: 33.7 cu. ft.

OPTIONS

1SA Firebird coupe option package includes vehicle with standard equipment (no cost). 1SB Firebird option group ($1,936). 1SA Formula coupe option package includes vehicle with standard equipment (no cost). 1SB Formula coupe option group ($1,121). 1SA Trans Am coupe option package, includes vehicle with standard equipment (no cost). 1SA Firebird and Formula convertible option package includes vehicle with standard equipment (no cost). 1SB Firebird and Formula convertible group ($435). 1SA Trans Am convertible option package, includes vehicle with standard equipment (no cost). R6A Firebird and Formula value package ($820). FE9 Federal emissions (no cost). YF5 50 California emissions (Firebird no cost; Formula/Trans Am $170). NG1 New York/Massachusetts Emissions (Firebird no cost; Formula/Trans Am $170). NB8 California/New York/Massachusetts Emissions override, requires FE9 (no cost). NC7 Federal emissions override, requires YF5 or NG1 (no cost). QCB P235/55R16 black sidewall touring tires for Firebird, standard Formula and Trans Am; not available on Trans Am convertible ($132). QFZ P245/50ZR16 black sidewall steel-belted radial all-weather performance tires for Formula and Trans Am coupe ($245). QLC P245/50ZR16 black sidewall steel-belted radial performance tires for Formula and Trans Am ($245). QFK P275/40ZR17 speed-rated tires for Formula and Trans Am coupe with WS6 only (no cost). 23/AN3 articulating bucket seats with Prado leather (Firebird and Formula $804). 28/AQ9 articulating bucket seats with Prado leather (Trans Am coupe $829; Trans Am convertible $804). Y82 Trans Am coupe option (standard). Y84 Trans Am convertible option (standard). W68 Sport Appearance package includes aero components, fog lamps, dual outlet exhausts for base models, requires QCB tires and automatic transmission ($1,449). Y87 3800 performance package includes limited-slip differential, four-wheel disc brakes, up-level steering, dual outlet exhausts, QCB tires and 3.42:1 axle if ordered with MXO transmission, base models only ($550). 1LE Performance Package includes special handling suspension, larger stabilizer bars, stiffer springs, Koni shocks ($1,175). WS6 Ram Air performance and handling package, includes Ram Air induction system; functional air scoops; 17-in. five-spoke aluminum wheels; P275/40ZR17 speed-rated tires and dual oval exhaust outlets ($3,345). UA6 content theft alarm ($90). K34 cruise control ($235). C49 electric rear window defogger ($180). CC1 hatch roof ($995). VK3 front license plate bracket (no cost). DG7 dual sport mirrors ($96). U75 power antenna, requires radio upgrade, standard on Trans Am convertible ($85). AU3 power door locks ($220). AG1 six-way power driver's seat ($270). A31 power windows ($290). W53 ETR AM/FM stereo with CD player, graphic equalizer, clock, seek up/down and four coaxial speakers ($100). W54 ETR AM/FM stereo with auto-reverse, graphic equalizer, clock, seek up/down, remote CD pre-wiring and 10-speaker sound system (coupes with 1SA $230; coupes with 1SB $130). W55 ETR AM/FM stereo with CD player, graphic equalizer, clock, seek up/down and 10-speaker sound system (coupes with 1SA $330; coupes with 1SB $230). W73 ETR AM/FM stereo with CD player, graphic equalizer, clock, seek up/down and six-speaker sound system ($100). U1S trunk mounted remote 12-disc CD changer ($595). GU5 performance axle ($225). AUO remote keyless entry ($150). UK3

steering wheel radio controls (Firebird/Formula $200; Trans Am $125). MN6 six-speed manual transmission in Formula/Trans Am (no cost). NW9 traction control ($450). MXO four-speed automatic transmission ($815). PO5 chrome aluminum wheels, not available with 1SA Firebird coupe ($595).

HISTORICAL FOOTNOTES

Roy S. Roberts remained Pontiac Motor Division's general manager in 1997. Total production in Canada included 32,692 Firebirds. The calendar year sales total was recorded as 32,524 Firebirds, which represented 5.8 percent of total Pontiac calendar year sales. Of 30,754 Firebirds built for the domestic market in the model year, 77.4 percent had the four-speed automatic transmission, 8.7 percent had a five-speed manual gearbox, 13.9 percent had the six-speed manual transmission, 7.0 percent had traction control, 58.1 percent had a limited-slip differential, 90.1 percent had power windows, 91.3 percent had power door locks, 12.4 percent had power seats, 32.9 percent had leather seats, 23.4 percent had memory seats, 92.8 percent had cruise control, 19.2 percent had chrome styled wheels, 81.8 percent had aluminum wheels, 83 percent had a rear window defogger, 90.1 percent had dual power rearview mirrors, 65 percent had hatch roofs, 23.3 percent had a premium sound system, 76.7 percent had a CD player, 68.3 percent had the keyless remote entry system and 35.3 percent had an anti-theft device.

The Ram Air Trans Ams were rated at 305 hp and came with 17-inch, five-spoke rims.

The "twin-nostril" hood was again a calling card of the WS6 Ram Air Package, seen here on a Bright Red Formula.

Bold New Firebird

For 1998, Pontiac Motor Division's stable of aggressively styled cars included a bold new Firebird with a new appearance guaranteed to up its legendary status among sports car enthusiasts. The base Firebird model now shared its front fascia design with the Formula model. The front end design incorporated twin center ports below the hood and restyled, round, outboard-mounted fog lamps.

Two new paint colors, Navy Metallic and Sport Gold Metallic, were available. The Formula Firebird also had new rear-end styling. Inside were gauges with clear white characters on black analog faces to help keep drivers informed of what was going on with their cars.

The hot, rear-drive 2+2 Firebird offered five model choices in 1998, since the Formula convertible was dropped. Previously, base, Formula and Trans Am convertibles were offered, but production failed to top 3,000 units in 1996-1997. Production numbers for 1998 were close to 2,100 ragtops out of 32,157 total cars. Coupes were again featured in base, Formula and Trans Am trim levels.

Formulas and Trans Ams got a new, all-aluminum 5.7-liter 305-hp V-8 with a six-speed manual transmission. A Ram Air package provided 320 hp.

Styling was freshened with a front fascia that incorporated a new headlamp design. There were updated taillights, too. Suspension tuning was revised and base models received a one-piece drive shaft. Firebird V-8s with four-speed automatic transmissions had a larger torque converter. All Firebirds got

standard four-wheel disc brakes. A midyear Formula option was an AutoCross package with a beefed-up suspension. A $1,125-delete option that turned the Formula into a stripped-down street performance car was also new.

I.D. NUMBERS

The vehicle identification number (VIN) is located on the top left-hand surface of the instrument panel and is visible through the windshield. The VIN has 17 symbols. The first symbol indicates the country of manufacture (1 or 4=United States, 2=Canada, 3=Mexico). The second symbol indicates the manufacturer (G=General Motors). The third symbol indicates the make/division (2=Pontiac and 7=GM of Canada). The fourth, fifth symbols indicate the car line and series (F/S=Firebird and convertible, F/V=Formula-Trans Am and convertible). The sixth symbol indicates body style (2=two-door model 87, 3=two-door convertible model 67). The seventh symbol indicates the restraint system: 2=Active manual belts with driver and passenger inflatable restraints, 4=Active manual belts front and side. The eighth symbol indicates the engine type: M=UPC L82 3.1-liter V-6, G=UPC LS1 5.7-liter V-8. The 10th symbol indicates model year (W=1998). The 11th symbol indicates the GM assembly plant (2=Ste. Therese, Canada). The last six symbols are the consecutive unit number at the factory.

COLORS

10=Bright White, 13=Bright Silver Metallic, 28=Navy Blue Metallic, 31=Bright Green Metallic, 41=Black, 63=Sport Gold Metallic, 79=Blue-Green

Chameleon, 81=Bright Red, 88=Bright Purple Metallic and 96=Red-Orange Metallic.

FIREBIRD – SERIES F/S – V-6/V-8

A hatchback coupe and a convertible were featured in the base Firebird series. Styling was freshened with a front fascia that incorporated a new headlamp design. There were updated taillights, too. Suspension tuning was revised and base models received a one-piece drive shaft. Firebird V-8s with four-speed automatic transmissions had a larger torque converter. All Firebirds got standard four-wheel disc brakes. Standard equipment on the base Firebird coupe included extensive acoustical insulation, dual front airbags, air conditioning, a black fixed-mast antenna at right rear, a brake/transmission shift interlock safety feature with automatic transmission, power four-wheel disc brakes with four-wheel ABS, the UPC L36 3800 Series II 200-hp SFI V-6 engine, cruise control, electric rear and side window defoggers, Solar-Ray tinted glass, instrumentation (including an electric analog speedometer, a tachometer, odometer, coolant temperature indicator, oil pressure gauge, voltmeter and LED trip odometer), sport exterior mirrors (left-hand remote controlled), a day/night inside rearview mirror with reading lamps, left- and right-hand covered visor vanity mirrors, a Delco AM/FM stereo ETR radio and cassette (with seven-band graphic equalizer, touch control, search-and-replay, Delco TheftLock, clock, seek up/down, remote CD pre-wiring and four-speaker coaxial sound system), reclining front bucket seats, four-way driver and passenger front seat manual adjusters, a rear two-passenger folding seat, a four-spoke sport tilt steering wheel with adjustable column, the PASS-Key II theft-deterrent system, P215/60R16 touring tires with a high-pressure compact spare, the UPC MM5 five-speed manual transmission, controlled-cycle windshield wipers and bright silver 16-inch five-spoke cast-aluminum wheels.

Model Number	Body/Style Number	Body Type & Seating	Factory Price	Shipping Weight	Production Total
F/S	S87V	2d hatchback-4P	$18,540	3,340 lbs.	15,869
F/S	S67V	2d convertible-4P	$24,830	3,492 lbs.	704

FORMULA FIREBIRD – CARLINE F V-6/V-8

The Formula Firebird convertible was gone. Previously base, Formula and Trans Am convertibles had been offered, but ragtop production failed to top 3,000 units in 1996-1997. Production numbers for 1998 were close to 2,100 ragtops. Formulas got a new, all-aluminum LS1 5.7-liter 305-hp V-8 with a six-speed manual transmission. The WS6 Ram Air package provided 320 hp. A midyear Formula option was an AutoCross package with a beefed-up suspension. A $1,125-delete option that turned the Formula into a stripped-down street performance car was also new. Standard equipment on the Formula Firebird coupe included extensive acoustical insulation, dual front airbags, air conditioning, a power antenna, a brake/transmission shift interlock safety feature with automatic transmission, power four-wheel disc brakes with four-wheel ABS, the UPC LS1 5.7-liter SFI V-8 engine, cruise control, power door locks, electric rear and side window defoggers, Solar-Ray tinted glass, instrumentation (including an electric analog speedometer, a tachometer, odometer, coolant temperature indicator, oil pressure gauge, voltmeter and LED trip odometer), a day/night inside rearview mirror with reading lamps, power automatic sport mirrors with blue glass, power window controls with driver's "express down" feature (power mirrors and door locks required), a Delco 500-watt peak power Monsoon AM/FM stereo (with CD, seven-band graphic equalizer, clock, Touch Control, seek up/down, search and replay, Delco TheftLock, high-performance 10-speaker sound system in coupe or six-speaker sound system in convertible, HSS speakers and tweeters in doors, 6.5-inch subwoofers in sail panels, subwoofer amp and four speakers, and tweeters in rear quarter panels), reclining front bucket seats, four-way driver and passenger front seat manual adjusters, a rear two-passenger folding seat, a leather-wrapped steering wheel with radio controls (including leather-wrapped steering wheel, shift knob and parking brake handle) and adjustable tilt column, the PASS-Key II theft-deterrent system, P245/50ZR16 speed-rated all-weather tires with a high-pressure compact spare, four-speed automatic transmission, controlled-cycle

The Firebird received a few updates for 1998, including new headlight and taillight assemblies.

windshield wipers and bright silver 16-in. five-spoke cast-aluminum wheels.

Model Number	Body/Style Number	Body Type & Seating	Factory Price	Shipping Weight	Production Total
FORMULA FIREBIRD - SERIES F/V - (V-8)					
F/V	87	2d hatchback-4P	$23,390	3,455 lbs.	2,123
FORMULA FIREBIRD - WS6 RAM AIR - SERIES F/V - (V-8)					
F/V	87	2d hatchback-4P	$26,490	3,455 lbs.	Note 1

NOTE 1: No separate breakout available.

TRANS AM – SERIES F/V – V-8

The 1998 Trans Am came as a coupe or a convertible. Like Formulas, Trans Ams got a new, all-aluminum LS1 5.7-liter 305-hp V-8 with a six-speed manual transmission. The WS6 Ram Air package provided 320 hp. Styling was freshened by the new front fascia that incorporated a new headlamp design and the updated taillights. Trans Ams with four-speed automatic transmissions had a larger torque converter. Standard equipment on the Trans Am coupe included extensive acoustical insulation, dual front airbags, air conditioning, a power antenna, a brake/transmission shift interlock safety feature with automatic transmission, power four-wheel disc brakes with four-wheel ABS, UPC LS1 5.7-liter SFI V-8 engine, cruise control, power door locks, electric rear and side window defoggers, Solar-Ray tinted glass, instrumentation (including an electric analog speedometer, a tachometer, odometer, coolant temperature indicator, oil pressure gauge, voltmeter and LED trip odometer), a day/night inside rearview mirror with reading lamps, power automatic sport mirrors with blue glass, power window controls with driver's "express down" feature (power mirrors and door locks required), a Delco 500-watt peak power Monsoon AM/FM stereo (with CD, seven-band graphic equalizer, clock, Touch Control, seek up/down, search and replay, Delco TheftLock, high-performance 10-speaker sound system in coupe or six-speaker sound system in convertible, HSS speakers and tweeters in doors, 6.5-in. subwoofers in sail panels, subwoofer amp and four speakers, and tweeters in rear quarter panels), reclining front bucket seats, four-way driver and passenger front seat manual adjusters, a rear two-passenger folding seat, a leather-wrapped steering wheel with radio controls (including leather-wrapped steering wheel, shift knob and parking brake handle) and adjustable tilt column, the PASS-Key II theft-deterrent system, P245/50ZR16 speed-rated all-weather tires with a high-pressure compact spare, four-speed automatic transmission, controlled-cycle windshield wipers and bright silver 16-in. five-spoke cast-aluminum wheels, an audible content theft-deterrent system, remote keyless entry and a six-way power front driver's seat.

Model Number	Body/Style Number	Body Type & Seating	Factory Price	Shipping Weight	Production Total
TRANS AM – SERIES F/V - (V-8)					
F/V	87	2d hatchback-4P	$26,500	3,477 lbs.	12,046
F/V	67	2d convertble-4P	$30,240	3,605 lbs.	1,413
TRANS AM – WS6 RAM AIR - SERIES F/V - (V-8)					
F/V	87	2d hatchback-4P	$29,600	3,477 lbs.	Note 2

Note 2: No separate breakout available.

ENGINES

Base V-6 [UPC L36]: Overhead valve. Displacement: 231 cid. (3.8-liter). Bore & stroke: 3.80 x 3.40 in. Compression ratio: 9.4:1. Brake horsepower: 200 at 5200 rpm. Torque: 225 ft. lbs. at 4000 rpm. Fuel system: SFI. VIN Code: K. UPC Code: L36.

5.7-liter V-8 [UPC LS1]: Overhead valve. Aluminum block and head. Aluminum intake manifold. Displacement: 350 cid. (5.7-liter). Bore & stroke: 3.90 x 3.62 in. Brake horsepower: 305 at 5200 rpm. Torque: 335 ft. lbs. at 4000 rpm. Compression ratio: 10.5:1. Fuel system: SFI. VIN Code: G.

5.7-liter Ram Air V-8 [UPC LS1]: Overhead valve. Ram Air. Eight-cylinder. Cast-iron block and head. Aluminum intake manifold. Displacement: 350 cid. Bore & stroke: 3.90 x 3.62 in. Brake horsepower: 320 at 5200 rpm. Torque: 345 ft. lbs. at 4400 rpm. Compression ratio: 10.5:1. Fuel system: SFI.

CHASSIS

Firebird: Wheelbase: 101.0 in. Overall length: 193.4 in. Width: 74.5 in. Height: (coupe) 52.0 in., (convertible) 52.7 in. Standard tires: steel-belted radial P215/60R16 black sidewall touring.

Formula: Wheelbase: 101.0 in. Overall length: 193.4 in. Width: 74.5 in. Height: 52.0 in. Standard tires: P245/50ZR16 speed-rated, all-weather.

Trans Am: Wheelbase: 101.0 in. Overall length: 193.8 in. Width: 74.5 in. Height: (coupe) 51.7 in., (convertible) 52.4 in. Standard tires: P245/50ZR16 speed-rated, all-weather.

Trans Ams received a new all-aluminum LSI 5.7-liter V-8.

TECHNICAL

Firebird: Chassis: Front engine/rear drive. Base transmission: Five-speed manual. Front suspension: Modified MacPherson strut with anti-roll bar. Rear suspension: Live axle with coil springs, control arms, torque arm, track bar and anti-roll bar. Steering: Power re-circulating ball. Brakes: Power four-wheel discs with ABS.

Formula Firebird: Front engine/rear drive. Base transmission: Five-speed manual. Front suspension: Modified MacPherson strut with anti-roll bar. Rear suspension: Live axle with coil springs, control arms, torque arm, track bar and anti-roll bar. Steering: Power re-circulating ball. Brakes: Power four-wheel discs with ABS.

Trans Am: Chassis: Front engine/rear drive. Base transmission: Five-speed manual. Front suspension: Modified MacPherson strut with anti-roll bar. Rear

Trans Am convertibles carried a price tag of $30,240 for 1998.

suspension: Live axle with coil springs, control arms, torque arm, track bar and anti-roll bar. Steering: Power re-circulating ball. Brakes: Power four-wheel discs with ABS.

OPTIONS

Firebird coupe 1SA package includes vehicle standard equipment only (no charge). Firebird coupe 1SB package includes 1SA package plus power door locks, power windows, dual power mirrors, power antenna and power seat ($1,610). Firebird coupe 1SC package includes 1SB plus power seat, security package with theft deterrent system and remote keyless entry ($2,450). Formula coupe 1SB package includes power seat, security package with theft deterrent system, remote keyless entry system and removable hatch roof ($1,505). Firebird convertible 1SA package includes security package with theft deterrent system and remote keyless entry system (no charge). Trans Am 1SA package includes same as Firebird convertible (no charge). VK3 front license plate bracket (no charge). FE9 Federal emissions (no charge). YF5 California emissions ($170). NG1 New York, Massachusetts and Connecticut emissions ($170). GU5 performance rear axle, not available on Firebird ($225). NW9 Traction control system, not available on base Firebird, requires QCB or QFZ tires ($450). WS6 Ram Air performance and handling package ($3,100). Y87 Firebird 3800 V-6 performance package ($440). P05 chromed 16-in. aluminum wheels ($595). W54 "Monsoon" ETR AM/FM stereo with auto reverse cassette, graphic equalizer, clock, seek up/down, remote CD pre-wiring and 10-speaker sound system; in coupes with 1SA ($230); in Trans Am coupes ($100 credit). W55 ETR AM/FM stereo with CD player, graphic equalizer, clock, seek up/down and 10-speaker sound system, in Firebird coupes with 1SC (no charge); in other Firebird coupes ($430). W59 ETR AM/FM stereo with auto-reverse cassette, graphic equalizer, clock, seek up/down, remote CD pre-wiring and six speakers, in convertible ($100 credit). CC1 removable hatch roof with locks and stowage, coupes only, included on Formula coupe with 1SB; in other Firebirds ($995). R7X security package for coupe, included with Firebird 1SC or Formula 1SB packages, otherwise ($240). AQ9 articulating custom bucket seats with adjustable lumbar supports ($155). AR9 leather trimmed front bucket seats ($650). AG1 six-way power driver's seat in coupes, no charge in Firebird with 1SB or Formula with 1SC, otherwise ($270). W68 Sport Appearance Package ($990). MN6 six-speed manual transmission, not available in base Firebird; in Formula and Trans Am (no charge). MM5 five-speed manual transmission, standard and only available on base Firebird coupe, no charge with 1SA; on coupe with 1SB/1SC, the following amount is a credit for deleting the automatic transmission ($815 credit). MXO four-speed automatic transmission, standard in Formula and Trans Am, no charge in base Firebird with 1SB or 1SC; in other base Firebirds ($815).

HISTORICAL FOOTNOTES

Total production in Canada included 33,299 Firebirds. The model-year sales total was 33,578 Firebirds, which represented 0.4 percent of total U.S. new car sales. Of 32,157 Firebirds built for the domestic market in the model year, 80.1 percent had the four-speed automatic transmission, 8.0 percent had a five-speed manual gearbox, 11.9 percent had the six-speed manual transmission, 17.3 percent had traction control, 60.4 percent had a limited-slip differential, 87.3 percent had power windows, 87.3 percent had power door locks, 71.4 percent had power seats, 48.3 percent had leather seats, 27.6 percent had memory seats, 30.6 percent had chrome styled wheels, 69.4 percent had aluminum wheels, 83 percent had a rear window defogger, 93.8 percent had dual power rearview mirrors, 76.8 percent had hatch roofs, 10.7 percent had a premium sound system, 89.3 percent had a CD player, 70 percent had the keyless remote entry system and 70 percent had an anti-theft device.

The 30th Anniversary Trans Am was a loaded model decked out in a striking white paint scheme and trimmed with a special interior.

The Big 3-0

A new 30th Anniversary Limited Edition Trans Am added a little distinction to the 1999 Firebird offerings. Otherwise, there were only minor changes. Formulas and Trans Ams now had a four-speed automatic transmission as standard equipment. Buyers could choose from it or a six-speed manual, which had a Hurst shifter. Traction control was available on V-6 Firebirds. Specific V-6 Firebirds also got a Torsen II slip-reduction rear axle as standard equipment. An Electronic Brake Force Distribution system and solenoid-based Bosch anti-lock brake system enhanced stopping capabilities. Also new was an upgraded sensing and diagnostic module to improve the passenger-protection system.

Part of the reason for little change was that "end-of-the-Firebird-line" rumors were floating around again. GM eventually said that the marque would be continued at least for a few more years with special-edition packages offered.

The 30th Anniversary Trans Am package was conceived as something very special. Each one of the cars was individually numbered to enhance its collectibility. The package also featured 30th Anniversary cloisonné door badges, striping and console emblems, floor mats with a metallic 30th Anniversary logo, specific blue-tinted, high-polished, 17-inch aluminum wheels, white leather seating surfaces and the buyer's choice of either a full ragtop or a T-top coupe. The anniversary edition Trans Ams were powered by the 5.7-liter Ram Air V-8.

Model year production reflected a substantial 28 percent increase to 41,226 units. Sales held fairly consistent at 32,899 cars versus 33,578 in 1998, 30,459 in 1997 and 36,546 in 1996. The Firebird registered a 0.4 percent share of total U.S. auto sales for the fourth year in a row.

I.D. NUMBERS

The vehicle identification number (VIN) is located on the top left-hand surface of the instrument panel and is visible through the windshield. The VIN has 17 symbols. The first symbol indicates the country of manufacture (1 or 4=United States; 2=Canada). The second symbol indicates the manufacturer (G=General Motors). The third symbol indicates the make/division (2=Pontiac and 7=GM of Canada). The fourth and fifth symbols indicate the car line and series: F/S=Firebird and convertible; F/V=Formula and convertible). The sixth symbol indicates body style (2=two-door coupe model 87; 3=two-door convertible model 67). The seventh symbol indicates the restraint system: 2=Active manual belts with driver and passenger inflatable restraints; 4=Active manual belts front and side. The eighth symbol indicates the engine type: G=LS1 5.7-liter V-8; K=L36 3.8-liter V-6. (Note: All Pontiac engines are MFI multi-point fuel-injected engines.) The ninth symbol is a check digit. The 10th symbol indicates model year (X=1999). The 11th symbol indicates the GM assembly plant (2=Ste. Therese, Canada). The last six symbols are the consecutive unit number at the factory.

COLORS

10=Artic White, 11=Pewter Metallic, 13=Silver Metallic, 20=Medium Blue Metallic, 28=Navy Blue Metallic, 31=Bright Green Metallic, 41=Black, 79=Blue-Green Chameleon and 81=Bright Red.

FIREBIRD - SERIES F/S - V-6

The availability of GM's Traction Control system was extended to V-6-powered Firebirds this year. All Firebirds with a V-8 and some with a V-6 had a Zexel Torsen II slip-reduction rear axle. An Electronic Brakeforce Distribution (EBD) system replaced the old hydraulic proportioning valve for improved brake performance. Also new was a solenoid-based Bosch antilock braking system. An enhanced Sensing and Diagnostic Module (SDM) recorded vehicle speed, engine rpm, throttle position and brake use in the last five seconds prior to airbag deployment. Standard equipment for the Firebird coupe included extensive acoustical insulation, dual front airbags, air conditioning, a black fixed-mast antenna at right rear, a brake/transmission shift interlock safety feature (with automatic transmission), power four-wheel disc brakes with four-wheel ABS, the UPC L36 3800 Series II 200-hp SFI V-6 engine, cruise control, electric rear and side window defoggers, Solar-Ray tinted glass, instrumentation (including electric analog speedometer, tachometer, odometer, coolant temperature indicator, oil pressure gauge, voltmeter and LED trip odometer), sport exterior mirrors (left-hand remote controlled, right-hand manual), a day/night inside rearview mirror with reading lamps, left- and right-hand covered visor-vanity mirrors, a Delco AM/FM stereo ETR radio and cassette (with seven-band graphic equalizer, touch control, search-and-replay, Delco TheftLock, clock, seek up/down, remote CD pre-wiring and four-speaker coaxial sound system), reclining front bucket seats, four-way driver and passenger front seat manual adjusters, a rear two-passenger folding seat, a four-spoke sport tilt steering wheel with adjustable column, the PASS-Key II theft-deterrent system, P215/60R16 touring tires with a high-pressure compact spare, the UPC MM5 five-speed manual transmission, controlled-cycle windshield wipers and bright silver 16-in. five-spoke cast-aluminum wheels.

Model Number	Body/Style Number	Body Type & Seating	Factory Price	Shipping Weight	Production Total
F/S	87	2d hatchback-4P	$18,700	3,340 lbs.	17,170
F/S	67	2d convertible-4P	$25,320	3,465 lbs.	1,245

FORMULA FIREBIRD - SERIES F/V V-8

Pontiac's 1999 sales catalog described the Formula as a car that "sports a functionally aggressive nose, a rumbling exhaust and tires wide enough to double as steamrollers." Standard equipment for the Formula Firebird coupe included extensive acoustical insulation, dual front airbags, air conditioning, power door locks, a power antenna, a brake/transmission shift interlock safety feature (with automatic transmission), power four-wheel disc brakes with four-wheel ABS, the UPC LS1 5.7-liter SFI V-8 engine, cruise control, electric rear and side window defoggers, Solar-Ray tinted glass, instrumentation (including electric analog speedometer, tachometer, odometer, coolant temperature indicator, oil pressure gauge, voltmeter and LED trip odometer), power automatic sport mirrors with blue glass, a day/night inside rearview mirror with reading lamps, left- and right-hand covered visor-vanity mirrors, a Delco 500-watt peak power Monsoon AM/FM stereo (with CD, seven-band graphic equalizer, clock, touch control, seek up/down, search and replay, Delco TheftLock, high-performance 10-speaker sound system in coupe, HSS speakers and tweeters in doors, 6.5-in. subwoofers in sail panels, subwoofer amplifier and four speakers and tweeters in rear quarter panels), reclining front bucket seats, four-way driver and passenger front seat manual adjusters, a rear two-passenger folding seat, a leather-wrapped tilt steering wheel with radio controls (including leather-wrapped shift knob and parking brake handle), power window controls with driver's express-down feature (requires power mirrors and door locks), the PASS-Key II theft-deterrent system, P245/50ZR16 speed-rated all-weather tires with a high-pressure compact spare, four-speed automatic transmission, controlled-cycle windshield wipers and bright silver 16-in. five-spoke cast aluminum wheels. Formulas with the WS6 Ram Air Performance and Handling package included a Ram Air induction system, functional air scoops, five-spoke 17-in. high-polish aluminum wheels, P275/40ZR17 speed-rated tires, a specific low-restriction dual outlet exhaust system and a specific tuned suspension. This year the WS6 cars had to have Artic White, Pewter Metallic, Navy Blue Metallic, Black or Bright Red finish and the optional UPC GU5 rear axle was required in cars with the four-speed automatic transmission. The price of the package was $3,150.

Model Number	Body/Style Number	Body Type & Seating	Factory Price	Shipping Weight	Production Total
FORMULA - SERIES F/V - (V-8)					
F/V	87	2d hatchback-4P	$23,600	3,455 lbs.	1,427
FORMULA – WS6 RAM AIR - SERIES F/V - (V-8)					
F/V	87	2d hatchback-4P	$26,750	3,455 lbs.	175

TRANS AM – SERIES F/V - V-8

The 1999 Pontiac sales catalog pictured a Navy Blue Metallic Trans Am convertible with the standard 300-plus-horsepower LS1 aluminum 5.7-liter V-8 and a black Trans Am coupe with the 320-hp WS6-equipped Ram Air LS1 V-8. It described the latter engine (also offered as a Formula option) as "the heart of the modern muscle car." Standard equipment for the Trans Am coupe included extensive acoustical insulation, dual front airbags, air conditioning, power door locks, a power antenna, a brake/transmission shift interlock safety feature (with automatic transmission), power four-wheel disc brakes with four-wheel ABS, the UPC LS1 5.7-liter SFI V-8 engine, cruise control, electric rear and side window defoggers, Solar-Ray tinted glass, instrumentation (including electric analog speedometer, tachometer, odometer, coolant temperature indicator, oil pressure gauge, voltmeter and LED trip odometer), power automatic sport mirrors with blue glass, a day/night inside rearview mirror with reading lamps, left- and right-hand covered visor-vanity mirrors, a Delco 500-watt peak power Monsoon AM/FM stereo (with CD, seven-band graphic equalizer, clock, touch control, seek up/down, search and replay, Delco TheftLock, high-performance 10-speaker sound system in coupe, HSS speakers and tweeters in doors, 6.5-in. subwoofers in sail panels, subwoofer amp and four speakers and tweeters in rear quarter panels), reclining front bucket seats, a six-way power front driver's seat, a rear two-passenger folding seat, a leather-wrapped tilt steering wheel with radio controls (including leather-wrapped shift knob and parking brake handle), power window controls with driver's express-down feature (requires power mirrors and door locks), the PASS-Key II theft-deterrent system, P245/50ZR16 speed-rated all-weather tires with a high-pressure compact spare, four-speed automatic transmission, controlled-cycle windshield wipers, bright silver 16-in. five-spoke cast aluminum wheels, an audible content theft-deterrent system and remote keyless entry. Trans Ams with the WS6 Ram Air Performance and Handling package included a Ram Air induction system, functional air scoops, five-spoke 17-in. high-polished aluminum wheels, P275/40ZR17 speed-rated tires, a specific low-restriction dual outlet exhaust system and a specific tuned suspension. This year the WS6 cars had to have Artic White, Pewter Metallic, Navy Blue Metallic, Black or Bright Red finish and the optional UPC GU5 rear axle was required in cars with the four-speed automatic transmission. The price of the package was $3,150.

Model Number	Body/Style Number	Body Type & Seating	Factory Price	Shipping Weight	Production Total
TRANS AM - SERIES F/V (V-8)					
F/V	87	2d hatchback-4P	$26,260	3,490 lbs.	10,343
F/V	67	2d convertible-4P	$30,330	3,580 lbs.	1,027
TRANS AM – WS6 RAM AIR - SERIES F/V (RAM AIR V-8)					
F/V	87	2d hatchback-4P	$29,410	3,490 lbs.	2,765
F/V	67	2d convertible-4P	$33,480	3,580 lbs.	467

30th ANNIVERSARY TRANS AM SERIES F/V - V-8

In March 1969 the first Trans Am made its debut at the Chicago Auto Show, so in February 1999, a special 30th Anniversary Trans Am was on display at the same event. The anniversary car was actually a joint effort of Pontiac Motor Division and the American Sunroof Corp. (ASC) and the cars were constructed in both firm's factories in St. Therese, Quebec, Canada. All 30th Anniversary models carried special features and included the WS6 Ram Air package. A limited run of 1,600 cars was made, of which 1,065 were coupes and 535 were convertibles. The United States market got 1,000 coupes and 500 ragtops and the balance were sold in Canada. A 30th Anniversary Trans Am also served as pace car for the Daytona 500 stock car race. The basis for the package was an Artic White WS6 Trans Am coupe or convertible carrying all standard Trans Am coupe or convertible equipment. The anniversary package included high-polished 17-in.

aluminum wheels with a medium blue color tint, dual two-tone blue racing stripes, white Prado leather seats with blue stitching, specially embroidered smooth headrests, white perforated vinyl door inserts with blue stitching, specific 30th Anniversary front floor mats, a specially embroidered cargo area mat, cloisonné blue 30th Anniversary emblems with a white Firebird logo, a white Firebird logo on the black rear taillight panel, unique blue WS6 emblems and a sequentially numbered instrument panel plaque below the radio. 30th Anniversary Trans Am convertibles also had a dark blue convertible top. The only options for the fully loaded cars were traction control, a Hurst shifter for the six-speed manual transmission and a 12-disc CD player.

Model Number	Body/Style Number	Body Type & Seating	Factory Price	Shipping Weight	Production Total
30th ANNIVERSARY TRANS AM – WS6 RAM AIR - SERIES F/V (RAM AIR V-8)					
F/V	87	2d hatchback-4P	$31,140	3,397 lbs.	1,065
F/V	67	2d convertible-4P	$35,210	3,514 lbs.	535

Note 4: The prices include custom lumbar support bucket seats ($155) the WS6 package ($3,150) and a $540 dealer destination charge.

ENGINES

Base V-6 [UPC L36]: Overhead valve. Displacement: 231 cid. (3.8-liter). Bore & stroke: 3.80 x 3.40 in. Compression ratio: 9.4:1. Brake horsepower: 200 at 5200 rpm. Torque: 225 ft. lbs. at 4000 rpm. Fuel system: SFI. VIN Code: K.

5.7-liter V-8 [UPC LS1]: Overhead valve. Aluminum block and head. Aluminum intake manifold. Displacement: 350 cid. (5.7-lter). Bore & stroke: 3.90 x 3.62 in. Brake horsepower: 305 at 5200 rpm. Torque: 335 ft. lbs. at 4000 rpm. Compression ratio: 10.5:1. Fuel system: SFI. VIN Code: G.

5.7-liter Ram Air V-8 [UPC LS1]: Overhead valve. Cast-iron block and head. Aluminum intake manifold. Displacement: 350 cid. Bore & stroke: 3.90 x 3.62 in. Brake horsepower: 320 at 5200 rpm. Torque: 345 ft. lbs. at 4400 rpm. Compression ratio: 10.5:1. Fuel system: SFI.

CHASSIS

Firebird: Wheelbase: 101.0 in. Overall length: 193.3 in. Width: 74.4 in. Height: (coupe) 51.2 in., (convertible) 51.8 in. Front tread: 60.7 in. Rear tread: 60.6 in. Front headroom: 37.2 in. Rear headroom: 35.2 in. Front legroom: 43.0 in. Rear legroom: 28.9 in. Front shoulder room: 57.4 in. Rear shoulder room: (coupe) 55.8 in.; (convertible) 43.5 in. Front hip room: 52.8 in. Rear hiproom: (coupe) 45.9 in.; (convertible) 43.7 in. Standard tires: steel-belted radial P215/60R16 black sidewall touring.

Formula: Wheelbase: 101.0 in. Overall length: 193.3 in. Width: 74.4 in. Height: 51.2 in. Front tread: 60.7 in. rear tread: 60.6 in. Front headroom: 37.2 in. Rear headroom: 35.2 in. Front legroom: 43.0 in. Rear legroom: 28.9 in. Front shoulder room: 57.4 in. Rear shoulder room: 55.8 in. 43.5 in. Front hip room: 52.8 in. Rear hip room: 45.9 in. Standard tires: P245/50ZR16 speed-rated, all-weather.

Trans Am: Wheelbase: 101.0 in. Overall length: 193.7 in. Width: 74.4 in. Height: (coupe) 51.8 in., (convertible) 51.8 in. Front tread: 60.7 in. rear tread:

60.6 in. Front headroom: 37.2 in. Rear headroom: 35.2 in. Front legroom: 43.0 in. Rear legroom: 28.9 in. Front shoulder room: 57.4 in. Rear shoulder room: (coupe) 55.8 in.; (convertible) 43.5 in. Front hip room: 52.8 in. Rear hiproom: (coupe) 45.9 in.; (convertible) 43.7 in. Standard tires: P245/50ZR16 speed-rated, all-weather.

TECHNICAL

Firebird: Overhead valve. Front engine/rear drive. Base transmission: Five-speed manual. Front suspension: Modified MacPherson strut with anti-roll bar. Rear suspension: Live axle with coil springs, control arms, torque arm, track bar and anti-roll bar. Steering: Power re-circulating ball. Brakes: Power four-wheel discs with ABS.

Formula Firebird: Chassis: Front engine/rear drive. Base transmission: Four-speed automatic. Front suspension: Modified MacPherson strut with anti-roll bar. Rear suspension: Live axle with coil springs, control arms, torque arm, track bar and anti-roll bar. Steering: Power re-circulating ball. Brakes: Power four-wheel discs with ABS.

Trans Am: Chassis: Front engine/rear drive. Base transmission: Four-speed automatic. Front suspension: Modified MacPherson strut with anti-roll bar. Rear suspension: Live axle with coil springs, control arms, torque arm, track bar and anti-roll bar. Steering: Power re-circulating ball. Brakes: Power four-wheel discs with ABS.

OPTIONS

1SA Firebird Coupe option package, includes vehicle with standard equipment (no cost). 1SB Plus Firebird Coupe option package, includes vehicle with standard equipment plus power door locks, power windows, power sport mirrors with blue tint, power antenna, automatic transmission and power seat ($1,510). 1SC Firebird option group ($2,450). 1SA Convertible option package, includes vehicle with standard equipment (no cost). GU5 3.23:1 performance axle ($300). FE9 Federal emissions (no cost). YF5 50 California emissions (no cost). NG1 New York/Massachusetts emissions (no cost). CC1 hatch roof ($995). Y87 3800 performance package ($490). 1LE Autocross Package for Formula, includes special handling suspension, larger stabilizer bars, stiffer springs, Koni shocks ($1,175). WS6 Ram Air performance and handling package ($3,150). R7Q 1LE standard equipment delete (credit of $1,125). U1S trunk-mounted, remote 12-disc CD changer ($595). W54 ETR AM/FM Monsoon stereo with auto-reverse, graphic equalizer, clock, seek up/down, remote CD pre-wiring and 10-speaker sound system ($330). W55 ETR AM/FM Monsoon stereo with CD player, graphic

equalizer, clock, seek up/down and 10-speaker sound system ($430). AQ9 articulating bucket seats with lumbar supports ($155). AG1 six-way power driver's seat ($270). W68 Sport Appearance package includes aero components, fog lamps, dual outlet exhausts for base models, requires QCB tires and automatic transmission ($1,040). QCB P235/55R16 black sidewall touring tires for Firebird, standard Formula and Trans

Only about 1,600 Formula Firebirds left the lot for model year 1999. This WS6 version is even rarer.

Am; not available Trans Am Convertible ($135). MW9 traction control system ($250-$450). MM5 five-speed manual transmission (no charge). MN6 six-speed manual transmission (no cost). MX0 four-speed automatic transmission, standard in Formula and Trans Am ($815). PO5 chrome aluminum 16-in. wheels ($595).

HISTORICAL FOOTNOTES

Total production in Canada included 36,219 Firebirds. The model-year sales total was 32,899 Firebirds, which represented 0.4 percent of total U.S. new car sales. Of 31,226 Firebirds built for the domestic market in the model year, 72.1 percent had the four-speed automatic transmission, 6.2 percent had a five-speed manual gearbox, 21.7 percent had the six-speed manual transmission, 41.9 percent had traction control, 33.6 percent had a limited-slip differential, 89 percent had power windows, 89 percent had power door locks, 78 percent had power seats, 49.9 percent had leather seats, 28 percent had memory seats, 23.9 percent had chrome styled wheels, 76.1 percent had aluminum wheels, 89.7 percent had a rear window defogger, 94.8 percent had dual power rearview mirrors, 78 percent had hatch roofs, 18.7 percent had a name brand CD changer, 81.3 percent had another CD player, 71.2 percent had the keyless remote entry system and 71.2 percent had an anti-theft device.

GM photo

The Trans Am was one of three F-Car models that accounted for a sales total of 31,826 for the 2000 model year. This one has the WS6 option.

New Millennium

The 2000 Firebird entered the new millennium with all the horsepower and performance it had been famous for. Both Formula and Trans Am models were available with new 17-in. wheels as part of a Ram Air package.

Also new was a Maple Red Metallic exterior color and ebony colored interior. On V-8s, the throttle linkage was revised to give cars with a manual transmission a more progressive "launch response." Child seat tethers were added to all models and all 2000 Firebirds complied with California low-emissions-vehicle (LEV) rules.

I.D. NUMBERS

The vehicle identification number (VIN) is located on the top left-hand surface of the instrument panel and is visible through the windshield. The VIN has 17 symbols. The first symbol indicates the country of manufacture (1 or 4=United States; 2=Canada). The second symbol indicates the manufacturer (G=General Motors). The third symbol indicates the make/division (2=Pontiac and 7=GM of Canada). The fourth and fifth symbols indicate the car line and series F/S=Firebird and convertible; F/V=Formula and convertible. The sixth symbol indicates body style: (2=two-door model 87; 3=two-door convertible model 67). The seventh symbol indicates the restraint system: 2=Active manual belts with driver and passenger inflatable restraints; 4=Active manual belts front and side; 6=Active manual belts with dual airbags and automatic passenger-side sensor; 7=Active manual belts with dual front-and-side airbags in front and rear. The eighth symbol indicates the engine type: G=UPC LS1 5.7-liter fuel-injected (MFI) V-8; K=UPC L36 3.8-liter fuel-injected (MFI) V-6. The ninth symbol is a check digit. The 10th symbol indicates model year (Y=2000). The 11th symbol indicates the GM

assembly plant (2=Ste. Therese, Canada). The last six symbols are the consecutive unit number at the factory.

COLORS

10=Artic White, 11=Pewter Metallic, 13=Silver Metallic, 20=Medium Blue Metallic; 28=Navy Blue Metallic, 31=Bright Green Metallic, 41=Black, 79=Blue-Green Chameleon and 81=Bright Red and Maple Red Metallic.

FIREBIRD - SERIES F/S - V-6/V-8

Two rear child seat tether anchors were added on all models. The throttle linkage on all V-8-powered Firebirds was revised. Standard Firebird coupe equipment included extensive acoustical insulation, dual front airbags, air conditioning, a black fixed-mast antenna, the brake/transmission shift interlock safety feature (with automatic transmission), power four-wheel disc brakes with four-wheel ABS, the UPC L36 3800 Series II 200-hp SFI V-6 engine, cruise control, electric rear and side window defoggers, Solar-Ray tinted glass, instrumentation (including electric analog speedometer, tachometer, odometer, coolant temperature indicator, oil pressure gauge, voltmeter and LED trip odometer), sport exterior mirrors (left-hand remote controlled), a day/night inside rearview mirror with reading lamps, left- and right-hand covered visor-vanity mirrors, a Delco AM/FM stereo ETR radio and cassette (with seven-band graphic equalizer, touch control, search-and-replay, Delco visor-vanity, clock, seek up/down, remote CD pre-wiring and four-speaker coaxial sound system), reclining front bucket seats, four-way driver and passenger front seat manual adjusters, a rear two-passenger folding seat, a four-spoke sport tilt steering wheel with adjustable column, the PASS-Key II theft-deterrent system, tilt steering column, P215/60R16 touring tires with a high-pressure compact spare, the UPC MM5 five-speed manual transmission, controlled-cycle windshield wipers and bright silver 16-in. five-spoke cast aluminum wheels.

Model Number	Body/Style Number	Body Type & Seating	Factory Price	Shipping Weight	Production Total
F/S	87	2d hatchback-4P	$19,140	3,323 lbs.	Note 1
F/S	67	2d convertible-4P	$25,760	3,402 lbs.	Note 1

NOTE 1: Production of 2000 Firebirds was 31,826 units in the U.S. and Canada.

FORMULA FIREBIRD SERIES F/V - V-8

Once again in 2,000 the Formula series offered only the two-door hatchback coupe. Although the basic body design had not changed since last year, the engine had new cast-iron exhaust manifolds, a better starter design, and an improved canister for the onboard refueling vapor recovery system. Formula Firebirds equipped with the WS6 Ram Air option package sported new 17-in. alloy wheel rims. Standard Formula Firebird coupe equipment included extensive acoustical insulation, dual front airbags, air conditioning, a black power antenna at right rear, the brake/transmission shift interlock safety feature (with automatic transmission), power four-wheel disc brakes with four-wheel ABS, the UPC LS1 5.7-liter 305-hp aluminum V-8 engine, cruise control, electric rear and side window defoggers, Solar-Ray tinted glass, instrumentation (including electric analog speedometer, tachometer, odometer, coolant temperature indicator, oil pressure gauge, voltmeter and LED trip odometer), power door locks, power automatic sport mirrors with blue glass, a day/night inside rearview mirror with reading lamps, left- and right-hand covered visor-vanity mirrors, a Delco 500-watt peak power Monsoon AM/FM stereo (with CD, seven-band graphic equalizer, clock, touch control, seek up/down, search and replay, Delco TheftLock, high-performance 10-speaker sound system in coupes, HSS speakers and tweeters in doors, 6.5-in. subwoofers in sail panels, subwoofer amp, four speakers and tweeters in rear quarter panels), reclining front bucket seats, four-way driver and passenger front seat manual adjusters, a rear two-passenger folding seat, a leather-wrapped tilt and adjustable steering wheel with radio controls (including leather-wrapped shift knob and parking brake handle), the PASS-Key II theft-deterrent system, a tilt steering column, P245/50ZR16 speed-rated all-weather tires with a high-pressure compact spare, a four-speed automatic transmission, controlled-cycle windshield wipers, power window controls with driver's express-down feature (requires power mirrors and door locks) and bright silver 16-in. five-spoke cast aluminum wheels.

Model Number	Body/Style Number	Body Type & Seating	Factory Price	Shipping Weight	Production Total
FORMULA FIREBIRD - SERIES F/V - (V-8)					
F/V	87	2d hatchback-4P	$24,320	3,341 lbs.	Note 2
FORMULA FIREBIRD – WS6 RAM AIR - SERIES F/V - (RAM AIR V-8)					
F/V	87	2d hatchback-4P	$27,470	3,341 lbs.	Note 2

NOTE 2: Production of 2000 Firebirds was 31,826 units in the U.S. and Canada.

TRANS AM – SERIES F/V - V-8

Standard Trans Am equipment included extensive

The Trans Am hatchback listed for about $27,400 in 2000. The price grew with the option list, which included a Ram Air V-8.

acoustical insulation, dual front airbags, air conditioning, a black power antenna at right rear, the brake/transmission shift interlock safety feature (with automatic transmission), power four-wheel disc brakes with four-wheel ABS, the UPC LS1 5.7-liter 305-hp aluminum V-8 engine, cruise control, electric rear and side window defoggers, Solar-Ray tinted glass, instrumentation (including electric analog speedometer, tachometer, odometer, coolant temperature indicator, oil pressure gauge, voltmeter and LED trip odometer), power door locks, power automatic sport mirrors with blue glass, a day/night inside rearview mirror with reading lamps, left- and right-hand covered visor-vanity mirrors, a Delco 500-watt peak power Monsoon AM/FM stereo (with CD, seven-band graphic equalizer, clock, touch control, seek up/down, search and replay, Delco TheftLock, high-performance 10-speaker sound system in coupes, HSS speakers and tweeters in doors, 6.5-in. subwoofers in sail panels, subwoofer amp, and four speakers and tweeters in rear quarter panels), reclining front bucket seats, a six-way power front driver's seat, a four-way passenger front seat manual adjuster, a rear two-passenger folding seat, a leather-wrapped tilt and adjustable steering wheel with radio controls (including leather-wrapped shift knob and parking brake handle), the PASS-Key II theft-deterrent system, a tilt steering column, P245/50ZR16 speed-rated all-weather tires with a high-pressure compact spare, a four-speed automatic transmission, controlled-cycle windshield wipers, power window controls with driver's express-down feature (requires power mirrors and door locks), bright silver 16-in. five-spoke cast aluminum wheels, an audible content theft-deterrent system and remote keyless entry.

Model Number	Body/Style Number	Body Type & Seating	Factory Price	Shipping Weight	Production Total
TRANS AM - SERIES F/V - (V-8)					
F/V	87	2d hatchback-4P	$27,430	3,397 lbs.	Note 3
F/V	67	2d convertible-4P	$31,500	3,514 lbs.	Note 3
TRANS AM – WS6 RAM AIR - SERIES F/V - (RAM AIR V-8)					
F/V	87	2d hatchback-4P	$30,580	3,397 lbs.	Note 3
F/V	67	2d convertible-4P	$34,650	3,514 lbs.	Note 3

NOTE 3: Production of 2000 Firebirds was 31,826 units in the U.S. and Canada.

ENGINES

Base V-6 [UPC L36]: Overhead valve. Displacement: 231 cid (3.8-liter). Bore & stroke: 3.80 x 3.40 in. Compression ratio: 9.4:1. Brake horsepower: 200

at 5200 rpm. Torque: 225 ft. lbs. at 4000 rpm. Fuel system: SFI. VIN Code: K.

5.7-liter V-8 [UPC LT1]: Overhead valve. Aluminum block and head. Aluminum intake manifold. Displacement: 350 cid (5.7-liter). Bore & stroke: 3.90 x 3.62 in. Brake horsepower: 305 at 5200 rpm. Torque: 335 ft. lbs. at 4000 rpm. Compression ratio: 10.5:1. Fuel system: SFI. VIN Code: G.

5.7-liter V-8 Ram Air [UPC LT1]: Eight-cylinder. Cast-iron block and head. Aluminum intake manifold. Displacement: 350 cid (5.7-liter). Bore & stroke: 3.90 x 3.62 in. Brake horsepower: 320 at 5200 rpm. Torque: 345 ft. lbs. at 4400 rpm. Compression ratio: 10.5:1. Fuel system: SFI.

CHASSIS

Firebird: Wheelbase: 101.0 in. Overall length: 193.3 in. Width: 74.4 in. Height: (coupe) 51.2 in., (convertible) 51.8 in. Front tread: 60.7 in. Rear tread: 60.6 in. Front headroom: 37.2 in. Rear headroom: 35.2 in. Front legroom: 43.0 in. Rear legroom: 28.9 in. Front shoulder room: 57.4 in. Rear shoulder room: (coupe) 55.8 in.; (convertible) 43.5 in. Front hip room: 52.8 in. Rear hip room: (coupe) 45.9 in.; (convertible) 43.7 in. Standard tires: steel-belted radial P215/60R16 black sidewall touring.

Formula: Wheelbase: 101.0 in. Overall length: 193.3 in. Width: 74.4 in. Height: 51.2 in. Front tread: 60.7 in. rear tread: 60.6 in. Front headroom: 37.2 in. Rear headroom: 35.2 in. Front legroom: 43.0 in. Rear legroom: 28.9 in. Front shoulder room: 57.4 in. Rear shoulder room: 55.8 in. 43.5 in. Front hip room: 52.8 in. Rear hip room: 45.9 in. Standard tires: P245/50ZR16 speed-rated, all-weather.

Trans Am: Wheelbase: 101.0 in. Overall length: 193.7 in. Width: 74.4 in. Height: (coupe) 51.8 in., (convertible) 51.8 in. Front tread: 60.7 in. rear tread: 60.6 in. Front headroom: 37.2 in. Rear headroom: 35.2 in. Front legroom: 43.0 in. Rear legroom: 28.9 in. Front shoulder room: 57.4 in. Rear shoulder room: (coupe) 55.8 in.; (convertible) 43.5 in. Front hip room: 52.8 in. Rear hip room: (coupe) 45.9 in.; (convertible) 43.7 in. Standard tires: P245/50ZR16 speed-rated, all-weather.

TECHNICAL

Firebird: Chassis: Front engine/rear drive. Base transmission: Five-speed manual. Front suspension: Modified MacPherson strut with anti-roll bar. Rear suspension: Live axle with coil springs, control arms, torque arm, track bar and anti-roll bar. Steering: Power re-circulating ball. Brakes: Power four-wheel discs with ABS.

Formula Firebird: Chassis: Front engine/rear drive. Base transmission: Four-speed automatic. Front suspension: Modified MacPherson strut with anti-roll bar. Rear suspension: Live axle with coil springs, control arms, torque arm, track bar and anti-roll bar. Steering: Power re-circulating ball. Brakes:

Power four-wheel discs with ABS.

Trans Am: Chassis: Front engine/rear drive. Base transmission: Four-speed automatic. Front suspension: Modified MacPherson strut with anti-roll bar. Rear suspension: Live axle with coil springs, control arms, torque arm, track bar and anti-roll bar. Steering: Power re-circulating ball. Brakes: Power four-wheel discs with ABS.

OPTIONS

1SA Firebird coupe option package, includes vehicle with standard equipment (no cost). 1SB Plus Firebird coupe option package, includes vehicle with standard equipment plus power door locks, power windows, power sport mirrors with blue tint, power antenna, automatic transmission and power seat ($1,510). 1SC Firebird option group ($2,450). 1SA convertible option package, includes vehicle with standard equipment (no cost). GU5 3.23:1 performance axle ($300). FE9 Federal emissions (no cost). YF5 50 California emissions (no cost). NG1 New York/Massachusetts emissions (no cost). CC1 hatch roof ($995). Y87 3800 performance package ($490). 1LE Autocross Package for Formula, includes special handling suspension, larger stabilizer bars, stiffer springs, Koni shocks ($1,175). WS6 Ram Air performance and handling package ($3,150). R7Q 1LE standard equipment delete (credit of $1,125). U1S trunk mounted remote 12-disc CD changer ($595). W54 ETR AM/FM Monsoon stereo with auto-reverse, graphic equalizer, clock, seek up/down, remote CD pre-wiring and 10-speaker sound system ($330). W55 ETR AM/FM Monsoon stereo with CD player, graphic equalizer, clock, seek up/down and 10-speaker sound system ($430). AQ9 articulating bucket seats with lumbar supports ($155). AG1 six-way power driver's seat ($270). W68 Sport Appearance package includes aero components, fog lamps, dual outlet exhausts for base models, requires QCB tires and automatic transmission ($1,040). QCB P235/55R16 black sidewall touring tires for Firebird, standard Formula and Trans Am; not available Trans Am convertible ($135). MW9 traction control system ($250-$450). MM5 five-speed manual transmission (no charge). MN6 six-speed manual transmission (no cost). MX0 four-speed automatic transmission, standard in Formula and Trans Am ($815). PO5 chrome aluminum 16-in. wheels ($595).

HISTORICAL FOOTNOTES

Total production in Canada was 31,826 Firebirds. Revel model company made a scale model of Al Hofmann's 2000 Firebird funny car. An option returning to the Firebird offerings in 2000 was the Firehawk package. It was now merchandised as a regular production option, although SLP Engineering produced the final vehicle. The 2000 Formula Firehawk included a unique hood, a 327-hp engine, an upgraded suspension and special wheels and tires.

The Trans Am convertible, like the coupe, came standard with the LSI V-8.

Modern Muscle Car

"Firebird: The muscle car lives," said Pontiac in 2001. The new F-Car took performance to new levels. The model lineup started with the Firebird coupe and convertible. Standard features included a hidden headlamp design, integrated fog lamps, fender-mounted air extractors and a sleek, aerodynamic body.

Pontiac celebrated its 75th anniversary in 2001. It released a hardcover book called *75 Years of Pontiac: The Official History* and transported a collection of historic vehicles and concept cars to events such as the Detroit Auto Show, Chicago Auto Show, New York Auto Show, Iola Old Car Show, Pontiac Oakland Club International Convention and Woodward Dream Cruise. At the latter event, held in the Detroit area in August, a "once-in-75-years" collection of 35 rare and unique Pontiacs was seen.

On Sept. 25, 2001, General Motors Corp. announced plans to drop the Pontiac Firebird and Chevrolet Camaro after 2002 and close the Canadian plant where they were made. GM termed the halt in production a "hiatus," rather than a final termination and said that the decision to drop the two cars was due to a drop in demand in the sporty car segment, which experienced a 53 percent decline in sales in the past decade.

I.D. NUMBERS

The vehicle identification number (VIN) is located on the top left-hand surface of the instrument panel and is visible through the windshield. The VIN has 17 symbols. The first symbol indicates the country of manufacture (1 or 4=United States; 2=Canada). The second symbol indicates the manufacturer (G=General Motors). The third symbol indicates the make/division (2=Pontiac and 7=GM of Canada). The fourth and fifth symbols indicate the car line and series F/S=Firebird and convertible, F/V=Formula and convertible. The sixth symbol indicates body style (2=two-door model 87; 3=two-door convertible model 67). The seventh symbol indicates the restraint system: 1=Active manual belts; 2=Active manual belts with driver and passenger inflatable restraints; 4=Active manual belts front and side; 5=Active manual belts with driver and passenger front and side airbags; 6=Active manual belts with driver and passenger front and side airbags and passenger sensor; 7=Active manual belts with driver and passenger front and side airbags and rear passenger compartment side airbags. The eighth symbol indicates the engine type: G=UPC LS1 5.7-liter fuel-injected (MFI) V-8; K=UPC L36 3.8-liter fuel-injected (MFI) V-6. (Note: All Pontiac engines made in U.S.). The ninth symbol is a check digit. The 10th symbol indicates model year (1=2001). The 11th symbol indicates the GM assembly plant (2=Ste. Therese, Canada). The last six symbols are the consecutive unit number at the factory.

COLORS

10=Artic White, 11=Pewter Metallic, 28=Navy Blue Metallic, 31=Bright Green Metallic, 41=Black, 44=Maple Red Metallic, 71=Sunset Orange 79=Blue-Green Chameleon, 81=Bright Red.

FIREBIRD – SERIES F/S - V-6/V-8

The F-Car remained true to its heritage while taking performance to new levels, although enthusiasts of the nameplate would be shocked by the announcement, in the fall of 2001, that General Motors would be stopping all Firebird (and Camaro) production after model year 2002. For more than three decades, the rear-wheel-drive Firebird had defined high-powered driving excitement. The 2001 lineup started with Firebird coupe and convertible. Firebird hood and rear quarter panels were made of two-sided galvanized steel, while the doors, hatch, roof, fenders and fascias were formed from composite materials that were lightweight and impervious to rust or corrosion. Base Firebird features included a hidden headlamp design, integrated fog lamps, fender-mounted air extractors and a sleek, aerodynamically shaped body. Standard equipment included air conditioning, cruise control, a fold-down rear seat and a center console with an auxiliary power outlet and dual cup holders. Standard for the base Firebird coupe and convertible was a 3800 V-6 that delivered 200 hp. It came hooked to a five-speed manual or available four-speed automatic transmission. A slick-shifting six-speed manual transmission was also available at no extra charge. An optional Hurst shifter was available on models equipped with the six-speed transmission. The Firebird's high-performance attitude was not limited to its engine compartment – it was also found in the wide selection of audio systems available. Base equipment for the Firebird coupe was a Delco 2001 Series electronically tuned radio with AM/FM stereo, a CD player, a seven-band graphic equalizer, four speakers, a clock and touch controls for seek, search and replay. All convertibles featured a standard Monsoon radio and eight speakers. Additional standard equipment on the Firebird coupe included safety-cage construction with side-door beams, manual lap/shoulder safety belts, driver and passenger frontal impact airbags and two rear compartment child safety seat top tether anchors, four-wheel disc brakes with EBD and ABS, a brake/transmission shift interlock system, automatic daytime running lamps, fog lamps and tires with built-in wear indicators and available traction control, a PASS-Key II theft-deterrent system, rear-wheel drive, 16 x 8-in. alloy rims, P215/60R16 tires, a Space Saver spare tire on a steel spare wheel, front independent suspension, a front stabilizer bar, a rear stabilizer bar, variable intermittent windshield wipers, a rear window defogger, four-person total seating capacity, bucket front seats with cloth upholstery, rear bucket seats, power door locks, power steering, a tilt-adjustable steering wheel with cruise control buttons on steering wheel, a remote-control left-hand outside rearview mirror, a manual control right-hand outside rearview mirror, a remote trunk release, front door pockets, front reading lights, front and rear floor mats and a tachometer. The Firebird convertible added (in addition to or in place of base equipment) a power convertible roof with a glass rear window, standard up-level Monsoon sound system with CD player and eight speakers, a six-way power driver's seat, a leather-wrapped steering wheel with redundant radio controls, leather trim on the shifter knob, remote keyless entry, an alarm system, power door locks, power windows, power outside rearview mirrors, a power radio antenna and a trunk light. The 3800 V-6 Performance package for the base Firebird models combined wider P235/55R16 touring tires with a Zexel Torsen II limited-slip differential, uplevel steering, dual exhaust outlets and a 3.42:1 axle ratio (available only with the automatic transmission). A Sports Appearance package offered for the base Firebird hatchback and base Firebird convertible included dual exhaust outlets, a distinctive chin spoiler, rocker panel extensions and a deeper rear valance. Base Firebirds with the optional V-8 engine had 5 more horsepower and 5 more ft. lbs. of torque than the 2000 base V-8. New exterior and interior colors were also available.

Model Number	Body/Style Number	Body Type & Seating	Factory Price	Shipping Weight	Production Total
F/S	S87V	2d hatchback-4P	$18,855	3,323 lbs.	Note 1
F/S	S67V	2d convertible-4P	$25,475	3,402 lbs.	Note 1

Note 1: Calendar-year production through Sept. 29, 2001 was 14,204 (all built in Canada).
Note 2: A $575 dealer destination charge applied.

FORMULA FIREBIRD SERIES F/V - V-8

The 2001 lineup included the Formula Firebird coupe. It had all of the Trans Ams performance features combined with much of the cleaner look of the base Firebird coupe. It no longer came with the WS6 Ram Air Formula option. Those who wanted a WS6 Firebird had to move up to the Trans Am series. Standard Formula Firebird equipment included the 5.7-liter 16-valve 310-hp LS1 V-8, four-speed automatic transmission, hood and rear quarter panels made of two-sided galvanized steel, additional composite body panels (doors, hatch, roof, fenders and fascias), a hidden halogen headlamp design, integrated fog lamps, fender-mounted air extractors, air conditioning, cruise control, a fold-down rear seat and a center console with an auxiliary power outlet and dual cupholders, safety-cage construction with side-door beams, manual lap/shoulder safety belts, driver and passenger frontal impact airbags and two rear compartment child safety seat top tether anchors, four-wheel disc brakes with EBD and ABS, a brake/transmission shift interlock system, automatic daytime running lamps, fog lamp, a PASS-Key II theft-deterrent system, rear-wheel drive, 16 x 8-in. alloy rims, P245/50ZR16 tires, a Space Saver spare tire on a steel spare wheel, front independent suspension, a front stabilizer bar, a rear stabilizer bar, variable intermittent windshield wipers, a rear window defogger, four-person total seating capacity, bucket front seats with cloth upholstery, rear bucket seats, power steering, a tilt-adjustable steering wheel with cruise control buttons on steering wheel, a remote-control left-hand outside rearview mirror, a manual control right-hand outside rearview mirror, a remote trunk release, front door pockets, front reading lights, front and rear floor mats, a tachometer and a clock, one-touch power windows, a standard up-level Monsoon sound system with CD player and eight speakers, a six-way power driver's seat, a leather-wrapped steering wheel with redundant radio controls, leather trim on the shifter knob and power outside rearview mirrors.

Model Number	Body/Style Number	Body Type & Seating	Factory Price	Shipping Weight	Production Total
FORMULA FIREBIRD - SERIES F/V - (V-8)					
F/V	87	2d hatchback-4P	$24,035	3,341 lbs.	Notes 3,4

Note 3: Calendar-year production through Sept. 29, 2001 was 14,204 (all built in Canada).
Note 4: A $575 dealer destination charge applied.

TRANS AM – SERIES F/V - V-8

The ultimate expression of Firebird muscle, the Trans Am, was offered in both coupe and convertible editions. Trans Am features included removable coupe roof panels, leather seat surfaces and an uplevel rear spoiler in the hatchback coupe. Bright Silver Metallic paint was re-placed with Sunset Orange Metallic. A new Camel Accent interior color was also added. To make the ride even better for those on the inside, the shock absorbers were improved on all models. A 5.7-liter Gen III LS1 V-8 was standard. It had the new camshaft and new intake manifold. The external EGR valve was also eliminated for a gain of 5 hp (to 310 hp). Standard

equipment on the Trans Am coupe and convertible also included the 5.7-liter 16-valve 310-hp V-8, four-speed automatic transmission, hood and rear quarter panels made of two-sided galvanized steel, additional composite body panels (doors, hatch, roof, fenders and fascias), a hidden halogen headlamp design, integrated fog lamps, fender-mounted air extractors, air conditioning, cruise control, a fold-down rear seat and a center console with an auxiliary power outlet and dual cupholders, safety-cage construction with side-door beams, manual lap/shoulder safety belts, driver and passenger frontal impact airbags and two rear compartment child safety seat top tether anchors, four-wheel disc brakes with EBD and ABS, a brake/transmission shift interlock system, automatic daytime running lamps, fog lamps, a PASS-Key II theft-deterrent system, rear-wheel drive, 16 x 8-in. alloy rims, P245/50ZR16 tires, a Space Saver spare tire on a steel spare wheel, front independent suspension, a front stabilizer bar, a rear stabilizer bar, variable intermittent windshield wipers, a rear window defogger, four-person total seating capacity, bucket front seats with leather upholstery, rear bucket seats, power steering, a tilt-adjustable steering wheel with cruise control buttons on steering wheel, a remote-control left-hand outside rearview mirror, a manual control right-hand outside rearview mirror, a remote trunk release, front door pockets, front reading lights, front and rear floor mats, a tachometer and a clock, one-touch power windows, a standard uplevel Monsoon sound system with CD player and eight speakers, a six-way power driver's seat, a leather-wrapped steering wheel with redundant radio controls, leather trim on the shifter knob, power outside rearview mirrors, remote power door locks and a six-way power driver's seat. Trans Am drivers who opted for the WS6 Ram Air Performance and Handling package enjoyed 15 additional horsepower and benefited from functional air scoops, Ram Air induction, a dual-outlet exhaust system, a power-steering cooler and a suspension tuned for maximum handling performance. The package included P275/40ZR17 performance radial tires on 9 x 17-in. highly polished alloy wheels featuring a

A Trans Am coupe with Ram Air sold for $30,535 in 2001.

five-spoke spoke design.

Model Number	Body/Style Number	Body Type & Seating	Factory Price	Shipping Weight	Production Total
TRANS AM – SERIES F/V – (V-8)					
F/V	87	2d hatchback-4P	$27,145	3,397 lbs.	Note 5
F/V	67	2d convertible-4P	$31,215	3,514 lbs.	Note 5
TRANS AM – WS6 RAM AIR – SERIES F/V – (V-8)					
F/V	87	2d hatchback-4P	$30,535	3,397 lbs.	Note 5
F/V	67	2d convertible-4P	$34,605	3,514 lbs.	Note 5

Note 5: Calendar-year production through Sept. 29, 2001 was 14,204 (all built in Canada).
Note 6: A $655 dealer destination charge applied.

ENGINES

Base V-6 [UPC L36]: Overhead valve. Cast-iron block. Cast-iron cylinder head. Displacement: 231 cid. (3.8L). Bore & stroke: 3.80 x 3.40 in. Compression ratio: 9.4:1. Brake horsepower: 200 at 5200 rpm. Torque: 225 ft. lbs. at 4000 rpm. Fuel system: SFI. VIN Code: K.

5.7-liter V-8 [UPC LS1]: Aluminum block and cylinder head. Aluminum intake manifold. Displacement: 350 cid. Bore & stroke: 3.90 x 3.62 in. Brake horsepower: 310 at 5200 rpm. Torque: 340 ft. lbs. at 4000 rpm. Compression ratio: 10.5:1. Fuel system: SFI. VIN Code: G.

5.7-liter Ram Air V-8 [UPC LS1]: Overhead valve. Aluminum block and cylinder head. Aluminum intake manifold. Ram Air induction. Displacement: 350 cid. Bore & stroke: 3.90 x 3.62 in. Brake horsepower: 325 at 5200 rpm. Torque: 350 ft. lbs. at 4000 rpm. Compression ratio: 10.5:1. Fuel system: SFI. VIN Code: G.

CHASSIS

Firebird: Wheelbase: 101.0 in. Overall length: 193.3 in. Width: 74.4 in. Height: coupe 51.2 in., convertible 51.8 in. Front tread: 60.7 in. Rear tread: 60.6 in. Front headroom: 37.2 in. Rear headroom: 35.2 in. Front legroom: 43.0 in. Rear legroom: 28.9 in. Front shoulder room: 57.4 in. Rear shoulder room: coupe 55.8 in.; convertible 43.5 in. Front hip room: 52.8 in. Rear hip room: coupe 45.9 in.; convertible 43.7 in. Standard tires: steel-belted radial P215/60R16 black sidewall touring.

Formula: Wheelbase: 101.0 in. Overall length: 193.3 in. Width: 74.4 in. Height: 51.2 in. Front tread: 60.7 in. rear tread: 60.6 in. Front headroom: 37.2 in. Rear headroom: 35.2 in. Front legroom: 43.0 in. Rear legroom: 28.9 in. Front shoulder room: 57.4 in. Rear shoulder room: 55.8 in. 43.5 in. Front hip room: 52.8 in. Rear hip room: 45.9 in. Standard tires: P245/50ZR16 speed-rated, all-weather.

Trans Am: Wheelbase: 101.0 in. Overall length: 193.7 in. Width: 74.4 in. Height: (coupe) 51.8 in., (convertible) 51.8 in. Front tread: 60.7 in. rear tread: 60.6 in. Front headroom: 37.2 in. Rear headroom: 35.2 in. Front legroom: 43.0 in. Rear legroom: 28.9 in. Front shoulder room: 57.4 in. Rear shoulder room: (coupe) 55.8 in.; (convertible) 43.5 in. Front hip room: 52.8 in. Rear hip room: (coupe) 45.9 in.; (convertible) 43.7 in. Standard tires: P245/50ZR16 speed-rated, all-weather.

TECHNICAL

Firebird: Chassis: Front engine/rear drive. Base transmission: Five-speed manual. Front suspension: SLA/coil over monotube gas-charged shocks, tubular stabilizer bars with links and 28-mm stabilizer bar. Rear suspension: Salisbury axle with torque arm, trailing arm, track bar, coil springs and 15mm stabilizer bar. Steering: Power rack and pinion, 16.9:1 ratio, 2.67 turns lock to lock, 37.9-ft. turn circle. Front brakes: 11.9-in. vented disc/302.3 mm. Rear brakes: 12-in. vented disc, power-assisted, 304.8 mm. Standard tires: P215/60R16 steel-belted radial black sidewall touring. Fuel tank: 16.8 gal.

Formula: Chassis: Front engine/rear drive. Base transmission: Four-speed automatic. Front suspension: SLA/coil over monotube gas-charged shocks, tubular stabilizer bar with links and 30-mm stabilizer bar. Rear suspension: Salisbury axle with torque arm, trailing arm, track bar, coil springs and 19mm stabilizer bar. Steering: Power rack and pinion, 14.4:1 ratio, 2.28 turns lock to lock, 37.75-ft. turn circle. Front brakes: 11.9-in. vented disc/302.3 mm. Rear brakes: 12-in. vented disc, power-assisted, 304.8 mm. Standard tires: P245/50ZR16 speed-rated, all-weather. Fuel tank: 16.8 gal.

Trans Am: Chassis: Front engine/rear drive. Base transmission: Four-speed automatic. Front suspension: SLA/coil over monotube gas-charged shocks, tubular stabilizer bar with links and 30-mm stabilizer bar. Rear suspension: Salisbury axle with torque arm, trailing arm, track bar, coil springs and 19mm stabilizer bar. Steering: Power rack and pinion, 14.4:1 ratio, 2.28 turns lock to lock, 37.75-ft. turn circle. Front brakes: 11.9-in. vented disc/302.3 mm. Rear brakes: 12-in. vented disc, power-assisted, 304.8 mm. Standard tires: P245/50ZR16 speed-rated, all-weather. Fuel tank: 16.8 gal.

OPTIONS

1SA Firebird coupe option package includes vehicle with standard equipment (no cost). 1SB Plus Firebird coupe option package, includes vehicle with standard equipment plus power door locks, power windows, power sport mirrors with blue tint, power antenna, automatic transmission and power seat ($1,505-$1,510). 1SC Firebird option group ($2,450). 1SH NHRA Special four-speed automatic edition For-

The 2001 Firebird interior was again lacking few creature comforts.

mula package, includes P245/50ZR16 high-performance tires, 3.23:1 rear axle, power steering cooler, four-speed automatic transmission and chrome wheels. ($1,170). 1SH NHRA Special six-speed manual edition Formula package, includes P245/50ZR16 high-performance tires, 3.23:1 rear axle, power steering cooler, Hurst shifter, six-speed manual transmission and chrome wheels. ($1,170). 1SX base Firebird 75th anniversary package, includes remote keyless entry, theft-deterrent system, six-way power driver's seat, 16 x 8-in. chrome five-spoke cast-aluminum wheels, 3.8-liter V-6, power antenna, power windows, power door locks and power mirrors ($4,530). 1SX Firebird Formula 75th anniversary (automatic) package includes remote keyless entry, theft-deterrent system, six-way power driver's seat, 16 x 8-in. chrome five-spoke cast-aluminum wheels, P245/50ZR16 performance tires, performance rear axle and four-speed automatic transmission. ($2,850). 1SX Firebird Formula 75th anniversary (manual) package, includes hatch roof, remote keyless entry, theft-deterrent system, six-way power driver's seat, traction control, 16 x 8-in. chrome five-spoke cast aluminum wheels, six-speed manual transmission and Hurst shifter ($2,875). AG1 six-way power driver's seat ($270). AQ9 Custom Prado leather bucket seats with adjustable lumbar support ($185). AR9 Front bucket seats with Prado leather seating surfaces in convertible ($575). AR9 Front bucket seats with Prado leather seating surfaces in Formula, requires 1SB ($575). AR9 Front bucket seats with Prado leather seating surfaces in Hatchback, requires 1SC ($575).

BBS Hurst Performance shift linkage in Formula or Trans Am ($325). CC1 removable hatch roof ($995). GU5 rear performance axle in Trans Am ($300). GU5 rear performance axle in Formula ($300). MM5 five-speed manual transmission in hatchback with 1SA, 1SB or 1SX required ($815 credit). MN6 six-speed manual transmission in Trans Am or Formula, includes "skip shift" feature (no charge). MX0 four-speed automatic transmission with overdrive in Firebird ($815). NW9 traction control in Formula or Trans Am ($450); in hatchback or convertible ($850). PQ5 16 x 8-in. chrome five-spoke cast-aluminum wheels on Formula ($595). QCB P235/55R16 touring tires on hatchback or convertible ($135). R6M New Jersey cost surcharge, required in New Jersey (no charge to customer). R7X protection group on Formula ($240). R9P power package for hatchback (no charge). UTS 12-disc CD player, trunk mounted ($595). V12 power steering cooler ($100). W53 Delco 2001 series ETR AM/FM stereo with CD player in hatchback with 1SA or 1SB (no charge). W54 Monsoon series ETR AM/FM stereo with auto-reverse cassette ($330-$430). W55 Monsoon series ETR AM/FM stereo with CD player ($430). W68 Sport Appearance package for convertible or hatchback ($1,040). WS6 Performance & Handling package for Trans Am ($3,390). X10 Monsoon series ETR AM/FM stereo with auto-reverse cassette in convertible ($100 credit). Y3C GT package for hatchback (no charge). Y87 3800 V-6 performance package for convertible ($490). YF5 California emissions requirements (no charge).

The 2001 Ram Air Trans Am.

Pontiac used the Trans Am Collector Edition as a send-off for the F-Cars. Production of the Firebird line was scheduled to halt after the 2002 model year.

Alive and Well

Changes in the 2002 Firebirds were very modest. A power antenna was made standard on all models, along with power remote mirrors, power automatic door locks and power windows with "express-down" driver's side window controls. A power steering cooler also became standard equipment on all cars with V-8 engines. A 3.8-liter V-6 and five-speed manual transmission were standard on the Firebird coupe. The Firebird convertible combined the same engine with a 4L60-E four-speed automatic transmission. The base Firebirds featured hidden headlamps, integrated fog lamps, fender-mounted air extractors and a sleek, aerodynamic body.

Pontiac introduced the yellow 2002 Firebird Trans Am "Collector Edition" model option in the fall of 2001. Available for both the coupe and the convertible, it featured a "screaming chicken" decal that put a contemporary spin on the eye-catching hood designs of the past, plus black painted WS6 wheels, black anodized front and rear brake calipers, black painted axles, Goodyear Eagle F1 performance tires and exclusive interior trim appointments. A specially issued Collector Edition owner's portfolio provided a crowning touch.

I.D. NUMBERS

The vehicle identification number (VIN) is located on the top left-hand surface of the instrument panel and is visible through the windshield. The VIN has 17 symbols. The first three symbols are the world make identifier code: 2G2=Canadian-built Pontiac. The fourth and fifth symbols (passenger cars) indicate the car line and series: (F/S=Firebird and Convertible; F/V=Formula and Convertible). The sixth symbol indicates body style (2=two-door model 87; 3=two-door Convertible model 67). The seventh symbol indicates the restraint system: 1=Active manual belts; 2=Active manual belts with driver and passenger inflatable restraints; 3=2=Active manual belts with driver inflatable restraints; 4=Active manual belts front and side; 5=Active manual belts with driver and passenger front and side airbags; 6=Active manual belts with driver and passenger front and side airbags and passenger sensor; 7=Active manual belts with driver and passenger front and side airbags and rear passenger compartment side airbags. The eighth symbol indicates the engine type: K=UPC L36 3.8-liter V-6 with MFI; G=LS1 5.7-liter aluminum V-8 with MFI. The ninth symbol is a check digit. The 10th symbol indicates model year (2=2002). The 11th symbol indicates the GM assembly plant (2=Ste. Therese, Canada). The last six symbols are the consecutive unit number at the factory.

COLORS

10=Artic White, 11=Pewter Metallic, 13=Bright Silver Metallic, 28=Navy Blue Metallic, 41=Black, 44=Maple Red Metallic, 71=Sunset Orange Metallic and 81=Bright Red. 54= The Collector Edition Trans Am featured exclusive Collector Yellow finish.

FIREBIRD – SERIES F/S - V-6/V-8

Changes in the 2002 Firebirds were very modest. A power antenna was made standard on all models, along with power remote mirrors, power automatic door locks and power windows with express-down driver's side window controls. A power steering cooler also became standard equipment on all cars with V-8 engines. A 3.8-liter V-6 and five-speed manual transmission were standard on the Firebird coupe. The Firebird convertible combined the same engine with a 4L60-E four-speed automatic transmission. The base Firebirds featured hidden headlamps, integrated fog lamps, fender-mounted air extractors and a sleek, aerodynamic body. Standard equipment included the

3.8-liter 200-hp V-6, a five-speed manual transmission, rear-wheel drive, 16 x 8-in. alloy rims, P215/60R16 all-season tires, a Space Saver spare tire, a steel spare wheel, front independent suspension, front and rear stabilizer bars, ventilated front disc/solid rear disc ABS brakes, child seat anchors, two front headrests, an anti-theft system, an engine immobilizer, daytime running lights, front fog lights, variable intermittent windshield wipers, a rear defogger, four-person total seating capacity, bucket front seats, cloth upholstery, folding bucket rear seats, power door locks, an AM/FM stereo (with CD and four-speaker sound system), cruise control, power steering with a four-spoke tilting and adjustable steering wheel (with cruise controls on leather-wrapped steering wheel), a remote-control left-hand outside rearview mirror, a manual right-hand outside rearview mirror, front cupholders, a remote trunk release, front door pockets, a front 12-volt power outlet, a front console with storage provisions, air conditioning, front reading lights, leather trim on the gear shift knob, front and rear floor mats, a trunk light, a tachometer and a clock. The base convertible had most of the same features with the following additions or substitutions: a four-speed automatic transmission, a remote anti-theft system, a power convertible top, a glass rear window, a six-way power driver's seat, a height-adjustable driver's seat, remote power door locks, one-touch power windows, power outside rearview mirrors, a Monsoon premium stereo system with 500 watts stereo output and eight speakers.

Model Number	Body/Style Number	Body Type & Seating	Factory Price	Shipping Weight	Production Total
F/S	87	2d hatchback-4P	$20,495	3,323 lbs.	Note 1
F/S	67	2d convertible-4P	$27,410	3,402 lbs.	Note 1

Note 1: Production not completed by publication date.
Note 2: Add $575 dealer destination charge to MSRP prices above to get delivered price.

FORMULA FIREBIRD SERIES F/V - V-8

The Formula Firebird hatchback coupe got four new standard features, including a removable hatch roof with sunshades, remote keyless entry, a six-way power driver's seat and an audible theft deterrent system. Formula coupe appointments included low-profile Z-speed-rated tires, silver 16-in. five-spoke sport wheels, a performance-oriented suspension and a 10-speaker version of the Monsoon CD audio system. Standard equipment included the 5.7-liter 310-hp V-6, a four-speed automatic transmission, rear-wheel drive, 16 x 8-in. alloy rims, P245/50ZR16 performance tires, a Space Saver spare tire, a steel spare wheel, front independent suspension, front and rear stabilizer bars, ventilated front disc/solid rear disc ABS brakes, child seat anchors, two front headrests, an anti-theft system, an engine immobilizer, daytime running lights, front fog lights, variable intermittent windshield wipers, a rear defogger, four-person total seating capacity, a six-way power height-adjustable driver's bucket seat and front passen-

ger bucket seat, cloth upholstery, folding bucket rear seats, power door locks, an AM/FM stereo (with CD and four-speaker sound system), cruise control, power steering with a four-spoke tilting and adjustable steering wheel (with cruise controls on leather-wrapped steering wheel), a remote-control left-hand outside rearview mirror, a manual right-hand outside rearview mirror, front cupholders, a remote trunk release, front door pockets, a front 12-volt power outlet, a front console with storage provisions, air conditioning, front reading lights, leather trim on the gear shift knob, front and rear floor mats, a trunk light, a tachometer, a clock, one-touch power windows, power outside rearview mirrors, a Monsoon premium brand stereo system with 500 watts stereo output and 10 speakers.

Model Number	Body/Style Number	Body Type & Seating	Factory Price	Shipping Weight	Production Total
F/V	V87V	2d hatchback-4P	$26,440	3,341 lbs.	Note 3

Note 3: Production not completed by publication date.
Note 4: Add $575 dealer destination charge to MSRP prices above to get delivered price.

TRANS AM – SERIES F/V - V-8

Trans Am models used the same standard drive train as the Formula coupe. The Trans Am came in coupe and convertible editions with standard removable roof panels with sunshades, leather seating surfaces and an uplevel rear spoiler for the coupe. Trans Am drivers got 310 hp and Trans Am drivers opting for Ram Air got 325 hp. Available transmissions for the LS1 V-8 included a six-speed manual transmission. Standard Trans Am equipment included the 5.7-liter 310-hp V-6, a four-speed automatic transmission, rear-wheel drive, 16 x 8-in. alloy rims, P245/50ZR16 performance tires, a Space Saver spare tire, a steel spare wheel, front independent suspension, front and rear stabilizer bars, ventilated front disc/solid rear disc ABS brakes, child seat anchors, two front headrests, a remote anti-theft system, an engine immobilizer, daytime running lights, front fog lights, variable intermittent windshield wipers, a rear defogger, four-person total seating capacity, a six-way power height-adjustable driver's bucket seat and front passenger bucket seat, leather upholstery, folding bucket rear seats, an AM/FM stereo (with CD and four-speaker sound system), cruise control, power steering with a four-spoke tilting and adjustable steering wheel (with cruise controls on leather-wrapped steering wheel), a remote-control left-hand outside rearview mirror, a manual right-hand outside rearview mirror, front cupholders, a remote trunk release, front door pockets, a front 12-volt power outlet, a front console with

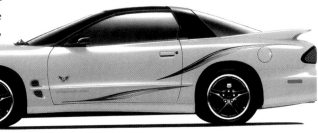

The Collector Edition T/A also came as a convertible.

storage provisions, air conditioning, front reading lights, leather trim on the gear shift knob, front and rear floor mats, a trunk light, a tachometer, a clock, 1-touch power windows, power outside rearview mirrors, a Monsoon premium brand stereo system with 500 watts stereo output and 10 speakers, remote power door locks, air-conditioning. The Trans Am convertible added a convertible top with glass window, front reading lights and a trunk light. Trans Am coupe and convertible models with the WS6 Ram Air Performance and Handling package benefited from functional air scoops, Ram Air induction, low-restriction dual-outlet exhaust and a suspension specifically tuned for maximum handling performance. The WS6 package also sported P275/40ZR17 performance radial tires mounted on 9 x 17-in. highly polished alloy wheels featuring a five-spoke spoke design.

Model Number	Body/Style Number	Body Type & Seating	Factory Price	Shipping Weight	Production Total
TRANS AM - SERIES F/V - (V-8)					
F/V	87	2d hatchback-4P	$28,470	3,397 lbs.	Note 5
F/V	67	2d convertible-4P	$32,540	3,514 lbs.	Note 5
TRANS AM – WS6 RAM AIR - SERIES F/V - (RAM AIR V-8)					
F/V	87	2d hatchback-4P	$31,760	3,397 lbs.	Note 5
F/V	67	2d convertible-4P	$35,830	3,514 lbs.	Note 5

Note 5: Production not completed by publication date.
Note 6: Add $575 dealer destination charge to MSRP prices above to get delivered price.

COLLECTOR YELLOW EDITION TRANS AM – SERIES F/V - V-8

To celebrate 35 years of Firebird, Pontiac introduced the 2002 Firebird Trans Am "Collector Edition" model option in the fall of 2001. Elements unique to the Collector Edition included a special Collector Yellow paint scheme, detailed interior appointments, special edition emblems and the WS6 Performance and Handling package. The package was available for both the coupe and the convertible. In addition to its paint scheme, the Collector Edition featured a special "screaming chicken" graphic package that put a contemporary spin on the eye-catching hood designs of classic '70s and '80s Firebird and Trans Am models. Two black "racing stripe" designs adorned the hood and wrapped themselves around the car's doors and rear quarter panels. The rear fascia also got special attention with a two-tone yellow and black treatment,

while both Collector Edition and Trans Am nameplates accented the lower doors. Staying true to the tradition of the WS6 performance and handling package's exterior appointments, the Collector Edition included black-painted WS6 wheels with a machined face surface, black anodized front and rear brake calipers and black painted axles. Goodyear Eagle F1 performance tires were standard. Inside were exclusive interior trim appointments that highlighted the design cues of Firebird and Trans Am through the years. The seats were wrapped in ebony leather with the headrests featuring embroidered Collector Edition logos. Also sporting the Collector Edition logo were the front floor mats and a trophy shelf mat. A specially issued Collector Edition owner's portfolio provided the finishing touch to the vehicle's interior. The standard Ram Air WS6 package featured the LS1 5.7-liter V-8 that churned out 325 hp and 350 ft. lbs. of torque (with WS6 package refinements). Standard equipment included a power antenna, power windows, power door locks, remote keyless entry, a theft-deterrent alarm system, a six-way power driver's seat, a Monsoon series AM/FM radio with CD player and a hatch roof with removable glass panels on Collector Edition coupes. Available options were Traction Control, a trunk-mounted 12-CD changer and a Hurst "short-throw" shifter in cars with six-speed manual transmission only.

Model Number	Body/Style Number	Body Type & Seating	Factory Price	Shipping Weight	Production Total
F/V	87	2d hatchback-4P	$34,760	3,397 lbs.	Note 5
F/V	67	2d convertible-4P	$38,830	3,514 lbs.	Note 5

Note 5: Production of 2,000 total units was publicized.
Note 6: Add $575 dealer destination charge to MSRP prices above to get delivered price.

ENGINES

Base V-6 [UPC L36]: Overhead valve. Cast-iron block and cylinder head. Displacement: 231 cid. Bore & stroke: 3.80 x 3.40 in. Compression ratio: 9.4:1. Brake horsepower: 200 at 5200 rpm. Torque: 225 ft. lbs. at 4000 rpm. Fuel system: SFI. VIN Code: K. Standard on Firebird coupe and convertible.

5.7-liter V-8 [UPC LS1]: Overhead valve. Aluminum block and cylinder head. Aluminum intake manifold. Displacement: 350 cid. Bore & stroke: 3.90 x 3.62 in. Brake horsepower: 310 at 5200 rpm. Torque: 340 ft. lbs. at 4000 rpm. Compression ratio: 10.5:1. Fuel system: SFI. VIN Code: G. Standard on Formula and Trans Am.

5.7-liter Ram Air V-8 [UPC LS1]: Overhead valve. Aluminum block and cylinder head. Aluminum intake manifold. Ram-air induction. Displacement: 350 cid. Bore & stroke: 3.90 x 3.62 in. Brake horsepower: 325 at 5200 rpm. Torque: 350 ft. lbs. at 4000 rpm. Compression ratio: 10.5:1. Fuel system: SFI. VIN Code: G.

The 2002 Collector Edition Trans Am paced the field at the Daytona 500.

Optional on Trans Am.

CHASSIS

Firebird: Wheelbase: 101.1 in. Overall length: 193.3 in. Width: 74.4 in. Height: (coupe) 51.2 in.; (convertible) 51.8 in. Front Tread: 60.7 in. Rear tread: 60.6 in.

Formula: Wheelbase: 101.1 in. Overall length: 193.3 in. Width: 74.4 in. Height: (coupe) 51.2 in.; (convertible) 51.8 in. Front Tread: 60.7 in. Rear tread: 60.6 in.

Trans Am: Wheelbase: 101.1 in. Overall length: 193.7 in. Width: 74.4 in. Height: (coupe) 51.2 in.; (convertible) 51.8 in. Front Tread: 60.7 in. Rear tread: 60.6 in.

TECHNICAL

Firebird: Chassis: Front engine/rear drive. Base transmission: Five-speed manual (except four-speed automatic in convertible). F41 front suspension: SLA/coil over monotube gas-charged shocks, tubular stabilizer bars with links and 28-mm stabilizer bar. F41 rear suspension: Salisbury axle with torque arm, trailing arm, track bar, coil springs and 15mm stabilizer bar. Steering: Power rack and pinion, 16.9:1 ratio, 2.67 turns lock to lock, 37.9-ft. turn circle. Front brakes: 11.9-in. vented disc/302.3 mm. Rear brakes: 12-in. vented disc, power-assisted, 304.8 mm. Standard tires: P215/60R16 steel-belted radial black sidewall touring. Fuel tank: 16.8 gal.

Formula: Chassis: Front engine/rear drive. Base transmission: Four-speed manual. FE2 front suspension: SLA/coil over monotube gas-charged shocks, tubular stabilizer bar with links and 30mm stabilizer bar. F41 rear suspension: Salisbury axle with torque arm, trailing arm, track bar, coil springs and 19mm stabilizer bar. Steering: Power rack and pinion, 14.4:1 ratio, 2.28 turns lock to lock, 37.75-ft. turn circle. Front brakes: 11.9-in. vented disc/302.3 mm. Rear brakes: 12-in. vented disc, power-assisted, 304.8 mm. Standard tires: P245/50ZR16 speed-rated, all-weather. Fuel tank: 16.8 gal.

Trans Am: Chassis: Front engine/rear drive. Base transmission: Four-speed manual. FE2 front suspension: SLA/coil over monotube gas-charged shocks, tubular stabilizer bar with links and 30mm stabilizer bar. F41 rear suspension: Salisbury axle with torque arm, trailing arm, track bar, coil springs and 19mm stabilizer bar. Steering: Power rack and pinion, 14.4:1 ratio, 2.28 turns lock to lock, 37.75-ft. turn circle. Front brakes: 11.9-in. vented disc/302.3 mm. Rear brakes: 12-in. vented disc, power-assisted, 304.8 mm. Standard tires: P245/50ZR16 speed-rated, all-weather. Fuel tank: 16.8 gal.

OPTIONS

[Firebird coupe] U1S trunk-mounted 12-disc CD changer ($595). P05 16 x 8-in. chrome five-spoke cast-aluminum wheels ($595). Y87 3.8-liter V-6 Performance package ($430). Y87 3.8-liter V-6 Performance package ($430). MX0 four-speed overdrive automatic transmission ($815). MM5 five-speed manual transmission ($815 credit). AG1 six-way power driver's seat ($270). 1SA base equipment group (no cost). NC7 Federal emissions override (no cost). FE9 Federal emissions requirements (no cost). AR9 front bucket seats with Prado leather seating surfaces ($575). W55 Monsoon series ETR AM/FM stereo with CD player ($430). R6M New Jersey cost surcharge (no cost). NB8 Northeast states emissions override (no cost). NG1 Northeast states emissions requirements (no cost). 1SB Option Group 2 ($1,755). CC1 removable hatch roof ($995). PDC security package ($240). W68 Sport Appearance package ($1,040). NW9 traction control ($250). **[Firebird convertible]** U1S trunk-mounted 12-disc CD changer ($595). P05 16 x 8-in. chrome five-spoke cast-aluminum wheels ($595). Y87 3.8-liter V-6 Performance package ($430). Y87 3.8-liter V-6 Performance package ($430). MM5 five-speed manual transmission (no cost). 1SA base equipment group (no cost). NC7 Federal emissions override (no cost). AR9 front bucket seats with Prado leather seating surfaces ($575). R6M New Jersey cost surcharge (no cost). NB8 Northeast states emissions override (no cost). NG1 Northeast states emissions requirements (no cost). W68 Sport Appearance package ($1,040). **[Firebird Formula coupe]** U1S trunk-mounted 12-disc CD changer ($595). P05 16 x 8-in. chrome five-spoke cast-aluminum wheels ($595). MN6 six-speed manual transmission (no cost). AG1 six-way power driver's seat ($270). 1SA base equipment group (no cost). NC7 Federal emissions override (no cost). FE9 Federal emissions requirements (no cost). AR9 front bucket seats with Prado leather seating surfaces ($575). BBS Hurst performance shift linkage ($325). 1SH NHRA Special four-speed automatic edition package ($1,070). 1SH NHRA special six-speed manual edition package ($1,095). R6M New Jersey cost surcharge (no cost). NB8 Northeast states emissions override (no cost). NG1 Northeast states emissions requirements (no cost). GU5 performance rear axle ($300). CC1 removable hatch roof ($995). NW9 traction control ($450). **[Trans Am coupe/convertible]** U1S trunk-mounted 12-disc CD changer ($595). P05 16 x 8-in. chrome five-spoke cast-aluminum wheels ($595). Z15 35th Anniversary Collector Edition ($3,000). MN6 six-speed manual transmission (no cost). 1SA base equipment group (no cost). 54U Collector Edition Yellow paint (no cost). NC7 Federal emissions override (no cost). FE9 Federal emissions requirements (no cost). BBS Hurst performance shift linkage ($325). 1SH NHRA Special four-speed automatic edition package ($1,070). 1SH NHRA special six-speed manual edition package ($1,095). R6M New Jersey cost surcharge (no cost). NB8 Northeast states emissions override (no cost). NG1 Northeast states emissions requirements (no cost). WS6 Performance and Handling package ($3,290). GU5 performance rear axle ($300). NW9 traction control ($450).

HISTORICAL FOOTNOTES

On Sept. 25, 2001, GM announced that the 2002 Firebird would be the last of the breed. However, the automaker left the gate open to use the Firebird name on a new type of car in the future.

Street Legal Performance (SLP) Firebirds

2000 Firehawk

Ex-Mopar drag racer Ed Hamburger started SLP Engineering, in Red Bank, New Jersey, to provide "street legal performance" to muscle car lovers. The firm's fortunes took off when it struck a deal with Pontiac to convert Firebirds into world-class supercars for the street and sell its SLP package, as a factory-approved option, through Pontiac dealerships. In 1991, this conversion evolved into the SLP Trans Am Firehawk, which became a dealer option in 1992.

Early SLP Firebirds were more or less based on the image of the black Trans Am that appeared in the *Smokey and the Bandit* flicks. As the package was refined the Firehawk Trans Ams got more powerful, more sophisticated and faster each year.

1991 Pontiac SLP Trans Am

The original 1991 SLP package was offered for all Tune-Port-Injected Firebirds and Trans Ams. It was made available through a partnership with General Motors' Service Parts Organization. The option represented an emissions-legal, OEM-quality, integrated group of go-fast goodies. It was designed for easy installation on a factory supplied new Firebird—and required no major modifications. The SLP kit could be ordered from Pontiac dealers through the *GM Performance Parts Catalog*.

The complete package provided 50 more horsepower at approximately 5,500 rpm and pushed the torque peak above 2,800 rpm. It promised a 1 second better 0-to-60 performance time and also improved quarter-mile performance by about 1 second or 6 mph.

The SLP hardware included cast-aluminum high-flow "siamesed" intake runners, "Tri-Y" stainless-steel tuned-length exhaust headers, a low-restriction stainless-steel exhaust system, revised engine calibration components (Cal-Pacs and PROMS) and a low-restriction cold-air-induction units.

High Performance Pontiac magazine reported on a 5.7-liter Trans Am with the Firebird SLP package that was offered through Pontiac dealers. The author of the article drove the car for a week and gave a good summary of its new-for-1991 technology. It produced 290 hp at 5,000 rpm and 350 ft. lbs. of torque. He compared the car with its bolt-on and plug-in modifications to a Royal Bobcat GTO of the 1960s.

A second SLP Trans Am tested by the magazine had the special header system with 1.75-inch primary tubes and 3-inch-wide collector pipes (dressed-up with styled tips). The tuned exhaust changed the torque and horsepower peaks to provide even a bit more performance. *High Performance Pontiac* reported a 5.7-second 0 to 60-mph time for the car with the special headers.

1992 Formula Firehawk

**1992 Formula Firehawk optional
competition interior**

1992 Formula Firehawk

1992 Pontiac Formula Firehawk

In 1992, Pontiac Motor Division and SLP Engineering teamed up to make the hot new Formula Firehawk available through the factory dealer network as a special 1992 Firebird model option. Representatives of Pontiac and SLP Engineering exhibited one of these cars at the Boston "World of Wheels" show during the first week of January 1992. They explained that Firehawks would be offered in "street" and "competition" versions. The street version produced 350 hp at 5,500 rpm and 390 ft. lbs. of torque at 4,400 rpm.

The factory-built Formula Firebird that served as the basis for SLP's Firehawk carried the 5.0-liter TPI V-8 and a four-speed automatic transmission (both upgraded to high-performance 1LE specs) plus air conditioning. Externally, the main differences from a stock Formula model were the use of five-spoke aluminum alloy wheels and a Firehawk decal on the right-hand side of the rear fascia.

The factory Formula had a $19,242 base price and the Firehawk Street package was $20,753 for a total delivered price of $39,995. The Firehawk Competition package was $9,905 additional, raising the total bill to $49,990 for the car displayed in Boston.

When a Firehawk was ordered, Pontiac shipped a new red Formula from its Van Nuys, California, factory to SLP Engineering in Toms River, New Jersey. SLP employees, under the direction of Ed Hamburger, then extracted the entire drive train and dropped in a much-modified, heavy-duty 350-cid Chevy engine block fitted with four-bolt mains, a forged steel crank, Gen II cast pistons, Ed Pink Racing con rods and a hydraulic roller cam. Bolted to this were aluminum heads with 2-in. intake and 1.56-in. exhaust stainless-steel valves.

A special downdraft port-injection manifold was also employed on the engine. Designed by Ray Falconer, it featured 11 1/2-in. runners, a 52-mm throttle-body, a high-flow dual filter system and stainless steel exhaust headers and exhaust pipes with dual catalytic converters and other performance refinements. SLP also added a Corvette ZF six-speed gearbox with computer-aide gear selection (CAGS), a Dana 44 rear axle with 3.54:1 gears, a shortened input shaft and a 16-lb. flywheel. The whole package was then made available to buyers through their local Pontiac dealers as RPO (Regular Production Option) B4U.

Formula Firehawk suspension modifications included revised spring rates, a lowered ride height, new struts, new rear shocks, larger front and rear anti-roll bars, special bushings and Corvette 11.85-inch disc brakes. Firestone 275/40ZR17 Firehawk tires were mounted on the 17 x 9.5-in. Ronal wheels.

Recaro seats were extra for $995 and the center console inside the cars was modified to give more space for shift throws.

The competition version of the Firehawk included the Recaro seats as standard equipment, plus 13-inch Brembo vented disc brakes with four-piston calipers, a roll cage and an aluminum hood. The rear seat was also left out.

High Performance Pontiac magazine reported that only 250 copies of what it called the "Quickest Street Pontiac Ever" were going to be made. The magazine found that its Formula Firehawk test car did 0 to 60 mph in 4.6 seconds and covered the quarter mile in 13.20 seconds at 107 mph.

SLP Engineering targeted production of five cars per week starting in July 1991, but really only produced actual cars on a build-to-order basis. A pre-production version of the Competition Firehawk was entered in the Bridgestone Petenza Supercar Series at Lime Rock Race Course on May 27, 1991. It took third place and the company soon had orders for three or four additional competition models.

The SLP kit was again made available through GM Service Parts Organization, but it was not shown in sales literature since there was some initial uncertainty about its being EPA certified. In the end, SLP Engineering wound up building only 25 street versions, at least one of which was a Trans Am convertible with serial No. 27. That could raise questions with future collectors, but the reason for the serial number being higher than the production total was that cars 18 and 25 were ordered but never built.

1994 Firehawk

1995 SLP Formula Firehawk

1995 Firehawk

1995 Pontiac/SLP Formula Firehawk

By 1995, SLP Engineering was operating as what General Motors called an "aftermarket partner company." It converted new Firebirds, which Pontiac shipped to its Garden State shop, into super high-performance cars. The 1995 Formula Firehawk was promoted as "an irresistible force that moves you." It now offered 300- and 315-hp versions of the 5.7-liter LT1 V-8, plus all-new features like optional chrome wheels. In addition, Ed Hamburger and his SLP engineers added a Hurst six-speed gear shifter. About 750 Formula Firehawks were sold in 1995.

Twin air scoops on the Formula Firehawk's snout were part of a special air-induction system that added 25 to 35 hp. The suspension was upgraded from Formula specifications to increase handling limits. Coupes benefited from bigger, better-handling Firestone 275/40/17 tires and 17-in. wide wheels. (Firehawk convertibles, however, came with narrower 16-inch wide Firestone tires and closed-lug 16-in.-wide alloy wheels. Other Formula Firehawk features included megaphone-style polished stainless-steel tailpipe tips, special exterior graphics and a sequentially numbered dash plaque. A sport suspension and performance exhaust system were optional.

A six-speed Firehawk coupe with the performance exhaust system went from 0 to 60 mph in 4.9 seconds and did the quarter mile in 13.5 seconds at 103.5 mph. Its top speed was 160 mph. The Formula Firehawk was available as an SLP alteration on '95 Formulas, which buyers had to order through Pontiac dealers. The Firehawks came with a three-year, 36,000-mile limited warranty. The base price for the alteration was $6,495, an increase of $500 over the 1993 and 1994 versions.

Since the six-speed Hurst shifter was a new accessory for the high-performance 1995 Formula Firehawk model, SLP Engineering promoted this feature by photographing a Firehawk coupe alongside a 1965 Pontiac Catalina 2 + 2 — an earlier high-performance Pontiac that also came with a Hurst shifter.

1997 Firehawk

1997 Pontiac Firebird special performance models

In 1997, Ed Hamburger's crew at SLP planned to build about 8,000 cars with Firehawk-type performance conversions. However, this approved aftermarket converter had now started doing conversions on both Firebirds and Camaros in 1996, which meant that not all of the 1997 Firehawks were Formula Firebirds. Nevertheless, GM continued to farm out specialty work to companies like SLP and this continued to result in some very interesting late-model muscle cars with instant collector-car status.

1999 Trans Am Firehawk

1999 Firehawk

2000 Firehawk

1999 Pontiac Trans Am Firehawk

Motor Trend's Jack Keebler (April 1999) described his bright red SLP Trans Am Firehawk as "All Detroit muscle all the time." The "Street Legal Performance" tuned Firebird's 16-valve 5.7-liter V-8 produced 327 hp at 5200 rpm and 345 ft. lbs. of torque at 4400 rpm. The car could do 0 to 60 mph in 5.3 seconds and covered the quarter mile in 13.6 seconds at 105.6 mph.

Keebler was comparing the $31,000 heated-up Firebird to nine other super cars, including the $140,000 Mercedes Benz CL600 and the $299,900 Bentley Continental R. It was the lowest-priced car in the pack, but was right up there with the top performing models.

The reworked 346-cid LS1 block was attached to a Borg-Warner T-56 six-speed manual transmission. A set of meaty P275/40ZR17 Firestone tires "attached" it to the road and helped it slide through a slalom course at 66 mph while pulling a strong 0.89 Gs on a skid pad. As usual, the car built by SLP Engineering could be ordered directly from an authorized Pontiac factory dealer.

2000 Pontiac Trans Am 10th Anniversary Firehawk

Like the original 1991 SLP Firebird, the 2000 SLP Trans Am 10th Anniversary Firehawk was based on a car used a motion picture. However, it was the current *X-Man* movie, rather than a Burt Reynolds's classic. Still, the car retained the overall look of a mean black machine with gold trim. It had gold-painted alloy wheels and gold body stripes.

Pontiac dealer order sheets listed the $3,999 Firehawk package as option number WU6. The $1,999 anniversary package was an additional add-on that the buyer had to specifically request. It came only in black and only on coupes and included gold stripe decals down the center of the body, gold alloy wheels, Firestone Firehawk radial tires (275/40ZR-17) and 10th anniversary logos.

The 2000 Firehawk relied on the Trans Am's LS1 V-8 fitted with a Ram Air induction system designed by SLP (not the factory's WS6 system). The composite hood, which was also designed by SLP and had smaller "nostrils" than the factory version, directed cold air to the hot engine. Other performance upgrades included a freer-flowing exhaust system with special gold, siamesed exhaust tips.

The 346-cid V-8 was tuned for 335 hp at 5200 rpm and 350 ft. lbs. of torque at 4000 rpm. It came mated to a six-speed manual gearbox. It took the $37,658 Firehawk about 5 seconds to zip from 0 to 60 mph. It could cover the quarter mile in 13.6 seconds at 106 mph.

2001 Pontiac Trans Am Firehawk

Having produced 34,000 vehicles through the end of the 2000 model year, SLP had gained recognition as the highest volume, niche vehicle producer in the U.S. It had also produced more Pontiac-GMC and Chevrolet niche vehicles than any company. Entering 2001, SLP said that it expected to build 32,000 Firebird and Camaro-based vehicles for the year and in 2002. Pontiac and SLP continued their long-term, muscle-car oriented relationship with another sleek, black, modified Firebird created as a modern interpretation of the car that actor Burt Reynolds drove in his old *Smokey and the Bandit* films.

The 2001 Firehawk was based on the Pontiac Trans Am with its all-aluminum 5.7-liter Corvette LS1

2001 Firehawk

V-8. It had a base price of just under $30,000, though most cars went out the door for about $36,000 when delivered with a typical assortment of options.

After reworking the 346-cid block a bit, the SLP shop squeezed 335 hp and 345 ft. lbs. of torque out of the TPI V-8, which was linked to a five-speed manual transmission.

The Firehawk rode a 101.1-inch wheelbase and tipped the scales at 3,487 lbs. The car's suspension featured long-and-short control arms, coil springs all around, a solid rear axle and fat front and rear anti-roll bars. The ABS brakes were vented discs 11.9 inches in diameter up front and 12 inches in diameter at the rear. The five-spoke cast-aluminum wheels carried P275/40ZR17 Firestone Firehawk tires front and rear.

Motor Trend (November 2000) liked the Firehawk's great value and strong power train, but criticized its huge, heavy doors, its tiny rear seats and its lack of storage space. The magazine felt that the heated-up Pontiac had a "teen machine" image. It also mentioned a "hip hopping" rear live axle as a problem on curvy roads. In a straight line, however, the 2001 Firehawk had no problem making it from 0 to 60 mph

Available only on V6 coupe and t-top coupe models*, Firebird GT is the perfect counterpart to its high horsepower cousin, SLP's legendary Firehawk. GT boasts a Pontiac designed and updated "Bird of Prey" logo that graces the hood and continues across the roofline to the rear of the vehicle. Along with that exterior enhancement,

Pontiac Excitement SLP Style

all GTs feature five additional horsepower and a more robust sound courtesy of its Trans Am Performance Exhaust with Dual-Dual Outlet Tips. For all this excitement and more, just add GM RPO Code Y3C to your Firebird order.

* GM RPO Y3C option is not offered on V6 Firebird convertible models.

2002 SLP Firebird GT

to SLP's new High Flow Induction System and proprietary Dual-Dual Performance Exhaust. Hooking up that much power is handled by Firestone's new and improved 17"

2002 Firehawk

in 5.16 seconds.

2002 Pontiac Firebird GT and Trans Am Firehawk

For 2002 — which was destined to be the Firebird's last year — SLP Engineering offered two models. The first was a $599 package (UPC Y3C) called the Firebird GT option that was available for the V-6 Firebird with the Y3B package. The Firebird GT package was not offered for the convertible and could not be ordered for the Trans Am, Formula or Firehawk or with several factory options, including Ram Air, ground effects, the Performance Enhancement group or the five-speed manual transmission.

Standard GT content included either a solid black stripe (except with navy blue or black exteriors) or a gradient silver stripe (except with Light Pewter or Sunset Orange exteriors), a pair of Firebird GT exterior decals on B-pillars and dual-dual exhaust outlets with high-performance mufflers (for five extra horsepower and a more "throaty" exhaust note).

The Firebird GT came in Arctic White, Pewter Metallic, Navy Blue Metallic, Black, Maple Red Metallic, Sunset Orange Metallic, Blue-Green Chameleon and Bright Red exterior colors.

A pair of options were available for $299 each. They included silver-painted 16 x 8-in. five-spoke Trans Am wheels and a performance suspension package with larger front and rear stabilizer bars.

The second SLP offering was the Firehawk package, which was available for the Trans Am coupe or convertible or Firebirds with the W66 Formula option in Arctic White, Pewter Metallic, Silver Metallic, Navy Blue Metallic, Black, Sunset Orange Metallic or Bright Red. The package price was $4,299 for cars with the factory WU6 package (345 hp) and $6,079 otherwise. Cars with the Firehawk package were also required to have a power steering cooler, Pontiac's QLC tires and 16-inch wheels. The package could not be teamed with several options, including the WS6 Ram Air package, Pontiac's PO5 chrome-plated aluminum wheels or Goodyear Eagle F1 tires.

Standard 2002 Firehawk content included a 335-hp LS1 V-8 with 350 ft. lbs. of torque (all cars built after Sept. 1, 2001, were slated to get SLP's High Flow Induction system that added 10 hp), an exclusive composite hood with functional air scoops, exclusive hood-mounted heat extractors, an underhood forced-air induction system, a special front fascia badge, a "Cat-Back" stainless steel performance exhaust system with twin dual tips, upgraded suspension components, 17 x 9-in. lightweight aluminum painted wheels, Firestone Firehawk 275/40ZR17 SZ50EP 17-in. tires, special Firehawk exterior graphics on the doors and rear fascia, a dash plaque and two Firehawk key fobs.

Options for the 2002 Firehawk included a rear deck lid spoiler with an extra-wide center high-mounted stoplight (not available on Trans Am convertible or Formula-based Firehawks), 17 x 9-inch chrome-plated five-spoke aluminum wheels, a custom rear deck mat with an embroidered Firebird logo, a commemorative portfolio to hold the GM owner's manual and supplemental SLP manual (including an SLP engraved pen, notepad, tire tread depth gauge and customized "Certificate of Authenticity"), a Bilstein Ultra Performance Suspension system, an Auburn High Torque Performance Differential with AAM cast-aluminum cooling cover, premium front floor mats with an embroidered Firehawk logo and a custom car cover with silk-screened Firehawk graphics.

As a reaction to GM's fall 2001 decision to drop the Firebird and Camaro after the 2002 model year, SLP Engineering began to look towards products based on other vehicles, so the company's 2002 offerings also included the GTX — a sporty compact based on the Pontiac Grand Prix — as well as the Thunderbolt, a "hot rod" mini pickup based on the latest rendition of the Ford Ranger. While Firebird and Camaro fans are unlikely to flock to these new SLP products in vast numbers, those who have come to love the Formula Firehawk, Trans Am Firehawk and Camaro SS will continue to cherish the thousands of examples that Hamburger's company has crafted over more than two decades.

2001 Firehawk

Firebird Price Guide

1967 Firebird

Vehicle Condition Scale

1: **Excellent:** Restored to current maximum professional standards of quality in every area, or perfect original with components operating and apearing as new. A 95-plus point show car that is not driven.

2: **Fine:** Well-restored or a combination of superior restoration and excellent original parts. Also, extremely well-maintained original vehicle showing minimal wear.

3. **Very Good:** Complete operable original or older restoration. Also, a very good amateur restoration, all presentable and serviceable inside and out. Plus, a combination of well-done restoration and good operable components or a partially restored car with all parts necessary to compete and/or valuable NOS parts.

4: **Good:** A driveable vehicle needing no or only minor work to be functional. Also, a deteriorated restoration or a very poor amateur restoration. All components may need restoration to be "excellent," but the car is mostly useable "as is."

5. **Restorable:** Needs complete restoration of body, chassis and interior. May or may not be running, but isn't weathered, wrecked or stripped to the point of being useful only for parts.

6. **Parts car:** May or may not be running, but is weathered, wrecked and/or stripped to the point of being useful primarily for parts.

1969 Trans Am

	6	5	4	3	2	1

1967 Firebird, V-8

	6	5	4	3	2	1
2d Cpe	720	2,160	3,600	7,200	12,600	18,000
2d Conv	880	2,640	4,400	8,800	15,400	22,000

NOTE: Deduct 25 percent for 6-cyl. Add 15 percent for 350 HO. Add 10 percent for 4-speed. Add 30 percent for the Ram Air 400 Firebird.

1968 Firebird, V-8

	6	5	4	3	2	1
2d Cpe	720	2,160	3,600	7,200	12,600	18,000
2d Conv	880	2,640	4,400	8,800	15,400	22,000

NOTE: Deduct 25 percent for 6-cyl. Add 10 percent for 350 HO. Add 10 percent for 4-speed. Add 25 percent for the Ram Air 400 Firebird.

1969 Firebird, V-8

	6	5	4	3	2	1
2d Cpe	720	2,160	3,600	7,200	12,600	18,000
2d Conv	880	2,640	4,400	8,800	15,400	22,000
2d Trans Am Cpe	760	2,280	3,800	7,600	13,300	19,000
2d Trans Am Conv	1,040	3,120	5,200	10,400	18,200	26,000

NOTE: Deduct 25 percent for 6-cyl. Add 15 percent for "HO" 400 Firebird. Add 10 percent for 4-speed. Add 20 percent for Ram Air IV Firebird. Add 50 percent for '303' V-8 SCCA race engine.

1972 Trans Am

1976 Esprit

1970 Firebird, V-8

2d Firebird	600	1,800	3,000	6,000	10,500	15,000
2d Esprit	620	1,860	3,100	6,200	10,850	15,500
2d Formula 400	640	1,920	3,200	6,400	11,200	16,000
2d Trans Am	760	2,280	3,800	7,600	13,300	19,000

NOTE: Deduct 25 percent for 6-cyl. Add 10 percent for Trans Am with 4-speed. Add 25 percent for Ram Air IV Firebird.

1971 Firebird, V-8

2d Firebird	620	1,860	3,100	6,200	10,850	15,500
2d Esprit	600	1,800	3,000	6,000	10,500	15,000
2d Formula	640	1,920	3,200	6,400	11,200	16,000
2d Trans Am	760	2,280	3,800	7,600	13,300	19,000

NOTE: Add 25 percent for Formula 455. Deduct 25 percent for 6-cyl. Add 40 percent for 455 HO V-8. Add 10 percent for 4-speed. (Formula Series - 350, 400, 455).

1972 Firebird, V-8

2d Firebird	580	1,740	2,900	5,800	10,150	14,500
2d Esprit	560	1,680	2,800	5,600	9,800	14,000
2d Formula	600	1,800	3,000	6,000	10,500	15,000
2d Trans Am	720	2,160	3,600	7,200	12,600	18,000

NOTE: Add 10 percent for Trans Am with 4-speed. Deduct 25 percent for 6-cyl. Add 40 percent for 455 HO V-8.

1973 Firebird, V-8

2d Cpe	560	1,680	2,800	5,600	9,800	14,000
2d Esprit	580	1,740	2,900	5,800	10,150	14,500
2d Formula	600	1,800	3,000	6,000	10,500	15,000
2d Trans Am	620	1,860	3,100	6,200	10,850	15,500

NOTE: Add 50 percent for 455 SD V-8 (Formula & Trans Am only). Deduct 25 percent for 6-cyl. Add 10 percent for 4-speed.

1974 Firebird, V-8

2d Firebird	340	1,020	1,700	3,400	5,950	8,500
2d Esprit	520	1,560	2,600	5,200	9,100	13,000
2d Formula	580	1,740	2,900	5,800	10,150	14,500
2d Trans Am	600	1,800	3,000	6,000	10,500	15,000

NOTE: Add 40 percent for 455-SD V-8 (Formula & Trans Am only). Deduct 25 percent for 6-cyl. Add 10 percent for 4-speed.

1975 Firebird, V-8

2d Cpe	300	900	1,500	3,000	5,250	7,500
2d Esprit	340	1,020	1,700	3,400	5,950	8,500
2d Formula	340	1,020	1,700	3,400	5,950	8,500
Trans Am	540	1,620	2,700	5,400	9,450	13,500

NOTE: Add 18 percent for 455 HO V-8. Deduct 25 percent for 6-cyl. Add 10 percent for 4-speed. Add $150 for Honeycomb wheels.

1976 Firebird, V-8

2d Cpe	248	744	1,240	2,480	4,340	6,200
2d Esprit Cpe	260	780	1,300	2,600	4,550	6,500
2d Formula Cpe	268	804	1,340	2,680	4,690	6,700
2d Trans Am Cpe	276	828	1,380	2,760	4,830	6,900

NOTE: Add 20 percent for 455 HO V-8. Deduct 25 percent for 6-cyl. Add 10 percent for 4-speed. Add $150 for Honeycomb wheels. Add 20 percent for Limited Edition.

1977 Firebird, V-8

2d Cpe	232	696	1,160	2,320	4,060	5,800
2d Esprit Cpe	240	720	1,200	2,400	4,200	6,000
2d Formula Cpe	252	756	1,260	2,520	4,410	6,300
2d Trans Am Cpe	260	780	1,300	2,600	4,550	6,500

NOTE: Add 10 percent for 4-speed.

1978 Firebird, V-8

2d Cpe	232	696	1,160	2,320	4,060	5,800
2d Esprit Cpe	240	720	1,200	2,400	4,200	6,000
2d Formula Cpe	252	756	1,260	2,520	4,410	6,300
2d Trans Am Cpe	260	780	1,300	2,600	4,550	6,500

NOTE: Add 10 percent for 4-speed.

1979 Firebird, V-8

2d Cpe	248	744	1,240	2,480	4,340	6,200
2d Esprit Cpe	256	768	1,280	2,560	4,480	6,400
2d Formula Cpe	264	792	1,320	2,640	4,620	6,600
2d Trans Am Cpe	320	960	1,600	3,200	5,600	8,000

NOTE: Add 15 percent for 10th Anniversary Edition. Add 10 percent for 4-speed.

1980 Firebird, V-8

2d Cpe	236	708	1,180	2,360	4,130	5,900
2d Cpe Esprit	240	720	1,200	2,400	4,200	6,000
2d Cpe Formula	244	732	1,220	2,440	4,270	6,100
2d Cpe Trans Am	252	756	1,260	2,520	4,410	6,300

NOTE: Deduct 15 percent for V-6. Add 10 percent for Indy Pace Car.

1981 Firebird, V-8

2d Cpe	240	720	1,200	2,400	4,200	6,000
2d Cpe Esprit	244	732	1,220	2,440	4,270	6,100
2d Cpe Formula	248	744	1,240	2,480	4,340	6,200
2d Cpe Trans Am	260	780	1,300	2,600	4,550	6,500
2d Cpe Trans Am SE	250	800	1,350	2,700	4,750	6,800

NOTE: Deduct 15 percent for V-6.

1982 Firebird, V-8

2d Cpe	252	756	1,260	2,520	4,410	6,300
2d Cpe SE	264	792	1,320	2,640	4,620	6,600
2d Cpe Trans Am	276	828	1,380	2,760	4,830	6,900

NOTE: Deduct 15 percent for V-6.

1983 Firebird, V-8

2d Cpe	252	756	1,260	2,520	4,410	6,300
2d Cpe SE	256	768	1,280	2,560	4,480	6,400
2d Cpe Trans Am	264	792	1,320	2,640	4,620	6,600

NOTE: Deduct 15 percent for V-6.

1984 Firebird
V-6

| 2d Cpe | 244 | 732 | 1,220 | 2,440 | 4,270 | 6,100 |
| 2d Cpe SE | 252 | 756 | 1,260 | 2,520 | 4,410 | 6,300 |

V-8

2d Cpe	264	792	1,320	2,640	4,620	6,600
2d Cpe SE	268	804	1,340	2,680	4,690	6,700
2d Cpe TA	272	816	1,360	2,720	4,760	6,800

1985 Firebird, V-8

2d Cpe	264	792	1,320	2,640	4,620	6,600
2d Cpe SE	268	804	1,340	2,680	4,690	6,700
2d Cpe Trans AM	272	816	1,360	2,720	4,760	6,800

NOTE: Deduct 30 percent for V-6 where available.

1986 Firebird

2d Cpe	264	792	1,320	2,640	4,620	6,600
2d SE V-8 Cpe	268	804	1,340	2,680	4,690	6,700
Trans Am Cpe	276	828	1,380	2,760	4,830	6,900

1987 Firebird
V-6

| 2d Cpe | 268 | 804 | 1,340 | 2,680 | 4,690 | 6,700 |

V-8

2d Cpe	276	828	1,380	2,760	4,830	6,900
2d Cpe Formula	280	840	1,400	2,800	4,900	7,000
2d Cpe Trans Am	288	864	1,440	2,880	5,040	7,200
2d Cpe GTA	296	888	1,480	2,960	5,180	7,400

NOTE: Add 10 percent for 5.7 liter V-8 where available.

1988 Firebird
V-6

| 2d Cpe | 240 | 720 | 1,200 | 2,400 | 4,200 | 6,000 |

V-8

2d Cpe	280	840	1,400	2,800	4,900	7,000
2d Formula Cpe	320	960	1,600	3,200	5,600	8,000
2d Cpe Trans Am	520	1,560	2,600	5,200	9,100	13,000
2d Cpe GTA	600	1,800	3,000	6,000	10,500	15,000

1989 Firebird
V-6

| 2d Cpe | 260 | 780 | 1,300 | 2,600 | 4,550 | 6,500 |

V-8

2d Cpe	280	840	1,400	2,800	4,900	7,000
2d Formula Cpe	300	900	1,500	3,000	5,250	7,500
2d Trans Am Cpe	560	1,680	2,800	5,600	9,800	14,000

1989 1/2 Firebird Trans Am Pace Car, V-6 Turbo

| Cpe | 760 | 2,280 | 3,800 | 7,600 | 13,300 | 19,000 |

1991 Trans Am

1990 Firebird
V-6
2d Cpe	260	780	1,300	2,600	4,550	6,500

V-8
2d Cpe	300	900	1,500	3,000	5,250	7,500
2d Formula Cpe	320	960	1,600	3,200	5,600	8,000
2d Trans Am Cpe	520	1,560	2,600	5,200	9,100	13,000
2d GTA Cpe	600	1,800	3,000	6,000	10,500	15,000

1991 Firebird
V-6
2d Cpe	260	780	1,300	2,600	4,550	6,500
2d Conv	560	1,680	2,800	5,600	9,800	14,000

V-8
2d Cpe	300	900	1,500	3,000	5,250	7,500
2d Conv	600	1,800	3,000	6,000	10,500	15,000
2d Formula Cpe	320	960	1,600	3,200	5,600	8,000
2d Trans Am Cpe	520	1,560	2,600	5,200	9,100	13,000
2d Trans Am Conv	660	1,980	3,300	6,600	11,550	16,500
2d GTA Cpe	600	1,800	3,000	6,000	10,500	15,000

1992 Firebird, V-8
2d Cpe	320	960	1,600	3,200	5,600	8,000
2d Conv	600	1,800	3,000	6,000	10,500	15,000
2d Formula Cpe	340	1,020	1,700	3,400	5,950	8,500
2d Trans Am Cpe	540	1,620	2,700	5,400	9,450	13,500
2d Trans Am Conv	620	1,860	3,100	6,200	10,850	15,500
2d GTA Cpe	580	1,740	2,900	5,800	10,150	14,500

NOTE: Deduct 10 percent for V-6.

1993 Firebird
2d Cpe, V-6	320	960	1,600	3,200	5,600	8,000
2d Formula Cpe, V-8	500	1,550	2,600	5,200	9,100	13,000
2d Trans Am Cpe, V-8	550	1,600	2,700	5,400	9,450	13,500

1994 Firebird
2d Cpe, V-6	420	1,260	2,100	4,200	7,350	10,500
2d Conv, V-6	540	1,620	2,700	5,400	9,450	13,500
2d Formula Cpe, V-8	500	1,450	2,400	4,800	8,400	12,000
2d Formula Conv, V-8	600	1,750	2,900	5,800	10,200	14,500
2d Trans Am Cpe, V-8	550	1,600	2,700	5,400	9,450	13,500
2d Trans Am GT Cpe, V-8	580	1,740	2,900	5,800	10,150	14,500
2d Trans Am GT Conv, V-8	620	1,860	3,100	6,200	10,850	15,500

Note: Add 15 percent for Trans Am with 25th Anniversary package.

1995 Firebird, V-6 & V-8
2d Cpe, V-6	400	1,250	2,100	4,200	7,350	10,500
2d Conv, V-6	550	1,600	2,700	5,400	9,450	13,500
2d Formula Cpe, V-8	500	1,450	2,400	4,800	8,400	12,000
2d Formula Conv, V-8	600	1,750	2,900	5,800	10,200	14,500
2d Trans Am Cpe, V-8	550	1,600	2,700	5,400	9,450	13,500
2d Trans Am Conv, V-8	600	1,850	3,100	6,200	10,900	15,500

1994 Firebird

2001 Trans Am

1991 GTA

Get Fired Up

WITH THESE NEW BOOKS FROM KRAUSE PUBLICATIONS

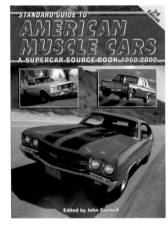
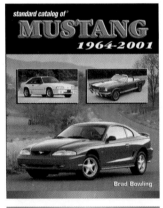
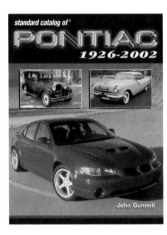

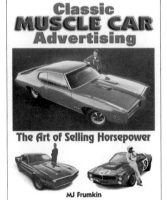